Numerical Sound Synthesis

1
2
3
4
5
6
7
8
9
10
11
12
13
14
15
16
17
18
19
20
21
22
23
24
25
26
27
28
29
30
31
32
33
34
35
36
37
38
39
40
41
42
43
44
45
46
47
48
49
50
51

Numerical Sound Synthesis

Finite Difference Schemes and Simulation in Musical Acoustics

Stefan Bilbao

Acoustics and Fluid Dynamics Group/Music,
University of Edinburgh, UK

A John Wiley and Sons, Ltd., Publication

This edition first published 2009
© 2009, John Wiley & Sons, Ltd

Registered office
John Wiley & Sons Ltd, The Atrium, Southern Gate, Chichester, West Sussex, PO19 8SQ, United Kingdom

For details of our global editorial offices, for customer services and for information about how to apply for permission to reuse the copyright material in this book please see our website at www.wiley.com.

Library of Congress Cataloguing-in-Publication Data

Bilbao, Stefan D.
  Numerical sound synthesis : finite difference schemes and simulation in musical acoustics / Stefan Bilbao.
      p. cm.
  Includes bibliographical references and index.
  ISBN 978-0-470-51046-9 (cloth)
  1. Musical instruments—Mathematical models. 2. Musical instruments—Computer simulation. 3. Finite differences. I. Title.
  ML3817.B55 2009
  781.2′3015118—dc22
                                                                          2009015955

A catalogue record for this book is available from the British Library.

ISBN: 978-0-470-51046-9 (Hbk)

Typeset in 9/11pt Times by Laserwords Private Limited, Chennai, India.

1
2
3
4
5
6
7
8
9
10
11
12
13
14
15
16
17
18
19
20
21
22
23
24
25
26
27
28
29
30
31
32
33
34
35
36
37
38
39
40
41
42
43
44
45
46
47
48
49
50
51

Contents

1
2
3
4
5
6
7
8
9
10
11
12
13
14
15
16
17
18
19
20
21
22
23
24
25
26
27
28
29
30
31
32
33
34
35
36
37
38
39
40
41
42
43
44
45
46
47
48
49
50
51

1
2
3
4
5
6
7
8
9
10
11
12
13
14
15
16
17
18
19
20
21
22
23
24
25
26
27
28
29
30
31
32
33
34
35
36
37
38
39
40
41
42
43
44
45
46
47
48
49
50
51

Preface

While this book was being written, digital sound synthesis reached something of a milestone—its 50th birthday. Set against the leisurely pace of the development and evolution of acoustic musical instruments in previous years, a half century is not a long time. But given the rate at which computational power has increased in the past decades, it is fair to say that digital sound is, if not old, at least enjoying a robust middle age. Many of the techniques that developed early on, during a 15-year burst of creativity beginning in the late 1950s, have become classics: wavetables, sinusoids, and FM oscillators are now the cornerstones of modern synthesis. All of these methods appeared at a time when operation counts and algorithmic simplicity were of critical importance. In the early days, these algorithms stretched the bounds of computing power, only to produce sound when shoehorned into the busy schedule of a university mainframe by a devoted and often sleep-deprived composer. Now, however, sounds of this nature may be produced quickly and easily, and are used routinely by musicians in all walks of life.

Beyond allowing musicians to do faster what was once grindingly slow, increased computational power has opened the door to research into newer, more demanding techniques. Certainly, in the last 20 years, the most significant effort has gone into a set of methods known, collectively, as "physical modeling." The hope is that by sticking to physical descriptions of musical objects, better synthetic sound quality may be achieved. There are many such methods available—all, however, may ultimately be viewed as numerical simulation techniques, applied to generate an approximate solution to the equations which describe an acoustic entity, such as a string, drum head, or xylophone bar. The interesting thing is that, in one way, this is a step backward; after all, modern numerical solution techniques are at least 80 years old, and predate the existence of not only the first digital sound synthesis methods, but in fact digital computers themselves! It is also a step backward in another sense—physical modeling techniques are far more computationally intensive than the classic methods, and, again, like the old days, algorithm efficiency has become a concern. Is physical modeling a step forward? This is a question that may only be answered subjectively—by listening to the sounds which may be produced in this way.

As mentioned above, physical modeling sound synthesis is an application of numerical simulation techniques. Regardless of the application, when one is faced with solving a problem numerically, many questions arise before any algebraic manipulations or computer coding are attempted. Or, rather, after one has made one or many such attempts, these questions are begged. There are many, but the most important are:

- How faithfully is the solution to be rendered? (Accuracy)

- How long should one reasonably expect to wait for the solution to be computed? (Efficiency)

- How bad is it if, for some unexpected reason, the simulation fails? (Stability)

Though the ideal answers are, of course, "very, not long, and bad," one might guess that rarely will one be able to design a method which behaves accordingly. Compromises are necessary, and the types of compromises to be made will depend on the application at hand. Regarding the first question above, one might require different levels of accuracy in, for instance, a routine weather prediction problem, as compared to the design of a nuclear reactor component. As for the second, though in all cases speedier computation is desirable, in most mainstream simulation applications the premium is placed rather on accuracy (as per the first question), though in some, such as for instance control systems built to reduce panel flutter, efficient on-line performance is essential. Finally, because many mainstream simulation applications are indeed intended to run off-line, many techniques have developed over the years in order to control the usual problems in simulation, such as oscillatory behavior and instability. In some applications, typically in an off-line scenario, such as in the design of an airfoil, if one encounters numerical results which suffer from these problems, one can adjust a parameter or two, and run the simulation again. But in an on-line situation, or if the application is to be used by a non-expert (such as might occur in the case of 3D graphics rendering), the simulation algorithm needs to produce acceptable results with little or no intervention from the user. In other words, it must be robust.

What about sound synthesis then? Numerical simulation methods have indeed, for some time, played a role in pure studies of the acoustics of musical instruments, divorced from sound synthesis applications, which are the subject of this book. For this reason, one might assume that such methods could be applied directly to synthesis. But in fact, the constraints and goals of synthesis are somewhat different from those of scientific research in musical acoustics. Synthesis is a rather special case of an application of numerical methods, in that the result is judged subjectively. Sometimes there is a target sound from a real-world instrument to be reproduced, but another, perhaps longer-term goal is to produce sounds from instruments which are wholly imaginary, yet still based on physical principles. Furthermore, these methods are destined, eventually, to be used by composers and musicians, who surely will have little interest in the technical side of sound synthesis, and who are becoming increasingly accustomed to working in a real-time environment. For this reason, it seems sensible to put more emphasis on efficiency and stability, rather than on computing extremely accurate solutions.

Such considerations, as well as the auxiliary concern of programming ease, naturally lead one to employ the simplest simulation methods available, namely finite difference schemes. These have been around for quite a long time, and, in many mainstream applications, have been superseded by newer techniques which are better suited to the complexities of real-world simulation problems. On the other hand, there are many advantages to sticking with a relatively simple framework: these methods are efficient, quite easy to program, and, best of all, one can use quite basic mathematical tools in order to arrive quickly at conclusions regarding their behavior. The trick in synthesis, however, is to understand this behavior in an audio setting, and, unfortunately, the way in which simulation techniques such as finite difference schemes are presented in many standard texts does not address the peculiarities of sound production. This has been one of the main motivations for writing this book.

Every book has a latent agenda. Frequency domain analysis techniques play a central role in both musical acoustics and numerical analysis, and such techniques are not neglected here. The reason for this is, of course, that many important features of real-world systems (such as musical instruments) may be deduced through linearization. But frequency domain techniques constitute only a single point of view—there are others. A dynamical systems viewpoint, in particular when energy concepts are employed, can also be informative. The use of energetic principles amounts to more than just a different slant on the analysis of numerical methods than that provided by frequency domain methods; it is in fact much more general, and at the same time less revealing—the dynamics of a system are compressed into the time evolution of a single scalar function. The information it does yield, however, is usually exactly what one needs in order to answer thorny questions

about, say, the stability of nonlinear numerical methods, as well as how to properly set numerical
boundary conditions. It is the key to solid design of numerical methods and of immense practical
utility, and for these reasons is given an elaborate treatment in this book. Besides—it's interesting!

This work is not really intended directly for musicians or practising acousticians, but rather for
working engineers and (especially) doctoral students and researchers working on the more technical
side of digital audio and sound synthesis. Nor is it meant as a collection of recipes, despite the
inclusion of a body of code examples. I realize that the audience for this book will be narrowed
somewhat (and maybe a little disappointed) because of this. The reason for this is that physical
modeling synthesis is really numerical simulation, a discipline which is somewhat more removed
from audio processing than many might like to believe. There is a need, I think, to step back from
the usual techniques which have been employed for this purpose, generally those which evolved
out of the language and tools of electrical engineers, namely digital signal processing, and to take a
look at things in the way a simulation specialist might. The body of techniques is different enough
to require a good deal of mathematics which may be unfamiliar to the audio engineer. At the same
time, the audio-informed point of view taken here may seem foreign to the simulation specialist.
It is my greatest hope that this book will serve to engender curiosity in both of these groups of
people—in the ultimate interest, of course, of producing new and beautiful sounds.

Book summary

Chapter 1 is a historical overview of digital sound synthesis techniques—though far from complete,
it highlights the (sometimes overlooked) links between abstract sound synthesis methods, based
essentially on signal processing manipulations, and more modern physical modeling sound synthesis
methods, as well as the connections among the various physical modeling methodologies.

In Chapter 2, time series and difference operators are introduced, and some time is spent on the
frequency domain interpretation of such operators, as well as on certain manipulations which are of
use in energy analysis of finite difference schemes. Special attention is paid to the correspondence
between finite difference operations and simple digital filter designs.

The simple harmonic oscillator is introduced in Chapter 3, and serves as a model for many
of the systems which appear throughout the rest of the book. Various difference schemes are
analyzed, especially with respect to numerical stability and accuracy, using both frequency domain
and energetic principles; the linear loss mechanism is also introduced.

Chapter 4 introduces various nonlinear excitation mechanisms in musical acoustics, many of
which reduce to nonlinear generalizations of the harmonic oscillator, as well as associated finite
difference schemes.

Chapter 5 is designed as a reference chapter for the remainder of the book, with a complete
introduction to the tools for the construction of finite difference schemes for partial differential
equations in time and one spatial dimension, including grid functions, difference operators, as well
as a description of frequency domain techniques and inner product formulations, which are useful
for nonlinear problems and the determination of numerical boundary conditions.

As a test problem, the 1D wave equation and a variety of numerical methods are presented in
Chapter 6. Various features of interest in musical simulations, including proper settings for boundary
conditions, readout, and interpolation, numerical dispersion and its perceptual significance, and
numerical stability conditions, are discussed. In addition, finite difference schemes are related to
modal methods, digital waveguides, and lumped networks, and relative strengths and weaknesses
are evaluated.

Chapter 7 deals with more musical extensions of the 1D wave equation and finite difference
schemes to the case of transverse vibration of bars and stiff strings, and considerable time is spent
on loss modeling as well as the coupling with hammer, mallet, and bow models, and coupling
with lumped elements and between bars. The chapter ends with an extension to helical springs and
spatially varying string and bar systems.

The first serious foray into numerical methods for distributed nonlinear systems occurs in
Chapter 8, with a discussion of nonlinear string vibration. Various models, of differing degrees
of complexity, are presented, and certain important perceptual effects of string nonlinearity, such
as pitch glides, phantom partial generation, and whirling, are described and simulated. Energetic
techniques play an important role in this case.

Chapter 9 picks up from the end of Chapter 6 to deal with linear wave propagation in an
acoustic tube, which is the resonating element in woodwind and brass instruments as well as
the vocal tract. Webster's equation and finite difference methods are introduced, followed by a
treatment of the vocal tract and speech synthesis, and finally reed-based woodwind instruments.
Features of musical interest such as tonehole modeling, bell radiation, and coupling to reed-like
excitation mechanisms are covered in detail.

Chapters 10, 11, 12, and 13 are analogous to Chapters 5, 6, 7, and 8 in two spatial dimensions.
Chapter 10 is a concise survey of difference operators and grid functions in both Cartesian and
radial coordinates. Chapter 11 deals with the important test case of the 2D wave equation, and
Chapter 12 constitutes the first discussion of 2D musical instruments, based on plate vibration.
Mallet and bow interaction, plate reverberation, 2D interpolation necessary for sound output, and
direction-dependent numerical dispersion in finite difference schemes, as well as loss modeling, are
also discussed. Chapter 13 continues with the topic of plate vibration and its extension to spherical
shells, in the nonlinear case, in order to simulate perceptually crucial effects such as crashes in
percussion instruments, and, as in Chapter 8, energy methods are developed.

Appendix A contains some rudimentary Matlab scripts which yield synthetic sound output
based on many of the models discussed in this book. A glossary of symbols is provided in
Appendix B.

As teaching aid

This book could be used as a teaching aid for students at the Master's or PhD level. A strong
background in digital signal processing, physics, and computer programming is essential. Topics
in applied mathematics which are assumed prerequisites are the usual ones found in a respectable
undergraduate program in the physical sciences or engineering: differential and integral calculus
(multivariable), linear algebra, complex analysis, ordinary and partial differential equations, Fourier,
Laplace, and z transforms, and some familiarity with functional analysis and in particular the notion
of L_2 inner product spaces. For a full-year course, one could comfortably cover the part of the
book which deals mainly with linear systems, namely Chapters 2, 3, 5, 6, 7, 9, 10, 11, and 12. The
material on nonlinear systems and other topics in the remainder of the book would perhaps be best
left to a subsequent seminar-based course. The programming exercises and examples are all based
around the use of the Matlab language, which is ideal for prototyping sound synthesis algorithms
but not for practical applications; the translation of some of these algorithms to a more suitable
(perhaps real-time) environment would make for an excellent, and practically useful independent
study project.

Other reading

For those new to sound synthesis and physical modeling, there are various texts which are worth
consulting, as follows.

The physics of musical instruments is covered in the texts by Fletcher and Rossing [136],
Rossing, Moore, and Wheeler [301], Campbell and Greated [70], and, especially, the text of
Chaigne and Kergomard [78], which is at present available only in French. A more advanced, but
less musical treatment of many of the systems encountered in this book is given in the classic texts
by Morse and Ingard [244], Graff [156], and Nayfeh and Mook [252]. Many interesting aspects

of musical instrument physics are detailed in the collection edited by Hirschberg, Kergomard, and
Weinreich [173].

For a general overview of digital sound synthesis, see the books by Roads [289], Dodge and
Jerse [107], and Moore [240], and various edited collections [290, 102, 291]. Special topics in
physical modeling sound synthesis are covered in various texts. For an exhaustive presentation
of digital waveguides, see the text by Smith [334], readily available on-line, and certainly the
best reference in existence on physical modeling. Functional transformation approaches, which are
similar to modal synthesis methods, are discussed in Trautmann and Rabenstein [361]. A variety
of sound synthesis techniques, including a good deal of material on both digital waveguides and
modal methods, are found in the book by Cook [91].

A good introduction to finite difference methods is the text by Strikwerda [342], which develops
frequency domain analysis in great detail, and from a point of view that will be accessible to those
with an audio signal processing background; indeed, some of the notation used here is borrowed
from Strikwerda's book. The text of Gustaffson, Kreiss, and Oliger [161], which is written at a
more advanced level, deals with energy techniques as well. The text by Ames [8], though much
older, is an invaluable reference.

Acknowledgments

Many people made the time to read drafts of this manuscript at various stages in its development.
I owe a great debt to John Chowning, John ffitch, Miller Puckette, Davide Rocchesso, Robert
Rowe, Tommy Rushton, Stefania Serafin, Julius Smith, Vesa Välimäki, Maarten van Walstijn, and
Jim Woodhouse. The editorial staff at Wiley were as sympathetic, flexible, and professional as
always—special thanks to Nicky Skinner and Simone Taylor.

The writing of this book was greatly facilitated through the generous support of the Lever-
hulme Trust, the Engineering and Physical Sciences Research Council UK, under grant number
C007328/1, and the Consonnes project, funded by the French AIP/GNR. Thanks also to the support of my many friends and colleagues at the School of Physics and the music subject area at the
University of Edinburgh. Special thanks to Elaine Kelly, for putting up with the long hours and
general chaos that went along with writing this book; I'll soon be returning the favor.

Edinburgh, February 27, 2009

1
2
3
4
5
6
7
8
9
10
11
12
13
14
15
16
17
18
19
20
21
22
23
24
25
26
27
28
29
30
31
32
33
34
35
36
37
38
39
40
41
42
43
44
45
46
47
48
49
50
51

1

Sound synthesis and physical modeling

Before entering into the main development of this book, it is worth stepping back to get a larger picture of the history of digital sound synthesis. It is, of course, impossible to present a complete treatment of all that has come before, and unnecessary, considering that there are several books which cover the classical core of such techniques in great detail; those of Moore [240], Dodge and Jerse [107], and Roads [289], and the collections of Roads et al. [290], Roads and Strawn [291], and DePoli et al. [102], are probably the best known. For a more technical viewpoint, see the report of Tolonen, Välimäki, and Karjalainen [358], the text of Puckette [277], and, for physical modeling techniques, the review article of Välimäki et al. [376]. This chapter is intended to give the reader a basic familiarity with the development of such methods, and some of the topics will be examined in much more detail later in this book. Indeed, many of the earlier developments are perceptually intuitive, and involve only basic mathematics; this is less so in the case of physical models, but every effort will be made to keep the technical jargon in this chapter to a bare minimum.

It is convenient to make a distinction between earlier, or abstract, digital sound synthesis methods, to be introduced in Section 1.1, and those built around physical modeling principles, as detailed in Section 1.2. (Other, more elaborate taxonomies have been proposed [328, 358], but the above is sufficient for the present purposes.) That this distinction is perhaps less clear-cut than it is often made out to be is a matter worthy of discussion—see Section 1.3, where some more general comments on physical modeling sound synthesis are offered, regarding the relationship among the various physical modeling methodologies and with earlier techniques, and the fundamental limitations of computational complexity.

In Figure 1.1, for the sake of reference, a timeline showing the development of digital sound synthesis methods is presented; dates are necessarily approximate. For brevity, only those techniques which bear some relation to physical modeling sound synthesis are noted—such a restriction is a subjective one, and is surely a matter of some debate.

Numerical Sound Synthesis: Finite Difference Schemes and Simulation in Musical Acoustics   Stefan Bilbao
© 2009 John Wiley & Sons, Ltd

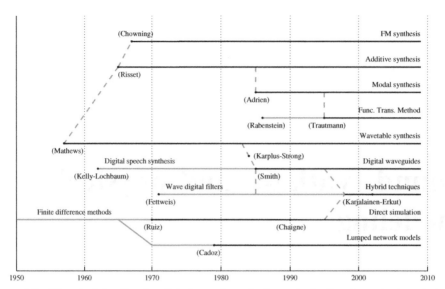

Figure 1.1   Historical timeline for digital sound synthesis methods. Sound synthesis techniques are indicated by dark lines, antecedents from outside of musical sound synthesis by solid grey lines, and links by dashed grey lines. Names of authors/inventors appear in parentheses; dates are approximate, and in some cases have been fixed here by anecdotal information rather than publication dates.

1.1   Abstract digital sound synthesis

The earliest synthesis work, beginning in the late 1950s[1], saw the development of abstract synthesis techniques, based primarily on operations which fit well into a computer programming framework: the basic components are digital oscillators, filters, and stored "lookup" tables of data, read at varying rates. Though the word "synthesis" is used here, it is important to note that in the case of tables, as mentioned above, it is of course possible to make use of non-synthetic sampled audio recordings. Nonetheless, such methods are often lumped in with synthesis itself, as are so-called analysis–synthesis methods which developed in the 1970s after the invention of the fast Fourier transform [94] some years earlier.

It would be cavalier (not to mention wrong) to assume that abstract techniques have been superseded; some are extremely computationally efficient, and form the synthesis backbone of many of the most popular music software packages, such as Max/MSP [418], Pd [276], Csound [57], SuperCollider [235], etc. Moreover, because of their reliance on accessible signal processing constructs such as tables and filters, they have entered the lexicon of the composer of electroacoustic music in a definitive way, and have undergone massive experimentation. Not surprisingly, a huge variety of hybrids and refinements have resulted; only a few of these will be detailed here.

The word "abstract," though it appears seldom in the literature [332, 358], is used to describe the techniques mentioned above because, in general, they do not possess an associated underlying physical interpretation—the resulting sounds are produced according to perceptual and mathematical, rather than physical, principles. There are some loose links with physical modeling, most notably between additive methods and modal synthesis (see Section 1.1.1), subtractive synthesis and

---

[1] Though the current state of digital sound synthesis may be traced back to work at Bell Laboratories in the late 1950s, there were indeed earlier unrelated attempts at computer sound generation, and in particular work done on the CSIRAC machine in Australia, and the Ferranti Mark I, in Manchester [109].

source-filter models (see Section 1.1.2), and wavetables and wave propagation in one-dimensional (1D) media (see Section 1.1.3), but it is probably best to think of these methods as pure constructs in digital signal processing, informed by perceptual, programming, and sometimes efficiency considerations. For more discussion of the philosophical distinctions between abstract techniques and physical modeling, see the articles by Smith [332] and Borin, DePoli, and Sarti [52].

1.1.1 Additive synthesis

Additive analysis and synthesis, which dates back at least as far as the work of Risset [285] and others [143] in the 1960s, though not the oldest digital synthesis method, is a convenient starting point; for more information on the history of the development of such methods, see [289] and [230]. A single sinusoidal oscillator with output $u(t)$ is defined, in continuous time, as

$$u(t) = A \cos(2\pi f_0 t + \phi) \qquad (1.1)$$

Here, t is a time variable, and A, f_0, and ϕ are the amplitude, frequency, and initial phase of the oscillator, respectively. In the simplest, strictest manifestation of additive synthesis, these parameters are constants: A scales roughly with perceived loudness and f_0 with pitch. For a single oscillator in isolation, the initial phase ϕ is of minimal perceptual relevance, and is usually not represented in typical symbolic representations of the oscillator—see Figure 1.2. In discrete time, where the sample rate is given by f_s, the oscillator with output u^n is defined similarly as

$$u^n = A \cos(2\pi f_0 n / f_s + \phi) \qquad (1.2)$$

where n is an integer, indicating the time step.

The sinusoidal oscillator, in computer music applications, is often represented using the symbolic shorthand shown in Figure 1.2(a). Using Fourier theory, it is possible to show that any real-valued continuous or discrete waveform (barring some technical restrictions relating to continuity) may be decomposed into an integral over a set of such sinusoids. In continuous time, if the waveform to be decomposed is periodic with period T, then an infinite sum of such sinusoids, with frequencies which are integer multiples of $1/T$, suffices to describe the waveform completely. In discrete time, if the waveform is periodic with integer period $2N$, then a finite collection of N oscillators yields a complete characterization.

The musical interest of additive synthesis, however, is not necessarily in exact decompositions of given waveforms. Rather, it is a loosely defined body of techniques based around the use

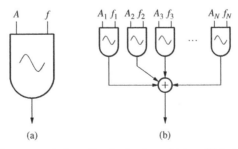

(a)   (b)

Figure 1.2 (a) Symbolic representation of a single sinusoidal oscillator, output at bottom, dependent on the parameters A, representing amplitude, and f, representing frequency. In this representation, the specification of the phase ϕ has been omitted, though some authors replace the frequency control parameter by a phase increment, and indicate the base frequency in the interior of the oscillator symbol. (b) An additive synthesis configuration, consisting of a parallel combination of N such oscillators, with parameters A_l, and f_l, $l = 1, \ldots, N$, according to (1.3).

of combinations of such oscillators in order to generate musical sounds, given the underlying
assumption that sinusoids are of perceptual relevance in music. (Some might find this debatable,
but the importance of pitch throughout the history of acoustic musical instruments across almost
all cultures favors this assertion.) A simple configuration is given, in discrete time, by the sum

$$u^n = \sum_{l=1}^{N} A_l \cos(2\pi f_l n/f_s + \phi_l) \tag{1.3}$$

where in this case N oscillators, of distinct amplitudes, frequencies, and phases A_l, f_l, and ϕ_l, for
$l = 1, \ldots, N$, are employed. See Figure 1.2(b). If the frequencies f_l are close to integer multiples
of a common "fundamental" frequency f_0, then the result will be a tone at a pitch corresponding
to f_0. But unpitched inharmonic sounds (such as those of bells) may be generated as well, through
avoidance of common factors among the chosen frequencies. With a large enough N, one can,
as mentioned above, generate any imaginable sound. But the generality of such an approach is
mitigated by the necessity of specifying up to thousands of amplitudes, frequencies, and phases. For
a large enough N, and taking the entire space of possible choices of parameters, the set of sounds
which will *not* sound simply like a steady unpitched tone is vanishingly small. Unfortunately,
using such a simple sum of sinusoids, many musically interesting sounds will certainly lie in the
realm of large N.

Various strategies (probably hundreds) have been employed to render additive synthesis more
musically tractable [310]. Certainly the most direct is to employ slowly time-varying amplitude
envelopes to the outputs of single oscillators or combinations of oscillators, allowing global control
of the attack/decay characteristics of the resulting sound without having to rely on delicate phase
cancellation phenomena. Another is to allow oscillator frequencies to vary, at sub-audio rates, so
as to approximate changes in pitch. In this case, the definition (1.1) should be extended to include
the notion of instantaneous frequency—see Section 1.1.4. For an overview of these techniques,
and others, see the standard texts mentioned in the opening remarks of this chapter.

Another related approach adopted by many composers has been that of analysis-synthesis,
based on sampled waveforms. This is not, strictly speaking, a pure synthesis technique, but it has
become so popular that it is worth mentioning here. Essentially, an input waveform is decomposed
into sinusoidal components, at which point the frequency domain data (amplitudes, phases, and
sometimes frequencies) are modified in a perceptually meaningful way, and the sound is then recon-
structed through inverse Fourier transformation. Perhaps the best known tool for analysis–synthesis
is the phase vocoder [134, 274, 108], which is based on the use of the short-time Fourier transformation, which employs the fast Fourier transformation [94]. Various effects, including pitch
transposition and time stretching, as well as cross-synthesis of spectra, can be obtained, through
judicious modification of frequency domain data. Even more refined tools, such as spectral modeling synthesis (SMS) [322], based around a combination of Fourier and stochastic modeling, as well
as methods employing tracking of sinusoidal partials [233], allow very high-quality manipulation
of audio waveforms.

1.1.2   Subtractive synthesis

If one is interested in producing sounds with rich spectra, additive synthesis, requiring a separate
oscillator for each desired frequency component, can obviously become quite a costly undertaking.
Instead of building up a complex sound, one partial at a time, another way of proceeding is
to begin with a very rich sound, typically simple to produce and lacking in character, such as
white noise or an impulse train, and then shape the spectrum using digital filtering methods. This
technique is often referred to as subtractive synthesis—see Figure 1.3. It is especially powerful
when the filtering applied is time varying, allowing for a good first approximation to musical tones
of unsteady timbre (this is generally the norm).

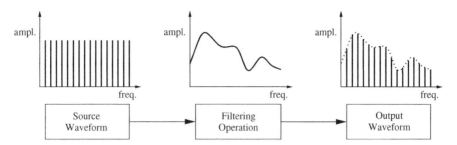

Figure 1.3 Subtractive synthesis.

Subtractive synthesis is often associated with physical models [240], but this association is a tenuous one at best.[2] What is meant is that many linear models of sound production may be broken down into source and filtering components [411]. This is particularly true of models of human speech, in which case the glottis is assumed to produce a wide-band signal (i.e., a signal somewhat like an impulse train under voiced conditions, and white noise under unvoiced conditions) which is filtered by the vocal tract, yielding a spectrum with pronounced peaks (formants) which indicate a particular vocal timbre. In this book, however, because of the emphasis on time domain methods, the source-filter methodology will not be explicitly employed. Indeed, for distributed nonlinear problems, to which frequency domain analysis is ill suited, it is of little use and relatively uninformative. Even in the linear case, it is worth keeping in mind that the connection of two objects will, in general, modify the characteristic frequencies of both—strictly speaking, one cannot invoke the notion of individual frequencies of components in a coupled system. Still, the breakdown of a system into a lumped/distributed pair representing an excitation mechanism and the instrument body is a very powerful one, even if, in some cases, the behavior of the body cannot be explained in terms of filtering concepts.

1.1.3 Wavetable synthesis

The most common computer implementation of the sinusoidal oscillator is not through direct calculation of values of the cosine or sine function, but, rather, through the use of a stored table containing values of one period of a sinusoidal waveform. A sinusoid at a given frequency may then be generated by reading through the table, circularly, at an appropriate rate. If the table contains N values, and the sample rate is f_s, then the generation of a sinusoid at frequency f_0 will require a jump of $f_s/f_0 N$ values in the table over each sample period, using interpolation of some form. Clearly, the quality of the output will depend on the number of values stored in the table, as well as on the type of interpolation employed. Linear interpolation is simple to program [240], but other more accurate methods, built around higher-order Lagrange interpolation, are also used—some material on fourth-order interpolation (in the spatial context) appears in Section 5.2.4. All-pass filter approximations to fractional delays are also possible, and are of special interest in physical modeling applications [372, 215].

It should be clear that one can store values of an arbitrary waveform in the table, not merely those corresponding to a sinusoid. See Figure 1.4. Reading through such a table at a fixed rate will generate a quasi-periodic waveform with a full harmonic spectrum, all at the price of a single table read and interpolation operation per sample period—it is no more expensive, in terms of computer arithmetic, than a single oscillator. As will be seen shortly, there is an extremely fruitful physical

---

[2] A link does exist, however, when analog synthesizer modules, often behaving according to principles of subtractive synthesis, are digitally simulated as "virtual analog" components.

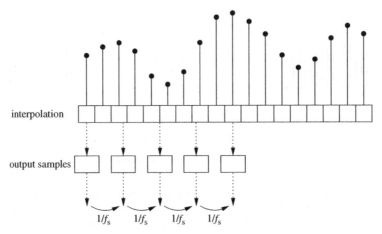

Figure 1.4 Wavetable synthesis. A buffer, filled with values, is read through at intervals of $1/f_s$ s, where f_s is the sample rate. Interpolation is employed.

interpretation of wavetable synthesis, namely the digital waveguide, which revolutionized physical modeling sound synthesis through the same efficiency gains—see Section 1.2.3. Various other variants of wavetable synthesis have seen use, such as, for example, wavetable stacking, involving multiple wavetables, the outputs of which are combined using crossfading techniques [289]. The use of tables of data in order to generate sound is perhaps the oldest form of sound synthesis, dating back to the work of Mathews in the late 1950s.

Tables of data are also associated with so-called sampling synthesis techniques, as a de facto means of data reduction. Many musical sounds consist of a short attack, followed by a steady pitched tone. Such a sound may be efficiently reproduced through storage of only the attack and a single period of the pitched part of the waveform, which is stored in a wavetable and looped [358]. Such methods are the norm in most commercial digital piano emulators.

1.1.4   AM and FM synthesis

Some of the most important developments in early digital sound synthesis derived from extensions of the oscillator, through time variation of the control parameters at audio rates.

AM, or amplitude modulation synthesis, in continuous time, and employing a sinusoidal carrier (of frequency f_0) and modulator (of frequency f_1), generates a waveform of the following form:

$$u(t) = (A_0 + A_1 \cos(2\pi f_1 t)) \cos(2\pi f_0 t)$$

where A_0 and A_1 are free parameters. The symbolic representation of AM synthesis is shown in Figure 1.5(a). Such an output consists of three components, as also shown in Figure 1.5(a), where the strength of the component at the carrier frequency is determined by A_0, and those of the side components, at frequencies $f_0 \pm f_1$, by A_1. If $A_0 = 0$, then ring modulation results. Though the above example is concerned with the product of sinusoidal signals, the concept of AM (and frequency modulation, discussed below) extends to more general signals with ease.

Frequency modulation (FM) synthesis, the result of a serendipitous discovery by John Chowning at Stanford in the late 1960s, was the greatest single breakthrough in digital sound synthesis [82]. Instantly, it became possible to generate a wide variety of spectrally rich sounds using a bare minimum of computer operations. FM synthesis requires no more computing power than a few digital oscillators, which is not surprising, considering that FM refers to the modulation

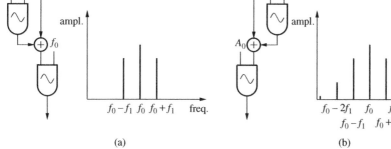

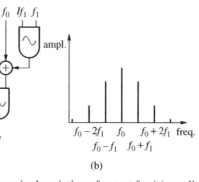

Figure 1.5   Symbolic representation and frequency domain description of output for (a) amplitude modulation and (b) frequency modulation.

of the frequency of a digital oscillator. As a result, real-time synthesis of complex sounds became possible in the late 1970s, as the technique was incorporated into various special purpose digital synthesizers—see [291] for details. In the 1980s, FM synthesis was very successfully commercialized by the Yamaha Corporation, and thereafter permanently altered the synthetic soundscape.

FM synthesis, like AM synthesis, is also a direct descendant of synthesis based on sinusoids, in the sense that in its simplest manifestation it makes use of only two sinusoidal oscillators, one behaving as a carrier and the other as a modulator. See Figure 1.5(b). The functional form of the output, in continuous time, is usually written in terms of sine functions, and not cosines, as

$$u(t) = A_0(t) \sin(2\pi f_0 t + I \sin(2\pi f_1 t)) \tag{1.4}$$

where, here, f_0 is the carrier frequency, f_1 the modulation frequency, and I the so-called modulation index. It is straightforward to show [82] that the spectrum of this signal will exhibit components at frequencies $f_0 + q f_1$, for integer q, as illustrated in Figure 1.5(b). The modulation index I determines the strengths of the various components, which can vary in a rather complicated way, depending on the values of associated Bessel functions. $A_0(t)$ can be used to control the envelope of the resulting sound.

In fact, a slightly better formulation of the output waveform (1.4) is

$$u(t) = A_0(t) \sin \left(2\pi \int_0^t f_0 + I f_1 \cos(2\pi f_1 t') dt' \right)$$

where the instantaneous frequency at time t may be seen to be (or rather defined as) $f_0 + I f_1 \cos(2\pi f_1 t)$. The quantity $I f_1$ is often referred to as the peak frequency deviation, and written as Δf [240]. Though this is a subtle point, and not one which will be returned to in this book, the symbolic representation in Figure 1.5(b) should be viewed in this respect.

FM synthesis has been exhaustively researched, and many variations have resulted. Among the most important are feedback configurations, useful in regularizing the behavior of the side component magnitudes and various series and parallel multiple oscillator combinations.

1.1.5   Other methods

There is no shortage of other techniques which have been proposed for sound synthesis; some are variations on those described in the sections above, but there are several which do not fall neatly into any one category. This is not to say that such techniques have not seen success; it is rather

that they do not fit naturally into the evolution of abstract methods into physically inspired sound
synthesis methods, the subject of this book.

One of the more interesting is a technique called waveshaping [219, 13, 288], in which case an
input waveform (of natural or synthetic origin) is used as a time-varying index to a table of data.
This, like FM synthesis, is a nonlinear technique—a sinusoid at a given frequency used as the
input will generate an output which contains a number of harmonic components, whose relative
amplitudes depend on the values stored in the table. Similar to FM, it is capable of generating rich
spectra for the computational cost of a single oscillator, accompanied by a table read; a distinction
is that there is a level of control over the amplitudes of the various partials through the use of
Chebyshev polynomial expansions as a representation of the table data.

Granular synthesis [73], which is very popular among composers, refers to a large body of
techniques, sometimes very rigorously defined (particularly when related to wavelet decompositions [120]), sometimes very loosely. In this case, the idea is to build complex textures using
short-duration sound "grains," which are either synthetic, or derived from analysis of an input waveform. The grains, regardless of how they are obtained, may then be rearranged and manipulated in
a variety of ways. Granular synthesis encompasses so many different techniques and methodologies
that it is probably better thought of as a philosophy, rather than a synthesis technique. See [287]
for a historical overview.

Distantly related to granular synthesis are methods based on overlap adding of pulses of short
duration, sometimes, but not always, to emulate vocal sounds. The pulses are of a specified form,
and depend on a number of parameters which serve to alter the timbre; in a vocal setting, the rate
at which the pulses recur determines the pitch, and a formant structure, dependent on the choice of
the free parameters, is imparted to the sound output. The best known are the so-called FOF [296]
and VOSIM [186] techniques.

1.2   Physical modeling

The algorithms mentioned above, despite their structural elegance and undeniable power, share
several shortcomings. The issue of actual sound quality is difficult to address directly, as it is
inherently subjective—it is difficult to deny, however, that in most cases abstract sound synthesis
output is synthetic sounding. This can be desirable or not, depending on one's taste. On the other
hand, it is worth noting that perhaps the most popular techniques employed by today's composers
are based on modification and processing of sampled sound, indicating that the natural quality of
acoustically produced sound is not easily abandoned. Indeed, many of the earlier refinements of
abstract techniques such as FM were geared toward emulating acoustic instrument sounds [241,
317]. The deeper issue, however, is one of control. Some of the algorithms mentioned above, such
as additive synthesis, require the specification of an inordinate amount of data. Others, such as FM
synthesis, involve many fewer parameters, but it can be extremely difficult to determine rules for
the choice and manipulation of parameters, especially in a complex configuration involving more
than a few such oscillators. See [53, 52, 358] for a fuller discussion of the difficulties inherent in
abstract synthesis methods.

Physical modeling synthesis, which has developed more recently, involves a physical description of the musical instrument as the starting point for algorithm design. For most musical
instruments, this will be a coupled set of partial differential equations, describing, for example, the
displacement of a string, membrane, bar, or plate, or the motion of the air in a tube, etc. The idea,
then, is to solve the set of equations, invariably through a numerical approximation, to yield an
output waveform, subject to some input excitation (such as glottal vibration, bow or blowing pressure, a hammer strike, etc.). The issues mentioned above, namely those of the synthetic character

and control of sounds, are rather neatly sidestepped in this case—there is a virtual copy of the musical instrument available to the algorithm designer or performer, embedded in the synthesis algorithm itself, which serves as a reference. For instance, simulating the plucking of a guitar string at a given location may be accomplished by sending an input signal to the appropriate location in computer memory, corresponding to an actual physical location on the string model; plucking it strongly involves sending a larger signal. The control parameters, for a physical modeling sound synthesis algorithm, are typically few in number, and physically and intuitively meaningful, as they relate to material properties, instrument geometry, and input forces and pressures.

The main drawback to using physical modeling algorithms is, and has been, their relatively large computational expense; in many cases, this amounts to hundreds if not thousands of arithmetic operations to be carried out per sample period, at a high audio sample rate (such as 44.1 kHz). In comparison, a bank of six FM oscillators will require probably at most 20 arithmetic operations/table lookups per sample period. For this reason, research into such methods has been slower to take root, even though the first such work on musical instruments began with Ruiz in the late 1960s and early 1970s [305], and digital speech synthesis based on physical models can be dated back even further, to the work of Kelly and Lochbaum [201]. On the other hand, computer power has grown enormously in the past decades, and presumably will continue to do so, thus efficiency (an obsession in the earlier days of digital sound synthesis) will become less and less of a concern.

1.2.1 Lumped mass–spring networks

The use of a lumped network, generally of mechanical elements such as masses and springs, as a musical sound synthesis construct, is an intuitively appealing one. It was proposed by Cadoz [66], and Cadoz, Luciani, and Florens in the late 1970s and early 1980s [67], and became the basis for the CORDIS and CORDIS-ANIMA synthesis environments [138, 68, 349]; as such, it constituted the first large-scale attempt at physical modeling sound synthesis. It is also the technique which is most similar to the direct simulation approaches which appear throughout the remainder of this book, though the emphasis here is entirely on fully distributed modeling, rather than lumped representations.

The framework is very simply described in terms of interactions among lumped masses, connected by springs and damping elements; when Newton's laws are employed to describe the inertial behavior of the masses, the dynamics of such a system may be described by a set of ordinary differential equations. Interaction may be introduced through so-called "conditional links," which can represent nonlinear contact forces. Time integration strategies, similar to those introduced in Chapter 3 in this book, operating at the audio sample rate (or sometimes above, in order to reduce frequency warping effects), are employed in order to generate sound output. The basic operation of this method will be described in more detail in Section 3.4.

A little imagination might lead one to guess that, with a large enough collection of interconnected masses, a distributed object such as a string, as shown in Figure 1.6(a), or membrane, as shown in Figure 1.6(b), may be modeled. Such configurations will be treated explicitly in Section 6.1.1 and Section 11.5, respectively. A rather large philosophical distinction between the CORDIS framework and that described here is that one can develop lumped networks which are, in a sense, only quasi-physical, in that they do not correspond to recognizable physical objects, though the physical underpinnings of Newton's laws remain. See Figure 1.6(c). Accurate simulation of complex distributed systems has not been a major concern of the designers of CORDIS; rather, the interest is in user issues such as the modularity of lumped network structures, and interaction through external control. In short, it is best to think of CORDIS as a system designed for artists and composers, rather than scientists—which is not a bad thing!

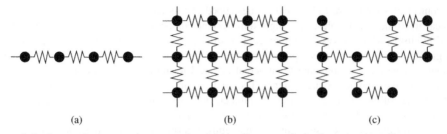

(a)   (b)   (c)

Figure 1.6   Lumped mass–spring networks: (a) in a linear configuration corresponding to a model of a lossless string; (b) in a 2D configuration corresponding to a model of a lossless membrane; and (c) an unstructured network, without a distributed interpretation.

1.2.2   Modal synthesis

A different approach, with a long history of use in physical modeling sound synthesis, is based on a frequency domain, or modal description of vibration of distributed objects. Modal synthesis [5, 4, 242], as it is called, is attractive, in that the complex dynamic behavior of a vibrating object may be decomposed into contributions from a set of modes (the spatial forms of which are eigenfunctions of the given problem at hand, and are dependent on boundary conditions). Each such mode oscillates at a single complex frequency. (For real-valued problems, these complex frequencies will occur in complex conjugate pairs, and the "mode" may be considered to be the pair of such eigenfunctions and frequencies.) Considering the particular significance of sinusoids in human audio perception, such a decomposition can lead to useful insights, especially in terms of sound synthesis. Modal synthesis forms the basis of the MOSAIC [242] and Modalys [113] sound synthesis software packages, and, along with CORDIS, was one of the first such comprehensive systems to make use of physical modeling principles. More recently, various researchers, primarily Rabenstein and Trautmann, have developed a related method, called the functional transformation method (FTM) [361], which uses modal techniques to derive point-to-point transfer functions. Sound synthesis applications of FTM are under development. Independently, Hélie and his associates at IRCAM have developed a formalism suitable for broad nonlinear generalizations of modal synthesis, based around the use of Volterra series approximations [303, 117]. Such methods include FTM as a special case. An interesting general viewpoint on the relationship between time and frequency domain methods is given by Rocchesso [292].

A physical model of a musical instrument, such as a vibrating string or membrane, may be described in terms of two sets of data: (1) the PDE system itself, including all information about material properties and geometry, and associated boundary conditions; and (2) excitation information, including initial conditions and/or an excitation function and location, and readout location(s). The basic modal synthesis strategy is as outlined in Figure 1.7. The first set of information is used, in an initial off-line step, to determine modal shapes and frequencies of vibration; this involves, essentially, the solution of an eigenvalue problem, and may be performed in a variety of ways. (In the functional transformation approach, this is referred to as the solution of a Sturm–Liouville problem [361].) This information must be stored, the modal shapes themselves in a so-called shape matrix. Then, the second set of information is employed: the initial conditions and/or excitation are expanded onto the set of modal functions (which under some conditions form an orthogonal set) through an inner product, giving a set of weighting coefficients. The weighted combination of modal functions then evolves, each at its own natural frequency. In order to obtain a sound output at a given time, the modal functions are projected (again through inner products) onto an observation state, which, in the simplest case, is of the form of a delta function at a given location on the object.

Though modal synthesis is often called a "frequency domain" method, this is not quite a correct description of its operation, and is worth clarifying. Temporal Fourier transforms are not

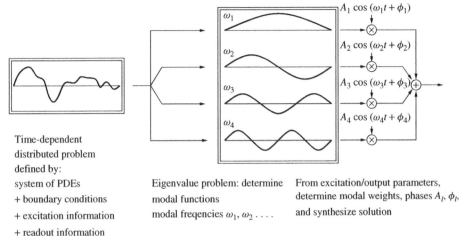

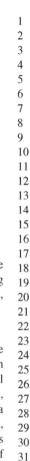

Time-dependent
distributed problem
defined by:

system of PDEs	Eigenvalue problem: determine	From excitation/output parameters,
+ boundary conditions	modal functions	determine modal weights, phases A_l, ϕ_l,
+ excitation information	modal freqencies $\omega_1, \omega_2 \ldots$	and synthesize solution
+ readout information		

Figure 1.7 Modal synthesis. The behavior of a linear, distributed, time-dependent problem can be decomposed into contributions from various modes, each of which possesses a particular vibrating frequency. Sound output may be obtained through a precise recombination of such frequencies, depending on excitation and output parameters.

employed, and the output waveform is generated directly in the time domain. Essentially, each mode is described by a scalar second-order ordinary differential equation, and various time-integration techniques (some of which will be described in Chapter 3) may be employed to obtain a numerical solution. In short, it is better to think of modal synthesis not as a frequency domain method, but rather as a numerical method for a linear problem which has been diagonalized (to borrow a term from state space analysis [101]). As such, in contrast with a direct time domain approach, the state itself is not observable directly, except through reversal of the diagonalization process (i.e., the projection operation mentioned above). This lack of direct observability has a number of implications in terms of multiple channel output, time variation of excitation and readout locations, and, most importantly, memory usage. Modal synthesis continues to develop—for recent work, see, e.g., [51, 64, 380, 35, 416].

Modal synthesis techniques will crop up at various points in this book, in a general way toward the end of this chapter, and in more technical detail in Chapters 6 and 11.

1.2.3 Digital waveguides

Physical modeling sound synthesis is, to say the least, computationally very intensive. Compared to earlier methods, and especially FM synthesis, which requires only a handful of operations per clock cycle, physical modeling methods may need to make use of hundreds or thousands of such operations per sample period in order to create reasonably complex musical timbres. Physical modeling sound synthesis, 20 years ago, was a distinctly off-line activity.

In the mid 1980s, however, with the advent of digital waveguide methods [334] due to Julius Smith, all this changed. These algorithms, with their roots in digital filter design and scattering theory, and closely allied to wave digital filters [127], offered a convenient solution to the problem of computational expense for a certain class of musical instrument, in particular those whose vibrating parts can be modeled as 1D linear media described, to a first approximation, by the wave equation. Among these may be included many stringed instruments, as well as most woodwind and brass instruments. In essence, the idea is very simple: the motion of such a medium may be

modeled as two traveling non-interacting waves, and in the digital simulation this is dealt with
elegantly by using two "directional" delay lines, which require no computer arithmetic at all!
Digital waveguide techniques have formed the basis for at least one commercial synthesizer (the
Yamaha VL1), and serve as modular components in many of the increasingly common software
synthesis packages (such as Max/MSP [418], STK [92], and Csound [57]). Now, some 20 years
on, they are considered the state of the art in physical modeling synthesis, and the basic design has
been complemented by a great number of variations intended to deal with more realistic effects
(discussed below), usually through more elaborate digital filtering blocks. Digital waveguides will
not be covered in depth in this book, mainly because there already exists a large literature on this
topic, including a comprehensive and perpetually growing monograph by Smith himself [334].
The relationship between digital waveguides and more standard time domain numerical methods
has been addressed by various authors [333, 191, 41], and will be revisited in some detail in
Section 6.2.11. A succinct overview is given in [330] and [290].

The path to the invention of digital waveguides is an interesting one, and is worth elab-
orating here. In approximately 1983 (or earlier, by some accounts), Karplus and Strong [194]
developed an efficient algorithm for generating musical tones strongly resembling those of strings,
which was almost immediately noticed and subsequently extended by Jaffe and Smith [179]. The
Karplus–Strong structure is no more than a delay line, or wavetable, in a feedback configuration,
in which data is recirculated; usually, the delay line is initialized with random numbers, and is
terminated with a low-order digital filter, normally with a low-pass characteristic—see Figure 1.8.
Tones produced in this way are spectrally rich, and exhibit a decay which is indeed characteristic
of plucked string tones, due to the terminating filter. The pitch is determined by the delay-line
length and the sample rate: for an N-sample delay line, as pictured in Figure 1.8, with an audio
sample rate of f_s Hz, the pitch of the tone produced will be at f_s/N, though fine-grained pitch
tuning may be accomplished through interpolation, just as in the case of wavetable synthesis. In
all, the only operations required in a computer implementation are the digital filter additions and
multiplications, and the shifting of data in the delay line. The computational cost is on the order
of that of a single oscillator, yet instead of producing a single frequency, Karplus–Strong yields
an entire harmonic series. The Karplus–Strong plucked string synthesis algorithm is an abstract
synthesis technique, in that in its original formulation, though the sounds produced resembled those
of plucked strings, there was no immediate physical interpretation offered.

There are two important conceptual steps leading from the Karplus–Strong algorithm to a
digital waveguide structure. The first is to associate a spatial position with the values in the
wavetable—in other words, a wavetable has a given physical length. The other is to show that the
values propagated in the delay lines behave as individual traveling wave solutions to the 1D wave
equation; only their sum is a physical variable (such as displacement, pressure, etc.). See Figure 1.9.
The link between the Karplus–Strong algorithm and digital waveguide synthesis, especially in the
"single-delay-loop" form, is elaborated by Karjalainen et al. [193]. Excitation elements, such as
bows, hammer interactions, reeds, etc., are usually modeled as lumped, and are connected to
waveguides via scattering junctions, which are, essentially, power-conserving matrix operations
(more will be said about scattering methods in the next section). The details of the scattering

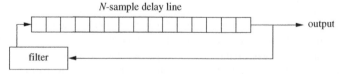

Figure 1.8 The Karplus–Strong plucked string synthesis algorithm. An N-sample delay line
is initialized with random values, which are allowed to recirculate, while undergoing a filtering
operation.

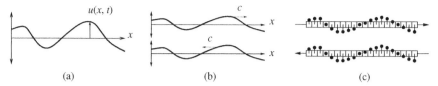

Figure 1.9   The solution to the 1D wave equation, (a), may be decomposed into a pair of traveling wave solutions, which move to the left and right at a constant speed c determined by the system under consideration, as shown in (b). This constant speed of propagation leads immediately to a discrete-time implementation employing delay lines, as shown in (c).

operation will be very briefly covered here in Section 3.3.3, Section 9.2.4, and Section 11.4. These were the two steps taken initially by Smith in work on bowed strings and reed instruments [327], though it is important to note the link with earlier work by McIntyre and Woodhouse [237], and McIntyre, Schumacher, and Woodhouse [236], which was also concerned with efficient synthesis algorithms for these same systems, though without an explicit use of delay-line structures.

Waveguide models have been successfully applied to a multitude of systems; several representative configurations are shown in Figure 1.10.

String vibration has seen a lot of interest, probably due to the relationship between waveguides and the Karplus–Strong algorithm. As shown in Figure 1.10(a), the basic picture is of a pair of waveguides separated by a scattering junction connecting to an excitation mechanism, such as a hammer or plectrum; at either end, the structure is terminated by digital filters which model boundary terminations, or potentially coupling to a resonator or other strings. The output is read from a point along the waveguide, through a sum of wave variables traveling in opposite directions. Early work was due to Smith [333] and others. In recent years, the Acoustics Group at the Helsinki University of Technology has systematically tackled a large variety of stringed instruments using digital waveguides, yielding sound synthesis of extremely high quality. Some of the target instruments have been standard instruments such as the harpsichord [377], guitar [218], and clavichord [375], but more exotic instruments, such as the Finnish kantele [117, 269], have been approached as well. There has also been a good deal of work on the extension of digital waveguides to deal with the special "tension modulation," or pitch glide nonlinearity in string vibration [378, 116, 359], a topic which will be taken up in great detail in Section 8.1. Some more recent related areas of activity have included banded waveguides [118, 119], which are designed to deal with systems with a high degree of inharmonicity, commuted synthesis techniques [331, 120], which allow for the interconnection of string models with harder-to-model resonators, through the introduction of sampled impulse responses, and the association of digital waveguide methods with underlying PDE models of strings [33, 34].

Woodwind and brass instruments are also well modeled by digital waveguides; a typical waveguide configuration is shown in Figure 1.10(b), where a digital waveguide is broken up by scattering junctions connected to models of (in the case of woodwind instruments) toneholes. At one end, the waveguide is connected to an excitation mechanism, such as a lip or reed model, and at the other end, output is taken after processing by a filter representing bell and radiation effects. Early work was carried out by Smith, for reed instruments [327], and for brass instruments by Cook [89]. Work on tonehole modeling has appeared [314, 112, 388], sometimes involving wave digital filter implementations [391], and efficient digital waveguide models for conical bores have also been developed [329, 370].

Vocal tract modeling using digital waveguides was first approached by Cook [88, 90]; see Figure 1.10(c). Here, due to the spatial variation of the cross-sectional area of the vocal tract, multiple waveguide segments, separated by scattering junctions, are necessary. The model is driven at one end by a glottal model, and output is taken from the other end after filtering to simulate

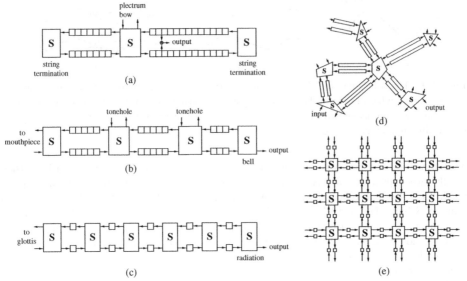

Figure 1.10 Typical digital waveguide configurations for musical sound synthesis. In all cases, boxes marked **S** represent scattering operations. (a) A simple waveguide string model, involving an excitation at a point along the string and terminating filters, and output read from a point along the string length; (b) a woodwind model, with scattering at tonehole junctions, input from a reed model at the left end and output read from the right end; (c) a similar vocal tract configuration, involving scattering at junctions between adjacent tube segments of differing cross-sectional areas; (d) an unstructured digital waveguide network, suitable for quasi-physical artificial reverberation; and (e) a regular waveguide mesh, modeling wave propagation in a 2D structure such as a membrane.

radiation effects. Such a model is reminiscent of the Kelly–Lochbaum speech synthesis model [201], which in fact predates the appearance of digital waveguides altogether, and can be calibrated using linear predictive techniques [280] and wave digital speech synthesis models [343]. The Kelly–Lochbaum model appears here in Section 9.2.4.

Networks of digital waveguides have also been used in a quasi-physical manner in order to effect artificial reverberation—in fact, this was the original application of the technique [326]. In this case, a collection of waveguides of varying impedances and delay lengths is used; such a network is shown in Figure 1.10(d). Such networks are passive, so that signal energy injected into the network from a dry source signal will produce an output whose amplitude will gradually attenuate, with frequency-dependent decay times governed by the delays and immittances of the various waveguides—some of the delay lengths can be interpreted as implementing "early reflections" [326]. Such networks provide a cheap and stable way of generating rich impulse responses. Generalizations of waveguide networks to feedback delay networks (FDNs) [293, 184] and circulant delay networks [295] have also been explored, also with an eye toward applications in digital reverberation. When a waveguide network is constructed in a regular arrangement, in two or three spatial dimensions, it is often referred to as a waveguide mesh [384–386, 41]—see Figure 1.10(e). In 2D, such structures may be used to model the behavior of membranes [216] or for vocal tract simulation [246], and in 3D, potentially for full-scale room acoustics simulation (i.e., for artificial reverberation), though real-time implementations of such techniques are probably decades away. Some work on the use of waveguide meshes for the calculation of room impulse responses has recently been done [28, 250]. The waveguide mesh is briefly covered here in Section 11.4.

1.2.4 Hybrid methods

Digital waveguides are but one example of a scattering-based numerical method [41], for which the underlying variables propagated are of wave type, which are reflected and transmitted throughout a network by power-conserving scattering junctions (which can be viewed, under some conditions, as orthogonal matrix transformations). Such methods have appeared in various guises across a wide range of (often non-musical) disciplines. The best known is the transmission line matrix method [83, 174], or TLM, which is popular in the field of electromagnetic field simulation, and dates back to the early 1970s [182], but multidimensional extensions of wave digital filters [127, 126] intended for numerical simulation have also been proposed [131, 41]. Most such designs are based on electrical circuit network models, and make use of scattering concepts borrowed from microwave filter design [29]; their earliest roots are in the work of Kron in the 1940s [211].

Scattering-based methods also play a role in standard areas of signal processing, such as inverse estimation [63], fast factorization and inversion of structured matrices [188], and linear prediction [280] for speech signals (leading directly to the Kelly–Lochbaum speech synthesis model, which is a direct antecedent to digital waveguide synthesis).

In the musical sound synthesis community, scattering methods, employing wave (sometimes called "W"), variables are sometimes viewed [54] in opposition to methods which employ physical (correspondingly called "K," for Kirchhoff) variables, such as lumped networks, and, as will be mentioned shortly, direct simulation techniques, which are employed in the vast majority of simulation applications in the mainstream world. In recent years, moves have been made toward modularizing physical modeling [376]; instead of simulating the behavior of a single musical object, such as a string or tube, the idea is to allow the user to interconnect various predefined objects in any way imaginable. In many respects, this is the same point of view as that of those working on lumped network models—this is reflected by the use of hybrid or "mixed" K–W methods, i.e., methods employing both scattering methods, such as wave digital filters and digital waveguides, and finite difference modules (typically lumped) [191, 190, 383]. See Figure 1.11. In some situations, particularly those involving the interconnection of physical "modules," representing various separate portions of a whole instrument, the wave formulation may be preferable, in that there is a clear means of dealing with the problem of non-computability, or delay-free loops—the concept of the reflection-free wave port, introduced by Fettweis long ago in the context of digital filter design [130], can be fruitfully employed in this case. The automatic generation of recursive structures, built around the use of wave digital filters, is a key component of such methods [268], and can be problematic when multiple nonlinearities are present, requiring specialized design procedures [309]. One result of this work has been a modular software system for physical modeling sound synthesis, incorporating elements of both types, called BlockCompiler [189]. More recently the scope of such methods has been hybridized even further through the incorporation of functional transformation (modal) methods into the same framework [270, 279].

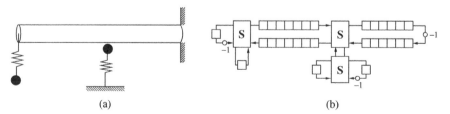

(a)   (b)

Figure 1.11 (a) A distributed system, such as a string, connected with various lumped elements, and (b) a corresponding discrete scattering network. Boxes marked **S** indicate scattering operations.

1.2.5   Direct numerical simulation

Digital waveguides and related scattering methods, as well as modal techniques, have undeniably become a very popular means of designing physical modeling sound synthesis algorithms. There are several reasons for this, but the main one is that such structures, built from delay lines, digital filters, and Fourier decompositions, fit naturally into the framework of digital signal processing, and form an extension of more abstract techniques from the pre-physical modeling synthesis era—note, for instance, the direct link between modal synthesis and additive synthesis, as well as that between digital waveguides and wavetable synthesis, via the Karplus–Strong algorithm. Such a body of techniques, with linear system theory at its heart, is home turf to the trained audio engineer. See Section 1.3.1 for more comments on the relationship between abstract methods and physical modeling sound synthesis.

For some time, however, a separate body of work in the simulation of musical instruments has grown; this work, more often than not, has been carried out by musical acousticians whose primary interest is not so much synthesis, but rather the pure study of the behavior of musical instruments, often with an eye toward comparison between a model equation and measured data, and possibly potential applications toward improved instrument design. The techniques used by such researchers are of a very different origin, and are couched in a distinct language; as will be seen throughout the rest of this book, however, there is no shortage of links to be made with more standard physical modeling sound synthesis techniques, provided one takes the time to "translate" between the sets of terminology! In this case, one speaks of time stepping and grid resolution; there is no reference to delays or digital filters and, sometimes, the frequency domain is not invoked at all, which is unheard of in the more standard physical modeling sound synthesis setting.

The most straightforward approach makes use of a *finite difference approximation* to a set of partial differential equations [342, 161, 284], which serves as a mathematical model of a musical instrument. (When applied to dynamic, or time-dependent systems, such techniques are sometimes referred to as "finite difference time domain" (FDTD) methods, a terminology which originated in numerical methods for the simulation of electromagnetics [351, 412, 352].) Such methods have a very long history in applied mathematics, which can be traced back at least as far as the work of Courant, Friedrichs, and Lewy in 1928 [95], especially as applied to the simulation of fluid dynamics [171] and electromagnetics [351]. Needless to say, the literature on finite difference methods is vast. As mentioned above, they have been applied for some time for sound synthesis purposes, though definitely without the success or widespread acceptance of methods such as

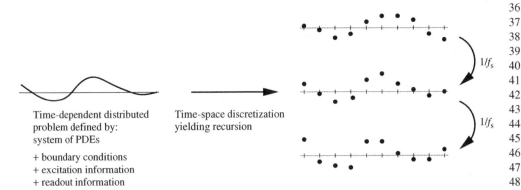

Figure 1.12   Direct simulation via finite differences. A distributed problem (at left) is discretized in time and space, yielding a recursion over a finite set of values (at right), to be updated with a given time step (usually corresponding to the inverse of the audio sample rate f_s).

digital waveguides, primarily because of computational cost—or, rather, preconceived notions about computational cost—relative to other methods.

The procedure, which is similar across all types of systems, is very simply described: the spatial domain of a continuous system, described by some model PDE, is restricted to a grid composed of a finite set of points (see Figure 1.12), at which values of a numerical solution are computed. Time is similarly discretized, and the numerical solution is advanced, through a recursion derived from the model PDE. Derivatives are approximated by differences between values at nearby grid points. The great advantage of finite difference methods, compared to other time domain techniques, is their generality and simplicity, and the wide range of systems to which they may be applied, including strongly nonlinear distributed systems; these cannot be readily approached using waveguides or modal synthesis, and by lumped models only in a very ad hoc manner. The primary disadvantage is that one must pay great attention to the problem of numerical instability—indeed numerical stability, and the means for ensuring it in sound synthesis algorithms, is one of the subjects that will be dealt with in depth in this book. Computational cost is an issue, but no more so than in any other synthesis method (with the exception of digital waveguides), and so cannot be viewed as a disadvantage of finite difference methods in particular.[3]

The most notable early finite difference sound synthesis work was concerned with string vibration, dating back to the work of Ruiz in 1969 [305] and others [169, 170, 19, 58]. Another very important contribution, in the context of vocal tract modeling and speech synthesis, was due to Portnoff [273]. The first truly sophisticated use of finite difference methods for musical sound synthesis was due to Chaigne in the case of plucked string instruments [74] and piano string vibration [75, 76]; this latter work has been expanded by others [232, 33], and extended considerably by Giordano through connection to a soundboard model [152, 154]. Finite difference methods have also been applied to various percussion instruments, including those based on vibrating membranes [139] (i.e., for drum heads), such as kettledrums [283], stiff vibrating bars such as those used in xylophones [77, 110] (i.e., for xylophones), and plates [79, 316]. Finite difference schemes for nonlinear musical systems, such as strings and plates, have been treated by this author [50, 42] and others [23, 22, 24]. Sophisticated difference scheme approximations to lumped nonlinearities in musical sound synthesis (particularly in the case of excitation mechanisms and contact problems) have been investigated [15, 282, 319] under the remit of the Sounding Object project [294]. A useful text, which employs finite difference methods (among other techniques) in the context of musical acoustics of wind instruments, is that of Kausel [196].

Finite difference methods, in the mainstream engineering world, are certainly the oldest method of designing a computer simulation. They are simply programmed, generally quite efficient, and there is an exhaustive literature on the subject. Best of all, in many cases they are sufficient for high-quality physical modeling sound synthesis. For the above reasons, they will form the core of this book. On the other hand, time domain simulation has undergone many developments, and some of these will be discussed in this book. Perhaps best known, particularly to mechanical engineers, is the finite element method (FEM) [121, 93] which also has long roots in simulation, but crystallized into its modern form some time in the 1960s. The theory behind FEM is somewhat different from finite differences, in that the deflection of a vibrating object is modeled in terms of so-called shape functions, rather than in terms of values at a given set of grid points. The biggest

---

[3] "Time domain" is often used in a slightly different sense than that intended here, at least in the musical acoustics/sound synthesis literature. The distinction goes back to the seminal treatment of McIntyre et al. [236], who arrived at a formulation suitable for a wide variety of musical instruments, where the instrument is considered to be made up of a lumped nonlinear excitation (such as a bow, reed, air jet, or a pair of lips) connected to a linear resonator. The resonator, assumed linear and time invariant, is completely characterized by its impulse response. As such, physical space disappears from the formulation entirely; the resonator is viewed in an input–output sense, and it is assumed that its impulse response is somehow available (it may be measured or calculated in a variety of ways). For time–space finite difference schemes, however, this is not the case. The spatial extent of the musical instrument is explicitly represented, and no impulse response is computed or employed.

benefit of FEMs is the ease with which relatively complex geometries may be modeled; this is of great interest for model validation in musical acoustics. In the end, however, the computational procedure is quite similar to that of finite difference schemes, involving a recursion of a finite set of values representing the state of the object. FEMs are briefly introduced on page 386. Various researchers, [20, 283] have applied finite element methods to problems in musical acoustics, though generally not for synthesis.

A number of other techniques have developed more recently, which could be used profitably for musical sound synthesis. Perhaps the most interesting are so-called spectral or pseudospectral methods [364, 141]—see page 388 for an overview. Spectral methods, which may be thought of, crudely speaking, as limiting cases of finite difference schemes, allow for computation with extreme accuracy, and, like finite difference methods, are well suited to problems in regular geometries. They have not, at the time of writing, found use in physical modeling applications, but could be a good match—indeed, modal synthesis is an example of a very simple Fourier-based spectral method.

For linear musical systems, and some distributed nonlinear systems, finite difference schemes (among other time domain methods) have a state space interpretation [187], which is often referred to, in the context of stability analysis, as the "matrix method" [342]. Matrix analysis/state space techniques will be discussed at various points in this book (see, e.g., Section 6.2.8). State space methods have seen some application in musical sound synthesis, though not through finite difference approximations [101].

1.3   Physical modeling: a larger view

This is a good point to step back and examine some global constraints on physical modeling sound synthesis, connections among the various existing methods and with earlier abstract techniques, and to address some philosophical questions about the utility of such methods.

1.3.1   Physical models as descended from abstract synthesis

Among the most interesting observations one can make about some (but not all) physical modeling methods is their relationship to abstract methods, which is somewhat deeper than it might appear to be. Abstract techniques, especially those described in Section 1.1, set the stage for many later developments, and determine some of the basic building blocks for synthesis, as well as the accompanying notation, which is derived from digital signal processing. This influence has had its advantages and disadvantages, as will be detailed below.

As mentioned earlier, digital waveguides, certainly the most successful physical modeling technique to date, can be thought of as a physical interpretation of wavetable synthesis in a feedback configuration. Even more important than the direct association between a lossless string and a wavetable was the recognition that systems with a low degree of inharmonicity could be efficiently modeled using a pair of delay lines terminated by lumped low-order digital filters—this effectively led the way to efficient synthesis algorithms for many 1D musical systems producing pitched tones. No such efficient techniques have been reported for similar systems in the mainstream literature, and it is clear that such efficiency gains were made possible only by association with abstract synthesis methods (and digital signal processing concepts in particular) and through an appreciation of the importance of human auditory perception to the resulting sound output. On the other hand, such lumped modeling of effects such as loss and inharmonicity is also a clear departure from physicality; this is also true of newer developments such as banded waveguides and commuted synthesis.

Similarly, modal synthesis may be viewed as a direct physical interpretation of additive synthesis; a modal interpretation (like that of any physical model) has the advantage of drastically reducing the amount of control information which must be supplied. On the other hand, it is restrictive in the sense that, with minor exceptions, it may only be applied usefully to linear and time-invariant systems, which is a side effect of a point of view informed by Fourier decomposition.

As mentioned above, there is not always a direct link between abstract and physical modeling techniques. Lumped network models and direct simulation methods, unlike the other techniques mentioned above, have distinct origins in numerical solution techniques and not in digital signal processing. Those working on hybrid methods have gone a long way toward viewing such methods in terms of abstract synthesis concepts [279, 191]. Similarly, there is not a strong physical interpretation of abstract techniques such as FM (see, though, [403] for a different opinion) or granular synthesis.

1.3.2   Connections: direct simulation and other methods

Because direct simulation methods are, in fact, the subject of this book, it is worth saying a few words about the correspondence with various other physical modeling methods. Indeed, after some exposure to these methods, it becomes clear that all can be related to one another and to mainstream simulation methods.

Perhaps the closest relative of direct techniques is the lumped mass–spring network methodology [67]; in some ways, this is more general than direct simulation approaches for distributed systems, in that one could design a lumped network without a distributed counterpart—this could indeed be attractive to a composer. As a numerical method, however, it operates as a large ordinary differential equation solver, which puts it in line with various simulation techniques based on semi-discretization, such as FEMs. As mentioned in Section 1.2.1, distributed systems may be dealt with through large collections of lumped elements, and in this respect the technique differs considerably from purely distributed models based on the direct solution of PDEs, because it can be quite cumbersome to design more sophisticated numerical methods, and to deal with systems more complex than a simple linear string or membrane using a lumped approach. The main problem is the "local" nature of connections in such a network; in more modern simulation approaches (such as, for example, spectral methods [364]), approximations at a given point in a distributed system are rarely modeled using nearest-neighbor connections between grid variables. From the distributed point of view, network theory may be dispensed with entirely. Still, it is sometimes possible to view the integration of lumped network systems in terms of distributed finite difference schemes—see Section 6.1.1 and Section 11.5 for details.

It should also come as no surprise that digital waveguide methods may also be rewritten as finite difference schemes. It is interesting that although the exact discrete traveling wave solution to the 1D wave equation has been known in the mainstream simulation literature for some time (since the 1960s at least [8]), and is a direct descendant of the method of characteristics [146], the efficiency advantage was apparently not exploited to the same spectacular effect as in musical sound synthesis. (This is probably because the 1D wave equation is seen, in the mainstream world, as a model problem, and not of inherent practical interest.) Equivalences between finite differences and digital waveguide methods, in the 1D case and the multidimensional case of the waveguide mesh, have been established by various authors [384, 386, 334, 333, 41, 116, 313, 312], and, as mentioned earlier, those at work on scattering-based modular synthesis have incorporated ideas from finite difference schemes into their strategy [190, 191]. This correspondence will be revisited with regard to the 1D wave equation in Section 6.2.11 and the 2D wave equation in Section 11.4. It is worth warning the reader, at this early stage, that the efficiency advantage of the digital waveguide method with respect to an equivalent finite difference scheme does not carry over to the multidimensional case [333, 41].

Modal analysis and synthesis was in extensive use long before it debuted in musical sound synthesis applications, particularly in association with finite element analysis of vibrating structures—see [257] for an overview. In essence, a time-dependent problem, under some conditions, may be reduced to an eigenvalue problem, greatly simplifying analysis. It may also be viewed under the umbrella of more modern so-called spectral or pseudospectral methods [71], which predate modal synthesis by many years. Spectral methods essentially yield highly accurate numerical approximations through the use of various types of function approximations to the desired solution; many different varieties exist. If the solution is expressed in terms of trigonometric functions, the method is often referred to as a Fourier method—this is exactly modal synthesis in the current context. Other types of spectral methods, perhaps more appropriate for sound synthesis purposes (and in particular collocation methods), will be discussed beginning on page 388.

Modular or "hybrid" methods, though nearly always framed in terms of the language of signal processing, may also be seen as finite difference methods; the correspondence between lumped models and finite difference methods is direct, and that between wave digital filters and numerical integration formulas has been known for many years [132], and may be related directly to the even older concept of absolute- or A-stability [148, 99, 65]. The key feature of modularity, however, is new to this field, and is not something that has been explored in depth in the mainstream simulation community.

This is not the place to evaluate the relative merits of the various physical modeling synthesis methods; this will be performed exhaustively with regard to two useful model problems, the 1D and 2D wave equations, in Chapters 6 and 12, respectively. For the impatient reader, some concluding remarks on relative strengths and weaknesses of these methods appear in Chapter 14.

1.3.3   Complexity of musical systems

In the physical modeling sound synthesis literature (as well as that of the mainstream) it is commonplace to see claims of better performance of a certain numerical method over another. Performance may be measured in terms of the number of floating point operations required, or memory requirements, or, more characteristically, better accuracy for a fixed operation count. It is worth keeping in mind, however, that even though these claims are (sometimes) justified, for a given system, there are certain limits as to "how fast" or "how efficient" a simulation algorithm can be. These limits are governed by system complexity; one cannot expect to reduce an operation count for a simulation below that which is required for an adequate representation of the solution.

System complexity is, of course, very difficult to define. Most amenable to the analysis of complexity are linear and time-invariant (LTI) systems, which form a starting point for many models of musical instruments. Consider any lossless distributed LTI system (such as a string, bar, membrane, plate, or acoustic tube), freely vibrating at low amplitude due to some set of initial conditions, without any external excitation. Considering the continuous case, one is usually interested in reading an output $y(t)$ from a single location on the object. This solution can almost always[4] be written in the form

$$y(t) = \sum_{l=1}^{\infty} A_l \cos(2\pi f_l t + \phi_l) \tag{1.5}$$

which is exactly that of pure additive synthesis or modal synthesis; here, A_l and ϕ_l are determined by the initial conditions and constants which define the system, and the frequencies f_l are assumed non-negative, and to lie in an increasing order. Such a system has a countably infinite number

---

[4] The formula must be altered slightly if the frequencies are not all distinct.

of degrees of freedom; each oscillator at a given frequency f_l requires the specification of two numbers, A_l and ϕ_l.

Physical modeling algorithms generally produce sound output at a given sample rate, say f_s. This is true of all the methods discussed in the previous section. There is thus no hope of (and no need for) simulating frequency components[5] which lie above $f_s/2$. Thus, as a prelude to a discrete-time implementation, the representation (1.5) may be truncated to

$$y(t) = \sum_{l=1}^{N} A_l \cos(2\pi f_l t + \phi_l) \tag{1.6}$$

where only the N frequencies f_1 to f_N are less than $f_s/2$. Thus the number of degrees of freedom is now finite: $2N$. Even for a vaguely defined system such as this, from this information one may go slightly farther and calculate both the operation count and memory requirements, assuming a modal-type synthesis strategy. As described in Section 1.2.2, each frequency component in the expression (1.5) may be computed using a single two-pole digital oscillator, which requires two additions, one multiplication, and two memory locations, giving, thus, $2N$ additions and N multiplications per time step and a necessary $2N$ units of memory. Clearly, if fewer than N oscillators are employed, the resulting simulation will not be complete, and the use of more than N oscillators is superfluous. Not surprisingly, such a measure of complexity is not restricted to frequency domain methods only; in fact, *any* method (including direct simulation methods such as finite differences and FEMs) for computing the solution to such a system must require roughly the same amount of memory and number of operations; for time domain methods, complexity is intimately related to conditions for numerical stability. Much more will be said about this in Chapters 6 and 11, which deal with time domain and modal solutions for the wave equation.

There is, however, at least one very interesting exception to this rule. Consider the special case of a system for which the modal frequencies are multiples of a common frequency f_1, i.e., in (1.5), $f_l = lf_1$. In this case, (1.5) is a Fourier series representation of a periodic waveform, of period $T = 1/f_1$, or, in other words,

$$y(t) = y(t - T)$$

The waveform is thus completely characterized by a single period of duration T. In a discrete setting, it is obvious that it would be wasteful to employ separate oscillators for each of the components of $y(t)$; far better would be to simply store one period of the waveform in a table, and read through it at the appropriate rate, employing simple interpolation, at a cost of $O(1)$ operations per time step instead of $O(N)$. Though this example might seem trivial, it is worth keeping in mind that many pitched musical sounds are approximately of this form, especially those produced by musical instruments based on strings and acoustic tubes. The efficiency gain noted above is at the heart of the digital waveguide synthesis technique. Unfortunately, however, for musical sounds which do not generate harmonic spectra, there does not appear to be any such efficiency gain possible; this is the case, in particular, for 2D percussion instruments and moderately stiff strings and bars. Though extensions of digital waveguides do indeed exist in the multidimensional setting, in which case they are usually known as digital waveguide meshes, there is no efficiency gain

---

[5] In the nonlinear case, however, one might argue that the use of higher sampling rates is justifiable, due to the possibility of aliasing. On the other hand, in most physical systems, loss becomes extremely large at high frequencies, so a more sound, and certainly much more computationally efficient, approach is to introduce such losses into the model itself. Another argument for using an elevated sample rate, employed by many authors, is that numerical dispersion (leading to potentially audible distortion) may be reduced; this, however, is disastrous in terms of computational complexity, as the total operation count often scales with the square or cube of the sample rate. It is nearly always possible to design a scheme with much better dispersion characteristics, which still operates at a reasonable sample rate.

relative to modal techniques or standard time differencing methods; indeed, the computational cost of solution by any of these methods is roughly the same.[6]

For distributed nonlinear systems, such as strings and percussion instruments, it is difficult to even approach a definition of complexity—perhaps the only thing one can say is that for a given nonlinear system, which reduces to an LTI system at low vibration amplitudes (this is the usual case in most of physics), the complexity or required operation count and memory requirements for an algorithm simulating the nonlinear system will be at least that of the associated linear system. Efficiency gains through digital waveguide techniques are no longer possible, except under very restricted conditions—one of these, the string under a tension-modulated nonlinearity, will be introduced in Section 8.1.

One question that will not be approached in detail in this book is of model complexity in the perceptual sense. This is a very important issue, in that psychoacoustic criteria could lead to reductions in both the operation count and memory requirements of a synthesis algorithm, in much the same way as they have impacted on audio compression. For instance, the description of the complexity of an LTI system in terms of the number of modal frequencies up to the Nyquist frequency is mathematically sound, but for many musical systems (particularly in 2D), the modal frequencies become very closely spaced in the upper range of the audio spectrum. Taking into consideration the concepts of the critical band and frequency domain masking, it may not be necessary to render the totality of the components. Such psychoacoustic model reduction techniques have been used, with great success, in many efficient (though admittedly non-physical) artificial reverberation algorithms. The impact of psychoacoustics on physical models of musical instruments has seen some investigation recently, in the case of string inharmonicity [180], and also for impact sounds [11], and it would be useful to develop practical complexity-reducing principles and methods, which could be directly related to numerical techniques.

The main point of this section is to signal to the reader that for general systems, there is no physical modeling synthesis method which acts as a magic bullet—but there certainly is a "target" complexity to aim for. There is a minimum price to be paid for the proper simulation of any system. For a given system, the operation counts for modal, finite difference, and lumped network models are always nearly the same; in terms of memory requirements, modal synthesis methods can incur a much heavier cost than time domain methods, due to the storage of modal functions. One great misconception which has appeared often in the literature [53] is that time domain methods are wasteful, in the sense that the entire state of an object must be updated, even though one is interested, ultimately, in only a scalar output, generally from a single location on the virtual instrument. Thus point-to-point "black-box" models, based on a transfer function representation, are more efficient. But, as will be shown repeatedly throughout this book, the order of any transfer function description (and thus the memory requirements) will be roughly the same as the size of the physical state of the object in question.

1.3.4 Why?

The question most often asked by musicians and composers (and perhaps least often by engineers) about physical modeling sound synthesis is: Why? More precisely, why bother to simulate the behavior of an instrument which already exists? Surely the best that can be hoped for is an exact reproduction of the sound of an existing instrument. This is not an easy question to answer, but, nonetheless, various answers do exist.

---

[6] It is possible for certain systems such as the ideal membrane, under certain conditions, to extract groups of harmonic components from a highly inharmonic spectrum, and deal with them individually using waveguides [10, 43], leading to an efficiency gain, albeit a much more modest one than in the 1D case. Such techniques, unfortunately, are rather restrictive in that only extremely regular geometries and trivial boundary conditions may be dealt with.

1
2
3
4
5
6
7
8
9
10
11
12
13
14
15
16
17
18
19
20
21
22
23
24
25
26
27
28
29
30
31
32
33
34
35
36
37
38
39
40
41
42
43
44
45
46
47
48
49
50
51

The most common answer is almost certainly: Because it can be done. This is a very good
answer from the point of view of the musical acoustician, whose interest may be to prove the
validity of a model of a musical instrument, either by comparing simulation results (i.e., synthesis)
to measured output, or by psychoacoustic comparison of recorded and model-synthesized audio
output. Beyond the academic justification, there are boundless opportunities for improvement in
musical instrument design using such techniques. From a commercial point of view, too, it would
be extremely attractive to have a working sound synthesis algorithm to replace sampling synthesis,
which relies on a large database of recorded fragments. (Consider, for example, the number of
samples that would be required to completely represent the output of an acoustic piano, with 88
notes, with 60 dB decay times on the order of tens of seconds, struck over a range of velocities and
pedal configurations.) On the other hand, such an answer will satisfy neither a composer of modern
electroacoustic music in search of new sounds, nor a composer of acoustic orchestral music, who
will find the entire idea somewhat artificial and pointless.

Another answer, closer in spirit to the philosophy of this author, is that physical modeling sound
synthesis is far more than just a means of aping sounds produced by acoustic instruments, and it
is much more than merely a framework for playing mix and match with components of existing
acoustic instruments (the bowed flute, the flutter-tongued piano, etc.). Acoustically produced sound
is definitely a conceptual point of departure for many composers of electroacoustic music, given
the early body of work on rendering the output of abstract sound synthesis algorithms less synthetic
sounding [241, 317], and, more importantly, the current preoccupation with real-time transformation
of natural audio input. In this latter case, though, it might well be true (and one can never really
guess these things) that a composer would jump at the chance to be freed from the confines of
acoustically produced sound if indeed an alternative, possessing all the richness and interesting
unpredictability of natural sound, yet somehow different, were available. Edgard Varèse said it
best [392]:

> I dream of instruments obedient to my thought and which with their contribution of
> a whole new world of unsuspected sounds, will lend themselves to the exigencies of
> my inner rhythm.

2

Time series and difference operators

In this short chapter, the basics of finite difference operations, as applied to time-dependent ordinary differential equations (ODEs) in the next two chapters, and subsequently to partial differential equations (PDEs), are presented. Though the material that appears here is rudimentary, and may be skipped by any reader with experience with finite difference schemes, it is advisable to devote at least a few minutes to familiarizing oneself with the notation, which is necessarily a bit of a hybrid between that used by those in the simulation field and by audio and electrical engineers (but skewed toward the former). There are many old and venerable texts [284, 8, 325] and some more modern ones which may be of special interest to those with a background in electrical engineering or audio [342, 161, 402, 121, 367] and which cover this material in considerably more detail, as well as the text of Kausel [196] which deals directly with difference methods in musical acoustics, but the focus here is on those aspects which will later pertain directly to physical modeling sound synthesis. Though the following presentation is mainly abstract and context free, there are many comments which relate specifically to digital audio.

The use of discrete-time series, taking on values at a finite set of time instants, in order to approximate continuous processes is natural in audio applications, but its roots far predate the appearance of digital audio and even the modern digital computer itself. Finite difference approximations to ODEs can be traced back to at least as far as work from the early twentieth century—see the opening pages of Ames [8] for a historical overview and references. Time series and simple difference operators are presented in Section 2.1 and Section 2.2, followed by a review of frequency domain analysis in Section 2.3, which includes some discussion of the z transform, and the association between difference operators and digital filter designs, which are currently the methodology of choice in musical sound synthesis. Finally, energy concepts are introduced in Section 2.4; these are rather non-standard and do not appear in most introductory texts on finite difference methods. They are geared toward the construction and analysis of finite difference schemes for nonlinear systems, which are of great importance in musical acoustics and physical modeling sound synthesis, and will be heavily used in the later sections of this book.

Numerical Sound Synthesis: Finite Difference Schemes and Simulation in Musical Acoustics   Stefan Bilbao
© 2009 John Wiley & Sons, Ltd

2.1   Time series

In a finite difference setting, continuously variable functions of time t, such as $u(t)$, are approximated by time series, often indexed by integer n. For instance, the time series u_d^n represents an approximation to $u(t_n)$, where $t_n = nk$, for a time step[1] k. In audio applications, perhaps more familiar is the sampling frequency f_s defined as

$$f_s = 1/k$$

Note that the symbol u has been used here to denote both the continuously variable function $u(t)$ and the approximating time series u_d^n; the "d" appended in the subscript for the time series stands for "discrete" and is simply a reminder of the distinction between the two quantities. In subsequent chapters, it will be dropped, in an attempt at avoiding a proliferation of notation; this ambiguity should lead to little confusion, as such forms rarely occur together in the same expression, except in the initial stages of definition of finite difference operators. The use of the same notation also helps to indicate the fundamental similarities in the bodies of analysis techniques which may be used in the discrete and continuous settings.

Before introducing these difference operators and examining discretization issues, it is worth making a few comments which relate specifically to audio. First, consider a function $u(t)$ which appears as the solution to an ODE. If some difference approximation to the ODE is derived, which generates a solution time series u_d^n, it is important to note that in all but a few pathological cases, u_d^n is *not* simply a sampled version of the true solution, i.e.,

$$u_d^n \neq u(nk)$$

Though obvious, it is especially important for those with an electrical or audio engineering background (i.e., those accustomed to dealing with sampled data systems) to be aware of this at the most subconscious level, so as to avoid arriving at false conclusions based on familiar results such as, for instance, the Shannon sampling theorem [261]. In fact, one can indeed incorporate such results into the simulation setting, but in a manner which may be counterintuitive (see Section 3.2.4). In sum, it is best to remember that in the strict physical modeling sound synthesis framework, there occurs no sampling of recorded audio material (though in practice, and particularly in commercial applications, there are many exceptions to this rule). Second, in audio applications, as opposed to standard simulation in other domains, the sample rate f_s and thus the time step k are generally set before run time, and are not varied; in audio, in fact, one nearly always takes f_s as constant, not merely over the duration of a single run of a synthesis algorithm, but over all applications (most often it is set to 44.1 kHz, sometimes to 32 kHz or 48 kHz). This, in contrast to the first comment above, is intuitive for audio engineers, but not for those involved with numerical simulation in other areas, who often are interested in developing numerical schemes which allow a larger time step with little degradation in accuracy. Though the benefits of such schemes may be interpreted in terms of numerical dispersion (see Section 6.2.3), in an audio synthesis application there is no point in developing a scheme which runs with increased efficiency at a larger time step (i.e., at a lower sampling rate), as such a scheme will be incapable of producing potentially audible frequencies in the upper range of human hearing. A third major distinction is that the duration of a simulation, in sound synthesis applications, is extremely long by most simulation standards (on the order of hundreds of thousands or millions of time steps). A variety of techniques which are commonly used in mainstream simulation can lead to audible distortion over such long durations. As an example, the introduction of so-called artificial viscosity [161] into a numerical

---

[1] Though k has been chosen as the symbol representing the time step in this book, the same quantity goes by a variety of different names in the various sectors of the simulation literature, including T, Δt, h_t, etc.

scheme in order to reduce spurious oscillations will result in long-time solution decay, which will
have an impact on the global envelope of the resulting sound output. Fourth, and finally, due to
the nature of the system of human aural perception, synthesis output is always scalar—that is, it
can be represented by a single time series, or, in the multichannel case, a small number of such
series, which is not the case in other applications. There are thus opportunities for algorithmic
simplification, with digital waveguides as a supremely successful example. Again, the perceptual
considerations listed above are all peculiar to digital audio.

2.2   Shift, difference, and averaging operators

In time domain simulation applications, just as in digital filtering, the fundamental operations which
may be applied to a time series u_d^n are shifts. The forward and backward shifts and the identity
operation "1" are defined as

$$e_{t+}u_d^n = u_d^{n+1} \qquad e_{t-}u_d^n = u_d^{n-1} \qquad 1u_d^n = u_d^n$$

and are to be regarded as applying to the time series u_d^n at all values of the index n. The identity
operator acts as a simple scalar multiplication by unity; multiples of the identity behave accordingly,
and will be indicated by multiplicative factors, such as "2" or "α," where α is a real constant.

A set of useful difference and averaging operations may be derived from these elementary
shifts. For example, various approximations to the first-derivative operator (the nature of this
approximation will be explained shortly) may be given as

$$\delta_{t+} \triangleq \frac{1}{k}(e_{t+} - 1) \cong \frac{d}{dt} \tag{2.1a}$$

$$\delta_{t-} \triangleq \frac{1}{k}(1 - e_{t-}) \cong \frac{d}{dt} \tag{2.1b}$$

$$\delta_{t\cdot} \triangleq \frac{1}{2k}(e_{t+} - e_{t-}) \cong \frac{d}{dt} \tag{2.1c}$$

These are often called forward, backward, and centered difference approximations, respectively.
The behavior of any such operator is most easily understood by expanding its action onto a time
series u_d^n, where the time index n is made explicit. For the operators defined above, for example,
one has

$$\delta_{t+}u_d^n = \frac{1}{k}\left(u_d^{n+1} - u_d^n\right) \qquad \delta_{t-}u_d^n = \frac{1}{k}\left(u_d^n - u_d^{n-1}\right) \qquad \delta_{t\cdot}u_d^n = \frac{1}{2k}\left(u_d^{n+1} - u_d^{n-1}\right) \tag{2.2}$$

Also useful, especially in the construction of so-called implicit schemes (which will be touched
upon briefly with regard to the oscillator in Section 3.3 and in much more detail in the distributed
setting in Section 6.3 and subsequently) and in energetic analysis (see Section 2.4), are various
averaging operators:

$$\mu_{t+} \triangleq \frac{1}{2}(e_{t+} + 1) \cong 1 \tag{2.3a}$$

$$\mu_{t-} \triangleq \frac{1}{2}(1 + e_{t-}) \cong 1 \tag{2.3b}$$

$$\mu_{t\cdot} \triangleq \frac{1}{2}(e_{t+} + e_{t-}) \cong 1 \tag{2.3c}$$

All of these averaging operators are approximations to the identity operation. (One might wonder
why one would introduce an approximation to the continuous-time identity operation, which, after

all, may be perfectly approximated through the identity in discrete time. The answer comes when
examining finite difference schemes in their entirety; in many cases, the accuracy of a scheme
involves the counterbalancing of the effects of various operators, not just one in isolation. See, for
example, Section 3.3.4 and Section 6.2.4.)

To avoid a doubling of terminology, averaging and difference operators will be referred to as
"difference" operators in this book, although "discrete" would probably be a better term. It should
be clear that all the operators defined in (2.1) and (2.3) commute with one another individually.
The Greek letters δ and μ are mnemonics for "difference" and "mean," respectively.

When combined, members of the small set of "canonical" simple difference operators in (2.1)
and (2.3) above can yield almost any imaginable type of approximation or difference scheme for
an ODE or system of ODEs. As an important example, an approximation to the second derivative
may be obtained through the composition of the operators δ_{t+} and δ_{t-}:

$$\delta_{tt} \triangleq \delta_{t+}\delta_{t-} = \frac{1}{k^2}(e_{t+} - 2 + e_{t-}) \cong \frac{d^2}{dt^2} \qquad (2.4)$$

Again, the constant "2" is to be thought of as twice the identity operation, under the application
of δ_{tt} to a time series.

In musical acoustics, the appearance of time derivatives of order higher than two is extremely
rare (one case is that of higher-order models of beam and plate vibration [156], another being that
of frequency-dependent loss in some models of string vibration [75, 305]), and, for this reason,
difference approximations to higher time derivatives will not be discussed further in any detail in
this book. See Problem 2.1. Approximations to higher spatial derivatives, however, play a central
role in various models of bar and plate vibration, but a treatment of the related difference operators
will be postponed until Chapter 5.

2.2.1 Temporal width of difference operators

Though the property of width, or stencil width of a difference operator, is usually discussed
with reference to spatial difference operators, this is a good place to introduce the concept. The
temporal width of an operator, such as any of those defined at the beginning of Section 2.2, is
defined as the number of distinct time steps (or levels) required to form the approximation. For
example, the operator δ_{t+}, as defined in (2.1a), when expanded out as in (2.2), clearly requires
two adjacent values of the time series u_d in order to be evaluated. The same is true of the operator
δ_{t-}, as well as the averaging operators μ_{t+} and μ_{t-}; all such operators are thus of width 2.
The operators $\delta_{t\cdot}$ and $\mu_{t\cdot}$, as well as δ_{tt}, will be of width 3. See Figure 2.1. In general, greater
accuracy (to be discussed in Section 2.2.3) is obtained at the expense of greater operator width,
which can complicate an implementation in various ways. For time difference operators, there
will be additional concerns with the initialization of difference schemes, as well as the potential
appearance of parasitic solutions, and stability analysis can become enormously complex. For
spatial difference operators, finding appropriate numerical boundary conditions becomes more
difficult. When accuracy is not a huge concern, it is often wise to stick with simple, low-width

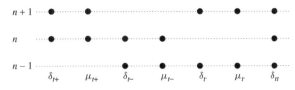

Figure 2.1 Illustration of temporal widths for various operators (as indicated above), when operating on a time series at time step n.

operators. In audio synthesis, the importance of greater accuracy may be evaluated with respect
to psychoacoustic criteria—this issue will be broached in more detail in Section 2.3.4 and in
Section 3.2.4.

2.2.2 Combining difference operators

For any collection of difference operators, each of which approximates the same continuous operator, any linear combination will approximate the same operator to within a multiplicative factor.
For instance, one may form a difference operator approximating a first derivative by

$$\alpha \delta_{t+} + (1 - \alpha)\delta_{t-}$$

for any α (generally constrained to be a real number). In this case, the operator $\delta_{t\cdot}$, defined in (2.1c),
can be obtained with $\alpha = 1/2$.

Similarly, for averaging operators, one may form the combination

$$\alpha \mu_{t+} + \phi \mu_{t-} + (1 - \alpha - \phi)\mu_{t\cdot}$$

for any scalar α and ϕ (again generally constrained to be real).

Difference operators may also be combined by composition (operator multiplication), as was
seen in the definition of the second difference δ_{tt}, in (2.4), which can be viewed as the composition
of the operators δ_{t+} and δ_{t-}. It is easy to show that any composition of averaging operators, such as

$$\mu_{t+}\mu_{t-}, \quad \mu_{t+}\mu_{t-}\mu_{t\cdot}, \quad \mu_{t-}\mu_{t\cdot}\mu_{t\cdot}\mu_{t\cdot}, \quad \cdots$$

is itself an averaging operator. See Problem 2.2. The first such combination above is useful
enough to warrant the use of a special symbol:

$$\mu_{tt} \triangleq \mu_{t+}\mu_{t-} \tag{2.5}$$

Any composition of averaging operators, which is itself composed with a single first difference
operator, such as

$$\mu_{t+}\delta_{t-}, \quad \mu_{t+}\mu_{t\cdot}\delta_{t\cdot}, \quad \mu_{t+}\mu_{t-}\mu_{t\cdot}\delta_{t+}, \quad \cdots$$

itself behaves as an approximation to a first derivative. See Problem 2.3. In general, the
composition of difference operators tends to increase temporal width.

2.2.3 Taylor series and accuracy

The interpretation of the various operators defined in the previous section as approximations to
differential operators is direct—indeed, the definitions of the first differences δ_{t+} and δ_{t-} are in
fact none other than the approximate forms (right-hand limit and left-hand limit) from which the
classical definition of the derivative follows, in the limit as k approaches 0. It is useful, however,
to be slightly more precise about the accuracy of these approximations, especially from the point
of view of sound synthesis.

A good starting point is in the standard comparison between the behavior of difference operators
and differential operators as applied to continuous-time functions, through simple Taylor series
analysis. In a slight abuse of notation, one may apply such difference operators to continuous-time
functions as well as to time series. For instance, for the forward time difference operator δ_{t+}
applied to the function u at time t, one may write

$$\delta_{t+}u(t) = \frac{1}{k}(u(t+k) - u(t))$$

Assuming $u(t)$ to be infinitely differentiable, and expanding $u(t + k)$ in Taylor series about t, one then has

$$\delta_{t+}u(t) = \frac{du}{dt} + \frac{k}{2}\frac{d^2u}{dt^2} + \cdots$$

where ... refers to terms which depend on higher derivatives of u, and which are accompanied by higher powers of k, the time step. The operator δ_{t+} thus approximates the first time derivative to an *accuracy* which depends on the first power of k, the time step; as k is made small, the difference approximation approaches the exact value of the derivative with an error proportional to k. Such an approximation is thus often called first-order accurate. (This can be slightly misleading in the case of operators acting in isolation, as the order of accuracy is dependent on the point at which the Taylor series is centered. See Problem 2.4. Such ambiguity is removed when finite difference schemes are examined in totality.) The backward difference operator is, similarly, a first-order accurate approximation to the first time derivative.

The centered difference operator, as might be expected, is more accurate. One may write, employing Taylor series centered about t,

$$\delta_{t\cdot}u(t) = \frac{1}{2k}\left(u(t + k) - u(t - k)\right) = \frac{du}{dt} + \frac{k^2}{6}\frac{d^3u}{dt^3} + \cdots$$

which illustrates that the centered approximation is accurate to second order (i.e., the error depends on the second power of k, the time step). Notice, however, that the width of the centered operator is three, as opposed to two for the forward and backward difference operators—in general, as mentioned in Section 2.2.1, the better the accuracy of the approximation, the more adjacent values of the time series will be required. This leads to the usual trade-off between performance and latency that one sees in, for example, digital filters. Fortunately, in physical modeling sound synthesis applications, due to perceptual considerations, it is probably true that only rarely will one need to make use of highly accurate operators. This issue will be discussed in a more precise way in Section 3.3.2, in the context of the simple harmonic oscillator.

The orders of accuracy of the various averaging operators may also be demonstrated in the same manner, and one has

$$\mu_{t+} = 1 + O(k) \qquad \mu_{t-} = 1 + O(k) \qquad \mu_{t\cdot} = 1 + O(k^2)$$

where again "1" refers to the identity operation, and $O(\cdot)$ signifies "order of." Similarly, the approximation to the second derivative δ_{tt} is second-order accurate; it will be useful later to have the full Taylor series expansion for this operator:

$$\delta_{tt} = \sum_{l=1}^{\infty} \frac{2k^{2(l-1)}}{(2l)!}\frac{d^{2l}}{dt^{2l}} = \frac{d^2}{dt^2} + O(k^2) \tag{2.6}$$

It is straightforward to arrive at difference and averaging approximations which are accurate to higher order. This is a subject which was explored extensively early on in the literature—see Problem 2.6 for an example.

It is important to keep in mind that though these discussions of accuracy of difference and averaging operators have employed continuous-time functions, the operators themselves will be applied to time series; in a sense, the analysis here is incomplete until an entire equation (i.e., an ODE) has been discretized, at which point one may determine the accuracy of the approximate solution computed using a difference scheme with respect to the true solution to the ODE. As a rule of thumb, the accuracy of an operator acting in isolation is indeterminate—in this section, it has been taken to refer to the order of the error term when an expansion is taken about the "reference" time instant $t = nk$.

2.2.4   Identities

Various equivalences exist among the various operators defined in this section. Here are a few of interest:

$$\mu_{t\cdot} = 1 + \frac{k^2}{2}\delta_{tt} \tag{2.7a}$$

$$\delta_{t\cdot} = \delta_{t+}\mu_{t-} = \delta_{t-}\mu_{t+} \tag{2.7b}$$

$$\delta_{tt} = \frac{1}{k}(\delta_{t+} - \delta_{t-}) \tag{2.7c}$$

$$1 = \mu_{t\pm} \mp \frac{k}{2}\delta_{t\pm} \tag{2.7d}$$

$$e_{t\pm} = \mu_{t\pm} \pm \frac{k}{2}\delta_{t\pm} \tag{2.7e}$$

$$e_{t\pm} = 1 \pm k\delta_{t\pm} \tag{2.7f}$$

$$\delta_{tt} = \frac{2}{k}(\delta_{t\cdot} - \delta_{t-}) \tag{2.7g}$$

$$\mu_{t\cdot} = k\delta_{t\cdot} + e_{t-} \tag{2.7h}$$

2.3   Frequency domain analysis

In this section, a very brief introduction to frequency domain analysis of finite difference operators is presented. As may be expected, such techniques can allow one to glean much perceptually important information from the model system, and also to compare the performance of a given difference scheme to the model system in an intuitive manner. It also allows a convenient means of analyzing numerical stability, if the model problem is linear and time invariant; this is indeed the case for many simplified systems in musical acoustics. For the same reason, however, one must be wary of any attempts to make use of such techniques in a nonlinear setting, though one can indeed come to some (generally qualitative) conclusions under such conditions.

2.3.1   Laplace and z transforms

For a continuously variable function $u(t)$, one definition of the Laplace transform $\hat{u}(s)$ is as follows:

$$\hat{u}(s) = \int_{-\infty}^{\infty} u(t)e^{-st}dt \tag{2.8}$$

where $s = j\omega + \sigma$ is a complex-valued frequency variable, with $\omega = 2\pi f$, for a frequency f in Hertz. The transformation may be abbreviated as

$$u(t) \overset{\mathcal{L}}{\Longrightarrow} \hat{u}(s)$$

If the transformation may be restricted to $s = j\omega$, then the Laplace transform reduces to a Fourier transform.

The definition of the Laplace transform above is two sided or bilateral, and useful in steady state applications. In many applications, however, a one-sided definition is employed, allowing initial conditions to be directly incorporated into the resulting frequency domain analysis:

$$\hat{u}(s) = \int_{0}^{\infty} u(t)e^{-st}dt \tag{2.9}$$

1
2
3
4
5
6
7
8
9
10
11
12
13
14
15
16
17
18
19
20
21
22
23
24
25
26
27
28
29
30
31
32
33
34
35
36
37
38
39
40
41
42
43
44
45
46
47
48
49
50
51

In general, for the analysis of well-posedness of differential equations and numerical stability, a two-sided definition may be used. Though it might be tempting to make use of Fourier transforms in this case, it is important to retain the complex frequency variable s in order to simplify the analysis of loss.

For a time series u_d^n, the z transform $\hat{u}_d(z)$, again two sided, may be defined as

$$\hat{u}_d(z) = \sum_{n=-\infty}^{\infty} z^{-n} u_d^n$$

where $z = e^{sk}$ is the discrete frequency variable, again with $s = j\omega + \sigma$, and where the superscript of z now indicates a power. The z transform may be abbreviated as

$$u_d^n \xrightarrow{z} \hat{u}_d(z)$$

Again, as for the case of the Laplace transform, a one-sided definition could be employed. (The symbol z is often written as g, and called the *amplification factor* in the analysis of finite difference recursions for distributed systems.) If z is restricted to $z = e^{j\omega k}$, the z transformation becomes a discrete-time Fourier transformation.

The Laplace and z transforms are covered in great detail in hundreds of other texts, and some familiarity with them is assumed—see, for example, [280] or [275] for more information. In particular, the subject of inverse Laplace and z transformations, though important in its own right, is not covered here, as it seldom appears in practical analysis and design of finite difference schemes.

Frequency domain ansatz

In PDE and numerical analysis, full Laplace and z transform analysis is usually circumvented through the use of an ansatz. For instance, for a continuous-time LTI problem, it is wholly sufficient to simplify the frequency domain analysis by examining a single-frequency solution

$$u(t) = e^{st}$$

Similarly, in discrete time, the ansatz

$$u_d^n = z^n$$

is also frequently employed. Various authors discuss the equivalence between this approach and full Laplace or z transform analysis [161, 342].

2.3.2 Frequency domain interpretation of differential and difference operators

The frequency domain interpretation of differential operators is well known to anyone who has taken an undergraduate course in electrical circuits. In continuous time, at steady state, one has, immediately from (2.8),

$$\frac{d^m}{dt^m} u(t) \xrightarrow{\mathcal{L}} s^m \hat{u}(s)$$

In discrete time, for the unit shift, one has

$$e_{t\pm} u_d^n \xrightarrow{z} z^{\pm 1} \hat{u}_d(z)$$

and for the various first differences and averaging operators, one has

$$\delta_{t+}u_{\mathsf{d}}^n \overset{z}{\Longrightarrow} \frac{1}{k}(z-1)\,\hat{u}_{\mathsf{d}}(z) \qquad \delta_{t-}u_{\mathsf{d}}^n \overset{z}{\Longrightarrow} \frac{1}{k}\left(1-z^{-1}\right)\hat{u}_{\mathsf{d}}(z) \qquad \delta_{t\cdot}u_{\mathsf{d}}^n \overset{z}{\Longrightarrow} \frac{1}{2k}\left(z-z^{-1}\right)\hat{u}_{\mathsf{d}}(z)$$

$$\mu_{t+}u_{\mathsf{d}}^n \overset{z}{\Longrightarrow} \frac{1}{2}(z+1)\,\hat{u}_{\mathsf{d}}(z) \qquad \mu_{t-}u_{\mathsf{d}}^n \overset{z}{\Longrightarrow} \frac{1}{2}\left(1+z^{-1}\right)\hat{u}_{\mathsf{d}}(z) \qquad \mu_{t\cdot}u_{\mathsf{d}}^n \overset{z}{\Longrightarrow} \frac{1}{2}\left(z+z^{-1}\right)\hat{u}_{\mathsf{d}}(z)$$

The second difference operator δ_{tt} transforms according to

$$\delta_{tt}u_{\mathsf{d}}^n \overset{z}{\Longrightarrow} \frac{1}{k^2}\left(z-2+z^{-1}\right)\hat{u}_{\mathsf{d}}(z)$$

Under some conditions, it is useful to look at the behavior of these discrete-time operators when z is constrained to be of unit modulus (in other words, when $z = e^{j\omega k}$). For instance, the operators δ_{tt} and $\mu_{t\cdot}$ transform according to

$$\delta_{tt}u_{\mathsf{d}}^n \Longrightarrow -\frac{4}{k^2}\sin^2(\omega k/2)\hat{u}_{\mathsf{d}}(e^{j\omega k}) \qquad \mu_{t\cdot}u_{\mathsf{d}}^n \Longrightarrow \cos(\omega k)\hat{u}_{\mathsf{d}}(e^{j\omega k})$$

where the $\Longrightarrow$ is now interpreted as referring to a discrete-time Fourier transform.

The Taylor series analysis of the accuracy of difference and averaging operators may be viewed simply in the frequency domain. Considering, for example, the operator δ_{t+}, one may write, by expanding $z = e^{sk}$ in powers of s about $s = 0$,

$$\delta_{t+}u_{\mathsf{d}}^n \overset{z}{\Longrightarrow} \frac{1}{k}(z-1)\,\hat{u}_{\mathsf{d}}(z) = \frac{1}{k}\left(e^{sk}-1\right)\hat{u}_{\mathsf{d}}(e^{sk}) = (s + O(k))\,\hat{u}_{\mathsf{d}}(e^{sk})$$

In other words, the difference operator δ_{t+} behaves, in the frequency domain, as a multiplication by a factor $s + O(k)$, corresponding to the first derivative plus a correction on the order of the time step k, and is thus first-order accurate.

2.3.3 Recursions and polynomials in z

Finite difference schemes are recursions. Though concrete examples of such recursions, as derived from ODEs, will appear at many instances in the following two chapters, a typical example is the following:

$$u_{\mathsf{d}}^n = -\sum_{n'=1}^{N} a^{(n')}u_{\mathsf{d}}^{n-n'} \tag{2.10}$$

The value of the time series u_{d}^n is calculated from a weighted combination of the last N values, and $a^{(n')}$ are the weighting coefficients. Such a recursion corresponds to an ODE without a forcing term, and, for those with a signal processing background, is no more than an all-pole digital filter operating under zero-input (transient) conditions. If the coefficients $a^{(n')}$ are constants (i.e., the underlying problem is LTI), the usual analysis technique here, as in standard filter design, is to take a z transform of (2.10) to get

$$P(z)\hat{u}_{\mathsf{d}} = 0 \qquad \text{with} \qquad P(z) = \sum_{n'=0}^{N} a^{(n')}z^{N-n'} \tag{2.11}$$

where $a^{(0)} = 1$. Frequency domain stability analysis of finite difference schemes is concerned with finding the roots of what is sometimes called the *amplification polynomial* $P(z)$, i.e.,

$$P(z) = 0 \tag{2.12}$$

These roots correspond to the natural frequencies of oscillation of the recursion (2.10). Polynomials such as the above arise when analyzing finite difference schemes for linear and shift-invariant PDEs as well, in which case the set of values $a^{(n')}$ may themselves be constant-coefficient functions of spatial frequency variables (or wavenumber). It is worth introducing some useful conditions on root locations here.

For numerical stability, it is usually the case that, just as for digital filters, one needs to bound any solution z to (2.11) by

$$|z| \leq 1 \quad \longrightarrow \quad \sigma \leq 0$$

In other words, the roots must have magnitude less than or equal to unity, corresponding to damped complex frequencies[2]. One way of proceeding is to find the roots z to (2.11) explicitly, but if one is interested in merely finding out the conditions under which the roots are bounded, simpler tests exist, such as the Schur–Cohn recursive procedure [342], which is analogous to the Routh–Hurwitz stability test [387] for checking root locations of polynomials associated with continuous-time systems. In many cases in physical modeling sound synthesis, however, the polynomial (2.11) is of second order, i.e.,

$$z^2 + a^{(1)}z + a^{(2)} = 0 \tag{2.13}$$

It is possible to show, either through an explicit calculation of the roots, or through the use of the Schur–Cohn recursion, that the roots of this quadratic will be bounded by unity if

$$|a^{(1)}| - 1 \leq a^{(2)} \leq 1 \tag{2.14}$$

See Problems 2.7 and 2.8. These conditions are plotted as a region in the $(a^{(1)}, a^{(2)})$ plane in Figure 2.2. This relatively simple pair of conditions will be used repeatedly throughout this book.

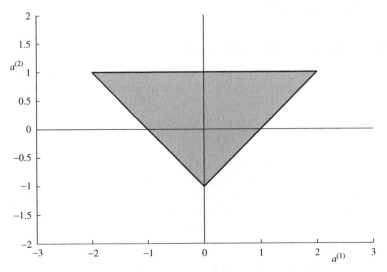

Figure 2.2   Region of the $(a^{(1)}, a^{(2)})$ plane (in grey) for which the roots of (2.13) are bounded by unity in magnitude.

---

[2] This condition is, in fact, a little too simple to catch many special cases which may occur in practice. For example, through analysis of finite difference schemes one can arrive at polynomials possessing double roots on the unit circle, leading, potentially, to linear growth of solutions; sometimes this is a natural consequence of the underlying model equations, sometimes not. Also, in some cases one may need to beware if the coefficients themselves are functions of parameters such as k, the time step, in order to ensure that roots are bounded in the limit as k becomes small.

It is also worth noting that under certain conditions (namely losslessness of the underlying model problem), polynomials occur in which $a^{(2)} = 1$, implying the simpler condition

$$|a^{(1)}| \leq 2 \tag{2.15}$$

2.3.4   Difference operators and digital filters

As discussed in Chapter 1, the most prominent current physical modeling sound synthesis techniques, such as digital waveguides and scattering methods, are based, traditionally, around the use of digital filters and the accompanying frequency domain machinery. It should be somewhat comforting then that, at least in the LTI case, many of the analysis methods used in the numerical simulation field (especially that of von Neumann, to be introduced in Chapter 5) are described in a nearly identical language, employing Fourier, Laplace, and z transforms, though spatial Fourier transforms and filters will be familiar only to those audio engineers with a familiarity with image processing or optics. In this short section, some connections between the difference operators described in the preceding sections and very simple digital filter designs are indicated.

Digital filters of high order play a central role in signal processing, including that of audio signals. Yet in physical modeling applications, due to the more strict adherence to an underlying model problem, higher-order difference operators, especially in time, are much more difficult to use. One reason for this has to do with numerical stability—though moderately higher-order schemes for ODEs, such as those of the Runge–Kutta variety, are commonly seen in the literature, for distributed problems, the coupling with spatial differentiation can lead to severe difficulties in terms of analysis, even in the linear case. Complex behavior in musical instrument simulations results from coupled low-order time differences—in digital filtering terminology, one might view such a configuration in terms of "banks of oscillators." Though a conventional analysis technique, particularly for finite element methods [121, 93], involves reducing a spatially distributed problem to a system of ODEs (i.e., through so-called semi-discretization), in the nonlinear case any stability results obtained in this way are generally not sufficient, and can be interpreted only as rules of thumb. Another reason is that in conventional audio filtering applications, the emphasis is generally on the steady state response of a given filter. But in physical modeling applications, in some cases one is solely interested in the transient response of a system (percussive sound synthesis is one such example). The higher the order of the time differentiation employed, the higher the number of initial conditions which must be supplied; as most systems in musical acoustics are of second order in time differentiation, time difference operators of degree higher than two will necessarily require the setting of extra "artificial" initial conditions.

It is useful to examine the difference operators defined in Section 2.2 in this light. Consider any LTI operator p (such as d/dt, the identity operator 1, or d^2/dt^2), applied to a function $x(t)$, and yielding a function $y(t)$. When viewed in an input output sense, one arrives, after Laplace transformation, at a transfer function form, i.e.,

$$y(t) = px(t) \overset{\mathcal{L}}{\Longrightarrow} \hat{y}(s) = h(s)\hat{x}(s)$$

where $h(s)$ is the transfer function corresponding to the operator p. When $s = j\omega$, one may find the magnitude and phase of the transfer function, as a function of ω, i.e.,

$$\text{magnitude} = |h(j\omega)| \qquad \text{phase} = \angle h(j\omega)$$

Similarly, for a discrete-time operator p_d applied to a time series x_d^n, yielding a time series y_d^n, one has, after applying a z transformation,

$$y_d^n = p_d x_d^n \overset{\mathcal{Z}}{\Longrightarrow} \hat{y}_d(z) = h_d(z)\hat{x}_d(z)$$

Table 2.1 Comparison between continuous-time operators d/dt, the identity 1, and d^2/dt^2, and various difference approximations, viewed in terms of transfer functions. For each operator, the continuous-time transfer function is given as a function of s and the discrete-time transfer function as a function of z. Magnitude and phase are given for $s = j\omega$ or $z = e^{j\omega k}$.

CT op.	$h(s)$	$\lvert h(j\omega)\rvert$	$\angle h(j\omega)$	DT op.	$h_{\mathrm d}(z)$	$\lvert h_{\mathrm d}(e^{j\omega k})\rvert$	$\angle h_{\mathrm d}(e^{j\omega k})$
				δ_{t+}	$\frac{1}{k}(z-1)$	$\frac{2}{k}\left\lvert\sin\left(\frac{\omega k}{2}\right)\right\rvert$	$\frac{\pi}{2}+\frac{\omega k}{2},\ \omega\ge 0$ $-\frac{\pi}{2}+\frac{\omega k}{2},\ \omega< 0$
$\frac{d}{dt}$	s	$\lvert\omega\rvert$	$\frac{\pi}{2},\ \omega\ge 0$ $-\frac{\pi}{2},\ \omega< 0$	δ_{t-}	$\frac{1}{k}\left(1-z^{-1}\right)$	$\frac{2}{k}\left\lvert\sin\left(\frac{\omega k}{2}\right)\right\rvert$	$\frac{\pi}{2}-\frac{\omega k}{2},\ \omega\ge 0$ $-\frac{\pi}{2}-\frac{\omega k}{2},\ \omega< 0$
				$\delta_{t\cdot}$	$\frac{1}{2k}\left(z-z^{-1}\right)$	$\frac{1}{k}\lvert\sin(\omega k)\rvert$	$\frac{\pi}{2},\ \omega\ge 0$ $-\frac{\pi}{2},\ \omega< 0$
				μ_{t+}	$\frac{1}{2}(z+1)$	$\left\lvert\cos\left(\frac{\omega k}{2}\right)\right\rvert$	$\frac{\omega k}{2}$
1	1	1	0	μ_{t-}	$\frac{1}{2}\left(1+z^{-1}\right)$	$\left\lvert\cos\left(\frac{\omega k}{2}\right)\right\rvert$	$-\frac{\omega k}{2}$
				$\mu_{t\cdot}$	$\frac{1}{2}\left(z+z^{-1}\right)$	$\lvert\cos(\omega k)\rvert$	$0,\ \lvert\omega\rvert<\frac{\pi}{2k}$ $\pi,\ \omega\ge\frac{\pi}{2k}$
$\frac{d^2}{dt^2}$	s^2	ω^2	π	δ_{tt}	$\frac{1}{k^2}\left(z-2+z^{-1}\right)$	$\frac{4}{k^2}\sin^2\left(\frac{\omega k}{2}\right)$	π

where $h_{\mathrm d}(z)$ is the transfer function corresponding to the operator $p_{\mathrm d}$. Again, one can find the magnitude and phase by restricting z to $z = e^{j\omega k}$, i.e.,

$$\text{magnitude} = \lvert h_{\mathrm d}(e^{j\omega k})\rvert \qquad\qquad \text{phase} = \angle h_{\mathrm d}(e^{j\omega k})$$

In Table 2.1, transfer functions for various differential and difference operators are given, as well as their magnitudes and phases. The discrete-time transfer functions are readily interpreted in terms of well-known filter structures. Leaving issues of causality aside, the operators δ_{t+} and δ_{t-} behave as high-pass filters with a single zero at the DC frequency $z = 1$, and $\delta_{t\cdot}$ is a two-zero filter with zeros at DC and the Nyquist frequency $z = -1$. The averaging operators μ_{t+} and μ_{t-} behave similarly as low-pass filters, each with a single zero at the Nyquist frequency $z = 1$, and $\mu_{t\cdot}$ is a two-zero filter with zeros at $z = \pm j$, or at one-quarter the sample rate. δ_{tt} behaves as a two-zero filter with a double zero at DC. See also Problem 2.9.

Notice that for all the difference operators presented in the table, the approximation to the magnitude response of the associated continuous-time operator is second-order accurate about $\omega = 0$—that is, if one expands the magnitude of $\lvert h(e^{j\omega k})\rvert$, for $\omega \ge 0$, in powers of ω, one has

$$\lvert h_{\mathrm d}(e^{j\omega k})\rvert = \lvert h(j\omega)\rvert + O(k^2)$$

But the same is not true of the phase response; for centered operators, such as $\delta_{t\cdot}$, $\mu_{t\cdot}$, and δ_{tt}, the phase response is exact, at least in some neighborhood around $\omega = 0$. For the other non-centered operators, it is not, and differs from the phase response of the associated continuous-time operator by a term of order k. Thus the "first-order accuracy" of such non-centered operators manifests itself in the phase behavior, which is to be expected. Such behavior may be directly related to the discussion of indeterminacy of accuracy of difference operators in isolation, from Section 2.2.3.

This behavior is perhaps more easily viewed in frequency domain plots of the magnitude and phase of these operators, as given in Figure 2.3, as are certain other interesting features. For example, note that, in terms of the magnitude response alone, the first-order accurate operators

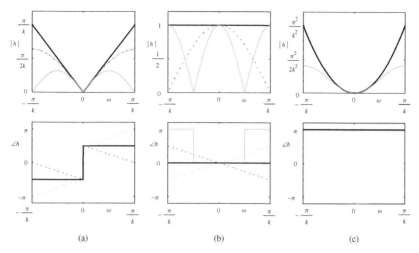

(a)   (b)   (c)

Figure 2.3   Magnitude (top) and phase (bottom) of difference approximations to (a) d/dt, (b) the identity operator 1, and (c) d^2/dt^2. In all cases, the exact response of the continuous operator is plotted as a thick black line, over the interval $\omega \in [-\pi/k, \pi/k]$. The responses of the centered operators $\delta_{t\cdot}$, $\mu_{t\cdot}$, and δ_{tt}, when distinct from those of the continuous-time operator, appear as solid grey lines. In the case of magnitude plots, the responses of the non-centered operators δ_{t+}, δ_{t-}, μ_{t+}, and μ_{t-} appear as dotted black lines, and in the case of phase plots as distinct dotted grey (forward operators) and black (backward operators) lines.

δ_{t+} and δ_{t-} better approximate the first derivative near $\omega = 0$ than the second-order accurate operator $\delta_{t\cdot}$, which might seem somewhat surprising. This is due to the fact that the simple forward and backward differences employ values of the time series which are only one time step apart, rather than two, in the case of the centered difference operator. Also note the "doubling" of the magnitude response in the case of $\delta_{t\cdot}$, about one-quarter the sampling rate; this is also surprising, but then the centered difference operator, which operates on values of the time series separated by two time steps, can be viewed as operating at a downsampled (by a factor of two) rate. This interesting doubling effect appears in finite difference schemes under certain conditions for various systems of interest in musical sound synthesis, such as the wave equation in 1D or 2D [382].

In the case of all the operators discussed here except for μ_{t-} and δ_{t-}, the resulting recursion appears to imply a non-causal relationship between an input sequence x_d^n and an output sequence y_d^n, but it is important to keep in mind that in numerical applications, this is not quite the correct interpretation. Generally, in a physical modeling sound synthesis application, there is not an input sequence as such (at least not at the audio rate), and no risk of the need for "looking into the future." But the use of such "non-causal" operations can lead to implicit behavior [342] in finite difference schemes in some cases—see Section 6.3.

The trapezoid rule

One difference approximation, of special importance in sound synthesis applications (and in particular those built around the use of scattering based methods—see Section 1.2.4), is the trapezoid rule. In operator form, it looks like

$$(\mu_{t+})^{-1}\,\delta_{t+} \tag{2.16}$$

where the $(\mu_{t+})^{-1}$ is to be understood here as an operator inverse. As $(\mu_{t+})^{-1}$ remains an approximation to the identity operator, the operator as a whole still behaves as an approximation to a first time derivative. Like the operators δ_{t+} and δ_{t-}, it can be viewed as second-order accurate about a midpoint between adjacent values of the time series. Operationally, the best way to examine it is in the input/output sense, for an input sequence x_d^n and output sequence y_d^n:

$$y_\mathrm{d}^n = (\mu_{t+})^{-1}\delta_{t+}x_\mathrm{d}^n \quad \text{or} \quad \frac{1}{2}\left(y_\mathrm{d}^{n+1} + y_\mathrm{d}^n\right) = \frac{1}{k}\left(x_\mathrm{d}^{n+1} - x_\mathrm{d}^n\right) \tag{2.17}$$

The trapezoid rule transforms as

$$y_\mathrm{d}^n = (\mu_{t+})^{-1}\delta_{t+}x_\mathrm{d}^n \quad \overset{z}{\Longrightarrow} \quad \hat{y}_\mathrm{d}(z) = \frac{2}{k}\frac{z-1}{z+1}\hat{x}_\mathrm{d}(z) \tag{2.18}$$

In the frequency domain form, the trapezoid rule is often referred to as a bilinear transformation.

As mentioned above, the trapezoid rule figures prominently in scattering-based approaches to synthesis, and is one of the cornerstones of wave digital filters [127]. An example of a wave digital structure employing the trapezoid rule, as well as a discussion of the relationship with other finite difference methods, appears in Section 3.3.3.

2.4   Energetic manipulations and identities

The frequency domain techniques presented in the previous section are of great utility in the analysis of linear and time-invariant (LTI) systems and difference schemes, and extend naturally to the distributed setting, in which case they are often referred to as von Neumann analysis [342]; such techniques can yield a great deal of important information regarding numerical stability, as well as the perceptual effects of discretization, in the form of so-called numerical phase and group velocity and dispersion. LTI systems, however, are only the starting point in musical sound synthesis based on physical models, and are not sufficiently complex to capture many of the more subtle and perceptually salient qualities of real musical sounds.

Frequency domain techniques do not apply directly to nonlinear systems, nor to finite difference schemes which approximate them. It is often tempting to view nonlinear systems in musical acoustics as perturbations of linear systems and to apply frequency domain analysis in a loose sense. If the perturbations are small, this approach is justifiable, and can yield additional information regarding, say, the evolution of natural frequencies of oscillation. In many cases, however, these perturbations are not small; the sound of percussion instruments such as gongs serves as an excellent example of the perceptual importance of highly nonlinear effects. Frequency domain techniques applied in such cases can be dangerous in the case of analysis, in that important transient effects are not well modeled, and potentially disastrous in the case of sound synthesis based on finite difference schemes, in that numerical stability is impossible to rigorously ensure in such a manner. Energetic techniques, which are based on direct time domain analysis of finite difference schemes, yield less information than frequency domain methods, but may be extended to nonlinear systems and difference schemes quite easily, and deal with many issues, including numerical stability analysis and the proper choice of numerical boundary conditions, in a straightforward way. In fact, though these techniques are, as a rule, far less familiar than frequency domain methods, they are not much more difficult to employ. In this section, some basic manipulations are introduced.

2.4.1   Time derivatives of products of functions or time series

Though, in this chapter, no systems have been defined as yet, and it is thus impossible to discuss quantities such as "energy," some algebraic manipulations may be introduced. Energetic quantities are always written in terms of products of functions or, in the discrete case, time series. Consider, for example, the following products:

$$\frac{du}{dt}\frac{d^2u}{dt^2} \qquad\qquad \frac{du}{dt}u \qquad\qquad (2.19)$$

In energetic analysis, whenever possible, it is useful to rewrite terms such as these as time derivatives of a single quantity (in this case, some function of u or its time derivatives). For instance, the terms above may be simply rewritten as

$$\frac{d}{dt}\left(\frac{1}{2}\left(\frac{du}{dt}\right)^2\right) \qquad\qquad \frac{d}{dt}\left(\frac{1}{2}u^2\right)$$

These are time derivatives of quadratic forms; in the context of the simple harmonic oscillator, which will be discussed in detail in Chapter 3, the quadratic forms above may be identified with the kinetic and potential energies of the oscillator, when u is taken as the dependent variable. Notice in particular that both quantities are squared quantities, and thus non-negative, regardless of the values taken by u or du/dt. It is useful to be able to isolate these energetic quantities, combinations of which are often conserved or dissipated, because, from them, one may derive bounds on the size of the solution itself. Arriving at such bounds in the discrete case is, in fact, a numerical stability guarantee.

For linear systems, the energetic quantities are always quadratic forms. For nonlinear systems, they will generally not be, but manipulations similar to the above may still be performed. For instance, it is also true that

$$\frac{du}{dt}u^3 = \frac{d}{dt}\left(\frac{1}{4}u^4\right) \qquad\qquad (2.20)$$

Note that the quantity under total differentiation above is still non-negative.

There are analogous manipulations in the case of products of time series under difference operators; the number is considerably greater, though, because of the multiplicity of ways of approximating differential operators, as seen in Section 2.2. Consider, for instance, the products

$$(\delta_t.u_d)\,\delta_{tt}u_d \qquad\qquad u_d\delta_t.u_d$$

where, now, $u_d = u_d^n$ is a time series; these are clearly approximations to the expressions given in (2.19). Expanding the first of these at time step n gives

$$(\delta_t.u_d^n)\,\delta_{tt}u_d^n = \frac{1}{2k}\left(u_d^{n+1} - u_d^{n-1}\right)\frac{1}{k^2}\left(u_d^{n+1} - 2u_d^n + u_d^{n-1}\right)$$

$$= \frac{1}{2k}\left(\left(\frac{u_d^{n+1} - u_d^n}{k}\right)^2 - \left(\frac{u_d^n - u_d^{n-1}}{k}\right)^2\right)$$

$$= \delta_{t+}\left(\frac{1}{2}(\delta_t._{-}u_d^n)^2\right)$$

Expanding the second gives

$$(\delta_t.u_d^n)\,u_d^n = \frac{1}{2k}\left(u_d^{n+1} - u_d^{n-1}\right)u_d^n = \frac{1}{2k}\left(u_d^{n+1}u_d^n - u_d^nu_d^{n-1}\right) = \delta_{t+}\left(\frac{1}{2}u_d^ne_{t-}u_d^n\right)$$

These instances of products of time series under difference operators can thus be reduced to total differences of quadratic forms; but when one moves beyond quadratic forms to the general case, it is not true that every such approximation will behave in this way. As an illustration, consider two approximations to the quantity given on the left of (2.20) above:

$$(\delta_t . u_{\mathrm{d}}^n)\,(u_{\mathrm{d}}^n)^3 \qquad\qquad (\delta_t . u_{\mathrm{d}}^n)\,(\mu_t . u_{\mathrm{d}}^n)\,(u_{\mathrm{d}}^n)^2$$

The first expression above cannot be interpreted as the total difference of a quartic form, as per the right side of (2.20) in continuous time. But the second can, and one may write

$$(\delta_t . u_{\mathrm{d}}^n)\,(\mu_t . u_{\mathrm{d}}^n)\,(u_{\mathrm{d}}^n)^2 = \frac{1}{2k}\left(u_{\mathrm{d}}^{n+1} - u_{\mathrm{d}}^{n-1}\right)\frac{1}{2}\left(u_{\mathrm{d}}^{n+1} + u_{\mathrm{d}}^{n-1}\right)(u_{\mathrm{d}}^n)^2 \qquad (2.21\text{a})$$

$$= \frac{1}{4k}\left((u_{\mathrm{d}}^{n+1})^2 (u_{\mathrm{d}}^n)^2 - (u_{\mathrm{d}}^n)^2 (u_{\mathrm{d}}^{n-1})^2\right) \qquad (2.21\text{b})$$

$$= \delta_{t+}\left(\frac{1}{4}(u_{\mathrm{d}}^n)^2 (e_{t-} u_{\mathrm{d}}^n)^2\right) \qquad (2.21\text{c})$$

These distinctions between methods of approximation turn out to be crucial in the stability analysis of finite difference schemes through conservation or energy-based methods.

2.4.2 Product identities and inequalities

For the sake of reference, presented here are various identities which are of use in the energetic analysis of finite difference schemes. For a time series u_{d}^n, it is always true that

$$(\delta_t . u_{\mathrm{d}})\,(\delta_{tt} u_{\mathrm{d}}) = \delta_{t+}\left(\frac{1}{2}(\delta_{t-} u_{\mathrm{d}})^2\right) \qquad (2.22\text{a})$$

$$(\delta_t . u_{\mathrm{d}})\,u_{\mathrm{d}} = \delta_{t+}\left(\frac{1}{2} u_{\mathrm{d}} e_{t-} u_{\mathrm{d}}\right) \qquad (2.22\text{b})$$

$$(\delta_{t+} u_{\mathrm{d}})\,\mu_{t+} u_{\mathrm{d}} = \delta_{t+}\left(\frac{1}{2} u_{\mathrm{d}}^2\right) \qquad (2.22\text{c})$$

$$(\mu_t . u_{\mathrm{d}})\,u_{\mathrm{d}} = \mu_{t+}\left(u_{\mathrm{d}} e_{t-} u_{\mathrm{d}}\right) \qquad (2.22\text{d})$$

$$(\mu_t . u_{\mathrm{d}})\,(\delta_t . u_{\mathrm{d}}) = \delta_t . \left(\frac{1}{2} u_{\mathrm{d}}^2\right) \qquad (2.22\text{e})$$

$$u_{\mathrm{d}} e_{t-} u_{\mathrm{d}} = (\mu_{t-} u_{\mathrm{d}})^2 - \frac{k^2}{4}(\delta_{t-} u_{\mathrm{d}})^2 \qquad (2.22\text{f})$$

For two time series, u_{d}^n and w_{d}^n, the following identity (which corresponds to the product rule of differentiation) is also useful:

$$\delta_{t+}(u_{\mathrm{d}} w_{\mathrm{d}}) = (\delta_{t+} u_{\mathrm{d}})\,(\mu_{t+} w_{\mathrm{d}}) + (\mu_{t+} u_{\mathrm{d}})\,(\delta_{t+} w_{\mathrm{d}}) \qquad (2.23)$$

Proofs of these identities are direct; see Problem 2.10. All these identities generalize in an obvious way to the distributed case—see the comment on page 110 for more on this.

An inequality of great utility, especially in bounding the response of systems subject to external excitations, is the following bound on the product of two numbers u and w:

$$|uw| \leq \frac{u^2}{2\alpha^2} + \frac{\alpha^2 w^2}{2} \qquad (2.24)$$

which holds instantaneously for any real number $\alpha \neq 0$ (u and w could represent values of a time series or of continuous functions).

2.4.3 Quadratic forms

In the energetic analysis of finite difference schemes for both linear and nonlinear systems, quadratic forms play a fundamental role—this is because the energy function for a linear system is always a quadratic function of the state, usually positive definite or semi-definite. Many nonlinear systems, some examples of which will be discussed in this book, may be written as linear systems incorporating extra nonlinear perturbation terms, and as a result the energy for such a system can be written as a quadratic form plus an additional perturbation, which may be non-negative.

Consider a particular such form in two real variables, x and y:

$$\mathfrak{H}(x, y) = x^2 + y^2 + 2axy \qquad (2.25)$$

where a is a real constant. It is simple enough to show that for $|a| < 1$, $\mathfrak{H}(x, y)$ is a paraboloid, and is positive definite (it is non-negative for all values of x and y, and possesses a unique minimum of zero at $x = y = 0$). For $a = \pm 1$, the form $\mathfrak{H}(x, y)$ is still non-negative, but not positive definite, i.e., it takes the value zero over the family of points given by $x = \mp y$. For $|a| < 1$, consider a level curve of $\mathfrak{H}$, at some value $\mathfrak{H} = \mathfrak{H}_0$, which is an ellipse oriented at 45 degrees with respect to the x or y axis. It should be clear, by visual inspection of Figure 2.4(a), that for a given value of $\mathfrak{H}_0$, the magnitudes of x and y are bounded, and in fact by

$$|x|, |y| \leq \sqrt{\frac{\mathfrak{H}_0}{1 - a^2}} \qquad (2.26)$$

See Problem 2.11. If $|a| > 1$, the level curves at $\mathfrak{H}(x, y) = \mathfrak{H}_0$ are hyperbolas, and it is simple to show that it is not possible to bound x or y in terms of $\mathfrak{H}_0$. The same is true of the borderline case of $|a| = 1$.

Quadratic forms such as $\mathfrak{H}(x, y)$, as mentioned above, appear naturally as energy functions of finite difference schemes for linear systems. For nonlinear systems, one almost always[3] has energy

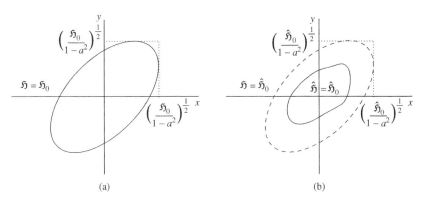

Figure 2.4   (a) A level curve of the quadratic form (2.25), for $\mathfrak{H} = \mathfrak{H}_0$. (b) A level curve of the nonlinear form (2.27) (solid line), and an associated level curve for the linear part (dashed line).

---

[3] While it is true that LTI systems always possess energy functions which are quadratic forms, the converse is not necessarily true—that is, there do exist nonlinear systems for which the energy is still a quadratic form. An interesting (and rare) example is the so-called simplified von Kármán model of plate vibration, discussed in depth in Section 13.2, which serves as an excellent model of strongly nonlinear behavior in percussion instruments such as cymbals and gongs, for which the Hamiltonian is indeed a quadratic form. Though this may be counterintuitive, it is worth recalling certain nonlinear circuit components which are incapable of storing energy (such as an ideal transformer with a nonlinear winding ratio). A closed circuit network, otherwise linear except for such elements, will also possess a stored energy expressible as a quadratic function in the state variables.

functions of the form

$$\hat{\mathfrak{H}}(x, y) = \mathfrak{H}(x, y) + \mathfrak{H}'(x, y) \tag{2.27}$$

where $\mathfrak{H}'(x, y)$ is another function of x and y, assumed non-negative, but not necessarily a quadratic form. Consider now a level curve of the function $\hat{\mathfrak{H}}(x, y)$, at $\hat{\mathfrak{H}} = \hat{\mathfrak{H}}_0$. Because $\mathfrak{H} \le \hat{\mathfrak{H}}$, one may deduce that

$$x^2 + y^2 + 2axy = \mathfrak{H}(x, y) \le \hat{\mathfrak{H}}(x, y) = \hat{\mathfrak{H}}_0$$

and thus, using the same reasoning as in the case of the pure quadratic form, one may obtain the bounds

$$|x|, |y| \le \sqrt{\frac{\hat{\mathfrak{H}}_0}{1 - a^2}}$$

This bound is illustrated in Figure 2.4(b). Thus even for extremely complex nonlinear systems, one may determine bounds on x and y provided that the additional perturbing energy term is non-negative, which is, in essence, no more than Lyapunov-type stability analysis [228]. This generality is what distinguishes energy-based methods from frequency domain techniques. Notice, however, that the bound is now not necessarily tight—it may be overly conservative, but through further analysis it might well be possible to determine more strict bounds on x and y. In the analysis of numerical schemes, these simple techniques allow one to deduce conditions for numerical stability for nonlinear systems, using no more than linear system techniques. See Problems 2.12 and 2.13.

In dynamical systems terminology, the level curves shown in Figure 2.4 may represent the path that a lossless system's state traces in the so-called phase plane; such a curve represents the constraint of constant energy in such a system. Though phase plane analysis is not used in this book, most of the lossless systems (and associated numerical methods) can and should be imagined in terms of such curves or surfaces of constant energy. A certain familiarity with phase plane analysis in the analysis of nonlinear systems is essential to an understanding of the various phenomena which arise [252], but in this book, only those tools that will be useful for practical robust algorithm design for sound synthesis will be developed. Symplectic numerical methods, very much related to energy techniques, are based directly on the analysis of the time evolution of numerical solutions in phase space [308].

2.5   Problems

Problem 2.1   *Show that the operators*

      (a) $\delta_{t+}\delta_{tt}$ *(b)* $\delta_{t-}\delta_{tt}$ *(c)* $\delta_{t\cdot}\delta_{tt}$

are all approximations to a third time derivative. For each, explicitly write the expression which results when applied to a time series u_d^n. What is the accuracy of such operators acting in isolation, when the expansion point is taken to be the instant $t = nk$? About which time instants should one expand in Taylor series in order to obtain a maximal order of accuracy in each case? What is the temporal width (see Section 2.2.1) for each operator?

Problem 2.2   *Prove that the composition of any number of operators of the form μ_{t+}, μ_{t-}, or $\mu_{t\cdot}$ is an approximation to the identity operator.*

Problem 2.3   *Prove that the composition of any number of operators of the form μ_{t+}, μ_{t-}, or $\mu_{t\cdot}$ with a single operator of type δ_{t+}, δ_{t-}, or $\delta_{t\cdot}$ is an approximation to a first time derivative.*

Problem 2.4   *Consider the difference operator δ_{t-}. When applied to a continuous function $u(t)$, it will require the values $u(t)$ and $u(t-k)$. Show that it is a second-order accurate approximation to the derivative du/dt by expanding in Taylor series about the time $t - (k/2)$.*

Problem 2.5   *In operator notation, a family of second-order accurate approximations to a second time derivative which operates over a width of five levels is*

$$(\alpha + (1-\alpha)\mu_{t.})\,\delta_{tt} \tag{2.28}$$

Using Taylor series expansions, find the unique value of α for which the operator is fourth-order accurate, when the expansion point is taken to be the central point of the five-point set of values.

Problem 2.6   *Show that the operator defined by*

$$\delta_{t.} - \frac{k^2}{6}\delta_{t+}\delta_{tt}$$

approximates a first time derivative to third-order accuracy, and find the appropriate time instant about which to perform a Taylor expansion. Show that this operator is of width 4, and that it is the only such operator of third-order accuracy.

Problem 2.7   *Consider the quadratic polynomial equation (2.13) in the variable z when $a^{(2)} = 1$, i.e.,*

$$z^2 + a^{(1)}z + 1 = 0$$

where $a^{(1)}$ is a real constant. Show that, depending on the value of $a^{(1)}$, the roots z_+ and z_- of the above equation will be either (a) complex conjugates or (b) real, and find the condition on $a^{(1)}$ which distinguishes these two cases. Also show that the product z_+z_- is equal to one in either case, without using the explicit forms of z_+ and z_-, and deduce that in case (a), z_+ and z_- are of unit modulus, and that in case (b), if the roots are distinct, one must be of magnitude greater than unity.

Problem 2.8   *Prove condition (2.14) for the quadratic (2.13). You should use the method described in the previous problem as a starting point.*

Problem 2.9   *For all the difference operators described in Problem 2.1 above, and for the operator given in Problem 2.5, for the special value of α which you determined, find the transfer function description $h_d(z)$. Where do the zeros lie in each case? What is the multiplicity of each zero? Plot the magnitude and phase response in each case.*

Problem 2.10   *Prove the identities given in (2.22) and (2.23).*

Problem 2.11   *Consider the quadratic form (2.25), and show that if $|a| \geq 1$, it is possible to find arbitrarily large values of x and y which solve the equation $\mathfrak{H} = \mathfrak{H}_0$, for any value of $\mathfrak{H}_0$.*

Problem 2.12   *Consider the function $\mathfrak{H}$ defined as*

$$\mathfrak{H} = \frac{1}{2}\left(\delta_{t-}u_d\right)^2 + \frac{\omega_0^2}{2}u_d e_{t-}u_d$$

where ω_0 is a real constant, and $u_d = u_d^n$ is a time series with time step k. Evaluating $\mathfrak{H}$ at time step n, show that it is a quadratic form as given in (2.25), in the variables u_d^n and u_d^{n-1}, except for a constant scaling. Find a condition on k, the time step, such that $\mathfrak{H}$ is positive definite. Under this condition, determine a bound on u_d^n in terms of $\mathfrak{H} = \mathfrak{H}_0$, ω_0, and k. ($\mathfrak{H}$ as defined here is an energy function for a particular finite difference scheme for the simple harmonic oscillator, which is discussed in Section 3.2. The analysis performed in this problem leads, essentially, to a numerical stability condition for the scheme.)

Problem 2.13 *Consider the function $\mathfrak{H}$ defined as*

$$\mathfrak{H} = \frac{1}{2}\,(\delta_t - u_d)^2 + \frac{\omega_0^2}{2}\,u_d e_{t-} u_d + \frac{b^2}{4}\,u_d^2 e_{t-}(u_d^2)$$

where ω_0 and b are real constants, and $u_d = u_d^n$ is a time series with time step k. Evaluating $\mathfrak{H}$ at time step n, show that it is a positive definite form as given in (2.27), in the variables u_d^n and u_d^{n-1}, except for a constant scaling. Find a condition on k, the time step, such that $\mathfrak{H}$ is positive definite; is it an improvement on the condition that you derived in the previous problem? Perform an analysis similar to that of the previous problem, determining a bound on the size of u_d^n in terms of $\mathfrak{H}$, ω_0, and k. ($\mathfrak{H}$ as defined here is an energy function for a particular finite difference scheme for a nonlinear oscillator, which is discussed in Section 4.2.1. The analysis performed in this problem leads, again, to a numerical stability condition for the scheme, now in the nonlinear case.)

3

The oscillator

An oscillator of some kind is the sound-producing mechanism in nearly every music-making device, including most Western acoustic orchestral instruments, many from outside the Western tradition, electromechanical instruments, analog synthesizers, and digital synthesis algorithms. In the context of the latter case, the oscillator was one of the first digital sound synthesis modules to appear (see Section 1.1.1), and continues to play a key role in physical modeling algorithms—indeed, every system described in this book is, at its most basic level, an oscillator.

It is interesting, however, that the reasons underlying the preeminence of the oscillator in digital sound synthesis are distinct in the case of early or abstract sound synthesis algorithms, outlined in Section 1.1, and physical modeling algorithms, described in Section 1.2. For abstract methods, sinusoids were seized upon at an early stage, apparently because of their perceptual significance in human audition: a sinusoid is perceived as a unit, characterized by a bare minimum of parameters, namely amplitude and frequency, which correlate well with perceived loudness and pitch. This is particularly true of additive and FM synthesis, but also of subtractive synthesis methods, in which case a non-sinusoidal oscillator is often used as the excitation, as well as wavetable methods, in which values are read periodically from a table. In physical modeling synthesis, which is based on descriptions of objects which are subject to the laws of physics, sinusoids (more properly, complex exponentials or damped sinusoids) occur naturally as eigenfunctions of linear and time-invariant systems, and many musical instruments can be well described to a first approximation as such. That sinusoids play such a dual perceptual/physical role is certainly not a coincidence—if the world is, to a first approximation, a linear system, then humans will be well adapted to perceive collections of sinusoids. Thus the distinction made above is not as clear-cut as it might first appear to be. Regardless of one's point of view, the linear oscillator is the obvious starting point for any description of sound synthesis, through physical modeling or any other method.

It is interesting to note that in many parts of the numerical simulation literature, the second-order simple harmonic oscillator is *not* the point of departure for descriptions of numerical methods—rather, a first-order linear ODE is usually taken to be the basic equation. The reason for this is that much research into numerical simulation is geared toward dealing with highly nonlinear fluid dynamics problems, which are often most easily expressed as systems of first-order equations. It would be simple enough to begin with such a first-order system here as well, and then progress to the second-order oscillator by writing it as a first-order system in two variables (see Section 3.1.3), but in fact most systems of interest in musical acoustics (and especially those involving the vibration of solids) can be described directly through second-order ODEs or PDEs in time; the finite element literature, also concerned first and foremost with the vibration of solids, shares this point of view.

This chapter is concerned with outlining the properties of the second-order linear oscillator, introduced in Section 3.1, as well as some simple and practically useful finite difference schemes in Section 3.2 and Section 3.3. There is an emphasis here on obtaining bounds on solution size; though this is of course a simple matter in the case of a linear oscillator, the tools and techniques introduced here will play a role in determining numerical stability conditions for simulations of musical systems which are far more complex. Both frequency domain analysis, which is familiar to most students of signal processing, and energetic methods, which will be much less so, are presented here. Lumped mass–spring networks are mentioned in passing in Section 3.4, and, finally, the simple harmonic oscillator with loss, and associated finite difference schemes, are discussed in Section 3.5.

3.1   The simple harmonic oscillator

The simple harmonic oscillator, perhaps the single most important ODE in physics, and of central importance to musical sound synthesis, is defined as

$$\frac{d^2u}{dt^2} = -\omega_0^2 u \tag{3.1}$$

It is a second-order ODE, and depends on the single parameter ω_0, also known as the angular frequency of oscillation. The frequency f_0, in Hertz, is given by $f_0 = \omega_0/2\pi$. The harmonic oscillator, as it is second order, requires the specification of two initial conditions, normally

$$u(0) = u_0 \qquad \frac{du}{dt}\bigg|_{t=0} = v_0$$

Equation (3.1) above may be arrived at in a variety of different contexts. In mechanics and acoustics, the canonical example is that of the mass–spring system, illustrated in Figure 3.1(a). A mass M is connected, via a linear spring of spring constant K, to a rigid support, and $u(t)$ represents the variation of the displacement of the mass about an equilibrium spring extension. Under these conditions, and if initial conditions such as u_0 and v_0 above are given, $u(t)$ satisfies (3.1) with $\omega_0 = \sqrt{K/M}$. The oscillator also occurs naturally in electrical circuit theory, as illustrated in Figure 3.1(b)—here, $u(t)$ represents the voltage across a linear capacitor, of capacitance C in series with an linear inductor of inductance L. Again, if appropriate initial conditions are supplied, the voltage will evolve according to (3.1), with $\omega_0 = 1/\sqrt{LC}$. Though electrical circuit theory

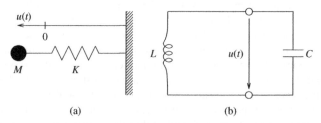

(a)   (b)

Figure 3.1   (a) Mass–spring system, with a mass M and a spring of stiffness K, for which the displacement $u(t)$, measured about an equilibrium distance (marked as 0), solves (3.1). (b) A connection of an inductor of inductance L, and a capacitor of capacitance C, for which the voltage $u(t)$ across the capacitor solves (3.1).

might seem to be a poor match for problems involving musical instrument modeling, and in fact will appear only fleetingly here, it is worth keeping in mind that scattering methods such as digital waveguides [334] and wave digital filters [127], which are heavily used in physical modeling sound synthesis, were all first developed using concepts borrowed from electrical network theory. See Section 1.2.4 for some general remarks on the use of scattering methods in synthesis, and Section 3.3.3 for a brief examination of wave digital filters. There is also, of course, a long tradition in acoustics of modeling lumped systems in terms of equivalent circuit elements, primarily for simplicity of representation [244].

3.1.1 Sinusoidal solution

It is well known that the solution to (3.1), if $u(t)$ is constrained to be real valued, and if $\omega_0 \neq 0$, has the form

$$u(t) = A \cos(\omega_0 t) + B \sin(\omega_0 t) \qquad (3.2)$$

where clearly, one must have

$$A = u_0 \qquad B = v_0/\omega_0$$

Another way of writing (3.2) is as

$$u(t) = C_0 \cos(\omega_0 t + \phi_0) \qquad (3.3)$$

where

$$C_0 = \sqrt{A^2 + B^2} \qquad \phi_0 = \tan^{-1}(-B/A) \qquad (3.4)$$

C_0 is the amplitude of the sinusoid, and ϕ_0 is the initial phase. See Figure 3.2.

From the sinusoidal form (3.3) above, it is easy enough to deduce that

$$|u(t)| = C_0 |\cos(\omega_0 t + \phi_0)| \leq C_0 \qquad \text{for} \qquad t \geq 0 \qquad (3.5)$$

which serves as a convenient bound on the size of the solution for all t, purely in terms of the initial conditions and the system parameter ω_0. Such bounds, in a numerical sound synthesis setting, are extremely useful, especially if a signal such as u is to be represented in a limited precision audio format. Note, however, that the bound above is obtained only through a priori knowledge of the form of the solution itself (i.e., it is a sinusoid). As will be shown in the next section, it is not really necessary to make such an assumption.

The use of sinusoidal, or more generally complex exponential, solutions of a given system in order to derive bounds on the size of the solution has developed, in the discrete setting, into a framework for determining the numerical stability of a simulation algorithm, also known as von Neumann analysis [342, 161]. Much more will be said about this from Chapter 5 onwards.

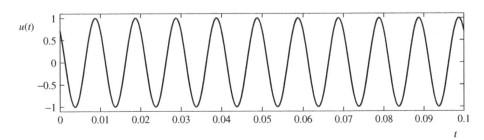

Figure 3.2 Sinusoid, of the form given in (3.3), with $C_0 = 1$, $f_0 = \omega_0/2\pi = 100$, and $\phi_0 = \pi/4$.

3.1.2 Energy

It is straightforward to derive an expression for the energy of the simple harmonic oscillator. Recalling the discussion at the beginning of Section 2.4.1, after multiplying (3.1) by du/dt, one arrives at

$$\frac{du}{dt}\frac{d^2u}{dt^2} + \omega_0^2 \frac{du}{dt}u = 0 \qquad \longrightarrow \qquad \frac{d}{dt}\left(\frac{1}{2}\left(\frac{du}{dt}\right)^2 + \frac{\omega_0^2}{2}u^2\right) = 0 \qquad (3.6)$$

Writing

$$\mathfrak{H} = \mathfrak{T} + \mathfrak{V} \qquad \text{with} \qquad \mathfrak{T} = \frac{1}{2}\left(\frac{du}{dt}\right)^2 \qquad \text{and} \qquad \mathfrak{V} = \frac{\omega_0^2}{2}u^2 \qquad (3.7)$$

one has

$$\frac{d\mathfrak{H}}{dt} = 0 \qquad \longrightarrow \qquad \mathfrak{H}(t) = \text{constant} \geq 0$$

When scaled by a constant with dimensions of mass, $\mathfrak{T}$, $\mathfrak{V}$, and $\mathfrak{H}$ are respectively the kinetic energy, potential energy, and total energy (or Hamiltonian) for the simple harmonic oscillator (SHO).

In order to arrive at a bound on solution size in this case, it may first be observed that

$$\mathfrak{H}(t) = \mathfrak{H}(0) = \frac{1}{2}v_0^2 + \frac{1}{2}\omega_0^2 u_0^2 = \frac{1}{2}\omega_0^2 C_0^2$$

where C_0 is defined in (3.4). Then, noting the non-negativity of $\mathfrak{T}$ and $\mathfrak{V}$, as defined in (3.7), it follows that

$$0 \leq \mathfrak{V}(t) \leq \mathfrak{H}(t) = \mathfrak{H}(0) = \frac{1}{2}\omega_0^2 C_0^2$$

and, using the form of $\mathfrak{V}(t)$, finally

$$|u(t)| \leq C_0 \qquad \text{for} \qquad t \geq 0 \qquad (3.8)$$

which is the same as the bound obtained in the previous section. In this case, however, one has made no a priori assumptions about the form of the solution. A bound on du/dt can also be obtained; though not so useful for the SHO given the strength of the above condition on u itself, such bounds do come in handy when dealing with distributed systems under free boundary conditions. See Problem 3.1.

This type of analysis, in which frequency domain analysis is avoided, has also been applied to the analysis of numerical simulation techniques, and is sometimes referred to as the energy method [284]. Here, although an energy has been "derived" from system (3.1), one could equally well begin from the expressions for kinetic and potential energy given in (3.7), and, through the application of variational principles, arrive at (3.1). This variational point of view dominates in the modern finite element simulation community.

3.1.3 As first-order system

In the literature, many numerical time-integration techniques are introduced with regard to first-order ODE systems. It is simple enough to expand the definition of the SHO, from (3.1), to a first-order system in two variables, i.e., in matrix form

$$\frac{d}{dt}\begin{bmatrix} u \\ v \end{bmatrix} = \begin{bmatrix} 0 & 1 \\ -\omega_0^2 & 0 \end{bmatrix}\begin{bmatrix} u \\ v \end{bmatrix}$$

All frequency domain and energy analysis can be applied to this equivalent system. Though first-order systems will come up only rarely in this book, it is worth being aware of such systems, as many time-integration techniques, including the ubiquitous Runge–Kutta family of methods and wave digital filters [127], are indeed usually presented with reference to first-order systems. In the distributed case, the important "finite difference time domain" family of methods [351] is also usually applied to first-order systems, such as the defining equations of electromagnetism.

3.1.4   Coupled systems of oscillators

Coupled second-order ODE systems occur frequently in finite element analysis, and, in musical sound synthesis, directly as descriptions of the dynamics of lumped networks, as per Section 1.2.1; what often remains, after spatial discretization of a distributed system, is a matrix equation of the form

$$\mathbf{M}\frac{d^2}{dt^2}\mathbf{u} = -\mathbf{K}\mathbf{u} \tag{3.9}$$

where $\mathbf{u}$ is an $N \times 1$ column vector, and $\mathbf{M}$ and $\mathbf{K}$ are known as, respectively, the $N \times N$ mass and stiffness matrices, which are (at least for linear and time-invariant problems) constants. $\mathbf{M}$ is normally diagonal, and $\mathbf{K}$ is usually symmetric, reflecting reciprocity of forces acting within the system defined by (3.9). If the product $\mathbf{M}^{-1}\mathbf{K}$ exists and is diagonalizable, with $\mathbf{M}^{-1}\mathbf{K} = \mathbf{U}\mathbf{\Lambda}\mathbf{U}^{-1}$, then the system may be immediately decoupled as

$$\frac{d^2}{dt^2}\mathbf{v} = -\mathbf{\Lambda}\mathbf{v} \tag{3.10}$$

where $\mathbf{u} = \mathbf{U}\mathbf{v}$, and $\mathbf{\Lambda}$ is the diagonal matrix containing the eigenvalues of $\mathbf{M}^{-1}\mathbf{K}$, which are normally real and non-negative. The system (3.9) will then have N frequencies ω_p (which are not necessarily distinct), given by

$$\omega_p = \sqrt{\mathbf{\Lambda}_{p,p}} \qquad \text{for} \qquad p = 1, \dots, N \tag{3.11}$$

Energy analysis also extends to systems such as (3.9). Left-multiplying by the row vector $d\mathbf{u}^T/dt$, where superscript T indicates a transposition operation, gives

$$\frac{d\mathbf{u}^T}{dt}\mathbf{M}\frac{d^2\mathbf{u}}{dt^2} + \frac{d\mathbf{u}^T}{dt}\mathbf{K}\mathbf{u} = 0$$

or, using the symmetry of $\mathbf{M}$ and $\mathbf{K}$,

$$\frac{d\mathfrak{H}}{dt} = 0 \quad \text{with} \quad \mathfrak{H} = \mathfrak{T} + \mathfrak{V} \quad \text{and} \quad \mathfrak{T} = \frac{1}{2}\frac{d\mathbf{u}^T}{dt}\mathbf{M}\frac{d\mathbf{u}}{dt} \quad \mathfrak{V} = \frac{1}{2}\mathbf{u}^T\mathbf{K}\mathbf{u}$$

If $\mathbf{M}$ and $\mathbf{K}$ are positive definite, then the energy $\mathfrak{H}$ will also be non-negative, and bounds on solution size may be derived as in the case of a single oscillator.

Lumped network approaches to sound synthesis, mentioned in Section 1.2.1, are built, essentially, around such coupled oscillator systems. The numerical treatment of such systems will appear later in Section 3.4. See Problems 3.2 and 3.3 for some simple concrete examples of coupled oscillators.

3.2   A finite difference scheme

The most basic finite difference scheme for the SHO (3.1) is obtained by introducing a time step k, a time series u^n intended to approximate the solution at time $t = nk$, and replacing the second time derivative by a second time difference, as defined in (2.4). One has, in operator form,

$$\delta_{tt} u = -\omega_0^2 u \qquad (3.12)$$

Note the compactness of the above representation, and in particular the absence of the time index, which is assumed to be n for each occurrence of the variable u. The finite difference scheme (3.12) is a second-order accurate approximation to (3.1)—see Section 3.2.5. For reference, a code example in the Matlab programming language is provided in Section A.1.

3.2.1   As recursion

By expanding out the behavior of the operator δ_{tt}, and reintroducing the time index n, one loses compactness of representation, but has a clearer picture of how to program such a scheme on a computer. One has

$$\frac{1}{k^2} \left(u^{n+1} - 2u^n + u^{n-1} \right) = -\omega_0^2 u^n \qquad (3.13)$$

which relates values of the time series at three levels $n + 1$, n, and $n - 1$. Rewriting (3.13) so that u^{n+1} is isolated gives

$$u^{n+1} = \left(2 - \omega_0^2 k^2 \right) u^n - u^{n-1} \qquad (3.14)$$

which is a two-step recursion in the time series u^n. This difference equation is identical in form to that of a two-pole digital filter under transient conditions [261].

3.2.2   Initialization

The difference equation (3.14) must be initialized with two values, typically u^0 and u^1. This pair of values is slightly different from what one would normally use to initialize the continuous-time harmonic oscillator, namely the values $u(0)$ and $du/dt|_{t=0}$. In the distributed case, especially under striking conditions, it is often the initial velocity which is of interest. Supposing that one has, instead of the two values u^0 and u^1, an initial value u_0 and an initial velocity condition (call it v_0), a very simple way of proceeding is to write

$$u^0 = u_0 \qquad \text{and} \qquad \delta_{t+} u^0 = v_0 \qquad \longrightarrow \qquad u^1 = u_0 + k v_0$$

This approximation is only first-order accurate. More accurate settings may be derived—see Problem 3.4—but, in general, there is not much point in setting initial conditions to an accuracy greater than that of the scheme itself. Since many of the schemes used in this book will be of relatively low accuracy, the above condition is wholly sufficient for most sound synthesis applications, especially if one is operating at an elevated audio sampling rate (i.e., for a small value of k), which is usually the case. In many situations, in fact, an initial condition is not employed, as the physical model is excited by an external source (such as a bow, or reed mechanism).

3.2.3   Numerical instability

It is easy enough to arrive at a numerical scheme such as (3.12) approximating the SHO, and, indeed, under some conditions it does generate reasonable results, such as the sinusoidal output shown in Figure 3.3(a). But this is not necessarily the case—sometimes, the solution exhibits explosive growth, as shown in Figure 3.3(b). Such explosive growth definitely does not correspond, in any sense, to an approximation to the SHO, and is referred to as unstable.

Stability analysis is a key aspect of all numerical methods, and is given an involved treatment throughout the rest of this book. It is of great importance in the case of physical models of musical

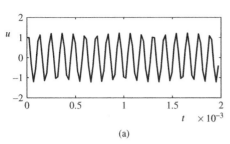
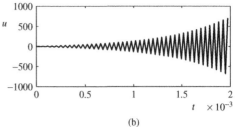

(a)   (b)

Figure 3.3   Output of scheme (3.12), running at a sample rate $f_s = 44\,100\,\text{Hz}$. In (a), sinusoidal output when $f_0 = \omega_0/2\pi = 8000\,\text{Hz}$, and in (b) unstable, explosive numerical behavior when $f_0 = \omega_0/2\pi = 14\,040\,\text{Hz}$.

instruments, which almost always operate under nearly lossless conditions, and which are thus especially prone to such instability. There are various ways of analyzing this behavior—in the present case of the SHO, frequency domain methods, described in the following section, are a natural choice. Energy methods, which extend well to more complex (nonlinear) problems, appear in Section 3.2.6.

3.2.4   Frequency domain analysis

The frequency domain analysis of scheme (3.12) is very similar to that of the SHO, as outlined in Section 3.1.1. Applying a z transformation, or, equivalently, inserting a test solution of the form $u^n = z^n$, where $z = e^{sk}$ (see comments on the frequency domain ansatz in Section 2.3), leads to the characteristic equation

$$z + (k^2\omega_0^2 - 2) + z^{-1} = 0$$

which has the solutions

$$z_\pm = \frac{2 - k^2\omega_0^2 \pm \sqrt{\left(2 - k^2\omega_0^2\right)^2 - 4}}{2} \qquad (3.15)$$

When $z_\pm$ are distinct, the solution to (3.12) will evolve according to

$$u^n = A_+ z_+^n + A_- z_-^n \qquad (3.16)$$

Under the condition

$$k < \frac{2}{\omega_0} \qquad (3.17)$$

the two roots $z_\pm$ will be complex conjugates of magnitude unity (see Section 2.3.3), in which case they may be written as

$$z_\pm = e^{\pm j\omega k}$$

where $\omega \neq \omega_0$, and the solution (3.16) may be rewritten as

$$u^n = A\cos(\omega nk) + B\sin(\omega nk) = C_0 \cos(\omega nk + \phi_0) \qquad (3.18)$$

where

$$A = u^0 \qquad B = \frac{u^1 - u^0\cos(\omega k)}{\sin(\omega k)} \qquad C_0 = \sqrt{A^2 + B^2} \qquad \phi_0 = \tan^{-1}(-B/A)$$

This solution is well behaved, and resembles the solution to the continuous-time SHO, from (3.2). From the form of the solution above, the following bound on the numerical solution size, in terms of the initial conditions and ω_0, may be deduced:

$$|u^n| \leq C_0 \tag{3.19}$$

Condition (3.17) may be violated in two different ways. If $k > 2/\omega_0$, then the two roots of (3.15) will be real, and one will be of magnitude greater than unity. Thus solution (3.16) will grow exponentially. If $k = 2/\omega_0$, then the two roots of (3.15) coincide, at $z_{\pm} = -1$. In this case, the solution (3.16) does not hold, and there will be a term which grows linearly. In neither of the above cases does the solution behave in accordance with (3.2), and its size cannot be bounded in terms of initial conditions alone. Such growth is called numerically unstable (and in the latter case marginally unstable), and condition (3.17) serves as a stability condition.

Stability conditions and sampling theory

Condition (3.17) may be rewritten, using sample rate $f_s = 1/k$ and the reference oscillator frequency $f_0 = \omega_0/2\pi$, as

$$f_s > \pi f_0$$

which, from the point of view of sampling theory, is counterintuitive—recall the comments on this subject at the beginning of Section 2.1. One might expect that the sampling rate necessary to simulate a sinusoid at frequency f_0 should satisfy $f_s > 2f_0$, and not the above condition, which is more restrictive. The reason for this is that the numerical solution does not in fact oscillate at frequency ω_0, but at frequency ω given by

$$\omega = \frac{1}{k} \cos^{-1} \left(1 - k^2 \omega_0^2/2\right)$$

This frequency warping effect is due to approximation error in the finite difference scheme (3.12) itself; such an effect will be generalized to numerical dispersion in distributed problems seen later in this book, and constitutes what is perhaps the largest single disadvantage of using time domain methods for sound synthesis. Note in particular that $\omega > \omega_0$. Perceptually, such an effect will lead to mistuning of "modes" in a simulation of a musical instrument. There are many means of combating this unwanted effect, the most direct (and crude) being to use a higher sampling rate (or smaller value of k)—the numerical frequency ω approaches ω_0 in the limit as k becomes small. This approach, however, though somewhat standard in the more mainstream simulation community, is not so useful in audio, as the sample rate is usually fixed,[1] though downsampling is a possibility. Another approach, which will be outlined in Section 3.3.2, involves different types of approximations to (3.1), and will be elaborated upon extensively throughout the rest of this book.

3.2.5   Accuracy

Scheme (3.12) employs only one difference operator, a second-order accurate approximation δ_{tt} to the operator d^2/dt^2. While it might be tempting to conclude that the scheme itself will generate a solution which converges to the solution of (3.1) with an error that depends on k^2 (which is in fact true in this case), the analysis of accuracy of an entire scheme is slightly more subtle than that

---

[1] In a distributed setting, when approximations in both space and time are employed, the spatial and temporal warping errors may cancel one another to a certain degree (indeed, perfectly, in the case of the 1D wave equation).

applied to a single operator in isolation. It is again useful to consider the action of the operator δ_{tt} on a continuous function $u(t)$. In this case, scheme (3.12) may be rewritten as

$$\left(\delta_{tt} + \omega_0^2\right) u(t) = 0 \tag{3.20}$$

or, using (2.6),

$$\left(\frac{d^2}{dt^2} + \omega_0^2\right) u(t) = O(k^2)$$

The left-hand side of the above equation would equal zero for $u(t)$ solving (3.1), but for approximation (3.12), there is a residual error on the order of the square of the time step k.

The accuracy of a given scheme will be at least that of the constituent operators and, in some rare cases, higher; two interesting case studies of great relevance to sound synthesis are presented in Section 3.3.4 and Section 6.2.4.

3.2.6 Energy analysis

Beginning from the compact representation of the difference scheme given in (3.12), one may derive a discrete conserved energy similar to that obtained for the continuous problem in Section 3.1.2. Multiplying (3.12) by a discrete approximation to the velocity, $\delta_t.u$, gives

$$(\delta_t.u)(\delta_{tt}u) + \omega_0^2 (\delta_t.u) u = 0$$

Employing the product identities given in Section 2.4.2 in the last chapter, one may immediately arrive at

$$\delta_{t+}\left(\frac{1}{2}(\delta_{t-}u)^2 + \frac{\omega_0^2}{2}ue_{t-}u\right) = 0$$

or

$$\delta_{t+}\mathfrak{h} = 0 \tag{3.21}$$

with

$$\mathfrak{h} = \mathfrak{t} + \mathfrak{v} \qquad \text{and} \qquad \mathfrak{t} = \frac{1}{2}(\delta_{t-}u)^2 \qquad \mathfrak{v} = \frac{\omega_0^2}{2}ue_{t-}u \tag{3.22}$$

Here, $\mathfrak{t}$, $\mathfrak{v}$, and $\mathfrak{h}$ are clearly approximations to the kinetic, potential, and total energies, $\mathfrak{T}$, $\mathfrak{V}$, and $\mathfrak{H}$, respectively, for the continuous problem, as defined in (3.7). All are time series, and could be indexed as $\mathfrak{t}^n$, $\mathfrak{v}^n$, and $\mathfrak{h}^n$, though it should be kept in mind that the above expressions are centered about time instants $t = (n-1/2)k$.

Equation (3.21) implies that the discrete-time series $\mathfrak{h}^n$, which approximates the total energy $\mathfrak{H}$ for the continuous-time problem, is constant. Thus the scheme (3.12) is energy conserving, in a discrete sense:

$$\mathfrak{h}^n = \text{constant} = \mathfrak{h}^0 \tag{3.23}$$

Though one might think that the existence of a discrete conserved energy would immediately imply good behavior of the associated finite difference scheme, the discrete approximation to the potential energy, given above in (3.22), is of indeterminate sign, and thus, possibly, so is $\mathfrak{h}$. The determination of non-negativity conditions on $\mathfrak{h}$ leads directly to a numerical stability condition. Expanding out the operator notation, one may write the function $\mathfrak{h}^n$ at time step n as

$$\mathfrak{h}^n = \frac{1}{2k^2}\left((u^n)^2 + (u^{n-1})^2\right) + \left(\frac{\omega_0^2}{2} - \frac{1}{k^2}\right)u^n u^{n-1}$$

which is no more than a quadratic form in the variables u^n and u^{n-1}. Applying the results given in Section 2.4.3, one may show that the quadratic form above is positive definite when

$$k < \frac{2}{\omega_0}$$

which is exactly the stability condition (3.17) arrived at through frequency domain analysis. See Problem 2.12. Under this condition, one further has that

$$|u^n| \leq \sqrt{\frac{2k^2\mathfrak{h}^n}{1 - (1 - \omega_0^2 k^2/2)^2}} = \sqrt{\frac{2k^2\mathfrak{h}^0}{1 - (1 - \omega_0^2 k^2/2)^2}} \qquad (3.24)$$

Just as in the case of frequency domain analysis, the solution may be bounded in terms of the initial conditions (or the initial energy) and the system parameters. In fact, the bound above is identical to that given in (3.19). See Problem 3.5.

Finite precision and round-off error

In infinite precision arithmetic, the quantity $\mathfrak{h}^n$ remains exactly constant, according to (3.23). That is, the discrete kinetic energy $\mathfrak{t}^n$ and potential energy $\mathfrak{v}^n$ sum to the same constant, at any time step n. See Figure 3.4(a). But in a finite precision computer implementation, there will be fluctuations in the total energy at the level of the least significant bit; such a fluctuation is shown, in the case of floating point arithmetic, in Figure 3.4(b). In this case, the fluctuations are on the order of 10^{-15} of the total energy, and the bit quantization of these variations is evident. Numerical energy is conserved to machine accuracy.

The analysis of conservative properties of finite difference schemes is younger than frequency domain analysis, and as a result, much less well known. It is, in some respects, far more powerful than the body of frequency domain analysis techniques which forms the workhorse of scheme analysis. The energy method [161] is the name given to a class of analysis techniques which do not employ frequency domain concepts. The study of finite difference schemes which furthermore possess conservation properties (of energy, and other invariants) experienced a good deal of growth in the 1980s [157, 307] and 1990s [225, 404, 145], and is related to more modern symplectic integration techniques [308, 324].

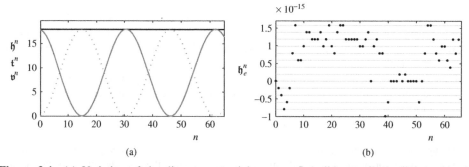

(a)   (b)

Figure 3.4 (a) Variation of the discrete potential energy $\mathfrak{v}^n$ (solid grey line), discrete kinetic energy $\mathfrak{t}^n$ (dotted grey line), and total discrete energy $\mathfrak{h}^n$ (solid black line), plotted against time step n, for the output of scheme (3.12). In this case, the values $\omega_0 = 1$ and $k = 1/10$ are used, and scheme (3.12) is initialized with the values $u^0 = 0.2$ and $u^1 = -0.4$. (b) Variation of the error in energy $\mathfrak{h}_e^n$, defined, at time step n, as $\mathfrak{h}_e^n = (\mathfrak{h}^n - \mathfrak{h}^0)/\mathfrak{h}^0$, plotted as black points. Multiples of single-bit variation are plotted as grey lines.

3.2.7 Computational considerations

The computational requirements of scheme (3.12) are most easily seen through an examination of the Matlab code in Section A.1. In each updating cycle, the algorithm requires one multiplication and one addition. Interestingly, this is nearly the same amount of computation required to generate values of a sinusoid through table reading, as is common practice in sound synthesis applications [240], as mentioned in Section 1.1.3, but with the advantage of a much reduced cost in terms of memory, as mentioned below. The use of recursive structures as a generator of sinusoids has been discussed by Smith and Cook [335]. In fact, with a small amount of additional work, a scheme can be developed which calculates exact values of the sinusoid—see Section 3.3.4. Though, for the sake of clarity of presentation, the algorithm in Section A.1 appears to make use of three memory locations, one for the current value of the computed solution and two for the previous two values, this may be reduced to two locations through overwriting. See Programming Exercise 3.1.

3.3 Other schemes

The difference scheme (3.12) is but the simplest form of approximation to (3.1), and, though it is indeed extremely useful, it does suffer from frequency warping error—the sinusoid generated by the scheme is of a frequency ω which may be different from ω_0, the frequency of the exact solution. The degree of warping becomes more pronounced for high values of ω_0 relative to $2\pi f_s$, where f_s is the sample rate. In this section, various techniques for the construction of improved finite difference schemes are detailed.

3.3.1 Using time-averaging operators

Another way to approximate (3.1) involves the use of temporal averaging operators, as introduced in Section 2.2. For example,

$$\delta_{tt}u = -\omega_0^2\mu_{t.}u \tag{3.25}$$

is also an approximation to (3.1), where it is to be recalled that the averaging operator $\mu_{t.}$ approximates the identity operation. Second-order accuracy is easy enough to determine by inspection of the centered operators δ_{tt} and $\mu_{t.}$, which are second-order accurate approximations to d^2/dt^2 and the identity operation, respectively. See Section 2.2.3.

This scheme, when the action of the operators δ_{tt} and $\mu_{t.}$ is expanded out, leads to

$$\frac{1}{k^2}\left(u^{n+1} - 2u^n + u^{n-1}\right) = -\frac{\omega_0^2}{2}\left(u^{n+1} + u^{n-1}\right) \tag{3.26}$$

which again involves values of the time series at three levels $n+1$, n, and $n-1$, and which can again be solved for u^{n+1}, as

$$u^{n+1} = \frac{2}{1 + \omega_0^2 k^2/2}u^n - u^{n+1} \tag{3.27}$$

The characteristic polynomial is now

$$z - \frac{2}{1 + \omega_0^2 k^2/2} + z^{-1} = 0$$

which has roots

$$z_\pm = \frac{1 \pm \sqrt{1 - \left(1 + \omega_0^2 k^2/2\right)^2}}{1 + \omega_0^2 k^2/2}$$

The solution will again evolve according to (3.16) when z_+ and z_- are distinct.

In this case, however, it is not difficult to show that the roots $z_\pm$ will be complex conjugates of unit magnitude for any choice of k. Thus $z_\pm = e^{\pm j\omega k}$, where ω, the frequency of the sinusoid generated by the scheme, is given by

$$\omega = \frac{1}{k} \cos^{-1} \left(\frac{1}{1 + \omega_0^2 k^2/2}\right)$$

Again $\omega \neq \omega_0$, but, in contrast to the case of scheme (3.12), one now has $\omega < \omega_0$. The result is a well-behaved sinusoidal solution of the form of (3.18) for any value of k; there is no stability condition of the form of (3.17). (This is typical of some types of implicit schemes for PDEs—see Section 6.3.2.) The energetic analysis mirrors this behavior. Multiplying (3.25) by $\delta_t . u$ and using identities (2.22a) and (2.22e) gives

$$(\delta_t . u)(\delta_{tt} u) + \omega_0^2 (\delta_t . u)(\mu_t . u) = \delta_{t+} \left(\frac{1}{2}(\delta_{t-} u)^2 + \frac{\omega_0^2}{2} \mu_{t-}(u^2)\right) = 0$$

or

$$\delta_{t+} \mathfrak{h} = 0 \quad \text{with} \quad \mathfrak{h} = \mathfrak{t} + \mathfrak{v} \quad \text{and} \quad \mathfrak{t} = \frac{1}{2}(\delta_{t-} u)^2 \quad \mathfrak{v} = \frac{\omega_0^2}{2} \mu_{t-} u^2 \quad (3.28)$$

Now, $\mathfrak{t}$ and $\mathfrak{v}$, and as a result $\mathfrak{h}$, are non-negative for any choice of k. A bound on solution size follows immediately. See Problem 3.6.

3.3.2   A second-order family of schemes

Though the stability condition inherent in scheme (3.12) has been circumvented in scheme (3.25), the problem of warped frequency persists. Using combination properties of the averaging operators (see Section 2.2.2), it is not difficult to see that any scheme of the form

$$\delta_{tt} u = -\omega_0^2 (\alpha + (1 - \alpha)\mu_t .) u \quad (3.29)$$

will also be a second-order accurate approximation to (3.1), for any choice of the real parameter α. In fact, it would be better to say "at least second-order accurate"—see Section 3.3.4 for more discussion. There is thus a one-parameter family of schemes for (3.1), all of which operate as two-step recursions: written out in full, the recursion has the form

$$u^{n+1} = \frac{2 - \alpha \omega_0^2 k^2}{1 + (1 - \alpha)\omega_0^2 k^2/2} u^n - u^{n-1}$$

Schemes (3.12) and (3.25) are members of this family with $\alpha = 1$ and $\alpha = 0$, respectively. See Programming Exercise 3.2.

The stability condition for the family of schemes (3.29) is now dependent on the free parameter α. Using frequency domain techniques, it may be shown that this condition is

$$k < \frac{2}{\omega_0 \sqrt{2\alpha - 1}} \quad \text{for} \quad \alpha \geq \frac{1}{2}, \quad \text{otherwise stable} \quad (3.30)$$

The scheme (3.29) also possesses a conserved energy, i.e.,

$$\delta_{t+}\mathfrak{h} = 0 \quad \text{with} \quad \mathfrak{h} = \mathfrak{t} + \mathfrak{v} \quad \text{and} \quad \mathfrak{t} = \frac{1}{2}(\delta_{t-}u)^2 \quad \mathfrak{v} = \frac{\omega_0^2}{2}\left(\alpha u e_{t-}u + (1-\alpha)\mu_{t-}(u^2)\right) \quad (3.31)$$

Finding a condition such that this energy is non-negative is again equivalent to the stability bound above obtained using frequency domain techniques. See Problem 3.7.

Frequency warping

It is interesting to examine the frequency warping characteristics of various members of this family, as a function of ω_0, the reference frequency for the SHO. See Figure 3.5(a). Notice that for small values of α, lower than about $\alpha = 0.7$, the difference scheme frequency is artificially low, and for values closer to $\alpha = 1$, artificially high. In fact, for high values of α, there is a certain "cutoff" frequency ω_0, for which the difference scheme becomes unstable—this is readily visible in the figure. In the middle range of values of α (between about $\alpha = 0.7$ and $\alpha = 0.8$), the difference scheme yields a good approximation over nearly the entire range of frequencies ω_0 up to the Nyquist limit. It is useful, from a musical point of view, to plot the frequency deviation in terms of cents, defined as

$$\text{deviation in cents} = 1200\log_2\left(\frac{\omega}{\omega_0}\right) \quad (3.32)$$

A deviation of 100 cents corresponds to a musical interval of a semitone. See Figure 3.5(b). For $\alpha = 0.7$, the maximum detuning is approximately two semitones and, if the sample rate is chosen sufficiently high, occurs in a region of the spectrum for which frequency discrimination in humans may not be of great importance [421]. See Programming Exercise 3.3. Note also the limited range of frequencies which can be simulated, for larger values of α, reflecting increased strictness of the stability condition for the family of schemes, from (3.30). See also Problem 3.8.

As mentioned earlier, the effect of frequency warping in discrete-time simulations of lumped systems generalizes to the issue of numerical dispersion and thus inharmonicity in schemes for PDEs. Though, as will be seen shortly, in Section 3.3.4, the problem may be dealt with neatly in the case of the oscillator in isolation, in general the only cure is through the use of more carefully designed schemes, such as those presented in this section.

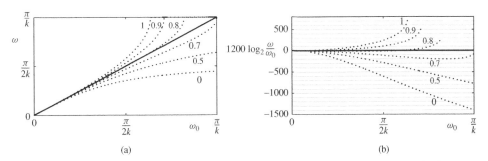

(a)   (b)

Figure 3.5 (a) Frequency ω of the parameterized difference scheme (3.29) for the SHO, plotted against $\omega_0 \in [0, \pi/k]$ as dotted lines, for various values of the free parameter α (indicated in the figure). The reference frequency is plotted as a solid black line. (b) Deviation in cents of ω from ω_0 for the same members of the family, as a function of $\omega_0 \in [0, \pi/k]$. Zero deviation is plotted as a solid black line. Successive deviations of a musical semitone are indicated by grey horizontal lines.

3.3.3   Wave digital filters

Because scattering methods have played such a dominant role in physical modeling sound synthesis for the past 20 years, it is worth making a short detour at this point to see how they fit into the standard framework of numerical methods. Wave digital filters, developed by Fettweis [127, 126], were the first such methods to appear, though not, admittedly, in the context of musical sound synthesis—see Section 1.2.4 for some comments on the history of such methods. Though based on ideas from circuit and network theory, in the end they can be rather simply viewed as finite difference schemes. Consider a parallel combination of an inductor and a capacitor, or LC circuit, as shown in Figure 3.6(a). An electrical network theorist would describe this system in the following way: supposing that the voltage across and current through the inductor (of inductance L) are u_1 and i_1, and the voltage across and current through the capacitor (of capacitance C) are u_2 and i_2, then the following four equations describe the dynamics of the parallel combination:

$$u_1 = L\frac{di_1}{dt} \qquad i_2 = C\frac{du_2}{dt} \qquad u_1 = u_2 \qquad i_1 + i_2 = 0 \tag{3.33}$$

The first two equations describe the internal behavior of the circuit elements themselves, and the last two are Kirchhoff's connection rules for a parallel combination of two circuit elements. The above system (3.33) of four equations in four unknowns can be reduced to the SHO (3.1) with $\omega_0 = 1/\sqrt{LC}$, with a dependent variable which is any of u_1, u_2, i_1, or i_2. (The analogy of the electrical network with an acoustical system such as that which might arise in a musical instrument model is direct: replacing currents with velocities, voltages with forces, and the inductance and capacitance with mass and the inverse of stiffness respectively, one arrives immediately at a simple mass–spring system.)

The wave digital discretization procedure relies on essentially two manipulations. The first is the discrete approximation of the first two of (3.33) through the trapezoid rule (see page 37); in terms of the difference operators that have been defined in this book, these discretized equations may be written as

$$\mu_{t+}u_1 = L\delta_{t+}i_1 \qquad \mu_{t+}i_2 = C\delta_{t+}u_2 \tag{3.34}$$

or, expanding out this notation and introducing a time index n,

$$u_1^{n+1} + u_1^n = \frac{2L}{k}\left(i_1^{n+1} - i_1^n\right) \qquad i_2^{n+1} + i_2^n = \frac{2C}{k}\left(u_2^{n+1} - u_2^n\right) \tag{3.35}$$

The connection rules are assumed to hold instantaneously in discrete time. The second manipulation is the introduction of wave variables:

$$a_1 = \frac{u_1 + R_1 i_1}{2\sqrt{R_1}} \qquad b_1 = \frac{u_1 - R_1 i_1}{2\sqrt{R_1}} \qquad a_2 = \frac{u_2 + R_2 i_2}{2\sqrt{R_2}} \qquad b_2 = \frac{u_2 - R_2 i_2}{2\sqrt{R_2}}$$

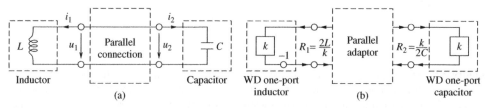

Figure 3.6   The LC circuit: (a) a parallel connection of an inductor of inductance L and a capacitor of capacitance C; and (b) the corresponding wave digital network.

Here, two positive constants, R_1 and R_2, called port resistances have been assigned to the inductor and capacitor, respectively. Under the special choices of $R_1 = 2L/k$ and $R_2 = k/(2C)$, the recursions (3.35) reduce to

$$b_1^{n+1} = -a_1^n \qquad b_2^{n+1} = a_2^n \tag{3.36}$$

These are the defining equations of the wave digital inductor and capacitor, respectively—notice that they involve only shifting operations (with sign inversion in the case of the inductor), and are thus strictly causal. They do, however, act in isolation, and must be connected through the equations which result from the substitution of wave variables into the connection rules:

$$\begin{bmatrix} a_1^n \\ a_2^n \end{bmatrix} = \begin{bmatrix} -1 + \frac{2R_2}{R_1+R_2} & \frac{2\sqrt{R_1 R_2}}{R_1+R_2} \\ \frac{2\sqrt{R_1 R_2}}{R_1+R_2} & -1 + \frac{2R_1}{R_1+R_2} \end{bmatrix} \begin{bmatrix} b_1^n \\ b_2^n \end{bmatrix} \tag{3.37}$$

This operation, called scattering, is at the heart of wave digital filtering, and is viewed as a two-port element in its own right, called an adaptor. Notice that the matrix operation above is orthogonal, preserving the "energy" or l_2 norm of wave variables through the scattering operation.[2] The scattering formulation may be extended to the connection of as many elements as desired, all the while maintaining this property of orthogonality, or losslessness. The wave digital discretization of the parallel inductor/capacitor combination is complete, and is illustrated in Figure 3.6(b); in each step in the recursion that the structure implies, there will occur a scattering step (at a wave digital adaptor), and a shifting of data. Such a mode of operation is also characteristic of digital waveguide networks.

One of the nice features of wave digital networks is that the energetic properties are fundamentally built in to the scattering and shifting operations. For example, using the orthogonality of the scattering matrix, in (3.37) and the simple shifting operations above in (3.36), it is simple to show, in this case, that

$$\left(a_1^{n+1}\right)^2 + \left(a_2^{n+1}\right)^2 = \left(b_1^{n+1}\right)^2 + \left(b_2^{n+1}\right)^2 = \left(a_1^n\right)^2 + \left(a_2^n\right)^2$$

or

$$\left(a_1^n\right)^2 + \left(a_2^n\right)^2 = \text{constant} \tag{3.38}$$

implying losslessness, using wave variables. This should come as no surprise—combining the two recursions in (3.34) leads immediately to the difference scheme (in, say, $u = u_1 = u_2$)

$$\delta_{tt}u = -\omega_0^2 \mu_{tt} u$$

which is a member of the family (3.29) of schemes for the SHO, with $\alpha = 1/2$ and $\omega_0^2 = 1/(LC)$. See also Programming Exercise 3.4. As was shown earlier, this scheme possesses a conserved energy, given in (3.31); this is in fact identical to the conserved quantity for the wave digital network, from (3.38). (Notice, however, that scheme (3.29) with $\alpha = 0.5$ behaves quite poorly with regard to frequency warping, as illustrated in Figure 3.5.)

---

[2] Though power-normalized waves, which give rise to orthogonal scattering matrices, have been used here, it is by no means necessary to use such wave variables. Simple "voltage waves" are in fact the norm in most applications of wave digital filters, including sound synthesis. In this case, scattering matrices are no longer orthogonal, but rather orthogonal with respect to a weighting of the port resistances—energy conservation holds in this case as well. For nonlinear networks, however, power-normalized waves are necessary in order to ensure passivity. See, for example, [128, 129, 41].

Energy conservation and the good stability properties that follow from it have been a primary selling point of wave digital filtering methods; another is the manner in which a complex system may be broken down into modular components, which behave strictly causally, leading to fully explicit methods. But, as has been seen throughout this chapter, at least in the case of the SHO, energy conservation follows from the simplest imaginable difference schemes; one need not restrict oneself to the use of a particular numerical integration method (such as the trapezoid rule) in order to obtain this property. Indeed, the entire apparatus of network theory and scattering is not necessary to show such conservation properties, or numerical stability. The modularity argument is also somewhat misleading: though for certain circuit networks, it is indeed possible to arrive at fully explicit methods using wave digital discretization principles, there are many (such as those involving nonlinearities) for which this is rather strenuous—a delicate juggling of port resistances, through the use of so-called reflection-free ports [130], will be necessary. This approach has been taken by some in sound synthesis applications—see Section 1.2.4 on hybrid methods. Often, however, simple finite difference schemes are explicit, such as those for the SHO. In short, wave digital filters are intuitively appealing but somewhat restrictive, and perhaps overly complicated, and do not lead to any real gains in terms of efficiency or ease of analysis, at least for simulation purposes. On the other hand, if one is making use of digital waveguides, which are genuinely more efficient than finite difference schemes for a certain range of applications, then wave digital filters are an excellent match when used in order to model, say, waveguide terminations, or connections with lumped elements.

3.3.4   An exact solution

For this very special case of the SHO, there is in fact a two-step recursion which generates the exact solution to (3.1), at times $t = nk$. It is simply given by

$$u^{n+1} - 2\cos(\omega_0 k)u^n + u^{n-1} = 0 \qquad (3.39)$$

This recursion may be more familiar to electrical and audio engineers as a two-pole filter operating under transient conditions. The z transformation analysis reveals

$$z - 2\cos(\omega_0 k) + z^{-1} = 0$$

which has solutions

$$z_\pm = \cos(\omega_0 k) \pm j\sin(\omega_0 k) = e^{\pm j\omega_0 k} \qquad \longrightarrow \qquad \omega = \omega_0$$

Thus the oscillation frequency ω of recursion (3.39) is exactly ω_0, the frequency of the continuous-time oscillator (3.1). In a sense, then, all the preceding analysis of difference schemes is pointless, at least in the case of (3.1). On the other hand, the SHO is pathological; more complex systems, especially when nonlinear, rarely allow for exact numerical solutions. One other case of interest, however, and the main reason for dwelling on this point here, is the 1D wave equation, to be introduced in Chapter 6, which is of extreme practical importance in models of musical instruments which are essentially 1D, such as strings and acoustic tubes. Numerical methods which are exact also exist in this case, and have been exploited with great success as digital waveguides [334].

Another question which arises here is that of accuracy. Consider again the one-parameter family of two-step difference schemes given by (3.29). Using identity (2.7a) relating μ_{tt} to δ_{tt}, it may be rewritten as

$$\delta_{tt}u = \frac{-\omega_0^2}{1 + \dfrac{\omega_0^2(1-\alpha)k^2}{2}}u$$

Under the special choice of

$$\alpha = \frac{2}{\omega_0^2} - \frac{\cos(\omega_0 k)}{1 - \cos(\omega_0 k)} \tag{3.40}$$

the difference scheme becomes exactly (3.39), or

$$\underbrace{\left(\delta_{tt} + \frac{2}{k^2}(1 - \cos(\omega_0 k))\right)}_{P} u = 0 \tag{3.41}$$

Consider the action of the operator P as defined above on a continuous function. Expanding the operator δ_{tt} and the function $\cos(\omega_0 k)$ in Taylor series leads to

$$P = \sum_{l=1}^{\infty} \frac{2k^{2(l-1)}}{(2l)!} \frac{d^{2l}}{dt^{2l}} + (-1)^{l-1} \frac{2\omega_0^{2l} k^{2(l-1)}}{(2l)!} = \sum_{l=1}^{\infty} \frac{2k^{2(l-1)}}{(2l)!} \left(\frac{d^{2l}}{dt^{2l}} + (-1)^{l-1}\omega_0^{2l}\right)$$

The various terms of the form

$$\left(\frac{d^{2l}}{dt^{2l}} + (-1)^{l-1}\omega_0^{2l}\right) \tag{3.42}$$

all possess a factor of $d^2/dt^2 + \omega_0^2$. Thus (3.41) may be rewritten as

$$\left(1 + O(k^2)\right)\left(\frac{d^2}{dt^2} + \omega_0^2\right)u = 0$$

which shows that the solution u indeed solves the equation of the SHO exactly.

This property of accuracy of a difference scheme beyond that of the constituent operators, under very special choices of the scheme parameters, is indeed a very delicate one. In the distributed setting, it has been exploited in the construction of so-called modified equation methods [181, 323, 259, 260, 98] and compact spectral-like schemes [222, 419, 203, 227].

3.3.5   Further methods

In this book, relatively simple difference strategies will be employed whenever possible. On the other hand, sometimes more accurate methods are necessary, especially when one is interested in more delicate modeling of musical instrument physics. There are a large variety of time differencing methods which are in use for the solutions of ODEs; normally, these are framed in terms of a first-order system, and so do not fit well into the main development here. Some of the better known are Adams–Bashforth, Adams–Moulton, and Runge–Kutta methods.

There do exist, however, some families of methods which have been developed directly for use with second-order systems, generally for application to problems in structural dynamics, such as those which occur in musical acoustics—among these are the Newmark family of schemes [256], as well as those proposed by Hilber, Hughes, and Taylor [168].

3.4   Lumped mass–spring networks

Similar principles of difference approximation may be applied to coupled systems of oscillators, introduced in Section 3.1.4. For an N-mass system defined by (3.9), one explicit approximation is

$$\mathbf{M}\delta_{tt}\mathbf{u} = -\mathbf{K}\mathbf{u} \tag{3.43}$$

where now $\mathbf{u} = \mathbf{u}^n$ is an N-vector time series. The resulting recursion is

$$\mathbf{u}^{n+1} = \left(2\mathbf{I} - k^2\mathbf{M}^{-1}\mathbf{K}\right)\mathbf{u}^n - \mathbf{u}^{n-1}$$

where $\mathbf{I}$ is the identity matrix. Stability analysis is similar to the scalar case; employing the ansatz $\mathbf{u}^n = \boldsymbol{\phi} z^n$ gives the following eigenvalue equation:

$$k^2\mathbf{M}^{-1}\mathbf{K}\boldsymbol{\phi} = -(z - 2 + z^{-1})\boldsymbol{\phi}$$

This equation possesses N solutions z; the condition that the scheme above is stable is similar to that of the scheme (3.12) for the SHO—in order to ensure that all roots z are bounded by 1 in magnitude, the condition

$$k \leq \frac{2}{\sqrt{\max(\text{eig}(\mathbf{M}^{-1}\mathbf{K}))}} \tag{3.44}$$

must be satisfied. Energy principles may be applied to scheme (3.43) to yield the same result. See Problem 3.9.

Though scheme (3.43) is explicit, and thus simple to implement, one difficulty is that of stiffness—if the natural frequencies of the coupled system are widely separated, then it will be necessary to use a relatively small time step (or high sampling frequency) in order to compute a solution. The flip side of this difficulty, in the realm of sound synthesis, where the sampling frequency is fixed, is that one can expect a good degree of frequency warping if the natural frequencies are in the upper range of the audio spectrum. One remedy is to apply a parameterized scheme such as that given in Section 3.3.2. For the coupled system (3.9), this will have the form

$$\mathbf{M}\delta_{tt}\mathbf{u} = -\mathbf{K}\left(\alpha + (1 - \alpha)\mu_{t\cdot}\right)\mathbf{u} \tag{3.45}$$

and will yield a much lower degree of frequency warping over the entire audio spectrum than scheme (3.43) for a properly chosen value of the parameter α. In the case of the single oscillator, there is no computational disadvantage to using such a scheme, but in the case of a coupled system, when $\mathbf{K}$ is not diagonal (this is the case for any interesting problem), linear system solution techniques will be necessary in order to perform an update. See Programming Exercise 3.5. Though, for sparse $\mathbf{K}$, many fast iterative techniques are available for linear system solution, computational cost is certainly heavier than for an explicit scheme, and programming complexity is undeniably greater. The deeper issue is that inherent to all implicit schemes: for most reasonably complex systems in musical acoustics, better accuracy usually comes with a price. Implicit methods (i.e., those involving a coupling among unknowns in a difference scheme update) will be revisited in more detail in the distributed setting—see Section 6.3.2. See Problem 3.10 for more on energy analysis of this scheme.

Another possibility is to diagonalize system (3.9) before discretization, or, for the coupled system (3.9), work with (3.10). In this case, the system consists of an uncoupled set of scalar oscillators, and one may employ a distinct exact scheme (see Section 3.3.4) to each component of the solution. This is an example of a modal method, and has the virtue of generating an exact solution with an explicit update. This is the approach taken by many in the finite element community, and also by some in modal sound synthesis [64]—one must be aware, however, that such a diagonalization can be prohibitively expensive if the system possesses a large number of degrees of freedom, and must be performed off-line. Depending on the application, one may also need to store the eigenvectors themselves—which can require an immense amount of computer memory!

3.5 Loss

Damping intervenes in any musical system, and, in the simplest case, may be modeled through the addition of a "linear loss" term to a given system. In the case of the SHO, one may add damping as

$$\frac{d^2u}{dt^2} = -\omega_0^2 u - 2\sigma_0 \frac{du}{dt} \tag{3.46}$$

where $\sigma_0 \geq 0$ is the damping parameter for the system. In terms of the mass–spring system or LC oscillator shown in Figure 3.1, the damping term corresponds to the addition of a linear dashpot or resistor, respectively.

The characteristic equation for (3.46), obtained through Laplace transformation, or through the insertion of a test solution $u = e^{st}$, is

$$s^2 + 2\sigma_0 s + \omega_0^2 = 0$$

which has solutions

$$s_\pm = -\sigma_0 \pm \sqrt{\sigma_0^2 - \omega_0^2}$$

If damping is small, i.e., if $\sigma_0 < \omega_0$, the roots may be written as

$$s_\pm = -\sigma_0 \pm j\omega_1 \quad \text{with} \quad \omega_1 = \sqrt{\omega_0^2 - \sigma_0^2}$$

In this case, the solution (3.3) may be generalized to

$$u(t) = e^{-\sigma_0 t}\left(A\cos(\omega_1 t) + B\sin(\omega_1 t)\right) = C_1 e^{-\sigma_0 t}\cos(\omega_1 t + \phi_1) \tag{3.47}$$

where A, B, C_1 and ϕ_1 are defined by

$$A = u_0 \qquad B = \frac{v_0 + \sigma_0 u_0}{\omega_1} \qquad C_1 = \sqrt{A^2 + B^2} \qquad \phi_1 = \tan^{-1}\left(-\frac{B}{A}\right)$$

See Figure 3.7.

It should be clear that the bound

$$|u(t)| \leq C_1 e^{-\sigma_0 t} \leq C_1 \tag{3.48}$$

holds for all $t \geq 0$.

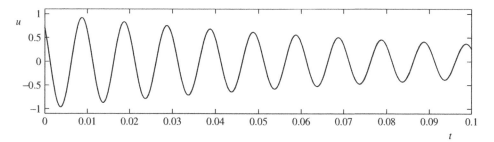

Figure 3.7 Damped sinusoid, of the form given in (3.47), with $C_1 = 1$, $\sigma_0 = 10$, $\omega_1 = 200\pi$, and $\phi_1 = \pi/4$.

The case of large damping, i.e., $\sigma_0 > \omega_0$, is of mainly academic interest in musical acoustics, but the solution will consist of two exponentially damped terms. For $\sigma_0 = \omega_0$, degeneracy of the roots of the characteristic solution leads to some limited solution growth. See Problem 3.11.

3.5.1   Energy

The energetic analysis of (3.46) is a simple extension of that for system (3.1). One now has, after again multiplying through by du/dt,

$$\frac{d\mathfrak{H}}{dt} = -2\sigma_0 \left(\frac{du}{dt}\right)^2 \leq 0 \quad \longrightarrow \quad \mathfrak{H}(t_1) \leq \mathfrak{H}(t_2) \leq \mathfrak{H}(0) \quad \text{for} \quad t_1 \geq t_2 \geq 0 \tag{3.49}$$

where $\mathfrak{H}$ is defined as in (3.7). The energy is thus a positive and monotonically decreasing function of time. This leads to the bound

$$|u(t)| \leq C_0 \tag{3.50}$$

which is identical to that obtained in the lossless case.

The bounds (3.48) and (3.50) obtained through frequency domain and energetic analysis, respectively, are distinct. Notice, in particular, that bound (3.50) is insensitive to the addition of loss, and, at the same time, is more general than bound (3.48), which requires the assumption of small damping (i.e., $\sigma_0 < \omega_0$). It is possible to reconcile this difference by extending the energetic analysis somewhat—see Problem 3.12.

3.5.2   Finite difference scheme

The damped oscillator (3.46) may be numerically integrated in a variety of ways. A simple scheme is the following:

$$\delta_{tt}u = -\omega_0^2 u - 2\sigma_0 \delta_{t\cdot}u \tag{3.51}$$

which, when the operator notation is expanded out, leads to the recursion

$$u^{n+1} = \frac{2 - \omega_0^2 k^2}{1 + \sigma_0 k} u^n - \frac{1 - \sigma_0 k}{1 + \sigma_0 k} u^{n-1}$$

This is again a recursion of temporal width three. See Programming Exercise 3.6.

The characteristic equation will now be

$$z - \frac{2 - \omega_0^2 k^2}{1 + \sigma_0 k} + \frac{1 - \sigma_0 k}{1 + \sigma_0 k} z^{-1} = 0 \tag{3.52}$$

The roots may be written explicitly as

$$z_\pm = \frac{1}{1 + \sigma_0 k} \left(1 - \frac{\omega_0^2 k^2}{2} \pm \sqrt{\left(1 - \omega_0^2 k^2/2\right)^2 - \left(1 - \sigma_0^2 k^2\right)}\right) \tag{3.53}$$

Though a direct analysis of the above expressions for the roots is possible, if one is interested in bounding the magnitudes of the roots by unity, it is much simpler to employ the conditions (2.14), which yield, simply,

$$k < \frac{2}{\omega_0} \tag{3.54}$$

The stability condition for scheme (3.51), which involves a centered difference approximation for the loss term, is thus unchanged from that of the undamped scheme (3.12). On the other hand, a more direct examination of the behavior of the roots given above can be revealing; see Problem 3.13.

Energetic analysis also yields a similar condition. Multiplying (3.51) by $\delta_{t \cdot} u$ gives, instead of (3.21),

$$\delta_{t+}\mathfrak{h} = -2\sigma_0 \left(\delta_{t \cdot} u\right)^2 \le 0 \qquad (3.55)$$

where $\mathfrak{h} = \mathfrak{t} + \mathfrak{v}$, with $\mathfrak{t}$ and $\mathfrak{v}$ defined as before in (3.22). From the previous analysis, it remains true that $\mathfrak{h}$ is non-negative under the condition (3.54), in which case one may deduce that

$$\mathfrak{h}^n \le \mathfrak{h}^0 \qquad (3.10)$$

for all $n \ge 1$. The discrete energy function is thus monotonically decreasing. As the expression for the energy is the same as in the lossless case, one may again arrive at a bound on solution size, i.e.,

$$|u^n| \le \sqrt{\frac{2k^2\mathfrak{h}^n}{1 - (1 - \omega_0^2 k^2/2)^2}} \le \sqrt{\frac{2k^2\mathfrak{h}^0}{1 - (1 - \omega_0^2 k^2/2)^2}} \qquad (3.56)$$

The scheme above makes use of a centered difference approximation to the loss term. Consider the following non-centered scheme:

$$\delta_{tt}u = -\omega_0^2 u - 2\sigma_0 \delta_{t-} u \qquad (3.57)$$

The characteristic equation will now be

$$z - \left(2 - \omega_0^2 k^2 - 2\sigma_0 k\right) + (1 - 2\sigma_0 k) z^{-1} = 0 \qquad (3.58)$$

The condition (2.14) now gives the following condition on k for numerical stability:

$$k \le \frac{2}{\omega_0^2} \left(-\sigma_0 + \sqrt{\sigma_0^2 + \omega_0^2}\right) \qquad (3.59)$$

See Problem 3.14. This non-centered scheme is only first-order accurate, but, if the loss parameter σ_0 is small, as it normally is for most systems in musical acoustics, the solution accuracy will not be severely degraded. Although in this case one can arrive at an explicit update using centered or non-centered difference approximations, in the distributed setting such backward difference approximations can be useful in avoiding implicit schemes, which are moderately more costly in terms of implementation—see comments on this topic in Section 3.4.

3.5.3 Numerical decay time

Like frequency, loss is an extremely important perceptual attribute of a musical system, in that it determines a characteristic decay time under transient conditions; as has been shown in the case of the SHO, frequency can be altered through numerical approximation, and, as one might expect, so can the decay time. It is thus worth spending a few moments here in determining just how much distortion will be introduced through typical finite difference approximations.

First consider the solution (3.47) to the SHO with loss, under normal (low-loss) conditions. The solution is exponentially damped, and the 60 dB decay time T_{60} (in amplitude) may be defined as

$$T_{60} = \frac{6 \ln 10}{\sigma_0} \qquad (3.60)$$

Considering now the simple difference scheme (3.51), if the stability condition (3.54) is respected, and again under low-loss conditions, the roots $z_\pm$ of the characteristic polynomial (3.52) will be complex conjugates, of magnitude

$$|z| = e^{-\sigma_d k} = \sqrt{\frac{1 - \sigma_0 k}{1 + \sigma_0 k}}$$

Here, σ_0 is the loss parameter for the model system (3.46), and σ_d is that corresponding to the finite difference scheme. One can then define a numerical 60 dB decay time $T_{d,60}$ by

$$T_{d,60} = \frac{6 \ln 10}{\sigma_d} = \frac{12k \ln 10}{\ln \left(\frac{1 + \sigma_0 k}{1 - \sigma_0 k} \right)} \tag{3.61}$$

For scheme (3.57), which uses a non-centered approximation to the loss term, the magnitudes of the solutions to the characteristic polynomial (3.58) will be, again under low loss conditions,

$$|z| = e^{-\sigma_d k} = \sqrt{1 - 2\sigma_0 k}$$

implying that

$$T_{d,60} = \frac{6 \ln 10}{\sigma_d} = \frac{12k \ln 10}{- \ln(1 - 2\sigma_0 k)}$$

It is useful to plot the relative decay time $T_{d,60}/T_{60}$ for the schemes mentioned above—see Figure 3.8.

For scheme (3.51), the numerical decay time is closer than 99% of the true decay time for $\sigma_0 k \leq 0.17$. For a sample rate of $f_s = 44.1$ kHz, this implies that for decay times greater than $T_{60} = 0.0018$ s, the numerical decay time will not be noticeably different than that of the model system. For scheme (3.57), the 99% threshold is met for $T_{60} \geq 0.031$ s. These decay times are quite short by musical standards, and so it may be concluded that numerical distortion of decay time is not of major perceptual relevance, at least at reasonably high sample rates.

Although in the two examples of numerical schemes above, the numerical decay time is independent of ω_0 (as it is for the model system), this is not always the case. See Problem 3.15.

3.5.4   An exact solution

Just as in the case of the SHO, an exact two-step numerical solution is available in the case of the SHO with loss. Considering the recursion

$$u^{n+1} = e^{-\sigma_0 k} \left(e^{\sqrt{\sigma_0^2 - \omega_0^2} k} + e^{-\sqrt{\sigma_0^2 - \omega_0^2} k} \right) u^n - e^{-2\sigma_0 k} u^{n-1} \tag{3.62}$$

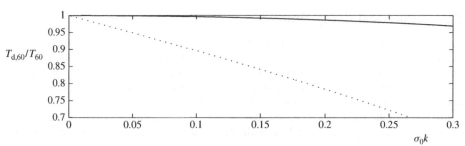

Figure 3.8   The relative 60 dB decay time $T_{d,60}/T_{60}$ for scheme (3.51), as a solid black line, and, for scheme (3.57), as a dotted black line, plotted against $\sigma_0 k$.

the characteristic polynomial is

$$z - e^{-\sigma_0 k}\left(e^{\sqrt{\sigma_0^2 - \omega_0^2}k} + e^{-\sqrt{\sigma_0^2 - \omega_0^2}k}\right) + e^{-2\sigma_0 k}z^{-1} = 0$$

which has roots

$$z_{\pm} = e^{\left(-\sigma_0 \pm \sqrt{\sigma_0^2 - \omega_0^2}\right)k}$$

The proof that the difference scheme (3.62) solves the loss SHO exactly may be carried out through the same series expansion methods used in Section 3.3.4. It is also possible to make a correspondence between scheme (3.62) and a parameterized finite difference scheme—see Problem 3.16.

3.6   Sources

So far in this chapter, only unforced oscillators have been discussed. Though uncoupled forcing terms almost never appear in the linear case in applications in musical acoustics, they play a rather important role in the case of nonlinear excitation mechanisms involving a continuous supply of energy, such as bow and reed models. See Section 4.3.1 and Section 9.3.

Considering the case of the oscillator with loss, a force term $F(t)$ may be added as

$$\frac{d^2 u}{dt^2} = -\omega_0^2 u - 2\sigma_0 \frac{du}{dt} + F(t) \tag{3.63}$$

In this case, it will be assumed that the force term $F(t)$ is known, though it should be kept in mind that in certain applications involving connections among objects, the force term may itself be a function of other unknowns in the system. (It should be noted that F, as it appears here and elsewhere in this book, does not in fact have dimensions of force, but of acceleration—in the case of a mass–spring system, it is the applied force divided by the mass. f will be used instead of F when a true force is intended.)

Frequency domain analysis of the forced oscillator is carried out in many textbooks—see, e.g., [244]. The main result, when the forcing function is sinusoidal, is that one obtains a solution which is a combination of a steady state response of the oscillator at the driving frequency, at a magnitude governed by the impedance of the oscillator, and the free or transient response, at the natural frequency of the oscillator—see Figure 3.9.

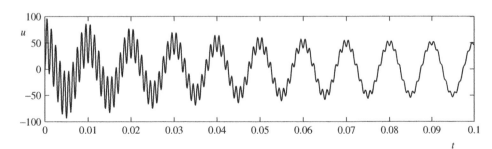

Figure 3.9   Response of the oscillator given in (3.63), with frequency $f_0 = \omega_0/2\pi = 1000\,\text{Hz}$ and $T_{60} = 0.5\,\text{s}$, when the forcing function F is given by $F = \cos(200\pi t)$, for $t \geq 0$. The transient response of the system at $f_0 = 1000\,\text{Hz}$ is superimposed onto the steady state response at $100\,\text{Hz}$.

Energy analysis leads immediately to

$$\frac{d\mathfrak{H}}{dt} = -2\sigma_0 \left(\frac{du}{dt}\right)^2 + \frac{du}{dt} F$$

Using inequality (2.24), with a choice of $\alpha = 1/\sqrt{4\sigma_0}$, gives the bound

$$\frac{d\mathfrak{H}}{dt} \leq \frac{F^2}{8\sigma_0} \quad \longrightarrow \quad \mathfrak{H}(t) \leq \mathfrak{H}(0) + \frac{1}{8\sigma_0} \int_0^t F^2 dt'$$

Thus the energy of the system may be bounded in terms of the initial conditions, through $\mathfrak{H}(0)$, and the external forcing function F, both of which are known a priori. This bound is, in most cases, rather conservative, but is useful especially in cases for which the forcing function $F(t)$ is of finite support of short duration. Notice, however, that in order to obtain such a bound, one must have a loss coefficient σ_0 which is strictly positive.

The number of possibilities for finite difference schemes is multiplied considerably by the presence of a forcing term—such is the interest of more involved techniques such as Newmark methods [256]. Keeping with two-step methods, one simple set is given by

$$\delta_{tt}u = -\omega_0^2 u - 2\sigma_0 \delta_{t.}u + [F] \tag{3.64}$$

where $[F] = [F]^n$ is some unspecified second-order accurate approximation to $F(t)$, such as F^n, $\mu_t.F^n$, $\mu_{tt}F^n$. In the case of the forcing term, there is much less difficulty in making use of multistep approximations, because F is assumed known (though in real-time sound synthesis applications, it may be sampled from data supplied by a performer). Energy analysis can be applied to a difference scheme in order to find bounds on the size of the solution in terms of the initial conditions, and the time series $[F]$—see Problem 3.18.

3.7   Problems

Problem 3.1   *For the simple harmonic oscillator, find a bound on du/dt in terms of the energy $\mathfrak{H}$. Use this to find another bound on $u(t)$, namely $|u(t)| \leq a_1 t + a_2$ for $t \geq 0$, and determine the positive constants a_1 and a_2 in terms of initial conditions. See Section 3.1.2.*

Problem 3.2   *Illustrated below are (a) a two-mass and (b) a three-mass lumped system. In each case, the masses are constrained to move longitudinally, and the displacement of the lth mass from its rest position is $u_l(t)$, as indicated by the distance from the vertical lines. The masses $M_1, M_2, \ldots,$ are connected to one another by linear springs, of stiffnesses $K_1, K_2, \ldots,$ as indicated. The series of masses and springs is terminated by rigid supports. Notice in particular that in each of (a) and (b), the masses M_l and spring stiffnesses K_l take on values which are distinct for each l (i.e., they are not all the same).*

Given that the forces acting on mass l from the right and left are $K_{l+1}(u_{l+1} - u_l)$ and $-K_l(u_l - u_{l-1})$, respectively, and that the total of all forces acting on mass l must be equal to $M_l d^2 u_l/dt^2$, derive coupled dynamical equations for all the masses. For each of (a) and (b) shown in the figure, write these equations in the vector–matrix form (3.9), with $\mathbf{u} = [u_1, u_2, \ldots]^T$, and give the explicit forms of the matrices $\mathbf{M}$ and $\mathbf{K}$.

(a)   (b)

Problem 3.3 *Consider the two-mass and three-mass systems of the previous problem, under the simplified conditions that $K_1 = K_2 = \cdots = K_0$ and $M_1 = M_2 = \cdots = M_0$, for positive constants K_0 and M_0. For each of cases (a) and (b) shown in the figure, explicitly find the eigenvalues of the matrix $\mathbf{M}^{-1}\mathbf{K}$ and, thus, the frequencies of the system, as per (3.11).*

Problem 3.4 *For the scheme (3.12), consider the following approach to initialization to second-order accuracy. For a continuous-time function $u(t)$ solving (3.1), it is true, through a Taylor series expansion, that*

$$u(k) = u(0) + k\frac{du}{dt}\Big|_{t=0} + \frac{k^2}{2}\frac{d^2u}{dt^2}\Big|_{t=0} + O(k^3)$$

Given the values $u(0) = u_0$ and $du/dt|_{t=0} = v_0$, determine, from the above approximation as well as the defining equation of the SHO, $u(k)$ in terms of u_0 and v_0. This can be used to set the value u^1 in the resulting difference scheme.

Problem 3.5 *For scheme (3.12), under the condition (3.17), prove that the bounds (3.19) and (3.24) obtained using frequency domain analysis and energetic techniques, respectively, are identical.*

Problem 3.6 *For the scheme (3.25), find a bound on the solution size in terms of the initial conditions and ω_0, through the expressions for the energy given in (3.28). The discussion of quadratic forms in Section 2.4.3 may be of use here.*

Problem 3.7 *For the scheme (3.29), (a) write the characteristic polynomial in z and prove the stability condition (3.30), and (b) show that the expression given in (3.31) is indeed a conserved energy and find conditions under which it is non-negative.*

Problem 3.8 *The deviation in cents of a frequency f (in Hertz) from a reference frequency f_0 is defined as*

$$\text{deviation in cents} = 1200 \, \log_2(f/f_0)$$

Find an explicit expression for this deviation in the case of schemes (3.12) and (3.25). Recall that $f = \omega/2\pi$ is the frequency of oscillation of the scheme, and $f_0 = \omega_0/2\pi$ is the "reference" frequency of the underlying SHO. For a sample rate of $f_s = 44\,100\,Hz$, find the lowest reference frequency f_0 at which the absolute value of this deviation is equal to 100 cents (one semitone) and 10 cents (one-tenth of a semitone). For scheme (3.29), with a value of $\alpha = 0.82$, what is the minimum value of this deviation over the band $f_0 \in [0, f_s/4]$?

Problem 3.9 *For difference scheme (3.43) for the coupled system of oscillators, left-multiply by the vector $\delta_t.\mathbf{u}^T$, and show that the following numerical energy is a conserved quantity:*

$$\mathfrak{h} = \mathfrak{t} + \mathfrak{v} \quad \text{with} \quad \mathfrak{t} = \frac{1}{2}(\delta_{t-}\mathbf{u}^T)\mathbf{M}(\delta_{t-}\mathbf{u}) \quad \mathfrak{v} = \frac{1}{2}\mathbf{u}^T\mathbf{K}e_{t-}\mathbf{u}$$

You may assume that $\mathbf{M}$ and $\mathbf{K}$ are symmetric.

Generalize the energy analysis of the simple difference scheme for the harmonic oscillator in Section 3.2.6. Can you show that the energy $\mathfrak{h}$ above is positive definite under the condition (3.44) obtained through frequency domain analysis?

Problem 3.10 *Consider the scheme (3.45) for the coupled system (3.9).*

(a) Show that it may be written in the form

$$\mathbf{u}^{n+1} = \mathbf{A}^{-1}\mathbf{B}\mathbf{u}^n - \mathbf{u}^{n-1}$$

1
2
3
4
5
6
7
8
9
10
11
12
13
14
15
16
17
18
19
20
21
22
23
24
25
26
27
28
29
30
31
32
33
34
35
36
37
38
39
40
41
42
43
44
45
46
47
48
49
50
51

and find the matrices **A** *and* **B** *explicitly in terms of* **M**, **K**, *the free parameter* α, *and the time step k.*

(b) Show that, for symmetric **K** *and* **M**, *an energy function of the form* $\mathfrak{h} = \mathfrak{t} + \mathfrak{v}$ *is conserved, with*

$$\mathfrak{t} = \frac{1}{2}(\delta_{t-}\mathbf{u}^T)\mathbf{M}(\delta_{t-}\mathbf{u}) \qquad \mathfrak{v} = \frac{\alpha}{2}\mathbf{u}^T\mathbf{K}e_{t-}\mathbf{u} + \frac{1-\alpha}{2}\mu_{t-}\left(\mathbf{u}^T\mathbf{K}\mathbf{u}\right)$$

Problem 3.11   *Find a general real-valued solution to (3.46) under the conditions (a) $\sigma_0 = \omega_0$ and (b) $\sigma_0 > \omega_0$. Determine the values of any constants in terms of initial conditions. Are these situations that you would expect to find in a practical acoustics setting? Discuss.*

Problem 3.12   *Consider the energetic analysis of the simple harmonic oscillator with loss, as described in Section 3.5.1. Note that although $\mathfrak{h}(t)$ will be monotonically decreasing in the case of linear loss, by (3.49), the specifics of its rate of decay are unclear. To this end, define the function $\bar{\mathfrak{h}}$ by*

$$\bar{\mathfrak{h}} = \mathfrak{h} + \sigma_0 u \frac{du}{dt} = \frac{1}{2}\left(\frac{du}{dt}\right)^2 + \frac{\omega_0^2}{2}u^2 + \sigma_0 u \frac{du}{dt} \tag{3.65}$$

Note that $\bar{\mathfrak{h}}$ approaches $\mathfrak{h}$ in the limit as $\sigma_0 \to 0$.

(a) Show that

$$\frac{d\bar{\mathfrak{h}}}{dt} = -\sigma_0\bar{\mathfrak{h}} \qquad \longrightarrow \qquad \bar{\mathfrak{h}}(t) = e^{-\sigma_0 t}\bar{\mathfrak{h}}(0) \tag{3.66}$$

Thus $\bar{\mathfrak{h}}$ decays exponentially, at decay rate σ_0, for any value of σ_0.

On the other hand, $\bar{\mathfrak{h}}$, in contrast to $\mathfrak{h}$, is not necessarily a non-negative function of the state u and du/dt. This non-negativity property is crucial in obtaining bounds such as (3.8).

(b) Show that the condition $\sigma_0 < \omega_0$ leads to

$$\bar{\mathfrak{h}} \geq \frac{\omega_0^2 - \sigma_0^2}{2}u^2$$

Show further that under such conditions, one has, from the above inequality, that

$$|u(t)| \leq \frac{1}{\omega_1}\sqrt{2\bar{\mathfrak{h}}(t)} \leq \frac{1}{\omega_1}\sqrt{2\bar{\mathfrak{h}}(0)} \qquad \text{for} \qquad t \geq 0$$

(c) Show that the bounding quantity on the right of the above inequality is in fact identical to C_1, and thus the bound above is identical to (3.48) obtained using frequency domain analysis.

Problem 3.13   *Consider the expression (3.53) for the roots of the characteristic polynomial for the difference scheme (3.51) of the simple harmonic oscillator with loss.*

(a) Supposing that the stability condition (3.54) is respected, find the conditions under which the solutions are either both real or complex conjugates.

(b) Again supposing that the stability condition (3.54) is respected, what form do the roots take when $\sigma_0 > 1/k$? What kind of solution will be produced, and will it be physically reasonable?

Problem 3.14   *Considering scheme (3.57) of the simple harmonic oscillator with loss, derive the stability condition (3.59) by using the condition (2.14). Derive the characteristic polynomial equation and a similar condition for the following scheme, which makes use of a forward difference approximation to the loss term:*

$$\delta_{tt}u = -\omega_0^2 u - 2\sigma_0\delta_{t+}u$$

Problem 3.15   *Consider the following approximation to the lossy simple harmonic oscillator (3.46):*

$$\delta_{tt}u = -\omega_0^2\mu_t.u - 2\sigma_0\delta_t.u$$

(a) Show that the scheme is unconditionally stable.

(b) Calculate the numerical decay time for this scheme, under low-loss conditions, and show that it will be dependent on ω_0.

Problem 3.16   *Considering the exact two-step recursion (3.62) for the simple harmonic oscillator with loss (3.46), it is reasonable to expect that it may be written in standard operator notation. Consider the following scheme, which depends on the two parameters ϕ and σ_0^*:*

$$\delta_{tt}u = -\omega_0^2 \left(\phi + (1-\phi)\mu_t.\right)u - 2\sigma_0^*\delta_t.u$$

Find settings for ϕ and σ_0^* in terms of ω_0, σ_0, and k and show that the scheme above is equivalent to (3.62) under low-loss conditions $\sigma_0 < \omega_0$.

Problem 3.17   *Consider the finite difference scheme for the oscillator given by*

$$u^{n+M} - 2u^n + u^{n-M} = -\omega_0^2(Mk)^2u^n$$

where $M \geq 1$ is an integer, and k, as before, is the time step.

(a) Show that this difference scheme approximates the simple harmonic oscillator to second-order accuracy in the time step k.

(b) Find the characteristic polynomial for this scheme, and a stability condition on k, the time step.

(c) Find the roots of the characteristic polynomial and thus the natural frequencies of the scheme. Show that one of these approaches ω_0.

(d) Is this a useful approximation to the simple harmonic oscillator? Discuss.

(This is an illustration of a digital structure which is capable of producing many frequency components, though the operation count is the same as that of a single oscillator. This is the same principle which underlies the digital waveguide—see Section 1.2.3.)

Problem 3.18   *For scheme (3.64), for the simple harmonic oscillator with a source term, perform energy analysis analogous to that of the model equation (3.63), and find a bound on the size of the solution u^n in terms of initial conditions, and the values of the time series $[F]$ at time steps between 0 and n.*

3.8   Programming exercises

Programming Exercise 3.1   *Adjust the code provided in Section A.1 such that only two memory locations are required in order to represent the state of the scheme (3.12) for the simple harmonic oscillator. This is slightly trickier than it appears to be—a hint is that you may wish to break the time series u^n into two sets, containing values for n odd and even.*

Programming Exercise 3.2   *Create two Matlab scripts which generate output according to the difference scheme family (3.29) and the exact scheme (3.39). The parameters which should be set in the preamble to your code should be: f_s, the sample rate, T_f, the total duration of the simulation, in seconds, f_0, the reference frequency of the simple harmonic oscillator, in Hertz, u_0, the initial displacement of the oscillator, and v_0, the initial velocity. For the script corresponding to the* *family* (3.29), *the additional parameter α must be specified. In this case, be sure to perform a test for numerical stability involving f_s, f_0, and α, and create an error message if it is violated. Your code should create plots of: the oscillator output as a function of n, the time step, the potential, kinetic, and total energy $\mathfrak{v}^n$, $\mathfrak{k}^n$, and $\mathfrak{h}^n$ as a function of n, as well as the variation in energy, i.e., $(\mathfrak{h}^n - \mathfrak{h}^0)/\mathfrak{h}^0$. You may wish to use the Matlab code provided for the simple scheme (3.12) in Section A.1 as a reference.*

Programming Exercise 3.3   *Adjust the code provided in Section A.1 such that, in addition to the output of the difference scheme, the exact solution to the differential equation (3.1) is generated, at the sample rate specified. Your code should play both outputs in succession. At a given sample rate such as f_s, find the smallest value of the reference frequency f_0 such that the frequency of the output of the difference scheme is perceptually distinct from that of the exact solution. Try typical values of the sample rate used in audio applications, such as $f_s = 32\,000$, $44\,100$, or $48\,000$ Hz.*

Programming Exercise 3.4   *Program the wave digital version of the simple harmonic oscillator, as per Section 3.3.3. Show that its behavior is identical to that of the scheme (3.29), under the choice of $\alpha = 1/2$. In order to do this, you will need to ensure that both methods are initialized in corresponding ways.*

Programming Exercise 3.5   *Consider the two-mass system shown at left in Problem 3.2 above, with $M_1 = 1$, $M_2 = 0.0001$, $K_1 = 1000$, $K_2 = 5000$, and $K_3 = 10\,000$. Write Matlab implementations of the schemes (3.43) and (3.45), running at $44\,100$ Hz, and using a parameter value of $\alpha = 0.82$ in the second case. Your code should calculate 1 s worth of output of the displacements u_1 and u_2, and plot the spectrum magnitude of each such output. Compare the characteristic frequencies of the output, in each case, to the exact frequencies of the system (3.9), calculated through (3.11).*

Programming Exercise 3.6   *Generalize the script provided in Section A.1 for the simple harmonic oscillator by introducing loss, according to scheme (3.51). In your code, you should have T_{60} as a global parameter, from which the parameter σ_0 is then derived.*

4

The oscillator in musical acoustics

Finite difference schemes for the simple harmonic oscillator (SHO) have been introduced in some detail in the last chapter. Though the SHO is not, by itself, an extremely interesting system, many excitation mechanisms in musical instruments may be modeled as nonlinear variants of it—indeed, the nonlinear excitation mechanism coupled with a linear resonator is at the heart of most current models of musical instruments [236, 297, 298]. Some examples which will be discussed in this chapter are the hammer or mallet interaction, the bow and (very briefly) reeds.

When designing a sound synthesis simulation, particularly for nonlinear systems, there are different ways of proceeding. It is sometimes easier, in the first instance, to make use of an ad hoc numerical method which is efficient and easily programmed, in order to generate sound output quickly, perhaps so as to uncover problems in the formulation of the underlying model system. On the other hand, with some extra work (and generally at some additional computational expense), better behaved numerical methods may be derived. Robustness, or numerical stability under a wide variety of possible playing conditions, is an especially useful property for a synthesis algorithm to possess, especially if the physical structure it simulates is to be virtually connected to other such structures. Other complications arise as well, such as the potential for non-uniqueness of computed solutions, which comes up in the case of the bow mechanism.

Frequency domain analysis may indeed be extended to deal with nonlinear systems, through perturbation techniques such as Linstedt–Poincaré methods, or harmonic balance techniques [252], or methods based on the use of Volterra series, and have been applied to the analysis of musical instruments [303, 167]. This is a very large topic, and one which is ill suited to time domain numerical methods; energy techniques will thus be employed here. It is worth noting that through the use of such techniques, though applicable to all the nonlinear systems discussed in this chapter, simple results are obtained only when the nonlinearities are of a smooth type, i.e., those which may be expressed as polynomials in the dependent variable. Though in the case of excitation mechanisms, the nonlinearities here are not of this form, some time will be spent on energy methods, mainly because the nonlinearities which arise in distributed problems, such as strings and plates, are sometimes quite smooth (see Chapters 8 and 13).

A nonlinear generalization of the SHO appears in Section 4.1, followed by various applications of interest in musical acoustics, such as lossless collision mechanisms (hammers), in Section 4.2, and continuous excitations involving loss, such as the bow and reed mechanisms, in Section 4.3. All of these systems are presented in a pure lumped form; connections to distributed models of instrument bodies are dealt with in subsequent chapters.

4.1 Nonlinear oscillators

Nonlinear oscillators of lumped type play a central role in conventional musical acoustics. Normally, such an oscillator is coupled to a distributed system, but, for the sake of analysis, it is instructive to look at the behavior of such systems when decoupled. The word "oscillator" employed here brings to mind an externally driven source, but, in this chapter, no distinction is made among driven oscillators, passive nonlinear systems, and nonlinear systems in musical acoustics which do not really oscillate at all in the musical sense (as in, say, the case of the hammer interaction). All can be described in roughly the same way.

A general uncoupled nonlinear oscillator may be written as

$$\frac{d^2u}{dt^2} = -F\left(u, \frac{du}{dt}\right) \tag{4.1}$$

Here, if $u(t)$ represents a position, then F has the interpretation, at least in a mechanical system, of a force, divided by the mass of the oscillating object—see the comments on page 67. The SHO (3.1) is a special case of such a form, with $F = \omega_0^2 u$. As in the linear case, this is a second-order ODE, and thus requires the specification of two initial conditions, namely $u(0)$ and $du/dt|_{t=0}$.

4.2 Lossless oscillators

A special case of great interest in musical acoustics is that for which F depends only on u,

$$\frac{d^2u}{dt^2} = -F(u) \tag{4.2}$$

which describes lossless systems. It is not difficult to see why—multiplying by du/dt gives

$$\frac{du}{dt}\frac{d^2u}{dt^2} + \frac{du}{dt}F(u) = 0 \qquad \longrightarrow \qquad \frac{d\mathfrak{H}}{dt} = 0$$

with

$$\mathfrak{H} = \mathfrak{T} + \mathfrak{V} \qquad \mathfrak{T} = \frac{1}{2}\left(\frac{du}{dt}\right)^2 \qquad \mathfrak{V} = \int_0^u F(\eta)d\eta \tag{4.3}$$

Thus, just as in the case of the linear oscillator, the ODE (4.2) possesses a conserved energy. Notice that the limit in the integral used to define $\mathfrak{V}$ could be changed, shifting the total energy by a constant. See Figure 4.1 for plots of some typical characteristics $F(u)$.

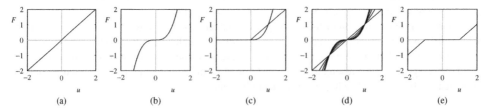

Figure 4.1 Some lossless characteristics $F(u)$: (a) linear; (b) cubic; (c) semi-linear and semi-cubic; (d) power law, under various choices of the exponent α; and (e) linear center limited.

The most obvious discretization of (4.2) is

$$\delta_{tt}u = -F(u) \tag{4.4}$$

This scheme is explicit, and trivial to implement. Unfortunately, however, its stability properties are somewhat obscure—see the following section on the special case of the cubic nonlinear oscillator for more comments on this topic. Still, it is a good first stab if one wants to put together a simulation in a hurry, though one should be alert to the potential for instability.

Given the discussion in the previous chapter on energy conservation in the case of the linear oscillator, one might wonder whether a conservative scheme for (4.2) exists. One way of proceeding is to write $F = d\mathfrak{V}/du = (d\mathfrak{V}/dt)/(du/dt)$, and thus obtain the scheme

$$\delta_{tt}u = -\frac{\delta_t.\mathfrak{v}}{\delta.u} \tag{4.5}$$

where $\mathfrak{v}^n$ is a discrete approximation to the potential energy $\mathfrak{V}(t)$ at time $t = nk$. This scheme is indeed conservative (see Problem 4.1), but, unfortunately, uniqueness and existence results are not forthcoming. There is much more to say about conservative schemes for this oscillator—see [157] for an introduction, and commentary. Numerical methods for Hamiltonian systems have undergone a large amount of work in recent years—of particular interest are symplectic methods [308]. A full treatment here would be rather lengthy, and it is better to examine several cases of relevance to musical acoustics and sound synthesis.

4.2.1   The cubic nonlinear oscillator

There is one special case of the nonlinear oscillator which is simply expressed and of extreme utility in musical acoustics, namely that in which the nonlinearity may be expressed as cubic, i.e.,

$$\frac{d^2u}{dt^2} = -\omega_1^4 u^3 \tag{4.6}$$

This equation goes by various names—Duffing's equation (without the linear, damping, and forcing terms) and also the stiffening or hard spring [234]. Though not entirely realistic, it serves as an excellent test problem—many distributed models of nonlinear string and plate vibration, of crucial importance in musical acoustics applications, can be expressed as third-order (i.e., cubic) systems. The third-order oscillator possesses many nice properties, and, by the standards of nonlinear systems, is comparatively easy to analyze—using perturbation analysis, one can say a great deal about interesting phenomena such as bifurcations etc. [252]. As this is relatively well documented, it is perhaps better to spend time looking at the properties of numerical simulation methods; the nice properties of this system also carry over to the discrete case.

The energy balance of this system may be found directly. It is

$$\frac{d\mathfrak{H}}{dt} = 0 \quad \text{with} \quad \mathfrak{H} = \mathfrak{T} + \mathfrak{V} \quad \mathfrak{T} = \frac{1}{2}\left(\frac{du}{dt}\right)^2 \quad \mathfrak{V} = \frac{1}{4}(\omega_1 u)^4 \tag{4.7}$$

Just as in the case of the linear oscillator, it is clear that, due to the non-negativity of $\mathfrak{H}$, $\mathfrak{T}$, and $\mathfrak{V}$, one can arrive at the following inequalities:

$$\left|\frac{du}{dt}\right| \le \sqrt{2\mathfrak{H}(0)} \qquad |u| \le \frac{\sqrt{2}(\mathfrak{H}(0))^{1/4}}{\omega_1}$$

Again, the solution size may be bounded in terms of the initial conditions, as well as the parameter ω_1.

The mixed linear/cubic oscillator and qualitative behavior

Useful, for conceptual purposes, as an illustration of some of the features which appear in much more complex vibrating systems, is the combined linear–cubic oscillator, of the form

$$\frac{d^2u}{dt^2} = -\omega_0^2 u - \omega_1^4 u^3 \tag{4.8}$$

This system, like (4.6), also possesses a well-behaved energy—the potential energy is the sum of that of the cubic oscillator and of the SHO itself. See Figure 4.2, which shows the solution to system (4.8), under initial conditions of increasing magnitude.

For small values of the initial condition, the solution approaches that of the SHO, giving a sinusoid at angular frequency ω_0. As the initial conditions are increased, two important phenomena are observed. First, under moderate-sized excitation, the solution remains approximately sinusoidal but at a frequency which is different from that of the solution to the SHO, and, in this case, higher. Second, under even stronger excitation, one begins to see other components appearing in the solution, with the most important contribution at (in this case) three times that of the "fundamental." Both these effects play an important perceptual role in musical acoustics, particularly in the case of string and percussion instruments, leading to phenomena such as pitch glides and phantom partials in strings plucked at high amplitudes (see Section 8.1.1 and Section 8.2.1) and to the spontaneous generation of high-frequency energy in instruments such as cymbals and gongs (see Section 13.3).

Finite difference schemes

There are a great variety of schemes available in the nonlinear case, even for a basic system such as the cubic nonlinear oscillator (4.6). Consider the following difference approximations:

$$\delta_{tt} u = -\omega_1^4 u^3 \qquad \longrightarrow \qquad u^{n+1} = \left(2 - \omega_1^4 k^2 (u^n)^2\right) u^n - u^{n-1} \tag{4.9a}$$

$$\delta_{tt} u = -\omega_1^4 u^2 \mu_{t.} u \qquad \longrightarrow \qquad u^{n+1} = \frac{2}{1 + \omega_1^4 k^2 (u^n)^2 / 2} u^n - u^{n-1} \tag{4.9b}$$

$$\delta_{tt} u = -\omega_1^4 \mu_{t.} (u^2) \mu_{t.} u \qquad \longrightarrow \qquad \text{no explicit update form} \tag{4.9c}$$

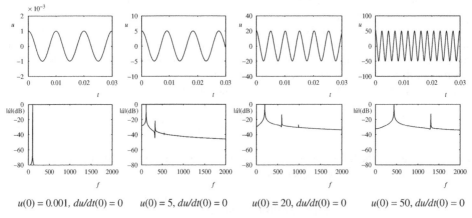

$u(0) = 0.001, \; du/dt(0) = 0$ $u(0) = 5, \; du/dt(0) = 0$ $u(0) = 20, \; du/dt(0) = 0$ $u(0) = 50, \; du/dt(0) = 0$

Figure 4.2 Output waveform (top), and spectrum (bottom), for the mixed linear–cubic nonlinear oscillator (4.8), with $\omega_0 = 200\pi$ and $\omega_1 = \sqrt{20\pi}$, under different initial conditions (given in the figure).

All three are centered and thus second-order accurate schemes. The approximation (4.9a) is perhaps the most natural and certainly the simplest in implementation. Unfortunately, it is difficult to say much about its stability behavior, as it does not possess a conserved energy analogous to (4.7). The schemes (4.9b) and (4.9c) are conservative. Through multiplication of these schemes by $\delta_t.u$, one may arrive at the energy balances

$$\delta_{t+}\mathfrak{h} = 0 \quad \text{with} \quad \mathfrak{h} = \mathfrak{t} + \mathfrak{v}, \quad \mathfrak{t} = \frac{1}{2}(\delta_{t-}u)^2 \quad \mathfrak{v} = \begin{cases} \dfrac{\omega_1^4}{4}u^2 e_{t-}u^2 & \text{for scheme (4.9b)} \\[2mm] \dfrac{\omega_1^4}{4}\mu_{t-}u^4 & \text{for scheme (4.9c)} \end{cases} \tag{4.10}$$

In both cases, the kinetic and potential energy terms are non-negative, and one can proceed to find a bound on solution size. For instance, one may immediately write, for either scheme,

$$|\delta_{t-}u| \le \sqrt{2\mathfrak{h}} \tag{4.11}$$

bounding the rate of growth of the solution. With a bit more work, bounds on the solution size itself may be obtained. See Problem 4.2. In fact, such schemes pose even less difficulty, in terms of stability analysis, than schemes for the linear oscillator—both schemes are unconditionally stable, for any choice of the time step k! Though one can use schemes such as (4.9a), there is the danger of instability, which shows itself in a much more obscure way than in the linear case. See Figure 4.3, which illustrates the unexpected instability of scheme (4.9a) after hundreds of thousands of time steps of stable behavior. A provably stable scheme is thus, for synthesis applications, a safe choice.

There is, however, a subtle, but extremely significant difference between the two conservative schemes. Scheme (4.9b) may be written as an explicit recursion, i.e., one may solve directly for u^{n+1} in terms of u^n and u^{n-1}, which are known. This is not the case for scheme (4.9c)—the unknown value u^{n+1} is coupled to the known values through a cubic equation, which must be solved at each time step. This is not difficult: one may employ a (somewhat formidable) formula for the roots of a cubic, or, better, use an iterative method. The problem is, however, that the cubic possesses, in general, three roots. Thus the issue of uniqueness of the numerical solution rears its head. One can of course go further and look for a condition on k, the time step, such that the cubic only possesses one real solution, but the point is that such difficulties do not arise for scheme (4.9b). These distinctions among nonlinear difference schemes become much more important in the distributed setting, as will be seen in the case of nonlinear string vibration in Section 8.2. Scheme (4.9a) corresponds to an explicit scheme, scheme (4.9b) to an implicit scheme, where updating may be done through the solution of a linear system, and scheme (4.9c) to an implicit scheme requiring algebraic nonlinear solution techniques.

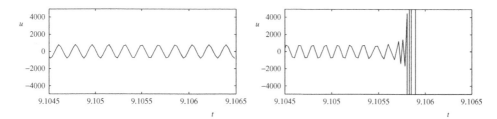

Figure 4.3 Numerical solutions to the cubic nonlinear oscillator, with $\omega_1 = \sqrt{20\pi}$ and with $f_s = 44\,100\,\text{Hz}$, for energy-conserving scheme (4.9b), and for scheme (4.9a), which becomes abruptly unstable after more than 9 seconds of run time (at time step $n = 401\,562$). The initial conditions used, in this case, are $u^0 = u^1 = 704.8165$.

4.2.2   Power law nonlinearities

Many models of nonlinearity in hammers and mallets [58, 75] are based around the use of a power law, of the form

$$F(u) = \omega_c^{\alpha+1}\text{sign}(u)|u|^\alpha \tag{4.12}$$

where α, the nonlinear exponent, is usually determined experimentally (through measurements, say, of a felt compression characteristic), though it is possible to arrive at a theoretical justification, such as Hertz's contact law [77]. See Figure 4.1(d). In fact, this nonlinearity most often occurs in musical acoustics in a "one-sided" form—see the next section. Explicit energy-conserving schemes for such a nonlinearity are not easily arrived at, except in the cases $\alpha = 1$ (linear) and $\alpha = 3$ (cubic). The difficulty is that the nonlinear characteristic F is not an analytic function of u unless α is an odd integer. Thus, the most direct approach is probably to use a scheme such as (4.4) in such cases. Drawing a lesson from the success of the partially implicit discretization of the cubic oscillator, one might guess that a scheme such as

$$\delta_{tt}u = -\omega_c^{\alpha+1}(\mu_t.u)|u|^{\alpha-1} \tag{4.13}$$

will possess better stability characteristics than the simple scheme (4.4)—see Programming Exercise 4.1.

4.2.3   One-sided nonlinearities and collisions: hammers and mallets

So far, the nonlinearities presented here have been two sided—the function $F(u)$ is antisymmetric, and thus, when interpreted as a force, acts in the direction opposite to that of u, when interpreted as a displacement. In many settings in musical acoustics involving collisions [282, 294], a one-sided definition is more appropriate—the force only acts when the displacement is positive (say), and acts so as to repel the colliding object. Such characteristics are illustrated in Figure 4.1(c).

The "oscillator" (4.2), in this case, serves as a model of a collision of a mass with a rigid object, such as a wall, and where $F(u)$ describes the stiffness of the mass. It is useful to adopt the following notation:

$$\frac{d^2u}{dt^2} = -[F(u)]^+ \qquad \text{where} \qquad [F(u)]^+ = \begin{cases} 0, & u \le 0 \\ F(u), & u > 0 \end{cases} \tag{4.14}$$

As an example, consider a comparison between the case of a collision where, in one case, the stiffening force is linear, i.e., $F(u) = \omega_0^2 u$, and in the other, the stiffening force is cubic, i.e., $F(u) = \omega_1^4 u^3$. Plots of the resulting behavior are shown in Figure 4.4. The most important thing to note is that in the case of the linear collision, regardless of the velocity with which the object approaches the barrier, the duration of the collision remains constant. For the stiffening object, the contact time becomes shorter as approach velocity is increased. Such effects of duration of contact time obviously have very important perceptual implications in sound synthesis: for a linear object, the resulting dynamics are simply scaled up in amplitude as collision velocity in increased—there will be no variation in timbre. For the nonlinear stiffening object, faster collision velocity leads to a sharper, brighter sound. There is little doubt that most collisions of interest in musical acoustics (such as, for example, piano hammer excitation) exhibit the latter behavior. Thus a good nonlinear model is necessary in any percussive instrument, otherwise the resulting sound will be rather uniform and insensitive to a player's gesture.

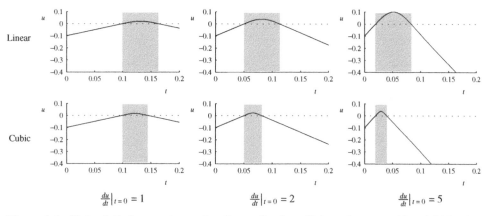

$$\frac{du}{dt}\Big|_{t=0} = 1 \qquad\qquad \frac{du}{dt}\Big|_{t=0} = 2 \qquad\qquad \frac{du}{dt}\Big|_{t=0} = 5$$

Figure 4.4 Plots of displacement u against time t, for the collision of a mass with a rigid barrier, in operation when u, the center of mass of the object, is positive. In this case, the mass approaches the barrier from below, with initial position $u(0) = -0.1$ and initial velocities as indicated. The top row shows the case of an object with linear stiffness, with $\omega_0 = 50$, and the bottom row that of an object with a cubic stiffening characteristic, with $\omega_1 = \sqrt{5000}$. The contact duration is indicated by the shaded grey area.

Partial conservation

As mentioned above, in Section 4.2.2, when the characteristic $F(u)$ is not analytic, it becomes much more difficult to design a numerical method for which numerical stability is easy to guarantee. The same is true of one-sided nonlinearities. One might expect, however, that if the one-sided nonlinearity is of linear or cubic type, conservative behavior can at least be ensured over intervals for which $u > 0$ or $u \leq 0$. Consider the following finite difference approximations to such one-sided nonlinearities:

$$\delta_{tt}u = -\omega_0^2[u]^+ \qquad\qquad \delta_{tt}u = -\omega_1^4([u]^+)^2\mu_{t\cdot}u \qquad\qquad (4.15)$$

where the $[\cdot]^+$ notation is as in (4.14). Such algorithms are not strictly conservative, and thus there is no global expression for energy. Consider, however, the energy-like functions

$$\mathfrak{h} = \frac{1}{2}(\delta_{t-}u)^2 + \frac{\omega_0^2}{2}[u]^+[e_{t-}u]^+ \qquad\qquad \mathfrak{h} = \frac{1}{2}(\delta_{t-}u)^2 + \frac{\omega_1^4}{4}\left([u]^+\right)^2\left([e_{t-}u]^+\right)^2$$

Such expressions are at least partially conserved by schemes (4.15) for intervals over which u does not change signs—on the other hand, an energy jump will be observed, as illustrated in Figure 4.5. The jump is larger in the case of the one-sided linear collision than for the one-sided cubic collision, for which the total jump is on the order of machine precision. One effect of such an energy jump is that an object undergoing a theoretically lossless collision will exhibit a difference in exit speed from entry speed. In general, however, such an effect is quite small over normal ranges of parameters. One could go further here, and look at possible ways around this problem (some of which are very involved), but for sound synthesis purposes, schemes such as the above are probably sufficient in practice.

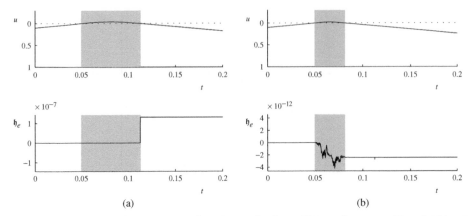

Figure 4.5 Plots of displacement u against time t, for the collision of a mass with a rigid barrier (top) and the variation in numerical energy $\mathfrak{h}_e = \left(\mathfrak{h} - \mathfrak{h}^0\right)/\mathfrak{h}^0$ (bottom), in the case of (a) a linear collision characteristic and (b) a cubic collision characteristic. In each case, the mass approaches the barrier from below, with initial position $u(0) = -0.1$ and an initial velocity of 2. The stiffness parameters are chosen as $\omega_0 = 50$ for the linear collision, and $\omega_1 = \sqrt{5000}$ for the cubic collision. The algorithms in (4.15) are employed, with a sample rate of $f_s = 44\,100\,\text{Hz}$.

Hammer and lumped oscillator

With a very slight added degree of complexity, the collision model above becomes very close to that which is often used in models of hammer or mallet interaction with a distributed object. Consider the case of a one-sided nonlinearity acting between a hammer-like object, with an inherent nonlinear stiffening characteristic, and a linear lumped mass–spring system, as shown at left in Figure 4.6. The equations of motion of this coupled system may be written as

$$M\frac{d^2u}{dt} = -Ku + f \qquad M_{\mathrm{H}}\frac{d^2u_{\mathrm{H}}}{dt} = -f \qquad f = K_{\mathrm{H}}\left(\left[u_{\mathrm{H}} - u\right]^+\right)^\alpha$$

where, here, u is the displacement of the "target," a mass–spring system of mass M and stiffness parameter K, and u_{H} is the displacement of the hammer, of mass M_{H}, and with a stiffness parameter K_{H}. Notice that the interaction force f only acts when the hammer position is greater than that of the target. The nonlinearity has been chosen to be of the form of a power law, a common choice in the musical acoustics of hammers [75]. More refined models take into account effects of hysteresis—see, e.g., [346].

For the sake of the musician–programmer, it is always a good idea to reduce the number of parameters which define a system to the bare minimum. In the above case, it is clear that not all of M, K, M_{H}, and K_{H} need be independently specified, and one may write

$$\frac{d^2u}{dt} = -\omega_0^2 u + \mathcal{M}F \qquad \frac{d^2u_{\mathrm{H}}}{dt} = -F \qquad F = \omega_{\mathrm{H}}^{\alpha+1}\left(\left[u_{\mathrm{H}} - u\right]^+\right)^\alpha \qquad (4.16)$$

where $\omega_0 = \sqrt{K/M}$, $\omega_{\mathrm{H}} = (K_{\mathrm{H}}/M_{\mathrm{H}})^{1/(\alpha+1)}$, the hammer mass/target mass ratio $\mathcal{M} = M_{\mathrm{H}}/M$, and $F = f/M_{\mathrm{H}}$. System (4.16) may be easily shown to be exactly lossless—see Problem 4.3.

As expected, the behavior of such a system is much more complex than that of the collision of a hammer with a rigid barrier—the force experienced by the mass can undergo oscillations due to the reaction of the mass–spring system back on the hammer, and recontact with the hammer is also possible—see Figure 4.6. Such complex behavior is also very much characteristic of the interaction between a hammer and a distributed object such as a string. See, e.g., [75] and the

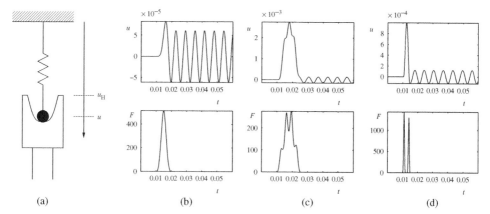

Figure 4.6 Collision between a hammer and a mass–spring system, as described by (4.16), illustrated in (a). Various resulting displacements (top) and interaction forces (bottom) are shown at right—in each case, the initial hammer velocity is 1, its initial displacement is 0.01 m below the target mass, and the mass–spring system has angular frequency $\omega_0 = 1000$ and the nonlinear exponent $\alpha = 3$. In (b) is shown a simple interaction, in the case of $\omega_H = \sqrt{100\,000}$ and $\mathcal{M} = 10$, in (c) a more complex force interaction showing the reaction of the mass–spring system on the hammer, for $\omega_H = \sqrt{100\,000}$ and $\mathcal{M} = 0.01$, and in (d) a contact/recontact phenomenon, when $\omega_H = \sqrt{2\,000\,000}$ and $\mathcal{M} = 1$.

comprehensive series of articles by Hall [163]. The subject of hammer–string interaction will be taken up here in Section 7.5. It is not difficult to extend this system to cover a collision between a hammer and multiple mass–spring systems—see Problem 4.4 and Programming Exercise 4.2; such multiple interactions are rather important in the case of, for instance, the piano, for which a hammer strikes several strings at once. See Section 7.6.

The simplest finite difference scheme for (4.16) is the following:

$$\delta_{tt}u = -\omega_0^2 u + \mathcal{M}F \qquad \delta_{tt}u_H = -F \qquad F = \omega_H^{\alpha+1}\left([u_H - u]^+\right)^\alpha \tag{4.17}$$

Such a scheme, which is entirely explicit, is very easy to implement—see the code example in Section A.2. The scheme is not conservative, but when $\alpha = 1$ or $\alpha = 3$, there is a modified form which is at least partially conservative—see Problem 4.5.

4.2.4 Center-limited nonlinearities

A musically interesting extension of the one-sided nonlinearity is the oscillator (4.2) under a center-limited lossless nonlinear characteristic—see Figure 4.1(e). In this case, the nonlinearity is only active when the magnitude of the displacement u is greater than some threshold—as such it serves as a crude model of an element which is able to rattle. The coupling of an element such as this to a string, as a form of preparation, is discussed in Section 7.7.2.

As an example of such a nonlinear characteristic, consider the following:

$$F(u) = \begin{cases} \omega_c^{\alpha+1}(u - \epsilon/2)^\alpha, & u \geq \epsilon/2 \\ 0, & |u| < \epsilon/2 \\ -\omega_c^{\alpha+1}(-u - \epsilon/2)^\alpha, & u \leq -\epsilon/2 \end{cases} \tag{4.18}$$

The object to which this characteristic corresponds can be thought of as a "dumbbell," of length ϵ (which is an extra design parameter), with a stiffness described by a power law nonlinearity. See

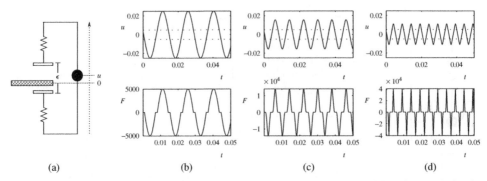

Figure 4.7   (a) Diagram representing a center-limited oscillating object, of length ϵ, and simulations of such an object, of length $\epsilon = 0.01$, and with nonlinear stiffness parameter $\omega_c = 500$, under different choices of the nonlinear exponent α: in (b), $\alpha = 1$; in (c), $\alpha = 2$; and in (d), $\alpha = 4$. The object displacement u is shown at top and the force F at bottom. In all cases, the initial position of the object is $u(0) = 0.003$, and the initial velocity is $du/dt|_{t=0} = -10$. Notice that the period of oscillation of the element depends strongly on the nonlinear exponent.

Figure 4.7(a). The system is conservative, with an energy given by (4.3), and one may develop finite difference schemes with a partial conservation property when $\alpha = 1$ or $\alpha = 3$, in a manner very similar to the one-sided collision model of the previous section. See Figure 4.7 for some typical simulation results, generated using a straightforward scheme of the type (4.4), and also Programming Exercise 4.3. Loss and the effect of gravity play a rather important role when one is dealing with rattling elements—see Programming Exercise 4.4 for some exploration of these features.

4.3   Lossy oscillators

One could easily introduce a linear loss term into the equation for the lossless oscillator (4.2), but, for collisions of short duration, this will yield results of minor perceptual significance. The real interest in lossy oscillator models in musical acoustics relates to the case of continuous forced excitation, as occurs in bowed string instruments, as well as in woodwind and brass instruments.

4.3.1   The bow

Before examining more realistic bow models, it is useful to look at an archetypical test problem of the form

$$\frac{d^2u}{dt^2} = -\alpha\phi\left(\frac{du}{dt}\right) \tag{4.19}$$

Here, $\alpha \geq 0$ is a free parameter, and the function ϕ is a given nonlinear characteristic. Normally, in models of bow friction, the function $\phi(\eta)$ is antisymmetric about $\eta = 0$, and possesses a region of steep positive slope near the origin (sticking regime), outside of which it is of negative slope (sliding regime). This feature will be explored further in some examples which follow and in Section 7.4, but for reference, some typical examples of such bow characteristics are shown in Figure 4.8. In many models [410], the sticking portion of the curve is in fact of infinite slope—two examples are shown in (a) and (b). A continuous curve, as shown in (c), though less physically justifiable, reasonably approximates this discontinuity, and is somewhat easier to work with numerically.

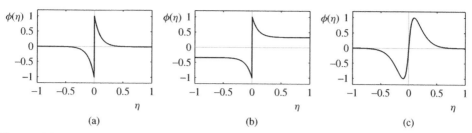

Figure 4.8 Some bow friction characteristics $\phi(\eta)$: (a) a hard characteristic defined by $\phi(\eta) = \text{sign}(\eta)e^{-a|\eta|}$, for some $a \geq 0$; (b) a hard characteristic with a non-zero limiting sliding friction value, defined by $\phi(\eta) = \text{sign}(\eta)\left(\epsilon + (1-\epsilon)e^{-a|\eta|}\right)$; and (c) a soft characteristic of the form $\phi(\eta) = \sqrt{2a}\eta e^{-a\eta^2 + 1/2}$.

This equation is of the form of an oscillator without a stiffness term. The variable u itself, undifferentiated, does not appear in the equation, implying a single mechanism for storing energy (through a kinetic term), and that furthermore it will not be possible to obtain bounds on u itself. Indeed, one could write the above equation in terms of du/dt alone, though it is simpler to retain the second-order form, especially when the above model of a nonlinear excitation is to be coupled to a distributed model. First-order forms equivalent to the above do occur in models of nonlinearities in nonlinear electrical circuit components used in analog synthesizers such as the Moog [165]—see Problem 4.6 for an example. As yet, this remains an unforced problem—the important forcing term will be introduced shortly.

Energy analysis indicates a constraint on ϕ: multiplying by du/dt, one obtains, immediately,

$$\frac{d\mathfrak{H}}{dt} = -\alpha \frac{du}{dt} \phi\left(\frac{du}{dt}\right) \quad \text{with} \quad \mathfrak{H} = \frac{1}{2}\left(\frac{du}{dt}\right)^2$$

Clearly then, if the quantity $\mathfrak{H}$ is to be monotonically decreasing, one must require that the characteristic $\phi(\eta)$ satisfy

$$\phi(\eta)\eta \geq 0 \quad \text{or} \quad \text{sign}(\phi(\eta)) = \text{sign}(\eta) \tag{4.20}$$

which is a requirement for passivity. If such a condition does not hold, it becomes possible for the nonlinearity to behave at certain instants as a source of energy, which is certainly not the case in any musical instrument.

As in the case of the lossless oscillator, various difference schemes are possible. Here are two:

$$\delta_{tt}u = -\alpha\phi(\delta_{t-}u) \tag{4.21a}$$

$$\delta_{tt}u = -\alpha\phi(\delta_{t\cdot}u) \tag{4.21b}$$

Scheme (4.21a), the simpler of the two, is clearly explicit, due to the use of a backward difference inside the nonlinear characteristic. As one might guess, however, it is rather difficult to say anything conclusive about its behavior, especially in terms of stability. The scheme (4.21b) permits some such analysis. Multiplying by $\delta_{t\cdot}u$ yields

$$\delta_{t+}\mathfrak{h} = -\alpha\left(\delta_{t\cdot}u\right)\phi(\delta_{t\cdot}u) \leq 0 \quad \text{with} \quad \mathfrak{h} = \frac{1}{2}(\delta_{t-}u)^2 \tag{4.22}$$

Thus, as in the continuous case, $\mathfrak{h}$ is non-negative and monotonically decreasing, and the behavior of scheme (4.21b) is thus stable, as long as the characteristic satisfies (4.20). On the other hand,

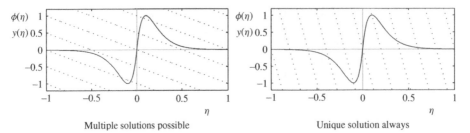

Multiple solutions possible   Unique solution always

Figure 4.9   Graphical representation of solutions to the equation $\phi(q) = -mq + b$, for a given bow-like characteristic $\phi(q)$ (shown as a solid black line). The lines $y(q) = -mq + b$, for $m > 0$, and for various values of b, are plotted as dotted black lines. Left, a choice of m for which multiple solutions may exist, for certain values of b; and right, a choice of m for which the solution is always unique, for any choice of b.

scheme (4.21b) is implicit. Using identity (2.7g), it may be rewritten in the following form:

$$-\frac{2}{\alpha k}\delta_{t\cdot}u + \frac{2}{\alpha k}\delta_{t-}u = \phi(\delta_{t\cdot}u)$$

Solutions may be examined graphically in terms of the unknown $\delta_{t\cdot}u$—see Figure 4.9.

There will always thus be at least one solution to this nonlinear equation, regardless of the form of ϕ. Though existence follows immediately, uniqueness does not—depending on the form of ϕ, there may be multiple solutions to the equation. The issue of multiple solutions in the case of the bow coupled to the string is an interesting one, and the continuous-time case has been discussed extensively by various authors, beginning with Friedlander [144], and most notably McIntyre and Woodhouse [237]. Here, in the discrete case, the following condition is sufficient:

$$k \leq -\frac{2}{\alpha \min_\eta \phi'(\eta)} \qquad \text{when} \qquad \min_\eta \phi'(\eta) \leq 0 \qquad (4.23)$$

This condition is a purely numerical one, and applies only to scheme (4.21b), though similar conditions exist for other schemes—see Problem 4.7. It is worth keeping in mind that the above condition *has no bearing on numerical stability*, which is already ensured for scheme (4.21b) under condition (4.20). That is, even when multiple solutions do exist, any choice will lead to strictly passive numerical behavior (though such a solution may be physically meaningless). It is, however, of the same form as stability conditions which typically arise in the design of explicit schemes for oscillators. See, e.g., Section 3.2.4 and the following example.

Connection to a mass–spring system and auto-oscillatory behavior

To get a better idea of how the bow actually functions, it is better to move to a more concrete setting involving a coupling of a bow model with a single mass–spring system, as shown in Figure 4.10(a). (In fact, it is only a small further step to connect the bow to a fully distributed string model—see Section 7.4.) Here, the motion of the mass is described by

$$\frac{d^2u}{dt^2} = -\omega_0^2 u - F_B\phi(v_{rel}) \qquad \text{where} \qquad v_{rel} = \frac{du}{dt} - v_B \qquad (4.24)$$

where $F_B \geq 0$ is a given control parameter (again, it is the bow force divided by the object mass, and has dimensions of acceleration), and v_B is a bow velocity. Notice that it is only the

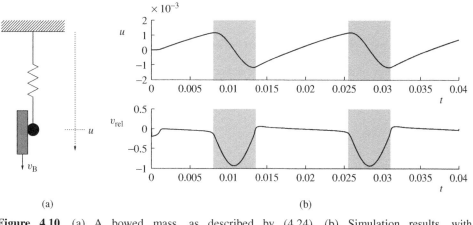

Figure 4.10 (a) A bowed mass, as described by (4.24). (b) Simulation results, with $f_0 = \omega_0/2\pi = 100$, $F_B = 4000$, and $v_B = 0.2$. The friction characteristic is of the form given in Figure 4.8(c), with $a = 100$. Displacement of mass (top), and relative velocity $v_{rel} = (du/dt) - v_B$ (bottom), with shaded regions illustrating intervals during which the mass slips from the bow—otherwise it "sticks."

relative velocity v_{rel} of the bow to the mass which appears in the model. Energy analysis now yields

$$\frac{d\mathfrak{H}}{dt} = -F_B \frac{du}{dt} \phi\,(v_{rel}) = \underbrace{-F_B v_{rel} \phi\,(v_{rel})}_{\text{power dissipated by bow}} \qquad \underbrace{-F_B v_B \phi\,(v_{rel})}_{\text{power supplied by bow}}$$

where $\mathfrak{H}$ is the Hamiltonian for a linear oscillator, as given in (3.7), and where the terms on the right-hand side of the energy balance may be interpreted as power dissipated and supplied by the bow, as indicated. Because, by (4.20), the dissipated power is negative, one has immediately

$$\frac{d\mathfrak{H}}{dt} \le -F_B v_B \phi\,(v_{rel}) \le |F_B v_B \phi\,(v_{rel})|$$

For many choices of bow characteristic (such as those pictured in Figure 4.8), F_B represents a maximum bow force—in other words, the characteristic ϕ is bounded such that

$$|\phi| \le 1 \qquad\qquad (4.25)$$

In this case, the energy inequality above may be weakened to

$$\frac{d\mathfrak{H}}{dt} \le |F_B v_B| \qquad \longrightarrow \qquad \mathfrak{H}(t) \le \mathfrak{H}(0) + t|F_B v_B|$$

This is a bound on the growth of the solution, purely in terms of the given numbers F_B and v_B. The above analysis changes very little if the values F_B and v_B are generalized to functions $F_B(t) \ge 0$ and $v_B(t)$, representing the gestural control signals of bow force/object mass and velocity.

The obvious generalization of scheme (4.21b) to the case of coupling to a mass–spring system is

$$\delta_{tt}u = -\omega_0^2 u - F_B \phi(v_{rel}) \qquad \text{where} \qquad v_{rel} = \delta_{t.}u - v_B \qquad (4.26)$$

The energy analysis of this scheme mirrors that of the continuous-time system above. Using familiar techniques, one arrives at the discrete energy balance

$$\delta_{t+}\mathfrak{h} = -F_B v_{rel}\phi(v_{rel}) - F_B v_B \phi(v_{rel}) \leq |F_B v_B|$$

where $\mathfrak{h}$ is the energy of the SHO, as discussed in Section 3.2.6. Again, energy growth is bounded in terms of the input values (or sequences) F_B and v_B. Two conditions on k, the time step, appear:

$$k < \frac{2}{\omega_0}, \qquad k \leq \frac{2}{-\max(F_B)\min_\eta \phi'(\eta)} \qquad \text{when} \qquad \min_\eta \phi'(\eta) \leq 0 \qquad (4.27)$$

The first condition is the familiar stability condition (3.17) for scheme (3.12) for the SHO, which ensures non-negativity of the numerical energy $\mathfrak{h}$. The second condition is that required for uniqueness of numerically computed solutions. One could go further and employ a more accurate difference strategy to the linear part of the system, along the lines of the scheme presented in Section 3.3.4, but the principle of stability analysis remains the same. An implementation of scheme (4.26) appears in Section A.3, and makes use of a Newton–Raphson iterative root finder (see Problem 4.8 and Programming Exercise 4.6). For simplicity, the continuous friction characteristic shown in Figure 4.8(c) is used—when a discontinuous characteristic is used, such root finders may also be used, though programming complexity increases somewhat.

The behavior of the bowed mass system is an example of an auto-oscillatory system—given a slowly varying input signal (such as that derived from a player's gesture), the system can reach a state of continuous oscillation. Even in this rudimentary case, a great variety of complex behavior results, and many of the key features of bowed string dynamics may be observed. The most crucial phenomenon is the stick–slip motion of the mass, as illustrated in Figure 4.10(b). The mass "sticks" to the bow for an interval as the spring is being extended or compressed, exhibiting little displacement relative to the bow, until the force of the spring is sufficient to set the mass into motion, in a direction opposing that of the bow motion, after which it then becomes stuck to the bow once again etc. The resulting displacement waveform is roughly of the form of an asymmetric triangle.

Some other phenomena are illustrated in Figure 4.11. As shown at left, an increase in bow force can lead to a characteristic "sharpening" of the displacement waveform and also an increased period of oscillation—this is a minor effect in bowed string dynamics, and is often referred to as pitch flattening [236]. At right, one may also observe a variation in the length of time necessary to reach steady oscillatory behavior which decreases with increased bow force.

4.3.2   Reed models

Given that the reed mechanism and coupling to an acoustic tube will be seen in great detail in Section 9.3, it is not necessary to present a full treatment in the lumped context—indeed, it may be viewed in terms of a (rather complex!) combination of the various nonlinear mechanisms already discussed in this chapter. At heart it behaves like a valve (see the descriptions in [136] and [78]) or as a lumped, driven, nonlinear oscillator subject to collisions; as in the case of the bow, when coupled to a resonator, auto-oscillations result. Here is a form incorporating many of the features which are by now standard [202]:

$$\frac{d^2 u}{dt^2} + 2\sigma_0 \frac{du}{dt} + \omega_0^2 u - \omega_1^\alpha \left(|[u+1]^-|\right)^{\alpha-1} = -F \qquad (4.28)$$

Reading through the terms from left to right, the first three terms, in the absence of the others, describe damped harmonic oscillations, with frequency ω_0 and damping parameter σ_0. If $u(t)$ represents the position of the reed, then the oscillations will occur about an equilibrium point at

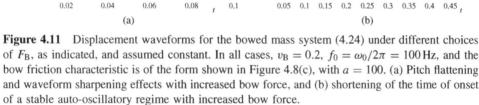

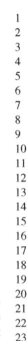

(a)   (b)

Figure 4.11 Displacement waveforms for the bowed mass system (4.24) under different choices of F_B, as indicated, and assumed constant. In all cases, $v_B = 0.2$, $f_0 = \omega_0/2\pi = 100\,\text{Hz}$, and the bow friction characteristic is of the form shown in Figure 4.8(c), with $a = 100$. (a) Pitch flattening and waveform sharpening effects with increased bow force, and (b) shortening of the time of onset of a stable auto-oscillatory regime with increased bow force.

$u = 0$. The next term introduces a lossless collision, when $u \leq -1$, using a power law characteristic (see Section 4.2.2). Such a collision models, in a rather ad hoc manner, the "beating" of the reed against the mouthpiece lay—notice that it will only become active under rather large oscillations. Finally, the term F on the right-hand side represents a driving term (i.e., it is related to the control mouth pressure), as well as a loss characteristic—it is similar to that of the bow (see Section 4.3.1), though the characteristic curve is of a very different form. It is, however, dependent on the state of the reed (as well as the tube to which it is coupled) in a rather involved way, and the full description is postponed until Section 9.3.

4.4 Problems

Problem 4.1 *Show that the scheme (4.5) for the lossless nonlinear oscillator is indeed conservative, with a conserved energy given by*

$$\mathfrak{h} = \frac{1}{2}\left(\delta_{t-}u\right)^2 + \mu_{t-}\mathfrak{v}$$

Problem 4.2 *Consider scheme (4.9b) for the cubic nonlinear oscillator. From the expression for the potential energy in (4.10), one may deduce that*

$$|ue_{t-}u| \leq \frac{2\sqrt{\mathfrak{h}}}{\omega_1^2}$$

A bound on $|u|$ itself does not immediately follow. Use the bound (4.11), along with the above, in order to find a bound on $|u|$. Hint: Square the bound in (4.11), and rewrite $\delta_{t-}u$ in terms of u and $e_{t-}u$.

Problem 4.3   *For the hammer–mass–spring collision defined in (4.16), prove that the following quantity,*

$$\mathfrak{H} = \frac{1}{2}\left(\frac{du}{dt}\right)^2 + \frac{\omega_0^2}{2}u^2 + \frac{M}{2}\left(\frac{du_H}{dt}\right)^2 + \frac{M}{\alpha+1}\left(\omega_H[u_H - u]^+\right)^{\alpha+1}$$

is conserved.

Problem 4.4   *Suppose that, instead of coming into contact with one mass–spring system, a hammer strikes two such systems simultaneously, as illustrated below.*

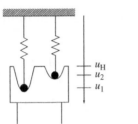

$$\frac{d^2u_1}{dt^2} = -\omega_1^2 u_1 + MF_1 \qquad F_1 = \omega_H^{\alpha+1}\left([u_H - u_1]^+\right)^\alpha$$

$$\frac{d^2u_2}{dt^2} = -\omega_2^2 u_2 + MF_2 \qquad F_2 = \omega_H^{\alpha+1}\left([u_H - u_2]^+\right)^\alpha$$

$$\frac{d^2u_H}{dt^2} = -F_1 - F_2$$

For this system, u_1 and u_2 are the displacements of the two masses, u_H is the hammer displacement, F_1 and F_2 are the forces/mass acting on the two target masses, ω_1 and ω_2 are the angular frequencies of the two mass–spring systems, ω_H is the stiffness parameter for the hammer (of nonlinearity exponent α), and M is the mass ratio of the hammer to either of the two target masses (assumed equal).

(a) *Find an expression for the energy of the system as a whole, and show that it is conserved.*

(b) *Extend the system above to the case of a hammer striking N equal masses.*

(c) *Extend the system above to the case of a hammer striking two unequal masses, and find a generalized expression for the conserved energy.*

Problem 4.5   *For the collision between a hammer and a mass–spring system described by (4.16), consider the following finite difference scheme:*

$$\delta_{tt}u = -\omega_0^2 u + MF \qquad \delta_{tt}u_H = -F \qquad F = \omega_H^{\alpha+1}\mu_t.\,(u_H - u)\left([u_H - u]^+\right)^{\alpha-1}$$

This is a variation on scheme (4.17), where the nonlinear discretization has a partially implicit character.

(a) *Show that this scheme exhibits partial energy conservation when $\alpha = 1$ or $\alpha = 3$ (i.e., show that the scheme possesses an energy function which is conserved except at instants when the hammer either comes into contact with or loses contact with the target mass–spring system).*

(b) *Show that the scheme allows for a unique update of u_H and u at each time step, regardless of the choice of $\alpha \geq 1$.*

Problem 4.6   *A single stage in a Moog ladder filter [165] is often modeled using a first-order differential equation similar to the following:*

$$\frac{du}{dt} = -\omega_c \tanh(u)$$

for some constant $\omega_c > 0$. This is the zero-input case—a single initial condition $u(0) = u_0$ must be specified.

(a) Show that if one defines the energy of this system as $\mathfrak{H} = \frac{1}{2}u^2$, then it must be true that $d\mathfrak{H}/dt \leq 0$, and thus that $|u(t)|$ is a monotonically decreasing function of time, and is bounded by $|u_0|$.

(b) Suppose that the differential equation is discretized as

$$\delta_{t-}u = -\omega_c \tanh(\mu_{t-}u)$$

where $u = u^n$ is a time series, initialized with a value u^0. Show that again, if one defines the energy as $\frac{1}{2}u^2$, $|u^n|$ is a monotonically decreasing function of time index n, and is bounded by $|u^0|$.

(c) The difference scheme above is implicit. Using identity (2.7e), it may be written as

$$\mu_{t-}u = -\frac{k\omega_c}{2} \tanh(\mu_{t-}u) + e_{t-}u$$

Using a diagram, and the fact that $e_{t-}u$ is known, show that the recursion possesses a unique solution in $\mu_{t-}u$ (from which u may be deduced) at each time step.

Problem 4.7   Consider the uncoupled bow-like oscillator, as given in (4.19). Instead of scheme (4.21b), examine the scheme given by

$$\delta_{tt}u = -\alpha\mu_{t-}\phi(\delta_{t+}u)$$

(a) Show that the above scheme, which is implicit, may be written as

$$\phi(\delta_{t+}u) = \frac{-2\alpha}{k}\delta_{t+}u + q$$

where q depends only on previously computed values of u. Show that a solution to the above implicit equation for $\delta_{t+}u$ possesses a unique solution under condition (4.23).

(b) Multiply the above scheme by $\delta_{t\cdot}u$, and show that the following energy balance results:

$$\delta_{t+}\mathfrak{H} = \frac{-\alpha}{4}(\delta_{t+}u + \delta_{t-}u)(\phi(\delta_{t+}u) + \phi(\delta_{t-}u))$$

where $\mathfrak{H}$ is again defined as in (4.22). It is difficult to find simple conditions under which the right-hand side of the above energy balance is non-positive (which is desirable in order to have passive behavior and thus numerical stability). Can you find a sufficient condition on ϕ such that the scheme is passive for any value of the time step k? Hint: The characteristics shown in the left and center panels of Figure 4.8 satisfy such a condition, but that shown at right does not.

Problem 4.8   Consider scheme (4.26) for the bowed mass–spring system. Show that it may be written as

$$\frac{2}{k}v_{\text{rel}} + F_B\phi(v_{\text{rel}}) + b = 0 \tag{4.29}$$

and determine b, which consists of known values (i.e., of previous computed values of the mass displacement and the values of the time series v_B). For the two friction characteristics

$$\phi(\eta) = \sqrt{2a}\eta e^{-a\eta^2+1/2} \qquad \phi(\eta) = \text{sign}(\eta)\left(\epsilon + (1-\epsilon)e^{-a|\eta|}\right) \tag{4.30}$$

where $0 \leq \epsilon \leq 1$, explicitly determine the bounds on k for the uniqueness of the solution to the equation in v_{rel} above.

4.5 Programming exercises

Programming Exercise 4.1 *For the lossless oscillator with a power law characteristic (4.12), compare the performance of difference schemes (4.4) and (4.13) at a given sample rate such as $f_s = 44.1\,kHz$. For a given value of the power law exponent $\alpha > 1$ (consider the values $\alpha = 1.5, 2, 2.5, 3, 3.5, 4$), and with initial conditions $u(0) = 1$, $du/dt(0) = 1$, find the value of ω for which each of the schemes becomes unstable. How does this instability manifest itself in the two cases? Can you conclude that one scheme possesses better stability properties than the other?*

Programming Exercise 4.2 *Consider the hammer–mass–spring interaction, discussed in Section 4.2.3. Generalize the finite difference approximation given in (4.17) to the case of a hammer striking two mass–spring systems, as described in Problem 4.4. Implement this scheme, using the code given in Section A.2 as a starting point. Your code should plot the displacements of the two masses, as well as the combined force $F_1 + F_2$ as a function of time.*

Programming Exercise 4.3 *Consider a rattling element coupled to a mass–spring system. Not surprisingly, this system and a finite difference scheme can be written in exactly the same way as the hammer–mass–spring interaction, as in (4.16) and (4.17), but where the nonlinear characteristic F is replaced by that which appears in (4.18). Modify the code example in Section A.2 so that it simulates such a rattle–mass–spring interaction. You will need to introduce the rattle length ϵ as an extra input parameter.*

Programming Exercise 4.4 *Extend the simulation of the rattle–mass–spring interaction in Programming Exercise 4.3 above to include the effects of gravity and loss (in the target mass–spring system). Now, the system must be generalized to*

$$\frac{d^2u}{dt^2} = -\omega_0^2 u - 2\sigma_0 \frac{du}{dt} + \mathcal{M}F(u - u_R) \qquad \frac{d^2u_R}{dt^2} = -F(u - u_R) - g \qquad (4.31)$$

where u and u_R are the displacements of the target mass–spring system and the rattle, respectively, σ_0 is the usual loss parameter for the SHO (see Section 3.5), and where $g = 9.8\,m/s^2$ is the acceleration due to gravity.

Develop and program a finite difference scheme for the above system. How would you introduce a loss mechanism into the rattling element itself?

Programming Exercise 4.5 *Modify the code example given in Section A.3 such that the bow force F_B and velocity v_B are time series $F_B = F_B^n$ and $v_B = v_B^n$. Experiment with different gestural profiles for both of these control parameter sets. For example, one choice of a control signal for, say, F_B might be, in continuous time and defined over the interval T_f,*

$$F_B(t) = F_{B,\,max} \begin{cases} t/\alpha, & 0 \le t \le \alpha \\ (T_f - t)/(T_f - \alpha), & \alpha \le t \le T_f \end{cases}$$

for some peak bow force $F_{B,max}$ and a parameter α, with $0 \le \alpha \le T_f$, which determines the time to the occurrence of the peak. A similar function could be defined for the velocity. Determine, if possible, the effect on the time taken for the mass–spring system to reach a stable oscillatory regime.

Programming Exercise 4.6 Newton–Raphson iterative root finding *In some numerical bow models, such as that given in (4.26) (as well as in a vast array of other non-musical applications), it is necessary to solve an equation of the form*

$$f(\eta) = 0$$

at each time step. The Newton–Raphson iterative root-finding procedure works as follows. Given some initial guess at the solution $\eta^{(0)}$, perform the following update

$$\eta^{(p+1)} = \eta^{(p)} - \frac{f(\eta^{(p)})}{f'(\eta^{(p)})}$$

successively until an adequately stable solution is found. (You might wish to measure convergence in terms of the error $|\eta^{(p+1)} - \eta^{(p)}|$, and terminate the algorithm when this error is sufficiently small.)

Referring to Problem 4.8, for the bowed mass–spring system, the nonlinear equation to be solved, in the relative velocity v_{rel}, is exactly (4.29). For given values of b, F_B, and k, write a Matlab function which returns v_{rel} for both choices of friction characteristic given in (4.30), using an input parameter to indicate the type of characteristic. In the second case, you will need to take care to separate your algorithm into cases, as the characteristic is not continuous. Your function should also perform a test to ensure that condition (4.23) is satisfied, and produce a warning if it is not. You may wish to refer to the code example in Section A.3, in which Newton–Raphson for the case of the continuous friction characteristic is employed.

Programming Exercise 4.7 *Modify the code example given in Section A.3 so that it uses the Matlab function for the Newton–Raphson iterative algorithm that you created in the previous exercise. Compare the behavior of the system under the distinct choices of friction characteristic from (4.30).*

1
2
3
4
5
6
7
8
9
10
11
12
13
14
15
16
17
18
19
20
21
22
23
24
25
26
27
28
29
30
31
32
33
34
35
36
37
38
39
40
41
42
43
44
45
46
47
48
49
50
51

1
2
3
4
5
6
7
8
9
10
11
12
13
14
15
16
17
18
19
20
21
22
23
24
25
26
27
28
29
30
31
32
33
34
35
36
37
38
39
40
41
42
43
44
45
46
47
48
49
50
51

5

Grid functions and finite difference operators in 1D

In this short chapter, the basic operations used in the construction of finite difference schemes for 1D distributed problems are introduced. The treatment will be somewhat abbreviated, partly because much of this material appears elsewhere, and partly because some of the underlying ideas have been dealt with in Chapter 2. As was the case in this earlier chapter, the presentation will again encompass both frequency domain analysis and pure time–space (energy) techniques. The full power of energy methods [161] will become evident here, not just because of their capability for arriving at stability conditions even for strongly nonlinear problems (some important musical examples of which will appear in subsequent chapters), but because of the ease with which appropriate numerical boundary conditions may be extracted; the proper setting of boundary conditions is always problematic, and is not at all well covered even in the best finite difference texts. This is not to say that frequency domain techniques are not useful; as was mentioned earlier, they are able to yield much important information regarding numerical dispersion, which, in musical simulations, may lead to perceptually audible deviations from the solution to a model system.

In Section 5.1, partial differential operators are introduced, followed by a brief discussion of the classification of partial differential equations in musical acoustics, transform techniques and the concepts of dispersion and phase velocity, and finally an introduction to inner product spaces and various manipulations of interest in PDE analysis. The extension of these techniques to the discrete case is given in Section 5.2, which introduces grid functions and difference operators, now in a distributed setting. Finally, some material on coordinate changes, useful when the problem under consideration exhibits some spatial variation, is covered in Section 5.3. The extension of these concepts to two spatial dimensions is postponed until Chapter 10.

5.1 Partial differential operators and PDEs

Some elements of musical instruments, and in particular strings, bars, and tubes, are well modeled by PDEs in time t and one spatial dimension x; such systems are often referred to as "1D." Various quantities, such as displacement, velocity, and pressure, are thus described by functions of two variables, such as $u(x, t)$. As in the case of lumped systems such as the harmonic oscillator (see Chapter 3), time t is usually defined for $t \geq 0$, though one may extend this definition to

---

Numerical Sound Synthesis: Finite Difference Schemes and Simulation in Musical Acoustics   Stefan Bilbao
© 2009 John Wiley & Sons, Ltd

$t \in [-\infty, \infty]$, for purposes of steady state (Laplace transform) analysis. One also normally takes $x \in \mathcal{D}$, where $\mathcal{D}$ represents some subset of the real line. There are essentially three domains $\mathcal{D}$ of interest in problems defined in 1D: the infinite domain $\mathcal{D} = \mathbb{R} = [-\infty, \infty]$, the semi-infinite domain $\mathcal{D} = \mathbb{R}^+ = [0, \infty]$, and the unit interval $\mathcal{D} = \mathbb{U} = [0, 1]$. The first two domains are of use in an analysis setting; in 1D problems in musical acoustics, $\mathcal{D} = \mathbb{U}$ is always chosen. It is worth noting that scaling techniques, employed whenever possible in this book (see Section 6.1.2 for a first example of this in the case of the 1D wave equation), render the use of other finite intervals unnecessary.

PDEs are equations relating partial temporal and spatial derivatives of one or more functions. In operator form, such derivatives are written as

$$\frac{\partial}{\partial t}, \quad \frac{\partial^2}{\partial t^2}, \quad \frac{\partial}{\partial x}, \quad \frac{\partial^2}{\partial x^2}, \quad \text{etc.}$$

When applied to a function such as $u(x, t)$, the abbreviated subscript notation will be frequently employed, i.e.,

$$\frac{\partial u}{\partial t} = u_t, \quad \frac{\partial^2 u}{\partial t^2} = u_{tt}, \quad \frac{\partial u}{\partial x} = u_x, \quad \frac{\partial^2 u}{\partial x^2} = u_{xx}, \quad \text{etc.}$$

For total time derivatives of a quantity without spatial dependence, such as those that occur in energy analysis or a lumped setting, the symbol d/dt is uniformly employed.

A PDE in a single variable $u(x, t)$, under zero-input conditions, may be simply written as

$$P\left(\frac{\partial}{\partial t}, \frac{\partial^2}{\partial t^2}, \frac{\partial}{\partial x}, \frac{\partial^2}{\partial x^2}, \ldots\right) u = 0 \tag{5.1}$$

where P is a partial differential operator which is a complete description of the behavior of the system at a given point—many of the systems under consideration in musical acoustics, both linear and nonlinear, may be written in this form. The notation above is somewhat loose; not indicated is the possibility of coefficients in the PDE which may depend on x, which may indeed occur in describing systems with a degree of variation in material parameters. Coefficients which depend on t (rendering the system time varying) are possible as well, but occur rarely in musical acoustics. For the systems of interest here, time derivatives of order greater than two occur infrequently, and for many (but not all), spatial derivatives are of even order, reflecting independence of the problem to direction. In some cases, a set of one or more coupled equations of the form (5.1) in several independent variables is necessary in describing a system; nonlinear systems such as strings and plates under high amplitude vibration conditions are two such examples—see Chapters 8 and 13. A description such as (5.1) is not complete until initial and boundary conditions have been supplied. Appropriate settings for such conditions will be dealt with on an as-needed basis, and the first description will occur with reference to the 1D wave equation, in the following chapter.

5.1.1   Classification of PDEs

In an abstract setting, there are established ways of classifying PDEs [146], which are useful in coming to conclusions about the form of the solution. One often speaks of a PDE as being time dependent or not, or of being hyperbolic, parabolic, or elliptic, or of being semi-linear versus quasi-linear. In the more specialized setting of musical acoustics, it is better to abandon this abstract view, and focus on the special types of systems (always time dependent and usually hyperbolic) which frequently occur: linear and shift-invariant (LSI) systems, linear and time-invariant (LTI) systems, more generally linear systems, and nonlinear systems. (In fact, nearly all systems in musical acoustics behave nonlinearly when coupled to an excitation mechanism—here, however, words such as "linear" etc. refer to the distributed resonator in isolation.)

As an example, consider the following equation:

$$u_{tt} = \gamma^2 u_{xx}$$

where $u(x, t)$ is the dependent variable to be solved for. If γ is a constant, this PDE is known as the 1D wave equation, and is LSI—the medium it describes behaves uniformly at all points in the domain and at all time instants. If γ depends on x, the system is still LTI, but not invariant with respect to the spatial variable, and not LSI. Its properties are different from one spatial location to another. If γ depends on x and t, it is simply linear. Finally, if γ depends on u itself, the equation is referred to as nonlinear. This classification follows through to any derived numerical simulation method. See Figure 5.1.

The analysis and numerical method construction techniques which are available are governed by the type of system under consideration. LSI systems, which form the majority of those under study in musical acoustics and employed until recently in physical modeling sound synthesis, are undeniably the easiest to deal with—the full scope of frequency domain and transform techniques is available, and as a result it is possible to obtain a very comprehensive picture of the resulting dynamics including information about wave propagation speeds and modes, as well as many features of associated numerical methods, such as stability conditions and dispersion. Such systems and the accompanying analysis machinery, as they occur in musical acoustics, will be examined in Chapters 6, 7, 11, and 12. Systems which are LTI but not LSI still allow a limited analysis: one may still speak of modes and frequencies, but one loses the convenient notion of a global wave velocity, and the most powerful analysis tools (von Neumann) for numerical simulation methods are no longer available. Some such systems will be seen in Section 7.10 and in Chapter 9. In the linear time-varying and nonlinear cases, the notion of frequency itself becomes unwieldy, though if the nonlinearity or time variation is weak, one may draw some (generally qualitative) conclusions through linearization, or, with much additional effort, through perturbation methods [252]. See Chapters 8 and 13. In all cases, however, it is possible and usually quite easy to arrive at a numerical simulation routine for synthesis, but, depending on the type of the original system, it will be more or less difficult to say or predict anything about the way in which it behaves.

One attribute of a system which persists in being clearly defined for any of the types of systems mentioned above is its energy. PDEs which occur in musical acoustics are not abstract concoctions—they correspond to real physical systems, and real physical systems always obey laws of conservation or dissipation of energy.

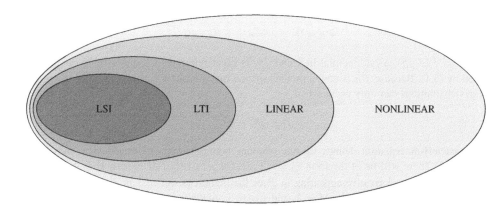

Figure 5.1   Classification of PDEs of interest in musical acoustics.

5.1.2 Laplace and Fourier transforms

As in the lumped case, the Laplace transform of a function such as $u(x, t)$ may be defined as

$$\hat{u}(x, s) = \int_{-\infty}^{\infty} u(x, t)e^{-st}dt \tag{5.2}$$

where $s = j\omega + \sigma$ is again the complex-valued frequency variable. See Section 2.3. As before, the definition is two sided, allowing one to ignore initial conditions. One may also define a spatial Fourier transform as

$$\tilde{u}(\beta, t) = \int_{-\infty}^{\infty} u(x, t)e^{-j\beta x}dx \tag{5.3}$$

where, here, β may be viewed as a real wavenumber; in general, spatial Fourier transforms are only used for problems defined over $\mathcal{D} = \mathbb{R}$, though Fourier series approximations for systems defined over a finite interval play a fundamental role in so-called modal synthesis methods—see, e.g., Section 6.1.11.

The actions of partial derivative operators applied to a function $u(x, t)$ transform according to

$$\frac{\partial^m u}{\partial t^m} \overset{\mathcal{L}}{\Longrightarrow} s^m \hat{u} \qquad \frac{\partial^l u}{\partial x^l} \overset{\mathcal{F}}{\Longrightarrow} (j\beta)^l \tilde{u}$$

where $\mathcal{L}$ or $\mathcal{F}$ accompanied by an arrow indicates a Laplace or Fourier transform, respectively.

Just as in the lumped case, as an alternative to full Laplace/Fourier analysis, it is often simpler to consider the effect of differential operators on a test function of the form

$$u(x, t) = e^{st + j\beta x} \tag{5.4}$$

which behaves as a single wavelike component, of temporal frequency s and wavenumber β. The use of this special function is often referred to in the literature as an *ansatz* [161]. See Section 2.3.

Dispersion relations

If the PDE under consideration is LSI, then both Laplace and Fourier transforms may be applied in order to arrive at a convenient algebraic description of the PDE in the frequency domain:

$$Pu = 0 \qquad \overset{\mathcal{L}, \mathcal{F}}{\Longrightarrow} \qquad \tilde{\hat{P}}\tilde{\hat{u}} = 0$$

where $\tilde{\hat{P}} = \tilde{\hat{P}}(s, j\beta)$, a multinomial in s and $j\beta$, is often referred to as the symbol of the PDE defined by (5.1). Because $\tilde{\hat{P}}\tilde{\hat{u}}$ is now a product of two functions of s and $j\beta$, it is easy to see that non-trivial solutions can only occur when

$$\tilde{\hat{P}}(s, j\beta) = 0$$

This characteristic equation defines various relations between temporal frequency s and spatial frequency β. These will be of the form $s_p = s_p(j\beta)$, for $p = 1, \ldots, M$, where M is the order of the highest temporal derivative appearing in P or the highest power of s in $\tilde{\hat{P}}(s, j\beta)$. (For most systems of interest in this book, $M = 2$, and the two solutions will be denoted by $s_\pm$.) These solutions are known as dispersion relations, and allow the extraction of information regarding propagation speeds.

1
2
3
4
5
6
7
8
9
10
11
12
13
14
15
16
17
18
19
20
21
22
23
24
25
26
27
28
29
30
31
32
33
34
35
36
37
38
39
40
41
42
43
44
45
46
47
48
49
50
51

Phase and group velocity

In lossless problems, it is typical to arrive at solutions $s_p(j\beta) = j\omega_p(j\beta)$ which are purely imaginary, so that one may write the dispersion relations as $\omega_p = \omega_p(\beta)$ for real frequencies ω_p. In this special case, for any such $\omega(\beta)$, the phase velocity v_ϕ and group velocity v_g are defined as

$$v_\phi = \frac{\omega}{\beta} \qquad v_g = \frac{d\omega}{d\beta} \qquad (5.5)$$

For a problem of order M in the time variable, there will be M dispersion relations. For second-order systems, these usually occur as a pair of opposite sign, representing wave propagation to the left and right. In this book, the positive solutions will be taken as the phase and group velocity. These velocities may be expressed most directly as functions of wavenumber, but more usefully perhaps as functions of frequency ω (or what is more directly comprehensible in musical acoustics, frequency $f = \omega/2\pi$) through the substitution of the dispersion relation itself; this is usually possible in 1D, but in higher dimensions only for problems which are isotropic. See Section 10.1.4.

For a given system, the phase velocity describes the speed of propagation of a single component of the solution, and the group velocity the gross speed of disturbances. For hyperbolic systems, such as the wave equation, it must be true that the group velocity is bounded from above (i.e., there is a maximum speed at which disturbances may propagate), though this is not necessarily true of the phase velocity—the case of Timoshenko beam theory is an interesting example of this [156]. See Problem 7.1. Most systems that will be examined in this book will be of hyperbolic type, with the exception of thin beams and plates, which do in fact allow infinite group velocities. Such anomalous behavior is a result of simplifying assumptions, and disappears when more accurate models are employed. If a system exhibits a small degree of loss—this is the majority of systems in musical acoustics—then one may loosely extend this idea of phase velocity by replacing ω in the definitions above by the imaginary part of s.

These concepts carry over to derived numerical methods in a natural way—finite difference schemes, at least for LSI systems, also possess phase and group velocities. Both are of use in coming to conclusions, in the musical sound synthesis context, about undesirable numerical inharmonicity, as well as stability [362].

5.1.3   Inner products and energetic manipulations

Energy analysis of PDE systems and boundary conditions is based, usually, around the definition of various types of spatial inner products [210]. An obvious choice in the continuous case is the L_2 inner product. In 1D, it, along with the accompanying norm, is defined as

$$\langle f, g \rangle_{\mathcal{D}} = \int_{\mathcal{D}} fg\, dx \qquad \|f\|_{\mathcal{D}} = \sqrt{\langle f, g \rangle_{\mathcal{D}}} \qquad (5.6)$$

for functions $f(x)$ and $g(x)$ defined over the interval $x \in \mathcal{D}$. For time-dependent problems such as those encountered in this book, such an inner product when applied to two functions $f(x, t)$ and $g(x, t)$ will itself be a function of time alone, i.e., $\langle f, g \rangle = \langle f, g \rangle(t)$.

Identities and inequalities

The following inequalities hold with regard to the above definition of the inner product and norm:

$$|\langle f, g \rangle_{\mathcal{D}}| \leq \|f\|_{\mathcal{D}} \|g\|_{\mathcal{D}} \qquad \text{Cauchy–Schwartz inequality} \qquad (5.7a)$$

$$\|f + g\|_{\mathcal{D}} \leq \|f\|_{\mathcal{D}} + \|g\|_{\mathcal{D}} \qquad \text{triangle inequality} \qquad (5.7b)$$

For any three functions f, g, and r, it is also true that

$$\langle f, gr \rangle_D = \langle fg, r \rangle_D$$

If the left and right endpoints of a given domain D are d_- and d_+, then the familiar integration by parts rule may be written, in inner product notation, as

$$\langle f, g_x \rangle_D = -\langle f_x, g \rangle_D + fg \big|_{d_-}^{d_+} \tag{5.8}$$

and thus boundary terms appear. The identity (5.8) may be extended to second derivatives as

$$\langle f, g_{xx} \rangle_D = \langle f_{xx}, g \rangle_D + (fg_x - f_x g) \big|_{d_-}^{d_+} \tag{5.9}$$

If $d_- = -\infty$ or $d_+ = \infty$, then the functions f and g are assumed to vanish when evaluated at such points. Thus, when $D = \mathbb{R}$, for example, one has simply

$$\langle f, g_x \rangle_{\mathbb{R}} = -\langle f_x, g \rangle_{\mathbb{R}} \qquad \langle f, g_{xx} \rangle_{\mathbb{R}} = \langle f_{xx}, g \rangle_{\mathbb{R}} \tag{5.10}$$

The total time derivative of an inner product is assumed to distribute to the constituent functions, i.e.,

$$\frac{d}{dt} \langle f, g \rangle_D = \langle f_t, g \rangle_D + \langle f, g_t \rangle_D$$

Notice the use of the symbol d/dt here to represent the total time derivative of a quantity without spatial dependence.

Vector form

In some cases, it may be necessary to make use of a vector form of the inner product: that is, for column vectors $\underline{f} = [f^{(1)}, \ldots, f^{(M)}]^T$ and $\underline{g} = [g^{(1)}, \ldots, g^{(M)}]^T$,

$$\langle \underline{f}, \underline{g} \rangle_D = \int_D \underline{f}^T \underline{g} \, dx$$

An application is to the analysis of non-planar string vibration—see Section 8.3.1. The above identities and inequalities generalize directly to the vector case in an obvious way.

5.2   Grid functions and difference operators

A grid function u_l^n, taking on values for integer n (usually $n \geq 0$), and for integer $l \in D$, is introduced in order to approximate a continuous function $u(x, t)$, at location $x = lh$ and at time $t = nk$. The quantity h is referred to as the grid spacing. Again, as in the case of time series, the same variable name (in this case u) will be used to represent both a grid function and the variable it is intended to approximate. See Figure 5.2.

As in the continuous case, there are essentially three domains D of interest for problems in one spatial dimension: $D = \mathbb{Z} = [-\infty, \ldots, \infty]$, $D = \mathbb{Z}^+ = [0, \ldots, \infty]$, and $D = \mathbb{U}_N = [0, \ldots, N]$. The finite domain $\mathbb{U}_N$ is the only domain of practical utility, and corresponds to the unit interval, provided one has chosen a grid spacing of $h = 1/N$, which one is always free to do through scaling techniques. For the moment, for simplicity, it will be assumed that grid functions are infinite in spatial extent, though the bounding of spatial domains will be introduced in Section 5.2.9. For reference, graphical representations of the behavior of the various operators described in this section are shown in Figure 5.3.

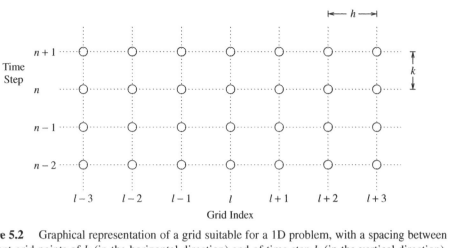

Figure 5.2   Graphical representation of a grid suitable for a 1D problem, with a spacing between adjacent grid points of h (in the horizontal direction) and of time step k (in the vertical direction).

5.2.1   Time difference and averaging operators

The definitions of time difference operators in the distributed setting are nearly unchanged from those covered in Section 2.2 and applied to time series. For a grid function u_l^n, the forward and backward shifts and the identity operation "1" are defined as

$$e_{t+}u_l^n = u_l^{n+1} \qquad e_{t-}u_l^n = u_l^{n-1} \qquad 1u_l^n = u_l^n$$

and are to be regarded as applying to the time series u_l^n at all values of the indices n and l. Approximations to a partial time derivative are defined as

$$\delta_{t+} \triangleq \frac{1}{k}(e_{t+} - 1) \approx \frac{\partial}{\partial t} \qquad \delta_{t-} \triangleq \frac{1}{k}(1 - e_{t-}) \approx \frac{\partial}{\partial t} \qquad \delta_{t\cdot} \triangleq \frac{1}{2k}(e_{t+} - e_{t-}) \approx \frac{\partial}{\partial t}$$

and averaging approximations to the identity operation as

$$\mu_{t+} \triangleq \frac{1}{2}(e_{t+} + 1) \approx 1 \qquad \mu_{t-} \triangleq \frac{1}{2}(1 + e_{t-}) \approx 1 \qquad \mu_{t\cdot} \triangleq \frac{1}{2}(e_{t+} + e_{t-}) \approx 1$$

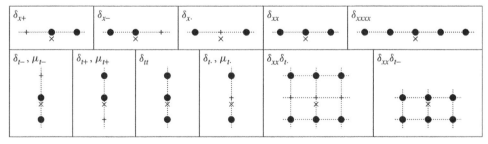

Figure 5.3   Footprints, or stencils of various 1D difference operators, as indicated. Time shifts of duration k are shown as vertical displacements, and spatial shifts of distance h by horizontal displacements. In each case, the grid points required for the approximation are indicated by black circles, and the central point at which the operator is applied is accompanied by a cross symbol.

An approximation to a second time derivative is, as before,

$$\delta_{tt} = \delta_{t+}\delta_{t-} \approx \frac{\partial^2}{\partial t^2}$$

5.2.2   Spatial difference operators

Approximations to spatial derivatives are based on the unit forward and backward spatial shift operations, defined as

$$e_{x+}u_l^n = u_{l+1}^n \qquad e_{x-}u_l^n = u_{l-1}^n$$

One has, immediately, the following forward, backward, and centered spatial difference approximations:

$$\delta_{x+} \triangleq \frac{1}{h}(e_{x+} - 1) \approx \frac{\partial}{\partial x} \qquad \delta_{x-} \triangleq \frac{1}{h}(1 - e_{x-}) \approx \frac{\partial}{\partial x} \qquad \delta_{x\cdot} \triangleq \frac{1}{2h}(e_{x+} - e_{x-}) \approx \frac{\partial}{\partial x}$$

and spatial averaging operators, similar to their temporal counterparts, can be defined accordingly:

$$\mu_{x+} = \frac{1}{2}(e_{x+} + 1) \qquad \mu_{x-} = \frac{1}{2}(1 + e_{x-}) \qquad \mu_{x\cdot} = \frac{1}{2}(e_{x+} + e_{x-}) \qquad \mu_{xx} = \mu_{x+}\mu_{x-}$$

Simple approximations to second and fourth spatial derivatives are given by

$$\delta_{xx} = \delta_{x+}\delta_{x-} \approx \frac{\partial^2}{\partial x^2} \qquad\qquad \delta_{xxxx} = \delta_{xx}\delta_{xx} \approx \frac{\partial^4}{\partial x^4} \qquad\qquad (5.11)$$

For ease of programming, it is useful to expand out the behavior of these compact operator representations in order to see directly the coefficients which should be applied to values of a given grid function u_l^n:

$$\delta_{xx}u_l^n = \frac{1}{h^2}\left(u_{l+1}^n - 2u_l^n + u_{l-1}^n\right) \qquad\qquad (5.12a)$$

$$\delta_{xxxx}u_l^n = \frac{1}{h^4}\left(u_{l+2}^n - 4u_{l+1}^n + 6u_l^n - 4u_{l-1}^n + u_{l-2}^n\right) \qquad\qquad (5.12b)$$

There are various identities which are of use in difference scheme analysis—here are two of interest:

$$\delta_{x+}(fg) = (\mu_{x+}f)(\delta_{x+}g) + (\delta_{x+}f)(\mu_{x+}g) \qquad\qquad (5.13)$$

$$\mu_{x\cdot} = 1 + \frac{h^2}{2}\delta_{xx} \qquad\qquad (5.14)$$

Just as in the case of temporal operators, spatial difference operators may be combined to yield more complex operators, generally of wider stencil. As an example, one form, dependent on a free parameter α, is the averaging operator

$$\alpha + (1 - \alpha)\mu_{x\cdot}.$$

which is an approximation to the identity for any value of α. A parameterized form such as the above can lead to a means of reducing the dispersive properties of finite difference schemes—see Section 6.3.

5.2.3   Mixed spatial–temporal difference operators

In some cases of interest in musical acoustics, and especially in models of frequency-dependent loss in strings (see Section 7.3), mixed derivative terms appear. It is straightforward to generate finite difference approximations to such operators using operator notation and principles of combining difference operators, as outlined in Section 2.2.2.

Considering, for example, the operator $\partial^3/\partial t\,\partial x^2$, two possible approximations are

$$\delta_{t-}\delta_{xx} \qquad\qquad \delta_{t\cdot}\delta_{xx}$$

The first approximation employs a backward time difference, and the second a centered time difference. Again, it is of use to examine the effect of such an operator applied to a grid function u_l^n:

$$\delta_{t-}\delta_{xx}u_l^n = \frac{1}{kh^2}\left(u_{l+1}^n - 2u_l^n + u_{l-1}^n - u_{l+1}^{n-1} + 2u_l^{n-1} - u_{l-1}^{n-1}\right)$$

$$\delta_{t\cdot}\delta_{xx}u_l^n = \frac{1}{2kh^2}\left(u_{l+1}^{n+1} - 2u_l^{n+1} + u_{l-1}^{n+1} - u_{l+1}^{n-1} + 2u_l^{n-1} - u_{l-1}^{n-1}\right)$$

In practical terms, there is a large distinction between the two approximations. That involving the backward time difference computes an approximation to $\partial^3/\partial t\,\partial x^2$ at grid location (l, n) using only values of the grid function at time steps n and $n-1$. That involving the centered time difference, however, requires access to values of the grid function at time step $n+1$. In a general two-step finite difference scheme (most of the systems to be discussed in this book may be dealt with in this way), the values of the grid function at time step $n+1$ constitute the unknowns. The use of such an operator then leads to a linear coupling among the unknown values of the grid function, and thus to the need for linear system solution techniques in order to arrive at a solution; such schemes are known as "implicit" [342]. Such implicit schemes will be employed at times in this book. Though they may require more effort at the programming stage, the actual computational work of performing (potentially large) linear system inversions is alleviated somewhat by the sparsity of the difference operators when viewed in matrix form—see Section 5.2.7.

5.2.4   Interpolation and spreading operators

Input and output are key attributes of physical modeling synthesis routines. The problem of applying inputs and taking output, though not extremely difficult, is not covered in most simulation texts.

Output and interpolation

In some cases in musical sound synthesis, one may be interested in accessing (listening to) a point in a distributed medium which lies between spatial grid points—some form of interpolation is thus necessary. If the listening or observation point is static, it is sufficient to truncate this position to a nearby grid location; if it is moving,[1] such truncation will inevitably lead to audible distortion (clicks) in the resulting sound output. See Section 6.2.9. Consider some 1D grid function u_l, consisting of values at locations lh for integer l, which represents the state of a simulated object at

---

[1] Moving output locations, though distinctly unphysical, can be employed as a very simple ad hoc means for rendering physical modeling sound synthesis output slightly more attractive, due to delicate phasing effects. Such effects do indeed occur in the real world (when, for example, a musical instrument moves slightly with respect to the listener), but are difficult to model directly.

some given instant. Supposing that the observation point is $x_o \in \mathcal{D}$, leftward truncation leads to an integer observation index $l_o = \text{floor}\,(x_o/h)$, and one may define an interpolation operator $I_0(x_o)$, acting on the grid function u_l, as

$$I_0(x_o)u_l = u_{l_o}$$

One could, as in sound synthesis methods employing wavetable interpolation [240], make use of a slightly improved interpolation operator which employs rounding rather than truncation. Better yet, if one also makes use of the fractional remainder of the truncation, defined by $\alpha_o = x_o/h - l_o$, one may define a linear interpolation operator $I_1(x_o)$ by

$$I_1(x_o)u_l = (1 - \alpha_o)u_{l_o} + \alpha_o u_{l_o+1}$$

One may of course go further along these lines, to develop interpolants of even better accuracy. For sound synthesis, linear interpolation is often sufficient, but Lagrange cubic interpolation is another possible choice. For a given observation index l_o and fractional part α_o, the cubic interpolant $I_3(x_o)$ is defined as

$$I_3(x_o)u_l = \frac{\alpha_o\,(\alpha_o - 1)\,(\alpha_o - 2)}{-6}u_{l_o-1} + \frac{(\alpha_o - 1)\,(\alpha_o + 1)\,(\alpha_o - 2)}{2}u_{l_o}$$
$$+ \frac{\alpha_o\,(\alpha_o + 1)\,(\alpha_o - 2)}{-2}u_{l_o+1} + \frac{\alpha_o\,(\alpha_o + 1)\,(\alpha_o - 1)}{6}u_{l_o+2}$$

This approximation makes use of four values of the grid function u_l neighboring the interpolation point, and requires more computational work than linear interpolation. It is, on the other hand, much more accurate than linear interpolation—see Section 5.2.5. The action of these interpolation operators is illustrated in Figure 5.4.

One programming concern is the behavior of such an interpolant when the observation point is within one grid spacing of the endpoint of the domain. Though not of major importance, there are several options: (1) restrict the observation point such that this cannot occur; (2) develop an asymmetric interpolant at such points; (3) revert to a simpler interpolant, such as I_1 for such locations; or (4) make use of virtual grid points (see Section 5.2.8) whose values are set by boundary conditions. Of these options, (1) is certainly the easiest to implement, and (4) the most general and least likely to lead to artifacts. See Programming Exercise 5.1.

Another approach which has been employed, particularly when the sound synthesis algorithm is based around the use of signal processing constructs such as delay lines, has been all-pass interpolation. See the article by Laakso et al. for an overview [215].

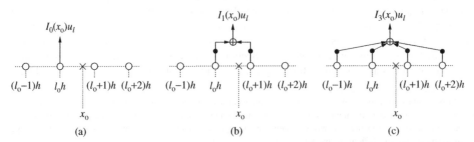

Figure 5.4 Schematic representation of various interpolation functions over a grid: (a) rounding; (b) linear interpolation; and (c) cubic interpolation. Multiplications by scaling factors, dependent on the interpolation point, are indicated by black circles.

Input and spreading operators

The flip side of output is, of course, input; exciting a given distributed object at a given location is a key feature of string instruments in particular, where the excitation may be a strike, pluck, or bow force. The excitation itself is often described as a lumped object, whose effect on a 1D system may be expressed in terms of a distribution of a given form. Beyond excitation, there is also the important issue of the pointwise interconnection of distributed objects, in which case one may imagine the objects receiving input information from one another at given locations.

The simplest such distribution corresponds to an excitation at a single location $x_i \in [0, 1]$. In the continuous case, this is exactly a Dirac delta function $\delta(x - x_i)$. As in the case of interpolation (see previous section), there are various ways of approximating such a distribution on a grid of spacing h. If $l_i = \text{floor}(x_i/h)$ is the nearest grid point to the left of x_i, then a zeroth-order distribution $J_{l,0}(x_i)$ is a grid function of the form

$$J_{l,0}(x_i) = \frac{1}{h} \quad \text{for} \quad l = l_i, \quad \text{otherwise } 0$$

Notice that the spreading function is scaled by $1/h$. Such a distribution is sufficient for many applications, especially if the grid is dense (i.e., h is small), and if the excitation remains stationary. But this is not always the case, and higher-order distributions may be necessary in some cases. In analogy with the interpolation operators I_1 and I_3, the linear and cubic spreading distributions, respectively $J_{l,1}$ and $J_{l,3}$, may be defined in terms of the fractional address $\alpha_i = x_i/h - l_i$ as

$$J_{l,1}(x_i) = \frac{1}{h} \begin{cases} 0, & l < l_i \\ (1 - \alpha_i), & l = l_i \\ \alpha_i, & l = l_i + 1 \\ 0, & l > l_i + 1 \end{cases} \qquad J_{l,3}(x_i) = \frac{1}{h} \begin{cases} 0, & l < l_i - 1 \\ \alpha_i (\alpha_i - 1)(\alpha_i - 2)/-6, & l = l_i - 1 \\ (\alpha_i - 1)(\alpha_i + 1)(\alpha_i - 2)/2, & l = l_i \\ \alpha_i (\alpha_i + 1)(\alpha_i - 2)/-2, & l = l_i + 1 \\ \alpha_i (\alpha_i + 1)(\alpha_i - 1)/6, & l = l_i + 2 \\ 0, & l > l_i + 2 \end{cases}$$

As in the case of interpolation, higher-order distribution functions are a possibility, though the higher the order, the wider the distribution function, and, again, one may need to make use of a specialized distribution or programming if x_i is within a very few grid points of an endpoint of the domain.

Some more comments on the relationship between interpolation and spreading operators, and on the gain of spreading operators, appear in Section 5.2.12.

Full grid interpolation

In certain applications, particularly involving systems possessing disparate wave speeds (see the case of coupled transverse–longitudinal string vibration in Section 8.2), it may be advantageous to perform interpolation on an entire grid function, rather than at a single location.

Suppose first that one has a grid function $u_l^{(1)}$ defined over a grid of spacing $h^{(1)}$, or at locations $x_l^{(1)} = lh^{(1)}$, and one would like to interpolate the values to a new grid function $u_m^{(2)}$, taking on values at locations $x_m^{(2)} = mh^{(2)}$, for some new grid spacing $h^{(2)}$. For the moment, assume that $h^{(2)} \leq h^{(1)}$, so that this is a spatial "upsampling" operation. An obvious way of proceeding is to simply employ the pointwise pth-order interpolant I_p to the grid function $u_l^{(1)}$ at locations $x_m^{(2)}$, and thus

$$u_m^{(2)} = I_p(x_m^{(2)})u^{(1)}$$

For two grids limited to a finite number of points, it is convenient to represent this operation in the following way:

$$u^{(2)} = \mathcal{I}_{h^{(1)} \longrightarrow h^{(2)}, p} u^{(1)}$$

where $\mathcal{I}_{h^{(1)} \to h^{(2)}, p}$ has the interpretation of a rectangular matrix; its exact form and dimensions will depend on the boundary conditions—see Programming Exercise 5.2.

Spatial downsampling may be carried out in a similar manner, but one must beware of the possibility of spatial aliasing. Instead of using a polynomial interpolator directly, the conjugate interpolant $\mathcal{I}^*_{h^{(2)} \to h^{(1)}, p}$ defined, using matrix transposition, as

$$\mathcal{I}^*_{h^{(2)} \to h^{(1)}, p} = \frac{h^{(1)}}{h^{(2)}} \mathcal{I}^T_{h^{(1)} \to h^{(2)}, p}$$

has excellent properties. See Programming Exercise 5.3 for some exploration of this operator, particularly with regard to aliasing.

5.2.5 Accuracy of difference operators

The concept of the accuracy of time–space difference operators is similar to that described in the case of pure time difference operators in Section 2.2.3, except that one must now take into account accuracy with respect to both dimensions. Generally, the difference operators described in the previous sections correspond to their continuous counterparts to within an additive factor which is dependent on powers of the time step k and the grid spacing h. Employing the same techniques as in Section 2.2.3, i.e., applying a difference operator to a continuous function and then making use of a 2D Taylor expansion about the grid point of operation, one may show that, for time difference operators,

$$\delta_{t+} = \frac{\partial}{\partial t} + O(k) \qquad \delta_{t-} = \frac{\partial}{\partial t} + O(k) \qquad \delta_{t\cdot} = \frac{\partial}{\partial t} + O(k^2)$$

$$\mu_{t+} = 1 + O(k) \qquad \mu_{t-} = 1 + O(k) \qquad \mu_{t\cdot} = 1 + O(k^2)$$

$$\delta_{tt} = \frac{\partial^2}{\partial t^2} + O(k^2)$$

and that, for spatial difference operators,

$$\delta_{x+} = \frac{\partial}{\partial x} + O(h) \qquad \delta_{x-} = \frac{\partial}{\partial x} + O(h) \qquad \delta_{x\cdot} = \frac{\partial}{\partial x} + O(h^2)$$

$$\delta_{xx} = \frac{\partial^2}{\partial x^2} + O(h^2) \qquad \delta_{xxxx} = \frac{\partial^4}{\partial x^4} + O(h^2)$$

For mixed time–space difference operators, such as approximations to $\partial^3/\partial t \partial x^2$, one has

$$\delta_{t-}\delta_{xx} = \frac{\partial^3}{\partial t \partial x^2} + O(k) + O(h^2) \qquad \delta_{t\cdot}\delta_{xx} = \frac{\partial^3}{\partial t \partial x^2} + O(k^2) + O(h^2)$$

Notice that, in all cases, centered difference operators lead to even-order accuracy.

The accuracy of a finite difference scheme may be linked to that of the constituent difference operators employed; one must be somewhat careful in coming to a direct conclusion, because in most cases the time step and grid spacing must also be related in a precise way so as to ensure numerical stability and convergence. This is a rather subtle point, and the reader is referred to the literature for more information [342].

The accuracy of the interpolation operators, as defined in Section 5.2.4, may also be deduced through the use of Taylor expansions—all are approximations to a Dirac delta function centered at the observation point x_0. When such operators are applied to a continuous function $u(x)$, one has

$$I_0(x_0)u(x) = u(x_0) + O(h) \qquad I_1(x_0)u(x) = u(x_0) + O(h^2) \qquad I_3(x_0)u(x) = u(x_0) + O(h^4)$$

5.2.6 Frequency domain interpretation

As for continuous problems, one may define transforms of discrete grid functions. Assuming for the moment that the grid function u_l^n is defined over $n = [-\infty, \ldots, \infty]$, and $l \in \mathcal{D} = \mathbb{Z}$, the discrete-time z transform and discrete spatial Fourier transform are defined by

$$\hat{u} = \sum_{n=-\infty}^{\infty} u_l^n z^{-n} \qquad \tilde{u} = \sum_{l=-\infty}^{\infty} u_l^n e^{-jl\beta h}$$

In the case of the z transform, the variable z may be viewed as a complex number of the form e^{sk}, with s a complex frequency $s = \sigma + j\omega$. The factor z, though completely analogous to that used in transform analysis of digital filters, is referred to as an amplification factor when employed in the context of finite difference scheme analysis (and is often denoted g instead of z [342]). In the spatial discrete Fourier transform, β is a real wavenumber.

As in the continuous case, it is sufficient to perform frequency domain analysis of difference operators and schemes with respect to the ansatz

$$u_l^n = z^n e^{jl\beta h}$$

For temporal operators, one has, as in the case of difference operators defined for lumped problems,

$$e_{t\pm} u \overset{\mathcal{Z}}{\Longrightarrow} z^{\pm 1} \hat{u}$$

and for the various first differences and averaging operators, one has

$$\delta_{t+} u \overset{\mathcal{Z}}{\Longrightarrow} \frac{1}{k}(z-1)\,\hat{u} \qquad \delta_{t-} u \overset{\mathcal{Z}}{\Longrightarrow} \frac{1}{k}\left(1-z^{-1}\right)\hat{u} \qquad \delta_{t\cdot} u \overset{\mathcal{Z}}{\Longrightarrow} \frac{1}{2k}\left(z-z^{-1}\right)\hat{u}$$

$$\mu_{t+} u \overset{\mathcal{Z}}{\Longrightarrow} \frac{1}{2}(z+1)\,\hat{u} \qquad \mu_{t-} u \overset{\mathcal{Z}}{\Longrightarrow} \frac{1}{2}\left(1+z^{-1}\right)\hat{u} \qquad \mu_{t\cdot} u \overset{\mathcal{Z}}{\Longrightarrow} \frac{1}{2}\left(z+z^{-1}\right)\hat{u}$$

The second difference δ_{tt} transforms according to

$$\delta_{tt} u \overset{\mathcal{Z}}{\Longrightarrow} \frac{1}{k^2}\left(z-2+z^{-1}\right)\hat{u}$$

Spatial difference operators behave in a similar way. One has

$$e_{x\pm} u \overset{\mathcal{F}}{\Longrightarrow} e^{\pm j\beta h}\tilde{u}$$

and for approximations to a first derivative

$$\delta_{x+} u \overset{\mathcal{F}}{\Longrightarrow} \frac{1}{h}\left(e^{j\beta h}-1\right)\tilde{u} \qquad \delta_{x-} u \overset{\mathcal{F}}{\Longrightarrow} \frac{1}{h}\left(1-e^{-j\beta h}\right)\tilde{u}$$

$$\delta_{x\cdot} u \overset{\mathcal{F}}{\Longrightarrow} \frac{1}{2h}\left(e^{j\beta h}-e^{-j\beta h}\right)\tilde{u} = \frac{j}{h}\sin(\beta h)\tilde{u}$$

Notice that the approximation to the operator $\delta_{x\cdot}$ acts as a pure imaginary multiplicative factor, a consequence of the centered antisymmetric footprint of $\delta_{x\cdot}$.

The operators δ_{xx} and δ_{xxxx} transform according to

$$\delta_{xx} u \overset{\mathcal{F}}{\Longrightarrow} \frac{1}{h^2}\left(e^{j\beta h}-2+e^{-j\beta h}\right)\tilde{u} = -\frac{4}{h^2}\sin^2(\beta h/2)\,\tilde{u} \tag{5.15a}$$

$$\delta_{xxxx} u \overset{\mathcal{F}}{\Longrightarrow} \frac{1}{h^4}\left(e^{j\beta h}-2+e^{-j\beta h}\right)^2\tilde{u} = \frac{16}{h^4}\sin^4(\beta h/2)\,\tilde{u} \tag{5.15b}$$

Notice that both operators behave as pure real multiplicative factors, a consequence of the centered symmetric footprint of both—furthermore, δ_{xx} is non-positive and δ_{xxxx} is non-negative for any choice of wavenumber β. See Problem 5.1.

Mixed temporal–spatial difference operators act as multiplicative factors involving both z and β. For the approximations to the third derivative $\partial^3/\partial t \partial x^2$, one has

$$\delta_{t-}\delta_{xx}u \xrightarrow{z,\mathcal{F}} \frac{-4}{kh^2}\left(1-z^{-1}\right)\sin^2(\beta h/2)\hat{u}$$

$$\delta_{t\cdot}\delta_{xx}u \xrightarrow{z,\mathcal{F}} \frac{-2}{kh^2}\left(z-z^{-1}\right)\sin^2(\beta h/2)\hat{u}$$

Recursions and amplification polynomials

The relationship between difference schemes and polynomials in the variable z has been discussed earlier in Section 2.3.3, in the case of ODEs. For finite difference schemes for LSI PDEs, the situation is similar.

Confining attention for the moment to 1D LSI problems defined over $\mathcal{D} = \mathbb{Z}$, finite difference schemes are recursions of the following form:

$$\sum_{l'\in\mathbb{M}}\sum_{n'=0}^{N}a_{l'}^{(n')}u_{l-l'}^{n-n'} = 0$$

where, as before, the scheme operates over $N+1$ adjacent time levels, and over a spatial width (or stencil) given by the set $\mathbb{M}$. The constants $a_{l'}^{(n')}$ are referred to as the scheme coefficients. One major distinction between the recursion above, operating over an entire grid function, and the recursion (2.10) in a time series is that it is not possible to isolate the unknowns unless all but one of the coefficients $a_{l'}^{(0)}$ are zero. If this is true, the scheme is referred to as explicit, and if not, as implicit (requiring more involved linear system solution techniques). Much more will be said about explicit and implicit schemes with regard to the 1D wave equation in the following chapter. Employing the ansatz $u_l^n = z^n e^{jl\beta h}$ in the above recursion leads to a polynomial of the form

$$P(z) = \sum_{n'=0}^{N}a^{(n')}(\beta)z^{N-n'} = 0 \qquad \text{where} \qquad a^{(n')}(\beta) = \sum_{l'\in\mathbb{M}}a_{l'}^{(n')}e^{-jl'\beta h} \qquad (5.16)$$

which is often referred to as an amplification polynomial [342] for the associated scheme. Again, the order of the polynomial relates to the number of time levels at which the scheme operates. Now, however, the effect of spatial difference operators is exhibited in the coefficients $a^{(n')}$, which are generally dependent on the wavenumber β. Thus a crude criterion for stability is that the roots of such a polynomial remain bounded in magnitude by unity *for all wavenumbers* β. In particular, when $N = 2$, as will be the case for most of the schemes here, the conditions (2.14) must hold for all β.

Numerical phase and group velocity

The definitions of phase and group velocities, for a scheme with a characteristic polynomial as defined by, say, (5.16), are directly analogous to those of the continuous case, as discussed briefly at the end of Section 5.1.2. For a lossless problem, behaving in a stable manner, one will have $|z| = 1$ or $z = e^{j\omega k}$. The N roots of the characteristic polynomial may then be written as $z_p = z_p(\beta)$, or, using $z_p = e^{j\omega_p k}$, as $\omega_p = \omega_p(\beta)$. The phase and group velocities are again given, for any such root, as

$$v_\phi = \frac{\omega}{\beta} \qquad\qquad v_g = \frac{d\omega}{d\beta}$$

The extent to which these quantities are different from those of the continuous model system is referred to as numerical dispersion. It is perhaps best to leave this (quite important) topic until concrete examples have been presented in subsequent chapters—see, e.g., Section 6.2.3.

5.2.7 Matrix interpretation of difference operators

It is sometimes useful, conceptually, and possibly for stability analysis or in an implementation, to have a picture of the behavior of various difference operators in matrix form. Leaving aside the consideration of boundary conditions, suppose a difference operator is to act on values of a grid function u_l, where the domain $\mathcal{D} = \mathbb{Z}$, so $l = -\infty, \ldots, \infty$, and where the time index n has been omitted. When these are arranged in an infinite column vector $\mathbf{u} = [\ldots, u_{-1}, u_0, u_1, \ldots]^T$, the operators δ_{x-}, δ_{x+}, and δ_{xx} can be expressed as the matrices $\mathbf{D}_{x-}$, $\mathbf{D}_{x+}$, and $\mathbf{D}_{xx}$, as follows:

$$
\mathbf{D}_{x-} = \frac{1}{h}
\begin{bmatrix}
\ddots & & & & \mathbf{0} \\
\ddots & 1 & & & \\
& -1 & 1 & & \\
& & -1 & 1 & \\
& & & -1 & 1 \\
\mathbf{0} & & & & \ddots & \ddots
\end{bmatrix}
\quad
\mathbf{D}_{x+} = \frac{1}{h}
\begin{bmatrix}
\ddots & \ddots & & & \mathbf{0} \\
& -1 & 1 & & \\
& & -1 & 1 & \\
& & & -1 & 1 \\
& & & & -1 & \ddots \\
\mathbf{0} & & & & & \ddots
\end{bmatrix}
\quad
\mathbf{D}_{xx} = \frac{1}{h^2}
\begin{bmatrix}
\ddots & \ddots & & & \mathbf{0} \\
\ddots & -2 & 1 & & \\
& 1 & -2 & 1 & \\
& & 1 & -2 & 1 \\
& & & 1 & -2 & \ddots \\
\mathbf{0} & & & & \ddots & \ddots
\end{bmatrix}
$$

$$(5.17)$$

Similarly, the averaging operators μ_{x-}, μ_{x+}, and $\mu_{x\cdot}$ take the forms $\mathbf{M}_{x-}$, $\mathbf{M}_{x+}$, and $\mathbf{M}_{x\cdot}$, as follows:

$$
\mathbf{M}_{x-} = \frac{1}{2}
\begin{bmatrix}
\ddots & & & & \mathbf{0} \\
\ddots & 1 & & & \\
& 1 & 1 & & \\
& & 1 & 1 & \\
& & & 1 & 1 \\
\mathbf{0} & & & & \ddots & \ddots
\end{bmatrix}
\quad
\mathbf{M}_{x+} = \frac{1}{2}
\begin{bmatrix}
\ddots & \ddots & & & \mathbf{0} \\
& 1 & 1 & & \\
& & 1 & 1 & \\
& & & 1 & 1 \\
& & & & 1 & \ddots \\
\mathbf{0} & & & & & \ddots
\end{bmatrix}
\quad
\mathbf{M}_{x\cdot} = \frac{1}{2}
\begin{bmatrix}
\ddots & \ddots & & & \mathbf{0} \\
\ddots & 0 & 1 & & \\
& 1 & 0 & 1 & \\
& & 1 & 0 & 1 \\
& & & 1 & 0 & \ddots \\
\mathbf{0} & & & & \ddots & \ddots
\end{bmatrix}
$$

$$(5.18)$$

Matrix representations of the other operators defined in Section 5.2.2, such as δ_{xxxx}, may be constructed in the same manner. See Problem 5.2.

The matrix representations shown above are infinite. For real-world problems, these operators are restricted to operate over a finite collection of grid points, such as $\mathbb{U}_N$, and boundary conditions come into play, usually affecting values in the matrices in the extreme rows and columns. For the most part in this book, such boundary conditions will be dealt with using operator notation, except in the case of implicit schemes, for which a finite matrix representation of a difference operator is an indispensable part of working code—see, e.g., Section 6.3.2.

5.2.8 Boundary conditions and virtual grid points

Though no physics has been mentioned as yet in this chapter, this is a good point to introduce the concept of numerical boundary conditions, which lead to implementation and analysis concerns which range from trivial to rather involved. The topic will be taken up in earnest in the next chapter, in the case of the 1D wave equation.

As an example, consider the operator δ_{xx}, applied to a grid function u_l, defined now not over $\mathcal{D} = \mathbb{R}$, but the $(N + 1)$-point unit interval $\mathcal{D} = \mathbb{U}_N = [0, 1, \ldots, N]$. At an interior point in the domain, all is well, and $\delta_{xx}u_l$ may be calculated as

$$
\delta_{xx}u_l = \frac{1}{h^2}(u_{l+1} - 2u_l + u_{l-1}) \qquad \text{for} \qquad l = 1, \ldots, N - 1
$$

But at $l = 0$, and $l = N$, the operator δ_{xx} appears to require values at locations which lie outside the domain of definition of the grid function, namely u_{-1} and u_{N+1}. Such locations are sometimes referred to as "virtual" (or "image" or "ghost" or "fictitious") grid points in a finite difference scheme—generally, though, boundary conditions come to the rescue, and allow the values at such points to be set in terms of the values in the interior.

For instance, one boundary condition which occurs frequently in musical acoustics, across a wide variety of applications, is the simple fixed condition, sometimes referred to as a Dirichlet-type boundary condition for which the values of the grid function at the endpoints are constrained to be zero, or, more generally, a constant. In the present case of the operator δ_{xx}, the result is trivial: the values u_0 and u_N are set to zero permanently, and in fact need not be calculated or even stored at all in an implementation. Slightly trickier is the case of zero spatial derivative conditions, often referred to as Neumann-type conditions. Here is one approximation:

$$\delta_x.u_0 = \delta_x.u_N = 0$$

The two conditions at $l = 0$ and $l = N$ are clearly second-order approximations to a zero-derivative condition. Written in terms of values at the image locations, they read as $u_{-1} = u_1$ and $u_{N+1} = u_{N-1}$, and thus the action of the operator δ_{xx} at the endpoints can now be given, purely in terms of values on the domain interior, as

$$\delta_{xx}u_0 = \frac{2}{h^2}(u_1 - u_0) \qquad \delta_{xx}u_N = \frac{2}{h^2}(-u_N + u_{N-1})$$

It is worth noting that this is but one type of approximation to a zero-derivative condition—the proper setting of numerical boundary conditions is an issue which will be taken up in greater detail in later chapters. See Problem 5.3 for another numerical variation on the zero-derivative condition, and Problem 5.4 for the more involved case of numerical boundary conditions applied to a fourth-order spatial difference operator.

It is also revealing to examine the effect of boundary conditions in the matrix form of the operator. In the Dirichlet and Neumann cases mentioned above, the matrix operations $\mathbf{D}_{xx}$ look like

$$\mathbf{D}_{xx}\begin{bmatrix} u_1 \\ u_2 \\ \vdots \\ u_{N-2} \\ u_{N-1} \end{bmatrix} = \frac{1}{h^2}\underbrace{\begin{bmatrix} -2 & 1 & & & \\ 1 & -2 & 1 & & \\ & \ddots & \ddots & \ddots & \\ & & 1 & -2 & 1 \\ & & & 1 & -2 \end{bmatrix}}_{u_0=u_N=0}\begin{bmatrix} u_1 \\ u_2 \\ \vdots \\ u_{N-2} \\ u_{N-1} \end{bmatrix}$$

$$\mathbf{D}_{xx}\begin{bmatrix} u_0 \\ u_1 \\ \vdots \\ u_{N-1} \\ u_N \end{bmatrix} = \frac{1}{h^2}\underbrace{\begin{bmatrix} -2 & 2 & & & \\ 1 & -2 & 1 & & \\ & \ddots & \ddots & \ddots & \\ & & 1 & -2 & 1 \\ & & & 2 & -2 \end{bmatrix}}_{\delta_x.u_0=\delta_x.u_N=0}\begin{bmatrix} u_0 \\ u_1 \\ \vdots \\ u_{N-1} \\ u_N \end{bmatrix}$$

(5.19)

As is natural, the boundary conditions affect only those matrix entries in the extreme rows. See Problem 5.5 and Programming Exercises 5.4 and 5.5. For difference operators defined over uniform grids, the bulk of the matrix representation is of sparse Toeplitz form, where the number of non-zero bands reflects the order of the difference operator and also, often, its accuracy.

Notice that the matrices are very sparse, implying that explicit storage of such matrices is not advisable (i.e., it is a huge waste of memory). Indeed, when such difference operators are applied in an explicit scheme, the matrix representation is entirely unnecessary. Even in an implicit setting, where linear systems involving such matrices are to be solved, various techniques are available—iterative methods are a natural choice [121, 342]. Indeed, when the grid functions are large, the direct inversion of a matrix operator is prohibitively expensive, in terms of both memory requirements and operation count (as the inverse of a sparse matrix is generally not sparse), and should be avoided at all costs. The Matlab language has a number of built-in iterative methods, which are very easy to use—see Programming Exercise 5.6 for a basic example. In fact, there are even more refined solution techniques which are specialized to the use of such sparse banded matrices, such as, for example, the Thomas algorithm. A full description of such methods would be rather lengthy, however, and the reader is referred to the literature [342, 354].

5.2.9   Inner products and identities

As one might gather, an essential step towards energy-based analysis of finite difference schemes for distributed problems is the introduction of a spatial inner product between two grid functions, which is analogous to the continuous definition given in (5.6). In the discrete setting, there are many ways of doing this, but the simplest is the following: an l_2 spatial inner product of two 1D grid functions, f_l^n and g_l^n, over the interval $l \in \mathcal{D}$, may be defined as

$$\langle f^n, g^n \rangle_{\mathcal{D}} = \sum_{l \in \mathcal{D}} h f_l^n g_l^n \tag{5.20}$$

In fact, this is none other than a Riemann sum approximation to a definite integral. The inner product is a scalar time series, dependent on n—note that for grid functions inside an inner product, the spatial index l is suppressed. An l_2 norm follows as

$$\| f^n \|_{\mathcal{D}} = \sqrt{\langle f^n, f^n \rangle_{\mathcal{D}}} \geq 0 \tag{5.21}$$

The Cauchy–Schwartz and triangle inequalities extend directly to such discrete inner products as

$$|\langle f^n, g^n \rangle_{\mathcal{D}}| \leq \| f^n \|_{\mathcal{D}} \| g^n \|_{\mathcal{D}} \tag{5.22a}$$

$$\| f^n + g^n \|_{\mathcal{D}} \leq \| f^n \|_{\mathcal{D}} + \| g^n \|_{\mathcal{D}} \tag{5.22b}$$

One may define other types of inner products [161], which vary slightly from the above definition in (5.20); these usually are distinct at the endpoints of the spatial interval over which the inner product is defined. Assuming that the endpoints of the interval $\mathcal{D}$ are given by d_- and d_+, one of particular interest is given by

$$\langle f^n, g^n \rangle_{\mathcal{D}}' = \sum_{l=d_-+1}^{d_+-1} h f_l^n g_l^n + \frac{h}{2} f_{d_-}^n g_{d_-}^n + \frac{h}{2} f_{d_+}^n g_{d_+}^n \tag{5.23}$$

A norm can again be defined in terms of this inner product, as per (5.21), and the Cauchy–Schwartz and triangle inequalities, from (5.22) above, also hold. This inner product may be interpreted as an approximation to the continuous inner product using trapezoids, rather than a Riemann sum, hence the factor of 1/2 which scales the values at the endpoints. As might be imagined, the use of such an inner product leads to variations in the way numerical boundary conditions are posed and implemented. Other, even more general inner products are available—see Problem 5.6. Some more comments appear in the next section.

Before looking at some of the manipulations which may be employed in the case of spatial difference operators, it is important to note that the identities involving only time difference or averaging operators applied to products of time series in the lumped context in Section 2.4.2 extend directly to the case of grid functions. For instance, identity (2.22a) for time series may be generalized, for a grid function u, as

$$\langle \delta_t.u, \delta_{tt}u \rangle_{\mathcal{D}} = \delta_{t+}\left(\frac{1}{2}\|\delta_t-u\|_{\mathcal{D}}^2\right) \tag{5.24}$$

(Notice that in this case the time difference δ_{t+} operates on a scalar time series, and not a grid function!) Such manipulations are of great use in the analysis in the following chapters, and generalizations of the identities (2.22) are readily proved—see Problem 5.7.

5.2.10   Summation by parts

Of extreme utility in energy analysis are various manipulations which correspond to integration by parts. For example, consider the inner product $\langle f, \delta_{x+}g \rangle_{\mathcal{D}}$, where, for brevity, the time index n has been suppressed. Assuming again that the endpoints of the interval $\mathcal{D}$ are given by d_- and d_+, an inner product representation of summation by parts may be derived as follows:

$$\langle f, \delta_{x+}g \rangle_{\mathcal{D}} = \sum_{l=d_-}^{d_+} hf_l\frac{1}{h}(g_{l+1} - g_l) = -\sum_{l=d_-}^{d_+} h\frac{1}{h}(f_l - f_{l-1})g_l + f_{d_+}g_{d_++1} - f_{d_--1}g_{d_-}$$

$$= -\langle \delta_{x-}f, g \rangle_{\mathcal{D}} + f_{d_+}g_{d_++1} - f_{d_--1}g_{d_-} \tag{5.25}$$

Notice that the boundary terms involve evaluations of the grid functions at points $d_+ + 1$ and $d_- - 1$, which are outside the domain of definition of the problem itself, at least when d_+ and d_- are finite. These are again instances of "virtual grid points," as discussed in Section 5.2.8. As was noted earlier, the values of grid functions at such virtual locations will always be set, through boundary conditions, in terms of values of the grid function over the domain interior. As such, in an implementation, it is unnecessary to store such values, though in some cases the explicit representation of such values can lead to algorithmic simplifications. Notice also that in the boundary terms, the grid functions f and g are evaluated at different (adjacent) locations. As in the continuous case, if $d_- = -\infty$ or $d_+ = \infty$, then the values of grid functions at these locations are assumed to vanish. For example, if $\mathcal{D} = \mathbb{Z}$, one has, simply, $\langle f, \delta_{x+}g \rangle_{\mathbb{Z}} = -\langle \delta_{x-}f, g \rangle_{\mathbb{Z}}$.

It is sometimes of use to rewrite identities such as summation by parts in terms of slightly different domains; this is a point of contrast with such identities in the continuous case. For example, for a given domain $\mathcal{D} = [d_-, \ldots, d_+]$, one may define related domains lacking one of the boundary points, such as $\underline{\mathcal{D}} = [d_-, \ldots, d_+ - 1]$ and $\overline{\mathcal{D}} = [d_- + 1, \ldots, d_+]$. One variant of summation by parts then looks like

$$\langle f, \delta_{x+}g \rangle_{\underline{\mathcal{D}}} = -\langle \delta_{x-}f, g \rangle_{\overline{\mathcal{D}}} + f_{d_+}g_{d_+} - f_{d_-}g_{d_-} \tag{5.26}$$

In this case, the boundary terms involve evaluations of the grid functions f and g at the same point.

It is of course possible to extend summation by parts to cover double spatial differences. Using the operator $\delta_{xx} = \delta_{x+}\delta_{x-}$, and summation by parts (5.25) or (5.26) twice, one has the following identities:

$$\langle f, \delta_{xx}g \rangle_{\mathcal{D}} = \langle \delta_{xx}f, g \rangle_{\mathcal{D}} - f_{d_-}\delta_{x-}g_{d_-} + g_{d_-}\delta_{x-}f_{d_-} + f_{d_+}\delta_{x+}g_{d_+} - g_{d_+}\delta_{x+}f_{d_+} \tag{5.27a}$$

$$\langle f, \delta_{xx}g \rangle_{\mathcal{D}} = \langle \delta_{xx}f, g \rangle_{\underline{\overline{\mathcal{D}}}} - f_{d_-}\delta_{x-}g_{d_-} + g_{d_-}\delta_{x+}f_{d_-} + f_{d_+}\delta_{x+}g_{d_+} - g_{d_+}\delta_{x-}f_{d_+} \tag{5.27b}$$

Again, if $\mathcal{D} = \mathbb{Z}$, the above identities simplify to

$$\langle f, \delta_{xx} g \rangle_{\mathbb{Z}} = \langle \delta_{xx} f, g \rangle_{\mathbb{Z}} \tag{5.28}$$

For the identities (5.27), notice that the boundary terms are not centered about the endpoints; this may be remedied with recourse to the primed inner product defined in (5.23), which can be useful in determining numerical boundary conditions which possess a higher degree of accuracy. See Problem 5.8.

5.2.11   Some bounds

It is also helpful to be able to relate norms of grid functions under spatial difference operations to norms of the grid functions themselves. For instance, consider the grid function $\delta_{x+} u$, defined over domain $\mathcal{D}$. One may write

$$\|\delta_{x+} u\|_{\underline{\mathcal{D}}}^2 = \sum_{l=d_-}^{d_+ - 1} h (\delta_{x+} u_l)^2 = \sum_{l=d_-}^{d_+ - 1} \frac{1}{h} (u_{l+1} - u_l)^2 = \sum_{l=d_-}^{d_+ - 1} \frac{1}{h} (u_{l+1}^2 + u_l^2 - 2 u_{l+1} u_l)$$

$$\leq \sum_{l=d_-}^{d_+ - 1} \frac{2}{h} (u_{l+1}^2 + u_l^2)$$

or

$$\|\delta_{x+} u\|_{\underline{\mathcal{D}}} \leq \frac{2}{h} \|u\|_{\mathcal{D}}' \leq \frac{2}{h} \|u\|_{\mathcal{D}} \tag{5.29}$$

Thus the norm of a grid function under a spatial difference is bounded from above by the norm of the grid function itself, times a factor of $2/h$. Notice that the bound is slightly tighter when the primed norm is used. Similarly, one has, for the grid function $\delta_{x-} u$,

$$\|\delta_{x-} u\|_{\overline{\mathcal{D}}} \leq \frac{2}{h} \|u\|_{\mathcal{D}}' \leq \frac{2}{h} \|u\|_{\mathcal{D}} \tag{5.30}$$

Bounds on higher differences of a grid function may be obtained through repeated use of the above bounds. For instance, for a grid function $\delta_{xx} u$, one has

$$\|\delta_{xx} u\|_{\underline{\overline{\mathcal{D}}}} = \|\delta_{x+} \delta_{x-} u\|_{\underline{\overline{\mathcal{D}}}} \leq \frac{2}{h} \|\delta_{x-} u\|_{\overline{\mathcal{D}}} \leq \frac{4}{h^2} \|u\|_{\mathcal{D}} \tag{5.31}$$

It is possible to relate the bounds presented here to the Fourier representation—see Problems 5.1 and 5.9.

For problems involving spatial variation, it is sometimes necessary to extend such identities to include a non-negative weighting grid function $\phi_l > 0$ (often representing a variation in material properties or geometry of an underlying problem, such as in the case of a bar, as discussed in Section 7.10, or an acoustic tube, as described in Chapter 9). In this case, the bound (5.29), for example, becomes

$$\|\sqrt{\phi} \delta_{x+} u\|_{\underline{\mathcal{D}}} \leq \frac{2}{h} \|\sqrt{\mu_{x-} \phi} u\|_{\mathcal{D}} \tag{5.32}$$

See Problem 5.10 for a sketch of the proof of this, as well as an extension to other inner product definitions.

5.2.12   Interpolation and spreading revisited

For a given system requiring both interpolation and spreading at the same location, it is useful to note the following. For a qth-order spreading function $J_{l,q}(x_0)$ operating at location x_0, and the associated interpolation function $I_q(x_0)$, it is true that for any grid function f,

$$\langle f, J_q(x_0)\rangle_{\mathcal{D}} = I_q(x_0)f \tag{5.33}$$

Note that this is only true when the interpolation and spreading functions are of the same order. This fact is important in proving stability for certain point-excited systems such as, for instance the bow–string interaction—see Section 7.4. Spreading of an input time series onto a grid is also associated with a slight change in gain. This gain for a spreading operator J may be written as

$$\mathrm{Gain}(J) = \sqrt{h}\|J\|_{\mathcal{D}}$$

and will depend on the fractional part α_i of the truncation to an integer grid point. For polynomial interpolants J_q of the type given in Section 5.2.4, one may show the following bound, which holds for all α_i:

$$\mathrm{Gain}(J_q) \leq 1 \tag{5.34}$$

See Problem 5.11.

5.3   Coordinate changes

In some problems, particularly those involving spatial variation of the vibrating material (such as strings of variable density, or bars of variable cross-section—see Section 7.10), it can be useful to employ changes of spatial coordinate which match, in some sense, the variation in the medium itself. In 1D, this is quite straightforward. For a given spatial coordinate x, define a new coordinate $\alpha = \alpha(x)$. In general, the map $x \to \alpha(x)$ should be smooth, one-to-one, and preserve the ordering of the points in the medium, i.e., if $x_1 \leq x_2$, then $\alpha(x_1) \leq \alpha(x_2)$. See Figure 5.5.

Partial derivatives may thus be transformed under such a mapping, i.e.,

$$\frac{\partial}{\partial x} \longrightarrow \alpha'\frac{\partial}{\partial \alpha} \qquad\qquad \frac{\partial^2}{\partial x^2} \longrightarrow \alpha'\frac{\partial}{\partial \alpha}\left(\alpha'\frac{\partial}{\partial \alpha}\right) \tag{5.35}$$

where, now, the function $\alpha' = \partial\alpha/\partial x$ intervenes. A PDE in a spatial variable x may thus be transformed to an equivalent PDE in the new coordinate α.

The interest in performing such changes of variables at the level of the PDE is to avoid the hassle of variable grid spacing in the original coordinates—once the transformation has been carried out, the grid spacing may again be chosen uniform, and all the difference scheme analysis then applies as usual. The most commonly occurring differential operator, at least in musical acoustics problems, is the second derivative, $\partial^2/\partial x^2$. In transformed coordinates, a centered approximation to the second derivative is

$$\delta_{xx} \qquad \longrightarrow \qquad \alpha'\delta_{\alpha+}\left((\mu_{\alpha-}\alpha')\delta_{\alpha-}\right) \tag{5.36}$$

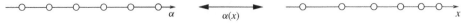

Figure 5.5   Coordinate change from coordinates x to coordinates α. A uniform grid in α coordinates maps to a variable grid in x coordinates.

which is second-order accurate, where the continuous form of α' is assumed known. See Problem 5.12 and Programming Exercise 5.7.

Integration by parts and summation by parts still hold, as long as a weighting function $1/\alpha'$ is inserted into the formulas. For example, in the continuous case,

$$\left\langle \frac{1}{\alpha'} f, \alpha' \left(\alpha' g_\alpha\right)_\alpha \right\rangle_{\mathbb{R}} = -\langle f_\alpha, \alpha' g_\alpha \rangle_{\mathbb{R}} = \left\langle \alpha' \left(\alpha' f_\alpha\right)_\alpha, \frac{1}{\alpha'} g \right\rangle_{\mathbb{R}}$$

and in the discrete case,

$$\left\langle \frac{1}{\alpha'} f, \alpha' \delta_{\alpha+} \left((\mu_{\alpha-}\alpha')(\delta_{\alpha-}g) \right) \right\rangle_{\mathbb{Z}} = -\langle \delta_{\alpha-}f, (\mu_{\alpha-}\alpha')(\delta_{\alpha-}g) \rangle_{\mathbb{Z}} = \left\langle \alpha' \delta_{\alpha+} \left((\mu_{\alpha-}\alpha')(\delta_{\alpha-}f) \right), \frac{1}{\alpha'} g \right\rangle_{\mathbb{Z}}$$

5.4   Problems

Problem 5.1   *From (5.15a), it is known that the application of the operator δ_{xx} to a grid function u_l corresponds, in the spatial frequency domain, to multiplication of the Fourier transform $\tilde{u}(\beta)$ by a factor $-4\sin^2(\beta h/2)/h^2$. For what value of β is the magnitude of this factor a maximum, and what is the value of the factor? Sketch the grid function $u_l = e^{jl\beta h}$ for this value of β.*

Problem 5.2   *Write the operator δ_{xxxx}, as defined in Section 5.2.2, in a matrix form over the infinite domain $\mathcal{D} = \mathbb{Z}$, similarly to those presented in Section 5.2.7.*

Problem 5.3   *Consider the difference operator δ_{xx} applied to the grid function u_l over $\mathbb{U}_N$, under the zero-derivative boundary approximations $\delta_{x-}u_0 = \delta_{x+}u_N = 0$, and express $\delta_{xx}u_0$ and $\delta_{xx}u_N$ purely in terms of values over the domain $\mathbb{U}_N$ (i.e., without using values at virtual points). Express the difference operator in matrix form, similar to that given at the end of Section 5.2.8.*

Problem 5.4   *Consider the operator δ_{xxxx}, as defined in (5.12b), applied to a grid function u_l, now defined over the semi-infinite domain $\mathcal{D} = \mathbb{Z}^+ = [0, 1, \ldots]$. At which grid points will the evaluation of this operator require access to grid points at virtual locations (i.e., outside of $\mathbb{Z}^+$)? Consider also the following three sets of boundary conditions, at $l = 0$:*

$$u = \delta_x.u = 0 \tag{5.37a}$$

$$u = \delta_{xx}u = 0 \tag{5.37b}$$

$$\delta_{xx}u = \delta_x.\delta_{xx}u = 0 \tag{5.37c}$$

In each case, use the conditions at $l = 0$ to arrive at expressions for $\delta_{xxxx}u_l$ over the entire domain $\mathbb{Z}^+$, purely in terms of values of u over the domain interior. (In the setting of bar vibration, which is the sound-producing mechanism in percussion instruments such as xylophones, these three types of conditions correspond to clamped, simply supported, and free conditions, respectively. See Section 7.1.2.) Do not forget that if $u_0 = 0$, it is not necessary to include it as part of the domain interior.

Problem 5.5   *Continuing from Problem 5.4, with the operator δ_{xxxx} applied to the grid function u_l over $\mathbb{Z}^+$, construct the semi-infinite matrix form of the operator under the three sets of boundary conditions described. Under the conditions described in (5.37a) and (5.37b), you may omit the evaluation at the endpoint $l = 0$. It is helpful to use the infinite form of the matrix operator you constructed in Problem 5.2 as a starting point.*

Problem 5.6   *Consider the discrete inner product defined, for simplicity, over $\mathcal{D} = \mathbb{Z}^+$ as*

$$\langle f, g \rangle_{\mathbb{Z}^+}^\epsilon = \sum_{l=1}^\infty h f_l g_l + \frac{\epsilon}{2} h f_0 g_0$$

with respect to a free parameter $\epsilon > 0$. (The primed inner product $\langle \cdot, \cdot \rangle'$ is a special case of this definition, with $\epsilon = 1$.) Show that the following summation by parts identity holds:

$$\langle f, \delta_{x+} g \rangle_{\mathbb{Z}^+}^\epsilon = \langle \delta_{x-} f, g \rangle_{\overline{\mathbb{Z}^+}} - f_0 \left((2 - \epsilon) \mu_{x+} + (\epsilon - 1) \right) g_0$$

where $\overline{\mathbb{Z}^+} = [1, 2, \ldots]$. Show also that the bound

$$\| \delta_{x+} u \|_{\mathbb{Z}^+} \leq \frac{2}{h} \| u \|_{\mathbb{Z}^+}^\epsilon$$

holds only for values of ϵ such that $\epsilon \geq 1$.

   For an interesting application of this definition of an inner product to the analysis of numerical boundary conditions, see Problem 6.8 in the next chapter.

Problem 5.7   *For each of the identities involving products of time series under the action of time difference operators, from (2.22), show that there is a corresponding identity for the case of a grid function $u = u_l^n$, defined over the domain $\mathcal{D}$. (As a starting point, you may wish to compare identity (2.22a) with its corresponding distributed form (5.24).)*

Problem 5.8   *Demonstrate, using the primed l_2 inner product defined in (5.23), over a domain $\mathcal{D}$, the summation by parts identity*

$$\langle f, \delta_{xx} g \rangle_{\mathcal{D}}' = \langle \delta_{xx} f, g \rangle_{\mathcal{D}}' - f_{d-} \delta_{x\cdot} g_{d-} + g_{d-} \delta_{x\cdot} f_{d-} + f_{d+} \delta_{x\cdot} g_{d+} - g_{d+} \delta_{x\cdot} f_{d+}$$

Thus the boundary terms involve difference approximations which are centered about the endpoints of the domain. This is in contrast with the corresponding identity (5.27a) in the case of the standard unprimed inner product.

Problem 5.9   *Find a grid function u_l defined over $\mathcal{D} = \mathbb{U}_N$ such that the first of bounds (5.29) (the one involving the primed inner product) is satisfied with equality. Your answer from Problem 5.1 may be of help here.*

Problem 5.10   *Prove the bound given in (5.32) for the case of the first difference of a grid function under a weighting.*

   Returning to the weighted norm introduced in Problem 5.6, consider an inner product defined over the finite interval $\mathcal{D} = \mathbb{U}_N$ as

$$\langle f, g \rangle_{\mathbb{U}_N}^{\epsilon_l, \epsilon_r} = \sum_{l=1}^{N-1} h f_l g_l + \frac{\epsilon_l}{2} h f_0 g_0 + \frac{\epsilon_r}{2} h f_N g_N \tag{5.38}$$

with respect to two free parameters $\epsilon_l, \epsilon_r > 0$. Such an inner product is of use, especially in deriving accurate boundary conditions for problems involving spatial variation—see Section 9.1.5, which deals with acoustic tube modeling.
   Show that a bound of the form

$$\left\| \sqrt{\phi} \delta_{x+} u \right\|_{\mathbb{U}_N} \leq \frac{2}{h} \left\| \sqrt{\mu_{x-} \phi} u \right\|_{\mathbb{U}_N}^{\epsilon_l, \epsilon_r} \tag{5.39}$$

only holds when $\epsilon_l \geq \phi_0 / \mu_{x-} \phi_0$ and $\epsilon_r \geq \phi_{N-1} / \mu_{x-} \phi_N$. Thus it is possible to build an inner product based on the parameters defining the problem, which can be useful—see Problem 9.5 for more on this topic.

Problem 5.11 *Prove bound (5.34) for the spreading functions J_0 and J_1, and also find the minimum value of the gain of each of the above operators, for any possible value of α_i.*

Problem 5.12 *Consider the second derivative under a coordinate transformation $\alpha(x)$, as given in (5.35). If $\alpha(x) = x^2$, rewrite the expression for the second derivative purely in terms of α (i.e., without any occurrence of x, which appears, for example, in $\alpha' = d\alpha/dx$).*

5.5   Programming exercises

Programming Exercise 5.1 *For an input vector of length $N + 1$ values (corresponding, ultimately, to values of a function $u(x)$ at locations $x = 0, 1/N, \ldots, 1$), create a Matlab script which interpolates a value $u(x_0)$, for some $0 \le x_0 \le 1$. The order of interpolation should be adjustable, through an input parameter, such that it performs zeroth-, first-, and third-order interpolation, as discussed in Section 5.2.4. In the case of third-order interpolation, you may revert to first-order interpolation when the observation point x_0 lies within a single grid point of either end of the domain.*

Programming Exercise 5.2 *(a) Consider a grid function $u_l^{(1)}$ defined over the unit interval over a grid of spacing $h^{(1)}$, and assume that it takes on zero values at the endpoints of the domain, so that only the values with $l = 1, \ldots, N^{(1)} - 1$, where $N^{(1)} = 1/h^{(1)}$, need be considered. Construct a pth-order upsampling interpolant $\mathcal{I}_{h^{(1)} \to h^{(2)}, p}$ in matrix form to a grid of spacing $h^{(2)} \le h^{(1)}$, again requiring that values of the resulting interpolated grid function $u_m^{(2)}$ take on values of zero at the endpoints of the unit interval. Your matrix should be of size $(N^{(2)} - 1) \times (N^{(1)} - 1)$, where $N^{(2)} = 1/h^{(2)}$. Construct the interpolant using both linear and cubic interpolation, and verify its performance by applying it to a sinusoidal vector of the form $u_l^{(1)} = \sin(q\pi l h^{(1)})$, for integer q. (In the case of the third-order interpolant, assume the grid function $u_l^{(1)}$ is antisymmetric about $l = 0$ and $l = N^{(1)}$.)*

(b) Sometimes it is necessary to interpolate values of a grid function defined between adjacent grid points. Suppose $u_{l+1/2}^{(1)}$ is a grid function defined for $l = 0, \ldots, N^{(1)} - 1$. Again construct linear and cubic upsampling interpolants to the new locations $x^{(2)} = (m + 1/2)/N^{(2)}$, for $m = 0, \ldots, N^{(2)} - 1$. For the cubic interpolant, assume that the grid function $u_{l+1/2}^{(1)}$ is symmetric about $x^{(1)} = 0$ and $x^{(1)} = 1$. Again test your interpolant by applying it to grid functions of the form $u_{l+1/2}^{(1)} = \cos(q\pi(l + 1/2)h^{(1)})$, for integer q.

Programming Exercise 5.3 *In the previous problem, you constructed upsampling matrix interpolants. Demonstrate that the conjugate downsampling interpolant, as defined by (5.2.4), indeed behaves as expected, by applying it to appropriate grid functions—for the interpolant in part (a) above, downsample functions $u_m^{(2)} = \sin(q\pi m h^{(2)})$, for integer q, and for that of part (b), downsample functions $u_{m+1/2}^{(2)} = \cos(q\pi(m + 1/2)h^{(2)})$, for integer q. Show also that neither interpolant produces a severe aliasing phenomenon.*

Programming Exercise 5.4 *Create a Matlab script which generates the matrix operator $\mathbf{D}_{xx}$, corresponding to the difference operator δ_{xx}, operating over the unit interval $\mathbb{U}_N = [0, 1, \ldots, N]$. Your code should operate under a combination of choices of numerical boundary conditions at either end of the domain, namely fixed (Dirichlet) or free (Neumann). You may use the fixed condition $u = 0$, and the centered numerical Neumann boundary condition $\delta_x.u = 0$. Make sure that your script generates sparse matrices (learn about the Matlab function $\mathtt{sparse}$ for this purpose), and that it generates matrices of the appropriate size—for example, under Neumann conditions at both ends, $\mathbf{D}_{xx}$ will be an $(N + 1) \times (N + 1)$ matrix, but for Dirichlet conditions, it will be $(N - 1) \times (N - 1)$.*

Programming Exercise 5.5   *Create a Matlab script which generates the matrix operator $\mathbf{D}_{xxxx}$, corresponding to the difference operator δ_{xxxx}, operating over the unit interval $\mathbb{U}_N = [0, 1, \ldots, N]$. Your code should be capable of setting any of the conditions (5.37) separately at each end of the boundary (i.e., at $l = 0$ or $l = N$), giving a total of nine possible outputs. Make sure that your script generates sparse matrices, and that it generates matrices of the appropriate size—for example, under conditions (5.37a) or (5.37b) at each end of the domain, $\mathbf{D}_{xxxx}$ will be an $(N - 1) \times (N - 1)$ matrix, but for conditions (5.37c) at both ends, it will be $(N + 1) \times (N + 1)$.*

Programming Exercise 5.6   *Using the Matlab script you created above which generates the matrix $\mathbf{D}_{xx}$, solve the equation $\mathbf{D}_{xx}\mathbf{x} = \mathbf{b}$, where $\mathbf{b}$ is a known vector, and where $\mathbf{x}$ is the unknown, in two different ways:*

(a) Explicitly compute the inverse $\mathbf{D}_{xx}^{-1}$, and solve for $\mathbf{x}$ as $\mathbf{x} = \mathbf{D}_{xx}^{-1}\mathbf{b}$.

(b) Use Matlab's standard iterative method to solve the equation. You may perform this calculation easily, as

```
x = Dxx\b
```

Using the tic *and* toc *commands, compare the performance of these two methods for a variety of sizes of the vectors $\mathbf{x}$ and $\mathbf{b}$. You may use the form of $\mathbf{D}_{xx}$ under fixed boundary conditions, and you may also wish to choose $\mathbf{b}$ in the form of a sinusoid or polynomial function, so that you can be sure that your calculated results are correct ($\mathbf{b}$ should be approximately the second derivative of $\mathbf{x}!$).*

Programming Exercise 5.7   *For a given function $u(x)$ defined over $\mathcal{D} = \mathbb{U}$, calculate the second derivative numerically in two different ways:*

(a) Directly, using the operator δ_{xx}, and $N + 1$ samples of the function $u(x)$ at locations $x = l/N$, for some integer N (the grid size).

(b) Under the coordinate transformation $\alpha(x) = x^2$. In this case, you will make use of samples of u which are equally spaced in the coordinate α—take $N + 1$ of them as well. Use the transformed difference operator in α given in (5.36). Be sure that you have written α' explicitly in terms of α, as per Problem 5.12.

In both cases, you need only calculate approximations to the second derivative at interior points in the domain. Plot both results together on the same set of axes. You may wish to choose your function u in the form of a sinusoid or polynomial function, so that you can be sure that your calculated results are correct.

6

The 1D wave equation

The 1D wave equation is, arguably, the single most important partial differential equation in musical acoustics, if not in physics as a whole. Though, strictly speaking, it is useful only as a test problem, variants of it serve to describe the behavior of strings, both linear and nonlinear, as well as the motion of air in an enclosed acoustic tube. It is well worth spending a good deal of time examining this equation as well as various means of arriving at a numerical solution, because the distinctions between well-known synthesis techniques such as lumped models, modal synthesis, digital waveguides, and classical time domain methods such as finite differences appear in sharp contrast.

In some respects, however, the 1D wave equation is a little too special to serve as a typical model problem. Though, as mentioned above, it is frequently used as a test problem for numerical methods, it is the rare example of a PDE which admits an exact numerical solution—furthermore, the solution may be computed in a very efficient manner. Though digital waveguide methods are built directly around such efficient numerical solutions, one must beware of the temptation to generalize such techniques to other problems. As a result, digital waveguides will be covered here, but the emphasis will be on those aspects of numerical techniques which do not rely on special behavior of a particular equation.

In Section 6.1, the 1D wave equation is defined, and in the first instance over the entire real line. Frequency domain analysis is introduced, followed by a discussion of phase and group velocity. The Hamiltonian formulation for the wave equation appears next, and is used in order to motivate the study of bounds on solution growth, as well as appropriate boundary conditions. Boundary conditions, coupled with frequency domain methods, lead to a representation of the solution in terms of modes. The section is concluded by a brief look at traveling wave solutions. A simple finite difference scheme is presented in Section 6.2, followed by frequency domain (or von Neumann) analysis, yielding the well-known Courant–Friedrichs–Lewy stability condition, and information regarding numerical dispersion, as well as its perceptual significance in sound synthesis. Energy analysis, applied to the problem of finding suitable numerical boundary conditions, appears next, followed by a look at the matrix form of the finite difference scheme, as well as the very important special case of the discrete traveling wave solution. Other varieties of finite difference schemes are sketched in Section 6.3. Modal synthesis methods are briefly touched upon in Section 6.4, and a treatment of loss follows in Section 6.5. Finally, in Section 6.6, various synthesis methods, specifically modal synthesis, lumped networks, and digital waveguides, are compared to difference schemes in this special case of the wave equation.

6.1 Definition and properties

The 1D wave equation is defined as

$$u_{tt} = c^2 u_{xx} \tag{6.1}$$

It is a second-order PDE in the dependent variable $u = u(x, t)$, where x is a variable representing distance, and t, as before, is time. The equation is defined over $t \geq 0$, and for $x \in \mathcal{D}$, where $\mathcal{D}$ is some simply connected subset of $\mathbb{R}$. c is a constant often referred to as the wave speed. See Section 5.1 for a description of the notation used here in representing partial differential operators.

As mentioned earlier, the 1D wave equation arises in a range of applications across all of physics, and occupies a privileged position in musical acoustics (see Figure 6.1). It is a crude first approximation, under low-amplitude conditions, to the transverse motion of strings, in which case $c = \sqrt{T_0/\rho A}$, where T_0 is the applied string tension, ρ is the material density, and A the string cross-sectional area. It is also an approximation to the longitudinal motion of a uniform bar [244], with $c = \sqrt{E/\rho}$ and where E and ρ are Young's modulus and again material density for the bar under consideration; longitudinal motion of a bar is of somewhat less interest in sound synthesis applications compared to transverse motion, which will be taken up in detail in Section 7.1. In the context of wind instrument modeling, it also describes the longitudinal vibration of an air column in a tube of uniform cross-section, with $c = \sqrt{B/\rho}$, and where B and ρ are the bulk modulus and material density of the air in the tube. The wave equation also applies to the case of the lossless electrical transmission line [80], where $c = \sqrt{1/LC}$, with L and C the inductance and capacitance per unit length of the line. The electrical transmission line, though not of intrinsic musical interest, has served as a conceptual basis for the construction of scattering-based numerical methods (digital waveguides and wave digital filters among them [41, 333]). Under musical conditions, the wave equation is a rather better approximation in the case of the acoustic tube than that of the string; string nonlinearities which lead to perceptually important effects will be dealt with in detail in Chapter 8.

The wave equation has been derived from first principles in countless works; perhaps the best treatment in the present context of acoustics appears in the classic texts of Morse [243] and Morse and Ingard [244]. Though such a derivation could well be skipped here, one form, based on the limiting behavior of an array of masses and springs, is of particular relevance in digital sound synthesis.

6.1.1 Linear array of masses and springs

Consider an equally spaced array of masses M, of spacing h, connected by linear springs of spring constant K and of equilibrium length h. Suppose that the masses are constrained to move only

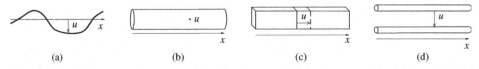

(a)   (b)   (c)   (d)

Figure 6.1   Different physical systems described by the wave equation (6.1). $u(x, t)$ may represent: (a) transverse displacement of a lossless string vibrating at low amplitude; (b) deviation in pressure about a mean in an acoustic tube, under lossless conditions; (c) deviation of a point from its position at rest for a uniform bar vibrating longitudinally; or (d) voltage across a lossless transmission line.

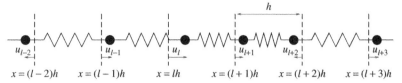

Figure 6.2   Linear array of masses and springs, constrained to move longitudinally. The displacement of the lth mass, located at equilibrium at spatial position $x = lh$, is written as u_l.

horizontally, and that the deviation of the lth mass from its rest position is written as $u_l(t)$. See Figure 6.2. The equation of motion of the lth mass will then be

$$M\frac{d^2u_l}{dt^2} = f_{l+\frac{1}{2}} - f_{l-\frac{1}{2}} \tag{6.2}$$

where, here, $f_{l+\frac{1}{2}}(t)$ represents the force exerted by the spring connecting the lth mass to the $(l+1)$th, where a positive force is assumed to act to the right. Under linear spring behavior, an expression for the force will be, in terms of the displacements u_l themselves,

$$f_{l+\frac{1}{2}} = K(u_{l+1} - u_l) \tag{6.3}$$

The defining equations (6.2) and (6.3) may be combined into a single equation as

$$M\frac{d^2u_l}{dt^2} = K(u_{l+1} - 2u_l + u_{l-1})$$

Now, defining $M = \rho Ah$, where ρ is a linear mass density and A is a constant with dimensions of area, and $K = EA/h$, where E is a stiffness parameter (actually, Young's modulus), the above may be written as

$$\frac{d^2u_l}{dt^2} = \frac{E}{\rho}\left(\frac{u_{l+1} - 2u_l + u_{l-1}}{h^2}\right) \tag{6.4}$$

In the limit as h becomes small, it is not difficult to see that, if the lumped displacements $u_l(t)$ are viewed as displacements of a continuous medium $u(x, t)$ at locations $x = lh$, then the right-hand side of the above equation is no more than a centered finite difference approximation to a second spatial derivative (see Section 5.2.2). The above equation then approaches the 1D wave equation (6.1), with $c = \sqrt{E/\rho}$, modeling, in this case, longitudinal vibrations of a stiff system, such as a bar.

Though the above is a method of deriving the wave equation from a linear array of masses and springs, it may be viewed, before the limit of small h is taken, in two separate ways, corresponding to separate philosophies of sound synthesis. The lumped network approach to sound synthesis, mentioned briefly in Section 1.2.1, would take a system of ODEs, defined by an equation such as (6.4) (or, more properly, the combined system of (6.2) and (6.3)) as the starting point for developing a numerical method. One can easily apply time-integration methods such as those outlined in Chapter 3. For a distributed system, such as that described by the wave equation, another way of proceeding is to take the distributed system as a starting point, thus bypassing any notion of a network of elements.[1] This is the point of view taken in this book. In the case presented here, as it turns out, the two approaches lead to very similar results. Indeed, if the second time derivative in (6.4) is approximated by a second time difference, a standard finite difference scheme for the wave equation results—see Section 6.2. For more complex systems, however, the correspondence is less direct. See Section 14.2.1 for some more comments on this subject.

---

[1] Indeed, for a distributed system, the entire apparatus of network theory is elegantly wrapped up in the PDE itself, and need never be explicitly employed!

6.1.2 Scaling

Non-dimensionalization, or scaling, is an extremely useful means of simplifying physical systems, especially in preparation for the application of numerical simulation techniques. In 1D, one may introduce the dimensionless coordinate $x' = x/L$, for some constant L with dimensions of length. In the case of the wave equation defined over a finite spatial domain, such as $x \in [0, x_0]$, it may be taken to be the length $L = x_0$, thus yielding a system defined over the domain $x' \in [0, 1]$. The wave equation (6.1) then becomes, in primed coordinates,

$$u_{tt} = \gamma^2 u_{x'x'} \qquad \text{with} \qquad \gamma = c/L \qquad (6.5)$$

Note that γ is a constant with dimensions of frequency. Such a description is useful in relating the wave equation to the simple harmonic oscillator, as described in Chapter 3. The term "wave speed" will still be used when referring to the constant γ.

This is a good example of a reduction in the number of parameters necessary to specify a system, which is of special importance in physical modeling sound synthesis—it is redundant to specify both the wave speed c and the length L, and the single parameter γ suffices. The fewer the number of parameters, the easier it will be for the musician working with a synthesis algorithm to navigate the space of possible timbres.[2] In general, forms in this book will be presented, whenever possible, in such a spatially scaled form, and the primed notation will be suppressed.

In the literature, it is commonplace to see a further temporal scaling, through the introduction of a temporal variable $t' = t/T$, for a characteristic time constant T. A judicious choice of $T = L/c$ leads to the form

$$u_{t't'} = u_{x'x'}$$

Though this form is apparently simpler than (6.5) above, in practice, especially when programming synthesis routines, there is no real advantage to such a further step (i.e., an extra parameter, namely the time step, will be reintroduced during the discretization procedure). In addition, the crucial frequency domain behavior of such a fully non-dimensionalized system is slightly obscured through the introduction of such temporal scaling. For this perceptual reason, namely that we are only interested in hearing the outputs of the resulting simulations, which themselves are time domain waveforms, only "half-way" spatial scaling will be employed in this book.

A further type of scaling, employed sometimes here, will be that of the dependent variable itself (in this case u); this becomes especially useful in nonlinear problems (see, e.g., the case of string vibration in Chapter 8 and plate vibration in Chapter 13), but can also lead to some simplification even for linear problems, as in the case of acoustic tubes—see Chapter 9.

6.1.3 Initial conditions

The 1D wave equation is a second-order (in time) PDE, and, just as for the SHO, requires the specification of two initial conditions. Normally these are the values of the variable u and its time derivative, at time $t = 0$, i.e.,

$$u(x, 0) = u_0(x) \qquad u_t(x, 0) = v_0(x)$$

which are now functions of x. Other equivalent choices (such as wave variables which are of use in a digital waveguide implementation) are possible. In some physical modeling synthesis applications, such as the modeling of struck or plucked strings, it is convenient in the first instance

---

[2] This replacement of physical parameters by a smaller set of perceptual parameters in some ways goes against the spirit of physical modeling synthesis, where one might want access to a full set of physical parameters. Notice, however, that in this case the physics itself remains unchanged under such data reduction.

to initialize the model itself using the above conditions. For a strike, for instance, one could choose a function v_0, perhaps peaked at a desired location corresponding to the strike center, and set u_0 to zero. For a pluck, one could make a similar choice for u_0, and set v_0 to zero. One commonly employed choice of initial displacement distribution, in the case of the string, is the triangular function, defined over the unit interval $\mathcal{D} = \mathbb{U}$ by

$$
c_{\text{tri}}(x) = \begin{cases} \dfrac{c_0}{x_0} x, & 0 \le x \le x_0 \\[2mm] \dfrac{c_0}{x_0 - 1}(x - 1), & x_0 < x \le 1 \end{cases} \tag{6.6}
$$

where c_0 and x_0 are the peak displacement and its location. For a strike, often localized to a very small region in the domain, one could use a delta function distribution, i.e., set $u_t(x, 0) = c_0 \delta(x - x_0)$, where c_0 and x_0 represent the amplitude and position of the strike.

One artificial (but physically reasonable) choice of initial condition profile, characterized by a small number of parameters, is the raised cosine distribution, defined by

$$
c_{\text{rc}}(x) = \begin{cases} \dfrac{c_0}{2}(1 + \cos(\pi(x - x_0)/x_{\text{hw}})), & |x - x_0| \le x_{\text{hw}} \\[2mm] 0, & |x - x_0| > x_{\text{hw}} \end{cases} \tag{6.7}
$$

Here, c_0 is the peak amplitude, x_0 the spatial center, and x_{hw} the half-width length of the distribution. See Figure 6.3. Such a function may be used in order to set either u_0 or v_0, and, depending on the choices of parameters, it may (very roughly) approximate the triangular and delta distributions mentioned above. It may also be extended in a natural way to two dimensions—see Section 11.1.

In a more complete physical modeling framework, however, such interactions are usually modeled not through initialization, but through applied forces, and in the case of string vibration, perhaps from a hammer or hand model; many examples of such interactions will be discussed in this book.

6.1.4 Strikes and plucks: time evolution of solution

Leaving aside the issue of boundary conditions, the wave equation (6.5), when supplemented by initial conditions, is complete. This is a good chance to look at some behavior exhibited under different types of initial excitation, and, in particular, assuming for the moment that the wave equation describes the time evolution of the displacement of a string, pluck-like excitations, in which case the initial position is set to a non-zero distribution, and the initial velocity to zero, and struck excitations, which are just the opposite. In Figure 6.4, the time evolution of the solution is shown at successive instants under both types of conditions, using the initializing function $c_{\text{rc}}(x)$ given in (6.7); the triangular initialization function will be employed slightly later, once boundary conditions have been introduced.

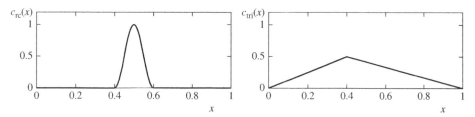

Figure 6.3 Different examples of initialization functions. Left, $c_{\text{rc}}(x)$ as defined in (6.7), with $c_0 = 1$, $x_0 = 0.5$, and $x_{\text{hw}} = 0.1$. Right, $c_{\text{tri}}(x)$ as defined in (6.6) with $c_0 = 0.5$ and $x_0 = 0.4$.

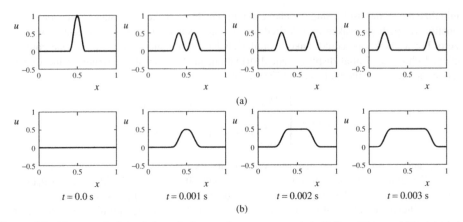

(a)

(b)

$t = 0.0$ s $t = 0.001$ s $t = 0.002$ s $t = 0.003$ s

Figure 6.4 Time evolution of the solution to the wave equation (6.5), with $\gamma = 100$: (a) under a plucked initial condition, with $u_0 = c_{rc}(x)$, and $x_0 = 0.5$, $c_0 = 1$, and $x_{hw} = 0.1$; and (b) under a struck initial condition of $v_0 = c_{rc}(x)$, with $x_0 = 0.5$, $c_0 = 1000$, and $x_{hw} = 0.1$. Successive snapshots of the solution profile are shown at the times indicated, over the interval $x \in [0, 1]$.

6.1.5 Dispersion relation

Frequency domain analysis is extremely revealing for LSI systems such as the wave equation. Considering the case of the 1D wave equation defined over the spatial domain $\mathcal{D} = \mathbb{R}$, a Fourier transform (in space) and a two-sided Laplace transform (in time) may be used. See Section 5.1.2 for more details. As a shortcut, one may analyze the behavior of the test solution

$$u(x, t) = e^{st + j\beta x}$$

where s is interpreted as a complex frequency variable, $s = \sigma + j\omega$, and β is a real wavenumber. The resulting characteristic equation (see Section 5.1.2) is

$$s^2 + \gamma^2 \beta^2 = 0 \tag{6.8}$$

which has roots

$$s_{\pm}(\beta) = \pm j\gamma\beta \qquad \longrightarrow \qquad \sigma = 0, \qquad \omega(\beta) = \pm\gamma\beta \tag{6.9}$$

This is the dispersion relation for the system (6.5); the frequency and wavenumber of a plane-wave solution are not independent. The two solutions correspond to left-going and right-going wave components.

6.1.6 Phase and group velocity

In the case of the wave equation above, the phase velocity and group velocity are both constant, i.e.,

$$v_\phi = v_g = \gamma \qquad \text{(1D wave equation)} \tag{6.10}$$

See Section 5.1.2. In particular, the phase and group velocities are independent of frequency ω. Thus any wavelike solution to the 1D wave equation travels at a constant speed. One might surmise, using arguments from Fourier theory, that if all components of a solution travel at the same speed, then any possible solution must travel with this speed—this is, in fact, true, and is one means of arriving at the so-called traveling wave solution to the wave equation, to be discussed next.

6.1.7   Traveling wave solutions

As is well known, the 1D wave equation possesses traveling wave solutions [244] of the form

$$u(x, t) = u^{(+)}(x - \gamma t) + u^{(-)}(x + \gamma t) \tag{6.11}$$

for arbitrary[3] functions $u^{(+)}$ and $u^{(-)}$, which represent rightward and leftward traveling waves of spatially non-dimensionalized speed γ, respectively. This decomposition, due to d'Alembert, may be arrived at directly in the time–space domain, through a change of variables, or through frequency domain analysis. Such a simple decomposition is peculiar to the 1D wave equation alone, and does not extend in general to more complex variants of the 1D wave equation (with some exceptions) or to the case of the wave equation in multiple dimensions. It is, however, the starting point for digital waveguide modeling, which is perhaps the best known of all physical modeling sound synthesis techniques, and will be described in more detail in Section 6.2.11. See Figure 6.5 for a graphical representation of the traveling wave decomposition.

Initialization is slightly more complex in the case of traveling wave components. The functions $u^{(+)}(x)$ and $u^{(-)}(x)$ may be related to $u_0(x)$ and $v_0(x)$ by

$$u^{(+)}(x) = \frac{1}{2}u_0(x) - \frac{1}{2\gamma} \int^x v_0(x')dx' \qquad u^{(-)}(x) = \frac{1}{2}u_0(x) + \frac{1}{2\gamma} \int^x v_0(x')dx' \tag{6.12}$$

The lower limit in the integration above has been left unspecified, but corresponds to the left endpoint of the domain $\mathcal{D}$ over which the wave equation is defined. In digital waveguide methods, it is these variables which must be initialized, rather than physically observable quantities such as, for example, displacement and velocity.

6.1.8   Energy analysis

The frequency domain analysis in Section 6.1.5 above has been applied to the case of the wave equation defined over an infinite domain $\mathcal{D} = \mathbb{R}$, and thus boundary conditions have not been taken into account. Another way of examining the behavior of the wave equation is similar to that which was discussed in Section 3.1.2, with regard to the oscillator, through the use of energetic techniques.

In the first instance, consider again the wave equation defined over the entire real line, i.e., for $\mathcal{D} = \mathbb{R}$. Taking the inner product of (6.5) with u_t over $\mathbb{R}$ (see Section 5.1.3 for the definition of

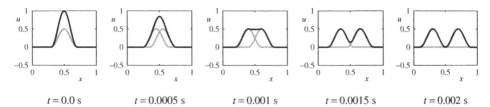

| $t = 0.0$ s | $t = 0.0005$ s | $t = 0.001$ s | $t = 0.0015$ s | $t = 0.002$ s |

Figure 6.5   Time evolution of the solution to the wave equation (6.5), with $\gamma = 100$, under a plucked initial condition, with $u_0 = c_{rc}(x)$, and $x_0 = 0.5$, $c_0 = 1$, and $x_{hw} = 0.2$. The solution is shown in black and traveling wave components in grey. Successive snapshots of the solution profile are shown at the times indicated, over the interval $x \in [0, 1]$.

---

[3] Arbitrary, barring technical considerations having to do with continuity of the functions themselves, and their derivatives.

the inner product and notational details) gives

$$\langle u_t, u_{tt} \rangle_{\mathbb{R}} = \gamma^2 \langle u_t, u_{xx} \rangle_{\mathbb{R}} \tag{6.13}$$

and, employing integration by parts, as per (5.10),

$$\langle u_t, u_{tt} \rangle_{\mathbb{R}} + \gamma^2 \langle u_{tx}, u_x \rangle_{\mathbb{R}} = 0 \tag{6.14}$$

Both of the terms in the above equation may be written as total derivatives with respect to time, i.e.,

$$\frac{d}{dt} \left(\frac{1}{2} \|u_t\|_{\mathbb{R}}^2 + \frac{\gamma^2}{2} \|u_x\|_{\mathbb{R}}^2 \right) = 0$$

or

$$\frac{d\mathfrak{H}}{dt} = 0 \quad \text{with} \quad \mathfrak{H} = \mathfrak{T} + \mathfrak{V} \quad \text{where} \quad \mathfrak{T} = \frac{1}{2} \|u_t\|_{\mathbb{R}}^2 \quad \mathfrak{V} = \frac{\gamma^2}{2} \|u_x\|_{\mathbb{R}}^2 \tag{6.15}$$

Here, $\mathfrak{T}$ and $\mathfrak{V}$ are, respectively, the kinetic and potential energy for the wave equation, and $\mathfrak{H}$ is the total energy, or Hamiltonian. (As in the case of the SHO, in order to arrive at a true energy, these quantities must be scaled by a constant with dimensions of mass.) Equation (6.15) and the non-negativity of the terms $\mathfrak{T}$ and $\mathfrak{V}$ above imply that

$$\mathfrak{H}(t) = \mathfrak{H}(0) \geq 0 \tag{6.16}$$

The non-negativity of $\mathfrak{T}$ and $\mathfrak{V}$ also imply that

$$\|u_t\|_{\mathbb{R}} \leq \sqrt{2\mathfrak{H}(0)} \qquad \|u_x\|_{\mathbb{R}} \leq \frac{\sqrt{2\mathfrak{H}(0)}}{\gamma} \tag{6.17}$$

Once boundary conditions are taken into account, it may be possible to improve upon these bounds—see Section 6.1.10.

6.1.9   Boundary conditions

The 1D wave equation involves second-order differentiation in space, and, as such, requires the specification of a single boundary condition at any endpoint of the spatial domain. A typical such condition often employed at an endpoint of the domain, such as $x = 0$, is the following:

$$u(0, t) = 0 \tag{6.18}$$

Such a condition is often referred to as being of Dirichlet type. If the 1D wave equation is intended to describe the displacement of a string, then this is a fixed termination. If $u(x, t)$ represents the pressure variation in an acoustic tube, such a condition corresponds (roughly) to an open end of the tube.

Another commonly encountered condition is the Neumann condition:

$$u_x(0, t) = 0 \tag{6.19}$$

Such a condition is easily interpreted in the context of the acoustic tube as corresponding to a closed tube end, and less easily in the case of the string, where it may be viewed as describing a string endpoint which is free to move in a transverse direction, but not longitudinally (it is best to visualize the end of such a string as constrained to move along a vertical "guide rail"). The Dirichlet and Neumann conditions are often generalized to include a non-zero constant on the right-hand side [161]. Both conditions are lossless—in order to get a better idea of what this means (and to gain some insights into how such conditions may be arrived at), energy techniques are invaluable. Consider now the wave equation defined not over the infinite domain $\mathcal{D} = \mathbb{R}$, but over the semi-infinite domain[4] $\mathcal{D} = \mathbb{R}^+ = [0, \infty]$. Taking an inner product of the wave equation with u_t, and employing integration by parts yields, instead of (6.14),

$$\langle u_t, u_{tt} \rangle_{\mathbb{R}^+} + \gamma^2 \langle u_{tx}, u_x \rangle_{\mathbb{R}^+} = \mathfrak{B} \triangleq -\gamma^2 u_t(0, t) u_x(0, t)$$

An extra boundary term $\mathfrak{B}$ has thus intervened, and one can not proceed to a statement of conservation of energy such as (6.15), but rather

$$\frac{d\mathfrak{H}}{dt} = \mathfrak{B} \tag{6.20}$$

where the definition of $\mathfrak{H}$ and its constituent terms are taken over $\mathbb{R}^+$ rather than $\mathbb{R}$. Now, the lossless interpretation of the Dirichlet and Neumann conditions above should be clear; the boundary term vanishes in either case, and one again has exact energy conservation,[5] as per (6.16). (Note, however, that in the case of the Dirichlet condition, the true losslessness condition, from the above, is rather that u_t vanish at the boundary, which is implied by the simpler condition that u itself vanish—in other words, u need only be specified as a constant, which can be chosen as zero.)

It follows directly that when the spatial domain of the problem at hand is finite, e.g., if $\mathcal{D} = \mathbb{U} = [0, 1]$, as is the case in all musical systems of interest, the energy balance becomes

$$\frac{d\mathfrak{H}}{dt} = \mathfrak{B} \triangleq \gamma^2 \left(u_t(1, t) u_x(1, t) - u_t(0, t) u_x(0, t) \right) \tag{6.21}$$

The boundary conditions at both ends of the domain come into play.

Lossy boundary conditions

The Dirichlet and Neumann conditions are by no means the only possible boundary conditions for the wave equation; there are an infinite number of possible terminations, some of which possess a reasonable physical interpretation. For example, a lossy condition is given by

$$u_t(0, t) = \alpha u_x(0, t) \tag{6.22}$$

for some constant $\alpha > 0$. In this case, over $\mathcal{D} = \mathbb{R}^+$, one has

$$\mathfrak{B} = -\alpha \gamma^2 (u_x(0, t))^2 \leq 0$$

implying that the energy is non-increasing. It becomes very simple, using energetic techniques, to categorize sources of loss according to whether they occur at the boundary or over the problem interior. When translated to a numerical setting, it becomes similarly possible to isolate potential sources of numerical instability—some are of global type, occurring over the problem interior, but often instability originates at an improperly set numerical boundary condition. The condition (6.22)

---

[4] One of the nice features of energy analysis is that it allows boundary conditions at different locations to be analyzed independently; this is a manifestly physical approach, in that one would not reasonably expect boundary conditions at separate locations to interact, energetically. The same simplicity of analysis follows for numerical methods, as will be seen in the first instance later in this chapter.

[5] For those with an engineering background, including those familiar with digital waveguides, the boundary term may be interpreted as the power supplied to the system due to interaction at the boundary.

above, under a special choice of α, can lead to a perfectly absorbing (i.e., impedance-matched) boundary condition—see Problem 6.1.

One can go much further along these lines, and analyze nonlinear boundary conditions as well. See Problem 6.2 for an example.

Energy-storing boundary conditions

The Dirichlet, Neumann, and lossy boundary conditions lead to conservation of energy, as a whole, or to instantaneous dissipation—they do not have "memory," and are incapable of storing energy. In some cases, one might expect a boundary termination to exhibit this property—some examples include termination of a string by a mass–spring system or also the open (radiative) termination of an acoustic tube.

One condition, often used in speech applications in order to model such radiation from the open end of a tube [280] at $x = 0$, is the following:

$$u_x(0, t) = \alpha_1 u_t(0, t) + \alpha_2 u(0, t) \tag{6.23}$$

for constants $\alpha_1 \geq 0$ and $\alpha_2 \geq 0$. Now, the energy balance (6.20) becomes

$$\frac{d\mathfrak{H}}{dt} = -\alpha_1 \gamma^2 (u_t(0, t))^2 - \alpha_2 \gamma^2 u_t(0, t) u(0, t)$$

or

$$\frac{d(\mathfrak{H} + \mathfrak{H}_b)}{dt} = -\mathfrak{Q} \leq 0 \qquad \text{where} \qquad \mathfrak{H}_b = \frac{\alpha_2 \gamma^2}{2} (u(0, t))^2 \qquad \mathfrak{Q} = \alpha_1 \gamma^2 (u_t(0, t))^2 \tag{6.24}$$

The total energy of the system is thus that of the problem over the interior, $\mathfrak{H}$, plus that stored at the boundary, $\mathfrak{H}_b$, and is again non-negative and non-increasing. The term with coefficient α_2 is often viewed, in the acoustic transmission line framework, as corresponding to the reactive (i.e., energy-storing) part of the terminating impedance of the tube, and that with coefficient α_1 to the resistive part.

This condition will be revisited in the context of tube modeling in Section 9.1.3.

Reflection of traveling waves at a boundary

The result of the choice of boundary conditions on the behavior of the solution to the wave equation is perhaps most easily approached using the traveling wave decomposition. Considering the wave decomposition (6.11), and a boundary condition at $x = 0$ of Dirichlet type, one immediately has that

$$u^{(+)}(-t) = -u^{(-)}(t)$$

Thus the traveling waves reflect, with sign inversion, at such a boundary. For the Neumann condition (6.19), one has that

$$u^{(+)}(-t) = u^{(-)}(t)$$

Under this condition, traveling waves reflect without sign inversion. It is useful to examine this behavior, as illustrated in Figure 6.6. The simple manner in which boundary conditions may be viewed using a traveling wave decomposition has been exploited with great success in digital waveguide synthesis. It is worth noting, however, that more complex boundary conditions usually will introduce a degree of dispersion into the solution, and traveling waves become distorted upon reflection.

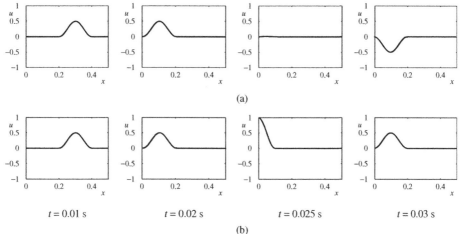

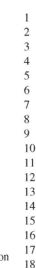

(a)

$t = 0.01$ s $t = 0.02$ s $t = 0.025$ s $t = 0.03$ s

(b)

Figure 6.6 Reflection of a leftward-traveling pulse at a boundary at $x = 0$, (a) with inversion under Dirichlet, or fixed conditions, and (b) without inversion under Neumann, or free conditions. In this case, the wave equation is defined with $\gamma = 20$, and the solution is plotted over the left half of the domain, at the times as indicated.

6.1.10 Bounds on solution size

Under conservative boundary conditions, the bounds (6.17) hold, regardless of whether $\mathcal{D}$, the spatial domain, is defined as the entire x axis, a semi-infinite domain, or a finite interval. It is important to note that both such bounds apply to derivatives of the dependent variable and not the dependent variable itself. This is in direct contrast to the case of the harmonic oscillator, and might seem counterintuitive, but follows directly from the definition of the 1D wave equation itself: note that only second derivatives appear, so that any solution of the form

$$u(x, t) = a_{00} + a_{01}t + a_{10}x + a_{11}xt$$

automatically satisfies the wave equation for any constants a_{00}, a_{10}, a_{01}, and a_{11}, and such a solution can clearly not be bounded for all t and all x. The wave equation, unless properly terminated, allows a solution which is capable of drifting.

Nevertheless, conditions may indeed be employed to derive bounds of a less strict type on the size of the solution itself. Take, for instance, the first of conditions (6.17). One may write, for any domain $\mathcal{D}$,

$$\|u\|_{\mathcal{D}} \frac{d}{dt} \|u\|_{\mathcal{D}} = \frac{1}{2} \frac{d}{dt} \|u\|_{\mathcal{D}}^2 = \langle u, u_t \rangle_{\mathcal{D}} \le \|u\|_{\mathcal{D}} \|u_t\|_{\mathcal{D}} \le \|u\|_{\mathcal{D}} \sqrt{2\mathcal{H}(0)}$$

where the first inequality above follows from the Cauchy–Schwartz inequality, and the second results from the first of bounds (6.17). One thus has

$$\frac{d}{dt} \|u\|_{\mathcal{D}} \le \sqrt{2\mathcal{H}(0)} \qquad \longrightarrow \qquad \|u\|_{\mathcal{D}}(t) \le \|u\|_{\mathcal{D}}(0) + \sqrt{2\mathcal{H}(0)}t \qquad (6.25)$$

and the norm of the solution at time t is bounded by an affine function of time t which depends only on initial conditions; growth is no faster than linear.

As one might expect, better bounds are possible if fixed boundary conditions are employed. Considering again the wave equation defined over the semi-infinite domain $\mathcal{D} = \mathbb{R}^+$, with the Dirichlet condition (6.18) applied at $x = 0$, one has, at any point $x = x_0$,

$$|u(x_0, t)| = \left| \int_{x=0}^{x=x_0} u_{x'} dx' \right| = |\langle u_x, 1 \rangle_{[0,x_0]}| \leq \|u_x\|_{[0,x_0]} \|1\|_{[0,x_0]} \leq \|u_x\|_{\mathbb{R}^+} \|1\|_{[0,x_0]} \leq \frac{1}{\gamma} \sqrt{2\mathcal{H}(0) x_0}$$

where in this case "1" represents a function of value 1. Here, again, the Cauchy–Schwartz inequality has been used as well as the second of bounds (6.17). The magnitude of the solution at any point x_0 in the semi-infinite domain may thus be bounded in terms of its distance from the endpoint. Notice that this is a much stronger condition than a bound on the norm of the solution (in fact, it is such a bound, but in a Chebyshev, or L_∞-type norm). If the spatial domain $\mathcal{D}$ above is changed to the finite interval $\mathbb{U} = [0, 1]$, the above analysis is unchanged, and, as long as the boundary condition at $x = 1$ is conservative, one may go further and write

$$|u(x_0, t)| \leq \frac{1}{\gamma} \sqrt{2\mathcal{H}(0)} \qquad \longrightarrow \qquad \|u\|_{\mathbb{U}} \leq \frac{1}{\gamma} \sqrt{2\mathcal{H}(0)} \tag{6.26}$$

which is indeed a bound on the L_2 norm of the solution. If the boundary condition at $x = 1$ is also of Dirichlet type, an improved bound is possible. See Problem 6.3.

6.1.11   Modes

As mentioned in Chapter 1, modal techniques appeared early on as a physical modeling sound synthesis method. The 1D wave equation is the usual point of departure in acoustics texts [244] for any discussion of the concept of modes of vibration. The procedure for determining the modal behavior of an LTI system such as the wave equation (6.5) is more general than dispersion analysis, in that boundary conditions are taken into account.

As a starting point, consider the behavior of a test solution of the form

$$u(x, t) = U(x)e^{j\omega t} \tag{6.27}$$

When inserted into the wave equation, the following ordinary differential equation results:

$$-\omega^2 U = \gamma^2 \frac{d^2 U}{dx^2}$$

which has solutions

$$U(x) = A \cos(\omega x / \gamma) + B \sin(\omega x / \gamma)$$

So far, boundary conditions have not been enforced—for an infinite domain, any frequency $\omega \neq 0$ yields a possible solution of the above form. Consider now the wave equation over the finite domain $\mathcal{D} = \mathbb{U}$, with fixed boundary conditions at $x = 0$ and $x = 1$. In order for $U(x)$ to vanish at $x = 0$, one must have $A = 0$; the condition at $x = 1$ leads, immediately, to

$$\omega_p = p\pi\gamma \qquad U_p(x) = B_p \sin(p\pi x) \qquad \text{for integer } p \neq 0 \tag{6.28}$$

where the subscript p on ω_p, $U_p(x)$, and B_p indicates the restriction of frequencies and solutions to a countably infinite set. Thus the test functions (6.27) solve the wave equation with fixed boundary conditions when they are of the form

$$u_p(x, t) = B_p \sin(p\pi x)e^{jp\pi\gamma t}$$

for some constants B_p. A general solution is then of the form

$$u(x,t) = \sum_{p=-\infty}^{\infty} B_p \sin(p\pi x) e^{jp\pi\gamma t}$$

Insisting on a real-valued solution leads to a semi-infinite expansion,

$$u(x,t) = \sum_{p=1}^{\infty} \left(a_p \cos(p\pi\gamma t) + b_p \sin(p\pi\gamma t)\right) \sin(p\pi x) \tag{6.29}$$

for some real constants a_p and b_p. These constants may be related to initial conditions by noting that

$$u(x,0) = \sum_{p=1}^{\infty} a_p \sin(p\pi x) \qquad u_t(x,0) = \sum_{p=1}^{\infty} p\pi\gamma b_p \sin(p\pi x)$$

From Fourier series arguments, and given two initial conditions $u(x,0) = u_0(x)$ and $u_t(x,0) = v_0(x)$, one may then deduce that

$$a_p = 2\int_U u_0(x) \sin(p\pi x)dx \qquad b_p = \frac{2}{\omega_p}\int_U v_0(x) \sin(p\pi x)dx, \qquad p = 1, \ldots, \infty \tag{6.30}$$

The above modal frequencies $\omega_p = p\pi\gamma$ and functions $U_p(x)$ hold for the wave equation under fixed or Dirichlet conditions, and must be recomputed as the boundary conditions are varied. Under free (Neumann) conditions at both ends, it is straightforward to show that the modal frequencies and functions are of the form

$$\omega_p = p\pi\gamma \qquad U_p(x) = A_p \cos(p\pi x) \qquad \text{for integer } p \tag{6.31}$$

The allowed frequencies are the same as in the case of fixed/fixed termination, with the minor exception that a zero-frequency solution is possible (with $p = 0$)—this follows immediately from rigid body motion, which is possible under free conditions. Under mixed conditions (i.e., fixed at $x = 0$ and free at $x = 1$), the frequencies and functions are given by

$$\omega_p = (p - 1/2)\pi\gamma \qquad U_p(x) = A_p \sin((p - 1/2)\pi x) \qquad \text{for integer } p \tag{6.32}$$

In this case, the lowest modal frequency is half of that in the case of fixed/fixed or free/free terminations. When such conditions are used to model the behavior of a musical instrument, the pitch will be an octave lower than in the other cases, and with only odd harmonics present. Such conditions are by no means unrealistic in a musical setting, and serve to describe, to a crude approximation, wind instruments which make use of a uniform cylindrical section of tubing, closed at one end and open at the other, such as the clarinet.

The modal functions for all three sets of boundary conditions are shown in Figure 6.7.

Though for such simple boundary conditions, the modal frequencies may be expressed in closed form, and the modal functions themselves may be written as trigonometric functions, it is worth keeping in mind that for even slightly more complex systems (such as, for example, the 1D wave equation under some other more involved boundary termination, or virtually any other system), modal frequencies and functions must be determined numerically. See Problem 6.4, and the musically relevant case of the vibrating bar in Section 7.1.3.

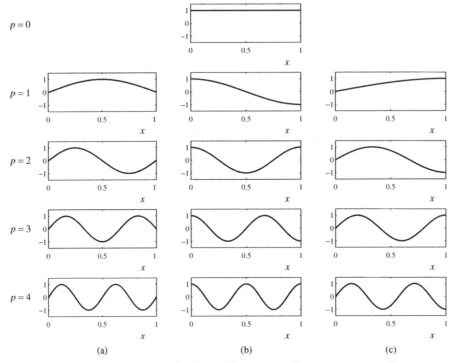

Figure 6.7 Modal functions for the 1D wave equation (6.5), as a function of $x \in \mathbb{U} = [0, 1]$, under various different boundary terminations: (a) fixed at both ends; (b) free at both ends; and (c) fixed at the left end and free at the right end. Modal functions are indexed by integer p—in cases (a) and (c) above, the first four modes are shown, and in case of free/free termination, an extra constant mode with $p = 0$ (which can be thought of as a DC offset, or in terms of rigid body motion) is also shown. All modal functions are normalized to the range $[-1, 1]$.

Modal density and degrees of freedom

As a prelude to discrete-time simulation of the 1D wave equation, it is important to say a word about the number of degrees of freedom of the system, which will ultimately determine computational complexity for any algorithm. See the comments on this topic in Section 1.3.3. The modal decomposition allows such information to be extracted in an especially easy way.

The modal description of the 1D wave equation is complete, in the sense that an expansion such as (6.29) is a general solution to the PDE formulation (6.5). The initial conditions may be expanded onto the various modes, yielding, at each frequency ω_p, two coefficients, a_p and b_p, corresponding to an initial displacement and velocity for a given mode. These two coefficients are sufficient to determine the time evolution of the mode, and thus each mode possesses two degrees of freedom. In any practical digital application (such as sound synthesis), the number of modes must be restricted to a finite set—a natural choice is those with frequencies which lie below half of the audio sampling rate, f_s. In other words, one needs only those (positive) frequencies for which $\omega_p < \pi f_s$. Considering, for example, the case of the 1D wave equation with Dirichlet conditions imposed at either end, the modal frequencies fall in a series given in (6.28) above. For the digital system operating at sample rate f_s, the total number of degrees of freedom N_m will be twice the number of frequencies which occur in the range $\omega_p \in [0, \pi f_s]$, or

$$N_m \approx 2 f_s / \gamma \tag{6.33}$$

The number N_{m} is a measure of the complexity of the 1D wave equation in a discrete-time simulation at sample rate f_{s}—it is, approximately, the number of units of computer memory that will be required in order to compute such a solution, and the number of arithmetic operations per time step also scales with N_{m}. It is important to note that this number remains roughly the same, regardless of the type of boundary conditions which are applied. (If, for instance, one makes use of Dirichlet conditions at one end of the domain and Neumann conditions at the other, the set of modal frequencies given in (6.32) results, leading to the same estimate of complexity as in (6.33) above.) Even more important, and as will be seen at various instances throughout this chapter, is that the complexity remains approximately the same for *any* numerical method which simulates the wave equation at a given sample rate f_{s}, with the interesting exception of digital waveguides—see Section 6.2.11.

6.2   A simple finite difference scheme

The most rudimentary finite difference scheme for the 1D wave equation (and in almost all respects, the best) is given, in operator form, as

$$\delta_{tt} u = \gamma^2 \delta_{xx} u \tag{6.34}$$

Here, as mentioned previously, u is shorthand notation for the grid function u_l^n, representing an approximation to the solution of the wave equation at $x = lh$, $t = nk$, where h is the spacing between adjacent grid points, and k is the time step. (See Chapter 5 for an overview of the difference operator notation used here and elsewhere in this chapter.) As the difference operators employed are second-order accurate, the scheme itself is in general second-order accurate in both time and space. (Under a special choice of h and k, its order of accuracy is infinite—in other words, it can yield an exact solution. This special case is characteristic of the wave equation alone, but forms the basis for digital waveguides—see Section 6.2.11.)

When the action of the operators is expanded out, a recursion results:

$$u_l^{n+1} = 2\left(1 - \lambda^2\right) u_l^n + \lambda^2 \left(u_{l-1}^n + u_{l+1}^n\right) - u_l^{n-1} \tag{6.35}$$

The important dimensionless parameter λ, often referred to as the Courant number, has been defined here by

$$\lambda \triangleq \gamma k / h \tag{6.35}$$

This scheme may be updated, explicitly, at each time step n, from previously computed values at the previous two time steps. It is perhaps easiest to see the behavior of this algorithm through a dependence plot showing the "footprint" of the scheme (6.34), shown in Figure 6.8.

For the moment, it is assumed that the spatial domain of the problem is infinite; the analysis of boundary conditions may thus be postponed temporarily, simplifying analysis somewhat.

6.2.1   Initialization

Scheme (6.34), like the wave equation itself, must be initialized with two sets of values. From the explicit form of the recursion (6.35), it should be clear that one must specify values of the grid function u_l^n at time steps $n = 0$ and $n = 1$, namely u_l^0 and u_l^1. Supposing that the initial displacement u_l^0 is given, and that one also has a grid function v_l^0 representing the initial velocity, one may then write for u_l^1

$$u_l^1 = u_l^0 + k v_l^0 \tag{6.36}$$

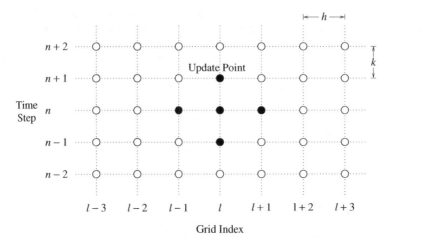

Figure 6.8 Computational footprint of scheme (6.34)—a value of the grid function u_l^n at the update location $(l, n + 1)$, as indicated, is updated using values at the previous two time steps. The set of points related under the scheme at this update location is indicated in black.

which is exactly the same procedure as in the case of the SHO. See Section 3.2.2 and Problem 3.4. This initialization strategy, however, can lead to unexpected results, especially when the initializing distribution is very sharply peaked—see Programming Exercise 6.1.

6.2.2   von Neumann analysis

Frequency domain analysis of the scheme (6.34) is similar to that applied to the continuous time–space wave equation. As a shortcut to full z transform, and spatial discrete Fourier transform analysis, consider again the behavior of a test solution of the form

$$u_i^n = z^n e^{jl\beta h} \tag{6.37}$$

where $z = e^{sk}$ (see Section 5.2.6). This again may be thought of as a wavelike solution, and in fact it is identical to that employed in the continuous case, sampled at $t = nk$ and $x = lh$. When substituted into the difference scheme (6.35), the following characteristic equation results:

$$z + 2(2\lambda^2 \sin^2(\beta h/2) - 1) + z^{-1} = 0 \tag{6.38}$$

which is analogous to (6.8) for the 1D wave equation. The roots are given by

$$z_{\pm} = 1 - 2\lambda^2 \sin^2(\beta h/2) \pm \sqrt{\left(1 - 2\lambda^2 \sin^2(\beta h/2)\right)^2 - 1}$$

Again, just as for the wave equation, there are two solutions (resulting from the use of a second difference in time), representing the propagation of the test solution in opposite directions.

One would expect that, in order for a solution such as (6.37) to behave as a solution to the wave equation, one should have $|z| = 1$ for any value of β, the wavenumber, otherwise such a solution will experience exponential growth or damping. This is not necessarily true for scheme (6.34). From inspection of the characteristic equation (6.38), and using the same techniques applied to the harmonic oscillator in Section 3.2.4, one may deduce that the roots are complex conjugates of unit magnitude when

$$|2\lambda^2 \sin^2(\beta h/2) - 1| \leq 1$$

which can be rewritten as

$$\lambda^2 \sin^2(\beta h/2) \leq 1 \qquad (6.39)$$

This inequality must be satisfied for any possible value of β. Because $\sin^2(\beta h/2)$ is bounded by one, the condition

$$\lambda \leq 1 \qquad (6.40)$$

is sufficient for stability. This is the famous Courant–Friedrichs–Lewy (CFL) condition [95], which has the interesting geometrical interpretation as illustrated in Figure 6.9.

Note that for λ slightly greater than unity, condition (6.39) will be violated near the maximum of the function $\sin^2(\beta h/2)$, which occurs at the wavenumber $\beta = \pi/h$, corresponding to a wavelength of $2h$—from basic sampling theory, this is the shortest wavelength which may be represented on a grid of spacing h. A typical manifestation of numerical instability is the explosive growth of such a component at the spatial Nyquist wavelength. See Figure 6.10.

The CFL condition as a bound on computational complexity

As seen above, the condition (6.40) serves as a bound which must be respected in order that scheme (6.34) remain stable. It does not, however, indicate how close to this bound λ should be chosen. In fact, in sound synthesis applications (and often not in others!) it is usually a good idea to choose λ as close to the stability limit as possible, as will be shown here.

First, consider the scheme (6.34), defined over the $N + 1$ point unit interval $\mathcal{D} = \mathbb{U}_N$. For a grid spacing h, the number of grid points covering the unit interval will be approximately $1/h$, and for a two-step scheme such as (6.34), the number of memory locations required, or degrees of freedom N_{fd}, will be twice this number. The stability condition (6.40) can then be rewritten as a bound on N_{fd}:

$$N_{fd} \leq \frac{2 f_s}{\gamma} \qquad (6.41)$$

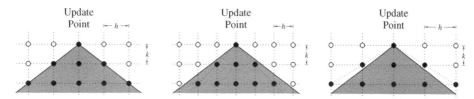

Figure 6.9 A geometrical interpretation of the Courant–Friedrichs–Lewy stability condition (6.40) for scheme (6.34). At a given update point (as indicated in the figures), the value of the solution to the continuous-time wave equation depends on values traveling on solution characteristics (solid dark lines), defined by $x - \gamma t = $ constant and $x + \gamma t = $ constant. The cone of dependence of the solution may be illustrated as the interior of this region (in grey). The scheme (6.34) at the update point possesses a numerical cone of dependence, illustrated by black points, and bounded by dashed black lines. At left, $h = \gamma k$, and the characteristics align exactly with values on the grid—in this case, the numerical solution is exact. At center, a value $h < \gamma k$ is chosen, violating stability condition (6.40)—the numerical cone of dependence lies strictly within the region of the dependence of the wave equation, and as such the scheme cannot compute an accurate solution, and is unstable. At right, with a choice of $h > \gamma k$, the numerical cone of dependence of the scheme includes that of the wave equation, and the scheme is stable.

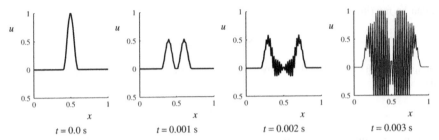

$t = 0.0$ s $t = 0.001$ s $t = 0.002$ s $t = 0.003$ s

Figure 6.10 Numerical instability. Left to right: successive outputs u of scheme (6.34), with a value of $\lambda = 1.0125$, violating condition (6.40). The sample rate is chosen as 8000 Hz, γ as 100, and the initial conditions are of a plucked raised cosine, amplitude 1, half-width 0.1, and centered at $x = 0.5$. As time progresses, components of the solution near the spatial Nyquist frequency quickly grow in amplitude; not long after the last plot in this series, the computed values of the solution become out of range.

Notice the similarity with the measure of the number of degrees of freedom N_m for a modal representation, from (6.33). When (6.41) holds with equality, the two measures are the same. What is interesting, however, is that N_{fd} may be chosen smaller than this: the CFL bound (6.40) specifies a lower bound on h in terms of k, which seems to imply that one could reduce the number of grid points at which a numerical solution is to be calculated, resulting in a reduced memory and operation count. One could do just this, but in fact one is merely cheating the dynamics of the wave equation itself, and wasting valuable audio bandwidth. It is easiest to see this after having a look at the effects of numerical dispersion.

6.2.3   Numerical dispersion

Consider now scheme (6.34) under the stability condition (6.40). Using $z = e^{j\omega k}$, the characteristic equation (6.38) may be written as

$$-4\sin^2(\omega k/2) = -4\lambda^2 \sin^2(\beta h/2) \qquad \longrightarrow \qquad \sin(\omega k/2) = \pm\lambda \sin(\beta h/2) \qquad (6.42)$$

or

$$\omega = \pm\frac{2}{k}\sin^{-1}(\lambda \sin(\beta h/2)) \qquad (6.43)$$

This is a dispersion relation for the scheme (6.34), relating frequency ω and wavenumber β in complete analogy with the relation (6.9) for the wave equation itself. Just as in the case of a continuous system, one may define phase and group velocities for the scheme, now in a numerical sense, exactly as per (6.10). (See the end of Section 5.2.6 for more on numerical phase and group velocities.) In the case of the wave equation, recall that these velocities are constant, and equal to γ for all wavenumbers. Now, however, both the phase and the group velocity are, in general, functions of wavenumber—in other words, different wavelengths travel at different speeds, and the scheme (6.34) is thus dispersive. Dispersion leads to a progressive distortion of a pulse as it travels, as illustrated in Figure 6.11. See Problem 6.5. This type of anomalous behavior is purely a result of discretization, and is known as numerical dispersion—it should be carefully distinguished from physical dispersion of a model problem itself, which will arise when systems are subject to stiffness; such systems will be examined shortly in Chapter 7. It is also true that the numerical velocities will also depend on the choice of the parameter λ, which may be freely chosen for scheme (6.34), subject to the constraint (6.40). The velocity curves, as functions of frequency for different values of λ, are shown in Figure 6.12.

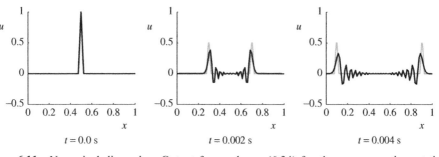

$t = 0.0$ s $t = 0.002$ s $t = 0.004$ s

Figure 6.11 Numerical dispersion. Output from scheme (6.34) for the wave equation, at times as indicated, for $\lambda = 1$ (in grey) and $\lambda = 0.5$ (in black). γ is chosen as 100, the sample rate is 16 000 Hz, and the initial conditions are set according to a narrow cosine distribution, of width 1/40. Notice that for λ away from 1, the higher-frequency components lag the wavefront, illustrating the phase velocity characteristic of the scheme. Notice also that the gross speed of the wave packet is slower as well, illustrating the group velocity characteristic.

Now, consider the very special case of $\lambda = 1$. Under this condition, the dispersion relation (6.43) reduces to

$$\omega = \frac{2}{k} \sin^{-1}(\sin(\beta h/2)) = \frac{\beta h}{k} = \gamma \beta$$

Now, the numerical dispersion relation is exactly that of the continuous wave equation, and the phase and group velocities are both equal to γ, independently of β. There is thus no numerical dispersion for this choice of λ—this is a reflection of the fact that the scheme (6.34) is exact when $\lambda = 1$, as will be shown in the next section.

Operation away from the CFL bound

This is a good opportunity to return to the question raised at the end of Section 6.2.2, namely that of the possibility of reduced computational complexity when $\lambda < 1$. One way of approaching this is to ask: what frequencies is scheme (6.34) capable of producing? The answer is most easily seen from (6.42) above. Considering only the positive solution, and using $\omega = 2\pi f$ and $f_s = 1/k$, the maximum such frequency f_{max} will be given by

$$\sin(\pi f_{max}/f_s) = \lambda \qquad \longrightarrow \qquad f_{max} = \frac{f_s}{\pi} \sin^{-1}(\lambda) < \frac{f_s}{2}$$

Thus, when $\lambda < 1$, scheme (6.34) is, in essence, not capable of filling the available audio bandwidth; the smaller the chosen λ, the lower the bandwidth of the scheme. See Figure 6.13. As a result, one

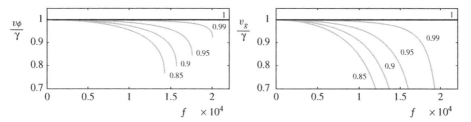

Figure 6.12 Numerical phase velocity (left) and group velocity (right) as a function of frequency f, normalized by the model velocity γ, for scheme (6.34), for a variety of values of λ, as indicated. The sample rate is chosen as 44 100 Hz.

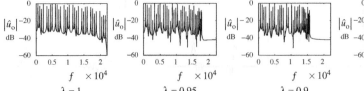
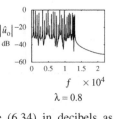

Figure 6.13 Typical magnitude spectra $|\hat{u}_o|$ of outputs from scheme (6.34) in decibels as a function of frequency f, under different choices of the parameter λ, as indicated in the figure. In this case, the initial condition is a raised cosine distribution $c_{rc}(x)$, with $x_0 = 0.3$, $x_{hw} = 0.05$, and $c_0 = 1$, and the readout location is $x = 0.6$. The sample rate is 44 100 Hz and $\gamma = 1102.5$. Notice in particular the reduction in the effective bandwidth of the computed solution, as λ becomes farther from the CFL bound at $\lambda = 1$. Also visible is the inharmonicity resulting from numerical dispersion, increasing as λ is moved away from the CFL bound.

can conclude that in order to reduce computational complexity, it is a far better idea to reduce the audio sample rate of the simulation, rather than to choose an unnaturally large value for the grid spacing (i.e., one which does not allow sufficient resolution of wavelengths at the desired sample rate). As mentioned above, such a choice also leads to undesirable numerical dispersion effects. This may be summarized in the following way:

Rule of Thumb #1

For an explicit numerical method, the best numerical behavior (i.e., the least numerical dispersion) is achieved when the stability condition is satisfied as near to equality as possible.

6.2.4   Accuracy

The difference operators δ_{xx} and δ_{tt} employed in scheme (6.34) are second-order accurate (see Section 5.2.5), and one might suspect that the solution generated will also exhibit this level of accuracy. Recall, however, from the analysis of a special scheme for the harmonic oscillator in Section 3.3.4, that accuracy of a scheme can, in some cases, be better than that of the constituent operators. Consider, now, the scheme (6.34) written in the following form:

$$P_d u = 0 \quad \text{with} \quad P_d = \delta_{tt} - \gamma^2 \delta_{xx}$$

where u is the grid function u_l^n. Supposing, now, that P_d operates on the continuous function $u(x, t)$, one may again expand the behavior of P_d in Taylor series, to get

$$P_d = \frac{\partial^2}{\partial t^2} - \gamma^2 \frac{\partial^2}{\partial x^2} + \sum_{p=2}^{\infty} \frac{2}{(2p)!} \left(k^{2(p-1)} \frac{\partial^{2p}}{\partial t^{2p}} - \gamma^2 h^{2(p-1)} \frac{\partial^{2p}}{\partial x^{2p}} \right)$$

$$= \frac{\partial^2}{\partial t^2} - \gamma^2 \frac{\partial^2}{\partial x^2} + O(k^2) + O(h^2)$$

Thus the difference operator P_d approximates the differential operator corresponding to the 1D wave equation to second order in both k and h. Note, however, that when $\lambda = 1$, or when $k\gamma = h$, the operator may be written as

$$P_d = \frac{\partial^2}{\partial t^2} - \gamma^2 \frac{\partial^2}{\partial x^2} + \sum_{p=2}^{\infty} \frac{2k^{2p-1}}{(2p)!} \left(\frac{\partial^{2p}}{\partial t^{2p}} - \gamma^{2p} \frac{\partial^{2p}}{\partial x^{2p}} \right)$$

Just as in the case of scheme (3.39), each term in the summation above possesses a factor of the form $\partial^2/\partial t^2 - \gamma^2\partial^2/\partial x^2$, showing that the difference scheme (6.34) does indeed generate an exact solution. Such delicate cancellation of numerical error has been exploited in the construction of highly accurate techniques often referred to as "modified equation" methods [323, 98].

6.2.5 Energy analysis

The energetic analysis of scheme (6.34) is very similar to that of the wave equation itself. It is easiest to begin with the scheme defined over the unbounded spatial domain $\mathcal{D} = \mathbb{Z}$. Taking the inner product of scheme (6.34) with the grid function defined by $\delta_t . u$, which is an approximation to the velocity, gives

$$\langle \delta_t . u, \delta_{tt} u\rangle_{\mathbb{Z}} = \gamma^2 \langle \delta_t . u, \delta_{xx} u\rangle_{\mathbb{Z}}$$

After employing summation by parts (see Section 5.2.10), one has

$$\langle \delta_t . u, \delta_{tt} u\rangle_{\mathbb{Z}} + \gamma^2 \langle \delta_{x+}\delta_t . u, \delta_{x+} u\rangle_{\mathbb{Z}} = 0$$

This may be written as the total difference

$$\delta_{t+}\left(\frac{1}{2}\|\delta_{t-}u\|_{\mathbb{Z}}^2 + \frac{\gamma^2}{2}\langle \delta_{x+}u, e_{t-}\delta_{x+}u\rangle_{\mathbb{Z}}\right)$$

or, after identifying the terms inside the parentheses above with kinetic and potential energy, as

$$\delta_{t+}\mathfrak{h} = 0 \qquad\qquad (6.44)$$

with

$$\mathfrak{t} = \frac{1}{2}\|\delta_{t-}u\|_{\mathbb{Z}}^2 \qquad \mathfrak{v} = \frac{\gamma^2}{2}\langle \delta_{x+}u, e_{t-}\delta_{x+}u\rangle_{\mathbb{Z}} \qquad \mathfrak{h} = \mathfrak{t} + \mathfrak{v} \qquad\qquad (6.45)$$

The total difference (6.44) above is a statement of conservation of numerical energy for the scheme (6.34), and it thus follows that

$$\mathfrak{h}^n = \mathfrak{h}^0$$

Scheme (6.34) is exactly conservative, in a numerical sense, for this special case of a spatial domain of infinite extent. This is true regardless of the values chosen for the time step k and the grid spacing h—and whether or not the scheme is stable! Just as in the case of the scheme for the SHO, discussed in Chapter 3, in an implementation, there will be variations in the energy on the order of "machine epsilon." See Figure 6.14 for an illustration of this.

6.2.6 Numerical boundary conditions

In order to examine boundary conditions, consider scheme (6.34) defined over the semi-infinite domain $\mathcal{D} = \mathbb{Z}^+$. Now, an inner product of scheme (6.34) with $\delta_t . u$ over $\mathbb{Z}^+$ gives

$$\langle \delta_t . u, \delta_{tt} u\rangle_{\mathbb{Z}^+} = \gamma^2 \langle \delta_t . u, \delta_{xx} u\rangle_{\mathbb{Z}^+}$$

After employing summation by parts, according to (5.25), boundary terms appear, i.e.,

$$\langle \delta_t . u, \delta_{tt} u\rangle_{\mathbb{Z}^+} + \gamma^2 \langle \delta_{x+}\delta_t . u, \delta_{x+} u\rangle_{\mathbb{Z}^+} = \mathfrak{b} \triangleq -\gamma^2 (\delta_t . u_0)(\delta_{x-}u_0)$$

or

$$\delta_{t+}\mathfrak{h} = \mathfrak{b}$$

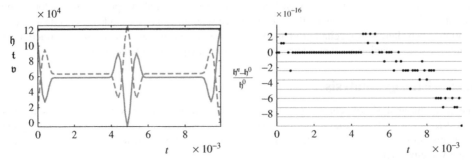

Figure 6.14 Numerical energy conservation for scheme (6.34), with $\gamma = 100$, $f_s = 8000$ and $\lambda = 1$, and where the initial condition is a plucked cosine distribution, centered at $x = 0.5$, of amplitude 1 and half-width 0.1. At left, the total energy $\mathfrak{h}$ (solid black line), $\mathfrak{v}$ (solid grey line), and $\mathfrak{t}$ (dotted grey line) are plotted against time; notice that it is possible, at certain instants, for the numerical potential energy $\mathfrak{v}$ to take on negative values. At right, the variation of the energy $(\mathfrak{h}^n - \mathfrak{h}^0)/\mathfrak{h}^0$ is also plotted against time; multiples of the bit quantization error are plotted as solid grey lines.

with

$$\mathfrak{t} = \frac{1}{2}\|\delta_{t-}u\|_{\mathbb{Z}^+}^2 \qquad \mathfrak{v} = \frac{\gamma^2}{2}\langle\delta_{x+}u, e_{t-}\delta_{x+}u\rangle_{\mathbb{Z}^+} \qquad \mathfrak{h} = \mathfrak{t} + \mathfrak{v} \tag{6.46}$$

One again has exact conservation under the conditions

$$u_0 = 0 \qquad \text{or} \qquad \delta_{x-}u_0 = 0 \longrightarrow u_0 = u_{-1} \tag{6.47}$$

The first condition above is exactly equivalent to the Dirichlet (or fixed) boundary condition at a left endpoint, and the second is a first difference approximation to the Neumann condition; although it refers to a virtual grid point at index $l = -1$, in fact the condition indicates how to eliminate this variable by setting it in terms of the values in the domain interior (in this case, the value of the grid function at u_0). Thus, at $l = 0$, scheme (6.35) may be modified to

$$u_0^{n+1} = (2 - \lambda^2)\,u_0^n - u_0^{n-1} + \lambda^2 u_1^n$$

Alternative inner products and boundary conditions

As mentioned in Section 6.1.9, there are many possibilities for boundary termination of the continuous-time–space wave equation beyond the simple Dirichlet and Neumann conditions. In the case of a numerical method, such as (6.34), the number of possible terminations becomes even greater, as there is a multiplicity of ways of approximating a given continuous boundary condition in a discrete setting. Indeed, with the right choice of inner product, one may prove numerical stability for other numerical boundary conditions, some of which may have benefits in terms of accuracy. The Dirichlet condition $u = 0$ at a boundary of the domain is relatively easy to deal with, numerically: a condition of $u_0 = 0$ falls immediately out of energy analysis, and is exact. The approximation to the Neumann condition arrived at in this way involves a non-centered first difference. One might wonder about the energetic behavior of a centered condition, such as $\delta_x.u_0$. To this end, the energy analysis of scheme (6.34) is performed as previously, but the alternative inner product $\langle\cdot, \cdot\rangle'_{\mathbb{Z}^+}$, as defined in Section 5.2.9, is used instead. In this case, one has

$$\delta_{t+}\mathfrak{h} = \mathfrak{b} \triangleq -\gamma^2 \delta_t.u_0 \delta_x.u_0 \tag{6.48}$$

with

$$t = \frac{1}{2} \left(\|\delta_{t-}u\|'_{\mathbb{Z}+} \right)^2 \qquad \mathfrak{v} = \frac{\gamma^2}{2} \langle \delta_{x+}u, e_{t-}\delta_{x+}u \rangle_{\mathbb{Z}+} \qquad \mathfrak{h} = t + \mathfrak{v}$$

One again has exact conservation under the conditions

$$u_0 = 0 \qquad \text{or} \qquad \delta_x.u_0 = 0 \longrightarrow u_1 = u_{-1}$$

The primed inner product also makes for a convenient analysis of the lossy boundary condition (6.22). Consider the numerical approximation

$$\delta_t.u_0 = \alpha \delta_x.u_0 \tag{6.49}$$

In this case, $\mathfrak{b} = -\alpha\gamma^2 (\delta_t.u_0)^2 \le 0$, so that numerical energy is non-increasing. (Under a particular choice of α, this boundary condition has the interesting property of being numerically perfectly absorbing—see Problem 6.6 and Programming Exercise 6.3.)

6.2.7   Bounds on solution size and numerical stability

One might wonder how the concept of numerical stability, which follows from frequency domain analysis, intervenes in the energetic framework for scheme (6.34). Take, as a starting point, the expressions for numerical energy in (6.46), in the case of scheme (6.34) defined over $\mathcal{D} = \mathbb{Z}^+$, under conservative numerical boundary conditions (6.47). The key point, just as for the case of the SHO, is that in contrast with the energy $\mathfrak{H}$ defined for the continuous system, $\mathfrak{h}$ is not necessarily positive definite, due to the indefinite nature of the numerical potential energy term $\mathfrak{v}$. To determine conditions under which the numerical energy $\mathfrak{h}$ is positive definite, one may proceed as in the case of the SHO, and write, for the potential energy,

$$\mathfrak{v} = \frac{\gamma^2}{2} \langle \delta_{x+}u, e_{t-}\delta_{x+}u \rangle_{\mathbb{Z}+} = \frac{\gamma^2}{2} \left(\|\delta_{x+}\mu_{t-}u\|^2_{\mathbb{Z}+} - \frac{k^2}{4} \|\delta_{x+}\delta_{t-}u\|^2_{\mathbb{Z}+} \right)$$

$$\ge \frac{\gamma^2}{2} \left(\|\delta_{x+}\mu_{t-}u\|^2_{\mathbb{Z}+} - \frac{k^2}{h^2} \|\delta_{t-}u\|^2_{\mathbb{Z}+} \right)$$

In the equality above, the identity (2.22f) for time difference operators has been used, and in the inequality, the bound (5.29) on spatial differences. Thus, one has for the total energy,

$$\mathfrak{h} = t + \mathfrak{v} \ge \frac{1}{2} \left(1 - \lambda^2 \right) \|\delta_{t-}u\|^2_{\mathbb{Z}+} + \frac{\gamma^2}{2} \|\delta_{x+}\mu_{t-}u\|^2_{\mathbb{Z}+}$$

This discrete conserved energy is thus non-negative under the condition $\lambda \le 1$, which is the CFL condition (6.40) arrived at using von Neumann analysis.

In order to obtain a general bound on the solution size, independent of boundary conditions, one may note that under the condition (6.40), one then has

$$\|\delta_{t-}u\|_{\mathbb{Z}+} \le \sqrt{\frac{2\mathfrak{h}^0}{1 - \lambda^2}}$$

which implies, further, that for the grid function u^n at any time step n, one must have

$$\|u^n\|_{\mathbb{Z}+} \le nk \sqrt{\frac{2\mathfrak{h}^0}{1 - \lambda^2}}$$

Thus, just as for the bound (6.25) in the case of the continuous wave equation, growth of the l_2 norm of the discrete solution is no faster than linear. If boundary conditions are of Dirichlet or fixed type, then, just as in the continuous case, better bounds are available. See Problem 6.7.

Instability at boundaries

The proper discretization of boundary conditions is a very delicate business, as far as stability is concerned—though, for a simple system such as the wave equation, the "obvious" numerical choices turn out to work properly, for more complex systems, there are many more choices, and thus many more ways to go astray.

As a rudimentary (though somewhat artificial) example of a "bad" choice of boundary condition in the present case of scheme (6.34) for the wave equation, consider the following Neumann-type condition at grid point $l = 0$:

$$\alpha\delta_{x-}u_0 + (1 - \alpha)\delta_{x.}u = 0$$

where α is a free parameter. This can be viewed as a weighted linear combination of the two conditions $\delta_{x-}u_0 = 0$ and $\delta_{x.}u_0 = 0$, both of which lead to stable simulation results. One might argue then that such a condition must also lead to stable results, but depending on the choice of α, it can become unstable, as illustrated in Figure 6.15, with a choice of $\alpha = -0.05$. Notice that this instability is of a different nature from that resulting from the violation of the CFL condition, as shown in Figure 6.10. Here, the unstable behavior originates from the boundary location itself, rather than over the entire domain. From a programming and debugging standpoint, it is obviously helpful to be able to classify such types of instability. It is interesting to note that the boundary condition above is conservative, provided one makes the right choice of inner product to build an energy function. Thus, again, energy conservation is not sufficient for numerical stability, but it is rather non-negativity of this conserved energy which is required. See Problem 6.8.

The analysis of numerical stability, including the effect of boundary conditions, has been carried out by many authors. One classic and very powerful technique, proposed by Gustaffson, Kreiss, and Sundstrom [162], Kreiss [209], and Osher [263], is based on frequency domain analysis of the combined scheme/boundary condition system, and reduces essentially to conditions on root locations in the complex plane. Another technique involves performing eigenvalue analysis of a scheme, when written in state space form—see the next section. This is often referred to as the "matrix method." As might be apparent, such a technique is generally applicable to systems which are LTI (and not merely LSI), though the extension to nonlinear systems becomes problematic. The greater difficulty, pointed out by Strikwerda [342] is that such analysis does not give much guidance as to how to how to proceed if, indeed, the eigenvalue analysis reveals a stray unstable mode. Energy analysis can give sufficient conditions for stability under a particular choice of boundary condition, in an insightful way. As an example, consider the wave equation defined over $\mathbb{R}^+$, with the radiation boundary condition (6.23) applied to the left end (this condition is crucial for brass and woodwind instrument modeling). Here is one possible numerical boundary condition:

$$\delta_{x.}u_0 = \alpha_1\delta_{t.}u_0 + \alpha_2u_0 \tag{6.50}$$

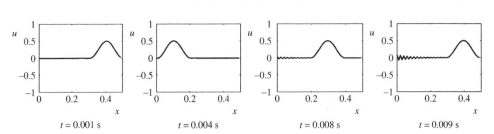

$t = 0.001$ s $t = 0.004$ s $t = 0.008$ s $t = 0.009$ s

Figure 6.15 Numerical instability at an improperly chosen boundary condition, using scheme (6.34), for the wave equation with $\gamma = 50$, and running at a sample rate of $10\,000$ Hz. In this case, as an approximation to the Neumann condition at $x = 0$, the condition $\alpha\delta_{x-}u_0 + (1 - \alpha)\delta_{x.}u_0 = 0$ is used with a value of $\alpha = -0.05$. The initial condition is of plucked type, using a raised cosine distribution. Not long after the plot shown in the last panel, the computed values are out of range.

From the numerical energy balance (6.48) in the primed inner product, one has, for the boundary term $\mathfrak{b}$,

$$\mathfrak{b} = -\gamma^2\alpha_1\,(\delta_t.u_0)^2 - \gamma^2\alpha_2\,(\delta_t.u_0)\,u_0 = -\gamma^2\alpha_1\,(\delta_t.u_0)^2 - \frac{\gamma^2\alpha_2}{2}\delta_{t+}\,(u_0e_t - u_0)$$

where, in the second step above, identity (2.22b) has been employed. Now, however, one may write, for energy balance (6.48),

$$\delta_{t+}\,(\mathfrak{h} + \mathfrak{h}_b) = -\gamma^2\alpha_1\,(\delta_t.u_0)^2 \qquad \text{where} \qquad \mathfrak{h}_b = \frac{\gamma^2\alpha_2}{2}u_0e_t - u_0 \tag{6.51}$$

This balance, involving a stored energy over the problem interior ($\mathfrak{h}$) and at the boundary ($\mathfrak{h}_b$), is completely analogous to (6.24) for the continuous system. The numerical energy of the system as a whole must decrease. But, as before, it is the positivity condition on the new combined numerical energy which leads to a stability condition. One may write, for $\mathfrak{h}$ and $\mathfrak{h}_b$, using steps similar to those employed previously,

$$\mathfrak{h} \geq \frac{1}{2}\left(1 - \lambda^2\right)\left(\|\delta_t - u\|'_{\mathbb{Z}+}\right)^2 \qquad \mathfrak{h}_b \geq -\frac{\gamma^2\alpha_2k^2}{8}\,(\delta_t - u_0)^2$$

or

$$\mathfrak{h} + \mathfrak{h}_b \geq \sum_{l=1}^{\infty}\frac{h}{2}\left(1 - \lambda^2\right)(\delta_t - u_l)^2 + \left(\frac{h}{4}\left(1 - \lambda^2\right) - \frac{\lambda^2\alpha_2h^2}{8}\right)(\delta_t - u_0)^2$$

The first term above is non-negative under the CFL condition (6.40). For the second term, however, the condition is more strict:

$$\lambda \leq \frac{1}{1 + \alpha_2h/2} \tag{6.52}$$

The above condition is sufficient for stability under the boundary condition (6.50). It is not, however, necessary, and there do exist other numerical boundary conditions which do not lead to an extra interfering condition—see Problem 6.9 and Programming Exercise 6.4. Similar issues arise when dealing with connections with lumped objects—see, e.g., Section 7.7.1 for an example, and a general principle behind ensuring numerical stability for connections of objects.

6.2.8   Matrix form and modes

For those with a background in electrical engineering, it may be helpful to rewrite the difference scheme (6.34) in state space, or vector–matrix form. Though in this book the difference operators are sparse, and thus not do not require full storage in matrix form, for implicit schemes it will be necessary to solve linear systems involving such matrices.

Suppose that the values of the grid function u_l^n to be computed at time step n are arranged in a finite-length column vector $\mathbf{u}$. (If it is necessary to compute values of the grid function at the endpoints, the vector will be of the form $\mathbf{u}^n = [u_0^n, \ldots, u_N^n]^T$; if not, then it will be of the form $\mathbf{u}^n = [u_1^n, \ldots, u_{N-1}^n]^T$.) The operator δ_{xx} in matrix form must be specialized from the infinite form given in (5.17), taking boundary conditions into account. Some examples of such forms include those given in (5.19).

Regardless of the exact form of $\mathbf{D}_{xx}$, difference scheme (6.34) may be written, in vector–matrix form, as

$$\mathbf{u}^{n+1} = \left(2\mathbf{I} + \gamma^2k^2\mathbf{D}_{xx}\right)\mathbf{u}^n - \mathbf{u}^{n-1} \qquad \text{or} \qquad \underbrace{\begin{bmatrix} \mathbf{u}^{n+1} \\ \mathbf{u}^n \end{bmatrix}}_{\mathbf{w}^{n+1}} = \underbrace{\begin{bmatrix} 2\mathbf{I} + \gamma^2k^2\mathbf{D}_{xx} & -\mathbf{I} \\ \mathbf{I} & 0 \end{bmatrix}}_{\mathbf{A}}\underbrace{\begin{bmatrix} \mathbf{u}^n \\ \mathbf{u}^{n-1} \end{bmatrix}}_{\mathbf{w}^n}$$

where, here, $\mathbf{I}$ and $\mathbf{0}$ indicate identity and zero matrices of the appropriate size. The first form above is a two-step recursion in the vector $\mathbf{u}^n$, and the second a one-step recursion in the expanded vector $\mathbf{w}^n = [(\mathbf{u}^n)^T, (\mathbf{u}^{n-1})^T]^T$, which can be thought of as the state of the finite difference scheme (6.34). The one-step form is known as a state space representation. Examining the first form above, and assuming solutions of the form $\mathbf{u} = \boldsymbol{\phi} z^n$, the characteristic equation

$$\frac{1}{k^2}(z - 2 + z^{-1})\boldsymbol{\phi} = \gamma^2 \mathbf{D}_{xx}\boldsymbol{\phi}$$

results. The solutions, $\boldsymbol{\phi}_p$, which are the eigenvectors of $\mathbf{D}_{xx}$, whatever form it takes, can be interpreted as the modal functions of difference scheme (6.34); due to discretization error, they will be distinct from the modes of the wave equation itself. The associated modal frequencies ω_p will then be given as solutions to the quadratic equations

$$z_p + (-2 - \gamma^2 k^2 \mathrm{eig}_p(\mathbf{D}_{xx})) + z_p^{-1} = 0$$

where $\mathrm{eig}_p(\mathbf{D}_{xx})$ signifies "pth eigenvalue of," and where $z_p = e^{j\omega_p k}$. If the eigenvalues of $\mathbf{D}_{xx}$ satisfy the condition $-4/\gamma^2 k^2 \leq \mathrm{eig}(\mathbf{D}_{xx}) \leq 0$ (this is similar to the CFL condition (6.40) for the scheme), then the roots of this characteristic equation will be on the unit circle, with the numerical frequencies given by

$$\omega_p = \frac{2}{k} \sin^{-1}\left(k\gamma\sqrt{-\mathrm{eig}_p(\mathbf{D}_{xx})}\right) \tag{6.53}$$

Numerical inharmonicity

In a musical setting, the perceptual counterpart to numerical dispersion, or the artifact of variation in wave speed with frequency, is a detuning of modal frequencies from those of the model equation itself; normally, for finite difference schemes, this will be an effect of increasing importance with higher frequencies.

As an example, consider the 1D wave equation, with parameter $\gamma = 882$, under fixed boundary conditions. The modal frequencies are integer multiples of $\gamma/2 = 441$. It is interesting to look at the behavior of the modal frequencies of scheme (6.34), operating at sample rate $f_s = 44\,100\,\mathrm{Hz}$, under different choices of the Courant number λ—these may be calculated from (6.53) above. See Table 6.1.

There are several things worth noting here. As expected, the frequencies are exact when $\lambda = 1$. For other values of λ, the frequencies become successively detuned from these exact values, both as the modal frequencies become higher and as λ is moved away from the stability condition at $\lambda = 1$. On the other hand, even under dispersive conditions, the detuning of modal frequencies is rather small and, in the worst case over the range of frequencies less than $3000\,\mathrm{Hz}$, a little under

Table 6.1 Modal frequencies, in Hertz, for scheme (6.34) for the wave equation, with $\gamma = 882$, and under fixed boundary conditions, operating at a sample rate of $f_s = 44\,100\,\mathrm{Hz}$.

Mode number	$\lambda = 1$	$\lambda = 0.98$	$\lambda = 0.94$	$\lambda = 0.9$	$\lambda = 0.8$
1	441.0	441.0	441.0	441.0	441.0
2	882.0	882.0	881.9	881.8	881.7
3	1323.0	1322.9	1322.7	1322.5	1321.9
4	1764.0	1763.8	1763.4	1762.9	1761.4
5	2205.0	2204.6	2203.8	2202.9	2199.9
6	2646.0	2645.3	2643.9	2642.3	2637.0

6 cents. This is a rather complex issue, psychoacoustically speaking. One might argue that, given that human frequency sensitivity is very limited beyond about 3000 Hz [421], numerical dispersion is thus not really of perceptual importance. This is partly true—in fact, the sound output generated using such an algorithm will indeed have a pitch of almost exactly 441 Hz, under various choices of λ, as the reader may wish to verify by running the code example provided in Section A.4. What the reader will also notice, however, for values of λ away from 1, is that the inharmonic upper partials tend to become very closely spaced in the upper range of the spectrum (see, e.g., Figure 6.13), generating a somewhat unpleasant noise-like component to the output! Though in more realistic models, of, for example, strings, such an effect will always be subsumed by losses which are strong at high frequencies, the conclusion here is that the question of the perceptual importance of numerical dispersion depends strongly on the problem at hand, and is an important design consideration if one is employing direct simulation techniques—indeed, modal methods, as well as digital waveguides in the 1D case, exhibit no such effect. Another source of detuning is the precise nature of the numerical boundary condition—although the numerical Dirichlet condition applied to the scheme (6.34) is indeed exact, this is not necessarily true of other conditions. The Neumann condition is one example—see Programming Exercise 6.5.

6.2.9   Output and interpolation

The generation of sound output is, obviously, the end goal of physical modeling synthesis. A complete consideration of the signal path from a vibrating object to the human eardrum is enormously complex, and depends not merely on the vibrating object itself, but also on the geometry and other properties of the room in which it is vibrating, the position of the listener with respect to the instrument, etc. In principle, one could attempt a full time domain simulation of the accompanying ambient system, but such a calculation is gargantuan, and dwarfs that of the vibrating object. Some comments on the feasibility of full 3D room acoustics simulations appear in Section 14.1.1. From the vantage point of synthesis (rather than pure musical acoustics), such models are overkill—if one is interested in ambient effects, one is far better off making use of standard reverberation models based on psychoacoustic considerations [334]. Indeed, as wave propagation in acoustic spaces is linear, the entire perceptual effect of the room on a generated musical sound can be well described using transfer function models, using as an input the vibration amplitude of the musical object at its surface. For these reasons, in this book, output will be limited to direct reading of vibration amplitude—if one wants to go further and add in room effects, one may do so in a subsequent step!

For a time domain method, certainly the easiest way to generate output is to merely read a value from the grid function as it is being updated, at a given observation point. In the case of scheme (6.34), and supposing that the output location is x_o, this may be done using interpolation—see Section 5.2.4. If $I_p(x_o)$ is the corresponding pth-order interpolation operator, an output time series u_o^n may be generated from the grid function u_l^n for scheme (6.34) as

$$u_o^n = I_p(x_o)u_l^n$$

This is a "feedforward" step, and there is thus no risk of instability, once u^n has been calculated. It is also extremely cheap—no more than a handful of operations are required for this computation, and certainly far fewer than the number required by the recursion (6.34) itself. Indeed, if the output location is fixed, it is probably a good idea to use zeroth-order interpolation (i.e., rounding of the output location to that of the grid point to its left), and avoid arithmetic altogether. One may wish to process the time series u_o^n with, for example, a low-order filter which crudely models radiation effects, similar to those which arise in speech synthesis applications [280].

As expected, there will be a spectral effect associated with the choice of output location—see Figure 6.16, where output waveforms and frequency spectra are plotted for distinct output locations.

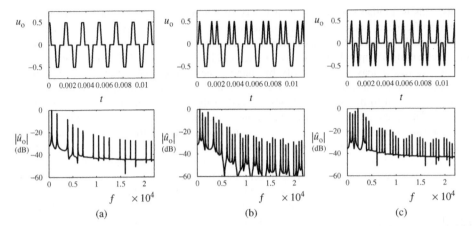

Figure 6.16 Output of scheme (6.34), with $f_s = 44\,100\,\text{Hz}$ and $\gamma = 1102.5$, with an initial "plucked" condition of the form of a sharp pulse centered at $x = 0.6$, at different locations: (a) at $x_0 = 0.5$; (b) at $x_0 = 0.3$; and (c) at $x_0 = 0.1$. In each case, the output waveform is shown at top, and the frequency spectrum at bottom.

In the present case of the 1D wave equation, this is perhaps easiest to understand by inspection of a modal representation, such as that given (6.29), where fixed boundary conditions are employed. If output is read from the domain center, at $x_0 = 1/2$, all even-numbered harmonics will necessarily be absent from the output spectrum, as can be seen clearly in Figure 6.16(a). More generally, the choice of output location leads to spectral windowing effects, or a "modulation" of the relative amplitudes of the various harmonics.

Moving output locations

For a time domain method, there is no reason why the output location cannot itself be moving—see the footnote on page 101 for some justification for this. Indeed, the idea of reading from a physical model at variable locations has been proposed as a synthesis technique known as "scanned synthesis" [401], though in that case the readout point may be moving at audio rates, effectively modulating the output of the physical model. Here, however, it will be assumed that the motion is slow relative to the speed of wave propagation, leading to a phasing effect, as various harmonics are cancelled. See Figure 6.17. In contrast to the case of a static output location, good interpolation will be necessary, otherwise audible distortions ("clicks," as well as potentially time-varying low passing) will occur in the output.

Multiple output locations

It is also straightforward, once one has computed a grid function u_l^n, to read output simultaneously at various points—these will exhibit some slight spectral variations. When mapped to different loudspeakers (possibly many), the spectral variations serve as a crude but effective means of spatializing physical modeling output. Reading outputs from multiple locations also serves to reduce, at least perceptually, the effects of spectral "holes" which follow inevitably from the choice of a single output location.

It is important to note that, for time domain methods, computational cost is approximately independent of the number of outputs, because the entire state of the virtual object is directly observable. In this sense, multiple outputs come "for free." The same is true for digital waveguide models, but not for methods based on modal synthesis—see the comments on this topic in

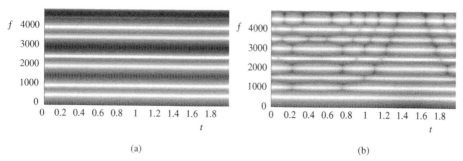

(a)   (b)

Figure 6.17   Spectrograms of output of scheme (6.34), with $f_s = 44\,100\,\text{Hz}$ and $\gamma = 1000$, under a "plucked" initial condition of the form of a sharp spike. In (a) the output location is fixed at $x = 1/3$, and in (b) the output location varies sinusoidally about $x = 1/3$, at a sub-audio rate.

Section 6.6. See also Programming Exercise 6.6, which deals with multiple moving output locations in the case of the wave equation.

6.2.10   Implementation details and computational requirements

Now that the finite difference scheme (6.34) has been examined from many different perspectives, it is worth discussing some of the practical considerations that arise when one settles down to program such a method for synthesis. Basic example code is provided in Section A.4 for reference on the points raised here.

One minor consideration is that of the choice of time step k and grid spacing h. For synthesis (in stark opposition to other mainstream applications), it is the time step which is chosen first, as $k = 1/f_s$, where f_s is a typical audio sample rate such as $f_s = 32\,000, 44\,100, 48\,000\,\text{Hz}$, etc. The grid spacing h must then be chosen according to the CFL condition (6.40). At least in the case of the 1D wave equation, a choice of $\lambda = 1$ is ideal, as it leads to an exact solution. But in real-world applications, the spatial domain will always be the unit interval $\mathcal{D} = \mathbb{U}$, and the grid spacing h must then divide this domain into an integer number of parts,[6], i.e., $h = 1/N$, for some integer N. As discussed in Section 6.2.3, however, it is always advantageous to choose the grid spacing such that the CFL condition is satisfied as near to equality as possible. Thus, in an initial step, one may choose N as

$$N := \text{floor}(1/\gamma k), \qquad \text{then} \qquad h := 1/N \qquad \text{and set} \qquad \lambda := \gamma k / h$$

For sufficiently high sample rates and low values of γ (or fundamental frequency), the dispersion introduced will be minimal. Another strategy is to choose $\lambda = 1$ and h accordingly, and allow the domain to be of a length slightly different from 1—this is less desirable, however, as it can lead to an audible mistuning of the fundamental, a phenomenon which does not occur if the previous method is employed. Digital waveguide methods on the other hand (see the next section) rely on the choice of $\lambda = 1$, and thus only this second method is viable; precise tuning must be carried out using filter terminations (such as fractional delays [215]).

In general, the computational requirements will depend on the choice of the sample rate, the grid spacing (mediated by the CFL condition), as well as the complexity of the scheme footprint. In this case, as may be read from the explicit form of the recursion (6.35), updating at a given grid point requires, for a general choice of λ, two multiplications and three additions, or five arithmetic operations. When the domain is limited to the unit interval, evaluations at approximately $1/h$ such

---

[6] This is not strictly true—one could choose $h = \gamma k$, and then develop a special interpolated boundary condition at a grid point which does not lie directly on the boundary.

points will be required—one says approximately because, depending on boundary conditions, one will have some minor variations in the number of grid points. Thus $5/h$ arithmetic operations are required per step in the recursion, and thus, in 1 second, $5/hk$ operations will be required. If h and k are chosen according to (6.40) close to equality, then the full count will be $5f_s^2/\gamma$ operations per second. Thus computational complexity scales as the square of the sample rate. The number N_{fd} of required units of memory is as given in (6.41), corresponding to two grid functions' worth of data. Note that in the implementation in Section A.4, for programming simplicity, three separate grid functions are used—these can be reduced to two, in the same way as for the SHO—see Section 3.2.7 and Programming Exercise 3.1.

6.2.11 Digital waveguide interpretation

Consider the scheme (6.34), for the special case of $\lambda = 1$. As noted in Section 6.2.3, the numerical phase and group velocities of the scheme are identical to those of the wave equation itself, and thus independent of frequency. The expanded recursion (6.35) reads, now, as

$$u_l^{n+1} = u_{l+1}^n + u_{l-1}^n - u_l^{n-1} \tag{6.54}$$

Notice, in particular, that (1) there are no longer any multiplications necessary to update the scheme, and (2) the center grid point in the scheme footprint (see Figure 6.8) is no longer used. It is straightforward to identify this simplified scheme as an exact traveling wave solution to the wave equation. First consider the traveling wave solutions themselves, defined by

$$w^{(+)}(x, t) = u^{(+)}(x - \gamma t) \qquad w^{(-)}(x, t) = u^{(-)}(x + \gamma t)$$

At a location $x = lh$, $t = nk$, one has, immediately, that

$$w^{(+)}(lh, nk) = u^{(+)}(lh - \gamma nk) = u^{(+)}(h(l - n)) = u^{(+)}(h(l - 1) - h(n - 1))$$
$$= w^{(+)}((l - 1)h, (n - 1)h)$$
$$w^{(-)}(lh, nk) = u^{(-)}(lh + \gamma nk) = u^{(-)}(h(l + n)) = u^{(-)}(h(l + 1) + h(n - 1))$$
$$= w^{(-)}((l + 1)h, (n - 1)h)$$

The above relations follow only under the condition that $\lambda = 1$, or, equivalently, that $h = \gamma k$. Notice that no approximations have been employed as yet. Replacing the functions $w^{(+)}$ and $w^{(-)}$ by grid functions, or wave variables, one has

$$w_l^{(+),n} = w_{l-1}^{(+),n-1} \qquad w_l^{(-),n} = w_{l+1}^{(-),n-1} \qquad u_l^n = w_l^{(+),n} + w_l^{(-),n} \tag{6.55}$$

The first two identities above indicate propagation of discrete wavelike variables to the right and left respectively, and the third that the observable physical variable u may be written as a sum of two such waves.

Given the three definitions above, one may then write

$$u_l^{n+1} = w_l^{(+),n+1} + w_l^{(-),n+1} = w_{l-1}^{(+),n} + w_{l+1}^{(-),n} = u_{l+1}^n + u_{l-1}^n - w_{l-1}^{(-),n} - w_{l+1}^{(+),n}$$
$$= u_{l+1}^n + u_{l-1}^n - w_l^{(-),n-1} - w_l^{(+),n-1}$$
$$= u_{l+1}^n + u_{l-1}^n - u_l^{n-1}$$

which is identical to the simplified scheme (6.54).

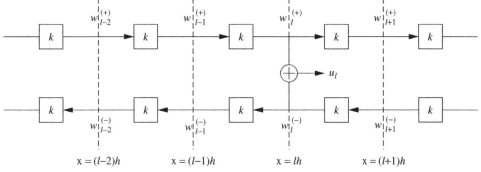

Figure 6.18 Schematic showing the delay-line or digital waveguide interpretation of (6.55). Here, delays of duration k seconds are indicated by boxes. The spacing between grid locations h must be related to the delay k by $h = \gamma k$.

The key to an efficient implementation is the recognition of the fact that the solution may be advanced purely though shifting operations applied to the wave variables $w^{(+)}$ and $w^{(-)}$. u itself need only be computed in a "feedforward" step at points at which an output is desired. See Figure 6.18. Typically, in audio, scalar outputs only are desired, and one does not need to observe the entire state of the object under consideration. There is thus a major distinction between sound synthesis and other applications, which perhaps explains why, although such exact discrete traveling wave solutions to the wave equation have been known for decades [8], this potential for increased efficiency was only seized upon later by Smith [334]. More will be said about this is Section 6.6.

In terms of the wave variables $w^{(+)}$ and $w^{(-)}$, as mentioned above, only shifting operations are required to advance the solution, leading to the well-known bidirectional delay-line form, as shown in Figure 6.18. For the sake of reference, an implementation of the digital waveguide is provided in Section A.5.

Initialization may be carried out through some discrete approximation to (6.12). That is, if the continuous initializing functions $u_0(x)$ and $q_0(x) = \int v_0(x')dx'$ are known, they may be sampled directly to yield the wave variables as

$$w_l^{(+),0} = \frac{1}{2}u_0(lh) - \frac{1}{2\gamma}q_0(lh) \qquad w_l^{(-),0} = \frac{1}{2}u_0(lh) + \frac{1}{2\gamma}q_0(lh)$$

This is clearly simpler when the excitation is of "plucked" type (i.e., $v_0(x) = 0$). If $q_0(x)$ is not expressible in closed form, then $v_0(x)$ may be integrated numerically—for instance, one could recursively generate the grid function $q_{0,l} = q_{0,l-1} + hv_0(lh)$, and use it in place of the samples $q_0(lh)$ in the above formula.

Boundary conditions

Boundary termination of digital waveguides can be quite straightforward. The most common types are as shown in Figure 6.19, in the case of a termination at the left end of the domain.

Termination with sign inversion, with the leftward-propagating delay line feeding back into the rightward propagating line, is particularly easy to analyze. If the termination point is situated directly on the boundary, at $x = 0$, then one has $w_0^{(+),n} = -w_0^{(-),n}$. This immediately implies, from summing of waves as per (6.55), that $u_0^n = w_0^{(+),n} + w_0^{(-),n} = 0$, corresponding to the Dirichlet-type numerical boundary condition (see Section 6.1.9).

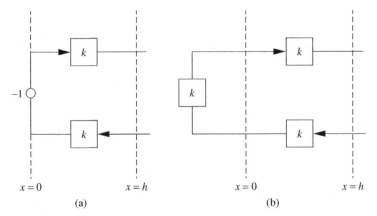

Figure 6.19 Terminations of a digital waveguide at a left end corresponding to (a) a fixed or Dirichlet boundary condition, and (b) a free or Neumann condition.

Another type of termination involves feeding back the signal from the leftward-propagating delay line into the rightward-propagating delay line, without sign inversion, and with an extra element of delay. It can be shown that this corresponds to a Neumann-type numerical boundary condition in scheme (6.34):

$$u_0^{n+1} = w_0^{(+),n+1} + w_0^{(-),n+1} = w_0^{(-),n} + w_1^{(-),n} = u_0^n - w_0^{(+),n} + u_1^n - w_1^{(+),n}$$

$$= u_0^n + u_1^n - w_0^{(-),n-1} - w_0^{(+),n-1}$$

$$= u_0^n + u_1^n - u_0^{n-1}$$

This is exactly the scheme (6.34), with $\lambda = 1$, at the grid point $l = 0$, under the condition that $\delta_{x-}u_0 = 0$.

Both these conditions have been shown, earlier, to conserve numerical energy, leading to stability conditions. In the waveguide picture, however, stability is obvious: the delay line is itself clearly lossless, and terminations such as sign inversions or delays cannot serve to cause solution growth. More elaborate settings for boundary conditions terminating digital waveguides are a central feature of waveguide modeling. See the text by Smith [334] for much more on this topic.

There is obviously a lot more to say about waveguides, and though there will be some further reference to scattering structures (see Section 6.6 in this chapter for some comments on waveguides and a comparison with other synthesis methods, Section 9.2.4 for the case of the Kelly–Lochbaum speech synthesis model, and Section 11.4 for the 2D extension of the digital waveguide), the present treatment must unfortunately end here. The interested reader is referred to the ample literature on this subject—see the references in Section 1.2.3.

6.3   Other schemes

Given that scheme (6.34) is exact for $\lambda = 1$, there is not practical interest in exploring more elaborate schemes for the 1D wave equation. On the other hand, few systems permit such an exact solution, and the 1D wave equation is thus quite singular in this regard and not at all representative of any other system of interest in musical acoustics. For this reason, some more complex finite difference constructions are briefly described in this section. For much more on finite difference constructions for the 1D wave equation, see, e.g., [365, 259, 260, 98, 40].

6.3.1 A stencil width of five scheme

An explicit generalization of scheme (6.34) employs a wider stencil-centered approximation to the spatial derivative term:

$$\delta_{tt} u = \gamma^2 \left(\alpha + (1 - \alpha)\mu_{x.}\right) \delta_{xx} u \tag{6.56}$$

This scheme involves a free parameter α, and reduces to scheme (6.34) when $\alpha = 1$; it is nominally second-order accurate in both space and time, which is immediately evident since all operators are centered. Notice the use of the operator $\alpha + (1 - \alpha)\mu_{x.}$, which is an approximation to the identity operation, as discussed at the end of Section 5.2.2. The form above may be expanded into the following recursion:

$$u_l^{n+1} = (2 + \lambda^2(1 - 3\alpha))u_l^n + \lambda^2(2\alpha - 1)\left(u_{l-1}^n + u_{l+1}^n\right) + \frac{\lambda^2}{2}(1 - \alpha)\left(u_{l+2}^n + u_{l-2}^n\right) - u_l^{n-1}$$

This scheme makes use of points two grid spacings removed from the update point, and thus has a stencil width of five. See Figure 6.20(a) for a representation of the stencil or "footprint" corresponding to this scheme.

The characteristic equation for scheme (6.56) is easily obtained, again through the insertion of a test solution of the form $u_l^n = z^n e^{jl\beta h}$:

$$z + \left(-2 + 4\lambda^2\left(1 - 2(1 - \alpha)\sin^2(\beta h/2)\right)\sin^2(\beta h/2)\right) + z^{-1} = 0$$

The condition that the roots of the characteristic equation be of unit magnitude is thus, from (2.15), that

$$0 \leq \lambda^2 \left(1 - 2(1 - \alpha)\sin^2(\beta h/2)\right)\sin^2(\beta h/2) \leq 1$$

for all values of β. In order to approach the analysis of this apparently unwieldy expression, note that what is really needed is to find the maximum and minimum values of a polynomial over an interval. Writing $p = \sin^2(\beta h/2)$, and noting that $0 \leq p \leq 1$, the conditions above may be written as

$$\min_{p\in[0,1]} F(p) \geq 0 \quad \text{and} \quad \lambda^2 \leq \frac{1}{\max_{p\in[0,1]} F(p)} \quad \text{where} \quad F(p) = p(1 - 2(1 - \alpha)p) \tag{6.57}$$

The left-hand inequality is satisfied for

$$\alpha \geq 1/2 \tag{6.58}$$

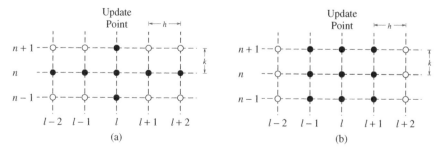

Figure 6.20 Computational stencil of (a) scheme (6.56), and (b) scheme (6.60).

Given the above restriction on α, the right-hand inequality yields a rather complex bound on λ, which is dependent on the chosen value of α:

$$\lambda \leq \begin{cases} \sqrt{8(1-\alpha)}, & \frac{1}{2} \leq \alpha \leq \frac{3}{4} \\ \sqrt{1/(2\alpha-1)}, & \alpha > \frac{3}{4} \end{cases} \tag{6.59}$$

See Problem 6.10.

One problem with the use of such a scheme is that because the stencil or footprint is now wider, it will be necessary to set an additional boundary condition when the scheme is restricted to a finite domain, such as $\mathbb{U}_N$. It is clear that updating u_l^{n+1} at grid points of index $l = 0$ and $l = 1$ requires access to values outside the domain interior, but the wave equation itself allows only a single boundary condition at the endpoint of the domain. This extra numerical boundary condition must thus be set very carefully—this is a general problem with numerical methods of high accuracy which do not operate locally. Energetic analysis for this scheme is also possible, and leads to the same stability conditions above, as well as to proper settings for the numerical boundary conditions; because this scheme is of academic interest only, such analysis will be not be presented here. Energy analysis of wider stencil schemes will, however, be dealt with at a later stage, in the case of the ideal bar, in Section 7.1.4. The choice of the parameter α has a rather large influence on the numerical phase and group velocities (and thus on the tuning of mode frequencies). See Figure 6.21(a).

6.3.2   A compact implicit scheme

A generalization of scheme (6.34) of an entirely different character is the following:

$$(\theta + (1 - \theta)\mu_{x.}) \, \delta_{tt} u = \gamma^2 \delta_{xx} u \tag{6.60}$$

This scheme also involves a free parameter, θ, and reduces to scheme (6.34) when $\theta = 1$, and is again nominally second-order accurate in both space and time. Variants of this scheme have indeed been used for sound synthesis [74] from models of vibrating strings, and xylophone bars [77], though the version presented here is slightly different from that used in the references above (see Problem 6.11). The symbol θ has been chosen to indicate the relationship with so-called

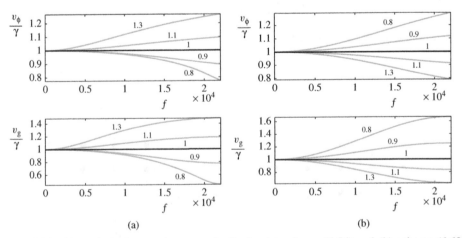

(a)   (b)

Figure 6.21   Numerical phase and group velocity for (a) scheme (6.56) and (b) scheme (6.60), under various choices of the free parameters α and θ, respectively, as indicated.

"θ-schemes," and fractional time-step methods used for simulating first-order equations, particularly in fluid dynamics applications [393].

The following recursion results:

$$\theta u_l^{n+1} + \frac{1-\theta}{2}\left(u_{l+1}^{n+1} + u_{l-1}^{n+1}\right) = \left(\lambda^2 + 1 - \theta\right)\left(u_{l+1}^n + u_{l-1}^n\right) + 2(\theta - \lambda^2)u_l^n - \theta u_l^{n-1}$$
$$+ \frac{\theta - 1}{2}\left(u_{l+1}^{n-1} + u_{l-1}^{n-1}\right)$$

In this case, the values of the grid function at the update time step $n + 1$, written on the left side of the above recursion, are coupled; this is the first instance in this book of a so-called implicit finite difference scheme. It is not possible to solve the above recursion without the use of linear system solution techniques, which are usually more costly than explicit updating. In order to better understand the implementation of such a scheme, matrix representations of difference operators as discussed in Section 5.2.7 are essential. Assuming the column vector $\mathbf{u}^n$ to contain the values of the grid function u_l^n, then the scheme may be written as

$$\mathbf{u}^{n+1} = \mathbf{A}^{-1}\mathbf{B}\mathbf{u}^n - \mathbf{u}^{n-1} \quad \text{with} \quad \mathbf{A} = \theta\mathbf{I} + (1-\theta)\mathbf{M}_x. \quad \mathbf{B} = \gamma^2 k^2 \mathbf{D}_{xx} + 2\mathbf{A}$$

where it is assumed that if the grid function is limited to a finite set of values, boundary conditions (to be discussed shortly) will be incorporated into the above matrices. $\mathbf{D}_{xx}$ and $\mathbf{M}_x$ are matrix representations of the difference operators δ_{xx} and μ_x, which appear, in infinite form, in Section 5.2.7. The real work involved here is in the solution of the linear system involving the matrix $\mathbf{A}$ at each time step. A full matrix inversion of $\mathbf{A}$ (or even full storage of the matrix $\mathbf{A}$ itself) is to be avoided in any implementation, as $\mathbf{A}$ is tridiagonal and thus very sparse, and various fast solution techniques, most notably the Thomas algorithm [354, 342], are often employed. See Programming Exercise 5.6 in the previous chapter, which illustrates the use of all-purpose iterative methods in the Matlab programming environment.

In exchange for this added complexity, such schemes are potentially much more accurate than explicit schemes, and often operate under much looser stability conditions (though it should be kept in mind that in this very special case, scheme (6.60) is exact when $\theta = 1$). To this end, it is worth again writing the characteristic polynomial corresponding to scheme (6.60), again employing the variable $p = \sin^2(\beta h/2)$:

$$(1 - 2(1 - \theta)p)z + (4\lambda^2 p - 2(1 - 2(1 - \theta)p)) + (1 - 2(1 - \theta)p)z^{-1} = 0$$

The stability analysis here is similar to that of the five-point scheme, except that now, one must determine the maximum and minimum values of a rational function over the unit interval; the stability conditions are then

$$\min_{p\in[0,1]} F(p) \geq 0 \quad \text{and} \quad \lambda^2 \leq \frac{1}{\max_{p\in[0,1]} F(p)} \quad \text{where} \quad F(p) = \frac{p}{1 - 2(1 - \theta)p} \tag{6.61}$$

which are satisfied when

$$\theta \geq \frac{1}{2} \quad \text{and} \quad \lambda \leq \sqrt{2\theta - 1} \tag{6.62}$$

See Problem 6.12. Notice here that as θ becomes large, λ can also be large as well, meaning that, for a given grid spacing h, the time step k can become large as well, leading to fewer recursion steps relative to the standard scheme (6.34), for which λ is bounded strictly by 1. This is the justification often given for using implicit methods—though each step in the recursion becomes more complex, computationally, than that of an explicit scheme, one may get away with fewer such steps. For sound synthesis, this is probably the wrong way of looking at the relative merits of explicit and implicit methods. The time step k is fixed, from the outset, from the audio sample rate. A better interpretation is that implicit methods, *operating at a given sample rate*, can allow for much lower numerical dispersion than an explicit scheme *operating at the same sample rate*. Some examples of this will be provided at later stages in this book, especially in the case of bar vibration in Section 7.1.5, but a good question is: in the context of musical sound synthesis, is the reduction of numerical dispersion of enough perceptual importance to justify the use of more complex schemes? The answer, however, can only be dependent on the specifics of the problem at hand. The reduction of numerical dispersion, however, is but one advantage of implicit methods; another is easier control over stability, one which will be seen to be of great utility in dealing with sound synthesis methods for nonlinear problems. See, for example, Chapter 8 for some examples of the use of implicit methods in the case of nonlinear string vibration.

One potential complication of the use of implicit methods is in setting boundary conditions—it can be far less clear how to do this properly when the update values at the boundaries themselves are coupled to other unknowns. Again, energy analysis is invaluable in this respect. For scheme (6.60), one may employ identity (5.14), and rewrite the scheme as

$$\left(1 + \frac{(1-\theta)h^2}{2}\delta_{xx}\right)\delta_{tt}u = \gamma^2\delta_{xx}u$$

Considering the scheme defined over the semi-infinite domain $\mathcal{D} = \mathbb{Z}^+$, taking an inner product with $\delta_t.u$ gives, as usual,

$$\delta_{t+}\mathfrak{h} = \mathfrak{b}$$

where, in this case, one has

$$\mathfrak{h} = \mathfrak{t} + \mathfrak{v} \quad \text{with} \quad \mathfrak{t} = \frac{1}{2}\|\delta_{t-}u\|_{\mathbb{Z}^+}^2 - \frac{(1-\theta)h^2}{4}\|\delta_{t-}\delta_{x+}u\|_{\mathbb{Z}^+}^2 \quad \mathfrak{v} = \frac{\gamma^2}{2}\langle\delta_{x+}u, e_{t-}\delta_{x+}u\rangle_{\mathbb{Z}^+}$$

and

$$\mathfrak{b} = -\gamma^2\left(\delta_t.u_0\right)\left(\delta_{x-}u_0\right) + \frac{(1-\theta)h^2}{2}\left(\delta_t.u_0\right)\left(\delta_{x-}\delta_{tt}u_0\right)$$

The scheme will be conservative when $\mathfrak{b}$ vanishes, and it is easy to see from the above expression that this will be true when, for example, $u_0 = 0$, or $\delta_{x-}u_0 = 0$, which are the same discrete Dirichlet and Neumann conditions as for the simple scheme (6.34).

6.4   Modal synthesis

The modal solution to the 1D wave equation given in Section 6.1.11 indicates a straightforward means of performing synthesis. Once the modal frequencies ω_p and functions $U_p(x)$ and, for a given pair of initial conditions $u(x, 0)$ and $u_t(x, 0)$, the weighting coefficients a_p and b_p have been determined, through a Fourier series decomposition such as (6.30), the solution at an output position such as $x = x_o$ may be written directly as

$$u(x_o, t) = \sum_p \left(a_p\cos(\omega_p t) + b_p\sin(\omega_p t)\right) U_p(x_o)$$

Leaving aside the issue of the infinite sum above, which must be truncated in any implementation, the main computational work will be in the generation of the time-dependent sinusoids above. Though this could, of course, be done using table lookup operations, as discussed in the context of abstract sound synthesis in Section 1.1.3, another way of proceeding is to express the system as a parallel combination of SHOs, as per

$$u(x_0, t) = \sum_p U_p(x_0)\Phi_p(t) \qquad \text{with} \qquad \frac{d^2\Phi_p(t)}{dt^2} = -\omega_p^2\Phi_p(t)$$

with $\Phi_p(0) = a_p$ and $d\Phi_p/dt = b_p\omega_p$.

This form is now suitable for discretization along the lines presented in Chapter 3. For each SHO in the sum above, one could use a simple scheme such as (3.12), but there is no reason not to use the exact scheme (3.39):

$$u^n(x_0) = \sum_{p=1}^{N_m/2} U_p(x_0)\Phi_p^n \qquad \Phi_p^{n+1} = 2\cos(\omega_p nk)\Phi_p^n - \Phi_p^{n-1} \quad \text{for} \quad p = 1, \dots, N_m \qquad (6.63)$$

The set of sinusoids, represented by Φ_p^n above, is truncated to $N_m/2$ (or the nearest integer below)—note, however, that this is the only approximation occurring in this discretization, as each oscillator generates an exact solution, provided that initialization is carried out carefully. A Matlab implementation of modal synthesis for the 1D wave equation appears in Section A.6. The scheme above may also be extended to the case of loss [380], where an exact scheme is also available, as per (3.60). See Problem 6.13 and Programming Exercise 6.8.

There are some minor subtleties relating to initialization here. Due to series truncation, if the input distributions are spatially band-limited (this is always the case), then some loss in information (and thus accuracy) will occur in the computation of a_p and b_p—for reasonably smooth excitations, this effect will be very small. Another slight issue crops up in determining a_p and b_p—if the input distributions are localized as Dirac delta functions, then these functions may be determined through sampling of the modal functions themselves, which is easy if these are available in closed form. Otherwise, one must perform the projections of (6.30) numerically (somehow). For the wave equation, the modal functions form a Fourier basis, and one may employ fast algorithms such as fast Fourier transforms (FFTs) in order to determine a_p and b_p—this is exactly what is done in the code example in Section A.6. But for more complex systems, the modal functions will not be expressible as such, and FFTs will not be available.

6.5 Loss

As in the case of the SHO, it is straightforward to extend the 1D wave equation through the addition of a term which models loss, or dissipation:

$$u_{tt} = \gamma^2 u_{xx} - 2\sigma_0 u_t \qquad (6.64)$$

where σ_0 is a non-negative constant. The loss term may be viewed as resulting from a variety of physical phenomena, including radiation and internal losses. This is a crude approximation, which may be improved upon in the case of strings—see Section 7.3.

The dispersion analysis applied to (6.64) yields the characteristic polynomial

$$s^2 + 2\sigma_0 s + \gamma^2\beta^2 = 0 \qquad (6.65)$$

with roots

$$s_\pm = -\sigma_0 \pm \sqrt{\sigma_0^2 - \gamma^2\beta^2}$$

For $\beta \geq \sigma_0/\gamma$, and writing $s_\pm = \sigma \pm \omega$, one has

$$\sigma = -\sigma_0 \qquad \omega = \sqrt{\gamma^2 \beta^2 - \sigma_0^2}$$

Thus the rate of loss is frequency independent and equal to σ_0, but the frequency is of a more complex form than in the lossless case. The phase and group velocity are now wavenumber dependent, and thus wave propagation is dispersive. An exact traveling wave solution to the lossy wave equation is thus ruled out (though it should be noted that lossy traveling wave solutions do exist for a slight variant of (6.64)—see Problem 6.15). The degree of dispersion is, however, quite small for realistic values of σ_0. See Problem 6.14. It should also be noted that for small values of the wavenumber, i.e., when $\beta < \sigma_0/\gamma$, the solutions $s_\pm$ will be purely real, indicating the presence of non-propagating solutions and a cutoff wavenumber.

The 60 dB decay time T_{60} for the lossy wave equation, which as noted above is frequency independent under low-loss conditions, may be written as

$$T_{60} = 6 \ln(10)/\sigma_0$$

and is a useful global parameter in a sound synthesis simulation.

From an energetic standpoint, the situation is again very similar to that of the SHO with loss—see Section 3.5. Considering the lossy 1D wave equation defined over the infinite domain $\mathcal{D} = \mathbb{R}$, one has, taking the inner product with u_t,

$$\langle u_t, u_{tt} \rangle_\mathbb{R} = \gamma^2 \langle u_t, u_{xx} \rangle_\mathbb{R} - 2\sigma_0 \|u_t\|_\mathbb{R}^2$$

or

$$\frac{d\mathfrak{H}}{dt} = -2\sigma_0 \|u_t\|_\mathbb{R}^2 \leq 0 \qquad \longrightarrow \qquad 0 \leq \mathfrak{H}(t_2) \leq \mathfrak{H}(t_1) \quad \text{for} \quad t_1 \leq t_2$$

where $\mathfrak{H}$ is defined as in the lossless case. Thus the energy is non-negative and decreases monotonically. It is not difficult to show that the boundary conditions given in Section 6.1.9 do not interfere with this strict dissipation—the energetic behavior of the wave equation is seen to be separated between contributions over the domain interior and at the boundary. See Problem 6.17. Though finite difference schemes will be examined here, it is of course possible to incorporate such loss modeling into modal methods (see Programming Exercise 6.8) and, with more difficulty, digital waveguides (see Problems 6.15 and 6.16, as well as Programming Exercise 6.9).

6.5.1   Finite difference scheme

An extension of scheme (6.34) to the case of linear loss is given by

$$\delta_{tt} u = \gamma^2 \delta_{xx} u - 2\sigma_0 \delta_{t\cdot} u \tag{6.66}$$

or, in the form of a recursion, as

$$u_l^{n+1} = \frac{2}{1 + \sigma_0 k} \left(\left(1 - \lambda^2\right) u_l^n + \frac{\lambda^2}{2} \left(u_{l-1}^n + u_{l+1}^n\right) \right) - \frac{1 - \sigma_0 k}{1 + \sigma_0 k} u_l^{n-1}$$

See Programming Exercise 6.7.

The characteristic polynomial for this scheme is

$$(1 + \sigma_0 k)z + \left(4\lambda^2 \sin^2(\beta h/2) - 2\right) + (1 - \sigma_0 k)z^{-1} = 0 \tag{6.67}$$

It is simple to show (see Problem 6.18) that the roots are bounded by unity for all wavenumbers β, under the condition (6.40), as for the scheme (6.34) for the lossless wave equation. Thus the addition of a centered difference approximation to the loss term does not affect the stability results obtained in the lossless case.

An easier way to see this is through energy analysis: one arrives immediately at

$$\delta_{t+}\mathfrak{h} = -2\sigma_0 \|\delta_{t\cdot}u\|_{\mathbb{Z}}^2 \leq 0$$

where the discrete energy is defined just as in the lossless case. Thus the energy of the scheme (6.66) is monotonically decreasing.

6.6   Comparative study I

Though this chapter has focused mainly on difference schemes for the 1D wave equation, various other well-known synthesis strategies have been briefly described as well—lumped methods in Section 6.1.1, digital waveguides in Section 6.2.11, and modal synthesis in Section 6.4. This is a good moment to step back to compare these techniques with respect to important practical issues in synthesis—the various programming, perceptual, and computational load issues become even more important for more complex systems, and it pays to keep one's mind's eye (or ear) on them at all times. As mentioned earlier, the 1D wave equation is a rather special case; the discussion here is continued with regard to the 2D wave equation in Section 11.8.

6.6.1   Accuracy

The accuracy with which a numerical solution is computed can have direct perceptual ramifications on sound output—numerical dispersion can lead to an undesirable mistuning of modes, and, in extreme cases, to a severe low-passing or band-limiting effect on sound output. These effects are illustrated in the present case of the 1D wave equation in Section 6.2.3. In general, all synthesis methods based on direct time–space simulation will be prey to such effects, including finite difference methods and lumped networks. It is possible, however, to design methods for which this effect is reduced, often greatly—see Section 6.3 for some examples—but such methods are always more computationally intensive, in the sense that they either must be implicit (requiring more computational work), or involve a wider stencil (requiring more care to be taken when setting boundary conditions). Another remedy, and not one which is advised here due to computational expense, is to make use of a simple scheme at a higher sample rate.

Modal methods, on the other hand, possess the great advantage of allowing an exact solution to be calculated, at least for LTI problems, and for sufficiently band-limited initial conditions. Once the problem has been decomposed into modes (somehow!), each of which behaves as an SHO, exact numerical methods exist. There is thus no mistuning of modes in a properly executed modal simulation. In this very special case of the 1D wave equation, digital waveguides also generate an exact solution, but, unlike the case of modal methods, this property extends to very few other systems.

6.6.2   Memory use

As should be clear from the discussion at various points in this chapter, memory requirements scale directly with the number of degrees of freedom of the system—this is true for finite difference methods (including lumped methods), modal methods, as well as digital waveguides. For the simple finite difference scheme (6.34) for the 1D wave equation defined over the unit interval, this number N_{fd} is bounded above by $N_{fd} \leq 2f_s/\gamma$, which corresponds to two grid functions' worth of "state." The number remains the same in the case of a lumped network representation, which yields the same difference scheme (see Section 6.1.1). It is indeed possible to develop schemes which require less memory, but at the expense of reduced solution bandwidth and increased numerical dispersion. The memory requirement for a digital waveguide, which is none other than a special case of scheme (6.34), is exactly $2f_s/\gamma$. For modal methods, the number of degrees of freedom required to fill the available audio bandwidth will be $N_m = 2f_s/\gamma$, corresponding to $N_m/2$ modes, each necessarily represented in discrete time by two units of memory. Again, one may attempt to reduce the number of modes in synthesis output, but only at the expense of reduced accuracy and bandwidth.

At the level of memory required to represent solution state, all these methods are thus equivalent—$2f_s/\gamma$ units should be considered to be a fundamental target. It is important to reiterate that this requirement does *not* depend significantly on the choice of boundary conditions—this is perhaps most easily understood in the case of finite difference schemes, for which boundary conditions are usually set by locally altering scheme coefficients, but even in the case of a modal representation, it is true that the modal density of an LTI problem remains the same, regardless of boundary conditions, at least in the high-frequency limit. The addition of loss, normally a very small effect in musical sound synthesis, leads only to a negligible change in these memory requirements.

Modal methods, however, can incur rather heavy costs if the modal frequencies and functions are not expressible in closed form (due, perhaps, to more complex boundary conditions). Keeping the frequency values, if they are not expressible in closed form, will amount to another $N_m/2$ worth of storage. If one were to attempt full storage of all $N_m/2$ modal shapes, at $N_m/2$ separate spatial locations (i.e., with enough values to allow resolution of all frequencies up to the Nyquist), the storage requirement balloons to $N_m^2/4$—this is, in fact, how modes are stored (via the so-called "shape matrix" [358]) in some modal synthesis software systems. (If one is only interested in the behavior of the system at, say, K separate output locations, one can get away with $K N_m/2$ worth of storage [380].) Clearly this imposes extra limitations on the number of degrees of freedom beyond those required of a time domain method.

6.6.3   Operation count

The run-time operation count per time step, for scheme (6.34) (including the lumped network representation), is $5N_{fd}/2$ additions/multiplications. For more complex schemes, such as those given in Section 6.3, the operation count will be higher, but will still scale as αN_{fd}, for some α which depends on the scheme—this remains true even for an implicit method, as long as the linear system to be solved is sparse. For modal methods, the operation count is N_m, which is normally less than that of the finite difference scheme, by a factor of about 2.5. Waveguides are the great exception: the operation count is $O(1)$ per time step—no calculations are performed except in order to obtain output and perhaps at non-trivial boundary terminations. This drastic cut in computational cost proved to be the key to the success of the digital waveguide modeling approach to sound synthesis.

6.6.4   Precomputation

Computation before run time for most finite difference schemes, including lumped methods and waveguides, is minimal. For modal methods, if the modal frequencies and shapes are not known, these must be determined through the solution of an eigenvalue problem. This can be quite costly, and potentially a very serious bottleneck if the number of modes is large—indeed, the determination of the eigenvalues can be more costly than the entire run-time calculation! Initialization also poses a problem, in that conditions posed in the spatial domain must be projected onto the modes, once determined—if the modes form a Fourier basis, one may make use of FFTs, but otherwise not.

6.6.5 Stability

Numerical stability is the great bugbear of time domain methods for synthesis, such as finite difference schemes and lumped networks, and is a real difficulty—if an instability can occur in a synthesis routine, it probably will, so it is well advised to do as much preparatory work as possible before plunging in and writing code. But powerful techniques for stability analysis (discussed at length in this chapter) do exist—with some practice, these are not extremely difficult to employ.

For entirely separate reasons, digital waveguides and modal methods are much less susceptible to stability problems. For LTI problems at least, once one has a representation in terms of decoupled modes, stability analysis reduces to the analysis of schemes for lumped oscillators, which is nearly trivial. Waveguides, on the other hand, are an example of a scattering method [41]—the hallmark of such methods is that they lead to simulation structures which are stable by construction, again under LTI conditions.

6.6.6 Output

One of the great benefits of a time domain implementation is that the entire state is calculated at each time step; it is also directly observable without any additional computational work or memory requirement. Changing a listening position amounts to no more than the adjustment of a reading position on the underlying grid function, perhaps with some minimal interpolation. Indeed, obtaining multiple outputs, at time-varying locations, is no more expensive than obtaining one. Modal methods are far less flexible in this regard—each output requires a separate set of modal weights, either drawn from a precomputed shape matrix, or computed on the fly (and necessarily recomputed upon any change in the output position).

6.7 Problems

Problem 6.1 *Consider the 1D wave equation, defined over the semi-infinite interval $\mathcal{D} = \mathbb{R}^+$. Show that when the lossy boundary condition (6.22) is employed at $x = 0$, with $\alpha = \gamma$, left-going traveling waves are completely absorbed. (You may substitute the traveling wave solution (6.11) directly into the boundary condition.)*

Problem 6.2 *Consider the 1D wave equation, defined over the semi-infinite interval $\mathcal{D} = \mathbb{R}^+$. Show that the nonlinear boundary condition*

$$u_x(0, t) = \alpha \, (u_t(0, t))^2 \, \text{sign}(u_t(0, t)) \qquad for \qquad \alpha \geq 0$$

is dissipative, i.e.,

$$\frac{d\mathfrak{H}}{dt} \leq 0$$

If this condition is generalized to

$$u_x(0, t) = f(u_t(0, t))$$

for some function f, what property must f satisfy in order that the system remain dissipative?

Problem 6.3 *Consider the 1D wave equation, defined over the finite interval $\mathcal{D} = \mathbb{U} = [0, 1]$, with fixed boundary conditions $u = 0$ at both boundary points. Show that under these conditions, bounds (6.26) may be improved to*

$$|u(x_0, t)| \leq \frac{1}{\gamma}\sqrt{\frac{\mathfrak{H}(0)}{2}} \qquad \longrightarrow \qquad \|u\|_{\mathcal{D}} \leq \frac{1}{\gamma}\sqrt{\frac{\mathfrak{H}(0)}{2}}$$

Problem 6.4 *Consider again the 1D wave equation, defined over the finite interval* $\mathbb{U} = [0, 1]$. *Under the boundary conditions*

$$u(0, t) = 0 \quad \text{and} \quad u_x(1, t) = -\alpha u(1, t)$$

for some constant $\alpha > 0$, *show that the modal frequencies* ω *must satisfy the equation*

$$\frac{\omega}{\gamma\alpha} = -\tan\left(\frac{\omega}{\gamma}\right)$$

and, as such, must be determined numerically. As ω *becomes large, show that the modal density approaches that of the wave equation under fixed/fixed, free/free, or fixed/free conditions.*

Problem 6.5 *Given the dispersion relation (6.43) for scheme (6.34) for the wave equation, show by direct calculation that the phase and group velocities, as functions of frequency* ω, *are equal to*

$$v_\phi(\omega) = \frac{h\omega}{2\sin^{-1}(\sin(\omega k/2)/\lambda)} \qquad v_g(\omega) = \frac{\gamma\sqrt{1 - \sin^2(\omega k/2)/\lambda^2}}{\cos(\omega k/2)}$$

Show that in the limit as ω *or* k *approaches zero, the limiting value of both these expressions is* γ, *the wave speed for the continuous-time–space wave equation.*

Problem 6.6 *For the lossy numerical boundary condition (6.49) for scheme (6.34) for the 1D wave equation, applied at grid point* $l = 0$, *show that when* $\lambda = 1$ *and* $\alpha = \gamma$, *the condition reduces to* $u_0^{n+1} = u_1^n$. *See also Programming Exercise 6.3.*

Problem 6.7 *As has been seen in Section 6.2.7, from the bound on the energy for scheme (6.34) defined over the semi-infinite domain* $\mathcal{D} = \mathbb{Z}^+$, *one may deduce that, under any conservative boundary condition at* $l = 0$, *and under stability condition (6.40), one has the conditions*

$$\|\delta_{t-}u\|_{\mathbb{Z}^+} \leq \sqrt{2\mathfrak{h}} \qquad \|\delta_{x+}\mu_{t-}u\|_{\mathbb{Z}^+} \leq \frac{\sqrt{2\mathfrak{h}}}{\gamma} \tag{6.68}$$

The first condition on its own serves to bound the rate of growth of the solution. If the condition at $l = 0$ *is of Dirichlet type, i.e.,* $u_0 = 0$, *then it is possible to determine a bound on* u_l^n *itself. This is a little trickier than in the continuous case, and requires a good number of the bounds and identities supplied in the previous chapter.*

(a) First, show that if $u_0 = 0$, *one may write* $u_l = \langle 1, \delta_{x+}u \rangle_{[0,l-1]}$, *where "1" indicates here a sequence of ones and, thus, using the Cauchy–Schwartz inequality, that*

$$|u_l| \leq \sqrt{lh}\|\delta_{x+}u\|_{[0,l-1]} \leq \sqrt{lh}\|\delta_{x+}u\|_{\mathbb{Z}^+}$$

(b) Using identity (2.7d), and the triangle inequality (5.22b), show furthermore that

$$|u_l| \leq \sqrt{lh}\left(\|\delta_{x+}\mu_{t-}u\|_{\mathbb{Z}^+} + \frac{k}{2}\|\delta_{x+}\delta_{t-}u\|_{\mathbb{Z}^+}\right) \leq \sqrt{lh}\left(\|\delta_{x+}\mu_{t-}u\|_{\mathbb{Z}^+} + \frac{k}{h}\|\delta_{t-}u\|_{\mathbb{Z}^+}\right)$$

(c) Use the separate bounds on $\|\delta_{t-}u\|_{\mathbb{Z}^+}$ *and* $\|\mu_{t-}\delta_{x+}u\|_{\mathbb{Z}^+}$ *given at the beginning of this problem to arrive at a final bound on* $|u_l|$ *in terms of* γ, λ, l, *and the energy* $\mathfrak{h}$.

Problem 6.8 *Caution: This is a difficult, but instructive problem, in that some rather more advanced energy-based techniques for the analysis of numerical boundary conditions are introduced.*

Consider scheme (6.34), defined over $\mathcal{D} = \mathbb{Z}^+$, under the generalized Neumann boundary condition at $l = 0$:

$$\alpha \delta_{x-} u_0 + (1 - \alpha) \delta_x . u_0 = 0$$

(Recall the example of numerical instability resulting from the use of this boundary condition, as described on page 140.) Using the results and definition in Problem 5.6 in the previous chapter, show that, by taking an ϵ inner product of the scheme with $\delta_t . u$, the following energy balance may be obtained:

$$\delta_{t+} \mathfrak{h} = -\gamma^2 (\delta_t . u_0) ((\epsilon - 1) \delta_{x-} u_0 + (2 - \epsilon) \delta_x . u_0)$$

where

$$\mathfrak{h} = \frac{1}{2} \left(\|\delta_{t-} u\|_{\mathbb{Z}+}^{\epsilon} \right)^2 + \frac{\gamma^2}{2} \langle \delta_{x+} u, e_{t-} \delta_{x+} u \rangle_{\mathbb{Z}+}$$

Thus the boundary condition above may be considered conservative under an ϵ inner product with $\alpha = \epsilon - 1$.

Go further, and show that

$$\mathfrak{h} \geq \frac{1}{2} \left(\|\delta_{t-} u\|_{\mathbb{Z}+}^{\epsilon} \right)^2 - \frac{\lambda^2}{2} \left(\|\delta_{t-} u\|_{\mathbb{Z}+}' \right)^2$$

Show that, for non-negativity, beyond the CFL condition, the condition $\lambda \leq \sqrt{\epsilon}$ must also be satisfied, and, given the relationship between α and ϵ, determine the range of α for which this additional condition interferes with the CFL bound.

Problem 6.9   *Consider, instead of the numerical radiation condition (6.50), the condition*

$$\delta_x . u_0 = \alpha_1 \delta_t . u_0 + \alpha_2 \mu_t . u_0 \qquad (6.69)$$

used in conjunction with scheme (6.34) over the domain $\mathcal{D} = \mathbb{Z}^+$. Show that the conserved numerical energy will be of the form $\mathfrak{h} + \mathfrak{h}_b$, but with a different definition of $\mathfrak{h}_b$ from that which appears in (6.51). Show that, in this case, the energy remains non-negative (and the scheme stable) under the CFL condition (6.40), without any interfering condition for the boundary.

Problem 6.10   *Considering the five-point stencil scheme (6.56) for the wave equation, show the stability conditions (6.58) and (6.59) through the determination of the maximum and minimum values of the function $F(p)$ over the unit interval $p \in [0, 1]$, as in (6.57).*

Problem 6.11   *Show that the two implicit schemes below for the 1D wave equation,*

$$(\theta + (1 - \theta) \mu_{x.}) \delta_{tt} u = \gamma^2 \delta_{xx} u \qquad \delta_{tt} u = \gamma^2 (\phi + (1 - \phi) \mu_{t.}) \delta_{xx} u$$

in the free parameters θ and ϕ, respectively, are equivalent when $\theta = 1 + \lambda^2 (1 - \phi)$. The identities (5.14) and (2.7a) may be of use here.

Problem 6.12   *Considering the implicit scheme (6.60) for the wave equation, show the stability conditions (6.62) through the determination of the maximum and minimum values of the function $F(p)$ over the unit interval $p \in [0, 1]$, as in (6.61).*

Problem 6.13   *Consider the wave equation with loss (6.64) defined over the domain $\mathcal{D} = \mathbb{U}$, under fixed boundary conditions. Extend the modal analysis of Section 6.1.11, and show that, for real wavenumbers $\beta_p = p\pi$, for integer p, a single solution is of the form*

$$u_p(x, t) = e^{\sigma_p t} \left(a_p \cos(\omega_p t) + b_p \sin(\omega_p t) \right) \sin(p\pi x) \qquad (6.70)$$

and determine σ_p and ω_p in terms of σ_0 and γ.

Problem 6.14   *Consider the lossy wave equation (6.64), defined over the unit interval $\mathcal{D} = \mathbb{U}$, with fixed boundary terminations.*

(a) Assume allowed wavenumbers β_p are of the form $\beta_p = p\pi$, and determine, from the dispersion relation (6.65), an expression for the frequency, in Hertz, of the pth mode. (Here, assume the "frequency" to refer to the imaginary part of the complex frequency variable s.)

(b) Assuming that $\gamma = 100$ and $T_{60} = 3$, calculate the frequency of the first mode (these parameters are typical of a musical string). By how many cents does it deviate from the frequency of the first mode in the lossless case?

Problem 6.15   *The wave equation with a loss term exhibits a (very slight) degree of dispersion, so clearly a strict traveling wave solution does not exist, ruling out an efficient solution by digital waveguides. But dispersionless wave propagation can extend to the case of loss, if a slightly different model is employed. Consider the so-called distortionless transmission line equation*

$$u_{tt} = \gamma^2 u_{xx} - 2\sigma_0 u_t - \sigma_0^2 u \tag{6.71}$$

defined over the real line $\mathcal{D} = \mathbb{R}$.

(a) Perform a dispersion analysis of this equation, by inserting a test solution of the form $u(x, t) = e^{st + j\beta x}$, and derive the characteristic equation relating s and β.

(b) Solve for the roots $s_\pm(\beta)$ of the characteristic equation, and express the real and imaginary parts of the roots separately, i.e., write $s_\pm(\beta) = \sigma(\beta) \pm j\omega(\beta)$. Show that, given this expression for $\omega(\beta)$, the phase and group velocity are again constant.

(c) Show, by direct substitution, that damped traveling wave solutions of the form $e^{-\sigma_0 t} u^{(+)}(x - \gamma t)$ and $e^{-\sigma_0 t} u^{(-)}(x + \gamma t)$ satisfy the distortionless transmission line equation (6.71), for arbitrary twice-differentiable distributions $u^{(+)}$ and $u^{(-)}$.

(d) By taking an inner product of (6.71) with u_t over $\mathcal{D} = \mathbb{R}$, find an expression for the energy $\mathfrak{H}$, and show that it is monotonically decreasing. Furthermore, find a bound on $\|u\|_\mathbb{R}$ in terms of the initial energy $\mathfrak{H}(0)$.

Problem 6.16   *Consider the following approximation to the distortionless wave equation (6.71) presented in the previous problem:*

$$\delta_{tt} u = \gamma^2 \delta_{xx} u - 2\sigma_0 \delta_t . u - \sigma_0^2 \mu_{tt} u \tag{6.72}$$

defined over the infinite domain $\mathcal{D} = \mathbb{Z}$.

(a) Write the characteristic polynomial corresponding to scheme (6.72). Show that the stability condition on λ, the Courant number, is unchanged from the Courant–Friedrichs–Lewy condition (6.40).

(b) Write the explicit recursion in the grid function u_l^n corresponding to the compact operator form given above. How does the computational footprint of the scheme simplify when $\lambda^2 = 1 - \sigma_0^2 k^2/4$?

(c) Show that, under the assumption that $\lambda^2 = 1 - \sigma_0^2 k^2/4$, a lossy discrete traveling wave solution exists. That is, given a traveling wave decomposition $u_l^n = u_l^{(+),n} + u_l^{(-),n}$, and where the wave variables $u_l^{(+),n}$ and $u_l^{(-),n}$ are updated according to $u_l^{(+),n} = r u_{l-1}^{(+),n-1}$, $u_l^{(-),n} = r u_{l+1}^{(+),n-1}$, for some constant r, show that the scheme (6.72) is implied, and find the value of r in terms of σ_0 and k.

(d) The rate of loss in the scheme (6.72) is not quite equivalent to that of the partial differential equation (6.71). Show that scheme (6.72) solves equation (6.71) exactly, with σ_0 replaced by a slightly different value σ_0^*, and find the value of σ_0^* in terms of σ_0 and k.

(e) Sketch a digital waveguide representation of the discrete traveling wave solution, where, now, each delay must be followed by multiplication by a factor r. Is it possible to use a single

bidirectional delay line, and consolidate these multiplications into a single multiplicative factor, applied at a given point in the delay line (such as the end)? See also Programming Exercise 6.9.

Problem 6.17   *Extend the energy analysis of the wave equation with loss (6.64) to the domain $\mathcal{D} = \mathbb{R}^+$, and show that under the Dirichlet, Neumann, or lossy boundary condition (6.22) at $x = 0$, the stored energy $\mathfrak{H}$ will be non-increasing.*

Problem 6.18   *Show that the roots of the characteristic equation (6.67) for the scheme (6.66) for the lossy wave equation are bounded by unity in magnitude under the condition $\lambda \leq 1$.*

6.8   Programming exercises

Programming Exercise 6.1   *Consider the 1D wave equation, under a sharp "plucked" excitation. In the most extreme case, one may write $u(x, 0) = \delta(x - x_i)$, $u_t(x, 0) = 0$, where $\delta(x - x_i)$ is a Dirac delta function at location $x = x_i$. The resulting solution should thus be, from the traveling wave decomposition, $u(x, t) = 0.5\left(\delta(x - x_i - \gamma t) + \delta(x - x_i + \gamma t)\right)$—in other words, it should be composed of two spikes traveling in opposite directions away from the excitation point.*

In the scheme (6.34), and assuming x_i to lie directly on a grid point at l_i, where $x_i = l_i h$, the first-order initializing strategy of (6.36) prescribes $u_{l_i}^0 = u_{l_i}^1 = 1/h$. Modify the code example given in Section A.4 such that the scheme is initialized in the above way, and examine the results after a few time steps. For simplicity, choose values of the wave speed and the sample rate such that the Courant condition may be satisfied with equality (i.e., $\lambda = 1$). Does the result correspond to the traveling wave solution given above?

Instead of the above setting for the initial conditions, choose $u_{l_i}^0 = 1/h$, $u_{l_i-1}^1 = u_{l_i+1}^1 = 1/2h$. Are the results more in line with the traveling wave solution? Can you explain what is going wrong with initialization strategy (6.36)?

Programming Exercise 6.2   *Modify the Matlab code provided in Section A.4 so that, in the main loop, the numerical energy $\mathfrak{h}^n$ is calculated. Now, with Dirichlet conditions at both ends of the domain (which is $\mathbb{U}_N$), the energy function is*

$$\mathfrak{h} = \frac{1}{2}\|\delta_{t-}u\|_{\mathbb{U}_N}^2 + \frac{\gamma^2}{2}\langle \delta_{x+}u, e_{t-}\delta_{x+}u\rangle_{\underline{\mathbb{U}_N}}$$

Verify that it is constant to machine accuracy (in double-precision floating point, about 15 decimal places), and plot the variation in the energy from the initial energy $\mathfrak{h}^0$, normalized by the initial energy as a function of time step.

Programming Exercise 6.3   *Consider the 1D wave equation, under the lossy condition (6.22) at the left end, and under a fixed Dirichlet condition at the right end. Modify the code example given in Section A.4 such that the numerical boundary condition (6.49) is employed at the left end. After appropriate initialization, show that when $\alpha = \gamma$ and $\lambda = 1$, the lossy boundary condition is perfectly absorbing (i.e., after a finite number of time steps, the state u of your recursion should consist entirely of zeros).*

Programming Exercise 6.4   *Consider the 1D wave equation, under the radiation condition (6.23) at the left end, and a Dirichlet condition at the right end. Modify the boundary condition in the code example in Section A.4 in two separate ways: according to the numerical condition (6.50), and that given in (6.69). For simplicity, consider the case for which $\alpha_1 = 0$ (i.e., the lossless case). For a given choice of γ and the sample rate f_s, experiment with both terminations for a variety of values of α_2 and λ. Demonstrate that for the boundary condition (6.50), the condition (6.52) is sufficient for stability, but not necessary—that is, show that for some values of λ which violate this*

1
2
3
4
5
6
7
8
9
10
11
12
13
14
15
16
17
18
19
20
21
22
23
24
25
26
27
28
29
30
31
32
33
34
35
36
37
38
39
40
41
42
43
44
45
46
47
48
49
50
51

condition, no instability is observed. How close to necessary is this condition for a given value of α_2? Demonstrate, to yourself, that the numerical boundary condition (6.69) is always stable as long as the CFL condition (6.40) is observed.

Programming Exercise 6.5   Consider the scheme (6.34), under two different types of numerical Neumann condition, applied at both ends of the domain:

$$\delta_{x-}u_0 = \delta_{x+}u_N = 0 \qquad\qquad \delta_{x\cdot}u_0 = \delta_{x\cdot}u_N = 0$$

Create a Matlab script which calculates the numerical modal frequencies for this scheme, under both termination types. (To do this, you will need to find the matrix operator $\mathbf{D}_{xx}$ corresponding to the difference operator δ_{xx}, under the above boundary conditions. It will be of size $(N + 1) \times (N + 1)$. You may then calculate the modal frequencies as per (6.53).) Experiment with different values of λ, and compare the resulting frequencies to the exact modal frequencies, from (6.31). Which type of condition leads to more accurate numerical frequencies?

Programming Exercise 6.6   Modify the code example in Section A.4, such that there are two output locations $x_o^{(1)}$ and $x_o^{(2)}$, which move sinusoidally according to

$$x_o^{(1)}(t) = 1/3 + A_{sw}\sin(2\pi f_{sw}t) \qquad\qquad x_o^{(2)}(t) = 2/3 - A_{sw}\sin(2\pi f_{sw}t)$$

where A_{sw}, the sweep depth, satisfies $0 \le A_{sw} < 1/3$, and where f_{sw} is the sweep frequency, generally under about 1 Hz—both should appear as additional global parameters. Implement truncation, linear, and cubic interpolation, where the choice is determined by an input flag. (The interpolation operations are described in Section 5.2.4.) Your code should write output to a two-column array, which can be played directly in stereo in Matlab. Experiment with your code for different fundamental frequencies $f_0 = \gamma/2$—is linear interpolation sufficient to eliminate audible clicks and time-varying low-passing effects?

Programming Exercise 6.7   Generalize the code example in Section A.4 to scheme (6.66) for the wave equation with a linear loss term. The decay time T_{60} should appear as an extra global parameter.

Programming Exercise 6.8   Generalize the code example in Section A.6 to the case of the wave equation with a linear loss term. The decay time T_{60} should appear as an extra global parameter. You will need to make use of a distinct set of modal frequencies ω_p, which are altered slightly with respect to those of the lossless case. The initialization strategy must be altered as well—see Problem 6.13.

Programming Exercise 6.9   Generalize the code example in Section A.5 to the case of the lossy distortionless wave equation, as described in Problem 6.15. A lossy discrete traveling wave formulation appears in Problem 6.16, where each traveling wave is attenuated by a factor r during a single time step. In an N-point delay line, these attenuation factors may be combined into a single factor of r^N acting at each end of the waveguide.

7

Linear bar and string vibration

In this chapter, the finite difference methods applied in the previous chapter to the 1D wave equation are extended to the more musically interesting case of bars and stiff strings. Linear or low-amplitude vibration is characteristic of a variety of instruments, including xylophones and marimbas, and, to a lesser extent, string instruments such as acoustic guitars and pianos, which can, under certain conditions, exhibit nonlinear effects (this topic will be broached in detail in Chapter 8). Linear time-invariant systems such as these, and the associated numerical methods, are still amenable to frequency domain analysis, which can be very revealing with regard to effects such as dispersion (leading to perceived inharmonicity). In the numerical setting, frequency domain analysis is useful in obtaining necessary stability conditions, and in analyzing dispersion which results from discretization error; energy analysis allows the determination of suitable numerical boundary conditions.

In Section 7.1, the idealized thin bar model is introduced—while too simple to use for sound synthesis purposes, many important ideas relating to discretization may be dealt with here in a compact manner. The more realistic stiff string model, incorporating stiffness, tension, and loss terms, is dealt with in Section 7.2 and Section 7.3. Various musical features are discussed in the following sections: namely, the coupling to a bow model in Section 7.4; to a hammer model in Section 7.5; the case of multiple strings in Section 7.6; the preparation of strings in Section 7.7 using lumped elements; and coupling between bars in Section 7.8. Simulation of helical spring structures is covered in Section 7.9. Finally, in Section 7.10, the more complex cases of strings of varying density and bars of variable cross-section are outlined; these are the first instances, in this book, of systems with spatial variation, and, as such, Neumann-type stability analysis for finite difference schemes no longer applies directly, though energetic methods remain viable.

7.1 The ideal uniform bar

Transverse vibrations of a thin bar[1] of uniform material properties and cross-section are covered by many authors [156, 244, 136]. In the lossless case, the defining PDE is

$$\rho A u_{tt} = -E I u_{xxxx} \tag{7.1}$$

---

[1] The use of the terms "bar," "beam," and "rod" is somewhat confused in the literature; they will be used interchangeably here, though in some cases, when one discusses a beam, it is assumed that one is referring to its transverse vibration alone, which is indeed the case in most parts of this book.

Numerical Sound Synthesis: Finite Difference Schemes and Simulation in Musical Acoustics Stefan Bilbao
© 2009 John Wiley & Sons, Ltd

where ρ is the material density of the medium, A is the cross-sectional area, E is Young's modulus, and I is a parameter often referred to as the bar moment of inertia, which depends on the geometry of the bar cross-section. In this section, it is assumed that these quantities are constants. More will be said about this in Section 7.10.2, which deals with bars of varying cross-section.

In spatially scaled form, where, as for the case of the wave equation, x has been replaced by x/L, for some constant L with dimensions of length, (7.1) becomes

$$u_{tt} = -\kappa^2 u_{xxxx} \tag{7.2}$$

where κ, a stiffness parameter, is defined by

$$\kappa = \sqrt{\frac{EI}{\rho A L^4}} \tag{7.3}$$

Again, one may note that several constants, E, ρ, I, A, and a characteristic length L, have been replaced by a single parameter κ, allowing for a substantial reduction in the parameter space faced by the programmer and eventual user (composer). This is, like the 1D wave equation, a second-order (in time) PDE in a single variable and, as before, two initial conditions, normally $u(x, 0)$ and $u_t(x, 0)$, must necessarily be specified. See Section 6.1.3 for more on these conditions—in short, one may imagine plucking or striking a stiff bar in exactly the same way as for a string described by the wave equation. This is the simplest possible model of transverse vibration of a uniform stiff medium, often referred to as the Euler–Bernoulli model; many other more complex models are available—see, e.g., [156, 252]. If the medium is not thin, then the linear Timoshenko theory of beam vibration may be suitable—see Problem 7.1 for a presentation of this system, and, for some investigation of its frequency domain behavior and range of applicability in musical acoustics, Programming Exercise 7.1.

7.1.1 Dispersion

Information about propagation speeds may be obtained through the insertion of a test solution of the form $u(x, t) = e^{st+j\beta x}$ into (7.2). One arrives at the characteristic equation

$$s^2 + \kappa^2 \beta^4 = 0$$

which has solutions or dispersion relations

$$s_\pm = \pm j\kappa\beta^2 \qquad \longrightarrow \qquad \omega_\pm = \pm\kappa\beta^2 \tag{7.4}$$

Thus, the frequency ω of a wave component scales as the square of the wavenumber β—this is in sharp contrast to the case of the wave equation, for which ω scales directly with β. Such behavior, which is referred to as dispersive, may be more readily understood with regard to the phase and group velocity (see Section 5.1.2), which, in this case, are given by

$$v_\phi(\beta) = \frac{\omega}{\beta} = \kappa\beta \qquad v_g(\beta) = \frac{d\omega}{d\beta} = 2\kappa\beta$$

In other words, components of large wavenumber (or short wavelength) travel faster than those of small wavenumber (long wavelength). These velocities may also be written in terms of frequency ω, using (7.4), as

$$v_\phi(\omega) = \sqrt{\kappa\omega} \qquad v_g(\omega) = 2\sqrt{\kappa\omega}$$

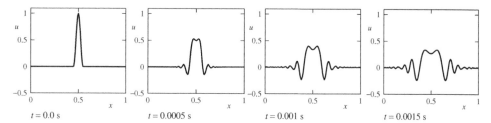

$t = 0.0$ s $t = 0.0005$ s $t = 0.001$ s $t = 0.0015$ s

Figure 7.1   Time evolution of the solution to the ideal bar equation (7.1), with $\kappa = 1$, under a plucked initial condition, with $u_0 = c_{rc}(x)$, and $x_0 = 0.5$, $c_0 = 1$, and $x_{hw} = 0.05$. Successive snapshots of the solution profile are shown at the times indicated, over the interval $x \in [0, 1]$.

See Figure 7.1 for an illustration of dispersive behavior in a thin bar. As one might expect, there will be a very pronounced effect (namely inharmonicity) on the natural frequencies of the bar, when the domain is limited to be finite. See Section 7.1.3. The phase and group velocity are unbounded—in the limit as β becomes large (or the wavelength small), these speeds become infinite. This is a consequence of the assumptions underlying the ideal bar vibration model, and was later corrected by Timoshenko—see Problem 7.2. It is important to note that in the case of the bar of infinite extent, only real wavenumbers β need be considered (if β has an imaginary part, the test solution will necessarily be unbounded). But when the domain is limited to be finite, such solutions are indeed possible, and have a complicating effect on modal analysis (not to mention synthesis!). See Section 7.1.3.

7.1.2   Energy analysis and boundary conditions

Energy techniques have already been presented with respect to the 1D wave equation in detail in Section 6.1.8. For the case in which the bar equation is defined over the real line, i.e., $\mathcal{D} = \mathbb{R}$, one may take the inner product of (7.2) with u_t, to get

$$\langle u_t, u_{tt} \rangle_{\mathbb{R}} + \kappa^2 \langle u_t, u_{xxxx} \rangle_{\mathbb{R}} = 0$$

and, using integration by parts twice, according to (5.10),

$$\langle u_t, u_{tt} \rangle_{\mathbb{R}} + \kappa^2 \langle u_{txx}, u_{xx} \rangle_{\mathbb{R}} = 0 \qquad \longrightarrow \qquad \frac{d\mathfrak{H}}{dt} = 0$$

where

$$\mathfrak{H} = \mathfrak{T} + \mathfrak{V} \qquad \text{and} \qquad \mathfrak{T} = \frac{1}{2} \|u_t\|_{\mathbb{R}}^2 \qquad \mathfrak{V} = \frac{\kappa^2}{2} \|u_{xx}\|_{\mathbb{R}}^2 \qquad (7.5)$$

Thus the bar equation (7.2), like the wave equation, possesses a conserved energy, and is thus lossless. As before, the energy is also non-negative, and bounds on solution growth may again be determined.

Lossless boundary conditions

In order to derive the usual boundary conditions [244, 156] for the ideal bar at a single endpoint, one may perform the above energy analysis for the case $\mathcal{D} = \mathbb{R}^+$. Again taking an inner product, one arrives immediately at

$$\langle u_t, u_{tt} \rangle_{\mathbb{R}^+} + \kappa^2 \langle u_t, u_{xxxx} \rangle_{\mathbb{R}^+} = 0$$

Integration by parts now gives

$$\frac{d\mathfrak{H}}{dt} = \mathfrak{B} \triangleq \kappa^2 \left(u_t(0, t) u_{xxx}(0, t) - u_{tx}(0, t) u_{xx}(0, t) \right) \tag{7.6}$$

with $\mathfrak{H}$ defined as in (7.5), but where inner products run over $\mathbb{R}^+$ instead of $\mathbb{R}$. The boundary term $\mathfrak{B}$ vanishes under the following pairs of conditions at $x = 0$:

$$u = u_x = 0 \qquad \text{clamped} \tag{7.7a}$$

$$u = u_{xx} = 0 \qquad \text{simply supported} \tag{7.7b}$$

$$u_{xx} = u_{xxx} = 0 \qquad \text{free} \tag{7.7c}$$

For any of the above choices, one again has energy conservation, i.e.,

$$\frac{d\mathfrak{H}}{dt} = 0$$

As in the case of the wave equation, many other lossless or lossy boundary terminations are possible—these are the three which arise most frequently in the literature. See Problem 7.3 for more on other types of termination. Such analysis may be extended directly to cover the case of the bar defined over a finite domain, such as $\mathcal{D} = \mathbb{U} = [0, 1]$, and the choice of any pair of conditions given in (7.7) at either end will lead to energy conservation.

7.1.3   Modes

The ideal bar, as defined in (7.2), is LTI, and thus an analysis in terms of modes is straightforward. One might expect that because the system is more generally LSI, such analysis would be as simple as in the case of the 1D wave equation, yet even for this rudimentary system, complications begin to appear.

Again assume oscillatory solutions of the form $u(x, t) = U(x)e^{j\omega t}$, which must now satisfy

$$-\omega^2 U = -\kappa^2 \frac{d^4 U}{dx^4}$$

and thus real-valued solutions are of the form

$$U(x) = A \cos\left(\sqrt{\frac{\omega}{\kappa}} x\right) + B \sin\left(\sqrt{\frac{\omega}{\kappa}} x\right) + C \cosh\left(\sqrt{\frac{\omega}{\kappa}} x\right) + D \sinh\left(\sqrt{\frac{\omega}{\kappa}} x\right)$$

When the ideal bar is defined over $\mathcal{D} = \mathbb{U}$, the possible values of the frequency ω, as well as three of the four constants A, B, C, and D, may be determined after two appropriate boundary conditions are set at either end of the bar (the fourth remains arbitrary, but may be set through normalization of the resulting modal function). For one very special choice, namely simply supported conditions at both ends (this is not very realistic in a musical acoustics setting), it is possible to show [244] that one will have $A = C = D = 0$, and a closed-form expression for the modal frequencies and shapes results:

$$\omega_{\pm p} = \pm \kappa \pi^2 p^2 \qquad \text{and} \qquad U_p(x) = \sin(p\pi x) \qquad \text{for} \qquad p = 1, \ldots \tag{7.8}$$

Thus the frequencies increase as the square of the mode number. Note that in this case, one can obtain the expression for the pth modal frequency through substitution of the wavenumber $\beta = p\pi$ into the dispersion relation, given in (7.4).

For nearly all other choices of boundary condition (including most of the useful forms given in (7.7) above), there is not a closed-form expression for the modal frequencies ω_p, and, furthermore, the values of A, B, C, and D will depend on the as-yet-unknown values of ω_p. For example, under simply supported conditions at $x = 0$ and clamped conditions at $x = 1$, there results $A = C = 0$, and the modal frequencies and shapes are given by

$$\tan\left(\sqrt{\frac{\omega_p}{\kappa}}\right) = \tanh\left(\sqrt{\frac{\omega_p}{\kappa}}\right) \quad \text{and} \quad U_p(x) = \sin\left(\sqrt{\frac{\omega_p}{\kappa}}x\right) - \frac{\sin\left(\sqrt{\frac{\omega_p}{\kappa}}\right)\sinh\left(\sqrt{\frac{\omega_p}{\kappa}}x\right)}{\sinh\left(\sqrt{\frac{\omega_p}{\kappa}}\right)}$$

$$(7.9)$$

While there is no conceptual or practical difficulty in determining the frequencies ω_p, it does become somewhat unwieldy from a synthesis point of view. The modal frequencies must first be determined, necessarily off-line, presumably through the solution of an eigenvalue problem or perhaps an iterative method applied directly to the implicit definition of frequency ω_p above. More difficult, here, is the question of storage. In addition to the memory required to store the frequencies themselves, it will be necessary to store the modal shapes. In this case, it is probably advisable to store the functions sin, cos, sinh, and cosh, with sufficient resolution, as well as the proper settings for the coefficients A, B, C, and D for each mode. For problems which are not LSI, however, these possibilities for simplification disappear—there will not be a convenient implicit definition of the modal frequencies, nor will there be a decomposition of the modal shapes into components such as trigonometric and hyperbolic trigonometric functions. All must necessarily be determined through the solution of an eigenvalue/eigenmode problem (again off-line), and stored. For reference, plots of modal functions under all combinations of the boundary conditions given in (7.7) are shown in Figure 7.2.

Modal density and pitch

As has been discussed with reference to the 1D wave equation at the end of Section 6.1.11, the determination of the distribution of modal frequencies is useful in that it gives a measure of the number of degrees of freedom necessary to describe the system. Considering again the case of simply supported conditions at either end of the bar, the frequencies, in Hertz, will be given by $f_{\pm p} = \pm \kappa \pi p^2/2$, and thus the number N_m which fall in the audio band $f_p \in [-f_s/2, f_s/2]$ will be approximately

$$N_m = 2\sqrt{\frac{f_s}{\kappa \pi}} \qquad (7.10)$$

This can be viewed as the number of degrees of freedom of the ideal bar. Again, it is important to note that this number will *not* depend in a significant way on the boundary conditions employed—any choice of boundary conditions will lead, in the high-frequency limit, to the same density of modes. For example, in the case of the simply supported/clamped conditions given above, the implicit definition of the modal frequencies given in (7.9) leads to the following distribution of modal frequencies, in the limit as ω_p becomes large:

$$\omega_{\pm p} \approx \pm \kappa \pi^2 \left(p + \frac{1}{4}\right)^2$$

so that, again, the number of degrees of freedom is given, approximately, by (7.10). The same is true of other choices of boundary condition—see Problem 7.4.

For the wave equation, which, depending on boundary conditions, possesses a uniformly spaced series of harmonics, or modal frequencies, it is easy to associate a musical pitch with the system parameters: under fixed conditions, for example, one has a fundamental frequency of $f_0 = \gamma/2$. In

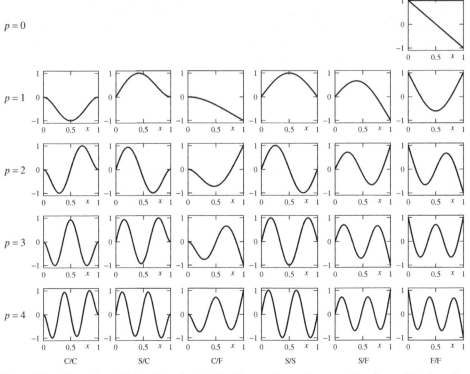

Figure 7.2 Plots of modal functions for the ideal bar, under various combinations of the boundary conditions of clamped (C), simply supported (S), and free (F) types given in (7.7), as indicated at bottom. The first four modal shapes are shown, in order of increasing frequency, down each column. In the case of free/free termination, an additional pair of modal shapes, of frequency 0, is also shown. The modal functions are all normalized so that they take on values between -1 and 1.

the case of a bar, this is not so, due to inharmonicity or dispersion. The lowest frequency will be in the range of $\kappa\pi/2$, with variations due to the type of boundary conditions. If this frequency is in the upper musical range (i.e., in, say, the right half of the piano keyboard), then a listener will associate a pitch with this frequency. If it is low, however, the series of frequencies will be comparatively dense, and pitch assignment can be difficult. Other factors, such as frequency-dependent loss, also intervene in this respect. For this reason, in implementations, it is perhaps simpler to leave the parameter κ as it is, and ask the user to learn its perceptual significance.

7.1.4   A finite difference scheme

The most straightforward finite difference scheme for the ideal bar equation (7.2) may be written, in operator form, as

$$\delta_{tt}u = -\kappa^2\delta_{xxxx}u \tag{7.11}$$

where the definition of δ_{xxxx} is given in (5.12b). When the operator notation is expanded out, the following two-step recursion results:

$$u_l^{n+1} = (2 - 6\mu^2)u_l^n + 4\mu^2\left(u_{l+1}^n + u_{l-1}^n\right) - \mu^2\left(u_{l-2}^n + u_{l+2}^n\right) - u_l^{n-1} \tag{7.12}$$

In order to be updated, the scheme requires access to values of the grid function two grid spacings away from the update point, and is parameterized by the single number μ,

$$\mu \triangleq \kappa k / h^2$$

μ plays a role similar to λ, the Courant number, which appears in schemes for the wave equation. Like the two-step scheme for the wave equation (6.34), scheme (7.11) must be initialized with values of the grid function u_l^n at time steps $n = 0$ and $n = 1$. Scheme (7.11) is, formally, second-order accurate in both time and space—unlike the case of scheme (6.34) for the wave equation, there is no special choice of the parameter μ which leads to improved accuracy.

von Neumann analysis

Just as for schemes for the wave equation, one may employ the test function $u_l^n = z^n e^{j\beta l h}$, which, when inserted in scheme (7.11), gives the following characteristic polynomial in z:

$$z + (16\mu^2 \sin^4(\beta h / 2) - 2) + z^{-1} = 0 \tag{7.13}$$

This equation possesses roots of magnitude unity under the condition

$$\mu \leq \frac{1}{2} \qquad \longrightarrow \qquad k \leq \frac{h^2}{2\kappa} \tag{7.14}$$

which is somewhat different from the condition (6.40) which arises in the scheme (6.34) for the 1D wave equation. Now, the time step is bounded by the square of the grid spacing, rather than the grid spacing itself. This condition has interesting ramifications with regard to computational complexity, as will be discussed next.

Degrees of freedom and computational complexity

Supposing that the bar equation is defined over the unit interval $\mathcal{D} = \mathbb{U}$, the number of degrees of freedom of the scheme will be, as in the case of schemes for the wave equation, twice the number of grid points over this interval (scheme (7.11) is again a two-step scheme). Given that this number of grid points is approximately $1/h$, and that the sample rate is defined as $f_s = 1/k$, the number of degrees of freedom will be bounded, from the stability condition (7.14), as

$$N_{\text{fd}} = \frac{2}{h} \leq \sqrt{\frac{2 f_s}{\kappa}}$$

which is very similar to the number of modes required to represent the solution of the ideal bar equation to frequencies up to f_s, from (7.10), but not the same—it is greater by a factor of $\sqrt{\pi/2}$ which is quite close to one, meaning that a modal representation and the finite difference scheme possess roughly the same number of degrees of freedom. This small discrepancy may be related to effects of numerical dispersion, as described in the next section. It is crucial to note that, in a comparison between the wave equation and the bar equation, for which both possess the same first non-zero modal frequency (or "fundamental," if one may indeed apply that term to an inharmonic system such as a bar), the bar will possess far fewer degrees of freedom—as a result, computations for dispersive systems such as bars are lighter than those for non-stiff systems such as strings. This may be counterintuitive, given that the bar equation itself *looks more complex* than the wave equation. Looks can be deceiving. Such an efficiency gain for stiff systems may be exploited to great benefit in, for instance, models of plate reverberation, which are far less computationally intensive than even 2D simulations of the wave equation, in the context of artificial reverberation.

See Section 12.3.3. On the other hand, the thin bar model is itself an idealization—when more
realistic models are employed, the number of degrees of freedom (and thus the memory and
operation count in simulation) creeps up again. See Problem 7.2.

Numerical dispersion

When the stability condition (7.14) is satisfied, the roots of the characteristic equation are of the
form $z = e^{j\omega k}$, and thus the characteristic polynomial (7.13) may be written as

$$\sin(\omega k/2) = \pm 2\mu \sin^2(\beta h/2)$$

which is analogous to the dispersion relation (7.4) for the continuous ideal bar equation. In contrast
with scheme (6.34) for the wave equation, this scheme exhibits numerical dispersion, beyond the
natural dispersion inherent in the bar equation itself, for any allowable choice of μ. See Figure 7.3
for plots of numerical phase and group velocity for different choices of μ—it remains true,
however, that numerical dispersion is minimized as μ approaches the bound given in (7.14), as
per Rule of Thumb #1, given on page 136.

It is also true in this case that when the scheme is operating away from the stability condition
(7.14) (i.e., when $\mu < 1/2$), there will be some loss in available bandwidth for the computed
solution. The dispersion relation above possesses solutions for real frequencies f only when

$$f \le f_{max} = \frac{1}{\pi k} \sin^{-1}(2\mu)$$

where f_{max} is a numerical cutoff frequency—this cutoff behavior is clearly visible in Figure 7.3.

Energy conservation and non-negativity

Just as for schemes for the wave equation, energy analysis is possible (and indeed quite straightforward) for scheme (7.11). Considering the problem defined over the infinite domain $\mathcal{D} = \mathbb{Z}$, taking
an inner product with the grid function $\delta_t.u$, and using the double summation by parts identity
(5.28), gives

$$\langle \delta_t.u, \delta_{tt}u \rangle_{\mathbb{Z}} = -\kappa^2 \langle \delta_t.u, \delta_{xxxx}u \rangle_{\mathbb{Z}} = -\kappa^2 \langle \delta_{xx}u, \delta_t.\delta_{xx}u \rangle_{\mathbb{Z}}$$

or

$$\delta_{t+}\mathfrak{h} = 0 \quad \text{with} \quad \mathfrak{h} = \mathfrak{t} + \mathfrak{v} \quad \text{and} \quad \mathfrak{t} = \frac{1}{2}\|\delta_t{-}u\|_{\mathbb{Z}}^2 \quad \mathfrak{v} = \frac{\kappa^2}{2}\langle \delta_{xx}u, e_{t-}\delta_{xx}u \rangle_{\mathbb{Z}} \quad (7.15)$$

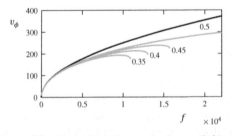
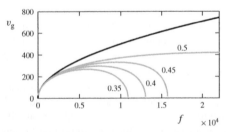

Figure 7.3   Numerical phase velocity v_ϕ (left) and group velocity v_g as functions of frequency f
for scheme (7.11) for the ideal bar equation, with $\kappa = 1$, under different choices of the parameter
μ (as indicated), plotted as grey lines. The curves for the continuous model system are plotted
as black lines. In this case, the time step has been chosen as $k = 1/44\,100$. Notice the numerical
cutoff visible in the curves for values of $\mu < 1/2$.

The total difference (7.15) above is a statement of conservation of numerical energy for the scheme (7.11), and it thus follows that

$$\mathfrak{h}^n = \mathfrak{h}^0$$

Just as in the case of schemes for the wave equation, in order to find conditions under which this energy is non-negative, one may write, using identity (2.22f) and inequality (5.31),

$$\mathfrak{h} = \frac{1}{2}\|\delta_{t-}u\|_{\mathbb{Z}}^2 + \frac{\kappa^2}{2}\|\mu_{t-}\delta_{xx}u\|_{\mathbb{Z}}^2 - \frac{k^2\kappa^2}{8}\|\delta_{t-}\delta_{xx}u\|_{\mathbb{Z}}^2$$

$$\geq \left(\frac{1}{2} - \frac{2k^2\kappa^2}{h^4}\right)\|\delta_{t-}u\|_{\mathbb{Z}}^2 + \frac{\kappa^2}{2}\|\mu_{t-}\delta_{xx}u\|_{\mathbb{Z}}^2$$

The energy is non-negative under condition (7.14), and under this condition a bound on solution size for all n follows immediately. Again, energy analysis leads to the same stability condition as von Neumann analysis.

Numerical boundary conditions

Numerical boundary conditions may be derived, again as in the case of schemes for the wave equation. Here, however, the analysis is slightly more delicate—different choices of inner product, as well as uses of summation by parts, can give rise to different conserved energies, accompanied by distinct numerical boundary conditions.

Consider now the scheme (7.11) defined over the semi-infinite domain $\mathbb{Z}^+$. Taking the inner product with $\delta_{t\cdot}u$, and using the summation by parts identity from (5.27b), gives

$$\delta_{t+}\mathfrak{h} = \mathfrak{b} \qquad \text{with} \qquad \mathfrak{h} = \mathfrak{t} + \mathfrak{v} \qquad \text{and} \qquad \mathfrak{t} = \frac{1}{2}\|\delta_{t-}u\|_{\mathbb{Z}^+}^2 \qquad \mathfrak{v} = \frac{\kappa^2}{2}\langle\delta_{xx}u, e_{t-}\delta_{xx}u\rangle_{\overline{\mathbb{Z}^+}}$$

and

$$\mathfrak{b} = -\kappa^2\,(\delta_{t\cdot}\delta_{x+}u_0)\,(\delta_{xx}u_0) + \kappa^2\,(\delta_{t\cdot}u_0)\,(\delta_{x-}\delta_{xx}u_0)$$

Thus numerical energy conservation follows under the following choices of numerical boundary condition at the left end point of a domain:

$$u = \delta_{x+}u \quad = 0 \qquad \text{clamped} \tag{7.16a}$$

$$u = \delta_{xx}u \quad = 0 \qquad \text{simply supported} \tag{7.16b}$$

$$\delta_{xx}u = \delta_{x-}\delta_{xx}u = 0 \qquad \text{free} \tag{7.16c}$$

These conditions are analogous to the conditions (7.7) for the ideal bar equation.

The particular form of summation by parts used above, namely that given in (5.27b), leads to a simple, tractable expression for the numerical conserved energy, if $\mathfrak{b} = 0$—tractable in the sense that non-negativity is easy to show, as the expression for the potential energy $\mathfrak{v}$ is limited strictly to the *interior* of the problem domain. Just as in the case of the infinite domain discussed in Section 7.1.2, one has

$$\mathfrak{h} = \frac{1}{2}\|\delta_{t-}u\|_{\mathbb{Z}^+}^2 + \frac{\kappa^2}{2}\|\mu_{t-}\delta_{xx}u\|_{\mathbb{Z}^+}^2 - \frac{k^2\kappa^2}{8}\|\delta_{t-}\delta_{xx}u\|_{\overline{\mathbb{Z}^+}}^2$$

$$\geq \left(\frac{1}{2} - \frac{2k^2\kappa^2}{h^4}\right)\|\delta_{t-}u\|_{\mathbb{Z}^+}^2 + \frac{\kappa^2}{2}\|\mu_{t-}\delta_{xx}u\|_{\overline{\mathbb{Z}^+}}^2$$

and the stability condition (7.14) again leads to non-negativity.

It is important to note that if one were to use the other form of the summation by parts identity, i.e., that given in (5.27a), the derived boundary conditions would be distinct, as would the expression for energy. In some cases, it is not so easy to show non-negativity as v may not be limited to the interior of the problem domain. See Problem 7.5 for some variations on energy analysis and numerical boundary conditions for the bar.

Implementation of numerical boundary conditions

It is useful to show how numerical boundary conditions such as (7.16), written in compact operator form, may be implemented directly in the scheme (7.11).

The clamped condition at $l = 0$ is the most straightforward: one may set

$$u_0 = u_1 = 0$$

at each pass through the recursion. Thus only values u_l of the solution at locations $l = 2, 3, \ldots$ need be computed; because the operator δ_{xxxx} is of width 5, its value may be computed directly using the settings above for u_0 and u_1.

The simply supported conditions are slightly more complicated. They may be rewritten as

$$u_0 = 0 \qquad\qquad u_{-1} = -u_1$$

Now, values at the grid locations $l = 1, \ldots$ must be updated; under the action of δ_{xxxx}, the value at $l = 1$ will require access to a value at a virtual grid point $l = -1$ (see Section 5.2.8). It is sufficient to examine the behavior of the operator δ_{xxxx} at locations near the boundary, and employ both conditions above:

$$\delta_{xxxx}u_1 = \frac{1}{h^4} (u_3 - 4u_2 + 6u_1 - 4u_0 + u_{-1}) = \frac{1}{h^4} (u_3 - 4u_2 + 5u_1)$$

Such conditions may be incorporated into a matrix form of the operator δ_{xxxx}, as outlined in Section 5.2.8.

The settings for the free boundary condition are left to Problem 7.6.

7.1.5   An implicit scheme

The problem of numerical dispersion does not arise in the case of the most straightforward scheme for the 1D wave equation. In the case of the bar, however, the rudimentary scheme presented in the previous section does indeed suffer from such dispersion. It has also been noted that the number of degrees of freedom of the scheme, N_{fd}, is slightly larger than the number which follows from modal analysis. As will be shown in this section, these two undesirable phenomena are related, and the discrepancy may be addressed using implicit methods.

An implicit scheme for the 1D wave equation, dependent on a single free parameter θ, has been presented in Section 6.3.2. Consider a similar implicit scheme for the ideal bar equation:

$$(\theta + (1 - \theta)\mu_{x\cdot}) \delta_{tt}u = -\kappa^2\delta_{xxxx}u \qquad\qquad (7.17)$$

In vector–matrix form, assuming as usual that the column vector $\mathbf{u}^n$ contains the values of the grid function u_l^n, then the scheme may be written as

$$\mathbf{u}^{n+1} = \mathbf{A}^{-1}\mathbf{B}\mathbf{u}^n - \mathbf{u}^{n-1} \qquad \text{with} \qquad \mathbf{A} = \theta\mathbf{I} + (1 - \theta)\mathbf{M}_x. \qquad \mathbf{B} = -\kappa^2 k^2\mathbf{D}_{xxxx} + 2\mathbf{A} \qquad (7.18)$$

where the various matrix operators incorporate boundary conditions. Again, a sparse (tridiagonal) linear system solution is required at each time step.

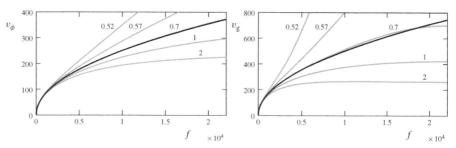

Figure 7.4 Numerical phase velocity v_ϕ (left) and group velocity v_g as functions of frequency f for scheme (7.17) for the ideal bar equation with $\kappa = 1$, under different choices of the parameter θ, are plotted as grey lines. The curves for the continuous model system are plotted as black lines. In this case, the time step is chosen as $k = 1/44\,100$, and μ is chosen so as to satisfy bound (7.19) with equality.

The von Neumann and energy methods yield the following stability conditions:

$$\theta \geq \frac{1}{2} \qquad \mu \leq \frac{\sqrt{2\theta - 1}}{2} \qquad\qquad (7.19)$$

See Problem 7.7. As usual, one may also make use of energy techniques in order to arrive at suitable numerical boundary conditions; the numerical clamped and simply supported conditions for the explicit scheme lead to conservative numerical behavior in this case as well, but the free condition must be altered slightly—see Problem 7.8.

It is instructive to plot the phase and group velocities for the scheme, for different values of the free parameter θ—see Figure 7.4. As usual, the scheme parameter μ is chosen as close to the stability bound as possible, so as to maximize the bandwidth of the scheme at a given sample rate $f_s = 1/k$, as discussed on page 170 with regard to the explicit scheme. Observe that for the choice of $\theta \cong 0.7$, the numerical phase velocity is nearly a perfect match to the phase velocity of the model system. This choice of θ can be viewed as resulting from a consideration of the number of degrees of freedom, in the following way. Supposing that the scheme is defined over the unit interval $\mathcal{D} = \mathbb{U}_N$, and that μ is chosen such as to satisfy the second of conditions (7.19) with equality, then the number of degrees of freedom for the scheme (i.e., twice the number of points on the grid) will be

$$N_{\mathrm{fd}} = 2/h = 2\sqrt{\frac{\mu}{k\kappa}} = \sqrt{\frac{2}{k\kappa}}(2\theta - 1)^{1/4} = \sqrt{\frac{\pi}{2}}(2\theta - 1)^{1/4} N_{\mathrm{m}}$$

where $N_{\mathrm{m}} = 2\sqrt{1/(k\kappa\pi)}$ is the number of degrees of freedom resulting from modal analysis, as given in (7.10). In order to have $N_{\mathrm{fd}} = N_{\mathrm{m}}$, one must then choose

$$\theta = \frac{1 + 4/\pi^2}{2} = 0.7026\ldots$$

The lesson here is that, for a parameterized scheme, the best numerical behavior (i.e., the least numerical dispersion) is obtained when the number of degrees of freedom of the scheme matches that of the physical system. Also note that even though implicit schemes are marginally more costly, computationally, than explicit schemes, the number of degrees of freedom of the scheme, and thus the number of grid points, is reduced from that of the explicit scheme under this choice of θ.

From a musical point of view, it is instructive to look at the effect of the use of an implicit scheme on the calculated numerical modal frequencies. From the vector–matrix form (7.18), the

Table 7.1 Comparison among modal frequencies of the ideal bar, under simply supported conditions, with a fundamental frequency of 100 Hz, and modal frequencies (as well as their cent deviations from the exact frequencies) of the explicit scheme (7.11), and the implicit θ scheme (7.17), with $\theta = 0.7026$, with a sample rate $f_s = 44\,100$ Hz, and where μ is chosen so as to satisfy (7.19) as close to equality as possible.

Mode number	Exact freq.	Explicit		Implicit	
		Freq.	Cent dev.	Freq.	Cent dev.
1	100.0	99.7	−4.4	100.0	−0.8
2	400.0	396.0	−17.4	399.3	−3.0
3	900.0	880.2	−38.5	896.7	−6.4
4	1600.0	1539.1	−67.1	1590.3	−10.5
5	2500.0	2356.4	−102.4	2478.5	−15.0
6	3600.0	3313.5	−143.6	3560.0	−19.4

set of such frequencies f_p, indexed by integer p, may be calculated as

$$f_p = \frac{1}{2\pi k} \cos^{-1} \left(\frac{1}{2} \mathrm{eig}_p \left(\mathbf{A}^{-1} \mathbf{B} \right) \right)$$

where eig_p signifies "pth eigenvalue of." Note that the modal frequencies for the explicit scheme may be calculated as well, by choosing $\theta = 1$.

From the results given in Table 7.1, one can immediately see that the accuracy of the implicit scheme is far superior to that of the explicit method—indeed, deviations of numerical frequencies from the exact values which are potentially audible for the explicit scheme are close to the threshold of inaudibility in the implicit case. What is more surprising, however, given the fidelity with which the numerical phase velocity of the implicit scheme with $\theta = 0.7026$ matches that of the model system, is that the numerical frequencies do not match even better! There are a couple of (admittedly extremely subtle) factors which account for this. The main one is that, due to the truncation of the number of grid points to an integer, it becomes difficult to satisfy the stability condition (7.19) exactly, so that μ undershoots its maximum allowed value by a very small amount. The other is that the numerical boundary condition, here chosen as being of simply supported type, is approximate as well, and not accounted for by dispersion analysis of the scheme over the infinite domain. One could thus go much further toward developing even more refined designs, but, for musical purposes, the above accuracy is probably sufficient for most cases.

The lesson here is:

Rule of Thumb #2

For a parameterized implicit numerical method, the best numerical behavior (i.e., the least numerical dispersion) is obtained when the stability condition is satisfied with equality, and when the free parameter(s) are chosen such that the number of degrees of freedom of the scheme matches that of the model system, at a given sample rate.

7.2   Stiff strings

In some musical instruments (in particular the piano), strings may be subject to a restoring force due not only to applied tension, but also to stiffness. Though the effect of stiffness is usually small

relative to that of tension, it does lead to an audible inharmonicity (which is usually desirable!). The
PDE model of such a string has been presented by many authors [244, 379], and, when spatially
scaled, has the form

$$u_{tt} = \gamma^2 u_{xx} - \kappa^2 u_{xxxx} \tag{7.20}$$

and may be viewed as a combination of the wave equation (6.5) and that of the ideal bar (7.2). It
is, again, a second-order (in time) PDE, and as such requires two initial conditions, of the form
mentioned in, for example, Section 6.1.3 and Section 7.1. The dispersion relation for the stiff
string, as defined by (7.20), is

$$s^2 + \gamma^2 \beta^2 + \kappa^2 \beta^4 = 0$$

implying that

$$\omega_\pm = \pm \beta \sqrt{\gamma^2 + \kappa^2 \beta^2}$$

and thus the phase and group velocity will be

$$v_\phi = \sqrt{\gamma^2 + \kappa^2 \beta^2} \qquad v_g = \frac{\gamma^2 + 2\kappa^2 \beta^2}{\sqrt{\gamma^2 + \kappa^2 \beta^2}}$$

Writing these expressions in terms of ω is tedious, but the results are as expected: for low frequencies, the velocities approach γ, and for high frequencies, the velocity of the ideal bar. "High"
and "low" here now must be taken with regard to the size of κ relative to γ. See Figure 7.5.

7.2.1 Energy and boundary conditions

The energy analysis of the stiff string, defined in (7.20), is similar to that performed for the wave
equation and for the ideal bar. Considering the stiff string defined over the semi-infinite domain
$\mathcal{D} = \mathbb{R}^+$, and taking the inner product with u_t, one arrives at

$$\frac{d\mathfrak{H}}{dt} = \mathfrak{B} \qquad \text{with} \qquad \mathfrak{H} = \mathfrak{T} + \mathfrak{V}$$

and

$$\mathfrak{T} = \frac{1}{2} \|u_t\|^2_{\mathbb{R}+} \qquad \mathfrak{V} = \frac{\gamma^2}{2} \|u_x\|^2_{\mathbb{R}+} + \frac{\kappa^2}{2} \|u_{xx}\|^2_{\mathbb{R}+}$$

$$\mathfrak{B} = -\gamma^2 u_t(0, t) u_x(0, t) + \kappa^2 u_t(0, t) u_{xxx}(0, t) - \kappa^2 u_{tx}(0, t) u_{xx}(0, t)$$

Here, the potential energy is merely the sum of the potential energies for the wave equation and
for the bar. The boundary term $\mathfrak{B}$ vanishes, implying losslessness, under the clamped and simply

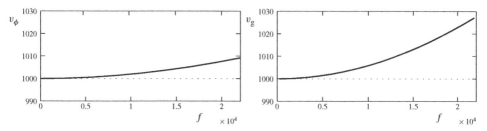

Figure 7.5 Phase velocity v_ϕ (left) and group velocity v_g (right) as functions of frequency f for
the stiff string equation (7.20), with $\gamma = 1000$ and $\kappa = 1$. The velocities of the system without
stiffness are plotted as dotted lines.

supported conditions (7.7a) and (7.7b), but the free termination (which is not often employed in the musical acoustics of strings) must be modified to

$$u_{xx}(0, t) = \kappa^2 u_{xxx}(0, t) - \gamma^2 u_x(0, t) = 0$$

7.2.2   Modes

Modal analysis is also similar. Over the domain $\mathcal{D} = \mathbb{U}$ and under simply supported conditions, the modal frequencies and functions are of the form

$$U_p(x) = \sin(p\pi x) \qquad \omega_p = \gamma p\pi \sqrt{1 + \frac{\kappa^2 \pi^2}{\gamma^2} p^2}$$

When the stiffness parameter κ is small, as in the case of most strings, the frequencies f in Hertz are sometimes written in terms of the fundamental frequency $f_0 = \gamma/2$ for the ideal lossless string, and an inharmonicity factor B [135]:

$$f_p = f_0 p \sqrt{1 + Bp^2} \qquad \text{with} \qquad B = \frac{\kappa^2 \pi^2}{\gamma^2} \tag{7.21}$$

Thus the harmonic series becomes progressively detuned, to a degree dependent on B.

Again, for other choices of boundary conditions, the modal functions must be expressed in terms of trigonometric and hyperbolic trigonometric functions, and there is not a closed-form expression for the modal frequencies. Under clamped conditions, for low stiffness, the modal frequencies are changed little from the above series—see Problem 7.9. The number of degrees of freedom will thus be, approximately,

$$N_m = \sqrt{\frac{2}{B} \left(\sqrt{1 + Bf_s^2/f_0^2} - 1 \right)} \tag{7.22}$$

7.2.3   Finite difference schemes

Finite difference schemes for (7.20) may be arrived at using the same construction techniques as in the case of the 1D wave equation and the ideal bar equation. The simplest is certainly the following:

$$\delta_{tt} u = \gamma^2 \delta_{xx} u - \kappa^2 \delta_{xxxx} u \tag{7.23}$$

The von Neumann stability condition for this scheme is

$$\lambda^2 + 4\mu^2 \leq 1 \tag{7.24}$$

and is expressed in terms of the Courant number $\lambda = \gamma k/h$, used in schemes for the 1D wave equation, and the parameter $\mu = \kappa k/h^2$, used in the case of schemes for the ideal bar. See Problem 7.10. Of more practical use is the equivalent form written directly in terms of k and h:

$$h^4 - \gamma^2 k^2 h^2 - 4\kappa^2 k^2 \geq 0 \qquad \longrightarrow \qquad h \geq h_{min} = \sqrt{\frac{\gamma^2 k^2 + \sqrt{\gamma^4 k^4 + 16\kappa^2 k^2}}{2}}$$

Thus, again, for a given k (or sample rate $f_s = 1/k$), there is a minimum grid spacing h_{min}.

One implicit generalization of the now-familiar θ type is

$$(\theta + (1 - \theta)\mu_{x.}) \delta_{tt} u = \gamma^2 \delta_{xx} u - \kappa^2 \delta_{xxxx} u \tag{7.25}$$

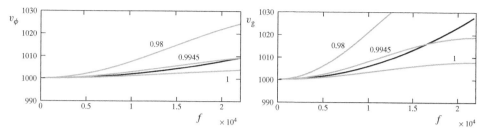

Figure 7.6 Phase velocity v_ϕ (left) and group velocity v_g (right) as functions of frequency f for the stiff string equation (7.20), with $\gamma = 1000$ and $\kappa = 1$, in black. Plotted in grey are the numerical phase velocities of the parameterized scheme (7.25), under different choices of the free parameter θ, as indicated. The sample rate is $f_s = 44\,100$ Hz, and the grid spacing h is chosen at the stability limit (7.26).

and stability analysis leads to the condition

$$\theta \geq \frac{1}{2} \quad \text{and} \quad \lambda^2 + 4\mu^2 \leq 2\theta - 1 \quad \longrightarrow \quad h \geq h_{\min} = \sqrt{\frac{\gamma^2 k^2 + \sqrt{\gamma^4 k^4 + 16\kappa^2 k^2 (2\theta - 1)}}{2(2\theta - 1)}}$$

(7.26)

The number of degrees of freedom N_{fd} will thus be, in the ideal case where the bound above is satisfied with equality,

$$N_{\text{fd}} = \frac{2}{h_{\min}}$$

(7.27)

As expected, the numerical phase and group velocities for the implicit scheme depend heavily on the choice of θ; it is more difficult to get a good match, in this case, across the entire frequency spectrum, especially under low-stiffness conditions. See Figure 7.6. Still, one can do fairly well, as long as θ is chosen properly. As before, the best fit occurs when the number of degrees of freedom of the scheme matches that of the model problem, and one can indeed determine in this way a value for θ, dependent now on γ, κ, and f_s—see Problem 7.11 and Programming Exercise 7.2.

In vector–matrix form, the scheme may be written as

$$\mathbf{u}^{n+1} = \mathbf{A}^{-1} \mathbf{B} \mathbf{u}^n - \mathbf{u}^{n-1}$$

with

$$\mathbf{A} = \theta \mathbf{I} + (1 - \theta) \mathbf{M}_x. \qquad \mathbf{B} = 2\mathbf{A} + k^2 \left(\gamma^2 \mathbf{D}_{xx} - \kappa^2 \mathbf{D}_{xxxx} \right)$$

Numerical boundary conditions for the stiff string may be determined through energy analysis; the conditions (7.16a) and (7.16b) hold as before, and are the most useful in the context of string modeling.

7.3 Frequency-dependent loss

Real strings exhibit a rather complex loss characteristic—the various frequency components do not all decay at the same rate. Loss generally increases with frequency, leading to a sound with a wide-band attack, decaying to a few harmonics. One model of frequency-dependent loss in linear strings is given by the following PDE [33]:

$$u_{tt} = \gamma^2 u_{xx} - \kappa^2 u_{xxxx} - 2\sigma_0 u_t + 2\sigma_1 u_{txx}$$

(7.28)

The term with coefficient $\sigma_0 \geq 0$ is the familiar loss term which was encountered earlier in the case of the wave equation in Section 6.5. On its own, it gives rise to a bulk frequency-independent loss (i.e., a constant T_{60} at all frequencies). The extra term with coefficient $\sigma_1 \geq 0$ is one means of modeling the frequency dependence of the loss characteristic. It is worth noting that this is not the original model of frequency-dependent loss (which employed a third time derivative term) which was proposed by Ruiz [305], and then later used in piano synthesis models by various authors [75]. See Problems 7.12 and 7.13.

The characteristic equation for (7.28) is

$$s^2 + 2\left(\sigma_0 + \sigma_1\beta^2\right)s + \gamma^2\beta^2 + \kappa^2\beta^4 = 0$$

which has roots

$$s_{\pm} = -\sigma_0 - \sigma_1\beta^2 \pm \sqrt{(\sigma_0 + \sigma_1\beta^2)^2 - (\gamma^2\beta^2 + \kappa^2\beta^4)}$$

For small σ_0 and σ_1, the term under the root above is negative for all wavenumbers over a very small cutoff, and one may write, using $s_{\pm} = \sigma \pm j\omega$,

$$\sigma(\beta) = -\sigma_0 - \sigma_1\beta^2 \qquad \omega(\beta) = \sqrt{\gamma^2\beta^2 + \kappa^2\beta^4 - (\sigma_0 + \sigma_1\beta^2)^2}$$

The loss $\sigma(\beta)$ thus decreases monotonically as a function of wavenumber, taking the value of $-\sigma_0$ in the limit as β approaches zero.

Practical settings for decay times

It can be somewhat difficult to get a grasp on the perceptual significance of the parameter σ_1. To this end, it is worth rewriting the expression for loss $\sigma(\beta)$ as a function of frequency, i.e., $\sigma(\omega)$. From the expression for $\omega(\beta)$ given above, it is reasonable to assume that when the loss parameters σ_0 and σ_1 are small (as they should be in any reasonable model of a bar or string used for musical purposes), then one may write

$$\omega(\beta) \cong \sqrt{\gamma^2\beta^2 + \kappa^2\beta^4} \qquad \longrightarrow \qquad \beta^2 = \frac{-\gamma^2 + \sqrt{\gamma^4 + 4\kappa^2\omega^2}}{2\kappa^2} \triangleq \xi(\omega)$$

which further implies that one may write $\sigma(\omega)$ as

$$\sigma(\omega) = -\sigma_0 - \sigma_1\xi(\omega)$$

With two parameters available to set the decay profile for the string, one could then specify T_{60} decay times at frequencies ω_1 and ω_2, and set σ_0 and σ_1, from the above formula, as

$$\sigma_0 = \frac{6\ln(10)}{\xi(\omega_2) - \xi(\omega_1)}\left(\frac{\xi(\omega_2)}{T_{60}(\omega_1)} - \frac{\xi(\omega_1)}{T_{60}(\omega_2)}\right) \qquad \sigma_1 = \frac{6\ln(10)}{\xi(\omega_2) - \xi(\omega_1)}\left(-\frac{1}{T_{60}(\omega_1)} + \frac{1}{T_{60}(\omega_2)}\right)$$

(7.29)

See Figure 7.7, showing a typical loss profile for a two-parameter model and a spectrogram of an output signal. For this model, in which loss increases monotonically with frequency, one must choose $T_{60}(\omega_2) \leq T_{60}(\omega_1)$ when $\omega_2 > \omega_1$. If one were interested in more a more complex decay profile, one could introduce additional terms in the model PDE involving higher spatial derivatives. See Problems 7.14 and 7.15. This, however, complicates the analysis of boundary conditions and stability, and will inevitably lead to a higher computational cost, though it may be useful in some applications, such as bar-based percussion instruments [77, 110].

One of the advantages of modal methods is that loss may be set separately for each mode, at virtually no additional computational cost—one could, for example, make use of loss parameters derived directly from measurement, in which case modal synthesis becomes a form of analysis–synthesis, allowing for very accurate reproduction of individual tones.

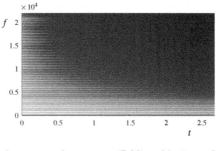

Figure 7.7   At left, a typical plot of T_{60} against frequency, for system (7.28), with $T_{60} = 5$ at 100 Hz, and $T_{60} = 3$ at 2000 Hz. At right, a spectrogram of sound output, for a stiff string with $\gamma = 800$ and $\kappa = 8$, with the loss parameters as specified above.

7.3.1   Energy and boundary conditions

The energy analysis of system (7.28) is similar to that of previous systems, except for the treatment of the frequency-dependent loss term. Again examining the system over the domain $\mathcal{D} = \mathbb{R}^+$, and taking an inner product with u_t, leads to the energy balance

$$\frac{d\mathfrak{H}}{dt} = \mathfrak{B} - \sigma_0 \|u_t\|_{\mathbb{R}^+}^2 - \sigma_1 \|u_{xt}\|_{\mathbb{R}^+}^2 \qquad \text{with} \qquad \mathfrak{H} = \mathfrak{T} + \mathfrak{V}$$

and where $\mathfrak{T}$ and $\mathfrak{V}$ are defined as for the lossless stiff string, and where the boundary term must be modified to

$$\mathfrak{B} = -\gamma^2 u_t(0, t) u_x(0, t) + \kappa^2 \left(u_t(0, t) u_{xxx}(0, t) - u_{tx}(0, t) u_{xx}(0, t)\right) - 2\sigma_1 u_t(0, t) u_{tx}(0, t)$$

Clamped and simply supported terminations, of the form given in (7.7), may again be viewed as lossless,[2] as $\mathfrak{B}$ vanishes. The free condition is more complex: one possibility is to write

$$u_{xx} = 0 \qquad \kappa^2 u_{xxx} - \gamma^2 u_x - 2\sigma_1 u_{tx} = 0$$

Under any of these conditions, and when $\sigma_0 \geq 0$ and $\sigma_1 \geq 0$, one has, just as in the case of the wave equation with loss, a monotonic decrease in energy, i.e.,

$$\frac{d\mathfrak{H}}{dt} \leq 0 \qquad \longrightarrow \qquad \mathfrak{H}(t_2) \leq \mathfrak{H}(t_1) \qquad \text{for} \qquad t_2 \geq t_1$$

7.3.2   Finite difference schemes

There are various ways of approximating the mixed derivative term in order to arrive at a finite difference scheme; two slightly different approximations have been introduced in Section 5.2.3. Two schemes are given, in operator form, as

$$\delta_{tt} u = \gamma^2 \delta_{xx} u - \kappa^2 \delta_{xxxx} u - 2\sigma_0 \delta_{t.} u + 2\sigma_1 \delta_{t-} \delta_{xx} u \qquad (7.30a)$$

$$\delta_{tt} u = \gamma^2 \delta_{xx} u - \kappa^2 \delta_{xxxx} u - 2\sigma_0 \delta_{t.} u + 2\sigma_1 \delta_{t.} \delta_{xx} u \qquad (7.30b)$$

Though these differ only in the discretization of the final term, there is a huge difference, in terms of implementation, between the two: scheme (7.30a) is explicit, and scheme (7.30b) is implicit.

---

[2] Lossless, in the sense that no additional loss is incurred at the boundaries, though the system is lossy as a whole.

Note also the use of a non-centered difference operator δ_{t-} in the explicit scheme, rendering it formally only first-order accurate, though as this term is quite small, it will not have an appreciable effect on accuracy as a whole, nor, even, a perceptual effect on sound output.

Because the implicit scheme employs centered operators only, stability analysis is far simpler—in fact, the loss terms have no effect on the stability condition, which remains the same as in the lossless case. The implicit scheme (7.30a) may be written in matrix form as

$$\mathbf{A}\mathbf{u}^{n+1} + \mathbf{B}\mathbf{u}^n + \mathbf{C}\mathbf{u}^{n-1} = 0$$

with

$$\mathbf{A} = (1 + \sigma_0 k)\mathbf{I} - \sigma_1 k\mathbf{D}_{xx} \qquad \mathbf{B} = -2\mathbf{I} - \gamma^2 k^2 \mathbf{D}_{xx} + \kappa^2 k^2 \mathbf{D}_{xxxx} \qquad \mathbf{C} = (1 - \sigma_0 k)\mathbf{I} + \sigma_1 k\mathbf{D}_{xx}$$

The reader may wish to look at the code provided in Section A.8. The matrix formulation makes for a remarkably compact recursion, at least in Matlab. See Programming Exercise 7.3 for a comparison of the performance to that of the explicit scheme (7.30a).

7.4   Coupling with bow models

As a first example of a coupling with an excitation mechanism, consider the case of a bow model, as described in Section 4.3.1. In this earlier section, the coupling of a bow model with a lumped mass–spring system has been considered. Coupling to a distributed object is not much more difficult to deal with. For a general presentation of the bow–string mechanism, and its use in synthesis, see, e.g., [410].

Suppose, first, that the bow acts on an ideal string, described by the wave equation defined over the unit interval $\mathcal{D} = \mathbb{U}$, at a location x_i, where x_i can be time varying, i.e., $x_i = x_i(t)$. If the spatial distribution of the bow is point-like, then the system is described, in scaled form, by

$$u_{tt} = \gamma^2 u_{xx} - \delta(x - x_i) F_B \phi(v_{rel}) \qquad \text{where} \qquad v_{rel} = u_t(x_i) - v_B \qquad (7.31)$$

Here, $F_B = F_B(t) \geq 0$ is the bow force/total string mass, $v_B = v_B(t)$ is the bow velocity, and ϕ is some friction characteristic assumed to satisfy properties (4.20) and (4.25). $\delta(x - x_i)$, it is to be recalled, is a spatial Dirac delta function centered at x_i.

Helmholtz motion

The earliest studies of bowed string dynamics, by Helmholtz and Raman in particular, focused on a phenomenological description of the motion, often referred to as Helmholtz motion—see [237] or [136] and the references therein for more on the history of the development of such models. See Figure 7.8 for the standard pictorial representation of auto-oscillations or Helmholtz motion. The principle is not extremely different from the case of the bowed mass (see Section 4.3.1), though in the case of the ideal string, roughly triangular waveforms are generated.

Energy balance

An inner product with u_t over $\mathbb{U}$ gives the energy balance

$$\frac{d\mathfrak{H}}{dt} = \mathfrak{B} - u_t(x_i) F_B \phi(v_{rel}) = \mathfrak{B} - v_{rel} F_B \phi(v_{rel}) - v_B F_B \phi(v_{rel})$$

where $\mathfrak{H}$ is, as before, the Hamiltonian for the ideal string, as given in (6.15) and taken over the interval $\mathcal{D} = \mathbb{U}$, $\mathfrak{B}$ is the usual boundary term as given in (6.21), and the other two terms

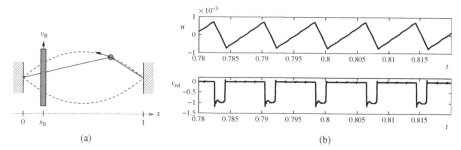

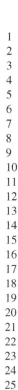

(a)   (b)

Figure 7.8 (a) Typical phenomenological description of bowed string motion (Helmholtz motion): a point on a string, assumed bent into a triangular shape, races around an envelope of parabolic shape; (b) the output waveform at the bowing point; and (c) relative velocity v_{rel} between string and bow, for an ideal string with a fundamental frequency of 125 Hz, under fixed end conditions, subject to bowing at constant speed $v_B = 0.2$, and with constant bow force $F_B = 50$, with the bowing point at $x_i = 0.25$. The bow characteristic shown in Figure 4.8(c) has been used, with $a = 100$. The above outputs have been produced using scheme (7.32) operating at a sample rate of 44 100 Hz.

represent dissipation in the bow mechanism, and power supplied by the bow, respectively. Under conservative or lossy boundary conditions, one has $\mathfrak{B} \leq 0$, and thus

$$\frac{d\mathfrak{H}}{dt} \leq -v_B F_B \phi(v_{rel}) \leq |F_B v_B| \qquad \longrightarrow \qquad \mathfrak{H}(t) \leq \mathfrak{H}(0) + \int_0^t |F_B v_B| dt'$$

Thus the state of the string is bounded in terms of initial conditions and energy provided by the bow.

Finite difference scheme

The case of the bow–string system, for which the bowing point may be moving during a player's gesture, requires a somewhat subtle numerical treatment—as one might expect, interpolation and spreading operators play a rather important role in the case of a difference scheme acting over a grid. Consider the following difference scheme analogous to (7.31):

$$\delta_{tt}u = \gamma^2 \delta_{xx}u - J(x_i^n)F_B\phi(v_{rel}) \qquad \text{where} \qquad v_{rel} = I(x_i^n)\delta_t.u - v_B \qquad (7.32)$$

Here, $F_B = F_B^n \geq 0$ and $v_B = v_B^n$ are now time series (perhaps sampled from data captured from a controller of some type). x_i^n is a time series representing the bow position at time step n. Notice now the appearance of the interpolator $I(x_i^n)$, used in order to obtain a value of string velocity at the bowing point, and the spreading function $J(x_i^n)$, which distributes the bow force over several neighbouring grid points on the string—see Section 5.2.4. The order of both is unspecified for the moment. An inner product with $\delta_t.u$ over the domain $\mathbb{U}_N$ yields the energy balance

$$\delta_{t+}\mathfrak{h} = \mathfrak{b} - \langle \delta_t.u, J(x_i^n) \rangle_{\mathbb{U}_N} F_B\phi(v_{rel})$$

where $\mathfrak{h}$ and $\mathfrak{b}$ are the Hamiltonian and boundary term for this scheme for the 1D wave equation, as discussed in Section 6.2.5 and Section 6.2.6.

For arbitrary interpolation and spreading operators, one cannot go further and find a stability condition. If, however, one chooses polynomial interpolants $I = I_p(x_i^n)$ and $J = J_{l,p}(x_i^n)$ of the same order, p, then using (5.33), one may write

$$\delta_{t+}\mathfrak{h} = \mathfrak{b} - F_B(I(x_i^n)\delta_t.u)\phi(v_{rel}) = \mathfrak{b} - F_B v_{rel}\phi(v_{rel}) - F_B v_B\phi(v_{rel})$$

In direct analogy with the continuous system, under lossless or dissipative numerical boundary conditions $\flat \leq 0$, one arrives, finally, at

$$\delta_{t+}\flat \leq |F_B v_B| \qquad \longrightarrow \qquad \flat^n \leq \flat^0 + \sum_{q=0}^{n-1} k |F_B^q v_B^q|$$

Again, one may bound the behavior of the scheme in terms of the known time series F_B and v_B. Notice in particular that the motion of the bowing position has no influence on stability.

Scheme (7.32) is implicit, and just as in the case of the bowed mass, there is the potential for non-uniqueness of numerical solutions. Taking an inner product with $J_{l,p}(x_i^n)$, and again using (5.33), gives

$$I_p(x_i^n)\delta_{tt}u = \gamma^2 I_p(x_i^n)\delta_{xx}u - \|J_p(x_i^n)\|_{\mathbb{U}}^2 F_B \phi\,(v_{rel}) \tag{7.33}$$

This equation may be solved uniquely for the relative velocity v_{rel} under the condition

$$k \leq -\frac{2}{\max(F_B)\max(\|J_p(x_i^n)\|_{\mathbb{U}}^2)\min(\phi')} \qquad \longrightarrow \qquad \lambda \leq \frac{2\gamma}{-\max(F_B)\min(\phi')} \tag{7.34}$$

which holds by virtue of the bound (5.34) on the interpolant J_p, and when $\min(\phi') \leq 0$, which is normally the case (when $\min(\phi') \geq 0$, the solution is always unique). The condition above must be satisfied in addition to the usual CFL condition (6.40) for this simple scheme for the wave equation. See Problem 7.16. Once the relative velocity has been determined, scheme (7.32) may be updated explicitly—see Programming Exercise 7.4.

Moving bowing point

When the bowing point is moving, extremely complex aural effects may be obtained, as the bowing point moves past the maximum of a particular mode—see Figure 7.9. In this case, good interpolation is crucial—zeroth-order truncation of the bowing position to a nearby grid point leads to very unpleasant audible artifacts. See Figure 7.10. Second-order (linear) interpolation vastly reduces the audibility of such motion, and fourth-order interpolation is an even safer choice, though it will probably only be necessary under sublime listening conditions.

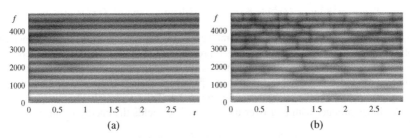

Figure 7.9   Spectrograms of synthetic sound output for a bowed string, with fundamental frequency 400 Hz, and for a bow acting with $F_B = 50$ and $v_B = 0.2$, with a friction characteristic of the form shown in Figure 4.8(c), with $a = 20$. Scheme (7.32) is used, at a sample rate of 44 100 Hz, and readout is taken at a point 0.45 of the way along the string from the left end. (a) String bowed at a location $x = 0.25$, and (b) with a bow location varying linearly between $x = 0.25$ and $x = 0.75$, illustrating the modulation of the amplitudes of the partials in the resulting sound.

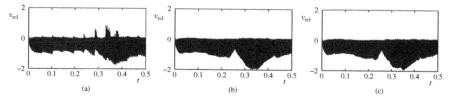

Figure 7.10   Relative velocity of the string to the bow, $v_{\mathrm{rel}} = \delta_t . u - v_{\mathrm{B}}$, for a difference scheme for an ideal string with fundamental frequency 400 Hz, and with constant bow force $F_{\mathrm{B}} = 150$, $v_{\mathrm{B}} = 0.2$, and where the bowing point moves from $x = 0.25$ to $x = 0.45$ over a duration of 1 second. Difference scheme (7.32) is used at sample rate 44 100 Hz, with interpolation of (a) zeroth order, (b) second order, and (c) fourth order. Notice the periodic jumps in (a) corresponding to hard truncations of the moving bowing point to a neighboring grid point. Output is read at $x = 0.7$.

Extensions

The model of bowed-string dynamics presented above is very crude, and may be extended in many ways. Given the material in the earlier part of this chapter, a direct extension is to the case of the bowed bar, which may be carried out fairly easily—see Problem 7.17 and Programming Exercise 7.5. Recently, there have been investigations into more delicate features of the bow–string interaction. Among the more interesting are the modeling of torsional wave propagation in bowed strings [151, 27], as well as the generalization of the bow to the case of finite width [272]. Both features have seen some investigation in the context of synthesis [321, 320, 319] and may be modeled using extensions of the finite difference methods described here, but as space is limited, these are left as an interesting exercise to the enterprising reader.

7.5   Coupling with hammer and mallet models

The hammer or mallet interaction forms the basis for many percussion instruments—in the 1D case, xylophones, marimbas, and other instruments are excited in this way (not to mention, of course, the piano itself). The interaction of a simple hammer model with a mass–spring system has been presented in Section 4.2.3, and, indeed, most of the important issues have already been described in detail. The extension to the case of an interaction with a 1D distributed system such as a string or bar is direct.

Consider, for simplicity, the case of a hammer, with a stiffness defined by a one-sided nonlinearity of some type, colliding with an ideal string whose dynamics are described by the 1D wave equation. Beginning from a dimensional form, and using a power law as the nonlinear characteristic (a common choice [154, 75]), one has

$$\rho A u_{tt} = T_0 u_{xx} + \epsilon(x) f \qquad f = -M_{\mathrm{H}} \frac{d^2 u_{\mathrm{H}}}{dt^2} = K_{\mathrm{H}} \left([u_{\mathrm{H}} - \langle \epsilon, u \rangle_{\mathcal{D}}]^+ \right)^\alpha$$

Here, ρ, A, and T_0 are the mass density, cross-sectional area, and tension in the string. The distribution $\epsilon(x)$, assumed fixed, represents the striking profile of the hammer, with position u_{H}, mass M_{H}, stiffness parameter K_{H}, and nonlinear stiffness exponent α—often set in the range between 1.5 and 3.5 [346]. $\epsilon(x)$ is usually sharply peaked, and, in the crudest model, could be idealized as a Dirac delta function. When spatially scaled over the interval $\mathcal{D} = \mathbb{U}$, the system has the form

$$u_{tt} = \gamma^2 u_{xx} + \epsilon(x) \mathcal{M} F \qquad F = -\frac{d^2 u_{\mathrm{H}}}{dt^2} = \omega_{\mathrm{H}}^{1+\alpha} \left([u_{\mathrm{H}} - \langle \epsilon, u \rangle_{\mathbb{U}}]^+ \right)^\alpha \qquad (7.35)$$

where the relevant parameters are now $\mathcal{M} = M_H/\rho AL$, the mass ratio of the hammer to the total string mass, and a frequency-like parameter $\omega_H = (K_H/M_H)^{1/(1+\alpha)}$. The hammer–string system, of course, preserves energy:

$$\frac{d\mathfrak{H}}{dt} = \mathfrak{B} \quad \text{with} \quad \mathfrak{H} = \mathfrak{H}_S + \mathfrak{H}_H$$

where $\mathfrak{H}_S$ is the energy of the string as given in (6.15) and limited to the domain $\mathcal{D} = \mathbb{U}$, $\mathfrak{B}$ is the usual boundary term, given in (6.21), and $\mathfrak{H}_H$, the energy of the hammer, is given by

$$\mathfrak{H}_H = \frac{\mathcal{M}}{2}\left(\frac{du_H}{dt}\right)^2 + \frac{\mathcal{M}\omega_H^{\alpha+1}}{1+\alpha}\left([u_H - \langle \epsilon, u\rangle_{\mathbb{U}}]^+\right)^{\alpha+1}$$

7.5.1   Force profiles and brightness

The key feature of the nonlinear hammer model in conjunction with a string is in the dependence of the resulting timbre on the hammer velocity—the harder the strike, the brighter the sound. This is easiest to understand by looking at simulated force interaction and output spectra, as in Figure 7.11. As velocity increases, the total interaction time tends to decrease, leading to a sharper "impulse"-like excitation and an overall brightening of the spectrum. Notice also the complexity of the interaction force profiles, which possess various peaks corresponding to the return of reflected waves to the hammer.

7.5.2   Finite difference schemes

The obvious finite difference scheme for (7.35) is

$$\delta_{tt}u = \gamma^2\delta_{xx}u + \epsilon \mathcal{M}F \qquad F = -\delta_{tt}u_H = \omega_H^{1+\alpha}\left([u_H - \langle \epsilon, u\rangle_{\mathbb{U}_N}]^+\right)^\alpha \qquad (7.36)$$

where, here, ϵ_l is some discrete approximation to the hammer profile $\epsilon(x)$—if $\epsilon(x)$ is localized as a Dirac delta function about a striking location x_H (which is a rather good choice in the case

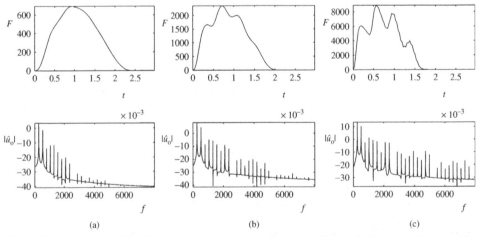

(a)   (b)   (c)

Figure 7.11   Force profiles (top) and output magnitude spectra (bottom) for a struck string. The string is of fundamental frequency 262 Hz, and is struck by a hammer, of mass ratio $\mathcal{M} = 0.75$, stiffness parameter $\omega_H = 3000$, and nonlinear stiffness exponent $\alpha = 2.5$, at position $x = 0.12$. Various hammer velocities are employed: (a) 0.5 m/s (piano); (b) 1.5 m/s (mezzoforte); and (c) 5 m/s (fortissimo).

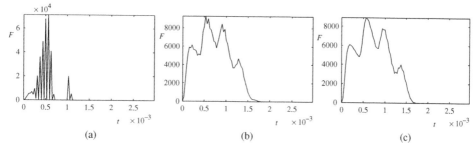

(a)   (b)   (c)

Figure 7.12 Numerical hammer–string force interaction profiles, for the hammer and string of parameters given in Figure 7.11, with a striking velocity of 5 m/s. In (a), scheme (7.36) is used, with a Courant number λ very close to 1, giving spurious oscillatory behavior. In (b), scheme (7.36) is again used, with a reduced Courant number close to $\lambda = 0.9$, and the oscillatory behavior is reduced somewhat. In (c), semi-implicit scheme (7.37) is used, at a Courant number close to 1, and oscillatory behavior is only barely evident.

of a hammer), then one may use the pth-order spreading function $\epsilon_l = J_{l,p}(x_H)$. The order of interpolation p is much less important here than in the case of the bow, as the hammer excitation generally is of very short duration, and not of time-varying location along the string, so zeroth-order truncation is a good bet. The scheme is entirely explicit, easy to implement, and is very similar to that presented in [75]. It does, however, exhibit some problems, the most serious of which is numerical oscillation—see Figure 7.12(a), showing the results of using this scheme directly, with a Courant number near 1. Such behavior is, of course, disastrous, perceptually. The usual remedy when unwanted oscillation occurs, at least in mainstream applications, is to reduce the Courant number away from the stability bound, and indeed, by $\lambda = 0.9$, the oscillatory behavior is attenuated significantly—see Figure 7.11(b). But, for synthesis applications, this is not a good idea, due to greatly reduced audio bandwidth and numerical dispersion—see Rule of Thumb #1 on page 136. Taking a cue from the analysis of schemes for power law nonlinearities in Section 4.2.2, one might try a semi-implicit approximation:

$$\delta_{tt}u = \gamma^2\delta_{xx}u + \epsilon\mathcal{M}F \qquad F = -\delta_{tt}u_H = \omega_H^{1+\alpha}\left([u_H - \langle\epsilon, u\rangle_{U_N}]^+\right)^{\alpha-1}\mu_{t\cdot}\left(u_H - \langle\epsilon, u\rangle_{U_N}\right) \tag{7.37}$$

This approximation is partially conservative (see Section 4.2.3) when $\alpha = 1$ or $\alpha = 3$. The behavior of this scheme is, indeed, much better, even near the Courant limit—the numerical oscillations have been largely suppressed. On the other hand, the implementation is slightly complicated by the implicit approximation—though more will be said about this in Section 7.7, which deals with connections between strings and passive lumped elements, the reader is referred to Problem 7.18 and Programming Exercise 7.6.

7.6 Multiple strings

Regardless of the type of synthesis method employed, once one has implemented one string or bar model, it is straightforward to make use of several at once, to synthesize different notes of a variety of bar or string-based instruments. More interesting is the case of several strings employed in order to generate a single note—such is the case, for example, for the piano, where two or three strings are struck at once, for each note, over most of the keyboard range. Normally, the strings differ little in their material properties, though depending on the tuning strategy (in synthesis, the algorithm designer has ultimate control over tuning) slight variations in tension give rise to desirable beating effects which go a long way toward rendering synthesis output more natural.

One may thus consider an (as yet) uncoupled system of M PDEs, of the 1D wave equation form

$$u_{tt}^{(q)} = \left(\gamma^{(q)}\right)^2 u_{xx}^{(q)} \qquad \text{for } q = 1, \ldots, M$$

Here, M is the number of strings, and $u^{(q)}$ is the transverse displacement of the Mth string. Though, for simplicity, the 1D wave equation has been used here, one could easily extend each PDE to include the usual stiffness and loss terms, and, potentially, nonlinear effects (see Chapter 8). The important point, however, is that the term involving $\gamma^{(q)}$, which incorporates tensioning effects, varies from one string to the next. In this spatially scaled form, all the strings are of unit length.

As far as tuning goes, recall that under low-stiffness and low-loss conditions, and under fixed boundary conditions, the pitch of the qth string will be almost exactly $\gamma^{(q)}/2$. Important design parameters in this case are f_0, the center pitch for the set of strings, and D, a detuning parameter, in cents. One can then set the values of $\gamma^{(q)}$ as

$$\gamma^{(q)} = 2^{1 + \frac{(2q-1-M)D}{2400(M-1)}} f_0 \qquad \text{for } q = 1, \ldots, M$$

Thus the M strings are detuned by a total of D cents from the highest pitch to the lowest.

A finite difference scheme follows immediately as

$$\delta_{tt} u^{(q)} = \left(\gamma^{(q)}\right)^2 \delta_{xx} u^{(q)} \qquad \text{for } q = 1, \ldots, M$$

A hitch arises here. The stability condition for the qth scheme will be, at least in the case of lossless non-stiff strings,

$$\lambda^{(q)} = \gamma^{(q)} k / h^{(q)} \leq 1 \qquad \longrightarrow \qquad h^{(q)} \geq \gamma^{(q)} k$$

where, here, $\lambda^{(q)}$ and $h^{(q)}$ are the Courant number and grid spacing for the qth string. If $\gamma^{(q)}$ exhibits some variation with q, then there will be distinct lower bounds on the grid spacings for the various strings. There are two ways of dealing with this: (1) take a uniform $h \geq \max_q(\gamma^{(q)}k)$ for all the strings; or (2) maintain a distinct $h^{(q)}$ for each string. For a low degree of variation in $\gamma^{(q)}$, option (1) is probably preferable, as it leads to great programming simplicity: the grid functions for all the strings will contain the same number of values. On the other hand, it is also clear that, under option (1), the grid spacing $h^{(q)}$ is chosen away from the Courant limit for some of the strings—thus there will be some reduction in audio bandwidth, and if this becomes noticeable, option (2) is perhaps preferable. The situation does not change much when loss and stiffness terms are included in the analysis, as there is always a lower bound on the grid spacing for any explicit scheme. See Programming Exercise 7.7.

Hammer interaction

In the case of the piano, multiple strings are excited at once by a single hammer; the situation is not that different from the case of a hammer striking multiple masses, which has been introduced briefly in Problem 4.4. In the case of strings, such an interaction may be written as follows:

$$u_{tt}^{(q)} = \left(\gamma^{(q)}\right)^2 u_{xx}^{(q)} + 2\sigma_0 u_t^{(q)} + \epsilon^{(q)}(x) \mathcal{M}^{(q)} F^{(q)} \qquad \text{for } q = 1, \ldots, M \qquad (7.38)$$

where for the qth string, $F^{(q)}$ is the force/mass of the hammer, $\mathcal{M}^{(q)}$ the mass ratio of the hammer to the string, and $\epsilon^{(q)}(x)$ the distribution of the hammer (these need not be identical). A loss term, of loss coefficient σ_0, has been added here for slightly more realism. The forces are related to the hammer displacement by

$$\frac{d^2 u_H}{dt^2} = -\sum_q F^{(q)} \qquad F^{(q)} = \omega_H^{1+\alpha} \left([u_H - \langle \epsilon^{(q)}, u^{(q)} \rangle_{\mathbb{U}}]^+\right)^\alpha$$

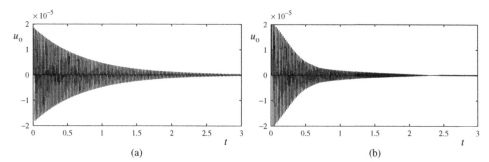

Figure 7.13   Output waveforms for system (7.38), for (a) a system with a single string, and (b) a system with three strings. In each case, the average fundamental frequency is 50 Hz and $T_{60} = 5$ s, but for the multiple string case, the strings are detuned by 5 cents relative to one another. In each case, the strings are struck at velocity 1 m/s with a hammer of mass ratio $\mathcal{M} = 1$ and with stiffness parameter $\omega_H = 200\pi$, at a position 0.1 of the way along the strings. Output is taken at $x = 0.3$.

Again, the system is strictly dissipative, and difference schemes such as (7.36) and (7.37) may be generalized directly.

Output and variation of temporal envelope

There are many ways of obtaining output. The most direct, considering that the strings in the set are all of equal perceptual importance, is to sum outputs from a given location:

$$u_o = \sum_{q=1}^{M} I(x_o^{(q)}) u^{(q)}$$

The most obvious effect of the use of multiple strings is on the temporal envelope of the resulting sound. If the strings are slightly detuned with respect to one another, cancellation will occur. Such cancellation plays a role in, for example, so-called two-stage decay of piano tones [136]—even for the very basic model given in (7.38), which possesses frequency-independent loss terms only, such behavior is audible; the output exhibits a rapid initial decay, and after phase differences among the various strings accumulate, the decay rate slows considerably. See Figure 7.13.

7.7   Prepared strings

The preparation of pianos, through the insertion of objects such as erasers, washers, etc., adjacent to the strings, was popularized by Cage [69]. It serves as an excellent case study for physical modeling synthesis for several reasons. First, the objects to be modeled (namely, the strings and the preparing objects) are all of a fairly well-understood nature—indeed the whole problem, barring the connection to a soundboard, can be described in terms of objects which are 1D or 0D (i.e., lumped). Second, this is the first appearance in this book of *modular* connections among physical modeling constructs, and thus the first step toward a flexible environment for the design of new virtual instruments, or modular synthesis. Some such work has been done using scattering-based numerical methods (see Section 1.2.4 and the references therein), and in a more limited fashion, using modal methods (see Section 1.2.2). Finally, the motivations of Cage and others who were interested in transforming the timbres of conventional instruments are exactly in line with the aesthetic spirit of physical modeling synthesis. In this section, and that which follows, such fanciful constructions will be examined from a numerical point of view.

As a starting point, consider again an ideal lossy string, modeled by the 1D wave equation accompanied by a loss term, with a lumped force f acting at a given location x_P. In scaled form, replacing f by $F = f/M_S$, where M_S is the total string mass, this may be written as

$$u_{tt} = \gamma^2 u_{xx} - 2\sigma_0 u_t + \delta(x - x_P)F \tag{7.39}$$

Here, $\delta(x - x_P)$ is a Dirac delta function peaked at $x = x_P$—as in the case of a hammer, it could be generalized to a finite-width distribution, but the localized connection is sufficient for the present purposes. So far, the form of the force term is unspecified—it could result from a constraint of some kind, dependent purely on the string state itself, or it could represent a coupling to another object. Even at this stage, it is worth noting that, if the force F depends linearly on properties of the string and/or other objects, the modal frequencies of the combined system cannot, in general, be related to those of the system in the absence of the force term—thus a modal approach to synthesis will require a complete recalculation of all the modal frequencies and shapes. If the connection is nonlinear, then one can expect a significant departure from the usual behavior of the ideal string.

An energy balance for this string may be written, under conservative boundary conditions, as

$$\frac{d\mathfrak{H}_S}{dt} = -2\sigma_0 \|u_t\|_{\mathbb{U}}^2 + Fu_t(x_P)$$

where $\mathfrak{H}_S$ is the usual Hamiltonian for the wave equation, as per (6.15). It is not difficult to add additional terms to the above model representing stiffness and frequency-dependent damping, but the above model suffices for an investigation of the main numerical issues.

7.7.1   Springs and dampers

Perhaps the simplest type of preparation involves massless springs and damping elements—see Figure 7.14. A combined model is described by

$$F = -\omega_0^2 u(x_P) - \omega_1^4 (u(x_P))^3 - 2\sigma_P u_t(x_P) \tag{7.40}$$

Here, there are two terms representing a linear spring and a cubic nonlinear spring, as well as a damping term—it is a crude model of, say, a piece of rubber wedged underneath a string. Using the usual techniques, the energy balance becomes

$$\frac{d\mathfrak{H}}{dt} = -2\sigma_0 \|u_t\|_{\mathbb{U}}^2 - 2\sigma_P(u_t(x_P))^2 \quad \text{with} \quad \mathfrak{H} = \mathfrak{H}_S + \mathfrak{H}_P \quad \text{and} \quad \mathfrak{H}_P = \frac{\omega_0^2}{2}(u(x_P))^2 + \frac{\omega_1^4}{4}(u(x_P))^4$$

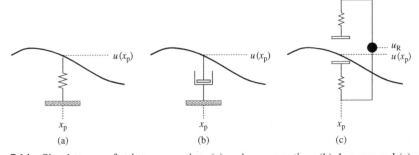

(a)   (b)   (c)

Figure 7.14   Simple types of string preparation: (a) spring connection; (b) damper; and (c) rattling element.

There is now an additional component to the stored energy, $\mathfrak{H}_P$, due to the spring. Notice that the energy for the combined system is non-negative, and, as before, monotonically decreasing.

There are, of course, many different choices now available for discretization—as in the case of the hammer, not all have the same properties! Suppose first that the wave equation (7.39) is discretized using the basic difference scheme,

$$\delta_{tt}u = \gamma^2 \delta_{xx}u - 2\sigma_0 \delta_t.u + J_p(x_P)F \tag{7.41}$$

where, here, $J_p(x_P)$ is a pth-order spreading operator (see Section 5.2.4). One way of discretizing the force equation is as

$$F = -\omega_0^2 \mu_t.\eta - \omega_1^4 \eta^2 \mu_t.\eta - 2\sigma_P \delta_t.\eta \quad \text{where} \quad \eta = I_p(x_P)u \tag{7.42}$$

and $I_p(x_P)$ is a pth-order interpolation operator (see Section 5.2.4). The system, though not linear, has been discretized in such a way as to indicate that the result will be strictly dissipative. Examining each of the terms in F separately: the linear spring term has been treated exactly as in the semi-implicit scheme for the oscillator, as discussed in Section 3.3.1, the cubic nonlinear oscillator term as per the method given in (4.9b), and the extra damping term by a centered difference, as per the lossy SHO—see Section 3.5.2.

As one might expect, under conservative boundary conditions the system as a whole possesses a discrete energy balance of the form

$$\delta_{t+}\mathfrak{h} = -2\sigma_0 \|\delta_t.u\|_{\mathbb{U}_N}^2 - 2\sigma_P \left(\delta_t.\eta\right)^2 \quad \text{with} \quad \mathfrak{h} = \mathfrak{h}_S + \mathfrak{h}_P \quad \text{and} \quad \mathfrak{h}_P = \frac{\omega_0^2}{2}\mu_{t-}\left(\eta^2\right) + \frac{\omega_1^4}{4}\eta^2 e_{t-}\eta^2$$

where $\mathfrak{h}_S$ is the stored energy for scheme (6.34) for the wave equation, as given in (6.45). Notice that the expression for the energy of the prepared string is non-negative—thus the total energy $\mathfrak{h}$ must also remain non-negative under the condition $\lambda \leq 1$, and the scheme is stable. Under this particular discretization, the addition of a lumped element has no effect on stability of the combined system, which is a very useful feature from the point of view of modular physical modeling. It is not true of all possible discretizations, however, as will be noted shortly.

Besides stability, the other crucial feature of a numerical method simulating an arbitrary connection among objects is that of computability—note that in the coupled expressions (7.41) and (7.42), there is a simultaneous dependence on u^{n+1}, the unknowns. Complicating matters is the use of interpolation and spreading operators, distributing the coupling over various nearby grid points. This may be analyzed in the following way. Taking an inner product of (7.41) with $J_p(x_P)$ (or, equivalently, interpolating the equation with $I_p(x_P)$) gives

$$\delta_{tt}\eta = \gamma^2 \zeta - 2\sigma_0 \delta_t.\eta + \|J_p(x_P)\|_{\mathbb{U}_N}^2 F \quad \text{with} \quad \eta = I_p(x_P)u \quad \zeta = I_p(x_P)\delta_{xx}u$$

Given that, at update step $n + 1$, ζ is known, then one may solve directly for η^{n+1} in terms of known values using (7.42):

$$a = 1 + \sigma_0 k + hk^2 \|J_p(x_P)\|_{\mathbb{U}_N}^2 \left(\omega_0^2/2 + \omega_1^4(\eta^n)^2/2 + \sigma_P/k\right)$$

$$b = -1 + \sigma_0 k - hk^2 \|J_p(x_P)\|_{\mathbb{U}_N}^2 \left(\omega_0^2/2 + \omega_1^4(\eta^n)^2/2 - \sigma_P/k\right)$$

$$\eta^{n+1} = \frac{1}{a}\left(\gamma^2 k^2 \zeta + 2\eta^n\right) + \frac{b}{a}\eta^{n-1}$$

Once η^{n+1} is determined, then F^n is known, from (7.42), and then, finally, the scheme (7.41) may be updated explicitly.

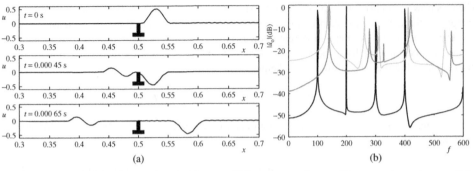

(a)   (b)

Figure 7.15 Ideal lossless string, with $\gamma = 200$, connected to a linear spring at $x_P = 0.5$. (a) Reflection and transmission of an incoming pulse from the spring, with stiffness parameter $\omega_0 = 4000$, at times as indicated. (b) Output spectrum for sound created using a plucked raised cosine initial condition of amplitude 1, with output read at $x = 0.8$, under different choices of the spring stiffness: $\omega_0 = 1000$ (in dark grey), $\omega_0 = 2000$ (in light grey), and without a spring connection (in black). Scheme (7.41) coupled to (7.42) is used, and the sample rate is 44 100 Hz.

The variety of timbres which can be generated using such a simple connection is surprisingly large. Beginning first with the case of a lossless linear spring connection (i.e., $\omega_1 = \sigma_P = 0$), the main effect will be, in the space–time domain, to induce reflection of traveling waves at the preparation location x_P—see Figure 7.15(a); the amount of reflection and transmission depends on the choice of the stiffness parameter ω_0. In the frequency domain, the result is a shifting of modal frequencies of the combined spring–string system—for the present case of the wave equation, this means that the resulting spectrum of sound output will be inharmonic, and increasingly so as the lumped stiffness increases in strength—see Figure 7.15(b). (Note that there will be an additional dependence on the positioning of the spring, i.e., on the choice of x_P.) As such, the resulting sounds will be far more like those of percussion instruments than typical stringed instruments—which is, of course, the whole point of undertaking string preparation to begin with!

Considering the case of a pure linear damper (i.e., $\omega_0 = \omega_1 = 0$), the most obvious effect will be that of increased loss, beyond that inherent in the string model itself. What is more interesting, however, is the frequency domain behavior of the damping introduced, which, again, will depend on the damper position, as well as the loss coefficient σ_P. If σ_P is large, the string is effectively divided into two, yielding completely different pitches from the unprepared string. See Figure 7.16(b), which shows a spectrogram of a typical output for such a point-damped string.

The most interesting case is that of the nonlinear spring (i.e., $\sigma_P = \omega_0 = 0$), especially in the case for which there is some damping in the string model itself. Initially, there will be a rather lively variation in the frequency components, as illustrated in Figure 7.16(a), but as damping intervenes, the behavior settles down to that of the unprepared string. Note that in the limiting case of low-amplitude vibration, the behavior of the combined system approaches that of the unprepared system; this is distinct from that of the linear spring connection, which always exhibits inharmonicity, regardless of the amplitude of excitation.

Numerical instability of connections

The scheme (7.42) which discretizes the connection with the spring–damper system has been specially chosen so as to be numerically stable always—the energy function for the combined string–spring–damper system is positive definite, and monotonically decreasing. But due to the

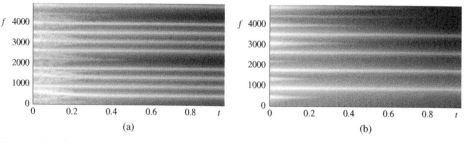

(a)   (b)

Figure 7.16 Spectrograms of output for a model of an ideal string with loss, with $\gamma = 880$ and $T_{60} = 2$, connected to: (a) a cubic nonlinear spring at $x_P = 0.5$, with $\omega_1 = 100$; and (b) a linear damper, again at $x_P = 0.5$, with $T_{60} = 1$. In this second case, the damper partially divides the string into two segments, yielding an effective pitch of twice the fundamental of the string after several hundred milliseconds. Scheme (7.41) coupled to (7.42) is used in both cases, and the sample rate is 44 100 Hz, with output taken at $x = 0.8$, and where the initial condition is of plucked type, using a raised cosine distribution centered at $x = 0.65$ and of amplitude 1.

implicit nature of the difference scheme, this is not the simplest scheme available. Indeed, considering the special case of the linear spring alone (i.e., with $\omega_1 = \sigma_P = 0$), one could use, instead of (7.42),

$$F = -\omega_0^2 I_p(x_P)u \qquad (7.43)$$

which leads to a completely explicit update of (7.41). Indeed, such a direct discretization of a stiffness term is in line with the stable discretization of the stiffness term in the SHO, as per (3.12), and one might expect that the combined spring–string system should remain stable as well. In fact, this is not necessarily the case—as shown in Figure 7.17, the solution can indeed become unstable, with the instability manifesting itself, as expected, by high-frequency oscillations emanating from the connection point which grow and eventually obliterate the solution.

In order to examine this, suppose, for the sake of simplicity, that the interpolation function is of zeroth order, so that the spring acts directly on the value of the grid function u_l at some grid

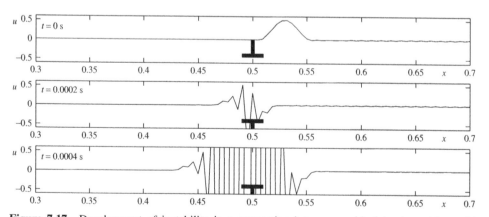

Figure 7.17 Development of instability in a connection between an ideal lossless string, with $\gamma = 200$, and a linear spring at $x_P = 0.5$, of stiffness $\omega_0 = 4000$, using finite difference scheme (7.41) along with (7.43). The sample rate is 44 100 Hz.

point located at $l = l_P$. Under lossless conditions, and for conservative boundary conditions on the string, the total conserved energy for this combined system will be

$$\mathfrak{h} = \underbrace{\frac{1}{2}\|\delta_{t-}u\|_{\mathbb{U}_N}^2 + \frac{\gamma^2}{2}\langle \delta_{x+}u, e_{t-}\delta_{x+}u\rangle_{\underline{\mathbb{U}}_N}}_{\mathfrak{h}_S} + \underbrace{\frac{\omega_0^2}{2}u_{l_P}e_{t-}u_{l_P}}_{\mathfrak{h}_P}$$

where $\mathfrak{h}_S$ indicates the energy of the string, and $\mathfrak{h}_P$ the added potential energy of the spring connection. Clearly, neither of the contributions is necessarily non-negative. One may bound them as follows:

$$\mathfrak{h}_S \geq \frac{1}{2}\left(1 - \lambda^2\right)\|\delta_{t-}u\|_{\underline{\mathbb{U}}_N}^2 \qquad\qquad \mathfrak{h}_P \geq -\frac{k^2\omega_0^2}{8}\left(\delta_{t-}u_{l_P}\right)^2$$

which implies, for the sum, that

$$\mathfrak{h} \geq \sum_{l\neq l_P} \frac{h}{2}\left(1 - \lambda^2\right)\left(\delta_{t-}u_l\right)^2 + \left(\frac{h}{2}\left(1 - \lambda^2\right) - \frac{k^2\omega_0^2}{8}\right)\left(\delta_{t-}u_{l_P}\right)^2$$

At grid points other than $l = l_P$, the non-negativity condition is, as before, the CFL condition $\lambda \leq 1$. But at $l = l_P$, there is another, stronger condition that must be enforced:

$$\frac{h}{2}\left(1 - \lambda^2\right) - \frac{k^2\omega_0^2}{8} > 0$$

In this case, the stability condition of the combination *interferes* with that of the systems in isolation, which is very different from the case of the discretization from (7.42). The lesson here is that the semi-implicit character of a scheme such as (7.42) allows for a modular connection without the additional worry of inducing instability—at the expense, of course, of a slightly more involved update. This is typical of many numerical methods for combined systems, and, in fact, is exactly the principle behind scattering-based numerical approaches—see Section 1.2.4 and the recent publication by Rabenstein et al. [279]. Indeed, in the case of a string–spring connection, if one were to use a digital waveguide for the string (corresponding exactly to scheme (7.41)), and a wave digital filter for the spring (which is also semi-implicit, like (7.42)), modular stability is also obtained. But, as illustrated here, it is not necessary to make use of scattering principles in order to arrive at such a result. When connecting a lumped object to a distributed object, a good rule of thumb is the following:

Rule of Thumb #3

Efficient modular numerical behavior is obtained when a semi-implicit method is used for lumped objects, and when an explicit method is used for distributed objects.

7.7.2   Rattling elements

Another type of preparation often used is the rattling element—such an element can be viewed as suspended on the string or bar and, perhaps, subject to gravity. The treatment of such an element is somewhat similar to that of the hammer, in that it must be considered to have mass. Rattle-like elements have been briefly introduced in the lumped context in Section 4.2.4.

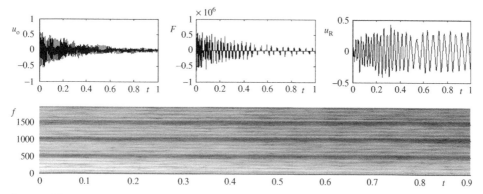

Figure 7.18 Typical behavior of a rattle connected to an ideal string with loss. In this case, the string has a fundamental frequency of 100 Hz and $T_{60} = 6$ s. The rattle is positioned at $x_P = 0.2$, is of length $\epsilon = 0.5$ and mass ratio $\mathcal{M} = 0.7$, and has stiffness parameter $\omega_R = 3000$, with nonlinear stiffness exponent $\alpha = 1$. Across the top row are plotted string displacement, at $x = 0.8$, force F, and rattle displacement u_R as functions of time t. A spectrogram of displacement output appears at bottom.

In scaled form, the situation is again described by (7.39), now employing a center-limited nonlinearity:

$$F = \begin{cases} -\omega_R^{\alpha+1} \left(u(x_P) - u_R - \epsilon/2 \right)^\alpha, & u(x_P) - u_R \geq \epsilon/2 \\ 0, & |u(x_P) - u_R| < \epsilon/2 \\ \omega_R^{\alpha+1} \left(u_R - u(x_P) - \epsilon/2 \right)^\alpha, & u(x_P) - u_R \leq -\epsilon/2 \end{cases} \quad \frac{d^2 u_R}{dt^2} = -\mathcal{M}F \quad (7.44)$$

Here, u_R is the vertical position of the center of the rattling element, acting at a point $x = x_P$ along the string, ω_R is the nonlinear stiffness parameter, with stiffness exponent α, $\mathcal{M}$ is the mass ratio of the entire string to the rattle, and ϵ is the rattle length. Some typical behavior is illustrated in Figure 7.18; notice the complex behavior of the temporal envelope, and the intervals during which the force on the string is zero.

Though simple, the rattling element changes the timbre of the struck string (or bar) in a variety of ways, depending on the choices of rattle parameters—indeed, the resulting sounds can be very far from those of plucked or struck strings. If, for example, the rattle length ϵ is large, the resulting individual collisions between string and rattle will be clearly audible—see Figure 7.19(a). If the rattle length is smaller, individual collisions will not necessarily be heard, and rather a high-frequency buzzing is imparted to the sound, not unlike that of, say, a sitar. If, in addition, the mass of the rattle is made large compared to that of the string, effects of detuning of the string, and possibly splitting of harmonics, will be heard, as the rattle acts, grossly speaking, as a lumped mass in partial contact with the string—see Figures 7.19(b) and 7.19(c).

As might be expected, as in the case of the hammer, developing a conservative scheme is not easy, but partial conservation may be ensured if the nonlinearity exponent α is equal to 1 or 3; a semi-implicit discretization, of the type discussed in Section 4.2.2, is a safe choice for the nonlinearity; exploration of such finite difference schemes, which are very similar to those presented in the previous sections, is left to Problem 7.19 and Programming Exercise 7.8.

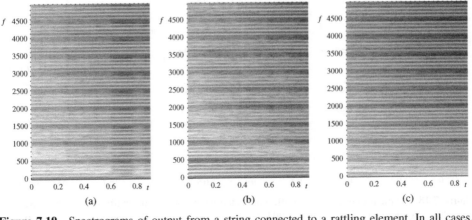

Figure 7.19   Spectrograms of output from a string connected to a rattling element. In all cases, the string has a fundamental frequency of 100 Hz and a decay time of $T_{60} = 6$ s, and is excited with a plucked raised cosine pulse, centered at $x = 0.65$, and of half-width 0.1. In all cases, the rattle has a nonlinearity exponent of $\alpha = 2$, and output is read from the string at $x = 0.8$. In (a), the rattle is positioned at $x_P = 0.2$, with $\omega_R = 5000$, $\epsilon = 0.5$, and a mass ratio of $\mathcal{M} = 100$. As the rattle is of relatively large dimensions, distinct "bounces" are visible here as wide-band disturbances in the spectrum. In (b), the rattle is much shorter and stiffer, with the parameters as before except with $x_P = 0.2$, with $\omega_R = 10\,000$ and $\epsilon = 0.01$, yielding a more buzzy output, easily seen as superimposed on the harmonic spectrum of the output. In (c), the rattling element is much heavier, and positioned at the string center; the parameters are $x_P = 0.5$, $\omega_R = 3000$, $\epsilon = 0.05$, and $\mathcal{M} = 1$, and in this case a distinctive "splitting" of the harmonics of the string is audible.

7.8   Coupled bars

Part of the fun of physical modeling (and, indeed, maybe the very point of it all) is to go beyond what can be done with an acoustic instrument. There are eminently physical ways of modifying a synthesis routine which would be difficult, if not impossible, to carry out in the real world—witness the caution with which an orchestra director will allow a Steinway grand to be prepared. Coupling of string and bar models is one such example, and in the virtual world no blowtorch is necessary.

Coupling between distributed systems and lumped objects has been discussed extensively in the last few sections. The same principles of analysis may be applied when distributed objects are coupled. For the sake of variety, consider the case of two ideal bars, coupled through some as yet unspecified mechanism, as illustrated in Figure 7.20.

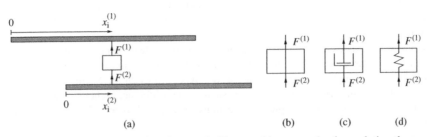

Figure 7.20   (a) A pair of bars, pointwise coupled by an arbitrary mechanism relating the resulting forces. (b) A rigid connection, (c) a damped connection, and (d) a spring-like connection.

Supposing that the bars are of differing material properties, the system may be written, in dimensional form, as

$$\rho^{(1)} A^{(1)} u_{tt}^{(1)} = -E^{(1)} I^{(1)} u_{x^{(1)} x^{(1)} x^{(1)} x^{(1)}} + \delta(x^{(1)} - x_i^{(1)}) f^{(1)}$$

$$\rho^{(2)} A^{(2)} u_{tt}^{(2)} = -E^{(2)} I^{(2)} u_{x^{(2)} x^{(2)} x^{(2)} x^{(2)}} + \delta(x^{(2)} - x_i^{(2)}) f^{(2)}$$

Here, the superscripts (1) and (2) refer to the first and second bar, respectively—notice that different spatial coordinates $x^{(1)}$ and $x^{(2)}$ are used for each. The bars are assumed to lie over the spatial intervals $x^{(1)} \in [0, L^{(1)}]$ and $x^{(2)} \in [0, L^{(2)}]$, respectively, and the connection points are $x_i^{(1)}$ and $x_i^{(2)}$, respectively. Using the techniques described earlier in this chapter, one could easily extend this model to the case of a stiff string, with frequency-dependent loss, or to the case of a distributed connection, or, using methods to be introduced in Section 7.10, to the case of bars of variable cross-sectional area or density. This model behaves somewhat like a tuning fork, depending on the type of connection (i.e., on the definition of the mechanism giving rise to the forces $f^{(1)}$ and $f^{(2)}$), and could serve as a starting point for physical models of certain electromechanical instruments such as the Fender–Rhodes electric piano. See Figure 7.21 for a picture of the typical behavior of a coupled bar system.

Using the first bar as a reference, scaling may be carried out, using coordinates $x^{(1)'} = x^{(1)}/L^{(1)}$ and $x^{(2)'} = x^{(2)}/L^{(2)}$, and subsequently removing primes, as

$$u_{tt}^{(1)} = -\left(\kappa^{(1)}\right)^2 u_{x^{(1)} x^{(1)} x^{(1)} x^{(1)}}^{(1)} + \delta(x^{(1)} - x_i^{(1)}) F^{(1)}$$

$$\mathcal{M} u_{tt}^{(2)} = -\mathcal{M} \left(\kappa^{(2)}\right)^2 u_{x^{(2)} x^{(2)} x^{(2)} x^{(2)}}^{(2)} + \mathcal{M} \delta(x^{(2)} - x_i^{(2)}) F^{(2)}$$

where

$$\kappa^{(1)} = \sqrt{\frac{E^{(1)} I^{(1)}}{\rho^{(1)} A^{(1)} (L^{(1)})^4}} \quad \kappa^{(2)} = \sqrt{\frac{E^{(2)} I^{(2)}}{\rho^{(2)} A^{(2)} (L^{(2)})^4}} \quad F^{(1)} = \frac{f^{(1)}}{\rho^{(1)} A^{(1)} L^{(1)}} \quad F^{(2)} = \frac{f^{(2)}}{\rho^{(2)} A^{(2)} L^{(2)}}$$

and where the mass ratio $\mathcal{M}$ of the second bar to the first is defined as

$$\mathcal{M} = \frac{\rho^{(2)} A^{(2)} L^{(2)}}{\rho^{(1)} A^{(1)} L^{(1)}}$$

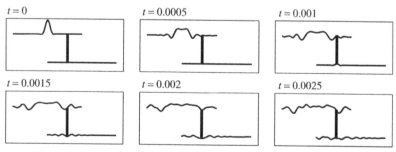

Figure 7.21 Time evolution of displacement profiles for a coupled bar system, at times as indicated. Here, the bars are of stiffnesses $\kappa^{(1)} = 2$ (bottom bar) and $\kappa^{(2)} = 3$ (top bar), of equal masses, and coupled via a rigid connection occurring at $x_i^{(1)} = 0.3$ and $x_i^{(2)} = 0.8$. Boundary conditions are of clamped type, and the second bar is initialized with a plucked raised cosine distribution at the bar center.

Now, both bars are defined over the unit interval $\mathcal{D} = \mathbb{U}$. The energy balance for this system, assuming conservative boundary termination (see Section 7.1.2 for the case of the ideal bar), is

$$\frac{d\mathfrak{H}}{dt} = F^{(1)} u_t^{(1)}(x_i^{(1)}) + \mathcal{M} F^{(2)} u_t^{(2)}(x_i^{(2)}) \quad \text{with} \quad \mathfrak{H} = \mathfrak{H}^{(1)} + \mathfrak{H}^{(2)}$$

and

$$\mathfrak{H}^{(1)} = \frac{1}{2}\|u_t^{(1)}\|_{\mathbb{U}}^2 + \frac{(\kappa^{(1)})^2}{2}\|u_{x^{(1)}x^{(1)}}\|_{\mathbb{U}}^2 \qquad \mathfrak{H}^{(2)} = \frac{\mathcal{M}}{2}\|u_t^{(2)}\|_{\mathbb{U}}^2 + \frac{\mathcal{M}(\kappa^{(2)})^2}{2}\|u_{x^{(2)}x^{(2)}}\|_{\mathbb{U}}^2$$

The system as a whole will be dissipative when

$$F^{(1)} u_t^{(1)}(x_i^{(1)}) + \mathcal{M} F^{(2)} u_t^{(2)}(x_i^{(2)}) \le 0 \tag{7.45}$$

or lossless when the above inequality is satisfied with equality. If the connection itself can store energy (i.e., if there are masses or springs involved), then dissipative behavior will occur if

$$F^{(1)} u_t^{(1)}(x_i^{(1)}) + \mathcal{M} F^{(2)} u_t^{(2)}(x_i^{(2)}) = -\frac{d\mathfrak{H}_C}{dt} - \mathfrak{Q}$$

where $\mathfrak{H}_C \ge 0$ and $\mathfrak{Q} \ge 0$, because, in this case, one will then have

$$\frac{d}{dt}(\mathfrak{H} + \mathfrak{H}_C) = -\mathfrak{Q} \le 0 \tag{7.46}$$

7.8.1 Connection types

The simplest type of connection is that of rigid type:

$$F^{(1)} = -\mathcal{M} F^{(2)} \quad \text{and} \quad u_t^{(1)}(x_i^{(2)}) = u_t^{(2)}(x_i^{(2)})$$

satisfying (7.45) with equality. Forces are equal and opposite, and the bars are constrained to move at the same velocity at the connection point. The resulting behavior of such a system is, from a spectral point of view, enormously complex—the modal frequencies will depend strongly on the relative stiffnesses of the bars, the mass ratio, as well as the connection points. See Figure 7.22. Even for such a connection, there are a huge variety of timbres available to the instrument designer.

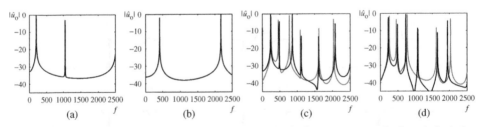

Figure 7.22 Output spectra for a coupled bar system. Typical output spectra for bars in isolation, under clamped conditions, for stiffness parameters (a) $\kappa^{(1)} = 50$ and (b) $\kappa^{(2)} = 100$. Shown in (c) are output spectra under variations in the connection point, for two bars of mass ratio $\mathcal{M} = 1$. The connection point on the first bar is at $x_i^{(1)} = 0.3$ and on the second bar at $x_i^{(2)} = 0.8$ (in grey) and 0.7 (in black). In (d), a similar comparison of spectra is shown, under variations in the mass ratio, for fixed connection points $x_i^{(1)} = 0.3$ and $x_i^{(2)} = 0.8$, where $\mathcal{M} = 1$ (grey) and 0.3 (black).

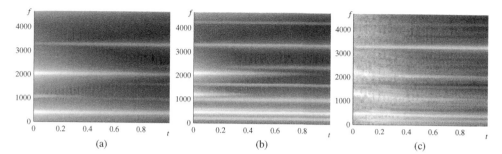

Figure 7.23   Spectrograms of audio output for two bars under a damped spring connection. The two bars are of stiffness coefficients $\kappa^{(1)} = 50$ and $\kappa^{(2)} = 100$, and of mass ratio $\mathcal{M} = 0.2$, and the connection points are $x_i^{(1)} = 0.3$ and $x_i^{(2)} = 0.8$. In (a), a pure damper of damping coefficient $\sigma_P = 1.4$ is employed; in (b), the same damper with a linear spring with $\omega_0 = 1000$; and in (c), the same damper again with a nonlinear spring with $\omega_1 = 70$. Output is taken from the second bar, at location $x^{(2)} = 0.5$.

A device involving both damping and a mixed linear–cubic spring is described by

$$F^{(1)} = -\mathcal{M}F^{(2)} = -\omega_0^2\eta - \omega_1^4\eta^3 - 2\sigma_C\frac{d}{dt}\eta \qquad \text{with} \qquad \eta = u^{(1)}(x_i^{(1)}) - u^{(2)}(x_i^{(2)})$$

Such a spring obviously possesses a potential energy $\mathfrak{H}_C$, given by

$$\mathfrak{H}_C = \frac{\omega_0^2}{2}\eta^2 + \frac{\omega_1^4}{4}\eta^4$$

which renders the system dissipative as a whole, with an energy balance of the form (7.46), with $\mathfrak{Q} = 2\sigma_C (d\eta/dt)^2$. Even more variability in timbre is now possible—see Figure 7.23. The linear spring action serves to further alter modal frequencies, as does the damping term, which also generally leads to frequency-dependent decay. Interestingly, depending on the connection points, and the strength of the damper, it can allow for energy to be traded back and forth between the bars, at potentially a very slow rate, leading to interesting sub-audio rate variations in amplitude, as is visible in Figures 7.23(a) and 7.23(b). Finally, the nonlinear spring term in conjunction with damping yields pitch changes and wide-band sound output, dependent on the strength of the excitation—see Figure 7.23(c).

7.8.2   Finite difference schemes

Finite difference schemes may be developed in the usual way for the coupled bar system—the one new feature here is that, because the bars may be of differing stiffnesses (i.e., $\kappa^{(1)} \neq \kappa^{(2)}$), it is not necessarily a good idea to use the same grid spacing for each. The reason for this is straightforward—if a global sample rate is chosen, then a distinct stability condition will arise for each bar in isolation. If the spacing is chosen the same for both bars, heavy numerical dispersion will necessarily be introduced. Recall, from Section 7.1.4, that if one wants to use an explicit scheme, numerical dispersion effects are very strong, especially in the case of the bar. It is thus wise to choose distinct grid spacings $h^{(1)}$ and $h^{(2)}$ for the first and second bars, respectively.

The simplest scheme is of the following form:

$$\delta_{tt}u^{(1)} = -\left(\kappa^{(1)}\right)^2\delta_{x^{(1)}x^{(1)}x^{(1)}x^{(1)}}u^{(1)} + J_p(x_i^{(1)})F^{(1)} \tag{7.47a}$$

$$\delta_{tt}u^{(2)} = -\left(\kappa^{(2)}\right)^2\delta_{x^{(2)}x^{(2)}x^{(2)}x^{(2)}}u^{(2)} + J_p(x_i^{(2)})F^{(2)} \tag{7.47b}$$

where, as before, J_p represents a spreading operator of order p. Notice that the two instances of J_p will be acting over distinct grids. The discrete energy balance, under conservative numerical boundary conditions, will be

$$\delta_{t+}\mathfrak{h} = \delta_{t\cdot}(I_p(x_i^{(1)})u^{(1)})F^{(1)} + \delta_{t\cdot}(I_p(x_i^{(2)})u^{(2)})\mathcal{M}F^{(2)} \quad \text{with} \quad \mathfrak{h} = \mathfrak{h}^{(1)} + \mathfrak{h}^{(2)} \qquad (7.48)$$

and where the discrete energies for the two bars are given for bars (1) and (2) by

$$\mathfrak{h}^{(1)} = \frac{1}{2}\|\delta_{t-}u^{(1)}\|^2_{\overline{U}_{N^{(1)}}} + \frac{(\kappa^{(1)})^2}{2}\langle \delta_{x^{(1)}x^{(1)}}u^{(1)}, e_t - \delta_{x^{(1)}x^{(1)}}u^{(1)}\rangle_{\overline{U}_{N^{(1)}}}$$

$$\mathfrak{h}^{(2)} = \frac{M}{2}\|\delta_{t-}u^{(2)}\|^2_{\overline{U}_{N^{(2)}}} + \frac{M(\kappa^{(2)})^2}{2}\langle \delta_{x^{(2)}x^{(2)}}u^{(2)}, e_t - \delta_{x^{(2)}x^{(2)}}u^{(2)}\rangle_{\overline{U}_{N^{(2)}}}$$

These are the same expressions as in the case of uncoupled bars (see Section 7.1.4), and are non-negative under the conditions

$$\mu^{(1)} = \frac{k\kappa^{(1)}}{(h^{(1)})^2} \le \frac{1}{2} \qquad \mu^{(2)} = \frac{k\kappa^{(2)}}{(h^{(2)})^2} \le \frac{1}{2} \qquad (7.49)$$

As mentioned above, the grid spacings $h^{(1)}$ and $h^{(2)}$ should be chosen to satisfy the above bounds as close to equality as possible.

The rigid connection is the simplest to deal with. One may use

$$F^{(1)} = -\mathcal{M}F^{(2)} \qquad I_p(x_i^{(1)})u^{(1)} = I_p(x_i^{(2)})u^{(2)} \qquad (7.50)$$

Here, the positions of the bars at the connection point are set equal—this is an especially easy way to enforce a condition of equal velocity (instead of adding an extra parameter representing the distance between the bars, which is of no consequence). Under these conditions, there is exact numerical energy conservation from (7.48), and thus numerical stability follows if conditions (7.49) are respected.

The damper and spring connection is more complex, but may be dealt with in a manner similar to the lumped spring connection discussed in Section 7.7.1. A semi-implicit discretization leads to

$$F^{(1)} = -\mathcal{M}F^{(2)} = -2\sigma_C\delta_{t\cdot}\eta - \omega_0^2\mu_{t\cdot}\eta - \omega_1^4\eta^2\mu_{t\cdot}\eta \qquad (7.51)$$

with

$$\eta = I_p(x_i^{(1)})u^{(1)} - I_p(x_i^{(2)})u^{(2)}$$

Explicit updating

Due to the implicit nature of the approximation to $F^{(1)}$ and $F^{(2)}$, it is not immediately clear how to go about performing an update. The forces depend on unknown values of the grid functions and conversely—a complicating factor is that due to the spreading functions, there is in fact a coupled region of interdependence of forces and displacements. An explicit update is indeed possible—as a first step, apply the interpolation operators $I_p(x_i^{(1)})$ and $I_p(x_i^{(2)})$ to (7.47a) and (7.47b), respectively, to get

$$\delta_{tt}I_p(x_i^{(1)})u^{(1)} = -\zeta^{(1)} + h^{(1)}\|J_p(x_i^{(1)})\|^2_{\overline{U}_{N_1}}F^{(1)}$$

$$\delta_{tt}I_p(x_i^{(2)})u^{(2)} = -\zeta^{(2)} + h^{(2)}\|J_p(x_i^{(2)})\|^2_{\overline{U}_{N_2}}F^{(2)}$$

where $\zeta^{(1)}$ and $\zeta^{(2)}$ are known, and given by

$$\zeta^{(1)} = \left(\kappa^{(1)}\right)^2 I_p(x_i^{(1)})\delta_{x^{(1)}x^{(1)}x^{(1)}x^{(1)}}u^{(1)} \qquad \zeta^{(2)} = \left(\kappa^{(2)}\right)^2 I_p(x_i^{(2)})\delta_{x^{(2)}x^{(2)}x^{(2)}x^{(2)}}u^{(2)}$$

Given $F^{(1)} = -\mathcal{M}F^{(2)}$, one may solve for the unknown forces (say, $F^{(1)}$), as

$$F^{(1)} = \frac{\zeta^{(1)} - \zeta^{(2)} + \delta_{tt}\eta}{h^{(1)}\|J_p(x_i^{(1)})\|_{\mathbb{U}_{N_1}}^2 + h^{(2)}\|J_p(x_i^{(2)})\|_{\mathbb{U}_{N_2}}^2/\mathcal{M}}$$

In the case of a rigid connection (i.e., when $F^{(1)} = -\mathcal{M}F^{(2)}$ and $I_p(x_i^{(1)}) = I_p(x_i^{(2)})$ implying $\eta = 0$, as per (7.50)), $F^{(1)}$ may be calculated immediately from known values of the grid functions. Once the forces are known, they may be inserted directly into the updates (7.47a) and (7.47b), which are fully explicit.

For spring–damper connections, the situation is slightly more complicated: η is as yet unknown in the expression for the force above. Note, however, that using (7.51), one may write

$$\frac{\zeta^{(1)} - \zeta^{(2)} + \delta_{tt}\eta}{h^{(1)}\|J_p(x_i^{(1)})\|_{\mathbb{U}_{N_1}}^2 + h^{(2)}\|J_p(x_i^{(2)})\|_{\mathbb{U}_{N_2}}^2/\mathcal{M}} = -\omega_0^2\mu_{t\cdot}\eta - \omega_1^4\eta^2\mu_{t\cdot}\eta - 2\sigma_P\delta_{t\cdot}\eta$$

which is a linear equation in the unknown value of η at time step $n + 1$, and which may be solved directly. Once η is determined, the forces may be determined, and, as before, inserted into the updates (7.47a) and (7.47b).

7.9   Helical springs

Though this book is mainly concerned with sound synthesis based on physical models of musical instruments, one can indeed apply the same techniques to simulate certain audio effects as well. At present there is an increasing amount of effort going into simulations of electrical circuits used in classic analog synthesis, both for filtering and for direct synthesis—as one might expect, virtual analog (as it is called) is again always based on numerical methods for solving systems of differential equations, normally ODEs, as the components are modeled as lumped. See, e.g., [165, 340, 413]. Slightly more relevant here are the wide variety of electromechanical effects which have been notoriously difficult to emulate digitally, as they rely on distributed components. Physical modeling offers an approach to digital versions of effects such as the Leslie speaker [337] and plate reverberation [44, 47, 12].

An interesting mechanical system which plays an important role in analog audio effects processing is the helical spring. Spring-based reverberation, originally intended as a low-cost means of applying reverberation to a dry audio input signal, has a characteristic sound all its own, and even in the digital age is still admired and emulated. Spring reverberation has been simulated using digital waveguides [1], and, more recently, using explicit finite difference methods by Parker [266].

The physics of springs is similar, in many respects, to that of the ideal bar; the motion of the spring is largely linear, and may be well described in 1D, and this is reflected by the PDE description. As such, it is an excellent candidate for simulation by physical modeling techniques. On the other hand, there are significant departures from the bar model, especially in that longitudinal motion of the spring may not be neglected, leading to a coupled longitudinal–transverse system resembling that which describes nonlinear string vibration—see Section 8.2.

7.9.1   A coupled PDE system

There are a variety of models of the dynamics of helical springs, of varying degrees of complexity. Perhaps the best known is the system due to Wittrick [409]. As, for springs of interest in musical acoustics, such a system describes phenomena which are far beyond the range of human audio perception, it is probably best to begin with a simple model, presented in [137]:

$$u_{tt} = -\frac{Er^2}{4\rho} \left(u_{xxxx} + 2\epsilon^2 u_{xx} + \epsilon^4 u\right) + \frac{E\epsilon}{\rho}\left(\zeta_x - \epsilon u\right) \qquad \zeta_{tt} = \frac{E}{\rho}\left(\zeta_{xx} - \epsilon u_x\right)$$

Here, x is a variable representing arc length along a spring of circular cross-section and radius r, and $u(x, t)$ and $\zeta(x, t)$ are the local displacements in the transverse and longitudinal directions. E and ρ are Young's modulus and material density, and the parameter $\epsilon \approx 1/R$ is a measure of spring curvature, where R is the radius of the coil. See Figure 7.24. Various approximations have been made in arriving at this simple form, the most important of which are that transverse displacement in only a single polarization is modeled, tension effects have been neglected, and the helix angle is very small (i.e., the spring is tightly wound). Notice that under low-curvature conditions (i.e., in the limit as ϵ becomes small), the system decouples into the ideal bar equation (in u) and the 1D wave equation (in ζ).

When spatially scaled, through the introduction of a coordinate $x' = x/L$, and scaling the dependent variables as $\zeta' = \zeta/L$ and $u' = u\epsilon$, and after removing primes, the system is of the form

$$u_{tt} = -\kappa^2 \left(u_{xxxx} + 2q^2 u_{xx} + q^4 u\right) + \gamma_1^2 q^2 \left(\zeta_x - u\right) \qquad \zeta_{tt} = \gamma_1^2 \left(\zeta_{xx} - u_x\right) \qquad (7.52)$$

where $\kappa = \sqrt{Er^2/4\rho L^4}$, $\gamma_1 = \sqrt{E/\rho L^2}$, and $q = \epsilon L$. The system is now defined over the unit interval $\mathcal{D} = \mathbb{U}$.

Dispersion relation

Given that system (7.52) is LSI, dispersion analysis is revealing. Because the system consists of two coupled second-order equations, there will be two separate dispersion relations. For springs

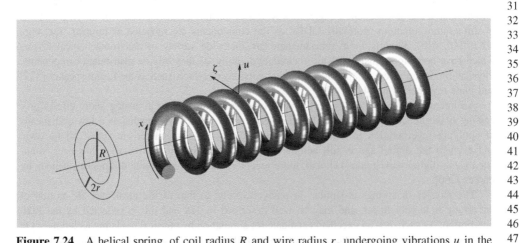

Figure 7.24 A helical spring, of coil radius R and wire radius r, undergoing vibrations u in the transverse direction, and ζ in the longitudinal direction, as a function of x, the arc length along the spring.

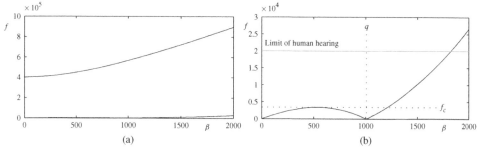

(a)   (b)

Figure 7.25 (a) Dispersion relations $f(\beta)$ for system (7.52), and (b) close-up view of primary dispersion curve in the audio range, with features determined by q and f_c. The spring has parameters $\kappa = 0.0625$, $q = 1000$, and $\gamma = 2511$.

of musical interest, one will lie in the range of very high frequencies (i.e., in the range above 100 kHz). (For higher-order theories of spring vibration, such as that due to Wittrick, there will be more such dispersion relations, but all will lie in an even higher range of frequencies.) It is not, however, possible to identify the two dispersion curves in terms of pure longitudinal or transverse motion—both sets of solutions are mixtures. See Figure 7.25(a), showing both dispersion relations for a spring of dimensions typical in audio reverberation. The lower dispersion curve, shown in Figure 7.25(b), which is of primary importance in the resulting sound, is not monotonically increasing (as it is in the case of strings and bars), and in fact reaches zero at $\beta = q$ and possesses a peak in the mid range of the audio spectrum, at a frequency f_c given by

$$f_c = \frac{3\kappa q^2}{8\pi \sqrt{5}} \qquad (7.53)$$

(f_c is a very useful design parameter, especially if one has access only to measured spring responses, from which the cutoff will be easily visible in a spectrogram.) There will be very complex behavior in terms of wave speeds, and thus transients in a resulting impulse response—such behavior is instrumental in determining the characteristic sound of spring reverberators.

Loss

As a simple ad hoc means of introducing loss into this system, consider the following generalization of (7.52):

$$u_{tt} = -\kappa^2 \left(u_{xxxx} + 2q^2 u_{xx} + q^4 u\right) + \gamma_1^2 q^2 \left(\zeta_x - u\right) - 2\sigma^{(t)} u_t \qquad \zeta_{tt} = \gamma_1^2 \left(\zeta_{xx} - u_x\right) - 2\sigma^{(l)} \zeta_t$$
$$(7.54)$$

where here, $\sigma^{(t)} \geq 0$ and $\sigma^{(l)} \geq 0$ are loss parameters (typically very small in a reverberation setting!) which should be set according to measured data.

Energy

System (7.54) is dissipative, and it is not difficult to arrive at an energy balance. Assuming the system to be defined over the unit interval $\mathcal{D} = \mathbb{U}$, it is of the form

$$\frac{d\mathfrak{H}_{spr}}{dt} = \mathfrak{B}_{spr,left} + \mathfrak{B}_{spr,right} - \mathfrak{Q}_{spr} \qquad \text{with} \qquad \mathfrak{H}_{spr} = \mathfrak{T}_{spr} + \mathfrak{V}_{spr,uc} + \mathfrak{V}_{spr,\times} \qquad (7.55)$$

and

$$\mathfrak{T}_{\mathrm{spr}} = \frac{1}{2}\|u_t\|_{\mathbb{U}}^2 + \frac{q^2}{2}\|\zeta_t\|_{\mathbb{U}}^2 \qquad \mathfrak{V}_{\mathrm{spr,uc}} = \frac{\kappa^2}{2}\|u_{xx} + q^2 u\|_{\mathbb{U}}^2 \qquad \mathfrak{V}_{\mathrm{spr,\times}} = \frac{\gamma_1^2 q^2}{2}\|\zeta_x - u\|_{\mathbb{U}}^2$$

$$\mathfrak{B}_{\mathrm{spr,left}} = \kappa^2 u_t(0,t)\left(u_{xxx}(0,t) + q^2 u_x(0,t)\right) - \kappa^2 u_{xt}(0,t)\left(u_{xx}(0,t) + q^2 u(0,t)\right)$$

$$+ q^2 \gamma_1^2 \zeta_t(0,t)\left(u(0,t) - \zeta_x(0,t)\right)$$

$$\mathfrak{B}_{\mathrm{spr,right}} = -\kappa^2 u_t(1,t)\left(u_{xxx}(1,t) + q^2 u_x(1,t)\right) + \kappa^2 u_{xt}(1,t)\left(u_{xx}(1,t) + q^2 u(1,t)\right)$$

$$- q^2 \gamma_1^2 \zeta_t(1,t)\left(u(1,t) - \zeta_x(1,t)\right)$$

$$\mathfrak{Q}_{\mathrm{spr}} = -2\sigma^{(0)}\|u_t\|_{\mathbb{U}}^2 - 2q^2\sigma^{(1)}\|\zeta_t\|_{\mathbb{U}}^2$$

Conservative boundary conditions (i.e., $\mathfrak{B}_{\mathrm{spr,left}} = \mathfrak{B}_{\mathrm{spr,right}} = 0$) follow immediately, but the analysis is postponed until the driving mechanism has been specified.

7.9.2 Finite difference schemes

System (7.54) poses some interesting problems from the point of view of time domain simulation. At the heart of these difficulties is the presence of two sets of solutions which lie in distinct frequency ranges—these correspond exactly to the two dispersion curves shown in Figure 7.25(a). One of these lies in the range of human audio perception, but the other is normally above. It would be useful to be able to simulate only the portion of the system which gives rise to audible frequencies, but the very special form of the dispersion relation in the audio range results precisely from the coupling between the two variables. In simulation, it will thus be necessary to simulate the full system.[3]

The upper dispersion relation, however, leads to difficulties. Clearly, if an explicit method is employed [266], such frequencies cannot be simulated unless the sample rate is chosen sufficiently high, leading to great computational expense. Since the phase velocity corresponding to such a curve is higher than that of the lower curve, an explicit method will lead to an excessively large grid spacing, which is insufficient to resolve all but the lowest range of frequencies corresponding to the lower dispersion relation (i.e., to extreme numerical dispersion and band-limiting). An implicit method is thus a good starting point. Here is a parameterized family of schemes for system (7.54):

$$(1 + \eta\kappa k\delta_{xx})\,\delta_{tt}u = -\kappa^2\left(\delta_{xxxx}u + 2\bar{q}^2\delta_{xx}u + \bar{q}^4 u\right)$$

$$+ \gamma_1^2 q^2\left(\alpha + (1-\alpha)\mu_{t\cdot}\right)\left(\delta_{x-}\zeta - u\right) - 2\sigma^{(0)}\delta_{t\cdot}u \qquad (7.56\mathrm{a})$$

$$\left(1 + \theta\gamma_1^2 k^2 \delta_{xx}\right)\delta_{tt}\zeta = \gamma_1^2\left(\alpha + (1-\alpha)\mu_{t\cdot}\right)\left(\delta_{xx}\zeta - \delta_{x+}u\right) - 2\sigma^{(1)}\delta_{t\cdot}u \qquad (7.56\mathrm{b})$$

Here, the free parameters are $\bar{q}$, α, θ, and η, which are of great use in tuning the frequency response of the scheme. The parameter $\bar{q}$ is an approximation to q, and the terms involving the parameters η and θ are of the same form as those which have already been examined in the case of the ideal bar, in Section 7.1.5, and the 1D wave equation, in Section 6.3.2.

Stability conditions

Stability conditions for the above scheme may be derived using energy methods—see Problem 7.20. A first condition, on α, which affects the coupling term between the two subsystems

---

[3] In the digital waveguide setting, it would be possible to use the lower dispersion relation as the starting point for the design of a terminating all-pass filter—this, however, is a quasi-physical manner of proceeding, and will necessarily obscure the nature of the all-important connection to the excitation element. Given that the resulting all-pass filter will necessarily be of very high order, thus eliminating the efficiency gain of a waveguide implementation, it is probably better to stick with a simulation of the full system.

in u and ζ, greatly simplifies the resulting analysis:

$$0 \leq \alpha \leq \frac{1}{2} \tag{7.57}$$

In fact, it is wise to choose $\alpha = 1/2$.

For consistency, the parameter $\bar{q}$ must be equal to q, to second order. Here is a good choice, the significance of which will be explained below:

$$\bar{q} = \frac{2}{h} \sin\left(\frac{qh}{2}\right) \tag{7.58}$$

Finally, given the above restrictions on $\bar{q}$ and α, the following conditions on θ and η need to be satisfied:

$$h \geq 2\gamma k\sqrt{\theta} \qquad h \geq \sqrt{\kappa k\left(2\eta + \sqrt{4\eta^2 + (1 + |\cos(qh)|)^2}\right)} \tag{7.59}$$

when $\theta > 0$ and $\eta > 0$ (this is the range of interest for good control over numerical dispersion).

Numerical dispersion and tuning

One might wonder why such an apparently complex scheme is necessary; it is thus useful to examine the effects of the various free parameters on the dispersion relation—see Figure 7.26. It is assumed here that $\alpha = 1/2$. First, assume that the remaining parameters take on their default values: $\bar{q} = q$ and $\eta = \theta = 0$. One notices immediately that the wavenumber at which the numerical dispersion relation reaches its minimum does not occur at $\beta = q$, as per the continuous system, as shown in Figure 7.26(a). The choice of $\bar{q}$ as in (7.58) rectifies this, as shown in Figure 7.26(b). Still, however, the dispersion relation is a very poor match to that of the model system at high wavenumbers—the scheme is as yet incapable of operating in the upper range of the audio spectrum, and any results generated using this scheme will have a very dull "low-passed" character.

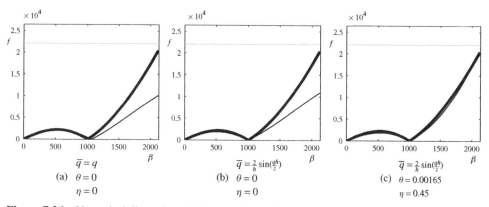

Figure 7.26 Numerical dispersion relations $f(\beta)$, for the family of schemes (7.56), under lossless conditions, for different choices of the free parameters $\bar{q}$, θ, and η: (a) under the default conditions; (b) when $\bar{q}$ is adjusted such that the zero of the numerical dispersion relation coincides with that of the model problem; and (c) for a choice of parameters leading to high accuracy. In all cases, the numerical dispersion relation is indicated by a black line, that of the model system by a thick black line, and $f_s/2$ by a grey line, where $f_s = 44.1\,\text{kHz}$. The spring has the parameters given in the caption to Figure 7.25.

To this end, the parameters η and θ may be adjusted, perhaps through an optimization procedure, so as to yield a numerical dispersion curve which very closely matches that of the system, over the entire audio spectrum—see Figure 7.26(c).

7.9.3   Excitation and reverberation

For a typical spring reverberation system, excitation occurs at one end of the spring. In some cases, a small permanent magnet attached to the end of the spring is driven by an external electromagnetic field. Similarly, at the opposite end, there is a connection to another magnet, the motion of which is captured as output. In some cases, the magnets are aligned with the longitudinal motion of the spring ends (i.e., with ζ) [1]. Assuming the magnets, of mass ratios $\mathcal{M}_{in}$ and $\mathcal{M}_{out}$ with respect to the total spring mass, behave as lumped oscillators of frequencies ω_{in} and ω_{out}, and with damping parameters $\sigma^{(in)}$ and $\sigma^{(out)}$, their dynamics may be described as

$$\frac{d^2 u_{in}}{dt^2} = -\omega_{in}^2 \left(u_{in} - \frac{1}{2}\zeta(0, t) \right) - 2\sigma^{(in)} \frac{du_{in}}{dt} + F(t) \tag{7.60a}$$

$$\frac{d^2 u_{out}}{dt^2} = -\omega_{out}^2 \left(u_{out} - \frac{1}{2}\zeta(1, t) \right) - 2\sigma^{(out)} \frac{du_{out}}{dt} \tag{7.60b}$$

Here, u_{in} and u_{out} are the positions of the magnets, and $F(t)$ is the driving force divided by the mass of the magnet at the left end. See Figure 7.27.

In order to connect these lumped oscillators, it is again useful to find an energy balance. For the oscillators above, it is true that

$$\frac{d\mathfrak{H}_{in}}{dt} = -\mathfrak{Q}_{in} + \mathfrak{B}_{in} + \mathcal{M}_{in}q^2 \frac{du_{in}}{dt} F \qquad \frac{d\mathfrak{H}_{out}}{dt} = -\mathfrak{Q}_{out} + \mathfrak{B}_{out} \tag{7.61}$$

where

$$\mathfrak{H}_{in} = \frac{\mathcal{M}_{in}q^2}{2}\left(\frac{du_{in}}{dt}\right)^2 + \frac{\mathcal{M}_{in}q^2\omega_{in}^2}{4}u_{in}^2 + \frac{\mathcal{M}_{in}q^2\omega_{in}^2}{4}(u_{in} - \zeta(0, t))^2$$

$$\mathfrak{H}_{out} = \frac{\mathcal{M}_{out}q^2}{2}\left(\frac{du_{out}}{dt}\right)^2 + \frac{\mathcal{M}_{out}q^2\omega_{out}^2}{4}u_{out}^2 + \frac{\mathcal{M}_{out}q^2\omega_{out}^2}{4}(u_{out} - \zeta(1, t))^2$$

$$\mathfrak{B}_{in} = -\frac{\mathcal{M}_{in}q^2\omega_{in}^2}{2}\zeta_t(0, t)(u_{in} - \zeta(0, t)) \qquad \mathfrak{Q}_{in} = 2\sigma^{(in)}\mathcal{M}_{in}q^2\left(\frac{du_{in}}{dt}\right)^2$$

$$\mathfrak{B}_{out} = -\frac{\mathcal{M}_{out}q^2\omega_{out}^2}{2}\zeta_t(1, t)(u_{out} - \zeta(1, t)) \qquad \mathfrak{Q}_{out} = 2\sigma^{(out)}\mathcal{M}_{out}q^2\left(\frac{du_{out}}{dt}\right)^2$$

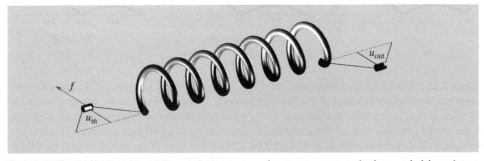

Figure 7.27   Helical spring, connected to mass–spring systems at endpoints and driven by an external force F.

Combining the energy balances (7.61) with that of the spring itself, from (7.55), a global energy balance may be obtained:

$$\frac{d\mathfrak{H}}{dt} = -\mathfrak{Q} + \mathfrak{B} + \mathcal{M}_{in}q^2\frac{du_{in}}{dt}F$$

with

$$\mathfrak{H} = \mathfrak{H}_{spr} + \mathfrak{H}_{in} + \mathfrak{H}_{out} \geq 0 \qquad \mathfrak{Q} = \mathfrak{Q}_{spr} + \mathfrak{Q}_{in} + \mathfrak{Q}_{out} \geq 0 \qquad \mathfrak{B} = \mathfrak{B}_{left} + \mathfrak{B}_{right} + \mathfrak{B}_{in} + \mathfrak{B}_{out}$$

Boundary conditions

When the boundary term $\mathfrak{B}$ vanishes, the energy balance above is dissipative under undriven conditions, and, when driven, the state of the system may be bounded in terms of supplied energy. The boundary term vanishes under the following conditions:

$$u = 0 \quad \text{or} \quad u_{xxx} + q^2u_x = 0 \quad \text{at} \quad x = 0, 1 \quad (7.62a)$$

$$u_x = 0 \quad \text{or} \quad u_{xx} + q^2u = 0 \quad \text{at} \quad x = 0, 1 \quad (7.62b)$$

$$\zeta = 0 \quad \text{or} \quad u - \zeta_x - \frac{\mathcal{M}_{in}\omega_{in}^2}{2\gamma_1^2}(u_{in} - \zeta) = 0 \quad \text{at} \quad x = 0 \quad (7.62c)$$

$$\zeta = 0 \quad \text{or} \quad u - \zeta_x + \frac{\mathcal{M}_{out}\omega_{out}^2}{2\gamma_1^2}(u_{out} - \zeta) = 0 \quad \text{at} \quad x = 1 \quad (7.62d)$$

The first two sets of conditions pertain only to the transverse displacement u—one may easily extrapolate clamped, simply supported, and free conditions from those of the ideal bar, from (7.7). The second two sets involve both the longitudinal displacement ζ and the transverse displacement u—it is the second of each pair that allows for coupling between the lumped mass–spring networks and the spring.

Scheme for mass–spring systems, and numerical boundary conditions

A convenient means of discretizing the mass–spring systems (7.60) is as follows:

$$\delta_{tt}u_{in} = -\omega_{in}^2(\alpha + (1-\alpha)\mu_{t\cdot})\left(u_{in} - \frac{1}{2}\zeta_0\right) - 2\sigma^{(in)}\delta_{t\cdot}u_{in} + F \quad (7.63a)$$

$$\delta_{tt}u_{out} = -\omega_{out}^2(\alpha + (1-\alpha)\mu_{t\cdot})\left(u_{out} - \frac{1}{2}\zeta_N\right) - 2\sigma^{(out)}\delta_{t\cdot}u_{out} \quad (7.63b)$$

where α is chosen as for the spring system, as per (7.57), and where $F = F^n$ is a sampled version of the input signal $F(t)$.

In this case, no further stability global conditions are required, and stable numerical boundary conditions analogous to (7.62) may be found using energy analysis. For example, at the driving end of the spring, a set of boundary conditions, corresponding to one of each pair in (7.62), is

$$u_0 = \delta_{x+}u_0 = 0 \qquad \theta k^2\delta_{x-}\delta_{tt}\zeta_0 - (\alpha + (1-\alpha)\mu_{t\cdot})\left(\delta_{x-}\zeta_0 - u_0 + \frac{\mathcal{M}_{in}\omega_{in}^2}{2\gamma_1^2}(u_{in} - \zeta_0)\right) = 0$$

$$(7.64)$$

See Problem 7.20.

Simulation results

The sound resulting from such a simulation may be matched very closely to that of an actual spring reverberation unit—see Figure 7.28, which shows an output spectrogram. Individual reflections are

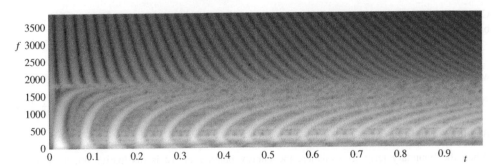

Figure 7.28 Spectrogram of output from scheme (7.56) for a spring, coupled to mass–spring systems at the ends, using schemes (7.63). The spring has the parameters given in the caption to Figure 7.25, with, additionally, $\sigma^{(1)} = \sigma^{(t)} = 1.65$, and the endpoint systems have mass ratios $\mathcal{M}_{in} = \mathcal{M}_{out} = 0.1$, frequencies $\omega_{in} = \omega_{out} = 1000$, and damping parameters $\sigma^{(in)} = \sigma^{(out)} = 275$. For the scheme, the free parameters are chosen as in Figure 7.26(c), and the scheme runs at 44.1 kHz. Output is taken directly as the position u_{out} of the mass at the right endpoint.

directly visible—they appear as curved arcs in the spectrogram due to strong dispersive effects. The confused appearance of the spectrum below the frequency f_c may be related directly to the dispersion curve for the spring, as illustrated in Figure 7.25(b), where, for a given frequency, solutions of differing wavenumbers are possible. Above this frequency, the behavior is essentially bar-like. Notice also the presence of a resonance, due to the mass–spring terminations.

7.10   Spatial variation and stretched coordinates

All the distributed systems discussed up to this point have been linear and shift invariant, or LSI (see Section 5.1.1). Some objects which occur in musical acoustics exhibit variations in material properties with position—in 1D, the most important example is certainly the acoustic tube of variable cross-section, which features prominently in wind instruments and the voice. Simulation for the acoustic tube will be covered in Chapter 9. In the arena of string and bar vibration, the main example is the bar of varying cross-section, which occurs in percussion instruments such as xylophones [77] and marimbas, and the string of variable density is a useful preliminary test problem.

In such cases, some of the analysis tools used up to this point lose their utility—there is no longer a well-defined notion of a phase or group velocity, and von Neumann analysis becomes unwieldy,[4] though the notions of a modal expansion and characteristic frequencies persist. A good treatment of energy analysis of finite difference schemes for systems similar to those which appear in this section is that of Cohen and Joly [84].

7.10.1   Strings of varying cross-section

As a first example, consider the equation of motion of a string, of length L, under tension T_0, with mass density ρ and a variable cross-sectional area $A(x) = A_0 \epsilon^2(x)$, in dimensional form:

$$\rho A_0 \epsilon^2(x) u_{tt} = T_0 u_{xx} \qquad \text{over} \qquad x \in [0, L]$$

---

[4] von Neumann stability analysis may be carried out using so-called frozen-coefficient analysis [341], but energy analysis is an elegant and informative alternative.

The spatial variation is thus consolidated in the factor $\epsilon(x)$. This equation can be spatially scaled as

$$\epsilon^2(x)u_{tt} = \gamma_0^2 u_{xx} \qquad \text{over} \qquad x \in \mathbb{U} \tag{7.65}$$

where $\gamma_0 = \sqrt{T_0/\rho A_0 L^2}$. One can think of this equation, in a very rough sense, as a wave equation with a wave speed $\gamma = \gamma_0/\epsilon(x)$ which varies with position. Now, the modal shapes and frequencies will depend wholly on the density profile, and, in general, can only be computed numerically, or determined experimentally. Energy analysis may be applied just as in previous examples. One arrives at

$$\frac{d\mathfrak{H}}{dt} = \mathfrak{B} \qquad \text{with} \qquad \mathfrak{H} = \mathfrak{T} + \mathfrak{V}$$

and where one now has

$$\mathfrak{T} = \frac{1}{2}\|\epsilon u_t\|_{\mathbb{U}}^2 \qquad \mathfrak{V} = \frac{\gamma_0^2}{2}\|u_x\|_{\mathbb{U}}^2 \qquad \mathfrak{B} = \gamma_0^2\left(u_t(1,t)u_x(1,t) - u_t(0,t)u_x(0,t)\right)$$

Thus one may come to the same conclusions regarding conservative boundary conditions as in the case of the 1D wave equation. In particular, the Dirichlet and Neumann conditions given in Section 6.1.9 continue to lead to energy conservation.

Consider now the obvious choice for a finite difference scheme for (7.65):

$$\epsilon^2 \delta_{tt} u = \gamma_0^2 \delta_{xx} u \tag{7.66}$$

Here, $\epsilon = \epsilon_l$ represents the grid function obtained through direct sampling of the given function $\epsilon(x)$ at the grid locations $x = lh$. Energy analysis, i.e., using an inner product with $\delta_t.u$, leads to the energy balance

$$\delta_{t+}\mathfrak{h} = \mathfrak{b} \qquad \text{with} \qquad \mathfrak{h} = \mathfrak{t} + \mathfrak{v}$$

and

$$\mathfrak{t} = \frac{1}{2}\|\epsilon\delta_{t-}u\|_{\mathbb{U}_N}^2 \qquad \mathfrak{v} = \frac{\gamma_0^2}{2}\langle \delta_{x+}u, e_{t-}\delta_{x+}u\rangle_{\underline{\mathbb{U}}_N} \qquad \mathfrak{b} = \gamma_0^2\left(\delta_t.u_N\delta_{x+}u_N - \delta_t.u_0\delta_{x-}u_0\right)$$

Under what conditions is this quantity non-negative? Assuming conservative boundary conditions, so that $\mathfrak{b} = 0$, one has, using the same techniques as in the case of the 1D wave equation,

$$\mathfrak{h} \geq \frac{1}{2}\|\epsilon\delta_{t-}u\|_{\mathbb{U}_N}^2 - \frac{\gamma_0^2 k^2}{8}\|\delta_{x+}\delta_{t-}u\|_{\underline{\mathbb{U}}_N}^2 \geq \frac{1}{2}\|\epsilon\delta_{t-}u\|_{\mathbb{U}_N}^2 - \frac{\gamma_0^2 k^2}{2h^2}\|\delta_{t-}u\|_{\mathbb{U}_N}^2$$

$$= \frac{1}{2}\sum_{l=0}^{N} h\left(\epsilon_l^2 - \lambda^2\right)(\delta_{t-}u_l)^2$$

where $\lambda = \gamma_0 k/h$. This expression can only be non-negative under the condition

$$\lambda \leq \epsilon_{\min} = \min_{l \in \mathbb{U}_N} \epsilon_l \tag{7.67}$$

Under such conditions, one can, as before, go further and find bounds on solution growth, and thus the above serves as a stability condition for scheme (7.66).

Frequency domain behavior

The scheme (7.66), even when condition (7.67) is satisfied with equality, behaves rather poorly, in that bandwidth is wasted, depending on the variation of the density—the larger the variation, the less of the spectrum is used. See Figure 7.29 for some plots of typical output spectra, under

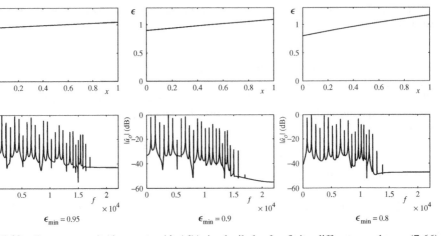

Figure 7.29   Output magnitude spectra $|\hat{u}_o(f)|$, in decibels, for finite difference scheme (7.66) for the string of variable cross-sectional area, under different profiles, as indicated in plots of $\epsilon(x)$, related to the cross-sectional area $A(x)$ and a nominal value A_0 through $A(x) = A_0\epsilon^2(x)$. The sample rate is chosen as $f_s = 44\,100\,\mathrm{Hz}$, $\gamma_0 = 1500$, and the bound (7.67) is satisfied as close to equality as possible. The initial condition is of plucked type, using a raised cosine of amplitude 1, centered at $x = 0.3$, of half-width 0.1, and the readout position is taken at $x = 0.8$.

different choices of the function $\epsilon(x)$. Such behavior is definitely audible, leading to a low-passing effect on the resulting sound output, and is to be avoided at all costs. One solution to this problem is to design implicit schemes; a better idea, however, given that the problem itself exhibits spatial variation, is to introduce coordinate changes.

Using stretched coordinates

In essence, the low-passing effect which occurs for the scheme (7.66) is another example of the same behavior which occurs in explicit schemes for LSI systems when the stability condition is not satisfied with equality—see, e.g., the case of schemes for the wave equation operating away from the CFL condition, as discussed in Section 6.2.3. It is possible to make sense of this geometrically in terms of the "regions of dependence" arguments used in this case, and as illustrated in Figure 7.30(a). (The reader may wish to refer to Figure 6.9 in the previous chapter, which deals with similar issues for schemes for the wave equation.)

Considering the model problem (7.65), one may say that at a given point x, the wave speed is, roughly, $\gamma = \gamma_0/\epsilon(x)$, and thus the region of dependence varies from point to point. At the point x at which ϵ takes its minimum value, the region of dependence is thus largest, and, as the numerical region of dependence of the scheme must include that of the model problem (for convergence, and stability), on a uniform grid, the minimum grid spacing is determined by ϵ at this point—energy analysis leads to exactly this result, as given in (7.67). At other grid points, however, the grid spacing is larger than this, and thus the scheme exhibits dispersive behavior over the majority of the domain.

The natural means of attacking this problem is to employ stretched coordinates which match the variation in the wave speed—see Section 5.3 for the relevant algebraic machinery. Consider a dimensionless coordinate $\alpha(x)$, defined in terms of x as

$$\alpha(x) = \frac{\int_0^x \epsilon(\eta)d\eta}{\int_0^1 \epsilon(\eta)d\eta}$$

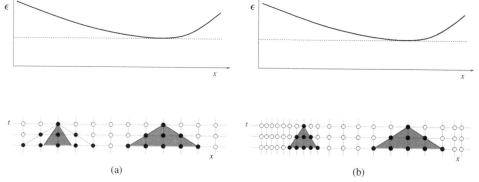

Figure 7.30   Coordinate transformation and regions of dependence (bottom) in a scheme for a string of variable cross-section (top). For such a string, the local wave speed, and thus the region of dependence, will be variable. For an explicit scheme over a uniformly sampled grid, as shown in (a), at bottom, the numerical region of dependence of the scheme only matches that of the model system (indicated in grey) at the location at which ϵ is a minimum. In (b), a coordinate transformation is applied such that the numerical and model regions of dependence coincide.

The spatially scaled form of (7.65) then becomes

$$\epsilon u_{tt} = \gamma_0^2 \left(\epsilon u_\alpha \right)_\alpha$$

A finite difference scheme for the above equation is

$$[\epsilon]\delta_{tt}u = \gamma_0^2 \delta_{\alpha+}\left((\mu_{\alpha-}\epsilon)(\delta_{\alpha-}u) \right) \tag{7.68}$$

Here, the exact form of the discrete approximation to ϵ on the left is left unspecified for the moment, and indicated as the grid function $[\epsilon] = [\epsilon]_l$. A discrete energy follows, as before, through an inner product with $\delta_t.u$, now in α coordinates, i.e.,

$$\delta_{t+}\mathfrak{h} = \mathfrak{b} \qquad \text{with} \qquad \mathfrak{h} = \mathfrak{t} + \mathfrak{v} \qquad \text{and} \qquad \mathfrak{b} = \gamma_0^2 \left(\delta_t.u_N \mu_{\alpha+}\epsilon_N \delta_{\alpha+}u_N - \delta_t.u_0 \mu_{\alpha-}\epsilon_0 \delta_{\alpha-}u_0 \right)$$

and

$$\mathfrak{t} = \frac{1}{2}\| \sqrt{[\epsilon]}\delta_{t-}u \|_{\overline{\mathbb{U}}_N}^2 \qquad \mathfrak{v} = \frac{\gamma_0^2}{2} \langle (\mu_{\alpha-}\epsilon)(\delta_{\alpha-}u), e_{t-}\delta_{\alpha-}u \rangle_{\overline{\mathbb{U}}_N}$$

It then follows, after manipulations similar to those performed previously, that under conservative or lossy conditions $\mathfrak{b} \le 0$,

$$\mathfrak{h} \ge \frac{1}{2}\| \sqrt{[\epsilon]}\delta_{t-}u \|_{\overline{\mathbb{U}}_N}^2 - \frac{\lambda^2}{2}\| \sqrt{\mu_{\alpha\alpha}\epsilon}\delta_{t-}u \|_{\overline{\mathbb{U}}_N}^2 = \frac{1}{2}\sum_{l=0}^{N} h \left([\epsilon] - \lambda^2 \mu_{\alpha\alpha}\epsilon \right) (\delta_{t-}u_l)^2$$

Here, then, the natural choice of $[\epsilon] = \mu_{\alpha\alpha}\epsilon$ leads to the stability condition

$$\lambda \le 1$$

which is independent of ϵ—the coordinate transformation has removed such a dependence. This scheme now exhibits much better behavior in the frequency domain—see Figure 7.31. The audio bandwidth is filled, barring the slight loss incurred near the Nyquist, due to quantization of the number of grid points to an integer (i.e., the condition $\lambda \le 1$ is satisfied close to equality).

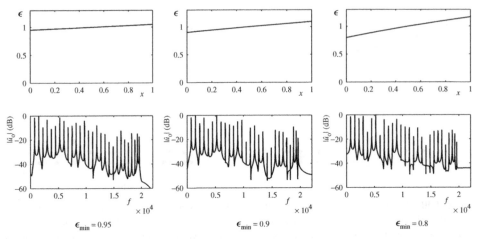

Figure 7.31 Output spectra for finite difference scheme (7.68) for the string of variable density, under different density profiles. The other conditions are the same as in the caption to Figure 7.29.

7.10.2   Bars of varying cross-section

Much more relevant, at least in musical acoustics, is the case of the bar of variable cross-sectional area. For some percussion instruments, e.g., the marimba, bars are tuned, often by cutting an arch-like shape into the bars. See, e.g., [136] for an overview. The effects of variations in cross-sectional area on the modal frequencies are complex, to say the least.

In the case of the uniform ideal bar, there is no need, from a simulation point of view, to enter into the details of various physical parameters—all the relevant parameters, including bar length, could be bundled into a single stiffness parameter κ. When the cross-section is varying, more care needs to be taken, and it is useful to begin again from a dimensional form, which is

$$\rho A(x)u_{tt} = -(EI(x)u_{xx})_{xx} \qquad (7.69)$$

In the spatially varying case, both A and the moment of inertia I will be functions of some characteristic thickness, which is dependent on x. It is assumed, here, that the material density ρ and Young's modulus E are not variable (though one could permit such variations as well).

It is easiest to concentrate on the case of a bar of rectangular cross-section, with width b and thickness $H(x) = H_0\phi(x)$. H_0 is a reference thickness, and $\phi(x)$ represents the variations about this value. For such a bar, the area and moment of inertia are given by

$$A = bH_0\phi(x) \qquad\qquad I = \frac{1}{12}bH_0^3\phi^3$$

Under these conditions, when scaled, (7.69) becomes

$$\phi u_{tt} = -\kappa_0^2\left(\phi^3 u_{xx}\right)_{xx} \qquad (7.70)$$

where

$$\kappa_0^2 = \frac{EH_0^2}{12\rho L^4}$$

and where, as previously, L is the physical length of the bar.

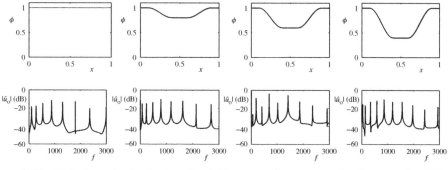

Figure 7.32   Output spectra for the bar of variable rectangular cross-sectional area, under different thickness profiles, as shown. Here, $\kappa_0 = 30$, and boundary conditions are of free type.

Arched bars

As an example of the effect of the variation in cross-sectional area, consider the effect of variation in the depth of an arch in a bar of rectangular cross-section, as shown in Figure 7.32. The gross effect of removing material from the bar is to decrease the modal frequencies—thus pitch is decreased. The ratios of the various modal frequencies, however, do not stay the same. In particular, the first two non-zero modal frequencies, which are primarily responsible for the perception of pitch, may be adjusted in this way so that their ratio becomes consonant (such as, say, 3:1). See Programming Exercise 7.9.

Energy

The variable bar system possesses a conserved energy as well. Over the real line, $\mathcal{D} = \mathbb{R}$, one has

$$\frac{d\mathfrak{H}}{dt} = 0 \qquad \text{with} \qquad \mathfrak{H} = \mathfrak{T} + \mathfrak{V} \tag{7.71}$$

with

$$\mathfrak{T} = \frac{1}{2}\|\sqrt{\epsilon}u_t\|_{\mathbb{R}}^2 \qquad \mathfrak{V} = \frac{\kappa_0^2}{2}\|\phi^{3/2}u_{xx}\|_{\mathbb{R}}^2$$

If the bar is defined over an finite interval, the fixed and clamped boundary conditions (7.7a) and (7.7b) continue to lead to exact conservation. The free condition, of great importance in mallet percussion instruments, must be modified to

$$u_{xx} = \left(\phi^3 u_{xx}\right)_x = 0$$

at an endpoint—the condition reduces to (7.7c) when ϕ is constant at an endpoint (which is commonly the case for percussion).

Loss in the spatially varying case will not be discussed here, though its effect on the energy balance above leads to strict dissipation—this effect carries over to the discrete case as well, and has no effect on numerical stability. See Problem 7.21.

Finite difference schemes

One can proceed immediately from (7.70) to a finite difference scheme:

$$[\phi]\delta_{tt}u = -\kappa_0^2\delta_{xx}\left(\phi^3\delta_{xx}u\right) \tag{7.72}$$

Again, some unspecified second-order approximation $[\phi]$ has been employed. This scheme also may be shown to be stable, using energy techniques, under the condition

$$\mu = \frac{k\kappa_0}{h^2} \leq \frac{1}{2} \min\left(\sqrt{\frac{[\phi]}{\mu_{xx}\,(\phi^3)}}\right) \approx \frac{1}{2\phi_{max}}$$

The approximate bound above may be made exact through the proper choice of the approximation $[\phi] = (\mu_{xx}\phi^3)/\phi^2$.

As might be gathered from the case of the string of variable density in the previous section, this scheme performs terribly! For even very small variations in thickness, the spectrum of the output can be band-limited to below one-quarter the sample rate. As such, this scheme is not attractive for synthesis—indeed, for larger variations in cross-sectional area, dispersion is so extreme that the scheme is practically useless—see Figure 7.32. Again, one may employ a stretched coordinate $\alpha(x)$, in order to accommodate the variations in cross-section. Under the coordinate transformation defined by

$$\alpha(x) = \frac{1}{\alpha_{av}} \int_0^x \frac{1}{\sqrt{\phi(\eta)}} d\eta \qquad \text{with} \qquad \alpha_{av} = \int_0^1 \frac{1}{\sqrt{\phi(\eta)}} d\eta$$

the system (7.70) becomes, using the transformed derivatives as introduced in Section 5.3,

$$\phi^{3/2} u_{tt} = -\frac{\kappa_0^2}{\alpha_{av}^4}\left(\phi^{-1/2}\left(\phi^{5/2}\left(\phi^{-1/2}u_\alpha\right)_\alpha\right)_\alpha\right)_\alpha$$

(Notice that the effect of the variation is now balanced on both side of the equation, in that an equal power of ϕ appears in both terms.) The related finite difference scheme is now

$$[\phi^{3/2}]\delta_{tt}u = -\frac{\kappa_0^2}{\alpha_{av}^4}\delta_{\alpha+}\left(\mu_{\alpha-}\phi^{-1/2}\delta_{\alpha-}\left(\phi^{5/2}\delta_{\alpha+}\left(\mu_{\alpha-}\phi^{-1/2}\delta_{\alpha-}u\right)\right)\right) \qquad (7.73)$$

and the stability condition, again following from energy analysis, is

$$\mu \leq \frac{\alpha_{av}^2}{2}\min\left(\sqrt{\frac{[\phi^{3/2}]}{\mu_{\alpha+}\left((\mu_{\alpha-}\phi^{5/2})(\mu_{\alpha-}\phi^{-1/2})^2\right)}}\right) \approx \frac{\alpha_{av}^2}{2}$$

Again, with a proper choice of $[\phi^{3/2}]$, namely $[\phi^{3/2}] = \mu_{\alpha+}\left((\mu_{\alpha-}\phi^{5/2})(\mu_{\alpha-}\phi^{-1/2})^2\right)$, the approximate bound above may be made exact.

The improvement, relative to scheme (7.72) is dramatic—see Figure 7.33. The bandwidth of the computed solution is nearly full, regardless of the degree of variation in cross-sectional

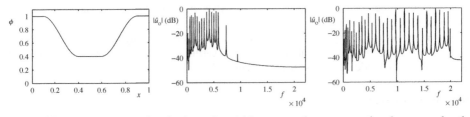

Figure 7.33 Output spectra for the bar of variable rectangular cross-sectional area, under the arched thickness profile, at left. Here, $\kappa_0 = 30$, boundary conditions are of free type, and the sample rate is $f_s = 44\,100$ Hz. In the center panel is shown the spectrum of sound output for scheme (7.72), and in the right panel, that of output from scheme (7.73).

area. The problem of numerical dispersion, i.e., modal mistuning, remains, however, just as in the case of the uniform bar (see page 170). For finer modeling, one could well employ an implicit generalization of either of schemes (7.72) or (7.73), as per the work of Chaigne and Doutaut [77].

7.11   Problems

Problem 7.1   *The Euler–Bernoulli model of bar vibration is valid when the bar thickness is small relative to its length. If this is not the case, then higher-order theories of bar vibration may be of interest. One such theory, due to Timoshenko, leads to a two-variable system [156, 195]:*

$$u_{tt} = -\frac{GK}{\rho}(\Psi_x - u_{xx}) \qquad \Psi_{tt} = \frac{E}{\rho}\Psi_{xx} + \frac{GAK}{\rho I}(u_x - \Psi)$$

Here, $u(x,t)$ is the transverse displacement of the bar, as before, and Ψ is a rotation of the bar cross-section relative to the normal. The parameters E, ρ, and A are as before—I is the bar moment of inertia, G is the shear modulus, and K is an empirically determined parameter. This is now a coupled system in two variables.

(a) Introduce the variables $x' = x/L$ and $u' = u/L$, for some characteristic length L, and simplify the system above (removing primes) to

$$u_{tt} = \gamma_s^2(u_{xx} - \Psi_x) \qquad \epsilon^2\Psi_{tt} = \epsilon^2\gamma_1^2\Psi_{xx} + \gamma_s^2(u_x - \Psi)$$

where $\gamma_s^2 = GK/\rho L^2$, $\gamma_1^2 = E/\rho L^2$, and $\epsilon^2 = I/AL^2$.

(b) Replacing time derivatives by factors $j\omega$ and spatial derivatives by factors $j\beta$, show that the dispersion relation for the Timoshenko system is

$$\omega^4 - \left((\gamma_s^2 + \gamma_1^2)\beta^2 + \gamma_s^2/\epsilon^2\right)\omega^2 + \gamma_s^2\gamma_1^2\beta^4 = 0 \qquad (7.74)$$

Solve this fourth-order equation for ω^2, and prove, by using series expansions, that one set of solutions behaves according to

$$\omega^2 = \kappa^2\beta^4 + O(\beta^6)$$

where κ is defined as for the Euler–Bernoulli equation, in (7.3). Thus, in the low-frequency limit, one solution to the Timoshenko system behaves as that of the thin bar model.

(c) From the expressions for $\omega(\beta)$ you derived above, show that for one set of solutions, the phase velocity $v_\phi = \omega/\beta$ can become unbounded, but that for all solutions, the group velocity $v_g = d\omega/d\beta$ remains bounded for all values of β.

(d) Suppose the Timoshenko system is defined over the semi-infinite domain $\mathcal{D} = \mathbb{R}^+$. Show that the following energy balance holds:

$$\frac{d\mathfrak{H}}{dt} = \mathfrak{B} \qquad \text{with} \qquad \mathfrak{H} = \frac{1}{2}\|u_t\|_{\mathbb{R}^+}^2 + \frac{1}{2}\|\epsilon\Psi_t\|_{\mathbb{R}^+}^2 + \frac{1}{2}\|\epsilon\gamma_1\Psi_x\|_{\mathbb{R}^+}^2 + \frac{\gamma_s^2}{2}\|u_x - \Psi\|_{\mathbb{R}^+}^2$$

and find the form of the boundary term $\mathfrak{B}$, which depends on the values of u and Ψ and their derivatives at $x = 0$. Propose some conditions under which the system remains lossless.

Problem 7.2   *Consider again the Timoshenko system, as defined in Problem 7.1. From the dispersion relation (7.74), show that in the high-frequency limit as β becomes large, the solutions approach*

$$\omega = \pm\gamma_s\beta \qquad \omega = \pm\gamma_1\beta$$

In this limit, what can you say about the density of modes? (You may assume that $\beta = p\pi$.) How does this differ from the behavior of the thin bar model? What can you conclude about the computational complexity of simulations for Timoshenko's system, in the limit of a high sample rate?

Problem 7.3   *Given the energy balance for the semi-infinite ideal bar from (7.6), show that the following conditions also imply losslessness. In all cases, the total conserved energy will be of the form $\mathfrak{H} + \mathfrak{H}_b$, where $\mathfrak{H}$ is as defined in (7.5) (limited to the domain $\mathcal{D} = \mathbb{R}^+$, and where $\mathfrak{H}_b$ is a term representing stored energy at the boundary point $x = 0$). The parameter α is constrained to be non-negative.*

(a) $u_{xx}(0, t) = 0$ and $u_{xxx}(0, t) + \alpha u(0, t) = 0$.
(b) $u(0, t) = 0$ and $u_{xx}(0, t) - \alpha u_x(0, t) = 0$.
(c) $u_{xx}(0, t) = 0$ and $u_{xxx}(0, t) + \alpha u_{tt}(0, t) = 0$.

Furthermore, show that the following termination is strictly dissipative:

(d) $u_{xx}(0, t) = 0$ and $u_{xxx}(0, t) + \alpha u_t(0, t) = 0$.

Problem 7.4   *An explicit formula for the modal frequencies of an ideal bar under simply supported conditions at each end is given in (7.8), and an implicit formula for those of the bar under clamped/simply supported conditions in (7.9). Derive implicit formulas for the remaining combinations of boundary conditions given in (7.7), namely: clamped/free, clamped/clamped, free/free, and simply supported/free. Show that in all cases the distribution of modal frequencies ω_p approaches $\omega_p = \kappa \pi^2 p^2$ in the limit as p becomes large. Deduce that the number of degrees of freedom of the bar, as given in (7.10), is approximately independent of the choice of boundary condition.*

Problem 7.5   *Show that, for scheme (7.11) for the ideal bar equation, defined over the semi-infinite interval $\mathcal{D} = \mathbb{Z}^+$, the following pairs of boundary conditions are conservative, and find the corresponding energy function. (Hint: Consider a primed inner product of the type given in (5.23).) Notice that the free boundary condition is centered, and thus more accurate than that given in (7.16c).*

$$u = \delta_{x+}u \quad = 0 \quad \text{clamped}$$

$$u = \delta_{xx}u \quad = 0 \quad \text{simply supported}$$

$$\delta_{xx}u = \delta_x.\delta_{xx}u = 0 \quad \text{free}$$

Problem 7.6   *Consider the action of the operator δ_{xxxx} applied to the grid function u_l, defined over $\mathbb{Z}^+$, under the free boundary condition (7.16c), and write $\delta_{xxxx}u_0$ and $\delta_{xxxx}u_1$ purely in terms of values of u_l over the domain interior.*

Problem 7.7   *Apply von Neumann stability analysis to the implicit scheme (7.17) for the ideal bar equation. Show that, by introducing the ansatz $u_l^n = z^n e^{j\beta lh}$, a characteristic polynomial of the form*

$$z + \left(-2 + \frac{16\mu^2 p^2}{1 - 2(1 - \theta)p^2}\right) + z^{-1} = 0$$

results. Here, as in the case of the simpler scheme (7.11), $p = \sin^2(\beta h/2)$ and takes on values between 0 and 1 only. Using the stability condition for second-order polynomials given in (2.14), show the stability conditions (7.19).

Problem 7.8   *Consider scheme (7.17), now from an energetic point of view. Assuming that it is defined over the semi-infinite interval $\mathcal{D} = \mathbb{Z}^+$, by taking an inner product with $\delta_t.u$, an energy balance of the following form results:*

$$\delta_{t+}\mathfrak{h} = \mathfrak{b} \quad \text{with} \quad \mathfrak{h} = \frac{1}{2}\|\delta_{t-}u\|_{\mathbb{Z}^+}^2 + \frac{\kappa^2}{2}\langle\delta_{xx}u, \delta_{xx}e_{t-}u\rangle_{\overline{\mathbb{Z}^+}} - \frac{(1-\theta)h^2}{4}\|\delta_{x+}\delta_{t-}u\|_{\mathbb{Z}^+}^2$$

(a) Show that the numerical energy above is non-negative under the conditions (7.19).
(b) Find the explicit form of the boundary term $\mathfrak{b}$, and show that it vanishes under the conditions (7.16a) and (7.16b) corresponding to the clamped and simply supported conditions.

Find new conditions, dependent on θ, *the free parameter, corresponding to the free conditions (7.7c).*

Problem 7.9   *Consider the stiff string equation (7.20). Assuming harmonic time dependence at frequency* ω, *the following differential equation results:*

$$\kappa^2 \frac{d^4 u}{dx^4} - \gamma^2 \frac{d^2 u}{dx^2} - \omega^2 u = 0$$

The general real-valued solution to the above equation is then

$$u = A \cos(\beta_1 x) + B \sin(\beta_1 x) + C \cosh(\beta_2 x) + D \sinh(\beta_2 x)$$

(a) Determine β_1 *and* β_2 *in terms of* κ, γ, *and* ω.
(b) Suppose that the string is defined over the unit interval $\mathcal{D} = \mathbb{U}$, *and clamped conditions (7.7a) are applied. Show that this leads to the condition*

$$2\beta_1\beta_2 (1 - \cos(\beta_1)\cosh(\beta_2)) + (\beta_2^2 - \beta_1^2) \sin(\beta_1)\sinh(\beta_2) = 0$$

(c) Show that for small values of κ *and* ω *relative to* γ, *the modal frequencies lie approximately in a harmonic series.*

Problem 7.10   *Using von Neumann analysis, prove stability condition (7.24) for scheme (7.23) for the equation of motion of a stiff string.*

Problem 7.11   *Consider the implicit* θ *scheme (7.25) for the stiff string equation. By equating the number of degrees of freedom of the model, from (7.22), and the number of degrees of freedom of the scheme, from (7.27), find an optimal setting for* θ *in terms of* γ, κ, *and the sample rate* f_s. *(You will need such an expression for the optimal* θ *in order to complete Programming Exercise 7.2 below.)*

Problem 7.12   *Consider the following variant of the stiff string model:*

$$u_{tt} = \gamma^2 u_{xx} - \kappa^2 u_{xxxx} - 2\sigma_0 u_t - b u_{ttt} \qquad (7.75)$$

which differs from the model (7.28) in the treatment of the frequency-dependent loss term.
(a) By inserting a test solution of the form $u = e^{st + j\beta x}$, *show that the characteristic equation for this model is*

$$bs^3 + s^2 + 2\sigma_0 s + \gamma^2 \beta^2 + \kappa^2 \beta^4 = 0$$

(b) Show that, for large values of the wavenumber β, *the roots of the characteristic equation must approach the roots of*

$$s^3 + \frac{\kappa^2}{b}\beta^4 = 0$$

(c) Prove that at least one of the roots of the characteristic equation must have a positive real part in the limit as β *becomes large. How does your analysis depend on the sign of* b? *What can you conclude about the validity of such a model?*

Problem 7.13   *Reconsider the stiff string model given in (7.75) above, defined over* $\mathcal{D} = \mathbb{R}$. *By taking an inner product with* u_t, *find an energy balance for the equation, of the form*

$$\frac{d\mathfrak{H}}{dt} = -\mathfrak{Q}$$

Are $\mathfrak{H}$ *and* $\mathfrak{Q}$ *non-negative?*

Problem 7.14 *Some physical models employ an even more refined model of frequency-dependent loss. Consider the following model of the stiff string, with three-parameter frequency-dependent loss:*

$$u_{tt} = \gamma^2 u_{xx} - \kappa^2 u_{xxxx} - 2\sigma_0 u_t + 2\sigma_1 u_{txx} - 2\sigma_2 u_{txxxx}$$

(a) By inserting a test solution of the form $u = e^{st+j\beta x}$, find the characteristic equation, and find the roots $s_{\pm}(\beta)$.

(b) Using $s_{\pm} = \sigma \pm j\omega$, find expressions for $\sigma(\beta)$ and $\omega(\beta)$, under the assumption that the parameters σ_0, σ_1, and σ_2 are small.

(c) The conditions

$$\sigma_0 \geq 0 \qquad \sigma_1 \geq 0 \qquad \sigma_2 \geq 0 \tag{7.76}$$

are sufficient for your expression for loss $\sigma(\beta)$ to be non-positive everywhere (i.e., so that all wavenumbers are damped). Derive necessary conditions. (Hint: Start by evaluating the expression $\sigma(\beta)$ for the limiting cases $\beta = 0$ and $\beta = \infty$.) Sketch $\sigma(\beta)$ for a representative case where the sufficient condition above is violated, but the necessary condition is satisfied; you should be able to produce loss curves which are non-monotonic as a function of wavenumber.

(d) Supposing that the equation above is defined over the infinite interval $\mathcal{D} = \mathbb{R}$, find an expression for the energy balance of the string of the form

$$\frac{d\mathfrak{H}}{dt} = -\mathfrak{Q}$$

and show that, under the sufficient conditions above, $\mathfrak{Q}$ is non-negative. Can you show that $\mathfrak{Q}$ is non-negative under the necessary conditions you derived in (c) above?

Problem 7.15 *Consider the following implicit scheme for the stiff string model with three-parameter frequency-dependent loss described in the previous problem:*

$$\delta_{tt}u = \gamma^2 \delta_{xx}u - \kappa^2 \delta_{xxxx}u - 2\sigma_0 \delta_{t\cdot}u + 2\sigma_1 \delta_{t\cdot}\delta_{xx}u - 2\sigma_2 \delta_{t\cdot}\delta_{xxxx}u$$

(a) Using von Neumann analysis (i.e., by inserting a test solution of the form $u_l^n = z^n e^{jl\beta h}$), find the characteristic polynomial for the scheme, which will be a quadratic in z.

(b) Show that, if the conditions (7.76) are satisfied, the stability condition for the scheme is unchanged from (7.24) for the stiff string without loss.

(c) Write the scheme in vector–matrix form

$$\mathbf{A}\mathbf{u}^{n+1} + \mathbf{B}\mathbf{u}^n + \mathbf{C}\mathbf{u}^{n-1} = 0$$

where $\mathbf{u}^n$ is a vector containing values of the grid function u_l^n. You may use the shorthand notations $\mathbf{D}_{xx}$ and $\mathbf{D}_{xxxx}$ to represent the matrix form of the operators δ_{xx} and δ_{xxxx}, thus assuming that boundary conditions are taken into account.

Problem 7.16 *Consider a difference scheme for the bow–string system, under the action of an interpolation operator, as in (7.33). Show that this equation may be written as the following non-linear equation in the relative velocity v_{rel}:*

$$\phi(v_{rel}) = \frac{-2}{k\|J_p(x_i)\|_{\mathbb{U}}^2 F_B} v_{rel} + q$$

where q consists of known values of the grid function u, and the time series v_B and F_B. Show that the uniqueness condition (7.34) results. Under what conditions on ϕ and F_B does this condition interfere with the stability condition $\lambda \leq 1$?

Problem 7.17   *Consider the case of the bowed bar with a loss term*

$$u_{tt} = -\kappa^2 u_{xxxx} - 2\sigma_0 u_t - \delta(x - x_i) F_B \phi (v_{rel}) \qquad \text{where} \qquad v_{rel} = u_t(x_i) - v_B$$

under conservative boundary conditions. A difference scheme is

$$\delta_{tt} u = -\kappa^2 \delta_{xxxx} u - 2\sigma_0 \delta_{t.} u - J_p(x_i) F_B \phi (v_{rel}) \qquad \text{where} \qquad v_{rel} = I(x_i)\delta_{t.} u - v_B$$

This scheme is, again, explicit, except for the determination of the relative bow velocity v_{rel}. By taking an inner product with $J_p(x_i)$, find a nonlinear equation of the form

$$\phi (v_{rel}) = b v_{rel} + q$$

and determine conditions under which the solution is unique.

Problem 7.18   *Consider the semi-implicit scheme (7.37) for the hammer–string interaction, and suppose the hammer distribution ϵ is localized at a single point $x = x_H$, giving $\epsilon_l = J_{l,p}(x_H)$, for a pth-order spreading function, as described in Section 5.2.4. Taking an inner product with $J_{l,p}(x_H)$, and defining the relative displacement $\eta = u_H - I_p(x_H)u$, the coupling may be written in terms of the two scalar updates*

$$\delta_{tt} I_p(x_H)u = \gamma^2 \delta_{xx} I_p(x_H)u + \|J_p(x_H)\|_{\mathbb{U}_N}^2 MF \qquad \delta_{tt} u_H = -F \qquad F = \omega_H^{1+\alpha} \left([\eta]^+\right)^{\alpha - 1} \mu_t.\eta$$

In the two updates, note that, due to the form of F, the coupling among the unknowns is linear. Combine the two updates into an explicit recursion for η. Show that once η is updated, F may be determined, and thus the system (7.37) may be explicitly updated.

Problem 7.19   *Consider the following semi-implicit discretization of the connection between an ideal string with loss and a rattling element, described by (7.44):*

$$\delta_{tt} u = \gamma^2 \delta_{xx} u - 2\sigma_0 \delta_{t.} u + J_p(x_P) F \tag{7.77}$$

with

$$\delta_{tt} u_R = -MF \qquad F = \begin{cases} -\omega_R^{\alpha+1} \mu_t. (\eta - \epsilon/2) (\eta - \epsilon/2)^{\alpha - 1}, & \eta \geq \epsilon/2 \\ 0, & |\eta| < \epsilon/2 \qquad \eta = I_p(x_P)u - u_R \\ \omega_R^{\alpha+1} \mu_t. (-\eta - \epsilon/2) (-\eta - \epsilon/2)^{\alpha - 1}, & \eta \leq -\epsilon/2 \end{cases}$$

Show that it is possible to obtain an explicit update in the scalar variable η, and that this may then be used in order to determine F, which can be used to update (7.77) directly.

Problem 7.20   *The analysis of complex multiparameter schemes such as scheme (7.56) for the helical spring is certainly possible through von Neumann analysis, but is rather strenuous (you may wish to attempt to prove stability conditions for this scheme in this way!). Energy methods lead to a far simpler analysis.*

   (a) Consider the scheme (7.56) defined, for simplicity, over the infinite domain $\mathcal{D} = \mathbb{Z}$, and show that the numerical conserved energy is of the form

$$\mathfrak{h}_{spr} = \mathfrak{t}_{spr} + \mathfrak{v}_{spr,uc} + \mathfrak{v}_{spr,\times}$$

where

$$\mathfrak{t}_{spr} = \frac{1}{2}\|\delta_{t-}u\|_{\mathbb{Z}}^2 + \frac{q^2}{2}\|\delta_{t-}\zeta\|_{\mathbb{Z}}^2$$

$$\mathfrak{v}_{spr,uc} = \frac{\kappa^2}{2}\langle(\delta_{xx}+\bar{q}^2)u, (\delta_{xx}+\bar{q}^2)e_{t-}u\rangle_{\mathbb{Z}} - \frac{\eta\kappa k}{2}\|\delta_{t-}\delta_{x-}u\|_{\mathbb{Z}}^2 - \frac{q^2\theta\gamma_1^2 k^2}{2}\|\delta_{t-}\delta_{x-}\zeta\|_{\mathbb{Z}}^2$$

$$\mathfrak{v}_{spr,\times} = \frac{\alpha\gamma_1^2 q^2}{2}\langle\delta_{x-}\zeta - u, e_{t-}(\delta_{x-}\zeta - u)\rangle_{\mathbb{Z}} + \frac{(1-\alpha)\gamma_1^2 q^2}{2}\mu_{t-}\|\delta_{x-}\zeta - u\|_{\mathbb{Z}}^2$$

Here, $\mathfrak{t}_{spr}$ is the kinetic energy, and $\mathfrak{v}_{spr,uc}$ and $\mathfrak{v}_{spr,\times}$ are the contributions to the potential energy due to uncoupled and coupled motion, respectively.

(b) Show that, under conditions (7.57) on α, a free parameter, it is true that $\mathfrak{v}_{spr,\times} \geq 0$, and thus

$$\mathfrak{h}_{spr} \geq \mathfrak{t}_{spr} + \mathfrak{v}_{spr,uc}$$

(c) Show that when $\theta > 0$ and $\eta > 0$, $\mathfrak{v}_{spr,uc}$ may be bounded as

$$\mathfrak{v}_{spr,uc} \geq -\frac{\kappa^2 k^2}{8h^4}\left(2 + |\bar{q}^2 h^2 - 2|\right)^2\|\delta_{t-}u\|_{\mathbb{Z}}^2 - \frac{2\eta\kappa k}{h^2}\|\delta_{t-}u\|_{\mathbb{Z}}^2 - \frac{2q^2\theta\gamma_1^2 k^2}{h^2}\|\delta_{t-}\zeta\|_{\mathbb{Z}}^2$$

and thus that the energy of the spring may be bounded as

$$\mathfrak{h}_{spr} \geq \frac{q^2}{2}\left(1 - \frac{4\theta\gamma_1^2 k^2}{h^2}\right)\|\delta_{t-}\zeta\|_{\mathbb{Z}}^2 + \frac{1}{2}\left(1 - \frac{4\eta\kappa k}{h^2} - \frac{\kappa^2 k^2}{4h^4}\left(2 + |\bar{q}^2 h^2 - 2|\right)^2\right)\|\delta_{t-}u\|_{\mathbb{Z}}^2$$

Finally, show that the energy $\mathfrak{h}_{spr}$ is non-negative under conditions (7.59), and when $\bar{q}$ is chosen according to (7.58). Can you go further and show a bound on solution growth?

(d) Extend this analysis in order to derive numerically stable boundary conditions, such as that given in (7.64). In the first instance, concentrate on the left boundary, and assume the problem to be defined over $\mathcal{D} = \mathbb{Z}^+$. The easiest way of proceeding is to derive an energy function which is defined strictly over the interior of this domain, in which case you may use the above analysis to find simple conditions under which the numerical energy is non-negative.

Problem 7.21   *Consider the spatially varying bar model in the scaled form given by*

$$\phi u_{tt} = -\kappa_0^2\left(\phi^3\left(u_{xx} + \sigma u_{txx}\right)\right)_{xx}$$

defined over the entire real line, $\mathcal{D} = \mathbb{R}$, where $\sigma \geq 0$ is a loss parameter. (Such a model has been used to describe the vibration of non-uniform xylophone bars [77].)

(a) Show that the energy balance (7.71) may be generalized to

$$\frac{d\mathfrak{h}}{dt} = -\mathfrak{Q}$$

and determine $\mathfrak{Q}$, showing that it is non-negative, and thus that the system is strictly dissipative.

(b) Design a scheme for the lossy model above, using a centered difference approximation $\delta_{t\cdot}$ for the extra time derivative in the loss term. Find conditions under which this scheme will be dissipative, and thus numerically stable, in the same way as for the model problem.

7.12   Programming exercises

Programming Exercise 7.1   *Consider the dispersion relation (7.74) for Timoshenko's system, which is a higher-order correction to the Euler–Bernoulli thin bar theory. Is such a higher-order* *theory necessary in musical acoustics? As a first step, consider a bar of rectangular cross-section, in which case $\gamma_1 = 4\gamma_s/3$, and $\epsilon = \eta/\sqrt{12}$, where η is the ratio of bar thickness to length. In order to investigate this, solve the Timoshenko dispersion relation numerically in Matlab, to give two curves $\omega(\beta)$, and plot these on top of the dispersion relation $\omega(\beta) = \kappa\beta^2$ for the thin bar theory, where $\kappa = \gamma_1\epsilon$. Your code should depend only on the parameters η and γ_s. You will need to make sure that you solve the dispersion relation over a range of wavenumbers β which yields results in the audio spectrum (assume $\omega \leq \pi f_s$, for some typical audio band such as $f_s = 44\,100\,Hz$).*

Determine the range of parameters η and γ_s over which the dispersion relation for the thin bar model is acceptably close to one of the dispersion relations for Timoshenko's system. You may wish to think about how to define acceptably close (perhaps through a measure of deviation, in cents). Also, one of the dispersion relations for Timoshenko's system normally yields very high frequencies—under what conditions on η and γ_s do such frequencies enter the audible range?

Programming Exercise 7.2   *Create a Matlab script which calculates and plots the phase velocity of the stiff string system (7.20), as well as the numerical phase velocity of the implicit scheme (7.25), for any values of κ, γ, and θ, over the band $f \in [0, f_s/2]$. You should assume that the grid spacing h_{min} is chosen at the stability limit, from (7.26). Assuming simply supported conditions, your code should also generate a list of the modal frequencies of the model system over the same band, as well as the modes of scheme (7.25). Verify, using the value for θ as a function of γ, κ, and f_s determined in Problem 7.11 above, that deviations in both the numerical phase velocity and scheme modal frequencies from those of the model system are minimized under these conditions.*

Programming Exercise 7.3   *Starting from the Matlab code example for the stiff string with frequency-dependent loss, given in Section A.8, which is a vector–matrix implementation of the implicit scheme (7.30b), modify it such that the explicit scheme (7.30a) is implemented in a direct form (i.e., without employing linear system solvers). Perform a comparison of performance of the two schemes, in terms of computation time, using the commands* tic *and* toc. *You may wish to examine the performance as it varies with the sample rate, or the parameter γ. (For your experiments, keep κ, σ_0, and σ_1 relatively small, so the system represents a nearly lossless string with slight detuning.)*

Programming Exercise 7.4   *Implement the finite difference bow–string model described in Section 7.4. You may wish to use the code examples corresponding to the difference scheme for the bowed mass and the 1D wave equation, given in Section A.3 and Section A.4 as starting points; you will also need an iterative solver—see Programming Exercise 4.6. Use the bow characteristic given in Figure 4.8(c), leaving a as an extra free parameter in your code, and make sure that your implementation produces an error message if the uniqueness condition (7.34) is violated. Set F_B and v_B as constants in your code, but allow the bowing position x_i to ramp linearly from start to end locations of your choice over the duration of the simulation. Make use of linear interpolation. (It may take some experimentation to find suitable values of F_B, v_B, and a such that you get sound output—you may wish to use values which appear in the figures in Section 7.4 as starting points.)*

Programming Exercise 7.5   *Alter the bow–string implementation above to perform bowed-bar synthesis, as per the model described in Problem 7.17, making note of the altered nonlinear equation to be solved. You may wish to use the finite difference scheme for the ideal bar, given in Section A.7, as a starting point.*

Programming Exercise 7.6   *Beginning from the explicit scheme for the stiff string which you implemented in Programming Exercise 7.4, implement a hammer interaction according to the semi-implicit scheme (7.37). In order to do this, you will need to generalize the update which you derived in Problem 7.18 to include loss and damping in the string model.*

Programming Exercise 7.7   *Extend the code you have created in Programming Exercise 7.5 above, which employs an explicit solver for a stiff string with loss, and a hammer excitation, to the case of multiple strings, as described in Section 7.6. Your new parameters will be M, the number of strings, and D, the detuning parameter. Make use of an equal number of grid points on each string.*

Programming Exercise 7.8   *Extend the code you have created in Programming Exercise 7.6 above to the case of preparation by multiple elements of the spring–damper type, as described in Section 7.7.1, and rattling elements, as described in Section 7.7.2. In both cases, you will need to extend your schemes to the case of stiffness and frequency-dependent damping—in the case of the rattle, a good starting point is the scheme given in Problem 7.19. You may also wish to develop a physical model involving preparation of multiple strings, for which the lumped hammer–multiple object collision described in Problem 4.4 is a good starting point.*

Programming Exercise 7.9   *Consider the case of a lossless bar of variable cross-sectional area, as described in Section 7.10.2. Implement scheme (7.73), over a stretched coordinate system; use an arched area variation function $\phi(x)$ which is of the following form:*

$$\phi(x) = \begin{cases} 1, & 0 \leq x \leq x^* \\ \phi_{\min} + \dfrac{(1-\phi_{\min})}{2}\left(1 + \cos(\pi(x-x^*)/b)\right), & x^* < x \leq x^* + b \\ \phi_{\min}, & x^* + b < x \leq 1 - x^* - b \\ \phi_{\min} + \dfrac{(1-\phi_{\min})}{2}\left(1 + \cos(\pi(x+x^*-1)/b)\right), & 1 - x^* - b < x \leq 1 - x^* \\ 1, & 1 - x^* < x \leq 1 \end{cases}$$

where $0 \leq x^* \leq 1/2$ describes the span of the arch, $0 \leq b \leq 1 - 2x^*$ its steepness, and $0 \leq \phi_{\min} \leq 1$ the depth. Use free boundary conditions at both ends of the bar.

   Experiment with the three parameters above in an attempt to tune the bar such that the first two harmonics are in a ratio as close to 1 : 3 as possible—in order to do this, it is probably best to excite the bar using, say, a sharp plucked initial condition, and look at a spectrum of sound output. You may wish to use the code example given in Section A.7 as a starting point.

8

Nonlinear string vibration

In Chapter 7, a general model of linear string motion has been presented. This model, which holds under low-amplitude vibration conditions, is sufficient in many cases of musical interest, but not all. If vibration amplitude becomes large (under, say, high-amplitude striking or plucking conditions), various nonlinear effects begin to appear, and can become perceptually dominant. The effect which is perhaps the most familiar to the reader will be that of the pitch glide, which is common across many instruments, and not merely strings (it occurs in struck percussion instruments as well—see Section 13.1). Under a high-amplitude strike or pluck, there is often a downward change in the pitch of the string, due to increased tension in the string. Such an effect, often called tension modulation [359, 378, 116], cannot be captured by a linear model, for which modal frequencies are, by linear system theory, fixed. Other more subtle phenomena also play an important perceptual role. The generation of audible so-called phantom partials [87, 24] in piano and guitar strings under high striking or plucking velocities is due to coupling between longitudinal and transverse vibration, and beating can result from the instability of motion of a nonlinear string in a single polarization, which is a purely three-dimensional effect known as "whirling."

The development here, proceeding from rudimentary models to the more complex, is the reverse of the usual treatment in acoustics. A useful starting point, and probably the simplest nonlinear distributed system in musical acoustics, is the Kirchhoff–Carrier equation describing large-amplitude string vibration, introduced in Section 8.1, which models the effect of tension modulation, and thus gives rise to pitch glide phenomena. Finite difference schemes and modal methods are discussed. In order to deal with more realistic cases of string vibration, more general models in both one and two polarizations are introduced in Section 8.2 and Section 8.3, respectively. Finite difference schemes are developed, and various effects of musical interest such as phantom partials and whirling are examined.

8.1 The Kirchhoff–Carrier string model

The simplest generalization of the dynamics of a string beyond the linear variants that have been detailed in the last chapter is that of Kirchhoff and Carrier [206, 72]:

$$\rho A u_{tt} = \left(T_0 + \frac{EA}{2L} \int_0^L u_x^2 dx \right) u_{xx} \qquad (8.1)$$

Here, as for the case of the linear string, ρ and T_0 are the material density and tension, respectively, and u represents string displacement in a single polarization. In contrast to the simple linear model, stiffness effects play a role, and thus Young's modulus E and the cross-sectional area A appear. The nonlinearity itself is of a very special form, involving an average of the squared string slope over the length of the string—as one might guess, this is a form arrived at through quite a number of assumptions, the most important of which are that $EA \gg T_0$, which is true in many cases of musical interest, and that the string is well defined only over a finite interval, in this case $x \in [0, L]$. The full derivation is readily available in the literature—see, e.g., the classic papers by Anand [9] and Narasimha [251]. Due to the simplicity of the nonlinear term, it is heavily used for the analysis of nonlinear phenomena [105, 106, 183, 302]. Such an equation has also been used as a starting point in many studies in musical acoustics—see, e.g., [155, 220] and, in sound synthesis, [117, 50, 264].

It is useful to spatially scale the system, using a coordinate $x' = x/L$, but, because the system is nonlinear (i.e., its response is amplitude dependent), a non-dimensionalization of the dependent variable itself, through a choice of $u' = u/L$, is also advisable.[1] The resulting system, now defined over the unit interval $\mathbb{U}$, is

$$u_{tt} = \gamma^2 \mathfrak{G} u_{xx} \qquad \text{with} \qquad \mathfrak{G} = 1 + \frac{\alpha^2}{2} \|u_x\|_{\mathbb{U}}^2 \tag{8.2}$$

where the parameters γ and α are defined by

$$\gamma = \frac{1}{L}\sqrt{\frac{T_0}{\rho A}} \qquad \alpha = \sqrt{\frac{EA}{T_0}} \tag{8.3}$$

The parameter γ should be familiar from the discussions in the previous two chapters, and α is a measure of the strength of stiffness versus tension effects in the string—observe that the effect is strong under low-tension conditions (hence the "boing"-like sound of loosely stretched strings). Notice also that the norm notation $\|\cdot\|$ has been introduced—see Section 5.1.3.

Given that effects of stiffness have appeared in this model, one might wonder what has happened to the linear fourth-order stiffness term which occurs, for example, in the model of the ideal bar, as discussed in Section 7.1. Such a term can indeed be included, to yield a basic model of nonlinear bar vibration—see Section 8.1.4.

Energy analysis and boundary conditions

Even though the Kirchhoff–Carrier equation (8.2) is the result of several very brutal approximations, it still possesses a conserved energy. It is possible to proceed as for the wave equation, and take an inner product with u_t, the velocity, over $\mathcal{D} = \mathbb{U}$, to get the energy balance

$$\frac{d\mathfrak{H}}{dt} = \mathfrak{B} = \gamma^2 \left(1 + \frac{\alpha^2}{2}\|u_x\|_{\mathbb{U}}^2\right) u_t u_x \Big|_0^1$$

with

$$\mathfrak{H} = \mathfrak{T} + \mathfrak{V} \qquad \text{and} \qquad \mathfrak{T} = \frac{1}{2}\|u_t\|_{\mathbb{U}}^2 \qquad \mathfrak{V} = \frac{\gamma^2}{2}\left(1 + \frac{\alpha^2}{4}\|u_x\|_{\mathbb{U}}^2\right)\|u_x\|_{\mathbb{U}}^2 \tag{8.4}$$

Under Dirichlet or Neumann conditions at either endpoint, the system is again exactly conservative. Note that the expression for the potential energy $\mathfrak{V}$ is no longer a quadratic form, reflecting the

---

[1] A better choice of scaling, for the Kirchhoff–Carrier equation, is $u' = u\sqrt{EA/2T_0}/L$, in which case the scaled system depends on the single parameter γ. In the interest of a uniform analysis of this system and more complex models of string vibration, the scaling $u' = u/L$ is preferable.

nonlinearity[2] of system (8.2). It remains true, however, that the energy is non-negative—notice, in particular, that it is *higher* than that of the associated linear system (the wave equation). As may be expected from the discussion in Section 2.4.3, such non-negativity of the nonlinear energy contribution will have a simplifying effect on numerical stability analysis for associated finite difference schemes.

For the remainder of this section, it will be assumed that Dirichlet conditions $u = 0$ hold at both ends of the string (which is very reasonable as a first approximation, but which must necessarily be revised if coupling to other structures is anticipated).

Loss

If a loss term is added to (8.2), i.e., if the equation is altered to

$$u_{tt} = \gamma^2 \mathfrak{G} u_{xx} - 2\sigma_0 u_t \tag{8.5}$$

with $\mathfrak{G}$ defined as before, then, under conservative boundary conditions, the energy $\mathfrak{H}$ will be monotonically decreasing, and the amplitude of vibration will thus decay just as in the linear case. What is more interesting, sonically, is the audible change in pitch, which is downward, from the moment of a strike or pluck—see the next section.

8.1.1   Amplitude-dependent pitch and pitch glides

For nonlinear systems in musical acoustics, it is rare to be able to come to any conclusions about perceptual effects through direct inspection, but the Kirchhoff–Carrier model, due to its extreme simplicity, does permit some observations to be made. From (8.2) it is clear that the entire effect of the nonlinearity is represented by the scalar factor $\mathfrak{G} \geq 1$. Assuming that the time variation of $\mathfrak{G}$ is slow (and it is always dangerous to make such assumptions), it can be viewed as a scaling factor to the parameter γ, and, thus, to the pitch. For instance, under fixed end conditions, the lowest frequency of vibration will be approximately $f_0 = \gamma\sqrt{\mathfrak{G}_{av}}/2$, where $\mathfrak{G}_{av}$ represents an average value of $\mathfrak{G}$ over several cycles. Note also that $\mathfrak{G}$ is always greater than one, and approaches this value in the limit as $\|u_x\|_U$ becomes small, or, in other words, when vibration amplitude is small (i.e., the linear case). Thus, the greater the energy of the string, the greater the frequency of vibration—see Figure 8.1 for some examples of this behavior.

One might expect, then, that loss will play an even more important role for such a nonlinear system than for linear strings, as discussed in the previous chapter. Not only will it determine the rate of decay of vibration, but in this case it will have the additional effect of altering the pitch over time, as the total energy of the system (and thus $\mathfrak{G}$) decreases.

If one accepts the factor $\sqrt{\mathfrak{G}}\gamma/2$, time averaged, as a crude estimate of instantaneous pitch, then it is not hard to deduce the following bound on $\mathfrak{G}$, purely from energetic considerations:

$$\mathfrak{G} \leq \sqrt{1 + \frac{2\alpha^2 \mathfrak{H}}{\gamma^2}} \tag{8.6}$$

Thus, $\mathfrak{G}$ is bounded by a function of $\mathfrak{H}$, which itself decreases monotonically. Even though $\mathfrak{G}$ itself is time varying in a complicated way, its average value will decrease smoothly, leading to the observed pitch glide. See Problem 8.1. Typical behavior is illustrated in the spectrogram shown in Figure 8.2.

---

[2] Though it is true that if the energy of a system is not expressed as a quadratic form of the state then the system must be nonlinear, the converse is not necessarily true. The von Kármán system, for instance, which describes high-amplitude vibration of a thin plate, is highly nonlinear, yet the expression for the energy remains a quadratic form. See Section 13.2.3.

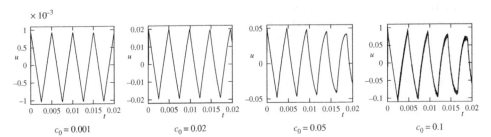

$$c_0 = 0.001 \qquad c_0 = 0.02 \qquad c_0 = 0.05 \qquad c_0 = 0.1$$

Figure 8.1 Plots of displacement of a string modeled by the Kirchhoff–Carrier equation (8.2), with $\gamma = 400$ and $\alpha = 10$, as a function of time t. In each case, the initial condition is a triangular function $c_{\text{tri}}(x)$, with $x_0 = 0.5$, and where the maximum displacements take on increasing values c_0 as indicated. The output displacement at the string center is plotted. Note in particular that the gross rate of oscillation increases with the initial displacement, and also the deformation of the waveform away from the pure triangular form, which is characteristic of lossless linear strings.

8.1.2   Finite difference schemes

A finite difference scheme for the Kirchhoff–Carrier equation is easily arrived at, through the methods described previously; indeed, the question is not so much how to construct a scheme, but how to make sure that the results are perceptually correct. As this is the first example in this book of a nonlinear PDE system, it is worth spending a bit of time examining the various ways in which the computed results can go astray. Stability is one concern, but there are others—for nonlinear systems, the range of pathological behavior is greater than in the linear case. It is worth noting that, for the Kirchhoff–Carrier equation, for which the nonlinearity is still of a relatively simple form, it is possible to arrive at digital waveguide structures which adequately capture effects such as pitch glides—see, e.g., [264, 269, 116]—normally through the use of variable-delay filter terminations, which effectively modulate string length or tension depending on the current string state.

A simple scheme

A direct finite difference approximation to the lossy form of the Kirchhoff–Carrier equation given in (8.5) is as follows:

$$\delta_{tt}u = \gamma^2[\mathfrak{g}]\delta_{xx}u - 2\sigma_0\delta_t.u \tag{8.7}$$

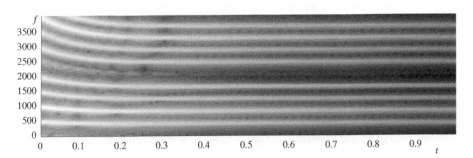

Figure 8.2 Spectrogram of output of a string modeled by the Kirchhoff–Carrier equation with a linear loss term (8.5), illustrating a typical pitch glide. Here, $\gamma = 400$, $\alpha = 10$, and $T_{60} = 2$ s. The initial condition is a raised cosine function $c_{\text{rc}}(x)$, with $x_0 = 0.8$, $x_{\text{hw}} = 0.1$, and $c_0 = 0.03$. The output displacement is taken at $x = 0.3$.

This scheme is assumed to be defined over the discrete unit interval $\mathcal{D} = \mathbb{U}_N$. Here, $[\mathfrak{g}] = [\mathfrak{g}]^n$ is a scalar time series, intended as an approximation to $\mathfrak{G}$; its form is left unspecified for the moment (this is indicated by the use of square brackets). There are obviously many ways of forming such an approximation; the most direct, by far, is

$$[\mathfrak{g}] = 1 + \frac{\alpha^2}{2} \|\delta_{x+}u\|_{\mathbb{U}_N}^2 \tag{8.8}$$

As it turns out, however, such a choice does not lead to an energy conservation or dissipation property for the finite difference scheme. As such, the stability properties of this scheme are somewhat obscure. (One thing which *must* remain true is that the Courant number $\lambda = \gamma k / h$ continue to satisfy $\lambda \leq 1$, for the simple reason that, in the limit of small-amplitude vibration and zero loss, this scheme reduces to scheme (6.34) for the 1D wave equation.)

For example, consider the example shown in Figure 8.3—stability depends now not just on the Courant number, but also on the amplitude of the initial condition. Indeed, for $\lambda = 0.9$, even a rather small initial condition leads to instability. The situation here is reminiscent of the case of the cubic oscillator, as discussed in Section 4.2.1. While the scheme does produce a pulse traveling with an increased speed for an initial condition at greater amplitude, high-frequency oscillations quickly appear and obliterate the solution.

One may note, however, that as the Courant number is lowered, the scheme will behave in a stable manner for a larger range of initial conditions—this is to be expected, perhaps, given the geometrical interpretation of the CFL condition (see Figure 6.9), and the fact that the "wave speed" will depend on the amplitude of the solution. For synthesis, however, this is not ideal—either one must choose one's Courant number depending on the strength of the excitation (leading to a necessary change in the grid spacing for each new excitation), or one may choose a low Courant number which can accommodate a wide range of amplitudes. This second option, however, leads to excessive numerical dispersion and loss of audio bandwidth, of the same nature as that mentioned in the linear case in Section 6.2.3. A better-behaved scheme is clearly desirable.

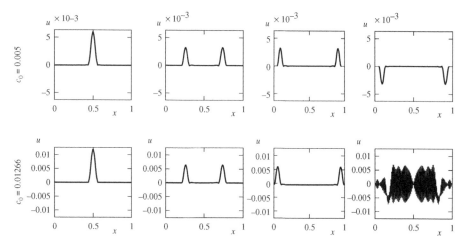

Figure 8.3 Amplitude-dependent numerical instability. The scheme (8.7) for the Kirchhoff–Carrier equation is used, with $[\mathfrak{g}]$ as defined in (8.8), with $\gamma = 100$ and $\alpha = 10$, and under lossless conditions, with $\sigma_0 = 0$. The scheme operates at 44 100 Hz, with a Courant number $\lambda = 0.9$. In each case, a raised cosine distribution c_{rc} is used to initialize the string state. In both cases, the distribution is centered at $x = 0.5$, and has a half-width of $x_{hw} = 0.05$. Under low amplitudes at a peak value of c_0 as indicated, the output is stable (at top), but at higher amplitudes, instabilities develop.

An improved scheme: numerical energy conservation

One might guess, given the treatment of the cubic nonlinear oscillator in Section 4.2.1, and the fact that the Kirchhoff–Carrier equation also involves a nonlinearity with third-order terms, that a stable scheme will necessarily have an implicit character. This is indeed true, and energy analysis of scheme (8.7) indicates a different setting for [g]. To find this, take the inner product of the scheme with $\delta_t.u$ over $\mathbb{U}_N$, to get

$$\langle \delta_t.u, \delta_{tt}u \rangle_{\mathbb{U}_N} = \gamma^2[g]\langle \delta_t.u, \delta_{xx}u \rangle_{\mathbb{U}_N} - 2\sigma_0 \|\delta_t.u\|_{\mathbb{U}_N}^2$$

$$= -\gamma^2[g]\langle \delta_t.\delta_{x+}u, \delta_{x+}u \rangle_{\underline{\mathbb{U}_N}} + b - q = -\gamma^2[g]\delta_{t+} \frac{1}{2}\langle \delta_{x+}u, e_{t-}\delta_{x+}u \rangle_{\underline{\mathbb{U}_N}} + b - q$$

where, here, the boundary term b and loss term q are given by

$$b = \gamma^2[g]\left(\delta_{x+}u_N \delta_t.u_N - \delta_{x-}u_0 \delta_t.u_0\right) \qquad q = 2\sigma_0\|\delta_t.u\|_{\mathbb{U}_N}^2$$

Clearly, regardless of the choice of [g], the boundary term vanishes when Dirichlet or Neumann conditions are applied at either end of the string, and the term q is non-negative.

An energy conservation (more generally dissipation) property, as mentioned earlier, does not follow for a choice of [g] such as the form given in (8.8). But consider the following choice:

$$[g] = g = 1 + \frac{\alpha^2}{2}\mu_{t+}\langle \delta_{x+}u, e_{t-}\delta_{x+}u \rangle_{\underline{\mathbb{U}_N}} \tag{8.9}$$

where the square brackets are removed, now that a choice of an approximation has been decided. This leads immediately to dissipation, i.e.,

$$\delta_{t+}\mathfrak{h} = -q \qquad \text{with} \qquad \mathfrak{h} = \mathfrak{t} + \mathfrak{v}$$

and

$$\mathfrak{t} = \frac{1}{2}\|\delta_{t-}u\|_{\mathbb{U}_N}^2 \qquad \mathfrak{v} = \frac{\gamma^2}{2}\left(\langle \delta_{x+}u, e_{t-}\delta_{x+}u \rangle_{\underline{\mathbb{U}_N}} + \frac{\alpha^2}{4}\langle \delta_{x+}u, e_{t-}\delta_{x+}u \rangle_{\underline{\mathbb{U}_N}}^2\right) \tag{8.10}$$

which is directly analogous to the energy of the Kirchhoff–Carrier system, from (8.4). Under lossless conditions, this energy will again be conserved, to machine accuracy, in a simulation—see Figure 8.4.

Clearly, the condition $\lambda \leq 1$ must be a necessary condition for stability for this scheme, which, again, reduces to scheme (6.34) for the 1D wave equation at low amplitudes and zero loss. Given these forms of the kinetic and potential energy for scheme (8.7) with the choice of g from (8.9), one important observation that one can make is that the potential energy $\mathfrak{v}$ consists of two terms: one due to linear effects and a second due to nonlinear effects, which is non-negative. Recalling the discussion of such terms in Section 2.4.3, it is not hard to see that if the energy for the linear scheme is non-negative under condition (6.40), then the addition of an extra non-negative term to the energy cannot affect this result. Thus condition (6.40) serves as a necessary and sufficient condition for non-negativity of energy, and, as one can show, a numerical stability condition—see [50] for a full exposition.

The quantity g defined above in (8.9), when used in (8.7), leads to an implicit scheme—g at time step n depends on values of u at time steps $n-1$, n, and $n+1$. Notice, however, that the unknown values at time step $n+1$ always appear quasi-linearly (i.e., with coefficients which depend on previously computed, and thus known, values of the grid function); as a result, existence

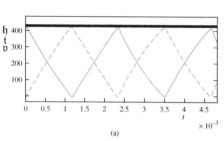
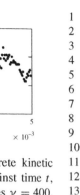

(a)   (b)

Figure 8.4 (a) Variation of the discrete potential energy $\mathfrak{v}$ (solid grey line), discrete kinetic energy $\mathfrak{t}$ (dotted grey line), and total discrete energy $\mathfrak{h}$ (solid black line), plotted against time t, for the output of scheme (8.7) using fixed boundary termination. In this case, the values $\gamma = 400$, $k = 1/44\,100$, and $\lambda = 0.9$ are used, and the scheme is initialized with the triangular distribution $c_{\text{tri}}(x)$, with $x_0 = 0.5$ and $c_0 = 0.035$. (b) Variation of the error in energy, defined, at time step n, as $\mathfrak{h}_e = \left(\mathfrak{h} - \mathfrak{h}^0\right)/\mathfrak{h}^0$, plotted as black points.

and uniqueness are assured. In vector–matrix form, where the column vector $\mathbf{u}^n$ contains the values of the grid function u_l^n at time step n, the scheme may be written as

$$\mathbf{A}^n\mathbf{u}^{n+1} + \mathbf{B}^n\mathbf{u}^n + \mathbf{C}^n\mathbf{u}^{n-1} = 0 \qquad (8.11)$$

where the update matrices $\mathbf{A}$, $\mathbf{B}$, and $\mathbf{C}$, under fixed boundary conditions, are as follows:

$$\mathbf{A} = (1 + \sigma_0 k)\mathbf{I} + \mathbf{q}\mathbf{q}^T \qquad \mathbf{B} = -2\mathbf{I} - \gamma^2 k^2 \mathbf{D}_{xx} \qquad \mathbf{C} = (1 - \sigma_0 k)\mathbf{I} + \mathbf{q}\mathbf{q}^T$$

where $\mathbf{I}$ is the identity operation, $\mathbf{D}_{xx}$ is the matrix form of the operator δ_{xx} (see Section 5.2.7), and the vector $\mathbf{q}$ is of the form

$$\mathbf{q} = \frac{\gamma \alpha k \sqrt{h}}{2} \mathbf{D}_{xx}\mathbf{u}$$

There is thus a linear system to be solved, involving the matrix $\mathbf{A}$ which itself depends on previously computed values of $\mathbf{u}$, at every time step. Interestingly, this scheme may be rewritten in an explicit form—when the boundary term is zero (it will be under fixed conditions), and under lossless conditions, $\mathfrak{g}$ itself may be rewritten as

$$\mathfrak{g} = \frac{1 + \frac{\alpha^2}{2}\|\delta_{x+}u\|_{\underline{U}_N}^2}{1 + \frac{\gamma^2 k^2 \alpha^2}{4}\|\delta_{xx}u\|_{\underline{U}_N}^2} \qquad (8.12)$$

This is something of a rarity among numerical methods—an explicit, conservative, and provably stable scheme for a nonlinear distributed system. It is the only such example to be discussed in this book (with the exception of schemes for the Berger model of plate vibration, described in Section 13.1). It is possible, in this case, due to the very simple form of the nonlinearity, which is scalar, putting it in line with explicit numerical methods for some lumped systems, particularly those where the nonlinearity is of third order—see Section 4.2.1. See also Problem 8.2.

Given that there is no longer any danger of instability, it is worth examining the behavior of this scheme, especially as λ approaches 1. See Figure 8.5, which compares the behavior of the scheme at $\lambda = 0.7$ and at $\lambda = 0.95$. In the former case, the solution is smooth and well behaved, and the characteristic pitch glide is observed, though there is a substantial reduction in the effective bandwidth of the scheme, as is to be expected when the scheme runs away from the stability limit.

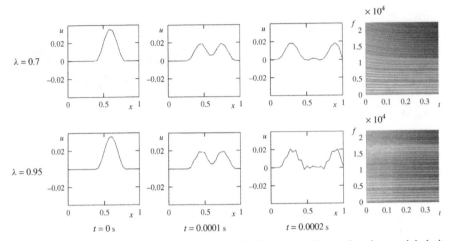

Figure 8.5   Output of scheme (8.7) for the Kirchhoff–Carrier equation, using the special choice of [g] given in (8.9), for a string with $\gamma = 1600$, $\alpha = 10$, and $T_{60} = 2$. The scheme runs at 44 100 Hz, and is initialized with a raised cosine pulse. Snapshots of the string profile are shown, at the times indicated, as well as a spectrogram of sound output, for two different cases: at top, for a value of the Courant number $\lambda = 0.7$ away from the stability bound; and at bottom, for $\lambda = 0.95$.

At $\lambda = 0.95$, however, oscillations begin to appear in the string profile, and the pitch glide is no longer present.

The reason for this anomalous behavior of the scheme near $\lambda = 1$ can be seen from the explicit form of g given in (8.12)—in effect, the denominator acts as a compensating mechanism, becoming large if numerical oscillations appear. This same effect, though, does not prevent the appearance of numerical oscillations, and indeed these do occur, at the spatial Nyquist frequency, though they do not grow. In this case, the denominator of g overcompensates for this behavior, and reduces the pitch glide effect as well! (Recall that g scales roughly with pitch.) See Programming Exercise 8.1.

Suppression of oscillatory behavior

The problem with the above schemes is the production of spurious oscillations at the spatial Nyquist frequency. In one case, it leads to instability and, in the other, to the suppression of the pitch glide effect; clearly, if one is to maximize bandwidth and produce the requisite perceptual effects, some additional means of controlling such oscillations is necessary.

The stable form of (8.7), with the choice of g as per (8.12), is a good starting point. Consider the following generalization of the scheme, which is similar in form to the compact implicit scheme for the 1D wave equation, as described in Section 6.3.2:

$$\left(1 + \theta\alpha^2\gamma^2k^2\delta_{xx}\right)\delta_{tt}u = \gamma^2 g\delta_{xx}u - 2\sigma_0\delta_{t.}u \tag{8.13}$$

This is a θ-type scheme. It is desirable that the scheme reduce to the explicit scheme (6.34) for the 1D wave equation at low amplitudes (this is the ideal case), so it is clear that θ cannot be a constant—it must depend on the string state, and must vanish in the linear limiting case. It also should balance the overcompensation effect caused by the choice of g, and, furthermore, for the sake of computability, it must be possible to obtain θ given known values of the string state. Here is one choice:

$$\theta = \theta_0 \|\delta_{x+}u\|^2_{\underline{U}_N} \tag{8.14}$$

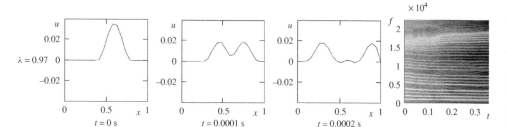

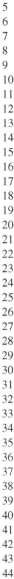

Figure 8.6 Output of scheme (8.13) for the Kirchhoff–Carrier equation, for a string with $\gamma = 1600$, $\alpha = 10$, and $T_{60} = 2$. The scheme runs at 44 100 Hz, with a choice of $\theta_0 = -0.125$, and is initialized with a raised cosine pulse. Snapshots of the string profile are shown, at the times indicated, for $\lambda = 0.97$.

for some constant θ_0 (a good range of values of θ_0 may be obtained through further analysis—see Problem 8.3).

Plotted in Figure 8.6 are simulation results to be compared with those for the uncompensated scheme shown in Figure 8.5; the numerical oscillations are greatly reduced, and, though there is still anomalous behavior high in the audio spectrum, the pitch glide has now reappeared, even for a Courant number very close to 1. The effect of introducing the extra compensating term in scheme (8.13) can be seen to increase numerical dispersion (and reduce bandwidth slightly) over the interval during which it is most active toward the beginning of the simulation. See also Programming Exercise 8.2.

A general rule

Given what has been observed in this section, i.e., the difficulties in obtaining reasonable results near the stability limit, the following rule of thumb may be deduced:

Rule of Thumb #4

For a scheme for a nonlinear system, anomalous behavior may be observed when the grid spacing is chosen close to the stability bound. Such behavior is reduced (and numerical dispersion increased) as the spacing is increased away from the bound.

This contradicts Rule of Thumb #1 (see page 136) which applies to linear systems.

8.1.3   A modal form

Though modal techniques are normally applied only to linear and time-invariant systems, in this case, because of the scalar nature of the nonlinearity, one might suspect that an extension of modal techniques might be possible. Modal techniques for synthesis for the Kirchhoff–Carrier equation have been discussed in [39], and are related to recent work on Volterra series representations [167, 303] for the same system.

Considering the Kirchhoff–Carrier equation with loss, suppose that fixed (Dirichlet) boundary conditions have been applied at either end of the string. It is valid, from Fourier theory arguments, to expand the solution $u(x, t)$ in the following series:

$$u(x, t) = \sum_{p=1}^{\infty} U_p(t) \sin(p\pi x)$$

Upon inserting this form in (8.5), it then results that

$$\sum_{p=1}^{\infty} \frac{d^2 U_p}{dt^2} \sin(p\pi x) = -\gamma^2 \mathfrak{G} \sum_{p=1}^{\infty} p^2 \pi^2 U_p \sin(p\pi x) - 2\sigma_0 \sum_{p=1}^{\infty} \frac{dU_p}{dt} \sin(p\pi x) \tag{8.15}$$

and, after multiplying through individually by the functions $\sin(p\pi x)$ and integrating over the domain $\mathcal{D} = \mathbb{U}$, one arrives at

$$\frac{d^2 U_p}{dt^2} = -\gamma^2 \mathfrak{G} p^2 \pi^2 U_p - 2\sigma_0 \frac{dU_p}{dt} \qquad \text{for} \qquad p = 1, 2, \dots$$

Through Parseval's relation, one may demonstrate that

$$\mathfrak{G} = 1 + \frac{\alpha^2}{2} \sum_{m=1}^{\infty} \frac{\pi^2 m^2}{2} U_m^2 \tag{8.16}$$

To this point, the modal description (8.15), accompanied by the alternative formulation of $\mathfrak{G}$ above, is equivalent to the time domain description (8.5); no approximations have been made. The PDE, defined over the unit interval $\mathbb{U}$, has been replaced by an infinite set of ODEs [105, 106]. In order to arrive at a formulation suitable for simulation, one may truncate the set to a finite number, say M:

$$\frac{d^2 U_p}{dt^2} + 2\sigma_0 \frac{dU_p}{dt} + \omega_p^2 U_p = -\omega_p^2 \frac{\alpha^2}{4\gamma^2} U_p \sum_{m=1}^{M} \omega_m^2 U_m^2 \qquad \text{for } p = 1, 2, \dots, M$$

Here, the set of base frequencies $\omega_p = p\gamma\pi$ has been introduced. Notice that this is no more than a set of SHOs with loss (on the left-hand side) coupled to one another through the nonlinearity (on the right-hand side). As expected, the system of ODEs satisfies an energy balance, now in the expansion coefficients U_p:

$$\frac{d\mathfrak{H}}{dt} = -\mathfrak{Q}$$

with

$$\mathfrak{H} = \sum_{p=1}^{M} \frac{1}{2} \left(\frac{dU_p}{dt} \right)^2 + \sum_{p=1}^{M} \frac{\omega_p^2}{2} U_p^2 + \frac{\alpha^2}{4\gamma^2} \left(\sum_{p=1}^{M} \frac{\omega_p^2}{2} U_p^2 \right)^2 \qquad \mathfrak{Q} = 2\sigma_0 \sum_{p=1}^{M} \left(\frac{dU_p}{dt} \right)^2$$

A family of finite difference schemes

Given the form above, and the fact that the system reduces to an uncoupled system of ODEs at low amplitudes, it is worthwhile to employ a parameterized scheme (see Section 3.3.2) for each member of the family:

$$\delta_{tt} U_p + \omega_p^2 \left(\phi_p + (1 - \phi_p)\mu_t. \right) U_p + 2\sigma_p \delta_t. U_p$$

$$= -\frac{\alpha^2 \omega_p^2}{4\gamma^2} U_p \sum_{m=1}^{M} \omega_m^2 U_m \mu_t. U_m \qquad \text{for } p = 1, 2, \dots, M \tag{8.17}$$

Here, $U_p = U_p^n$ is a time series, and the coefficients ϕ_p and σ_p may be set separately for each equation. The nonlinearity itself has been approximated using a semi-implicit operator. It is worth noting that, here, only the time derivative has been approximated; spatial derivatives have been approximated, through Fourier series, to what is sometimes called "spectral accuracy," which is, for all practical purposes, exact. In fact, this is an example of a spectral method [364]—these methods, and their potential in sound synthesis, will be discussed briefly beginning on page 388.

It is not difficult to show that the above system of equations is strictly dissipative, and thus numerically stable, under the following condition:

$$(2\phi_p - 1)k^2\omega_p^2 \leq 4 \tag{8.18}$$

Part of the stability argument relies on the special form of the discretization of the nonlinear terms—see Problem 8.4. As one might expect, from the discussion in Section 3.3.4, Section 3.5.4, and particularly Problem 3.16, there are special choices of ϕ_p and σ_p which allow that at least the linear part of the system is solved exactly:

$$\phi_p = \frac{1}{k^2\omega_p^2}\left(2 - \frac{\omega_p^2k^2\cos\left(\sqrt{\omega_p^2 - \sigma_0^2}k\right)}{\cosh(\sigma_0 k) - \cos(\sqrt{\omega_p^2 - \sigma_0^2}k)}\right) \qquad \sigma_p = \frac{\omega_p^2 k}{2}\frac{\sinh(\sigma_0 k)}{\cosh(\sigma_0 k) - \cos\left(\sqrt{\omega_p^2 - \sigma_0^2}k\right)}$$

The above settings hold under low-loss conditions $\sigma_0 \leq \omega_p$.

One question which arises is: how is the set of modal equations to be truncated, or, how does one choose M? Obviously, from consideration of the linear part of the system alone, and using the sampling theorem, one must enforce $\omega_p = p\gamma\pi \leq \pi/k$ for all p, and thus $M \leq 1/k\gamma$. But one might guess that as the set of base frequencies approaches filling the spectrum (i.e., spanning the full bandwidth up to half the sample rate), the distortion familiar from the discussion of finite difference schemes in the last section will reappear. This is indeed the case, as shown in Figure 8.7. When just a few components are modeled, the behavior is extremely good, and in fact much better than that of the finite difference scheme discussed earlier, in that there is no numerical dispersion at all under linear conditions, and thus no detuning of modal frequencies. On the other hand, as the number of modal components increases, other components begin to appear in the spectrum, and a type of spectral foldover or aliasing occurs. For a large number of components, the pitch glide effect again disappears. Again, a form of Rule of Thumb #4 is in force—instead of increasing the grid spacing, the number of modal components should be reduced. In either case, it is the number of degrees of freedom which is decreased. See also Programming Exercise 8.3.

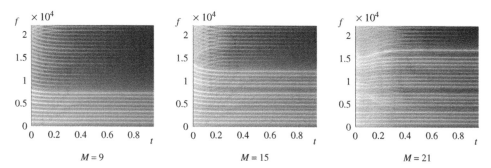

Figure 8.7 Spectrograms of output of the modal scheme (8.17) for the Kirchhoff–Carrier equation, under parameters and initialization as given in the caption to Figure 8.6. The scheme runs at a sample rate of 44 100 Hz, with a number M of modal components as indicated.

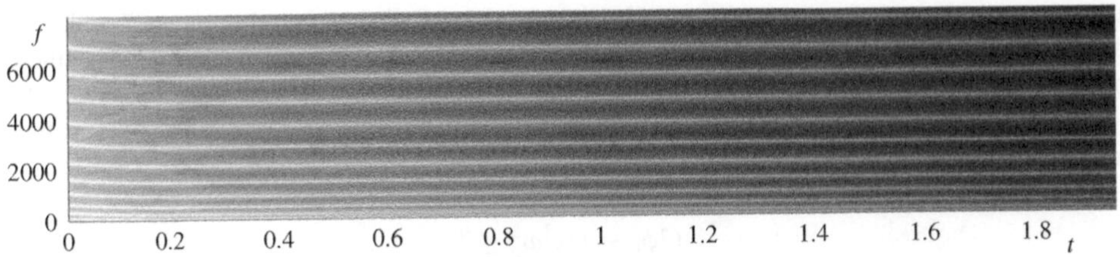

Figure 8.8   Spectrogram of output of the scheme (8.20) for the nonlinear bar model (8.19). Here, $\kappa = 10$, $\gamma_1 = 900$, $T_{60} = 2$, and the bar is terminated with clamped boundary conditions. The bar is excited with a plucked raised cosine distribution, centered at $x = 0.5$, of half-width $x_{hw} = 0.1$ and of amplitude $c_0 = 0.05$. The scheme is run at 44.1 kHz.

8.1.4   A nonlinear bar model

In the preceding treatment of nonlinear string vibration, effects of stiffness have intervened via the nonlinearity, which is averaged over the extent of the string. Similar models may be applied to bar vibration [160], in which case the resulting PDE description becomes that corresponding to the Kirchhoff bar model described in Section 7.1, with an additional term:

$$u_{tt} = -\kappa^2 u_{xxxx} + \frac{\gamma_1^2}{2}\|u_x\|_{\mathbb{U}}^2 u_{xx} - 2\sigma_0 u_t \tag{8.19}$$

where $\gamma_1^2 = E/\rho L^2$. Under conservative boundary conditions (these differ slightly from the case of the ideal bar—see Problem 8.5), it is not difficult to show that this system, as well as the following scheme, is strictly dissipative and numerical stable under condition (7.14):

$$\delta_{tt} u = -\kappa^2 \delta_{xxxx} u + \frac{\gamma_1^2}{2}\langle \delta_{x+} u, \mu_t . \delta_{x+} u \rangle_{\underline{\mathbb{U}_N}} \delta_{xx} u - 2\sigma_0 \delta_t . u \tag{8.20}$$

The general result is rather similar to the case of the string—a pitch glide is audible (see Figure 8.8), with the modal frequencies settling down to those characteristic of linear bar vibration as the overall amplitude decreases.

8.2   General planar nonlinear string motion

The Kirchhoff–Carrier model (8.1) is certainly the simplest model of the nonlinear distributed string—it adequately reproduces the important pitch glide effect, and can be simulated with relatively simple finite difference schemes. It is worth noting, however, that in this model, only transverse motion is explicitly modeled, and the longitudinal motion is averaged over the length of the string. While under certain conditions this approximation is acceptable (see [21] for a discussion of its range of validity), coupling between longitudinal and transverse motion does, in fact, lead to perceptually important effects such as so-called phantom partials (see Section 8.2.1), and a more complex model is necessary to capture these. A quite general model of string vibration (see, e.g., [244, 379]), including both longitudinal and transverse motion in a single plane (in dimensional form), is the following:

$$\rho A u_{tt} = E A u_{xx} - (EA - T_0)\left(\frac{\partial \Phi}{\partial u_x}\right)_x \qquad \rho A \zeta_{tt} = E A \zeta_{xx} - (EA - T_0)\left(\frac{\partial \Phi}{\partial \zeta_x}\right)_x \tag{8.21}$$

Here, $u(x, t)$ is again the transverse displacement of the string, and $\zeta(x, t)$ is the longitudinal displacement from its rest—see Figure 8.9(a) for a graphical representation of these quantities.

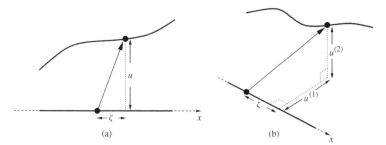

Figure 8.9 (a) Representation of the transverse displacement $u(x, t)$ and longitudinal displacement $\zeta(x, t)$ in the case of planar string motion, and (b) a similar diagram in the non-planar case, where the two transverse displacements are written as $u^{(1)}(x, t)$ and $u^{(2)}(x, t)$.

The constants ρ, A, E, and T_0 are as for the Kirchhoff–Carrier model, and the function Φ, which nonlinearly couples the two equations, is

$$\Phi = \sqrt{(1 + \zeta_x)^2 + u_x^2} - 1 - \zeta_x$$

Notice that the final term $-1 - \zeta_x$ has no influence on the dynamics of system (8.21)—it is included here so as to adjust the zero-point energy of the system as a whole. Even more general models are available—see, e.g., [251, 213, 405].

Using the same scaling strategy as for the Kirchhoff–Carrier system (i.e., substituting $x' = x/L$, $u' = u/L$, and $\zeta' = \zeta/L$ in the above system, and removing primes), one arrives at

$$u_{tt} = \gamma^2 \alpha^2 u_{xx} - \gamma^2 \left(\alpha^2 - 1\right) \left(\frac{\partial \Phi}{\partial q}\right)_x, \qquad \zeta_{tt} = \gamma^2 \alpha^2 \zeta_{xx} - \gamma^2 \left(\alpha^2 - 1\right) \left(\frac{\partial \Phi}{\partial p}\right)_x, \qquad (8.22)$$

where, for notational simplicity, the auxiliary variables

$$p = \zeta_x \qquad\qquad q = u_x \qquad\qquad (8.23)$$

have been introduced, and γ and α are as for the Kirchhoff–Carrier model, from (8.3). For Φ, one has

$$\Phi(p, q) = \sqrt{(1 + p)^2 + q^2} - 1 - p$$

8.2.1 Coupling between transverse and longitudinal modes and phantom partials

One should expect, given the discussion of the cubic nonlinear oscillator in Section 4.2.1, that for a string vibrating under nonlinear conditions, new frequency components will appear of a strength dependent on that of the excitation. This behavior does indeed occur for the tension-modulated nonlinearity [220], but in a much more pronounced way for the system described by system (8.22). Indeed, new components appear not merely at multiples of the fundamental (as in the case of the cubic nonlinear oscillator), but at frequencies which depend, in a very complex manner, on sum and difference frequencies between the linear modal frequencies of transverse and longitudinal motion. It is impossible to describe fully here the "rules" governing the locations of these new partials—see, e.g., [21] for much more on this topic. The important thing is that the new components appear inharmonically, and in dense clusters, lending a great richness to the resulting sound, especially in

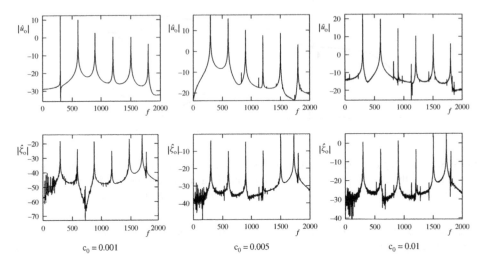

Figure 8.10 Output spectra for the nonlinear string system (8.22), under a plucked excitation. The string has parameters $\gamma = 600$ and $\alpha = 5.83$, and the excitation is of triangular type c_{tri}, with maximum displacement c_0 as indicated above, and is peaked at $x = 0.14$. Magnitude spectra are shown for transverse displacement u (top) and longitudinal displacement ζ (bottom), and output is read at $x_o = 0.7$.

instruments such as the guitar and piano. A particularly prevalent such component is often referred to as a "phantom" partial [87].

As a simple test case, consider system (8.22) excited by a plucked triangular distribution—plots of the magnitude spectrum of both the transverse displacement and the longitudinal displacement are shown in Figure 8.10. Under low-amplitude plucking conditions, the transverse displacement spectrum possesses evenly spaced peaks (here, the fundamental frequency is 300 Hz), and the longitudinal displacement spectrum also possesses such peaks, as it is driven by the transverse displacement, though at a much lower amplitude; also visible is the first harmonic in the longitudinal direction, at 1750 Hz. As the plucking amplitude rises, first isolated peaks, then clusters of peaks, begin to appear in the transverse displacement spectrum. Note that although the first longitudinal modal frequency does not have a strong presence in the transverse spectrum, in many instruments, such as the guitar and piano, longitudinal vibrations are passed via the bridge to the soundboard or resonating cavity of the instrument, so such frequencies will indeed be audible [87].

8.2.2 Energy

Finding an expression for the energy of system (8.22) is straightforward. Considering the problem defined over the infinite domain $\mathcal{D} = \mathbb{R}$, taking the inner product of the first of (8.22) with u_t, the second with ζ_t, and adding the result leads to:

$$\mathfrak{H} = \mathfrak{T} + \mathfrak{V} = \text{constant}$$

with

$$\mathfrak{T} = \frac{1}{2}\|u_t\|_{\mathbb{R}}^2 + \frac{1}{2}\|\zeta_t\|_{\mathbb{R}}^2 \qquad \mathfrak{V} = \frac{\gamma^2\alpha^2}{2}\|q\|_{\mathbb{R}}^2 + \frac{\gamma^2\alpha^2}{2}\|p\|_{\mathbb{R}}^2 - \gamma^2\left(\alpha^2 - 1\right)\langle\Phi, 1\rangle_{\mathbb{R}} \quad (8.24)$$

The energy $\mathfrak{H}$ is non-negative (though this is slightly tricky to show—see Problem 8.6).

8.2.3   Series approximations

Series approximated forms have played a significant role in the analysis of nonlinear systems such as the string model presented above; approximations to third or fourth order are commonly employed [244]. Recall also from the earlier discussion of the nonlinear oscillator in Section 4.2.1 that such approximated forms can lead to efficient and provably stable numerical methods. Such is the case here as well, but one must take great care in the choice of the type of approximation.

The function to be approximated is $\Phi(p,q)$. Consider three approximations, to second, third, and fourth order in p and q:

$$\Phi_2 = \frac{1}{2}q^2 \qquad \Phi_3 = \frac{1}{2}q^2 - \frac{1}{2}pq^2 \qquad \Phi_4 = \frac{1}{2}q^2 - \frac{1}{2}pq^2 + \frac{1}{2}q^2p^2 - \frac{1}{8}q^4$$

Approximation Φ_2, to second order, leads immediately to an uncoupling of longitudinal and transverse motion—u and ζ individually satisfy the 1D wave equation, with speeds of γ and $\gamma\alpha$, respectively.

More interesting, in the present context, are the approximations Φ_3 and Φ_4. It should be obvious that system (8.22), under the series approximations above, will also lead to a conservative system, with a modified energy function $\mathfrak{H}_3 = \mathfrak{T} + \mathfrak{V}_3$ or $\mathfrak{H}_4 = \mathfrak{T} + \mathfrak{V}_4$, where the modified expressions for the potential energy will be, in terms of p and q,

$$\mathfrak{V}_3 = \frac{\gamma^2}{2}\|q\|_{\mathbb{R}}^2 + \frac{\gamma^2\alpha^2}{2}\|p\|_{\mathbb{R}}^2 + \frac{\gamma^2(\alpha^2-1)}{2}\langle p,q^2\rangle_{\mathbb{R}} \tag{8.25a}$$

$$\mathfrak{V}_4 = \frac{\gamma^2}{2}\|q\|_{\mathbb{R}}^2 + \frac{\gamma^2}{2}\|p\|_{\mathbb{R}}^2 + \frac{\gamma^2(\alpha^2-1)}{8}\|q^2+2p\|_{\mathbb{R}}^2 - \frac{\gamma^2(\alpha^2-1)}{2}\|qp\|_{\mathbb{R}}^2 \tag{8.25b}$$

The third-order approximation in particular has been used in finite difference piano sound synthesis applications [23], and the fourth-order approximation (or variants—see below) is often used in studies of mode interaction [244].

Though useful for analysis purposes, the third- and fourth-order approximations are quite unphysical when it comes to the underlying Hamiltonian—in fact, due to series truncation, the potential energy terms can become negative, and unboundedly so! See Problem 8.7. This is obviously bad news if one is interested in developing a robust simulation routine, for if one cannot bound the behavior of the model system, it certainly will not be possible to do so for any derived numerical method.

A special series approximation

The problem above is one of Hamiltonian truncation. As an alternative, consider the following approximation to $\Phi(p,q)$, similar to Φ_4, but lacking one of the fourth-order terms:

$$\Phi_4^* = \frac{1}{2}q^2 - \frac{1}{2}pq^2 - \frac{1}{8}q^4$$

Now, the associated potential energy is

$$\mathfrak{V}_4^* = \frac{\gamma^2}{2}\|q\|_{\mathbb{R}}^2 + \frac{\gamma^2}{2}\|p\|_{\mathbb{R}}^2 + \frac{\gamma^2(\alpha^2-1)}{8}\|q^2+2p\|_{\mathbb{R}}^2$$

which is clearly non-negative if $\alpha \geq 1$ (which, again, is the case of most interest in the musical context). One might well ask in what sense the use of the approximation Φ_4^* is justified. One answer follows from the energetic analysis above; another relates to the relative orders of magnitude of p and q in system (8.22). As noted by Anand [9] and Morse and Ingard [244], under some conditions,

p can be considered to be of the same order of magnitude as q^2, and it is perhaps more natural, then, to use a homogeneous approximation, truncated to powers of, say, q. Given that the term p^2q^2 in $\mathfrak{V}_4$ is clearly of sixth order in q, it is then justified to neglect it with respect to the term in q^4. See [42] for more comments on this topic.

The system (8.22), under the choice Φ_4^*, reduces to

$$u_{tt} = \gamma^2 u_{xx} + \gamma^2 \frac{\alpha^2 - 1}{2}\left(q^3 + 2pq\right)_x \qquad\qquad \zeta_{tt} = \gamma^2\alpha^2\zeta_{xx} + \gamma^2\frac{\alpha^2 - 1}{2}\left(q^2\right)_x \qquad (8.26)$$

This system will be used as the starting point for the finite difference methods to be developed in the next section.

Wave speeds and computational implications

A fundamental difficulty with system (8.26) arises from the differing speeds of the two coupled equations: in the absence of the nonlinear terms, the system reduces to two 1D linear wave equations, one of speed γ and the other of speed $\gamma\alpha$—for applications in musical acoustics, α can be on the order of 10 or larger. Such a system with differing wave speeds, and thus operating over distinct ranges of frequencies, is often referred to as (in a very vague way) as "stiff." From the interpretation of the CFL condition in terms of a region of dependence (see Figure 6.9), an explicit scheme will clearly be strongly impacted by this. Consider, for example, *any* scheme for system (8.26) of the form

$$\delta_{tt}u = \gamma^2\delta_{xx}u + \cdots \qquad\qquad \delta_{tt}\zeta = \gamma^2\alpha^2\delta_{xx}\zeta + \cdots \qquad (8.27)$$

Regardless of the type of discretization applied to the nonlinear part, the scheme must still be capable of integrating the underlying linear system in a stable manner. Thus two CFL-type conditions on the time step k and grid spacing h must be enforced:

$$h \geq \gamma k \qquad\qquad h \geq \gamma\alpha k \qquad (8.28)$$

The second condition is more strict than the first—it is clear that both conditions cannot be satisfied near their respective stability limits, and thus numerical dispersion and, potentially, a very severe numerical cutoff will result. See Section 6.2.3 for a discussion of the effects of operation of such schemes away from the CFL limit. The ramifications of such issues, as well as potential solutions, will be explored in the remainder of this section.

8.2.4   A conservative finite difference scheme

Disregarding the dire warning above about schemes of the form (8.27), such a scheme does form a good starting point for the development and analysis of schemes which are stable in the fully nonlinear case. The discretization of the nonlinear terms in (8.26) is extremely delicate, but, one may note that the nonlinear terms are at most cubic. One may suspect a link with the schemes for the cubic nonlinear oscillator discussed in Section 4.2. This is in fact the case, and, indeed, the extension to distributed systems such as the present case of the nonlinear string has been one of the main motivations for the earlier preoccupation with such forms here.

There are many possibilities for conservative schemes for system (8.26). Here is a particularly simple one:

$$\delta_{tt}u = \gamma^2\delta_{xx}u + \gamma^2\frac{\alpha^2 - 1}{2}\delta_{x+}\left(q^2\mu_{t\cdot}q + 2q\mu_{tt}p\right) \qquad (8.29a)$$

$$\delta_{tt}\zeta = \gamma^2\alpha^2\delta_{xx}\zeta + \gamma^2\frac{\alpha^2 - 1}{2}\delta_{x+}\left(q\mu_{t\cdot}q\right) \qquad (8.29b)$$

where, in analogy with the continuous case, the quantities p and q are defined as

$$p = \delta_{x-}\zeta \qquad\qquad q = \delta_{x-}u$$

Notice in particular the use of time averaging operators on the right-hand side of both updates—such a scheme is implicit, but, notice also that, just as in the case of schemes such as (4.9b) for the cubic nonlinear oscillator, the unknowns appear only linearly, and thus there is no issue of existence or uniqueness of solutions. The full matrix update form will be given shortly.

Energy analysis

To see the conservative property of this scheme, it is useful to perform the calculation explicitly. Taking the inner products of the two schemes (8.29) with $\delta_t.u$ and $\delta_t.\zeta$ respectively, over $\mathcal{D} = \mathbb{Z}$, and using summation by parts leads to

$$\langle \delta_t.u, \delta_{tt}u\rangle_{\mathbb{Z}} = \gamma^2\langle \delta_t.u, \delta_{xx}u\rangle_{\mathbb{Z}} + \gamma^2\frac{\alpha^2-1}{2}\langle \delta_t.u, \delta_{x+}\left(q^2\mu_t.q + 2q\mu_{tt}p\right)\rangle_{\mathbb{Z}}$$

$$= -\gamma^2\langle \delta_t.q, q\rangle_{\mathbb{Z}} - \gamma^2\frac{\alpha^2-1}{2}\langle \delta_t.q, q^2\mu_t.q + 2q\mu_{tt}p\rangle_{\mathbb{Z}}$$

$$\langle \delta_t.\zeta, \delta_{tt}\zeta\rangle_{\mathbb{Z}} = \gamma^2\alpha^2\langle \delta_t.\zeta, \delta_{xx}\zeta\rangle_{\mathbb{Z}} + \gamma^2\frac{\alpha^2-1}{2}\langle \delta_t.\zeta, \delta_{x+}\left(q\mu_t.q\right)\rangle_{\mathbb{Z}}$$

$$= -\gamma^2\alpha^2\langle \delta_t.p, p\rangle_{\mathbb{Z}} - \gamma^2\frac{\alpha^2-1}{2}\langle \delta_t.p, q\mu_t.q\rangle_{\mathbb{Z}}$$

Adding the two equations, one arrives at

$$\delta_{t+}\left(\mathfrak{t} + \mathfrak{v}_{\text{lin}}\right) + \gamma^2\frac{\alpha^2-1}{2}\underbrace{\left(\langle \delta_t.q, q^2\mu_t.q + 2q\mu_{tt}p\rangle_{\mathbb{Z}} + \langle \delta_t.p, q\mu_t.q\rangle_{\mathbb{Z}}\right)}_{\Theta} = 0 \qquad (8.30)$$

where the kinetic energy $\mathfrak{t}$, and the part $\mathfrak{v}_{\text{lin}}$ of the potential energy corresponding to the underlying system (i.e., the second-order terms above), have been extracted as

$$\mathfrak{t} = \frac{1}{2}\|\delta_{t-}u\|_{\mathbb{Z}}^2 + \frac{1}{2}\|\delta_{t-}\zeta\|_{\mathbb{Z}}^2 \qquad \mathfrak{v}_{\text{lin}} = \frac{\gamma^2}{2}\langle q, e_{t-}q\rangle_{\mathbb{Z}} + \frac{\gamma^2\alpha^2}{2}\langle p, e_{t-}p\rangle_{\mathbb{Z}} \qquad (8.31)$$

Notice that the remaining terms depend only on the grid functions q and p, under the application of time difference and averaging operators—one may thus make liberal use of the identities (2.22) and (2.23), in order to write the term Θ, as indicated in (8.30) as the difference of a nonlinear potential energy contribution, as

$$\Theta \quad = \quad \langle q\delta_t.q, q\mu_{tt}.q\rangle_{\mathbb{Z}} + \langle q\delta_t.q, 2\mu_{tt}p\rangle_{\mathbb{Z}} + \langle \delta_t.p, q\mu_t.q\rangle_{\mathbb{Z}}$$

$$\stackrel{(2.22b),(2.22d)}{=} \frac{1}{2}\langle \delta_{t+}(qe_{t-}q), \mu_{t+}(qe_{t-}q)\rangle_{\mathbb{Z}} + \langle \delta_{t+}(qe_{t-}q), \mu_{t+}\mu_{t-}p\rangle_{\mathbb{Z}} + \langle \mu_{t+}(qe_{t-}q), \delta_{t+}\mu_{t-}p\rangle_{\mathbb{Z}}$$

$$\stackrel{(2.23),(2.22c)}{=} \delta_{t+}\left(\frac{1}{4}\|qe_{t-}q\|_{\mathbb{Z}}^2 + \langle qe_{t-}q, \mu_{t-}p\rangle_{\mathbb{Z}}\right)$$

Thus, finally, one has numerical energy conservation, i.e.,

$$\delta_{+}\mathfrak{h} = 0 \qquad \text{with} \qquad \mathfrak{h} = \mathfrak{t} + \mathfrak{v}_{\text{lin}} + \mathfrak{v}_{\text{nonlin}}$$

where t and v_{lin} are as given in (8.31) above, and where v_{nonlin} is defined as

$$v_{nonlin} = \gamma^2 \frac{\alpha^2 - 1}{2} \left(\frac{1}{4} \| q e_t - q \|_{\mathbb{Z}}^2 + \langle q e_t - q, \mu_t - p \rangle_{\mathbb{Z}} \right)$$

Scheme (8.29) is but one among many in a family of conservative methods for the system (8.26)—see [42]. Stability properties vary greatly, and one may lose the linear updating property. See Problem 8.8.

Non-negativity of energy and stability

As in the case of the systems examined in the previous chapters, once one has a numerical conservation property, the route to a stability condition is to find conditions under which the energy remains non-negative. To this end, note that by using identity (2.22f), the total potential energy may be written as

$$v = v_{lin} + v_{nonlin} = \frac{\gamma^2}{2} \langle q, e_t - q \rangle_{\mathbb{Z}} - \frac{\gamma^2 \alpha^2 k^2}{8} \| \delta_t - p \|_{\mathbb{Z}}^2 + \frac{\gamma^2}{2} \| \mu_t - p \|_{\mathbb{Z}}^2$$

$$+ \gamma^2 \frac{\alpha^2 - 1}{2} \left\| \mu_t - p + \frac{1}{2} q e_t - q \right\|_{\mathbb{Z}}^2$$

When $\alpha \geq 1$, one may go further and bound the potential energy from below, using inequalities (2.22f) and (5.30), as

$$v \geq \frac{\gamma^2}{2} \langle q, e_t - q \rangle_{\mathbb{Z}} - \frac{\gamma^2 \alpha^2 k^2}{8} \| \delta_t - p \|_{\mathbb{Z}}^2 \geq -\frac{\gamma^2 k^2}{8} \| \delta_t - q \|_{\mathbb{Z}}^2 - \frac{\gamma^2 \alpha^2 k^2}{8} \| \delta_t - p \|_{\mathbb{Z}}^2$$

$$\geq -\frac{\gamma^2 k^2}{2h^2} \| \delta_t - u \|_{\mathbb{Z}}^2 - \frac{\gamma^2 \alpha^2 k^2}{2h^2} \| \delta_t - \zeta \|_{\mathbb{Z}}^2$$

Finally, from the expression for total energy $\mathfrak{h}$, one arrives at

$$\mathfrak{h} \geq \frac{1}{2} \left(1 - \frac{\gamma^2 k^2}{h^2} \right) \| \delta_t - u \|_{\mathbb{Z}}^2 + \frac{1}{2} \left(1 - \frac{\gamma^2 \alpha^2 k^2}{h^2} \right) \| \delta_t - \zeta \|_{\mathbb{Z}}^2$$

which is non-negative under conditions (8.28). These are stability conditions for scheme (8.29)—notice that these are the same as the conditions which would be necessary for two linear wave equations in u and ζ. Not all schemes for the nonlinear string system possess this nice property! (See Problem 8.8.)

Vector–matrix update form

As the unknown grid functions u_l^{n+1} and ζ_l^{n+1} appear linearly in scheme (8.29), it is clear that the implicit scheme may be written in a vector–matrix form yielding a unique solution at each time step. Suppose the scheme is defined over the domain $\mathcal{D} = \mathbb{U}_N$, and that the values of the grid functions are set to zero at the endpoints of the interval at $l = 0$ and $l = N$. Defining the vector $\mathbf{w}^n$ as $\mathbf{w}^n = [u_1, \ldots, u_{N-1}, \zeta_1, \ldots, \zeta_{N-1}]^T$, the update is of the form

$$\mathbf{A}^n \mathbf{w}^{n+1} + \mathbf{B}^n \mathbf{w}^n + \mathbf{A}^n \mathbf{w}^{n-1} = \mathbf{0} \qquad (8.32)$$

where

$$\mathbf{A}^n = \begin{bmatrix} \mathbf{I} - \phi^2 \mathbf{D}_{x+} (\mathbf{\Lambda}^n)^2 \mathbf{D}_{x-} & -\phi^2 \mathbf{D}_{x+} \mathbf{\Lambda}^n \mathbf{D}_{x-} \\ -\phi^2 \mathbf{D}_{x+} \mathbf{\Lambda}^n \mathbf{D}_{x-} & \mathbf{I} \end{bmatrix} \quad \mathbf{B}^n = \begin{bmatrix} -2\mathbf{I} - \gamma^2 k^2 \mathbf{D}_{xx} & -2\phi^2 \mathbf{D}_{x+} \mathbf{\Lambda}^n \mathbf{D}_{x-} \\ 0 & -2\mathbf{I} - \gamma^2 \alpha^2 \mathbf{D}_{xx} \end{bmatrix}$$

where $\phi^2 = \gamma^2 k^2 (\alpha^2 - 1)/4$, and $\mathbf{I}$ and $\mathbf{0}$ are the $(N-1) \times (N-1)$ identity and zero matrices, respectively, $\mathbf{D}_{xx}$ is the $(N-1) \times (N-1)$ approximation to the second derivative, under Dirichlet conditions, and $\mathbf{D}_{x+} = -\mathbf{D}_{x-}^T$ is the $(N-1) \times N$ approximation to the first derivative—see Section 5.2.7 for more on these matrix forms. $\mathbf{\Lambda}^n$ is the diagonal $N \times N$ matrix defined as $\mathbf{\Lambda}^n = \mathrm{diag}(\mathbf{D}_{x-}[u_1, \ldots, u_{N-1}]')$. Notice, in particular, that the matrices $\mathbf{\Lambda}^n$ and $\mathbf{B}^n$ may be computed explicitly from known values of $\mathbf{w}^n$, and furthermore are sparse, allowing for efficient solution techniques.

Numerical behavior

The stability conditions (8.28) are, as mentioned, rather restrictive. Using a typical audio sample rate f_s such as 44 100 Hz leads to trouble—$k = 1/f_s$ must be chosen so as to satisfy the second condition, leading normally to a very large grid spacing. As the grid spacing is used for both the transverse displacement as well as the longitudinal displacement, the number of degrees of freedom necessary for the transverse displacement (the modes of which, in the audio range, are far more numerous than for the longitudinal displacement) is grossly insufficient, and a very severe numerical cutoff is evident. In fact, for most values of α which occur in practice, such a scheme is unusable at a typical audio sample rate. See Figure 8.11, which illustrates one such poor result, at 44.1 kHz: in this case, in theory, the transverse modal frequencies are at multiples of 100 Hz and the longitudinal modes at multiples of approximately 2500 Hz. Only the longitudinal modal frequencies are fairly well resolved, and, due to the severity of the stability condition, the transverse vibration is band-limited to about 500 Hz!

One obvious solution to this difficulty, and one taken by Bank and Sujbert [22], is to use a very high audio sample rate (often on the order of 400 000 Hz). But given that computational complexity scales with the square of the sample rate, this is obviously a technique of limited utility in synthesis. As a way around this difficulty, Bank has proposed using a modal representation for the longitudinal displacement [21], in conjunction with a finite difference scheme for the transverse displacement, which appears to work quite well. On the other hand, various more elaborate schemes for the wave equation and the ideal bar have been discussed in Section 6.3 and

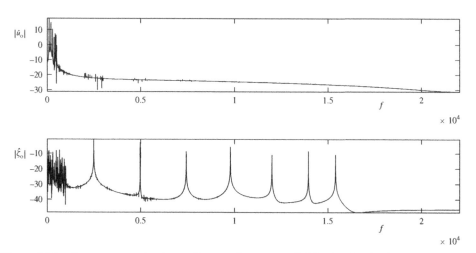

Figure 8.11   Output spectra for the nonlinear string system (8.26), simulated using scheme (8.29), running at 44.1 kHz; the spectrum of transverse motion is shown at top and that of longitudinal motion at bottom. The string has parameters $\gamma = 199.6$, $\alpha = 25.04$, and is excited using a plucked triangular distribution, of maximum amplitude 0.005; readout is taken at $x = 0.6$.

Section 7.1.5, respectively, and one may put such techniques to use here as well, with the goal
of reducing numerical dispersion and computational complexity, while retaining the nice stability
property mentioned above, and the more general ability to allow for modular interconnection with
other objects, even in the nonlinear case.

8.2.5   Improved finite difference schemes

The problem with scheme (8.29), as mentioned above, is that the stability conditions (8.28) conflict.
In addition, as it is the transverse displacement which is of primary importance in string vibration,
one would like to be able to use a scheme which is of high accuracy for at least this part of the
problem. To this end, consider the scheme

$$\delta_{tt}u = \gamma^2 \delta_{xx}u + \gamma^2 \frac{\alpha^2 - 1}{2}\delta_{x+}\left(q^2 \mu_{t\cdot}q + 2q\mu_{tt}p\right) \tag{8.33a}$$

$$(\theta + (1-\theta)\mu_{x\cdot})\,\delta_{tt}\zeta = \gamma^2\alpha^2\delta_{xx}\zeta + \gamma^2\frac{\alpha^2-1}{2}\delta_{x+}\left(q\mu_{t\cdot}q\right) \tag{8.33b}$$

which differs from scheme (8.29) through an added implicit treatment of the equation for longitudinal displacement, parameterized by θ. Under low-amplitude (or linear) conditions, this scheme
decouples into two independent schemes in u and ζ, the second of which is exactly the compact
implicit method for the 1D wave equation as discussed in Section 6.3.2.

From the earlier treatment of this scheme, one may deduce that the stability conditions for
scheme (8.33) are, in addition to the requirement $\theta \geq 1/2$, that

$$h \geq \gamma k \qquad h \geq \frac{\gamma\alpha k}{\sqrt{2\theta - 1}} \tag{8.34}$$

Though this condition has been derived using von Neumann methods, it may be shown to hold in
the case of the nonlinear coupled scheme above. See Problem 8.9. The free parameter θ may now
be set so that the bounds are identical, as

$$\theta = \frac{1 + \alpha^2}{2} \tag{8.35}$$

If the common bound is satisfied with equality, the result is very low dispersion in the "transverse"
wave equation approximation (8.33a) and considerable dispersion in the longitudinal approximation (8.33b); in particular, there is not a severe numerical cutoff, as in the case of (8.29)—see
Figure 8.12(a), which shows simulation results using this scheme at 44.1 kHz.

Still, however, the above solution is not entirely satisfying—when the two equations are uncoupled, the grid spacing h is appropriate for the transverse equation, but for the longitudinal equation
is too small. Thus, the number of degrees of freedom is too large—the fundamental longitudinal
modal frequency is usually quite high for musical strings (in the range of 1–2 kHz), so the number
of degrees of freedom for the longitudinal part of the system is quite low, compared to the number
required for the transverse part. As a result, rather severe dispersion is present in the longitudinal spectrum, which contains many spurious modes (these are clearly visible in Figure 8.12(a)).
A more natural approach, but one which is slightly more involved from a programming standpoint,
is to make use of distinct grids for the transverse and longitudinal displacements, and then interpolate back and forth between them. Recalling the discussion of full grid interpolants in Section 5.2.4,
one may generalize scheme (8.29) as

$$\delta_{tt}u = \gamma^2 \delta_{xx}^{(t)}u + \gamma^2\frac{\alpha^2-1}{2}\delta_{x+}^{(t)}\left(q^2\mu_{t\cdot}q + 2q\mu_{tt}p\right) \tag{8.36a}$$

$$\delta_{tt}\zeta = \gamma^2\alpha^2\delta_{xx}^{(l)}\zeta + \gamma^2\frac{\alpha^2-1}{2}\delta_{x+}^{(l)}\mathcal{I}_{h^{(l)}\to h^{(l)},p}^{*}\left(q\mu_{t\cdot}q\right) \tag{8.36b}$$

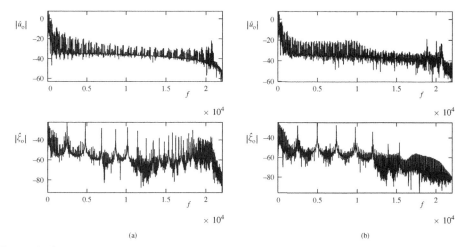

Figure 8.12 Output spectra for the nonlinear string system (8.26), simulated using (a) scheme (8.33) and (b) scheme (8.36) running at 44.1 kHz; the spectrum of transverse motion is shown at top and that of longitudinal motion at bottom. The string has parameters and excitation as given in the caption to Figure 8.11; readout is taken at $x = 0.7$.

Here, u and ζ are defined over grids of spacing $h^{(t)}$ and $h^{(l)}$, respectively, and the (t) and (l) superscripts of the difference operators indicate that the operator is applied over the transverse displacement or longitudinal displacement grid, respectively. Now, the grid functions p and q are defined as

$$p = \delta_{x-}^{(t)} \mathcal{I}_{h^{(l)} \to h^{(t)}, p} \zeta \qquad q = \delta_{x-}^{(t)} u$$

In the above system, $\mathcal{I}_{h^{(l)} \to h^{(t)}, p}$ and $\mathcal{I}_{h^{(l)} \to h^{(t)}, p}^{*}$ are the pth-order upsampling interpolant and its downsampling conjugate—see Section 5.2.4, as well as Programming Exercises 5.2 and 5.3 for the definition of these operations.

This algorithm is both cheaper, computationally, than scheme (8.33), due to the reduced number of grid points necessary to resolve the longitudinal displacement, and better behaved in terms of numerical dispersion—indeed, when the two equations are uncoupled, each is the simple scheme (6.34) for the 1D wave equation operating near its respective stability limit, and thus with very low dispersion. When coupled, this behavior is evident in the placement of the longitudinal modes, as can be seen in Figure 8.12(b).

Both the θ scheme (8.33) and the interpolated scheme (8.36) possess associated vector–matrix update forms similar to (8.32); see Problem 8.10 and Programming Exercise 8.4.

8.2.6 Stiff string modeling

In the musical context, it is stiff strings, such as those of guitars and pianos, that are of interest. As such, the nonlinear string model presented in this section needs to be generalized to include effects of stiffness, as well as frequency-dependent loss. The obvious way of proceeding, given that the string should behave linearly at low amplitudes, is to make use of a generalization of (7.28). Here is a resulting system:

$$u_{tt} = -\kappa^2 u_{xxxx} + \gamma^2 u_{xx} + \gamma^2 \frac{\alpha^2 - 1}{2} \left(q^3 + 2pq \right)_x - 2\sigma_0^{(t)} u_t + 2\sigma_1^{(t)} u_{txx} \qquad (8.37a)$$

$$\zeta_{tt} = \gamma^2 \alpha^2 \zeta_{xx} + \gamma^2 \frac{\alpha^2 - 1}{2} \left(q^2 \right)_x - 2\sigma_0^{(l)} \zeta_t + 2\sigma_1^{(l)} \zeta_{txx} \qquad (8.37b)$$

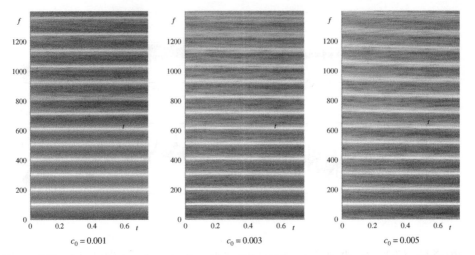

Figure 8.13 Spectrograms of synthesis using a finite difference scheme for system (8.37), for a nonlinear string with stiffness and frequency-dependent loss. In this case, the string has $\gamma = 199.6$, $\kappa = 1.48$, and $\alpha = 25.04$, and loss parameters $\sigma_0^{(t)} = \sigma_0^{(l)} = 0.498$ and $\sigma_1^{(t)} = \sigma_1^{(l)} = 0.0002$. The string is excited with a plucked triangular distribution c_{tri}, peaked at $x = 0.14$, and of amplitude c_0 as given in the panels above. Output is taken from the transverse displacement at $x_o = 0.92$. The scheme is run at 32 kHz.

Here, κ is as defined in (7.3) for the ideal bar, and the frequency-dependent loss is modeled by the terms of coefficients $2\sigma_0^{(t)}$, $2\sigma_1^{(t)}$, $2\sigma_0^{(l)}$, and $2\sigma_1^{(l)}$, which generally must be determined experimentally. This system is very similar to that employed by Bank and Sujbert [23] in their work on nonlinear piano string vibration, but can also be used to describe guitar string vibration. Finite difference schemes may be arrived at using the methods described in the previous section, with the new terms treated as in the linear case in Section 7.3.2—see Problem 8.10 and Programming Exercise 8.5.

As an illustration of such a scheme, see Figure 8.13, which reproduces the experimental results of Conklin [87], in which a stiff string is plucked at varying amplitudes. At low amplitudes, the behavior is essentially linear, but at higher amplitudes, phantom partials begin to appear—these are visible in the center panel, and begin to be distinct from the base set of partials from about the ninth partial onward. At even higher amplitudes, the tension modulation, or pitch glide effect, becomes apparent as well. This example, though instructive in that it illustrates the variety of effects possible in strings under nonlinear conditions, may be a bit extreme when it comes to synthesis, especially if one is willing to sacrifice the pitch glide effect, which is often not extremely strong, except in the case of very loosely strung guitar strings, and which is only barely evident in piano tones. A fully modal approach can be a good alternative, especially in a fixed (i.e., non-modular) configuration in which one is really interested in targeting a particular static instrument design. For such a modal method applied to piano modeling (incorporating some very clever corner-cutting to allow for the generation of phantom partials), and one yielding sound of exceptionally natural character, see the recent article by Zambon, Lehtonen, and Bank [415].

8.3   Non-planar string motion

In the previous sections, nonlinear string vibration models have been examined, where the motion is assumed to lie in a single plane. The extension to the case of non-planar motion is direct, at least on paper, but entirely new phenomena appear, related to the inherent instability of planar motion of a string—"instability" is used here not in the dynamic or numerical sense (referring to explosive behavior), but rather to mean that string motion which is initially planar will become largely non-planar under very small non-planar perturbation. The resulting effect is often referred to as "whirling," and has been studied by various authors [183, 304, 262], including in musical contexts [155]. In this section, only the generalization of the Kirchhoff–Carrier equation will be discussed, though system (8.22), as well as series approximated forms, may be extended as well.

8.3.1 Model equations

The Kirchhoff–Carrier system with loss (8.5) may be extended easily to the non-planar case as

$$\underline{\mathbf{u}}_{tt} = \gamma^2 \mathfrak{G} \underline{\mathbf{u}}_{xx} - 2\sigma_0 \underline{\mathbf{u}}_t \qquad \text{where} \qquad \mathfrak{G} = 1 + \frac{\alpha^2}{2} \|\|\underline{\mathbf{u}}_x\|\|_{\mathbb{U}}^2 \tag{8.38}$$

which is again in spatially scaled form and defined over the unit interval $\mathcal{D} = \mathbb{U}$, where γ and α are again as defined in (8.3). The transverse displacement $\underline{\mathbf{u}} = [u^{(1)}, u^{(2)}]$ is now a vector quantity with components $u^{(1)}$ and $u^{(2)}$ in two directions orthogonal to the string axis at rest. See Figure 8.9. Recall also the discussion of the vector generalization of the inner product and norm on page 98.

The above system (as well as the finite difference scheme below) is dissipative, as in the planar case; one may also show strict dissipation of angular momentum. The conservation and dissipation of quantities other than energy has been studied by various authors (see, e.g., [225, 404]). See also Problem 8.11.

8.3.2 Finite difference schemes

It is not difficult to extend the schemes presented in Section 8.1.2 to the non-planar case. For simplicity, consider the scheme corresponding to (8.7),

$$\delta_{tt}\underline{\mathbf{u}} = \gamma^2 \mathfrak{g} \delta_{xx}\underline{\mathbf{u}} - 2\sigma_0 \delta_t . \underline{\mathbf{u}} \qquad \text{where} \qquad \mathfrak{g} = 1 + \frac{\alpha^2}{2} \langle \delta_{x+}\underline{\mathbf{u}}, \mu_t . \delta_{x+}\underline{\mathbf{u}} \rangle_{\mathbb{U}_N} \tag{8.39}$$

which again is stable when $\lambda \leq 1$.

In order to put this scheme in a vector–matrix form suitable for implementation, it is useful to reorder the state $\underline{\mathbf{u}}$ as a single column vector $\mathbf{u} = [u_1^{(1)}, \ldots, u_{N-1}^{(1)}, u_1^{(2)}, \ldots, u_{N-1}^{(2)}]^T$. The update then is again of the form (8.11), where now the matrices $\mathbf{A}$, $\mathbf{B}$, and $\mathbf{C}$, under fixed boundary conditions, are

$$\mathbf{A} = (1 + \sigma_0 k)\mathbf{I} + \mathbf{q}\mathbf{q}^T \qquad \mathbf{B} = -2\mathbf{I} - \gamma^2 k^2 \begin{bmatrix} \mathbf{D}_{xx} & \mathbf{0} \\ \mathbf{0} & \mathbf{D}_{xx} \end{bmatrix} \qquad \mathbf{C} = (1 - \sigma_0 k)\mathbf{I} + \mathbf{q}\mathbf{q}^T$$

where

$$\mathbf{q} = \frac{\gamma \alpha k \sqrt{h}}{2} \begin{bmatrix} \mathbf{D}_{xx} & \mathbf{0} \\ \mathbf{0} & \mathbf{D}_{xx} \end{bmatrix} \mathbf{u}$$

As might be expected, this scheme will suffer from the same problems with spurious numerical oscillations when λ is close to 1—a solution to this difficulty follows along the lines of the schemes developed in Section 8.1.2.

8.3.3 Whirling

In the linear case, the two string polarizations vibrate independently. This is not so under non-linear conditions—energy is transferred back and forth between the two. As an example of this,

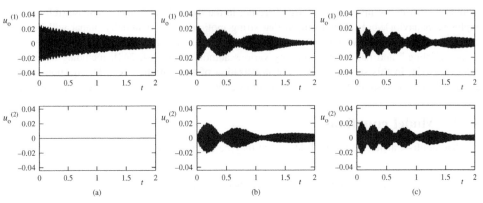

Figure 8.14 Whirling effect in a non-planar string model. In this case, $\gamma = 800$, $\alpha = 10$, and $T_{60} = 20$ s, and the string is initialized using a raised cosine distribution c_{rc}, with $x_0 = 0.5$, $x_{\text{hw}} = 0.3$, and $c_0 = 0.02$ as an initial displacement condition in the $u^{(1)}$ direction, and another such distribution similar to the first, but with increasing values of (a) $c_0 = 0$, (b) $c_0 = 20$, and (c) $c_0 = 40$, as an initial velocity distribution in the $u^{(2)}$ direction. Scheme (8.39) is used, at a sample rate of 22 050 Hz and with $\lambda = 0.8$. In each case, the displacements are read from the location $x = 0.3$ in both polarizations.

consider a string plucked precisely in the (1) polarization, under different levels of initial velocity perturbation in the (2) polarization, as illustrated in Figure 8.14. When no such perturbation is present, the motion is planar, and identical to that generated by the planar model (8.5). As the level of perturbation is increased, energy is transferred periodically to the (2) polarization, where the period is dependent on the amplitude of the excitation—in particular, notice that the period increases as the vibration is damped. While this may seem to be a slightly artificial example, such effects have been studied and found to be audible in certain stringed instruments—see, e.g., [155].

8.4 Problems

Problem 8.1 *Prove the bound (8.6) on $\mathfrak{G}$, which describes the pitch glide for the Kirchhoff–Carrier system with a linear loss term in the following way:*
(a) Given that $0 \leq \mathfrak{V} \leq \mathfrak{H}$, find a bound on $\|u_x\|_{\mathbb{U}}^2$ in terms of $\mathfrak{H}$.
(b) Given the bound on $\|u_x\|_{\mathbb{U}}^2$, and the fact that $\mathfrak{G}$ is a strictly increasing function of $\|u_x\|_{\mathbb{U}}^2$, show the bound (8.6).

Problem 8.2
(a) For scheme (8.7) for the Kirchhoff–Carrier equation, under lossless and fixed boundary conditions, show the equivalence between the two forms of $\mathfrak{g}$ given in (8.9) and (8.12).
(b) When there is loss, i.e., when $\sigma_0 > 0$, the expression $\mathfrak{g}$ as given in (8.9) again leads to stable numerical behavior, but the explicit expression given in (8.12) is no longer valid. Find a new expression allowing the explicit calculation of $\mathfrak{g}$ from known values of the grid function u.
(c) Another way to see the essentially explicit character of scheme (8.7), using $\mathfrak{g}$ as given in (8.9), is from the matrix update form (8.11). At each time step, one must solve a linear system involving the matrix $\mathbf{A}$, which is of the form $\mathbf{A} = \epsilon \mathbf{I} + \mathbf{q}\mathbf{q}^T$ for some constant ϵ. Show that the inverse of $\mathbf{A}$ may be written in closed form in terms of $\mathbf{q}$ and ϵ. (This is a very simple application of the matrix inversion lemma [176] to a rank 1 perturbation of a matrix with a known inverse.) Hint: Try to generalize from the scalar case; that is, if q is a scalar, $\mathbf{A}^{-1} = \left(1 - q^2/(\epsilon + q^2)\right)/\epsilon$.

Problem 8.3   *Though frequency domain analysis is not directly applicable to nonlinear finite difference schemes, it is possible to arrive at some (generally qualitative) conclusions about numerical oscillations.*

(a) First, consider scheme (8.7) for the Kirchhoff–Carrier equation under lossless conditions, and assume that $\mathfrak{g}$ is equal to some constant $\mathfrak{g}_0$. Thus,

$$\delta_{tt}u = \gamma^2 \mathfrak{g}_0 \delta_{xx} u$$

Using von Neumann analysis, the characteristic equation for this scheme will be

$$z - 2 + 4\lambda^2 \mathfrak{g}_0 p + z^{-1} = 0$$

where $p = \sin^2(\beta h/2)$. Under what conditions on λ will the scheme possess purely real roots? Show that when the roots are real, both are negative. Explain why negative real roots lead to oscillatory behavior in the underlying finite difference scheme. (Notice that nothing is being said here about stability—this is ensured by a choice of $\mathfrak{g}$ as given in (8.9).)

(b) Now consider the θ scheme (8.13), under lossless conditions, with the choice of θ as given in (8.14). Show that if one again takes $\mathfrak{g}$ to be a constant equal to $\mathfrak{g}_0$, the scheme looks approximately like

$$(1 + 2\gamma^2 k^2 \theta_0 (\mathfrak{g}_0 - 1)\,\delta_{xx})\delta_{tt}u = \gamma^2 \mathfrak{g}_0 \delta_{xx} u$$

Using von Neumann analysis, again find a characteristic polynomial for this scheme, and show that when $\theta_0 = -1/8$, the roots are complex conjugate pairs of unit magnitude for all spatial frequencies β, for all $\lambda \leq 1$. What can you conclude about numerical oscillatory behavior in this case?

Problem 8.4   *Show stability conditions (8.18) for the modal scheme (8.17) for the Kirchhoff–Carrier equation with loss. In order to do this, multiply each equation by $\delta_t.U_p$, and sum over $p = 1, \ldots, M$. You should show first that the energy contribution due to nonlinear effects is non-negative. Once you have done this, the analysis reduces to determining non-negativity conditions for quadratic forms individually in U_p; each of these is, essentially, an uncoupled simple harmonic oscillator with loss.*

Problem 8.5   *For the nonlinear bar model given in (8.19), show that conservative boundary conditions generalizing those of clamped or simply supported type are as per the linear case, in (7.7a) and (7.7b), but that the free condition (7.7c) must be altered to*

$$u_{xx} = \kappa^2 u_{xxxx} - \frac{\gamma_l^2}{2}\|u_x\|_{\mathbb{U}}^2 u_x = 0 \qquad \text{free}$$

at either end of the bar. Do you anticipate difficulties in the implementation of the free boundary condition, which now depends on the entire state of the bar, in a numerical method? Discuss.

Problem 8.6   *To show non-negativity of the energy $\mathfrak{H}$ for the nonlinear string system (8.22), it suffices to show that the expression for the potential energy $\mathfrak{V}$, given in (8.24), is non-negative. Show that $\mathfrak{V}$ may be rewritten as*

$$\mathfrak{V} = \gamma^2 \langle \Phi, 1 \rangle_{\mathbb{R}} + \frac{\gamma^2 \alpha^2}{2}\|\Phi + p\|_{\mathbb{R}}^2$$

and argue that both terms are individually non-negative.

Problem 8.7   *Show that the potential energy terms corresponding to the truncation of the nonlinearity in the string system (8.22) to third and fourth order can take on negative unbounded values, under any choice of $\alpha \neq 0$.*

1
2
3
4
5
6
7
8
9
10
11
12
13
14
15
16
17
18
19
20
21
22
23
24
25
26
27
28
29
30
31
32
33
34
35
36
37
38
39
40
41
42
43
44
45
46
47
48
49
50
51

Problem 8.8   *A scheme for the nonlinear string system (8.22) is given in (8.29). There are many other choices of scheme available. Here are three:*

(a) $\delta_{tt}u = \gamma^2\delta_{xx}u + \gamma^2\frac{\alpha^2-1}{2}\delta_{x+}\left(q^3 + 2qp\right)$ $\delta_{tt}\zeta = \gamma^2\alpha^2\delta_{xx}\zeta + \gamma^2\frac{\alpha^2-1}{2}\delta_{x+}\left(q^2\right)$

(b) $\delta_{tt}u = \gamma^2\delta_{xx}u + \gamma^2\frac{\alpha^2-1}{2}\delta_{x+}\left((\mu_{t.}q)(q^2 + 2p)\right)$ $\delta_{tt}\zeta = \gamma^2\alpha^2\delta_{xx}\zeta + \gamma^2\frac{\alpha^2-1}{2}\delta_{x+}\left(q^2\right)$

(c) $\delta_{tt}u = \gamma^2\delta_{xx}u + \gamma^2\frac{\alpha^2-1}{2}\delta_{x+}\left((\mu_{t.}q)\mu_{t.}(q^2 + 2p)\right)$ $\delta_{tt}\zeta = \gamma^2\alpha^2\delta_{xx}\zeta + \gamma^2\frac{\alpha^2-1}{2}\delta_{x+}\left(\mu_{t.}q^2\right)$

For each scheme, answer the following questions: Does the scheme possess a conserved energy? If so, can it be shown to be non-negative under some condition on h in terms of k, γ, and α? Can the scheme be solved uniquely for the unknown grid values at each time step?

Problem 8.9   *Consider the scheme (8.33) for the nonlinear string system (8.26); recall that this is a variant of scheme (8.29), in which the linear part of the scheme for longitudinal displacement is treated implicitly, with a free parameter θ. Show that the energetic analysis performed in pages 237 to 238 for scheme (8.29) extends to this case as well, with the difference that the linear part of the potential energy $\mathfrak{v}_{\text{lin}}$ must now be written as*

$$\mathfrak{v}_{lin} = \frac{\gamma^2}{2}\langle q, e_{t-}q\rangle_{\mathbb{Z}} + \frac{\gamma^2\alpha^2}{2}\langle p, e_{t-}p\rangle_{\mathbb{Z}} - \frac{h^2(1-\theta)}{4}\|\delta_{t-}p\|_{\mathbb{Z}}^2$$

Deduce conditions on non-negativity of conserved energy in this case, and show that they are in fact those given in (8.34).

Problem 8.10

   (a) Rewrite the scheme (8.33) for the nonlinear string vibration system (8.26) in a vector–matrix update form (8.32), where the state vector $\mathbf{w}^n$ again consists of values of the transverse displacement followed by values of the longitudinal displacement at time step n. You will thus need to find expressions for the matrices $\mathbf{A}^n$ and $\mathbf{B}^n$ in terms of operators such as $\mathbf{D}_{xx}$, $\mathbf{D}_{xxxx}$, etc. Assume θ is chosen according to (8.35), so that the number of values of the longitudinal displacement will be the same as that for the transverse displacement.

   (b) Rewrite scheme (8.36) in vector–matrix form. You may make explicit use of the operators $\mathcal{I}$ and $\mathcal{I}^*$ (which are themselves generally rectangular matrices), and make sure that you have defined your difference operators to be of appropriate sizes. (For example, the operators $\delta_{xx}^{(t)}$ and $\delta_{xx}^{(l)}$ become square matrices $\mathbf{D}_{xx}^{(t)}$ and $\mathbf{D}_{xx}^{(l)}$ of distinct sizes, corresponding to the differing grid spacings $h^{(t)}$ and $h^{(l)}$!) The full matrices $\mathbf{A}^n$ and $\mathbf{B}^n$ will, nonetheless, be square.

   (c) Consider the following difference approximation to system (8.37) for the nonlinear string with stiffness and frequency-dependent loss:

$$\delta_{tt}u = -\kappa^2\delta_{xxxx}^{(t)}u - 2\sigma_0^{(t)}\delta_{t.}u + 2\sigma_1^{(t)}\delta_{t.}\delta_{xx}^{(t)}u + \cdots$$

$$\delta_{tt}\zeta = -2\sigma_0^{(l)}\delta_{t.}\zeta + 2\sigma_1^{(l)}\delta_{t.}\delta_{xx}^{(l)}\zeta + \cdots$$

where the ellipsis $\cdots$ indicates the terms which appear in the schemes (8.33) and (8.36) for the lossless non-stiff, nonlinear string. Now, the vector–matrix update form will be

$$\mathbf{A}^n\mathbf{w}^{n+1} + \mathbf{B}^n\mathbf{w}^n + \mathbf{C}^n\mathbf{w}^{n-1} = \mathbf{0} \tag{8.40}$$

for the state vector $\mathbf{w}$. Determine the matrices $\mathbf{A}^n$, $\mathbf{B}^n$, and $\mathbf{C}^n$. Can you infer a stability condition for this scheme?

Problem 8.11   *Consider the non-planar Kirchhoff–Carrier system (8.38) and the finite difference scheme (8.39).*

1
2
3
4
5
6
7
8
9
10
11
12
13
14
15
16
17
18
19
20
21
22
23
24
25
26
27
28
29
30
31
32
33
34
35
36
37
38
39
40
41
42
43
44
45
46
47
48
49
50
51

(a) Find an expression of the total energy for both the continuous system and the finite difference scheme, and show that it is conserved when $\sigma_0 = 0$, and strictly dissipated when $\sigma_0 > 0$.

(b) Consider the following quantity, which scales with the total angular momentum of the string about the axis which defines its rest state:

$$\mathfrak{A} = \langle u^{(2)}, u_t^{(1)} \rangle_{\mathbb{U}} - \langle u^{(1)}, u_t^{(2)} \rangle_{\mathbb{U}}$$

Show that under conservative conditions ($\sigma_0 = 0$), and under Dirichlet boundary conditions at either end of the string, this quantity is conserved. Show that when $\sigma_0 > 0$, it follows that $d\mathfrak{A}/dt = -2\sigma_0\mathfrak{A}$, and thus $\mathfrak{A}$ decreases exponentially (in contrast to the case of energy, which decreases monotonically, but not exponentially).

(c) Show that for scheme (8.39), the following discrete angular momentum is conserved when $\sigma_0 = 0$ and under Dirichlet boundary conditions:

$$\mathfrak{a} = \langle \mu_{t-}u^{(2)}, \delta_{t-}u^{(1)} \rangle_{\mathbb{U}_N} - \langle \mu_{t-}u^{(1)}, \delta_{t-}u^{(2)} \rangle_{\mathbb{U}_N}$$

Show that it decreases geometrically when $\sigma_0 > 0$.

8.5   Programming exercises

Programming Exercise 8.1   The code example given in Section A.9 is an implementation of scheme (8.7) for the Kirchhoff–Carrier equation, under lossless conditions. As such, it is quite far from being a useful synthesis algorithm, but is worth getting familiar with its properties in this very simple form.

(a) Perform a study of pitch versus excitation strength. Use a plucked triangular excitation, a value of $\alpha = 10$, a relatively small value of λ, such as $\lambda = 0.7$, and increase the amplitude of the excitation as high as you can without generating high-frequency spurious oscillations (these will be audible as a high-pitched buzzing, and directly visible on plots of the output waveform).

(b) For a given α and λ, determine the maximum excitation strength which may be applied without generating spurious numerical oscillations. Does this confirm the analysis you performed in Problem 8.3?

(c) Verify that the algorithm conserves numerical energy to machine accuracy.

Programming Exercise 8.2   (a) Rewrite the code example given in Section A.9 in matrix update form, as per (8.11), using the generic linear system solution routine provided in Matlab. Loss should be introduced, so you should have T_{60} as another global parameter in your code (from which σ_0 may be derived).

(b) Extend the algorithm to the θ scheme (8.13). Experiment with different values of θ (keeping in mind the results of Problem 8.3), and convince yourself that it does indeed perform better (i.e., with less spurious numerical oscillation) for values of λ near 1. When this scheme becomes unstable (it can!), how does the instability manifest itself?

Programming Exercise 8.3   Program the "modal" algorithm simulating the Kirchhoff–Carrier equation given in (8.17). You may wish to use the code provided for modal solution to the 1D wave equation in Section A.6 as a starting point. Compare its performance, especially in terms of numerical oscillation, computational efficiency, and the capability of generating appropriate pitch glides, to the θ-type finite difference scheme you programmed in the previous exercise.

Programming Exercise 8.4   Program the nonlinear string vibration algorithms (8.33) and (8.36) which simulate (8.26). In order to do this, you will need to have written the schemes in a vector–matrix update form similar to (8.32) for scheme (8.29)—see Problem 8.10. For scheme (8.33), be sure to choose the scheme free parameter θ according to (8.35), so that the

1
2
3
4
5
6
7
8
9
10
11
12
13
14
15
16
17
18
19
20
21
22
23
24
25
26
27
28
29
30
31
32
33
34
35
36
37
38
39
40
41
42
43
44
45
46
47
48
49
50
51

numbers of grid points for the transverse and longitudinal displacements are the same. In the
case of scheme (8.36), which involves interpolation, you will need to generate appropriate-sized
interpolation matrices—see Programming Exercise 5.2. Choose the grid spacings in both cases to
be as close to the stability limit as possible.

(a) Perform a study of phantom partial generation, using, as an excitation, a triangular plucked
distribution c_{tri}, for a string of parameters as given in the caption to Figure 8.11. Be alert to
distinctions between the two schemes—do they generate the same results?

(b) Perform a study of aliasing phenomena, and the effect of increasing grid spacing away from
the stability bound in both cases. How does aliasing manifest itself perceptually?

Programming Exercise 8.5   Extend the code you have written in the previous exercise to include
the effects of stiffness and frequency-dependent damping. This should be rather easy to do; the only
things you will need to do will be to generalize the update matrices, and alter the stability condition.

1
2
3
4
5
6
7
8
9
10
11
12
13
14
15
16
17
18
19
20
21
22
23
24
25
26
27
28
29
30
31
32
33
34
35
36
37
38
39
40
41
42
43
44
45
46
47
48
49
50
51

9

Acoustic tubes

Wave propagation in acoustic tubes forms the basis of musical sound production in wind and brass instruments, as well as in the human voice. For various reasons, synthesis based on models of such instruments has seen a lot of activity—chief among these, perhaps, are the links with speech analysis and synthesis, the relative ease with which such systems may be analyzed and the extensive work in musical acoustics, and the use of waveguides which deal with some special cases with extreme efficiency.

The key concepts which are employed in the acoustical analysis of tube-based instruments are impedance, as well as ideas from scattering theory, such as reflectance, wave decompositions, and so forth—these are, of course, of extreme utility in model validation, given that measurements of tube responses are often best understood in the frequency domain. As in the rest of this book, this point of view is incorporated here, but to a lesser degree than is usual in pure musical acoustics. One can design time domain simulations without invoking any notion of frequency; the big bonus of a finite difference formulation is that the resulting implementation can be almost embarrassingly simple—see the code example given in Section A.10.

A general model of 1D wave propagation, Webster's equation, is presented in Section 9.1, along with a discussion of boundary conditions (particularly the radiation condition), modes, associated finite difference schemes, and the special cases of tubes of cylindrical and conical profile. As an application, such difference schemes are applied to the case of the vocal tract in Section 9.2, where one may find a direct correspondence between rudimentary difference schemes and scattering-based synthesis methods along the lines of the famous Kelly–Lochbaum model [201]. Finally, the more difficult case of the coupling of a tube to a nonlinear reed-like mechanism is covered in Section 9.3, from which follows a completely discrete wind instrument synthesis method.

9.1 Webster's equation

There are various ways of defining what is meant by the word "tube." In general, it can be described as an enclosure for which the length scale in one coordinate is significantly greater than in the others. In linear problems, the dynamics of the material filling the tube (air in musical applications) will satisfy the wave equation in 3D. If it is true that the wavelengths of interest are longer than the length scale in the two "short" coordinate directions, then it is possible to simplify the dynamics to one dimension, which will be called here, as in the case of bars and strings, x. A general tube-like object in musical acoustics, then, is characterized by the material properties of air, as well as

---

Numerical Sound Synthesis: Finite Difference Schemes and Simulation in Musical Acoustics Stefan Bilbao
© 2009 John Wiley & Sons, Ltd

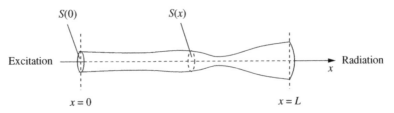

Figure 9.1   A 1D acoustic tube, with excitation at the left end, and radiated sound produced at the right end.

the function $S(x)$, representing, grossly, the cross-sectional area[1] of the tube at position x, where $x \in [0, L]$. See Figure 9.1.

A good model of the dynamics of such a tube, in terms of the variables $p(x, t)$ and $u(x, t)$, the pressure and volume velocity respectively at any point x and time t, may be derived through linearization of the equations of fluid dynamics:

$$\frac{S}{\rho c^2} p_t = -u_x \qquad \frac{\rho}{S} u_t = -p_x \qquad (9.1)$$

where ρ is density, and c is wave speed. The first equation above corresponds to pointwise conservation of mass and the second to conservation of momentum. From this first-order system, one may derive what is often referred to as Webster's equation [406]:

$$S\Psi_{tt} = c^2 (S\Psi_x)_x \qquad \text{with} \qquad p = \rho\Psi_t, \quad u = -S\Psi_x \qquad (9.2)$$

The assumptions which lead to this compact form are many: linearity, an equation of state of a special form relating pressure and density, and also that variations in u and p (and thus Ψ) are larger in scale than the tube width—these are all roughly valid in the case of the human voice, and in wind instruments except under high-amplitude playing conditions, or when bell flare becomes large. Such assumptions are discussed in detail by Benade and Jansson [32]. It is also worth pointing out that the first-order system (9.1), in the power conjugate variables p and u, is of the same form as the transmission line or telegrapher's equations [80], when p and u are replaced by a voltage and current, respectively, and the material constants by inductances and capacitances. The transmission line point of view is at the heart of many synthesis algorithms, including the Kelly–Lochbaum model [201], as well as digital waveguides and other scattering-based methods [344, 343]. For time domain synthesis, however, a second-order form such as (9.2) is perhaps simpler to deal with. Sometimes, as in the case of speech synthesis [280], Webster's equation is written directly in terms of the pressure variable through time differentiation of (9.2), but (9.2) is more fundamental, in that a correct energy balance is preserved—see Section 9.1.3.

Webster's equation appears in slightly different (equivalent) forms in the literature; one variant of particular interest is

$$\Phi_{tt} = c^2 (\Phi_{xx} - a(x)\Phi) \qquad \text{with} \qquad \Phi = \sqrt{S}\Psi, \quad a(x) = \frac{S_{xx}S - \frac{1}{2}S_x^2}{2S^2} \qquad (9.3)$$

Notice that the second spatial derivative term appears with a constant coefficient in this case; the quantity $a(x)$ is an expression for the curvature of the tube at x—see Problem 9.1.

---

[1] In fact, it represents the area of an isophase surface of the pressure distribution in the tube [38, 32].

Scaled form

It is again useful to scale variables, through the introduction of the dimensionless coordinate $x' = x/L$; another simplification is the scaling of the surface area function S, through a variable $S' = S(x)/S_0$, where S_0 is a reference surface area. A good choice of S_0 is $S_0 = S(0)$, so that the scaled area function always has $S'(0) = 1$. The dependent variables p and u in system (9.1) may also be scaled as $p' = p/\rho c^2$, $u' = u/c S_0$, to yield, after removing primes,

$$S p_t = -\gamma u_x \qquad \frac{1}{S} u_t = -\gamma p_x \qquad \text{for} \qquad x \in \mathbb{U} \tag{9.4}$$

whereas in the case of the 1D wave equation (see Section 6.1.2), $\gamma = c/L$.

The resulting systems corresponding to (9.2) and (9.3) are, after introducing the variables $\Psi' = \Psi/cL$ and $\Phi' = \Phi/cL\sqrt{S_0}$, and removing primes, of the form

$$S \Psi_{tt} = \gamma^2 (S \Psi_x)_x \qquad \Phi_{tt} = \gamma^2 (\Phi_{xx} - a(x)\Phi) \qquad \text{for} \qquad x \in \mathbb{U} \tag{9.5}$$

where, now, the non-dimensional variables p and u may be recovered from non-dimensional Ψ as

$$p = \frac{1}{\gamma} \Psi_t \qquad u = -S \Psi_x \tag{9.6}$$

9.1.1 Dispersive behavior

Webster's equation, like the equations defining the string of variable density and bar of variable cross-section (see Section 7.10), is linear and time invariant, but not more generally shift invariant. In this case the group and phase velocity are difficult to define properly, but one could attempt to examine such quantities on a "local" basis, assuming that the variation in $S(x)$ is not too large. The second form given in (9.5) is a good starting point. Suppose one examines a test solution of the form $\Phi(x, t) = e^{j\omega t + j\beta_{x_0} x}$, where the quantity β_{x_0} indicates a wavenumber in the neighborhood of x_0. One then arrives at the local dispersion relation

$$\omega^2 = \gamma^2 \left(\beta_{x_0}^2 + a(x_0) \right)$$

from which one can derive local phase and group velocities v_{ϕ, x_0} and v_{g, x_0}:

$$v_{\phi, x_0} = \gamma \frac{\sqrt{\beta_{x_0}^2 + a(x_0)}}{\beta_{x_0}} \qquad v_{g, x_0} = \gamma \frac{\beta_{x_0}}{\sqrt{\beta_{x_0}^2 + a(x_0)}}$$

Obviously, then, just as in the case of the ideal bar (see Section 7.1.1), wave propagation is dispersive to an extent which depends on the size of a. In contrast with the case of the bar, however, one may remark that, in the limit of high wavenumbers (or high frequencies), one has $v_{\phi, x_0}, v_{g, x_0} \to \gamma$, regardless of position x_0. Also, it is evident that dispersion will be greatest for low frequencies.

A graphical example is in order at this point—see Figure 9.2. The phenomenon of wave propagation in an acoustic tube is indeed dispersive—notice, however, that compared to the similar case of a pulse in a vibrating ideal bar, as illustrated in Figure 7.1, the transit of the pulse is relatively coherent. There is no cascade of ripples which precedes the main body of the pulse, but there is a pronounced low-frequency backscatter as the pulse passes through a constriction (i.e., a region of high tube curvature). This reflects the limiting behavior of the group and phase velocities, as discussed above. In addition, even as the pulse passes through the constriction, the overall speed of the pulse remains constant.

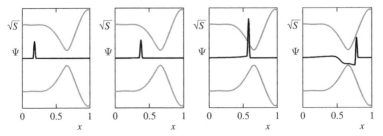

Figure 9.2   Dispersion of a pulse in an acoustic tube described by Webster's equation (9.5). The pulse travels from left to right, and the tube profile is shown as grey contours.

The distinctions among various types of spatial variation will have consequences on the numerical methods which result. One might expect that in this case, because the group and phase velocities approach a constant value, regardless of the extent of the spatial variation of the tube cross-section, stability analysis will be greatly simplified with respect to the case of the bar, and that computational complexity will also be independent of the tube cross-section[2]—these hunches are indeed borne out, and will be discussed in Section 9.1.5.

9.1.2   Cylinders and cones

Two special cases of the acoustic tube, often exploited in physical modeling sound synthesis for wind instruments, are the cylindrical tube and the conical tube. In the first case, one has a cross-sectional area function of the form $S(x) = 1$ (recall that the surface area function has been non-dimensionalized), and in the second, one has $S(x) = (1 + \epsilon x)^2$, for some constant $\epsilon > -1$, but normally assumed positive, so that the tube opens outward toward the bell. In both cases, Webster's equation can be reduced to the 1D wave equation, allowing the use of efficient digital waveguide structures.

For the cylinder, this is obvious from inspection of the first form given in (9.5). Because the digital waveguide in this case has been treated previously in Section 6.2.11, there is little more to be said here at the fundamental level, though there is, of course, a large body of techniques which has grown up around more sophisticated variations on the basic waveguide structure—see [334] and the references therein. A waveguide cylindrical tube model is a good first approximation to an instrument such as the clarinet, and was indeed the very first application of the technique in musical sound synthesis [327].

For the cone, the second form given in (9.5) is a better starting point. When $S(x) = (1 + \epsilon x)^2$, the curvature $a(x)$ vanishes, so that the 1D wave equation holds in the variable $\Phi = \sqrt{S}\Psi$. Thus, one is free to use a digital waveguide in order to propagate wavelike solutions which combine to form a physical variable Φ, and in an additional step, one must scale the output by $1/\sqrt{S}$ in order to obtain perceptually meaningful variables such as pressure and velocity. The existence of a digital waveguide form in the case of conical tubes expands considerably the utility of the waveguide technique in physical modeling synthesis, allowing for efficient solutions to be computed in the case of instruments such as the saxophone [314] and brass instruments with a conical bore. See [334] for much more on this topic.

---

[2] The astute reader here might argue that any conclusions reached regarding high-wavenumber limiting values of the phase and group velocity are in conflict with the very assumptions which lead to Webster's equation in the first place—and would be right! Here, as elsewhere, one must be very clear with oneself about which system one is taking to be "correct." This is a necessary choice if one wishes to arrive at any conclusions at all about the resulting numerical methods, which is, of course, the main goal here.

Much attention has been paid in the literature to tubes composed of cylindrical and conical segments, especially when each such segment is analyzed from an input/output (reflectance/
transmission) point of view [150, 232]—this has carried over, in a natural way, to synthesis
algorithms based on scattering structures [314, 368]. Here, however, where the emphasis is on
direct simulation, it is entirely sufficient to work with an arbitrary cross-section $S(x)$. Indeed, for
finite difference schemes, once one has made a choice of $S(x)$, the resulting algorithm is, from a
programming standpoint, completely insensitive to this choice. For this reason, and also because
cylindrical and conical waveguides are covered in great detail elsewhere, the present investigation
of these special cases will end here, though some comments will appear in Section 9.2.4, in which
finite difference schemes are related back to classic scattering structures used in articulatory speech
synthesis.

9.1.3   Energy and boundary conditions

An energy balance follows for Webster's equation. Proceeding immediately to the case of Webster's
equation defined over the unit interval $\mathcal{D} = \mathbb{U}$, one has, after taking an inner product with u_t,

$$\frac{d\mathfrak{H}}{dt} = \mathfrak{B} \quad \text{with} \quad \mathfrak{H} = \mathfrak{T} + \mathfrak{V} \quad \mathfrak{T} = \frac{1}{2}\|\sqrt{S}\Psi_t\|_{\mathbb{U}}^2 \quad \mathfrak{V} = \frac{\gamma^2}{2}\|\sqrt{S}\Psi_x\|_{\mathbb{U}}^2 \quad (9.7)$$

The energy $\mathfrak{H}$ is identical to that of the 1D wave equation, but in a norm weighted by S, and the
boundary term $\mathfrak{B}$ is given by

$$\mathfrak{B} = \gamma^2 \left(S(1)\Psi_t(1, t)\Psi_x(1, t) - S(0)\Psi_t(0, t)\Psi_x(0, t) \right)$$

The boundary terms represent the power supplied to the tube at the boundaries. (Recalling the
relationship between the derivatives of Ψ and the state variables p and u, from (9.6), both terms
are of the form pressure $\times$ volume velocity. Note that if one were to work with Webster's equation
written in terms of pressure instead of the potential function Ψ, this interpretation of the energy
balance would be lost.)

In musical instrument models, it is conventional to deal with the left boundary condition, at
$x = 0$, through an excitation mechanism—see Figure 9.1. For preliminary analysis of modes (see
the next section), it is useful to leave the excitation condition at $x = 0$, and assume a closed
tube end—in terms of the conditions discussed in Section 6.1.9, this amounts to $\Psi_x(0, t) = 0$, or a
Neumann (zero-velocity) condition. At the radiating end, there are various levels of approximation.
The simplest condition is of Dirichlet type (zero pressure), i.e.,

$$\Psi_t(1, t) = 0 \qquad \text{open end} \qquad (9.8)$$

Such a condition is, clearly, lossless. A more realistic condition which includes the effects of loss
and inertial mass has been introduced briefly in the case of the 1D wave equation in Section 6.1.9.
In the present case of Webster's equation in the variable Ψ, a simple form may be written as

$$\Psi_x(1, t) = -\alpha_1 \Psi_t(1, t) - \alpha_2 \Psi(1, t) \qquad \text{open end with inertia and loss} \qquad (9.9)$$

where the constants α_1 and α_2 depend on the tube parameters. In the case of a tube terminating
on an infinite plane, for instance, the constants may be calculated [14] as

$$\alpha_1 = \frac{1}{2(0.8216)^2\gamma} \qquad \alpha_2 = \frac{L}{0.8216\sqrt{S_0 S(1)/\pi}} \qquad (9.10)$$

which is useful in the case of, for example, vocal synthesis (these constants vary slightly in the literature—see [280] for different values). Another case of interest is the unflanged tube, for which the constants α_1 and α_2 take on moderately different values:

$$\alpha_1 = \frac{1}{4(0.6133)^2\gamma} \qquad\qquad \alpha_2 = \frac{L}{0.6133\sqrt{S_0 S(1)/\pi}} \qquad\qquad (9.11)$$

Normally, in the literature, this condition is expressed as an impedance relationship between pressure and volume velocity. The above condition corresponds, in the frequency domain, to a first-order rational approximation [280] to a more general complex function, which is a little different from the usual polynomial form [14, 136]—in simulation, one must take great care when approximating such an impedance, which must remain positive real in order for it to correspond to a passive termination (which a radiating end of a tube certainly is!). This is a fact well known to electrical network specialists [30, 407], but less so to musical acousticians. See Problems 9.2 and 9.3. Notice that in the low-frequency limit (i.e., as γ becomes small), the simpler boundary condition (9.8) is recovered. This condition also marks the appearance of another necessary dimensionless parameter, namely $L/\sqrt{S_0 S(1)/\pi}$, which is precisely the ratio of tube length to the radius at the radiating end.

Under condition (9.9) at the right end, and the Neumann condition at the left end, the energy balance for the tube becomes

$$\frac{d}{dt}(\mathfrak{H} + \mathfrak{H}_b) = -\mathfrak{Q}_b \le 0 \qquad \mathfrak{H}_b = \frac{\gamma^2\alpha_2 S(1)}{2}(\Psi(1, t))^2 \ge 0 \qquad \mathfrak{Q}_b = \gamma^2\alpha_1 S(1)(\Psi_t(1, t))^2 \ge 0$$

which again shows strictly dissipative behavior of a non-negative energy function, once the stored inertial energy for the termination is taken into account.

When the tube is driven at the left end (somehow!), the above energy balance is generalized to

$$\frac{d}{dt}(\mathfrak{H} + \mathfrak{H}_b) = -\mathfrak{Q}_b - \gamma^2\Psi_t(0, t)\Psi_x(0, t) = -\mathfrak{Q}_b + \gamma^3 p_{in}u_{in} \qquad\qquad (9.12)$$

where $p_{in}(t)$ and $u_{in}(t)$ are the non-dimensional pressure and volume velocity at the driving end.

9.1.4   Modes

As the tube cross-section $S(x)$ is arbitrary, there is, in general, no closed-form expression for the modes of a 1D acoustic tube. Still, before continuing to the more complete scenario involving radiation and connections to an excitation mechanism, it is useful to gain some insights about how the modes vary with the area function $S(x)$. One important observation is that, regardless of the tube cross-section $S(x)$, or of the type of boundary condition, the number of degrees of freedom N_m (twice the number of modes whose frequencies occur over a band $f \in [0, f_s/2]$, for a given f_s) will always be approximately

$$N_m \cong 2f_s/\gamma$$

which is unchanged from the case of the 1D wave equation, as discussed in Section 6.1.11. See Figure 9.3. It also remains true that computational complexity for numerical methods for Webster's equation is independent of the bore profile as well, as will be shown shortly.

This behavior of the modes of the acoustic tube in the limit of high frequencies follows from the analysis of phase and group velocity in Section 9.1.1. As noted earlier, however, dispersion can be a large effect at low frequencies, and one might expect that, as a result, there will be a considerable variation in the positions of the low modal frequencies depending on $S(x)$, which is indeed true—see Figure 9.3. This variation is of considerable timbral importance in musical acoustics, particularly in the case of the human voice, in which case the frequencies of the low modes become associated with so-called formants. See Section 9.2.2.

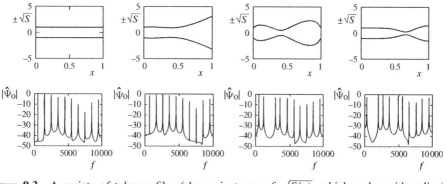

Figure 9.3 A variety of tube profiles (shown in terms of $\sqrt{S(x)}$, which scales with radius), at top, and typical distributions of harmonics for Webster's equation, under a Neumann (closed end) condition at $x = 0$ and a Dirichlet (open end) condition at $x = 1$. In this case, $\gamma = 2000$, and the average distance between harmonics is 1000 Hz, regardless of the tube profile, though a high degree of variation in the frequencies of the lowest modes is apparent. In this case, the tube is excited with a volume velocity impulse at the left end, and output is read at a point 0.2 of the way along the tube.

9.1.5 Finite difference schemes

As in the case of the bar of variable cross-section and the string of variable density (see Section 7.10), the number of choices of even simple varieties of finite difference schemes increases enormously, due to the spatial variation of the area function $S(x)$. It is again important to distinguish between the grid function S_l, which consists of sampled values of the continuous function $S(x)$ at locations $x = lh$, and a grid function $[S]_l$, which is some approximation to the continuous function $S(x)$, of an exact form yet to be determined—it is assumed that $[S]_l$ is a second-order accurate approximation to $S(x)$. A finite difference scheme for Webster's equation can then be written as

$$[S]\delta_{tt}\Psi = \gamma^2 \delta_{x+}((\mu_{x-}S)(\delta_{x-}\Psi)) \tag{9.13}$$

which may be expanded to give

$$\Psi_l^{n+1} = \frac{\lambda^2(S_{l+1}+S_l)}{2[S]_l}\Psi_{l+1}^n + \frac{\lambda^2(S_l+S_{l-1})}{2[S]_l}\Psi_{l-1}^n + \left(2 - \frac{\lambda^2(S_{l+1}+2S_l+S_{l-1})}{2[S]_l}\right)\Psi_l^n - \Psi_l^{n-1}$$

where $\lambda = \gamma k/h$ is again the Courant number for the scheme. It is straightforward to show that (9.13) is a second-order accurate approximation to Webster's equation. See Problem 9.4. The scheme above is similar to that presented in [381].

Energy analysis and boundary conditions

Energy analysis is direct, and similar to that carried out for the spatially varying systems in Section 7.10. Again, moving directly to the case $\mathcal{D} = \mathbb{U}_N$, the numerical energy balance is obtained, using familiar techniques, as

$$\delta_{t+}\mathfrak{h} = \mathfrak{b} \quad \text{with} \quad \mathfrak{h} = \mathfrak{t} + \mathfrak{v} \quad \mathfrak{t} = \frac{1}{2}\|\sqrt{[S]}\delta_{t-}\Psi\|_{\mathbb{U}_N}^2 \quad \mathfrak{v} = \frac{\gamma^2}{2}\langle(\mu_{x+}S)\delta_{x+}\Psi, e_{t-}\delta_{x+}\Psi\rangle_{\underline{\mathbb{U}_N}} \tag{9.14}$$

and where the boundary term is

$$\mathfrak{b} = \gamma^2(\delta_t.\Psi_N)(\mu_{x+}S_N)(\delta_{x+}\Psi_N) - \gamma^2(\delta_t.\Psi_0)(\mu_{x-}S_0)(\delta_{x-}\Psi_0)$$

These expressions are completely analogous to those which occur in the energy balance for the continuous system, in (9.7). Note, however, that the boundary term depends on values of the grid function S_l which are outside of $\mathbb{U}_N$—these values must be set judiciously.

First, consider boundary conditions corresponding to a closed tube end (left) and a radiating boundary (right):

$$\delta_{x-}\Psi_0 = 0 \qquad\qquad \delta_{x+}\Psi_N = -\alpha_1\delta_t.\Psi_N - \alpha_2\mu_t.\Psi_N \tag{9.15}$$

Under these conditions,

$$\mathfrak{b} = -\gamma^2\alpha_1(\delta_t.\Psi_N)^2 - \frac{\gamma^2\alpha_2}{2}\delta_{t+}(\mu_{t-}\Psi_N)^2$$

which are strictly dissipative, such that

$$\delta_{t+}(\mathfrak{h}+\mathfrak{h}_\mathfrak{b}) = -q_\mathfrak{b} \qquad \mathfrak{h}_\mathfrak{b} = \frac{\gamma^2(\mu_{x+}S_N)\alpha_2}{2}\mu_{t-}(\Psi_N)^2 \geq 0 \qquad q_\mathfrak{b} = \gamma^2(\mu_{x+}S_N)\alpha_1(\delta_t.\Psi_N)^2 \geq 0$$

Again, as in the context of lumped element/string modeling as described in Section 7.7, and following Rule of Thumb #3 given on page 192, a semi-implicit approximation to the radiating boundary condition has been employed and leads immediately to the non-negativity guarantees above.

Given that the scheme is strictly dissipative under boundary conditions (9.15), in order to arrive at a stability condition, it is as before necessary to find a condition under which the numerical energy is non-negative. The next step is to bound the potential energy term using various identities given in Chapter 5, and especially (5.32):

$$\mathfrak{v} = \frac{\gamma^2}{2}\langle(\mu_{x+}S)\delta_{x+}\Psi, e_{t-}\delta_{x+}\Psi\rangle_{\underline{\mathbb{U}_N}} \geq -\frac{\gamma^2 k^2}{8}\|\sqrt{\mu_{x+}S}\delta_{x+}\delta_{t-}\Psi\|^2_{\underline{\mathbb{U}_N}} \geq -\frac{\lambda^2}{2}\|\sqrt{\mu_{xx}S}\delta_{t-}\Psi\|^2_{\underline{\mathbb{U}_N}}$$

Now, a bound for the total energy $\mathfrak{h}$ is

$$\mathfrak{h} \geq \frac{1}{2}\|\sqrt{[S]}\delta_{t-}\Psi\|^2_{\mathbb{U}_N} - \frac{\lambda^2}{2}\|\sqrt{\mu_{xx}S}\delta_{t-}\Psi\|^2_{\mathbb{U}_N}$$

which is a quadratic form in the grid function $\delta_{t-}\Psi$. One arrives immediately at the following condition:

$$\lambda \leq \min\left(\sqrt{\frac{[S]}{\mu_{xx}S}}\right) \approx 1$$

Note that the stability condition is approximately independent of the area function $S(x)$; this is quite distinct from the cases of the string of variable density, or the bar of variable cross-sectional area. The reason for this distinction is that the limiting wave speed at high wavenumbers remains γ everywhere within the tube, though dispersion does intervene—see the comments in Section 9.1.1.

The numerical boundary conditions given in (9.15) are one possibility; through more extensive analysis (see Problem 9.5), centered, provably stable conditions may be derived:

$$\delta_{x.}\Psi_0 = 0 \qquad\qquad \delta_{x.}\Psi_N = -\alpha_1\delta_t.\Psi_N - \alpha_2\mu_t.\Psi_N \tag{9.16}$$

A special form

The approximate stability condition above may be made exact under a particular choice of $[S]$, i.e.,

$$[S] = \mu_{xx}S \qquad \longrightarrow \qquad \lambda \leq 1$$

This setting for [S] will thus be used in the remainder of this chapter. In this case, it is also worth looking at the special form of the recursion when $\lambda = 1$:

$$\Psi_l^{n+1} = \frac{2\,(S_{l+1} + S_l)}{S_{l-1} + 2S_l + S_{l+1}}\,\Psi_{l+1}^n + \frac{2\,(S_l + S_{l-1})}{S_{l-1} + 2S_l + S_{l+1}}\,\Psi_{l-1}^n - \Psi_l^{n-1} \tag{9.17}$$

This form, for which the value of Ψ at the grid point l, n has disappeared from the recursion, hints at the special case of the digital waveguide, as discussed in Section 6.2.11. And indeed it should, for this scheme may be viewed in terms of the Kelly–Lochbaum speech synthesis model, probably the first example of a scattering-based numerical method. See Section 9.2.4.

Numerical modes and accuracy

One of the interesting things about scheme (9.13) is that, in contrast with schemes for other spatially varying systems such as the arched bar (see Section 7.10), which are naturally very dispersive and thus require a good deal of improvement at the algorithmic level, it performs remarkably well.

As an example, consider the representative tube cross-sections shown in Figure 9.4. For a tube of relatively mild curvature, representing a wind instrument body, and for a typical value of γ, the modal frequencies calculated by scheme (9.13) are nearly exact; the deviation is far below the threshold of pitch discrimination. For larger values of γ, and for a more extreme cross-section, the scheme still performs very well. So good are the results that, in fact, it makes little sense to look for a better scheme, given that the inaccuracy in the assumptions underlying Webster's equation to begin with is probably much larger than the numerical inaccuracy introduced by the scheme.

Most interesting is the observation that the dispersive effects are evenly distributed over the audio spectrum—modal detuning does not deteriorate as one moves into the upper frequency range,

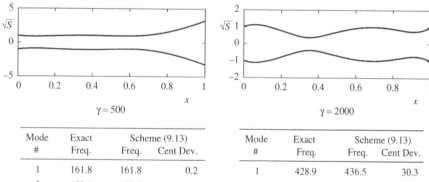

Mode #	Exact Freq.	Scheme (9.13) Freq.	Cent Dev.
1	161.8	161.8	0.2
2	459.1	459.0	−0.4
3	656.7	656.6	−0.4
4	890.6	890.5	−0.2
12	2880.3	2879.9	−0.2
13	3129.9	3129.4	−0.3

Mode #	Exact Freq.	Scheme (9.13) Freq.	Cent Dev.
1	428.9	436.5	30.3
2	1072.0	1092.1	32.2
3	2870.0	2851.7	−11.1
4	3829.9	3785.5	−20.1
12	11597.9	11483.5	−17.2
13	12586.8	12456.4	−18.0

Figure 9.4 Tube profiles, and comparisons between exact modal frequencies and numerical modes resulting from the use of scheme (9.13), running at 44.1 kHz, and for a value of λ chosen as close to 1 as possible. At left, a tube profile grossly characteristic of wind and brass instruments with a relatively low value of γ, and, at right, a more extreme profile resembling a vocal tract configuration, with a higher value of γ. In each case, a zero-velocity (Neumann) condition is used at the tube's left end and a zero-pressure (Dirichlet) condition at its right end. ("Exact" values for the modal frequencies are obtained by examining the same scheme for a very small time step, typically $k \leq 10^{-6}$.)

as it does in, for example, schemes for stiff systems such as bars (see Section 7.1.4). Qualitatively, the reason for this behavior may be viewed in terms of the limiting behavior of the phase and group velocities, as described in Section 9.1.1—physical dispersion (and thus mode detuning) is greatest at low frequencies, and in the high-frequency limit the solution behaves essentially like that of the 1D wave equation. But the difference scheme (9.13), from the standpoint of conventional accuracy analysis, performs well at low frequencies, and, at high frequencies, becomes equivalent to scheme (6.34) for the 1D wave equation, which is numerically exact, at least when $\lambda = 1$. These competing tendencies tend to cancel dispersion in a way that they do not in the case of a stiff system such as the ideal bar, where physical dispersion and numerical dispersion reinforce one another.

9.2   The vocal tract and speech synthesis

Vocal synthesis was, in some respects, the starting point for all digital sound synthesis; indeed, the first physical models of the vocal tract [201] were devised at roughly the same time that Max Mathews was performing his early experiments with computerized sound. From a modern perspective, one of the nice things about vocal synthesis is that it is very cheap, computationally; in fact, it is perhaps the least costly application that appears in this book. Even in the sluggish Matlab programming language, vocal synthesis using a 1D model is now far faster than real time—see the code example in Section A.10.

The body of work in speech synthesis is many times larger than that concerned with the totality of musical sound synthesis applications, and there is no hope of doing justice to this huge topic in a short section. The focus here is on methods derived from physical considerations of the dynamics of the vocal tract. The electrical transmission line analogy to the acoustic tube (see, e.g., [123]) has been and still is a popular means of representing the vocal tract, and has had a profound influence on the types of simulation strategies which have been employed—see, e.g., [280, 231]. The scattering interpretation, first introduced by Kelly and Lochbaum in 1962 [201], fits in very easily to the digital waveguide framework (indeed, it is a direct antecedent), and was one of the early applications of the technique to singing voice synthesis by Cook [90]. Waveguide meshes have also been used in 2D models of the vocal tract [247, 246].

Of course, it is always possible to view a scattering method in terms of finite difference methods, without employing wave concepts explicitly—see, e.g., [41], and in the present context of vocal synthesis, the article by Strube [345]—though relatively little work has been done on direct simulation in the absence of a circuit/scattering/transmission line point of view. Some exceptions are, for instance, [226], the recent work of van den Doel and Ascher [381], and, especially, the early treatment of Portnoff [273], far ahead of its time in 1973, which deals with Webster's equation directly, including many features discussed here, such as time variation and loss, leading to a finite difference approximation. On the other hand, modern articulatory speech systems (see, e.g., [125]) require a more detailed model of the vocal tract in 2D or 3D, and the transmission line analogy breaks down. Direct methods such as FDTD [96] or finite elements are really the only option—see [164] and the references therein.

9.2.1   Glottal excitation

In the discussion of Webster's equation in the previous section, the excitation is left unspecified. In the synthesis of vocal sounds, there are various ways of generating input. One, probably the most scientifically rigorous, is to make use of a model of the glottis itself. This is a large open research area, especially in the speech community—see, e.g., the early paper by Ishizaka and Flanagan [178] which set the stage for a large body of subsequent work. Usually, the glottis mechanism is modeled as a low-order mass–spring network, necessarily involving collisions; as such, most models are not extremely different from typical models of the reed or lips in woodwind and brass

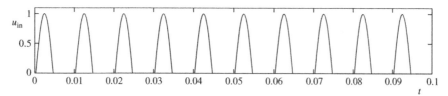

Figure 9.5 A crude synthetic glottal input waveform u_{in}, here with a period of 0.01s, and with a 45% duty cycle. This particular example has been generated by clipping of a sine wave.

instruments, which will appear shortly in Section 9.3. A standard approach in speech synthesis, and one which will be adopted here, is to assume minimal coupling between the glottis and the vocal tract [280], and to simply drive the tube with a specified waveform, normally expressed as an input volume velocity. There are many waveform types which pepper the literature—see, e.g., [124] for an overview; for the present purposes, the exact form of the input is not extremely important, but it should behave as a periodic series of pulses, with each pulse occupying a given fraction of the period (the duty cycle), corresponding to intervals during which the vocal folds are open. See Figure 9.5. Generally, the shorter the duty cycle, the more wide band the input spectrum. This is a prime example of the source-filter approach to sound synthesis—see Section 1.1.2.

Such a signal is useful in reproducing voiced (i.e., pitched) sounds; for unvoiced sounds, a noise signal can be employed, as a qualitative approximation to turbulence effects at the glottal opening. Such choices, however important they may be in practice, have no bearing on the operation or analysis of a source-filter physical model of the vocal tract, and will not be explored further here—for more information, see any standard text on speech synthesis [280], and refer to Programming Exercise 9.1, which explores some of the variations in source signal models, including vibrato effects, and the introduction of an amplitude envelope; these features are crucial, especially in singing voice synthesis.

In order to input any such waveform u_{in} into scheme (9.13), which is written in terms of Ψ, one may use (9.6) and then set, at grid point $l = 0$, using a time series u_{in},

$$\delta_{x\cdot}\Psi_0 = -u_{\text{in}} \qquad \longrightarrow \qquad \delta_{tt}\Psi_0 = \frac{2\gamma^2}{h}\left(\delta_{x+}\Psi_0 + \frac{\mu_{x-}S_0 u_{\text{in}}}{\mu_{xx}S_0}\right)$$

9.2.2 Formants

The well-known effect of the tube on the input excitation is to impose a formant structure in the frequency domain—see Figure 9.6. The formants are the tube resonances—due to the radiation condition, they possess a finite bandwidth and serve to emphasize spectral regions, allowing the listener to distinguish among various vowel sounds. For more on formant structure, and various vowel configurations, see Programming Exercise 9.2.

9.2.3 Wall vibration and loss

Webster's equation is somewhat more of an idealization in the case of the vocal tract than when applied to wind instruments; loss is an important consideration, especially when it comes to accurately reproducing formant bandwidths. The major source of loss, namely radiation, is already taken care of by the boundary condition (9.9). There are two other contributions, however, which will have a noticeable effect [339]. First, there is a viscous boundary layer at the walls of the tube; this leads to a root–frequency loss dependence, and is quite difficult to model properly using a time domain model—fractional derivatives intervene in an extension of Webster's equation. Such loss effects have indeed been approached in the context of wind instrument synthesis, in the scattering

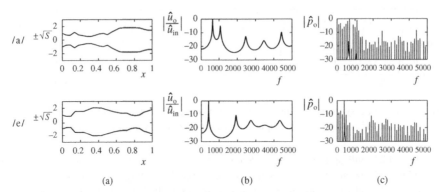

(a)   (b)   (c)

Figure 9.6   Formant structure. (a) Tube cross-sections corresponding to vocal tract configurations for the vowels /a/ and /e/ (Russian, adapted from measured data given in [280].). (b) Formant structure, here shown as a plot of the acoustic output velocity/input velocity transfer function $|\hat{u}_o/\hat{u}_{in}|$, and (c) spectrum of the output pressure waveform $|\hat{p}_o|$. In both cases, output is calculated using scheme (9.13) operating at 44.1 kHz. In (c), the input waveform is of the type shown in Figure 9.5, with a fundamental frequency of 100 Hz and with a 50% duty cycle.

framework [166, 2], but, as the topic is a rather large one, it will not be discussed further here. The other effect, that of vibration and damping in the tube walls themselves, is much more amenable to a finite difference treatment, as was carried out early on by Portnoff [273] and more recently by others [381].

A simple model of locally reacting walls [133] involves Webster's equation, coupled to another equation in a separate dimensionless function $w(x, t)$, which scales with the fractional change in local tube radius. In scaled form, and for a tube of cylindrical cross-section, the system may be written as

$$S\Psi_{tt} = \gamma^2 (S\Psi_x)_x - \epsilon S^{1/4}w_t \qquad w_{tt} + 2\sigma_0 w_t + \omega_0^2 w = \epsilon S^{1/4}\Psi_t \qquad (9.18)$$

Here, σ_0 and ω_0 are damping and fundamental frequency parameters for the vocal tract walls, and ϵ, a coupling coefficient, may be written as

$$\epsilon = c\sqrt{\frac{2\rho}{M}} \left(\frac{\pi}{S_0}\right)^{1/4}$$

where ρ is the density of air, c the speed of sound, and M the mass per unit area of the vocal tract walls. Notice in particular that the equation in w involves time derivatives only, simplifying analysis enormously. System (9.18) may easily be shown to be strictly dissipative—see Problem 9.6.

A finite difference scheme for this coupled system follows immediately:

$$\mu_{xx}S\delta_{tt}\Psi = \gamma^2\delta_{x+}((\mu_{x-}S)\delta_{x-}\Psi) - \epsilon S^{1/4}\delta_{t\cdot}w \qquad \delta_{tt}w + 2\sigma_0\delta_{t\cdot}w + \omega_0^2 w = \epsilon S^{1/4}\delta_{t\cdot}\Psi \quad (9.19)$$

This scheme, though apparently implicit, may be easily resolved into an explicit update in the grid functions w and Ψ—see Problem 9.7.

The main effect of using such a model is easily seen by examining the change to the formant structure, as shown in Figure 9.7. The lower formants are broadened, leading to a significant perceptual difference in resulting sound output, especially when the input pitch is changing, or under time-varying vocal tract conditions—in either case, if the lower formants are too sharply peaked, the resulting synthetic sound will ring unnaturally as frequency components approach a peak (or vice versa). See Programming Exercise 9.3.

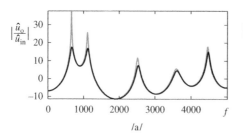

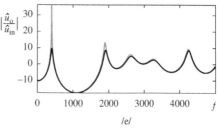

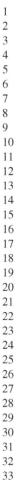

/a/   /e/

Figure 9.7 Formant structure, in decibels, for two vocal tract configurations (as illustrated in Figure 9.6), with a wall damping model (in black) and without (in grey). For the case of the wall model, curves are generated using scheme (9.19) for system (9.18), with parameters $\omega_0 = 0$, $\sigma_0 = 8125$, and $\epsilon = 2718$, and the sample rate is $f_s = 44.1\,\mathrm{kHz}$.

9.2.4 Scattering methods and finite difference schemes

As mentioned earlier (see Section 1.2), the Kelly–Lochbaum speech synthesis algorithm was perhaps the first instance of a sound-producing physical model. What is more, it is a scattering method, allying it to other methods such as digital waveguides and wave digital filters (see Section 1.2.4) which are heavily used in modern physical modeling synthesis for a great variety of musical instrument types. As has been shown in Section 6.2.11, however, digital waveguides may be rewritten as finite difference methods, and the same is true of scattering methods for voice synthesis.

A typical scattering structure may be arrived at in the following way. First, assume that the tube profile is approximated by a series of cylindrical segments, of length h, such that $N = 1/h$ is an integer (again, the tube is assumed to be of length 1). The left and right ends of the lth tube are located at $x = lh$ and $x = (l+1)h$, for $l = 0, \ldots, N-1$. See Figure 9.8. In each such tube, the system (9.4) is satisfied, with a constant surface area $[S]_{l+\frac{1}{2}}$, which is some approximation to $S(x)$ at the tube center. In this constant-coefficient case, the system may be reduced to the 1D wave equation, which admits traveling wave solutions, in both pressure and volume velocity. Thus,

$$p(x, t) = p^{(+)} + p^{(-)} \qquad \text{and} \qquad u(x, t) = u^{(+)} + u^{(-)} \tag{9.20}$$

where, as before, the superscripts $(+)$ and $(-)$ indicate solutions traveling to the right and left, respectively, with speed γ, according to

$$p^{(+)}(x, t) = p^{(+)}(x - \gamma\xi, t - \xi) \quad p^{(-)}(x, t) = p^{(-)}(x + \gamma\xi, t - \xi)$$
$$u^{(+)}(x, t) = u^{(+)}(x - \gamma\xi, t - \xi) \quad u^{(-)}(x, t) = u^{(-)}(x + \gamma\xi, t - \xi)$$

for some time-like parameter ξ. But the two sets of wavelike solutions are not independent—they are related by

$$u^{(\pm)} = [S]_{l+\frac{1}{2}} p^{(\pm)} \qquad \text{in } l\text{th tube}$$

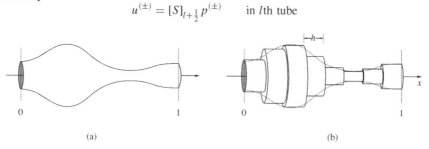

(a)   (b)

Figure 9.8 (a) An acoustic tube, and (b) a piecewise cylindrical approximation, where the length of each tube segment is $h = 1/N$, for some integer N (here, $N = 8$).

Here, $[S]_{l+\frac{1}{2}}$ serves as the admittance of the lth tube. Thus, one may choose to propagate pressure variables alone (though velocity variables are often used [280]).

Moving to the discrete setting, because the tube length is h, and the wave speed is uniformly γ over all tubes, one may take the unit delay to be $k = h/\gamma$. The wave variables, at times which are integer multiples n of k at the left and right ends of the lth tube, may then be labeled according to the junction (l) at which they are either impinging or scattered, and the side of the junction where they lie, as $p_{l,\text{left}}^{(+),n}$, $p_{l,\text{left}}^{(-),n}$, $p_{l,\text{right}}^{(+),n}$, and $p_{l,\text{right}}^{(-),n}$. A diagram is in order at this point—see Figure 9.9(a). In discrete form, wave propagation may be written as

$$p_{l,\text{left}}^{(+),n+1} = p_{l-1,\text{right}}^{(+),n} \qquad p_{l,\text{right}}^{(-),n+1} = p_{l+1,\text{left}}^{(+),n} \qquad (9.21)$$

purely in terms of what are now grid functions indexed by n and l.

The scattering operation follows, as in the case of wave digital filters, from equal pressures and velocities at the junctions between tubes. Between the lth and $(l+1)$th tubes, at junction index l, and at time step n, one must have

$$p_{l,\text{left}}^{(+),n} + p_{l,\text{left}}^{(-),n} = p_{l,\text{right}}^{(+),n} + p_{l,\text{right}}^{(-),n} \qquad [S]_{l-\frac{1}{2}}\left(p_{l,\text{left}}^{(+),n} - p_{l,\text{left}}^{(-),n}\right) = [S]_{l+\frac{1}{2}}\left(p_{l,\text{right}}^{(+),n} - p_{l,\text{right}}^{(-),n}\right)$$

This pair of equations may be rewritten in scattering form, relating junction outputs to inputs in terms of a single reflection parameter r_l:

$$\begin{bmatrix} p_{l,\text{left}}^{(-),n} \\ p_{l,\text{right}}^{(+),n} \end{bmatrix} = \underbrace{\begin{bmatrix} -r_l & 1+r_l \\ 1-r_l & r_l \end{bmatrix}}_{S_l} \begin{bmatrix} p_{l,\text{left}}^{(+),n} \\ p_{l,\text{right}}^{(-),n} \end{bmatrix} \qquad r_l = \frac{[S]_{l+\frac{1}{2}} - [S]_{l-\frac{1}{2}}}{[S]_{l+\frac{1}{2}} + [S]_{l-\frac{1}{2}}} \qquad (9.22)$$

Here, the scattering operation at junction l, again a 2×2 matrix multiplication, is indicated by S_l. The complete structure, involving the scattering operation above as well as the delays implied by (9.21), is illustrated in Figure 9.9(b).

Sometimes, in the setting of vocal synthesis, this scattering structure is extended to the time-varying case (see Section 9.2.5) by allowing the reflection coefficients r_l to depend on time, i.e., one uses r_l^n. It is worth noting that the nice stability properties of scattering networks disappear in this case [345], although if the rate of time variation is slow, there is little risk of such instability appearing. One idea is to make use of power-normalized scattering, as described in

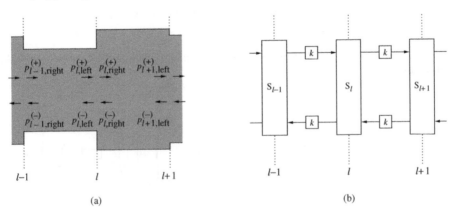

(a)   (b)

Figure 9.9   (a) A sequence of cylindrical tube sections, illustrating the traveling wave decomposition of the solution, and (b) the discrete scattering method, consisting of scattering junctions (labeled S_l) interleaved with pairs of digital unit sample (duration k) delay lines.

Section 3.3.3 in the context of wave digital filters, rendering each scattering matrix orthogonal, regardless of time variation in r_l. The problem here, however, is that such a lossless structure cannot possibly solve Webster's equation, for the simple reason that Webster's equation is *not* lossless in the time-varying case. The deeper issue is that, while scattering methods allow for very robust algorithm design (indeed, numerical energy conservation, described at great length in this book, is an in-built property of such methods), it may not always be clear what system they solve when one begins to fiddle with them in the absence of an underlying physical model!

Equivalence with a difference scheme

Just as in the case of digital waveguides (see Section 6.2.11), it is not difficult to show that this scattering structure is indeed equivalent to a finite difference scheme. Beginning from the definition of the pressure at the junction at location l (say on the left side), one may proceed as follows:

$$p_l^{n+1} \overset{(9.20)}{=} p_{l,\text{left}}^{(+),n+1} + p_{l,\text{left}}^{(-),n+1}$$

$$\overset{(9.22)}{=} (1 - r_l)p_{l,\text{left}}^{(+),n+1} + (1 + r_l)p_{l,\text{right}}^{(-),n+1}$$

$$\overset{(9.21)}{=} (1 - r_l)p_{l-1,\text{right}}^{(+),n} + (1 + r_l)p_{l+1,\text{left}}^{(-),n}$$

$$\overset{(9.20)}{=} (1 - r_l)p_{l-1}^{n} + (1 + r_l)p_{l+1}^{n} - (1 - r_l)p_{l-1,\text{right}}^{(-),n} - (1 + r_l)p_{l+1,\text{left}}^{(+),n}$$

$$\overset{(9.21)}{=} (1 - r_l)p_{l-1}^{n} + (1 + r_l)p_{l+1}^{n} - (1 - r_l)p_{l,\text{left}}^{(-),n-1} - (1 + r_l)p_{l,\text{right}}^{(+),n-1}$$

$$\overset{(9.20)}{=} (1 - r_l)p_{l-1}^{n} + (1 + r_l)p_{l+1}^{n} - p_l^{n-1}$$

Given the definition of r_l, from (9.22), this may be rewritten in terms of the area function $[S]$ as

$$p_l^{n+1} = \frac{2[S]_{l+\frac{1}{2}}}{[S]_{l-\frac{1}{2}} + [S]_{l+\frac{1}{2}}} p_{l+1}^{n} + \frac{2[S]_{l-\frac{1}{2}}}{[S]_{l-\frac{1}{2}} + [S]_{l+\frac{1}{2}}} p_{l-1}^{n} - p_l^{n-1}$$

and, when $[S]$ is defined as $[S]_{l+\frac{1}{2}} = (S_l + S_{l+1})/2$, this is exactly the special form of scheme (9.13), when $\lambda = 1$, as given in (9.17). It is, however, expressed here in terms of a pressure variable instead of Ψ, the potential.

Computational requirements

There is very little difference, in terms of computational complexity, between the Kelly–Lochbaum structure and difference scheme (9.17). Both require $2N$ units of memory—in the difference scheme, to hold the previous two grid functions in Ψ, and for the scattering structure, to hold the values in the delay elements as per Figure 9.9(b). The operation count is also very similar, depending on the implementation—see Problem 9.8.

It is important to point out, however, that the Kelly–Lochbaum structure requires that an integer number of segments of length h subdivide the unit interval, whereas scheme (9.13) in general does not; this allows for a much better tuning of formant frequencies for the difference scheme. It is possible to extend a scattering structure, using extra self-terminated delay elements at each junction, in order to account for such effects (see [41]), but at the expense of introducing three-port scattering. A "signal processing" approach, popular in digital waveguide modeling, is to make use of fractional delay terminations to the scattering structure, which are essentially all-pass structures—see, e.g., [372, 215].

A compromise between performance and efficiency, for scattering methods, is to use a more crude approximation to the vocal tract shape, employing multiple sample delay waveguides and

fewer scattering junctions, where all calculation is consolidated—see, e.g., [88], where such a
technique was employed in one of the first instances of real-time singing voice synthesis; though a
useful structure, it should be kept in mind that, even at high audio sample rates such as 44.1 kHz,
the total number of tube segments necessary even for a full simulation is roughly 20; this leads to
very low computational costs by today's standards. The need for such efficient structures in vocal
synthesis is thus much less urgent than it once was. When applied to wind instrument synthesis,
which involves much longer (and less dispersive) tubes, it is a much more justifiable simplification,
and a very powerful one indeed.

9.2.5 Time-varying vocal tract models

The production of any interesting vocal sounds necessarily requires some temporal variation of
the properties of the vocal tract—in standard models, the variation is consolidated in the surface
area function S, which becomes a function $S(x, t)$ of space and time. (Another type of variation,
and one which will not be explored here, is that of change in length of the vocal tract itself
[341, 371, 381].) This is the first example in this book of a time-varying system, though it remains
linear—see the classification of musical systems given in Section 5.1.1. In some ways, the analysis
of numerical methods for linear time-varying systems can be more difficult than for fully nonlinear
systems (at least those of autonomous type, for which time dependence only intervenes through
the dependent variable itself). The reason for this is that the conservation properties are obscured
by the assumption of time-varying coefficients—in reality, such a system is being driven by an
(unmodeled) source. As such, energy is injected into the system. In practice, however, the rate of
change of the area function is quite slow, and numerical schemes do perform as expected. Because
the system remains linear, there is no issue of uniqueness/existence for difference schemes as
occurs in the nonlinear setting.

A time-varying generalization of the first-order system (9.4) has been presented by various
authors [280, 344]. In non-dimensionalized form, it is

$$(Sp)_t = -\gamma u_x \qquad \left(\frac{u}{S}\right)_t = -\gamma p_x$$

where scaling has been carried out exactly as in the time-invariant case. (One must be careful
here in the choice of S_0, the reference area, which is not $S(0, t)$, but a constant such as $S(0, 0)$.)
A time-varying version of Webster's equation follows as

$$(S\Psi_t)_t = \gamma^2 (S\Psi_x)_x \tag{9.23}$$

See [381] for a different form of Webster's equation in the time-varying case, as well as a description of finite difference strategies. An energy analysis of this equation is useful in order to see the
effect of the time variation, which may be viewed as a driving term—see Problem 9.9. There are,
predictably, many possible discretizations of (9.23). Here is one rather well-behaved explicit form:

$$\delta_{t+} ((\mu_{t-}\mu_{xx}S)\delta_{t-}\Psi) = \gamma^2\delta_{x+} ((\mu_{tt}\mu_{x-}S)\delta_{x-}\Psi)$$

Stability, for this scheme, is difficult to show, at least using the present energy framework—frozen
coefficient analysis [342] is one other option. There are other, safer, and provably stable schemes
(see Problem 9.10), but this one suffices for a demonstration.

Formant transitions

The interest in a time-varying model is obvious—one may begin to approximate intelligible speech,
or singing. Loosely speaking, one may consider the resonances of the vocal tract, or formants, to

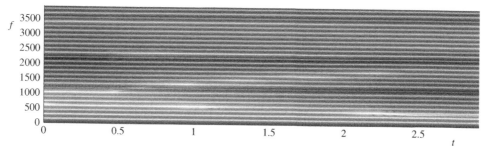

Figure 9.10 Spectrogram of output from the time-varying scheme (9.23), under a transition from an /a/ configuration to an /e/, effected between $t = 0.5$ and $t = 2.5$ s. The tube profiles shown in Figure 9.6 are interpolated linearly. The sample rate is 44.1 kHz, and the input is a waveform of the type shown in Figure 9.5, with a fundamental frequency of 120 Hz.

move when the tract configuration is changed—see Figure 9.10 for an example. Much has been written on this topic—see, e.g., [280]. While, from a numerical standpoint, there is not a lot to say here, it should be stressed that the precise trajectory of the change in vocal tract configurations is quite important in determining its perceptual correlate, the formant transitions. In the example above, the transition is effected in the most crude manner imaginable, i.e., by linearly interpolating between two configurations over the duration of the transition, and the result is only marginally natural sounding. The interested reader may wish to experiment with this—see Programming Exercise 9.4.

9.3   Reed wind instruments

Physical modeling synthesis for reed instruments has seen a relatively large amount of activity, and there are a great variety of methods—all, however, owe a great deal to the theoretical treatment of the musical self-sustained oscillator due to McIntyre et al. [236], which cast the standard model of the reed/bore interaction in a form which suggested efficient time domain digital realizations. The reed is modeled as a lumped oscillator and the bore in terms of its impulse response (or Green's function). Such time domain techniques (to be distinguished from the time–space methods employed here—see the footnote on page 17), written as a lumped nonlinear system coupled to an input/output model of the bore characterized by an impulse response, have been widely investigated—see, e.g., [25], and, for applications in synthesis, [158, 159].

Slightly later, and probably independently, Smith realized that such an impulse response could be efficiently generated for certain bore profiles by using delay lines—thus the first application of digital waveguides to synthesis [327]. For a good introduction to wave-based methods such as wave digital filters and digital waveguides for wind instruments, see [390, 388] and the references which appear in Section 1.2.3.

More closely allied to the finite difference exposition which follows here, adapted from [45], is the "K"-variable formulation of Avanzini and Rocchesso [15], as well as purely time domain characterizations of the reed mechanism using wave digital filters [41].

9.3.1   The single reed

The reed mechanism has been very briefly introduced, in an abstract form, in Section 4.3.2. A relatively standard approach, for the single reed, is to treat it as a lumped linear oscillator,

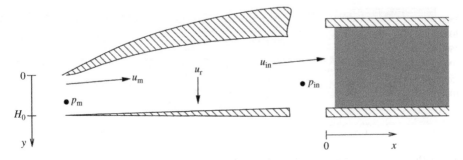

Figure 9.11 Illustration of a single reed model.

driven by a pressure drop across the mouthpiece—see Figure 9.11. The equation of motion, in dimensional form, is

$$\frac{d^2y}{dt^2} + 2\sigma_0 \frac{dy}{dt} + \omega_0^2(y - H_0) - \frac{\omega_1^{\alpha+1}}{H_0^{\alpha-1}}\left(|[y]^-|\right)^\alpha = -\frac{S_r p_\Delta}{M_r} \tag{9.24}$$

Here, $y(t)$ is the displacement of the reed relative to an equilibrium position H_0, M_r is the reed mass, S_r an effective surface area of the reed, ω_0 the resonant frequency, and σ_0 a damping parameter. The nonlinear term involving the coefficient ω_1 models the collision of the reed with the mouthpiece. It becomes active when $y < 0$, and acts as a one-sided repelling force, modeled as a power law nonlinearity of exponent α—see Section 4.2.2. Here, $[y]^- = (y - |y|)/2$. The reed displacement y is thus permitted to be negative. This term, inspired by collision models used in hammer–string dynamics [75], is the sole distinguishing feature of the model, which is otherwise identical to that which appears in the literature [159, 202, 350, 100, 389, 16].

The more important nonlinearity involves the pressure difference p_Δ across the mouthpiece, defined as

$$p_\Delta = p_m - p_{in}$$

where $p_m(t)$ is the mouth pressure (which is external control data, supplied by the player) and $p_{in}(t)$ the pressure at the entrance to the acoustic tube. This pressure difference is related to the flow in the mouthpiece u_m through Bernoulli's law,

$$u_m = w[y]^+ \sqrt{\frac{2|p_\Delta|}{\rho}} \operatorname{sign}(p_\Delta) \tag{9.25}$$

where, here, w is the width of the reed channel. The flow is non-zero only when the reed is not in contact with the mouthpiece, or when $y > 0$. As such, the quantity y^+ is given by $[y]^+ = (y + |y|)/2$. Neglected here is an inertia term—see, e.g., [136]. The square root dependence of flow on velocity could be generalized to a power law [17] with few resulting complications in the discretization procedure to be outlined below.

The flow variables themselves are related by a conservation law

$$u_{in} = u_m - u_r$$

where u_{in} is the flow entering the acoustic tube, and where u_r is related to reed displacement y by

$$u_r = S_r \frac{dy}{dt}$$

In order to facilitate the eventual coupling with an acoustic tube, defined by Webster's equation, it is useful to introduce scaled or non-dimensional variables as follows:

$$y' = \frac{y}{H_0} - 1 \qquad p'_. = \frac{p_.}{\rho c^2} \qquad u'_. = \frac{u_.}{c S_0}$$

for any pressure variable $p_.$ or velocity variable $u_.$, where c, ρ, and S_0 are the wave speed, air density, and left-hand cross-sectional area for the tube. When inserted in the above equations (and primes subsequently removed) the following system results:

$$\frac{d^2 y}{dt^2} + 2\sigma_0 \frac{dy}{dt} + \omega_0^2 y - \omega_1^{\alpha+1} \left(|[y+1]^-| \right)^\alpha = -\mathcal{Q} p_\Delta \qquad (9.26a)$$

$$p_\Delta = p_m - p_{in} \qquad (9.26b)$$

$$u_m = \mathcal{R}[y+1]^+ \sqrt{|p_\Delta|} \, \text{sign}(p_\Delta) \qquad (9.26c)$$

$$u_{in} = u_m - u_r \qquad (9.26d)$$

$$u_r = \mathcal{S} \frac{dy}{dt} \qquad (9.26e)$$

where

$$\mathcal{Q} = \frac{\rho c^2 S_r}{M_r H_0} \qquad \mathcal{R} = \sqrt{2} \frac{w H_0}{S_0} \qquad \mathcal{S} = \frac{S_r H_0}{c S_0} \qquad (9.27)$$

9.3.2   Energy balance

An energy balance follows immediately from system (9.26). Multiplying (9.26a) by dy/dt leads to

$$\frac{d\mathfrak{H}_r}{dt} = -\mathfrak{Q}_r - \mathcal{Q} \frac{dy}{dt} p_\Delta$$

where $\mathfrak{H}_r$, the stored energy of the reed (including collision effects), and the reed dissipation $\mathfrak{Q}_r$ are

$$\mathfrak{H}_r = \frac{1}{2} \left(\frac{dy}{dt} \right)^2 + \frac{\omega_0^2}{2} y^2 + \frac{(\omega_1 |[y+1]^-|)^{\alpha+1}}{\alpha+1} \geq 0 \qquad \mathfrak{Q}_r = 2\sigma_0 \left(\frac{dy}{dt} \right)^2 \geq 0$$

But, using the other members of system (9.26), one may continue as

$$\frac{d\mathfrak{H}_r}{dt} \overset{(9.26e)}{=} -\mathfrak{Q}_r - \frac{\mathcal{Q}}{\mathcal{S}} u_r p_\Delta \overset{(9.26d)}{=} -\mathfrak{Q}_r - \frac{\mathcal{Q}}{\mathcal{S}} u_m p_\Delta + \frac{\mathcal{Q}}{\mathcal{S}} u_{in} p_\Delta$$

$$\overset{(9.26c)}{=} -\mathfrak{Q}_r - \frac{\mathcal{Q} \mathcal{R}}{\mathcal{S}} [y+1]^+ |p_\Delta|^{3/2} + \frac{\mathcal{Q}}{\mathcal{S}} u_{in} p_\Delta$$

$$\overset{(9.26b)}{=} -\mathfrak{Q}_r - \mathfrak{Q}_m + \frac{\mathcal{Q}}{\mathcal{S}} u_{in} p_m - \frac{\mathcal{Q}}{\mathcal{S}} u_{in} p_{in}$$

where

$$\mathfrak{Q}_m = \frac{\mathcal{Q} \mathcal{R}}{\mathcal{S}} [y+1]^+ |p_\Delta|^{3/2} \geq 0$$

is the loss corresponding to the pressure drop in the mouthpiece.

At this point, one may note that the term $u_{in} p_{in}$ corresponds, in the coupled tube system with a radiating boundary condition, from (9.12) to

$$u_{in} p_{in} = \frac{1}{\gamma^3} \frac{d(\mathfrak{H} + \mathfrak{H}_b)}{dt} + \frac{1}{\gamma^3} \mathfrak{Q}_b$$

Thus, one arrives at

$$\frac{d}{dt}\left(\mathfrak{H}_r + \frac{\mathcal{Q}}{S\gamma^3}(\mathfrak{H} + \mathfrak{H}_b)\right) = -\mathfrak{Q}_r - \mathfrak{Q}_m - \frac{\mathcal{Q}}{S\gamma^3}\mathfrak{Q}_b + \frac{\mathcal{Q}}{S}u_{in}p_m \tag{9.28}$$

which relates the rate of change of the total energy stored in the reed, the acoustic tube, and at the radiating end of the tube to the various loss mechanisms and the supplied power. Here, it is clear that under zero-input (or transient) conditions, or when $p_m = 0$, the system is strictly dissipative—one may bound the various state variables corresponding to the tube and reed accordingly. Interestingly, under driven conditions, it is not clear that one may find a corresponding bound on the state in terms of p_m; this is in direct contrast to the situation for linear systems—see, e.g., the case of the driven SHO in Section 3.6. See Problem 9.11 for some exploration of this.

9.3.3   Finite difference schemes

A difference scheme for Webster's equation, including the radiating boundary condition, has been presented in Section 9.1.5. What remains is to devise a scheme for the reed system (9.26), and to couple it to the scheme for Webster's equation (9.13) at its left boundary. A simple scheme for the harmonic oscillator-like system (9.26a) is rather similar to those which are employed in Chapters 3 and 4:

$$\delta_{tt}y + 2\sigma_0\delta_{t\cdot}y + \omega_0^2\mu_{t\cdot}y - \omega_1^{\alpha+1}(\mu_{t\cdot}(y+1))\left(|[y+1]^-|\right)^{\alpha-1} = -\mathcal{Q}p_\Delta \tag{9.29}$$

Notice the use of semi-implicit approximations for both the linear reed stiffness term and the collision term—such an approach has been described at length in Chapter 4, and leads to very robust numerical behavior. The other members of system (9.26) involve no time differentiation, and thus may be left as they are, with the exception of (9.26e), which may be discretized as

$$u_r = S\delta_{t\cdot}y \tag{9.30}$$

In order to connect the difference scheme above to scheme (9.13) for Webster's equation, at $x = 0$, one may use

$$p_{in} = \frac{1}{\gamma}\delta_{t\cdot}\Psi_0 \qquad u_{in} = -\delta_{x\cdot}\Psi_0 \tag{9.31}$$

Implementation

The finite difference update (9.29), along with the other time-independent members of system (9.26), as well as (9.30), coupled with scheme (9.13) for Webster's equation, is at first sight rather complex. Notice that updating of y according to (9.29) depends on p_Δ, and thus eventually on y itself; it also depends on (as yet unknown) values of Ψ, which themselves depend on y! Furthermore, the coupling is nonlinear. Interestingly, in this case, a fully explicit solution is available, as will be detailed below.

Beginning from (9.29) at time step n, one may employ identities (2.7g) and (2.7h) in order to isolate $\delta_{t\cdot}y$ and p_Δ as

$$a_1^n + a_2^n\delta_{t\cdot}y^n = -\mathcal{Q}p_\Delta^n$$

where the time series a_1^n and a_2^n depend only on previously computed values of y. In addition, by virtue of the use of semi-implicit discretizations of the stiffness and collision terms, one also has $a_2^n \geq 0$. Then, using (9.30), (9.26d), and (9.26c), one ends up with a relationship between p_Δ and u_{in}:

$$p_\Delta^n + b_1^n\sqrt{|p_\Delta^n|}\,\text{sign}(p_\Delta^n) + b_2^n = b_3^n u_{in}^n \tag{9.32}$$

where $b_1^n \geq 0$ and $b_3^n \geq 0$ again depend only on known values of the grid function y.

Turning now to scheme (9.13) at the connection point with the reed model, using identity (2.7g), the scheme may be rewritten as

$$\frac{2(\mu_{xx} S_0)}{k} \left(\delta_{t \cdot} \Psi_0^n - \delta_{t-} \Psi_0^n \right) = \frac{2\gamma^2}{h} \left(\mu_{xx} S_0 \delta_{x+} \Psi_0^n - \mu_{x-} S_0 \delta_{x \cdot} \Psi_0^n \right)$$

Employing (9.31), as well as (9.26b), this may be written as

$$u_{\text{in}}^n = c_1^n p_\Delta^n + c_2^n \tag{9.33}$$

where c_1^n and $c_2^n \geq 0$ again depend on previously computed values of the grid function Ψ, as well as the external control signal p_{m}^n. Finally, (9.32) and (9.33) may be combined to given a single equation in p_Δ:

$$|p_\Delta| + d_1^n \sqrt{|p_\Delta|} + \frac{d_2^n}{\text{sign}(p_\Delta)} = 0 \tag{9.34}$$

where $d_1^n \geq 0$ and d_2^n are known. In order to have a real solution, one must have $\text{sign}(p_\Delta^n) = -\text{sign}(d_2^n)$—the above equation may then be solved uniquely in $\sqrt{|p_\Delta^n|}$.

Given that values of the grid function Ψ and the time series y are known up through time step n, the following order of operations is thus implied:

- Calculate p_Δ^n through the solution of (9.34).
- Calculate y^{n+1} through (9.29).
- Calculate p_{in}^n using (9.26b) and the known value of p_{m}^n.
- Calculate $\delta_{t \cdot} \Psi_0^n$, and thus Ψ_0^{n+1}, using the first of the boundary conditions (9.31).
- Calculate the remaining values of Ψ_l^{n+1}, $l > 0$, using scheme (9.13).

At this point, the calculation cycle is repeated. It is important to note that this explicit computability of the solution depends on the use of the semi-implicit approximations in (9.29); such computability (or modularity) is often reported to be a benefit of scattering methods such as wave digital filters [279, 190] and other wave-based methods [389]. Here, however, it has been carried out without any explicit reference to wave variables. See Problem 9.12 and Programming Exercise 9.5.

9.3.4   Self-sustained oscillation

The reed–bore system exhibits self-sustained oscillations, just as in the case of the bow–string interaction, as discussed in Section 7.4. See Figure 9.12 which shows the envelope of the output pressure waveform from the reed–bore model in a clarinet configuration, under various constant input pressures p_{m}, as indicated.

9.3.5   Reed beating effects

A very important effect, perceptually, is that of the collision, or beating, of the reed against the mouthpiece lay. In this lumped model, when the reed is in contact with the lay, it undergoes an elastic collision, and the flow u_{m} is identically zero. It is instructive to examine both the reed displacement and the output pressure spectrum under such conditions—see Figure 9.13. The reed displacement waveform becomes more square, with a Gibbs-like oscillatory effect at the leading edge of each period—note that the non-dimensional reed displacement takes on values <-1; the extent of such "penetration" may be controlled through the choice of ω_1 and α, but the general results are in agreement with other published simulation results (see, e.g., [200]). The output spectrum exhibits a marked relative increase in the strength of high-frequency components,

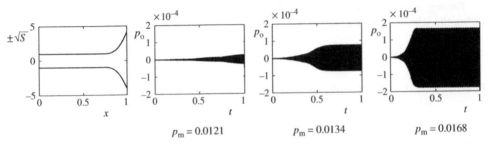

$$p_m = 0.0121 \qquad p_m = 0.0134 \qquad p_m = 0.0168$$

Figure 9.12   Self-sustained oscillation in the reed–bore model. At left, a non-dimensional clarinet-like bore profile, and in the three subsequent plots the output pressure waveform under increasing values of non-dimensional input pressure p_m, as indicated. At $p_m = 0.0121$, the model is at the threshold of oscillation, and as the pressure becomes higher, the note onset time becomes shorter. The reed model parameters, in this case, are, referring to system (9.26), $M_r = 3.37 \times 10^{-6}$ kg, $\omega_0 = 23\,250$ rad/s, $\sigma_0 = 1500$ s^{-1}, $H_0 = 4 \times 10^{-4}$ m, $\omega_1 = 316$, $\alpha = 3$, $S_r = 1.46 \times 10^{-4}$ m^2, and, for the bore, $L = 0.664$ m and $S_0 = 1.72 \times 10^{-4}$ m^2.

leading to a brighter sound [389]. Indeed, the realism of the resulting sound is greatly enhanced by such a beating model.

On the other hand, the lumped reed model is not wholly sufficient to capture the full behavior of such a system—in reality, the reed may not collide with the lay per se, but can curl up progressively against it. Clearly a one-mass model cannot represent such behavior, and a more refined model of the reed might allow for more degrees of freedom, or even distributed (i.e., bar-like) behavior. See, e.g., [16], where finite difference methods are used to simulate a distributed model of a reed.

9.3.6   Time-varying reed equilibrium displacement

In the model given in (9.26), there is a single external control signal, the mouth pressure p_m. In more elaborate models, there are often others—one perceptually salient one is the time variation

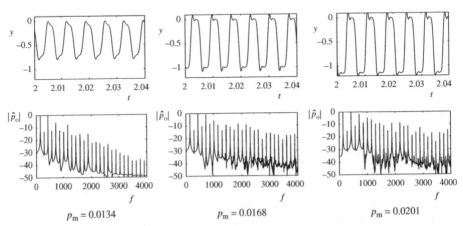

$$p_m = 0.0134 \qquad p_m = 0.0168 \qquad p_m = 0.0201$$

Figure 9.13   Beating effects in the reed model. Top, non-dimensional reed displacement y; bottom, non-dimensional output pressure spectrum $|\hat{p}_o|$, in decibels. Here, the bore and reed parameters are for a clarinet-like model, as in the caption to Figure 9.12, and scheme (9.29) is used, at a sample rate of 44.1 kHz. The input pressure waveform p_m is a constant, of a value indicated below the plots.

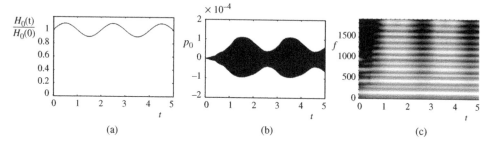

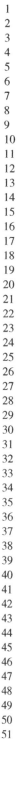

Figure 9.14 Time variation of the reed equilibrium displacement, for a reed–bore system of parameters as given in the caption to Figure 9.12: (a) the time variation of the displacement itself, plotted as $H_0(t)/H_0(0)$; (b) the resulting envelope of the non-dimensional pressure output; and (c) its spectrogram.

of the equilibrium displacement H_0 itself, due to increased embouchure force. The use of such a time-varying control $H_0(t)$ has been employed in the synthesis model of Guillemain et al. [159], and leads to important variations in timbre and loudness in the resulting sound output—see Figure 9.14.

From a systems point of view, variation of $H_0(t)$ is of a very different nature from that of the mouth pressure p_m, and is similar in many respects to time variation in the vocal tract cross-sectional area (see Section 9.2.5). As might be expected, a full analysis is very complex, in that though H_0 is treated as a parameter, variations are capable of injecting energy into the system; furthermore, it is used as a scaling parameter in arriving at the non-dimensional system (9.26). Given that the rate of change of H_0 will normally be very slow compared to audio rates, it seems reasonable to neglect such a complete analysis, and allow the parameters Q, R, and S to be slowly time varying as well. A choice such as this allows the difference scheme developed in Section 9.3.3 to continue to be used, though one must be alert to the possibility of instability if one begins varying H_0 at faster rates. See Programming Exercise 9.6.

9.3.7 Squeaks and multiphonics

Even with this very simple model of a single-reed wind instrument, it is possible to create a very wide variety of sounds, using merely a constant mouth pressure p_m and reed equilibrium displacement H_0, and crude bore profiles such as cylinders and cones. Indeed, the tones can evolve over long durations, warble, squeak, and exhibit a "multiphonic" character [18] (though this word is often used in conjunction with specialized fingerings—toneholes will be introduced in the next section). Indeed, the sounds generated, when one is first experimenting with such an algorithm, often resemble those made by beginners. This is exactly what one should expect from a true physical model—one must learn to play it.

For some typical (though somewhat artificial) examples of such complex timbres, see the spectrograms given in Figure 9.15. In the three cases, all that is altered is the bore profile (from cylindrical to conical) and the constant mouth pressure. At top is a typical clarinet-like note produced using a cylindrical bore, consisting of odd-numbered partials—note the rise time to self-sustained oscillation, as described earlier in Section 9.3.4. In the middle panel, the bore has been chosen conical, corresponding, very roughly, to that of a saxophone. At the indicated blowing pressure, rather complex behavior is observed over perhaps 3 s. Oscillatory behavior is set up initially, now with evenly spaced harmonics, followed by a stuttering tone occurring between 1.5 and 2 s, followed by a final settling down to a tone of a pitch slightly lower than that at the beginning of the sound. The warbling portion of the sound, in particular, is precisely a multiphonic.

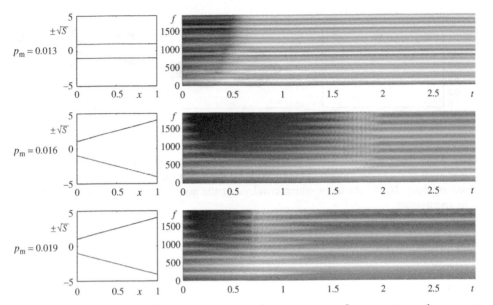

Figure 9.15 Bore profiles (left) and spectrograms of output pressure, for constant mouth pressures, as indicated. In all cases, the other system parameters are as in the caption to Figure 9.12. Results generated using scheme (9.29), at 44.1 kHz.

For the same configuration, raising the blowing pressure yields a very different behavior, as shown at bottom—the pitch of the tone makes a jump to the octave.

As one can imagine, the space of possible timbres becomes far larger when toneholes (to be discussed shortly) are introduced.

9.3.8   Toneholes

The tonehole is the primary means by which pitch changes are effected in a reed wind instrument. In musical acoustics, it is often referred to as a branched side tube, of a given radius b and height[3] τ, which may be open, closed, or partly open—see Figure 9.16(a). The obvious effect of an open hole is to change the effective tube length, and thus the sounding pitch of the wind instrument, to a degree which depends on the hole dimensions and placement, but more subtle effects result from the behavior of the mass of air enclosed in the hole volume, whether it is open or closed. The most important early technical work on the tonehole was due to Benade [31].

In the literature, the tonehole is almost invariably represented in terms of an equivalent electrical N-port, using the analogy between the acoustic bore and an electrical transmission line, and characterized in terms of an impedance or scattering matrix, linking pressures and volume velocities at the bore on either side of the branch. See, e.g., [253], and especially the pair of articles by Keefe [198, 197] (as well as subsequent corrections and refinements [199, 111, 255]), which set the stage for many later developments in experimental musical acoustics as well as synthesis algorithms for wind instruments. In particular, the circuit representation is a natural fit for scattering methods such as digital waveguides, and especially wave digital filters, which were originally devised as digital counterpart to analog circuit elements—see, e.g., [314, 336, 374, 391].

---

[3] The height τ, as shown in Figure 9.16(a), does not take into account the effect of curvature of the bore at the junction with the tonehole. A better definition of the tonehole height is the volume enclosed by the hole divided by the surface area πb^2—see [199] for an explicit calculation of this effective tonehole height.

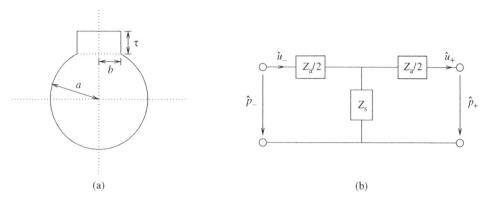

(a)   (b)

Figure 9.16   A single woodwind tonehole. (a) Bore cross-section at tonehole location. τ is the physical height of the tonehole, and b is the radius of the tonehole opening. The dimensionless parameters ξ and S_T are defined as $\xi = \tau/L$, where L is the length of the bore, and $S_T = \pi b^2/S(0)$, where $S(0)$ is the surface area of the bore at its left end. (b) Symmetric two-port circuit representation, with a series imedance Z_a and a shunt impedance Z_s.

As might be expected, however, there is no reason why the tonehole cannot be treated directly in a time–space finite difference scheme; in fact, the tonehole behaves exactly as a lumped element with mass and stiffness, in a way which is not extremely different from that of the preparation of strings using masses and springs, as discussed in Section 7.7. In fact, the case of the tonehole is easier to deal with in some respects, as in most models the lumped element is linear (though this not the case when a more refined model, taking into account the effects of nonlinear loss, is employed [112]). On the other hand, new complications arise, due to the particulars of the circuit representation and the essentially time-varying character of the tonehole in a playing situation. Again, the time domain approach to toneholes discussed here is quite distinct from, for example, those involving multiple convolutions with reflection functions from toneholes [232] with feedback to the reed mechanism [26].

Circuit representation

It is useful to take, as a starting point, the two-port representation shown in Figure 9.16(b), which includes impedances $Z_a(s)/2$ on the series branches and $Z_s(s)$ on the shunt branch. This symmetric "T" two-port is the usual form encountered in the literature, where there are slight variations in the exact forms of the shunt and series impedances. Even more general forms are possible—see, e.g., [111]. For the moment, the exact form of the impedances is left unspecified. $\hat{p}_-$ and $\hat{p}_+$ are the Laplace-transformed pressures to the left and right of the tonehole, and $\hat{u}_-$ and $\hat{u}_+$ the Laplace-transformed volume velocities—again, all dependent variables are assumed non-dimensionalized here.

In order to relate such a structure to a form of Webster's equation, it is useful to extract the pressure and volume velocity drops $\hat{p}_{\text{diff}} = \hat{p}_+ - \hat{p}_-$ and $\hat{u}_{\text{diff}} = \hat{u}_+ - \hat{u}_-$. Applying Kirchhoff's connection rules to the diagram shown in Figure 9.16(b), one arrives immediately at

$$\hat{p}_{\text{diff}} = -\epsilon(x)\frac{Z_a}{2}\,(\hat{u}_+ + \hat{u}_-) \qquad \hat{u}_{\text{diff}} = -\epsilon(x)\frac{1}{2Z_s + Z_a/2}\,(\hat{p}_+ + \hat{p}_-)$$

Here, $\epsilon(x)$ is a distribution peaked at the location of the tonehole $x = x_T$ along the bore, and is assumed to integrate to unity (it will shortly be represented by a Dirac delta function). Assuming that the pairs $\hat{p}_+, \hat{p}_-$ and $\hat{u}_+, \hat{u}_-$ approach common values of $\hat{p}$ and $\hat{u}$ (i.e., they are spatially continuous), one arrives at

$$\hat{p}_{\text{diff}} = -\epsilon(x) Z_a \hat{u} \qquad \hat{u}_{\text{diff}} = -\epsilon(x) \frac{1}{Z_s + Z_a/4} \hat{p}$$

Now, consider the first-order system (9.4) in the presence of such a lumped element and after Laplace transformation; the quantities $\hat{p}_{\text{diff}}$ and $\hat{u}_{\text{diff}}$ contribute directly to the expressions for $\hat{p}_x$ and $\hat{u}_x$, respectively, to yield

$$Ss\hat{p} = -\gamma \hat{u}_x - \frac{\gamma \epsilon(x)}{Z_s + Z_a/4} \hat{p} \qquad \frac{s}{S}\hat{u} = -\gamma \hat{p}_x - \gamma \epsilon(x) Z_a \hat{u} \qquad (9.35)$$

At this point, it is useful to introduce specific forms for the impedances Z_a and Z_s.

Keefe's tonehole model

Keefe [198] gives the following forms for the impedances Z_a and Z_s:

$$Z_a(s) = -\frac{s\xi_a^{o,c}}{\gamma S_T} \quad \text{(open, closed)} \qquad Z_s = \begin{cases} \dfrac{1}{S_T} \coth(\dfrac{s\xi}{\gamma}), & \text{(closed)} \\[2mm] \dfrac{s\xi_e}{\gamma S_T}, & \text{(open)} \end{cases} \qquad (9.36)$$

Here, the dimensionless parameters S_T and various forms of ξ have appeared; S_T is the ratio of the tonehole cross-sectional area to the area of the bore at its left end (not at the hole!), and ξ is the ratio of the tonehole height to the tube physical tube length L. The various forms for ξ, which depend on whether the hole is opened or closed, are effective lengths, and exact expressions appear in various publications [198, 199, 391]. In fact, the effective lengths themselves are frequency dependent to a slight degree—such frequency dependence is ignored here, for the sake of simplicity.

Missing in the above expression for Z_s, when the hole is open, is a loss term which, for the sake of simplifying analysis, will also be ignored for the moment; this is a rather important effect, in that it allows for sound radiation from the open hole. Unfortunately, its full characterization is rather complex—frequency dependence [199] and perhaps even nonlinear effects at the edges of the hole may need to be modeled [112]. A very crude model is, however, explored in Problem 9.13. Consider first the effect of Z_a on the second of (9.35)—when the resulting expression is inverse transformed back to the time domain, the following PDE results:

$$\frac{1}{S^*} u_t = -\gamma p_x \qquad \text{where} \qquad S^*(x) = \frac{S(x)}{1 - \dfrac{S(x)\xi_a \epsilon(x)}{S_T}} \qquad (9.37)$$

The area function $S^*(x)$ is equal to $S(x)$ except in the neighborhood surrounding the tonehole, where $\epsilon(x)$ is peaked. Notice, however, that this effective area can itself become negative—this is another interpretation of the so-called "negative length correction" which the impedance Z_a implies.[4] In fact, Z_a itself is not a positive real function, and thus does not correspond to a strictly passive circuit element! Such an feature leads, as might be expected, to some numerical difficulties when it comes to synthesis, as will be discussed shortly.

---

[4] One might argue that the function S^* is not well defined in the limit as $\epsilon(x)$ approaches a Dirac delta function distribution—this is the reason why a function ϵ taking on finite values has been employed here, though in the discrete setting such analytical questions can be sidestepped.

Given the above PDE relating pressure to volume velocity, it is useful to introduce a velocity potential, again called Ψ, which takes into account the effective surface area S^*, i.e., if

$$u = -S^*\Psi_x \qquad\qquad p = \frac{1}{\gamma}\Psi_t \tag{9.38}$$

then (9.37) is solved exactly. For the series impedance, it is useful, as a prelude to developing finite difference schemes, to approximate it as

$$Z_s = \begin{cases} \dfrac{\gamma}{s\xi\,S_T}, & \text{(closed)} \\[2mm] \dfrac{s\xi_e}{\gamma\,S_T}, & \text{(open)} \end{cases}$$

(Interestingly, the form involving the coth function implies a discrete-time relationship directly—see Problem 9.14.) Thus, when the hole is closed, it behaves as a capacitance, or stiffness, and when open, as an inductance, or mass. Now, the first of (9.35) may be written as

$$Ss\,\hat{p} = -\gamma\hat{u}_x - \frac{\gamma\epsilon(x)}{a_1 s + a_2/s}\,\hat{p} \quad \text{where} \quad a_1 = \begin{cases} -\dfrac{\xi_a^c}{4\gamma\,S_T}, & \text{(closed)} \\[2mm] \dfrac{\xi_e - \xi_a^c/4}{\gamma\,S_T}, & \text{(open)} \end{cases} \qquad a_2 = \begin{cases} \dfrac{\gamma}{\xi\,S_T}, & \text{(closed)} \\[2mm] 0, & \text{(open)} \end{cases}$$

or, using (9.38), and taking an inverse Laplace transformation, as the system

$$S\Psi_{tt} = \gamma^2\left(S^*\Psi_x\right)_x - \epsilon(x)\frac{dm}{dt} \qquad a_1\frac{d^2m}{dt^2} + a_2 m = \gamma\langle\Psi_t, \epsilon\rangle_{\mathbb{U}} \tag{9.39}$$

The new function $m(t)$ allows for the storage of energy in the lumped element. One can indeed work from this coupled form to arrive at a simulation routine. The difficulty, however, again relates back to the negative series impedance Z_a, which leads to a negative stored energy term in the above system, which leads, in turn, to somewhat tricky analysis of the resulting finite difference scheme. See Problem 9.15 for more on this topic. In the digital waveguide framework, it is possible [336] to "extract" the negative impedance from the lumped circuit representation, and append it as a "negative delay" to neighboring waveguides; in essence, the non-passive behavior of the element is subsumed by neighboring passive elements. This option, however, is not available in the difference setting, and is perhaps a disadvantage of a fully time–space discrete method, where it is not possible to commute the effects of a lumped element to other spatial locations.

The important point above, however, is that there is a simple coupled system (9.39) which describes the tonehole connection to the bore, which is a good starting point for the development of synthesis methods based on, perhaps, simplified models of the tonehole, such as that given below.

A simplified form and finite difference scheme

A great simplification (and one which may not be entirely justifiable) is to set the series impedance $Z_a = 0$. Van Walstijn and Scavone [391], in their treatment of the wave digital tonehole, and Scavone, using a pure waveguide construction [314], do essentially this while leaving the negative inductance to be subsumed as a "length correction" by neighboring delay lines. These authors go further, and propose a model which allows more generally for the effects of open and closed holes at once, through a parallel combination of an inductance (or mass) and capacitance (or stiffness):

$$Z_s = \frac{s\xi_e}{\phi\gamma\,S_T}\,\|\,\frac{\gamma}{(1-\phi)s\xi\,S_T} = \frac{1}{\dfrac{\phi\gamma\,S_T}{s\xi_e} + \dfrac{(1-\phi)s\xi\,S_T}{\gamma}} \tag{9.40}$$

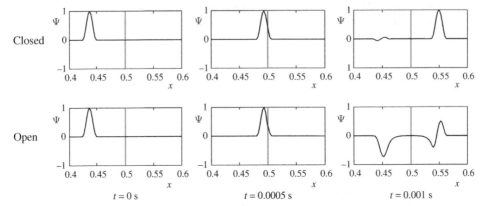

Figure 9.17 Scattering of a narrow pulse by a tonehole, when closed (top) and open (bottom), at the times indicated. The tonehole is located at $x_T = 0.5$, as indicated by the grey line. The tube is cylindrical, and the tonehole parameters are $S_T = 0.799$, $\xi = 0.0011$, and $\xi_e = 0.0026$.

When the parameter $0 \leq \phi \leq 1$ is equal to one, the tonehole is open, and when equal to zero, it is closed. In this case, it is not difficult to show that the following generalization of Webster's equation results:

$$S\Psi_{tt} = \gamma^2 (S\Psi_x)_x - \delta(x - x_T)m \qquad m = \frac{\phi\gamma^2 S_T}{\xi_e}\Psi + (1 - \phi)\xi S_T\Psi_{tt} \qquad (9.41)$$

Notice now that, because $Z_a(s)$ has been neglected, the area function $S^* = S$, and, furthermore, the distribution $\epsilon(x)$ has been approximated as a Dirac delta function. Again, an extra variable m has been introduced, though note that the system could be combined to a single equation in the velocity potential Ψ alone—this is only possible when Z_s results from a parallel combination of elements, which is not the case, for example, when losses intervene—see Problem 9.13.

The total energy for the system will thus be $\mathfrak{H} = \mathfrak{H}_{\text{tube}} + \mathfrak{H}_{\text{tonehole}}$, where $\mathfrak{H}_{\text{tube}}$ is the energy corresponding to the tube, as per (9.7), and the extra stored energy at the tonehole is

$$\mathfrak{H}_{\text{tonehole}} = \frac{\phi\gamma^2 S_T}{2\xi_e}(\Psi(x_T, t))^2 + \frac{(1 - \phi)\xi S_T}{2}(\Psi_t(x_T, t))^2 \geq 0 \qquad (9.42)$$

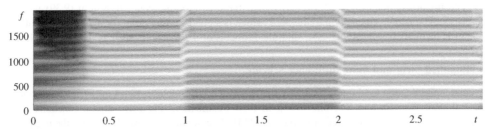

Figure 9.18 Spectrogram of sound output from a reed instrument model under a time-varying tonehole gesture. The reed model corresponds approximately to that of a clarinet, with bore profile and reed parameters as given in Figure 9.12, and with a blowing pressure which ramps linearly from $p_m = 0.013$ to $p_m = 0.027$ over a duration of 3 s. The tonehole is placed at $x_T = 0.8$, with $S_T = 0.1644$, $\xi = 0.0075$, and $\xi_e = 0.0134$, and is opened over a duration of 50 ms at $t = 1$ s, and closed over the same duration at $t = 2$ s. Scheme (9.43) is used, at a sample rate of 44 100 Hz. Output pressure is read from the end of the tube, at $x = 1$.

Thus, as before in the case of string preparation, the energetic effect of the tonehole, at least under the simplified model here, is to introduce an additional non-negative component to the total energy.

A useful finite difference approximation to (9.41) is as follows:

$$\mu_{xx} S \delta_{tt} \Psi = \gamma^2 \delta_{x+} \left((\mu_{x-} S) \delta_{x-} \Psi \right) - J_p(x_T) m \tag{9.43a}$$

$$m = \frac{\phi \gamma^2 S_T}{\xi_e} \left(\alpha I_p(x_T) \Psi + (1 - \alpha) \mu_t. I_p(x_T) \Psi \right) + (1 - \phi) \xi S_T \delta_{tt} I_p(x_T) \Psi \tag{9.43b}$$

Again, as in the case of the prepared string (see Section 7.7), the pth-order interpolation and spreading functions $I_p(x_T)$ and $J_p(x_T)$ have been employed—as such, the tonehole may be placed at any location along the bore. See Programming Exercises 9.7 and 9.8. Notice also the use of the free parameter α, which allows for a certain degree of tuning of the algorithm; this is an extra degree of freedom not available when, for example, methods such as wave digital filters are employed. Simple sufficient stability conditions for the above scheme follow, from energy analysis, as

$$\lambda \leq 1 \qquad\qquad \alpha \leq \frac{1}{2} \tag{9.44}$$

though it is possible to improve on this bound—see Problem 9.16.

Reflections

The gross effect of the tonehole is to induce frequency-dependent scattering; when open, the tonehole reflects low frequencies, and generally passes high-frequencies—see the example shown at bottom in Figure 9.17. In this case, the pulse is a traveling wave, and is unnaturally narrow, by musical standards, in order to exhibit the reflection and transmission characteristics. If the hole is closed, low frequencies are passed, with a slight high-frequency backscatter.

Partly open holes and time variation

The feature of interest in the model given in (9.41) is that it allows the tonehole to be partly open; furthermore, if the parameter ϕ is allowed to be time varying, it is possible to effect a change of state between open and closed. The obvious effect is, of course, to change the sounding pitch of the instrument—see Figure 9.18, which is generated using a clarinet-like model, using scheme (9.43) for the bore/tonehole connection.

More interesting, sonically, than the simple change of pitch, are the wide variety of multiphonics which may be generated though judicious placement of toneholes. If, for instance, a single tonehole is opened a good distance away from the bell, one is likely to generate a sound with a multiphonic character, exhibiting, perhaps, distinct sounding pitches and a slowly time-varying amplitude envelope—see Figure 9.19.

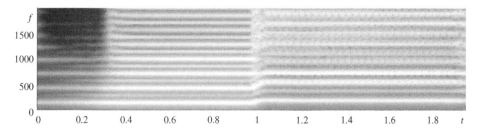

Figure 9.19 Spectrogram of sound output from a reed instrument model under a time-varying tonehole gesture. The reed, bore, and tonehole parameters are as in Figure 9.18, but the tonehole is located at $x_T = 0.6$, and opened at $t = 1$ s. The resulting tone sounds at two distinct pitches, and "warbles."

9.4 Other wind instruments

Due to space considerations, only single-reed wind instruments have been described in this chapter. There are, of course, other families of instruments based on acoustic tubes, many of which have been simulated for synthesis, including double-reed instruments, the flute family, and brass instruments. Many features are shared with the reed model, as detailed below, and indeed synthesis methods based on difference schemes, or digital waveguides may be readily applied to such instruments.

Double-reed instruments, such as the oboe and bassoon, though they have seen less research at the level of musical acoustics (see, e.g., [397, 6]), differ mainly in the treatment of the reed mechanism—due to the length and geometry of the reed, finer attention to the details of the flow nonlinearity is necessary. Still, the resulting lumped representation of the reed is not extremely different from that presented in Section 9.3, and sound synthesis algorithms have resulted [7, 158].

Brass instrument synthesis has also seen a lot of activity, and again, just as in the case of the reed, the typical model is composed of a linear bore connected to a lumped valve-like excitation. In this case, however, the "reed" (the player's lips) is in a configuration such that it is blown open at higher pressures, rather than shut—see, e.g., [136] for a standard explanation of the distinction between the two types of reed behavior. Simple models used in the studies in musical acoustics and in synthesis, however, are again nearly identical to the reed model presented in Section 9.3—see, e.g., [3, 297, 398]. Real-time synthesis has been available for some time, using digital waveguides [89], and methods based on nonlinear ODEs incorporating delays [297]; perhaps the most polished result has been the BRASS physical modeling software package recently released by IRCAM [400]. One significant departure in the model of the bore has involved looking at wave propagation in the bore at high blowing pressures, in which case shock waves may be produced, leading to a brighter timbre. In this case, Webster's equation no longer suffices, and a full model of nonlinear wave propagation must be simulated. See, e.g., [172, 245, 399]. Another departure from Webster's equation results from the relatively wide flare of the bell in brass instruments relative to woodwinds, in which case a 1D model may be insufficient to describe effects at high frequencies. See, e.g., the work of Noreland [258] in which finite difference methods in higher dimensions are employed in order to simulate such behavior.

More complex still is the case of flute- and recorder-like instruments; the interaction between the jet of air and the sharp-edged mouthpiece, beyond exciting the instrument body at its resonant frequencies, introduces turbulence which is audible as a noise-like component to the resulting sound. Synthesis applications employ a greatly simplified model of this interaction, along the lines of the model proposed by McIntyre et al. [236]—see, e.g., [85]. This is also true of digital waveguide models—see, e.g., [373, 369], and especially the work of Verge [395, 394].

9.5 Problems

Problem 9.1 *Find conditions on the surface area $S(x)$ such that $a(x)$, in the transformed form of Webster's equation given in (9.3), vanishes. Relate $a(x)$ to local tube curvature.*

Problem 9.2 *Recall the form of the radiating boundary condition for Webster's equation, given in (9.9). Such a condition is usually encountered in an impedance form in the literature, such as*

$$\hat{p}(s) = Z(s)\hat{u}(s) \quad \text{with} \quad Z(s) = \frac{s}{S(1)\gamma \, (\alpha_2 + \alpha_1 s)} \quad (9.45)$$

Here, p and u are dimensionless pressure and volume velocity, respectively, and the impedance is expressed in terms of the parameters α_1 and α_2 given in (9.10) or (9.11). The hat (i.e., circumflex) notation indicates a Laplace transformation in the frequency variable s.

(a) By replacing factors of s by partial time derivatives, show that the impedance relation above implies the radiation boundary condition (9.9) in the variable Ψ at $x = 1$. You may use the settings $p(1, t) = \Psi_t(1, t)/\gamma$ and $u(1, t) = -S(1)\Psi_x(1, t)$.

(b) Using a series expansion, show that the impedance $Z(j\omega)$ given above may be approximated as

$$Z(s) = \frac{s}{S(1)\gamma\alpha_2} \left(1 - \frac{\alpha_1}{\alpha_2}s\right) \qquad (9.46)$$

which is the form encountered frequently in the literature. As in part (a) above, convert this impedance into a boundary condition in Ψ at $x = 1$. Can you show, using energy methods, that this condition does not correspond to a strictly dissipative termination?

Problem 9.3 In order to represent a passive system, or one which dissipates energy, an impedance $Z(s)$ must satisfy the property of positive realness:

$$\text{Re}\,(Z(s)) \geq 0 \qquad \text{for} \qquad \text{Re}(s) > 0$$

See, e.g., [30, 387].

Show that the transfer function corresponding to the radiation boundary condition given in (9.45) above is positive real, but that the form in (9.46) is not. (Positive realness of an impedance corresponds exactly to strict dissipativity in the energy framework, and is used as a defining property in the design of stable wave digital filter networks.)

Problem 9.4 Consider scheme (9.13) for Webster's equation, and recall that the approximation [S] is second-order accurate. Show that it may be rewritten as

$$[S]\delta_{tt}u = \gamma^2\,(\delta_x.S\delta_x.u + \mu_{x+}\mu_{x-}S\delta_{xx}u)$$

Every approximation to either S or u in the above scheme is second-order accurate in space or time, so therefore deduce that the scheme is second-order accurate as a whole.

Problem 9.5 Showing numerical stability for the more accurate numerical boundary conditions (9.16) for Webster's equation is slightly tricky—the key is to define an appropriate inner product. To this end, consider the weighted inner product defined in (5.38), in which the endpoint weightings ϵ_l and ϵ_r are left unspecified for the moment.

Show that, by applying this inner product in the energy analysis of scheme (9.13), the following energy balance results, generalizing (9.14):

$$\delta_{t+}\mathfrak{h} = \mathfrak{b} \quad \text{with} \quad \mathfrak{h} = \mathfrak{t} + \mathfrak{v} \quad \mathfrak{t} = \frac{1}{2}\left(\|\sqrt{[S]}\delta_{t-}\Psi\|_{\mathbb{U}_N}^{\epsilon_l,\epsilon_r}\right)^2 \quad \mathfrak{v} = \frac{\gamma^2}{2}\langle(\mu_{x+}S)\delta_{x+}\Psi, e_{t-}\delta_{x+}\Psi\rangle_{\underline{\mathbb{U}}_N}$$

and where the boundary term is now

$$\mathfrak{b} = \gamma^2\delta_{t\cdot}\Psi_N\left(\frac{\epsilon_r}{2}\mu_{x+}S_N\delta_{x+}\Psi_N + \left(1 - \frac{\epsilon_r}{2}\right)\mu_{x-}S_N\delta_{x-}\Psi_N\right)$$

$$- \gamma^2\delta_{t\cdot}\Psi_0\left(\frac{\epsilon_l}{2}\mu_{x-}S_0\delta_{x-}\Psi_0 + \left(1 - \frac{\epsilon_l}{2}\right)\mu_{x+}S_0\delta_{x+}\Psi_0\right)$$

Show that under the special choices of $\epsilon_l = \mu_{x+}S_0/\mu_{xx}S_0$ and $\epsilon_r = \mu_{x-}S_N/\mu_{xx}S_N$, the boundary conditions (9.16) are strictly dissipative.

Can you continue and show that under these conditions, the energy itself is non-negative? Your answer to Problem 5.10 should be of use here.

Problem 9.6   *Consider Webster's equation, with a locally reacting wall vibration condition, as described in system (9.18).*

   (a) Show that this system is dissipative, i.e., that

$$\frac{d(\mathfrak{H} + \mathfrak{H}_w)}{dt} = -\mathfrak{Q}$$

where $\mathfrak{H}$ is the stored energy in the tube, given in (9.7), $\mathfrak{H}_w \geq 0$ is the stored energy of the walls, and where $\mathfrak{Q} \geq 0$ is the total wall loss. Assume conservative boundary conditions.

   (b) Suppose, furthermore, that the tube is cylindrical (i.e., $S = 1$) and of infinite extent (i.e. the system is defined over $\mathcal{D} = \mathbb{R}$), and that the wall is lossless (i.e., $\sigma_0 = 0$). Insert test solutions of the form $e^{st+j\beta x}$ for both Ψ and w, and determine a characteristic equation relating frequency s and wavenumber β. Show that there will be two separate dispersion relations, and that in both cases s is purely imaginary.

Problem 9.7   *Show that the coupled difference scheme (9.19) may be written in an explicit update form. In order to do this, you can either expand out the operator form as given, or employ identity (2.7g).*

Problem 9.8   *Show that both the simplified difference scheme (9.17) for Webster's equation and the scattering structure discussed in Section 9.2.4 may be implemented in a form requiring one multiplication per grid point (or junction), where for the scattering method, all arithmetic is performed according to (9.22). How does the number of additions vary?*

Problem 9.9   *Consider the time-varying generalization of Webster's equation (9.23). Suppose that one defines the "time-varying" stored energy of the system as*

$$\mathfrak{H} = \frac{1}{2}\|\sqrt{S}\Psi_t\|_{\mathbb{U}}^2 + \frac{\gamma^2}{2}\|\sqrt{S}\Psi_x\|_{\mathbb{U}}^2$$

   (a) Show that one may derive the following energy balance (assuming conservative boundary conditions):

$$\frac{d\mathfrak{H}}{dt} = -\frac{1}{2}\langle S_t\Psi_t, \Psi_t\rangle_{\mathbb{U}} + \frac{\gamma^2}{2}\langle S_t\Psi_x, \Psi_x\rangle_{\mathbb{U}}$$

   (b) Show that

$$\frac{d\mathfrak{H}}{dt} \leq \frac{1}{2}\|\sqrt{|S_t|}\Psi_t\|_{\mathbb{U}}^2 + \frac{\gamma^2}{2}\|\sqrt{|S_t|}\Psi_x\|_{\mathbb{U}}^2$$

and find a function $\alpha(t) \geq 0$, depending on the properties of S alone, such that

$$\frac{d\mathfrak{H}}{dt} \leq \alpha\mathfrak{H}$$

(Your function $\alpha(t)$ should be zero when S is time invariant.)

   (c) Finally, show that

$$\mathfrak{H}(t) \leq e^{\int_0^t \alpha(t')dt'}\mathfrak{H}(0)$$

Thus there is an bound on the rate of growth of the solution in terms of the variation in S.

   (d) How loose is the bound in (c) above? Estimate the growth in $\mathfrak{H}$ using common-sense assumptions about the rate of variation of S in typical speech.

Problem 9.10   *Consider the following implicit finite difference scheme for Webster's equation under time-varying conditions:*

$$\delta_{t+}\left((\mu_{t-}-\mu_{xx}S)\delta_{t-}\Psi\right) = \gamma^2\delta_{x+}\left((\mu_{tt}\mu_x - S)\mu_{t\cdot}\delta_{x-}\Psi\right)$$

It is possible to obtain a bound on solution growth in the same way as in the continuous case discussed above.

(a) Under conservative boundary conditions, show that the following energy balance holds:

$$\delta_{t+}\mathfrak{h} = -\frac{1}{2}\langle \delta_{t\cdot}\mu_{xx}S, (\delta_{t+}\Psi)(\delta_{t-}\Psi)\rangle_{U_N} + \frac{\gamma^2}{2}\langle \delta_{t\cdot}\mu_{x+}S, \mu_{tt}(\delta_{x+}\Psi)^2\rangle_{U_N}$$

where

$$\mathfrak{h} = \frac{1}{2}\|\sqrt{\mu_{t-}\mu_{xx}S}\delta_{t-}\Psi\|_{U_N} + \frac{\gamma^2}{2}\langle \mu_{t-}\mu_{x+}S, \mu_{t-}(\delta_{x+}\Psi)^2\rangle_{U_N}$$

(b) Prove that

$$\delta_{t+}\mathfrak{h} \leq \alpha\mu_{t+}\mathfrak{h}$$

for some scalar time series $\alpha = \alpha^n$, *which depends only on the grid function S. Show, furthermore, that*

$$\delta_{t+}\mathfrak{h} \leq \alpha^*\mu_{t+}\mathfrak{h}$$

where $\alpha^* = \max_n \alpha^n$.

(c) Given that $\mathfrak{h} \geq 0$ *unconditionally (such is the interest in using an implicit scheme here), show that there is a constant* ϵ, *such that*

$$\mathfrak{h}^n \leq \epsilon^n \mathfrak{h}^0$$

(d) Do you think this scheme will perform well, especially in terms of numerical dispersion? Consider its behavior in the simple time- and shift-invariant case when $S = 1$.

Problem 9.11   *Consider the energy balance for the single-reed system, as given in (9.28). It is not obvious that one may use this balance in order to bound the size of the state in terms of the control input* p_m. *In this problem, the idea is to show why this is difficult, and perhaps to inspire you to solve the problem!*

(a) Rewrite the energy inequality, neglecting the radiation loss term $\mathfrak{Q}_b$, *as*

$$\frac{d\mathfrak{H}_{total}}{dt} \leq -\left(\frac{2\sigma_0 u_r^2}{S^2} + \frac{\mathfrak{Q}}{S}p_m u_r\right) - \frac{\mathfrak{Q}\mathcal{R}}{S}\left([y+1]^+|p_\Delta|^{3/2} - [y+1]^+|p_\Delta|^{1/2}\text{sign}(p_\Delta)p_m\right)$$

(b) Consider the following inequality [210]: for any two positive numbers A, B, and for p, q such that $1/p + 1/q = 1$, *and* $1 < q < \infty$,

$$AB \leq \frac{A^p}{p} + \frac{B^q}{q} \tag{9.47}$$

Make use of this inequality (twice!) in order to rewrite the energy balance above as

$$\frac{d\mathfrak{H}_{total}}{dt} \leq a_1 p_m^2 + a_2[y+1]^+|p_m|^{3/2}$$

and find the corresponding values of the constants a_1 *and* a_2.

(c) Were it not for the factor of $[y+1]^+$, *one would be able to proceed to a bound on the growth of the energy, and thus the state variables, directly (how?). Here is a less satisfying way of proceeding: again using the inequality (9.47), rewrite the energy balance as*

$$\frac{d\mathfrak{H}_{total}}{dt} \leq a_1 p_m^2 + a_2|p_m|^{3/2} + b_1\left([y]^+\right)^2 + b_2|p_m|^3$$

and find the constants b_1 *and* b_2.

(d) Use the fact that $([y]^+)^2 \leq 2\mathfrak{H}_{\text{total}}/\omega_0^2$ to rewrite the inequality as

$$e^{\alpha t} \frac{d\left(e^{-\alpha t}\mathfrak{H}_{\text{total}}\right)}{dt} \leq f(p_m)$$

and determine the value of α and the form of $f(p_m)$. Show that this leads to the bound

$$\mathfrak{H}_{\text{total}}(t) \leq e^{\alpha t}\mathfrak{H}_{\text{total}}(0) + \int_0^t e^{\alpha(t-t')} f(p_m)dt'$$

How big is α for reasonable choices of the parameters for a reed–bore system? Is this a useful bound?

Problem 9.12   Referring to the implementation of the finite difference scheme for the reed–bore system, as discussed in Section 9.3.3, find expressions for the intermediate variables a^n, b^n, c^n, and d^n. Given that these will be used to advance the solution from time step n to time step $n+1$, they may only depend on values of y and the grid function Ψ up through time step n, as well as the sampled input mouth pressure p_m.

Problem 9.13   Consider the simplified model of the tonehole, as described on page 275, with $Z_a = 0$, but where now $Z_s(s)$ is generalized from the form given in (9.40) to include loss as

$$Z_s = \left(\frac{s\xi_e}{\phi\gamma S_T} + R\right) \,||\, \frac{\gamma}{(1-\phi)s\xi S_T}$$

where, as before, $||$ indicates a parallel combination, and where R is a non-negative constant.

  Show that using this impedance, a PDE system which generalizes (9.41) may be derived. Find also an associated finite difference scheme. Will the inclusion of the extra loss term have any bearing on numerical stability?

Problem 9.14   Consider the impedance relationship

$$\hat{p} = Z(s)\hat{u} \qquad \text{with} \qquad Z(s) = \coth(\alpha s/2)$$

for some positive constant α. Show that, in the time domain, this corresponds not to a differential equation, but to a relationship among values of $p(t)$ and $u(t)$ at two time instants separated by α seconds. Given that one of the impedances which appears in the tonehole model described in Section 9.3.8 is of this form, do you think it is a good idea to approximate $Z(s)$ as $Z(s) \approx 2/(s\alpha)$? (Take sample rate considerations into account!)

Problem 9.15   Consider the general PDE form of the coupling between an acoustic tube and Keefe's tonehole model, as per (9.39).

  (a) Show that, under conservative boundary conditions for the tube, the total stored energy is of the form $\mathfrak{H} = \mathfrak{H}_{\text{tube}} + \mathfrak{H}_{\text{tonehole}}$, where

$$\mathfrak{H}_{\text{tube}} = \frac{1}{2}\|S\Psi_t\|_\mathbb{U}^2 + \frac{\gamma^2}{2}\|S^*\Psi_x\|_\mathbb{U}^2 \qquad \mathfrak{H}_{\text{tonehole}} = \frac{a_1}{2}\left(\frac{dm}{dt}\right)^2 + \frac{a_2}{2}m^2$$

when $S^* \geq 0$ (find a condition under which this is true). Notice that a_1, which depends on the series impedance Z_a, is negative when the hole is closed.

  (b) Consider the following finite difference scheme:

$$\mu_{xx}S\delta_{tt}\Psi = \gamma^2\delta_{x+}\left(\mu_{x-}S^*\delta_{x-}\Psi\right) - \epsilon\delta_t.m \qquad a_1\delta_{tt}m + a_2\mu_t.m = \gamma\langle\delta_t.\Psi, \epsilon\rangle_{\mathbb{U}_N}$$

Here, the grid function ϵ_l is obtained through sampling of the continuous distribution $\epsilon(x)$. Assuming conservative boundary conditions, show that the scheme is conservative, with a numerical stored energy of $\mathfrak{h} = \mathfrak{h}_{\text{tube}} + \mathfrak{h}_{\text{tonehole}}$, where

$$\mathfrak{h}_{\text{tube}} = \frac{1}{2} \| \sqrt{\mu_{xx} S} \delta_{t-} \Psi \|_{\bar{\mathbb{U}}_N}^2 + \frac{\gamma^2}{2} \langle \mu_{x+} S^* \delta_{x+} \Psi, e_{t-} \delta_{x+} \Psi \rangle_{\underline{\mathbb{U}}_N}$$

and find the expression for $\mathfrak{h}_{\text{tonehole}}$ (which will depend only on the time series m).

(c) Show that the term $\mathfrak{h}_{\text{tube}}$ is non-negative if the following condition is satisfied:

$$\lambda \leq \sqrt{\frac{\mu_{xx} S}{\mu_{xx} S^*}}$$

and, given the expression for S^*, rewrite this as a bound $\lambda \leq r \leq 1$, and give the explicit expression for r. Can you interpret this bound in terms of a reduced effective length of the tube? Explain.

(d) From your expression for $\mathfrak{h}_{\text{tonehole}}$, and under the closed-hole condition, show that, though there is a range of values of k, the time step, over which the expression is non-negative, in the limit of small k the term must become negative. Thus, though the scheme may operate in an apparently stable manner, it is not convergent in the strict sense.

Problem 9.16 *Consider scheme (9.43) for the simplified tonehole model (9.41), and assume that the boundary conditions at both ends of the tube are conservative.*

(a) Show that the scheme possesses a conserved energy of the form

$$\mathfrak{h} = \mathfrak{h}_{\text{tube}} + \mathfrak{t}_{\text{tonehole}} + \mathfrak{v}_{\text{tonehole}}$$

where $\mathfrak{t}_{\text{tonehole}}$ and $\mathfrak{v}_{\text{tonehole}}$ are kinetic and potential energy terms for the tonehole analogous to those which appear in (9.42). Recall that $\mathfrak{h}_{\text{tube}} \geq 0$ under the condition that $\lambda \leq 1$.

(b) Show that the potential energy term $\mathfrak{v}_{\text{tonehole}}$ is non-negative under the second of conditions (9.44).

(c) By considering conditions under which the sum of $\mathfrak{t}_{\text{tonehole}}$ and $\mathfrak{v}_{\text{tonehole}}$ is non-negative, determine a more general condition relating α, ϕ, the time step k, and the various material parameters for the tonehole. This condition, combined with $\lambda \leq 1$, is a stronger stability condition for the scheme.

(d) Find an explicit update for both the grid function Ψ and the time series m.

9.6 Programming exercises

Programming Exercise 9.1 *Using the vocal synthesis Matlab code provided in Section A.10 as a starting point, generalize the glottal excitation function* uin. *(These manipulations are not physical modeling per se, but rather abstract synthesis techniques, as discussed in Section 1.1, which are very useful in the source-filtering context.) Here are some ways you could proceed. In the code example, the glottal waveform is crudely generated as*

$$u_{\text{in}} = [y(t)]^+ \qquad \text{where} \qquad y = \sin(2\pi f_0 t)$$

Here, $[\cdot]^+$, the clipping operation, indicates the "positive part of."

(a) Generalize the waveform $y(t)$ as follows:

$$y(t) = A(t) \sin \left(2\pi \int_0^{t'} (1 + \Delta f \sin(2\pi f_1 t')) f_0(t') dt' \right)$$

Here, $f_0(t)$ is the instantaneous frequency, f_1 a vibrato frequency, normally between 3 and 5 Hz, $0 \leq \Delta f \leq 1$ the vibrato depth, and $0 \leq A(t) \leq 1$ is an amplitude envelope. You can define these, in Matlab, by breakpoint functions, then interpolate to the sampling instants nk, for integer n (learn about the function `interp1` *for this purpose). You will also need to perform the integration in the argument of the sine function above numerically. See if you can generate a sung major scale, with the vowel /a/.*

(b) In the code example, the excitation is zero mean and positively clipped—thus its "duty cycle" is 50%. Try instead a waveform of the following form, which depends on a free parameter ϵ:

$$u_{\text{in}}(t) = \frac{[y(t) - \epsilon]^+}{1 - \epsilon} \qquad \text{with} \qquad 0 \leq \epsilon < 1$$

Have a listen to the differences in timbre as you play with this parameter. Try, also, squaring the waveform above, rendering it differentiable. (Try to guess what the perceptual result of such a squaring operation will be before listening to the output.)

Programming Exercise 9.2 *In the code example, only two vocal tract forms are provided, corresponding, roughly, to the Russian vowels /a/ and /e/ given by Fant [123]; this data, as well as forms for other vowels, appears in many texts, such as, e.g., [280]. Track down some other vocal tract configurations, and extend the Matlab code to include these. In the code example, the data is specified as position/surface area pairs $(x, S(x))$, and the data is then interpolated to the finite difference grid using* `interp1`. *Note that you must scale any data that you find such that it is non-dimensionalized, i.e., $0 \leq x \leq 1$, and $S(0) = 1$.*

In addition to generating sound examples, you may also wish to generate pictures of the formant structure corresponding to various vocal tract configurations. In order to do this, you may use, as your input function `uin`, *an impulse sequence consisting of a one followed by zeros. The formant structure may then be obtained by taking the magnitude of the Fourier transform of the output sequence of volume velocities read at the right end of the tube. Referring to difference scheme (9.13), you may obtain this sequence from the grid function Ψ, by taking $u_{\text{out}} = -S_N \delta_{x\cdot} \Psi_N$.*

Programming Exercise 9.3 *Introduce wall losses to the model, by using the coupled scheme (9.19), in the explicit update form you derived in Problem 9.7. In order to set the parameters for the wall itself, you may wish to begin from those given in the caption to Figure 9.7; if you are more ambitious, try to track down some data from the literature—try [273] as a starting point.*

Programming Exercise 9.4 *Implement the explicit scheme (9.23) in the case of a time-varying vocal tract model. In order to generate a simple time-varying function $S(x, t)$, start from the two static vocal tract configurations $S_{/a/}(x)$ and $S_{/e/}(x)$ (as given in the code example), and define $S(x, t)$ as*

$$S(x, t) = \alpha(t)S_{/a/}(x) + (1 - \alpha(t))S_{/e/}(x) \qquad \text{with} \qquad 0 \leq \alpha(t) \leq 1$$

Here, the function $\alpha(t)$ controls the degree of interpolation. Note that you should not construct $S(x, t)$ off-line, outside the main loop, as it is a huge waste of memory—rather, $\alpha(t = nk)$ should be generated in its entirety off-line, and then the function $S(x, t = nk)$ constructed in the main loop at time step n.

Programming Exercise 9.5 *Using the vocal synthesis code example provided in Section A.10 as a starting point, modify the code such that it performs reed instrument synthesis. There are various changes you need to make:*

- *Introduce, as global parameters, the reed mass M_r, effective surface area S_r, resonant frequency ω_0, collision parameters ω_1 and α, reed loss paramater σ_0, channel width w, and reed equilibrium displacement H_0, as well as air density ρ.*

- *Derive parameters Q, R, and S, as per (9.27).*

- *Adjust the radiation parameters, so as to correspond to condition (9.11), for an unflanged tube.*

- *Create a mouth pressure excitation p_m—this can be, in the simplest case, a constant vector, but could be generalized to a breakpoint function, interpolated to the sampling instants using the Matlab function* `interp1`.

- *Adjust the bore profile, given as* s, *such that it corresponds to various typical choices of interest in wind instrument synthesis, such as: a cylinder, a cone, or a cylinder with a bell-like termination. Allow the user to specify the type of profile, as well as extra parameters, when necessary. (If the profile is cylindrical, no parameters need be supplied, but if it is a cone, for example, an extra parameter, such as the ratio of surface area at the right end of the tube to that at the left end, will be necessary.)*

- *Implement the coupling of the excitation with the tube, using the scheme as outlined in Section 9.3.3, and the various intermediate variables for which you derived expressions in Problem 9.12.*

Programming Exercise 9.6   *Extend the single-reed synthesis algorithm which you programmed above to allow the reed equilibrium displacement to be time varying. As a starting point, just in order to hear the effects of such variation, you may wish to model such variation as a constant plus a sinusoidal offset, such as*

$$H_0(t) = H_0 \left(1 + \epsilon \sin(2\pi f_H t)\right)$$

where H_0 is an average value, and where $\epsilon \leq 1$ describes the depth of the variation, and f_H its frequency.

Programming Exercise 9.7   *For the single-reed instrument model you have developed over the last two exercises, introduce a static tonehole according to the simplified model (9.41) and the associated scheme (9.43). (You should have worked out an explicit update for the scheme in Problem 9.16.) In order to do this, you will need an expression for ξ_e, the effective tonehole length in the open-hole case. A simple approximation, in terms of the physical tonehole radius b and height τ, and where the bore radius is a at the location of the tonehole, is given as*

$$\xi_e = \frac{\tau}{L} + \frac{b}{L}\left(1.4 - 0.58\frac{b^2}{a^2}\right)$$

Your code will thus require the following new parameters: ξ, S_T (the ratio of tonehole cross-sectional area to that of the bore at its left end), x_T (the position of the tonehole), ϕ, between 0 and 1, which determines the state of the hole, as well as the free scheme parameter α.

Programming Exercise 9.8   *Extend the simulation of toneholes in the following ways:*
    (a) Allow the specification of a number Q of distinct toneholes, each characterized by a set of parameters as given in the previous exercise. This extension is relatively straightforward, assuming minimal interaction between holes. First, convince yourself that the dynamics of any single tonehole

may be simulated independently of those of any other, using a natural extension of scheme (9.43), which will now be of the form

$$\mu_{xx} S \delta_{tt} \Psi = \gamma^2 \delta_{x+} ((\mu_{x-} S) \delta_{x-} \Psi) - \sum_{q=1}^{Q} J_p(x_T^{(q)}) m^{(q)}$$

$$m^{(q)} = \frac{\phi^{(q)} \left(\gamma^{(q)}\right)^2 S_T^{(q)}}{\xi_e^{(q)}} \left(\alpha^{(q)} I_p(x_T^{(q)}) \Psi + (1 - \alpha^{(q)}) \mu_t . I_p(x_T) \Psi \right)$$

$$+ (1 - \phi^{(q)}) \xi^{(q)} S_T^{(q)} \delta_{tt} I_p(x_T^{(q)}) \Psi$$

In Matlab, it is probably best to vectorize the tonehole states, so that a loop over the Q toneholes may be avoided.

(b) Allow the tonehole state ϕ for each such tonehole to be time varying. In order to make your code "playable," you might wish to begin by specifying a list of events, characterized by: start time, hole number, duration, terminal state ϕ.

1
2
3
4
5
6
7
8
9
10
11
12
13
14
15
16
17
18
19
20
21
22
23
24
25
26
27
28
29
30
31
32
33
34
35
36
37
38
39
40
41
42
43
44
45
46
47
48
49
50
51

10

Grid functions and finite difference operators in 2D

This chapter is concerned with the extension of the difference operators introduced in Chapter 5 to two spatial dimensions. The 2D case is one of great interest in musical acoustics, given that many key components of musical instruments may be well described as such—for various percussion instruments such as drums, cymbals, and gongs, a 2D structure serves as the main resonating element, whereas in keyboard instruments and some stringed instruments it behaves as an auxiliary radiating element which imparts its own characteristic to the resulting sound. Perceptually speaking, the sound output from a 2D simulation is far richer than that of a 1D simulation. Part of this is due to the number of degrees of freedom, or modes, which, in the linear case, is considerably larger and of less regular a distribution than in 1D—sounds generated by 2D objects are generally inharmonic by nature. Beyond this, there are mechanisms at work, in particular in the nonlinear case, which lead to perceptual phenomena which have no real analogue in 1D; cymbal crashes are an excellent example of such behavior.

At the time of writing, there has been, so far, relatively little work on 2D problems in sound synthesis (with some exceptions: [139, 46, 140, 385, 384]), partly because, until recently, real-time synthesis from such systems on small computers was not possible. Another reason has been that percussion instruments have seen much less fundamental investigation from the point of view of musical acoustics than other instruments, though there is a growing body of work by Rossing and his collaborators (see [299, 136] for an overview), concerned mainly with experimental determination of modal frequencies, as well as considerable related work on time domain characterizations and nonlinear phenomena [283, 300]. On the other hand, such problems have a long research history in mainstream simulation, and, as a result, there is a wide expanse of literature and results which may be adapted to sound synthesis applications. Difference schemes are again a good choice for synthesis, and much of the material presented in Chapter 5 may be generalized in a natural way. The presentation here will be as brief as possible, except when it comes to certain features which are particular to 2D.

Partial differential operators in 2D, in both Cartesian and radial coordinates, are presented in Section 10.1, accompanied by frequency domain and energy analysis concepts and tools. Difference operators are then introduced in Cartesian coordinates in Section 10.2 and in radial coordinates in Section 10.3.

Numerical Sound Synthesis: Finite Difference Schemes and Simulation in Musical Acoustics   Stefan Bilbao
© 2009 John Wiley & Sons, Ltd

10.1 Partial differential operators and PDEs in two space variables

The single largest headache in 2D, both at the algorithm design stage and in programming a working synthesis routine, is problem geometry. Whereas 1D problems are defined over a domain which may always be scaled to the unit interval, in 2D no such simplification is possible. As such, the choice of coordinates becomes important. Here, to keep the emphasis on basic principles, only two such choices, namely Cartesian and radial coordinates (certainly the most useful in musical acoustics), will be discussed. Despite this, it is worth keeping in mind that numerical simulation methods are by no means limited to such coordinate choices, though as the choice of coordinate system (generally governed by geometry) becomes more complex, finite difference methods lose a good deal of their appeal, and finite element methods (see page 386) become an attractive option.

10.1.1 Cartesian and radial coordinates

Certainly the simplest coordinate system, and one which is ideal for working with problems defined over square or rectangular regions, is the Cartesian coordinate system, where a position is defined by the pair (x, y). For problems defined over circles, radial coordinates (r, θ) defined in terms of Cartesian coordinates by

$$r = \sqrt{x^2 + y^2} \qquad \theta = \tan^{-1}(y/x) \qquad (10.1)$$

may be more appropriate. See Figure 10.1 for an illustration of such coordinate systems.

In finite difference applications, Cartesian coordinates are undeniably much simpler to deal with, due to the symmetry between the x and y coordinate directions. Radial coordinates are trickier in some respects, especially due to the existence of a coordinate center, and also because differential operators exhibit a dependence on radius r.

10.1.2 Spatial domains

As in 1D, a 2D problem is defined over a given domain $\mathcal{D}$, a subset of the plane $\mathbb{R}^2$—see Figure 10.1 for an illustration of some of the regions to be discussed here. For analysis purposes, it is often convenient to work over the entire plane, or with $\mathcal{D} = \mathbb{R}^2$. In Cartesian coordinates,

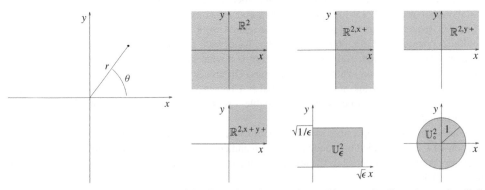

Figure 10.1   Coordinates (x, y), and (r, θ), and various regions of interest in Cartesian and radial coordinates.

sometimes, for the analysis of boundary conditions, it is useful to examine a semi-infinite domain, or half plane, of the form $\mathbb{R}^{2,x+} = \{(x, y) \in \mathbb{R}^2, x \geq 0\}$, or $\mathbb{R}^{2,y+} = \{(x, y) \in \mathbb{R}^2, y \geq 0\}$, and in order to deal with corner conditions, the quarter plane $\mathbb{R}^{2,x+y+} = \{(x, y) \in \mathbb{R}^2, x \geq 0, y \geq 0\}$.

In practice, however, at least in Cartesian coordinates, it is the $L_x \times L_y$ rectangular region, of the form $\{(x, y) \in \mathbb{R}^2, 0 \leq x \leq L_x, 0 \leq y \leq L_y\}$, which is of most interest. Through scaling of spatial variables, i.e., setting coordinates

$$x' = x/\sqrt{L_x L_y} \qquad\qquad y' = y/\sqrt{L_x L_y}$$

this region may always be reduced to the unit area rectangle of dimensions $\sqrt{\epsilon} \times \sqrt{1/\epsilon}$, where $\epsilon = L_x/L_y$ is the aspect ratio for the rectangle. This region will henceforth be called $\mathbb{U}^2_\epsilon$, and scaled coordinates will always be assumed (with the primed notation dropped). When $\epsilon = 1$ (i.e., the region is a square), the symbol $\mathbb{U}^2$ will be used.

In radial coordinates, the main region of interest is the circle of radius R, i.e., $\{(r, \theta) \in \mathbb{R}^2, 0 \leq r \leq R\}$. Again, through the introduction of a scaled coordinate this region may be reduced to the circle of radius 1, $\mathbb{U}^2_\circ$.

10.1.3 Partial differential operators

In Cartesian coordinates, the differential operators which appear, beyond partial time derivatives, which have already been discussed in Chapter 5, are of the form $\partial/\partial x$, $\partial/\partial y$, $\partial^2/\partial x^2$, $\partial^2/\partial y^2$, $\partial^2/\partial x \partial y$, etc. When applied to a function $u(x, y, t)$, the following notation will be used:

$$\frac{\partial u}{\partial x} = u_x \qquad \frac{\partial u}{\partial y} = u_y \qquad \frac{\partial^2 u}{\partial x^2} = u_{xx} \qquad \frac{\partial^2 u}{\partial y^2} = u_{yy} \qquad \frac{\partial^2 u}{\partial x \partial y} = u_{xy} \qquad \text{etc.}$$

Technical considerations having to do with interchanging the order of derivatives will be neglected here, so it may be assumed, for example, that $u_{xy} = u_{yx}$.

In radial coordinates, similar operators and accompanying notation are used, i.e.,

$$\frac{\partial u}{\partial r} = u_r \qquad \frac{\partial u}{\partial \theta} = u_\theta \qquad \frac{\partial^2 u}{\partial r^2} = u_{rr} \qquad \frac{\partial^2 u}{\partial \theta^2} = u_{\theta\theta} \qquad \frac{\partial^2 u}{\partial r \partial \theta} = u_{r\theta} \qquad \text{etc.}$$

For isotropic systems in musical acoustics, the most commonly occurring differential operator is not any of the above operators in isolation, but rather the 2D Laplacian Δ, defined in terms of its action on a function u as

$$\Delta u = u_{xx} + u_{yy} \qquad\qquad \Delta u = \frac{1}{r}(ru_r)_r + \frac{1}{r^2}u_{\theta\theta} \qquad (10.2)$$

in Cartesian and radial coordinates, respectively. Also important, especially in problems in plate dynamics, is the fourth-order operator known as the bi-Laplacian, or biharmonic operator $\Delta\Delta$, a double application of the Laplacian operator. In Cartesian coordinates, for example, when applied to a function u, it behaves as

$$\Delta\Delta u = u_{xxxx} + 2u_{xxyy} + u_{yyyy} \qquad (10.3)$$

10.1.4 Differential operators in the spatial frequency domain

Just as in 1D, it is possible to view differential operators in terms of their behavior in the spatial frequency domain—in general, this is only simple in Cartesian coordinates, where differential

operators remain shift invariant. (Notice that in radial coordinates, operators such as the Laplacian
show an explicit dependence on the coordinate r.)

In 2D, the frequency domain ansatz (5.4) is generalized to

$$u(x, y, t) = e^{st + j\beta_x x + j\beta_y y}$$

When $s = j\omega$, this corresponds to a wave traveling in direction $\beta = (\beta_x, \beta_y)$ in the Cartesian
plane, of wavelength $2\pi/|\beta|$, where $|\beta| = (\beta_x^2 + \beta_y^2)^{1/2}$ is the wavenumber magnitude, and where
β_x and β_y are the individual components. For such a test function, the various differential operators
above act as

$$\frac{\partial u}{\partial x} = j\beta_x u \qquad \frac{\partial u}{\partial y} = j\beta_y u \qquad \frac{\partial^2 u}{\partial x^2} = -\beta_x^2 u \qquad \frac{\partial^2 u}{\partial y^2} = -\beta_y^2 u \qquad \frac{\partial^2 u}{\partial x \partial y} = -\beta_y \beta_x u$$

and

$$\Delta u = -(\beta_x^2 + \beta_y^2)u = -|\beta|^2 u \qquad \Delta\Delta u = |\beta|^4 u$$

Notice in particular that the operators Δ and $\Delta\Delta$ lead to multiplicative factors which depend only
on the wavenumber magnitude $|\beta|$, and not on the individual components β_x and β_y—this is a
reflection of the isotropic character of such operations, which occur naturally in problems which
do not exhibit any directional dependence. The same is not true, however, of the discrete operators
which approximate them; see Section 10.2.2.

10.1.5   Inner products

The definition of the L_2 inner product in 2D is a natural extension of that in 1D. For two functions
f and g, dependent on two spatial coordinates, and possibly time as well, one may write

$$\langle f, g \rangle_D = \iint_D fg\, dx dy \qquad\qquad \langle f, g \rangle_D = \iint_D fgr\, dr d\theta \qquad\qquad (10.4)$$

in Cartesian and radial coordinates, respectively; the same notation will be used for both coordinate systems, though one should note the presence of the factor r implicit in the definition
in the radial case. The norm of a function f may be defined, as in the 1D case, as $\|f\|_D = \langle f, f \rangle_D$.

Integration by parts follows; in Cartesian coordinates, for example, over $D = \mathbb{R}^2$,

$$\langle f, g_x \rangle_{\mathbb{R}^2} = -\langle f_x, g \rangle_{\mathbb{R}^2} \qquad\qquad \langle f, g_y \rangle_{\mathbb{R}^2} = -\langle f_y, g \rangle_{\mathbb{R}^2} \qquad\qquad (10.5)$$

The following identity also holds for inner products involving the Laplacian:

$$\langle f, \Delta g \rangle_{\mathbb{R}^2} = \langle \Delta f, g \rangle_{\mathbb{R}^2} \qquad\qquad (10.6)$$

This holds in Cartesian coordinates, and in radial coordinates, provided that f and g and their
radial derivatives are bounded near the origin.

The Cauchy–Schwartz inequality (5.7a) and triangle inequality (5.7b) hold as in 1D, over any
domain D.

Edges

As in 1D, when the domain D possesses a boundary, or, in this case, an edge, extra terms appear
in the above identities. Consider first the half plane $D = \mathbb{R}^{2,x+}$. Now, the first of the integration

by parts identities (10.5) becomes

$$\langle f, g_x \rangle_{\mathbb{R}^{2,x+}} = -\langle f_x, g \rangle_{\mathbb{R}^{2,x+}} - \{f, g\}_{(0,\mathbb{R})}$$

where $\{f, g\}_{(0,\mathbb{R})}$ indicates a 1D inner product over the domain boundary at $x = 0$, i.e.,

$$\{f, g\}_{(0,\mathbb{R})} = \int_{y=-\infty}^{\infty} f(0, y)g(0, y)dy \tag{10.7}$$

This special notation for the 1D inner product used to indicate boundary terms arising in 2D problems is distinct from that employed in previous chapters—see Section 5.1.3.

Additional terms appear when higher derivatives are involved. For the case of the Laplacian, over the same domain, (10.6) becomes

$$\langle f, \Delta g \rangle_{\mathbb{R}^{2,x+}} = \langle \Delta f, g \rangle_{\mathbb{R}^{2,x+}} - \{f, g_x\}_{(0,\mathbb{R})} + \{f_x, g\}_{(0,\mathbb{R})}$$

The case of the quarter plane, $\mathcal{D} = \mathbb{R}^{2,x+y+}$, is of particular interest in problems defined over rectangular regions. Now, in the case of the Laplacian, boundary terms appear along both edges:

$$\langle f, \Delta g \rangle_{\mathbb{R}^{2,x+y+}} = \langle \Delta f, g \rangle_{\mathbb{R}^{2,x+y+}} - \{f, g_x\}_{(0,\mathbb{R}^+)} + \{f_x, g\}_{(0,\mathbb{R}^+)} - \{f, g_y\}_{(\mathbb{R}^+,0)} + \{f_y, g\}_{(\mathbb{R}^+,0)}$$

Circular domains

The circular domain $\mathcal{D} = \mathbb{U}_\circ^2$ is of great practical utility in sound synthesis applications for certain percussion instruments, such as cymbals and gongs. There is only a single edge, at $r = 1$, though, in difference approximations, an artificial "edge" appears at $r = 0$, which must be treated carefully—see the discussion of the discrete Laplacian beginning on page 300. In order to examine boundary conditions, integration by parts is again a necessary tool. Here is an identity of great utility:

$$\langle f, \Delta g \rangle_{\mathbb{U}_\circ^2} = -\langle f_r, g_r \rangle_{\mathbb{U}_\circ^2} - \langle (1/r)f_\theta, (1/r)g_\theta \rangle_{\mathbb{U}_\circ^2} + \{f, g_r\}_{(1,[0,2\pi))} \tag{10.8a}$$

$$= \langle \Delta f, g \rangle_{\mathbb{U}_\circ^2} + \{f, g_r\}_{(1,[0,2\pi))} - \{f_r, g\}_{(1,[0,2\pi))} \tag{10.8b}$$

Of slight concern are the factors of $(1/r)$ which appear in the inner products above; it must further be assumed that f and g are bounded and single valued at $r = 0$.

10.2 Grid functions and difference operators: Cartesian coordinates

The extension of the definitions in Section 5.2.2 to two spatial coordinates is, in the Cartesian case, immediate. A grid function $u_{l,m}^n$, for $(l, m) \in \mathcal{D}$, and $n \geq 0$, represents an approximation to a continuous function $u(x, y, t)$, at coordinates $x = lh_x$, $y = mh_y$, $t = nk$. Here, $\mathcal{D}$ is a subset of the set of pairs of integers, $\mathbb{Z}^2$, and h_x and h_y are the grid spacings in the x and y directions. The semi-infinite domains, or half planes corresponding to $\mathbb{R}^{2,x+}$ and $\mathbb{R}^{2,y+}$, are $\mathbb{Z}^{2,x+} = \{(l, m) \in \mathbb{Z}^2, l \geq 0\}$ and $\mathbb{Z}^{2,y+} = \{(l, m) \in \mathbb{Z}^2, m \geq 0\}$. For the quarter plane, one can define $\mathbb{Z}^{2,x+y+} = \{(l, m) \in \mathbb{Z}^2, l, m \geq 0\}$. Most important, in real-world simulation, is the rectangular region $\mathbb{U}_{N_x,N_y}^2 = \{(l, m) \in \mathbb{Z}^2, 0 \leq l \leq N_x, 0 \leq m \leq N_y\}$.

Temporal operators behave exactly as those defined in 1D, in Section 5.2.1, and it is not worth repeating these definitions here. Spatial shift operators in the x and y directions may be defined as

$$e_{x+}u_{l,m}^n = u_{l+1,m}^n \qquad e_{x-}u_{l,m}^n = u_{l-1,m}^n \qquad e_{y+}u_{l,m}^n = u_{l,m+1}^n \qquad e_{y-}u_{l,m}^n = u_{l,m-1}^n$$

1
2
3
4
5
6
7
8
9
10
11
12
13
14
15
16
17
18
19
20
21
22
23
24
25
26
27
28
29
30
31
32
33
34
35
36
37
38
39
40
41
42
43
44
45
46
47
48
49
50
51

and forward, backward, and centered difference operators as

$$\delta_{x+} \triangleq \frac{1}{h_x}(e_{x+} - 1) \approx \frac{\partial}{\partial x} \qquad \delta_{x-} \triangleq \frac{1}{h_x}(1 - e_{x-}) \approx \frac{\partial}{\partial x} \qquad \delta_{x\cdot} \triangleq \frac{1}{2h_x}(e_{x+} - e_{x-}) \approx \frac{\partial}{\partial x}$$

$$\delta_{y+} \triangleq \frac{1}{h_y}(e_{y+} - 1) \approx \frac{\partial}{\partial y} \qquad \delta_{y-} \triangleq \frac{1}{h_y}(1 - e_{y-}) \approx \frac{\partial}{\partial y} \qquad \delta_{y\cdot} \triangleq \frac{1}{2h_y}(e_{y+} - e_{y-}) \approx \frac{\partial}{\partial y}$$

Centered second derivative approximations follow immediately as

$$\delta_{xx} = \delta_{x+}\delta_{x-} \approx \frac{\partial^2}{\partial x^2} \qquad\qquad \delta_{yy} = \delta_{y+}\delta_{y-} \approx \frac{\partial^2}{\partial y^2}$$

and various mixed derivative approximations, such as $\delta_{x+}\delta_{y-}$ approximating $\partial^2/\partial x \partial y$, may be arrived at through composition. It is also possible to define averaging operators in the x and y directions, such as μ_{x+}, μ_{y-}, etc., generalizing those presented in Section 5.2.2. See Figure 10.2 and Problem 10.1.

Equal grid spacings

Though, in general, one can choose unequal grid spacings h_x and h_y in the two Cartesian coordinates x and y, for simplicity of analysis and programming it is often easier to set them equal to a single constant, i.e., $h_x = h_y = h$. This is natural for problems which are isotropic (i.e., for which wave propagation is independent of direction). This simplification is employed in much of the remainder of this book. There are cases, though, for which such a choice can lead to errors which can become perceptually important when a very coarse grid is used (i.e., typically in simulating musical systems of high pitch). For some examples relating to the 2D wave equation, see Problem 11.7 and Programming Exercise 11.1 in the following chapter. When the system itself exhibits significant anisotropy, however (such as in the case of certain plates used as soundboards—see Section 12.5), this simplification must be revisited.

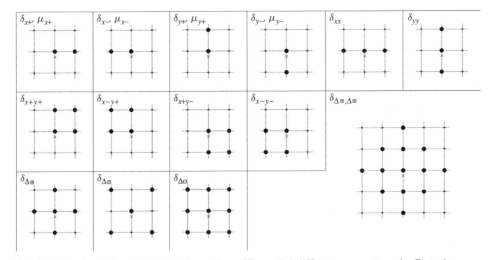

Figure 10.2   Stencils or footprints for various 2D spatial difference operators, in Cartesian coordinates, as indicated. In each case, the point at which the operator acts is indicated by a × symbol.

The discrete Laplacian and biharmonic operators

Quite important in musical sound synthesis applications is the approximation to the Laplacian operator, as given in (10.2)—there are clearly many ways of doing this. The simplest, by far, is to make use of what is known as the five-point Laplacian. Here are two possible forms of this operator, one making use of points adjacent to the center point, and another employing points diagonally adjacent:

$$\delta_{\Delta\boxplus} = \delta_{xx} + \delta_{yy} = \Delta + O(h^2) \qquad \delta_{\Delta\boxtimes} = \delta_{xx} + \delta_{yy} + \frac{h^2}{2}\delta_{xx}\delta_{yy} = \Delta + O(h^2) \tag{10.9}$$

These two operators may be combined in a standard way (see Section 2.2.2) to yield a so-called nine-point Laplacian, depending on a free parameter α:

$$\delta_{\Delta\alpha} \triangleq \alpha\delta_{\Delta\boxplus} + (1-\alpha)\delta_{\Delta\boxtimes} = \Delta + O(h^2) \tag{10.10}$$

Though it involves more grid points, it may be used in order to render an approximation more isotropic—see Section 11.3 for an application of this in the case of the 2D wave equation.

Also important, in the case of the vibrating stiff plate, is the discrete biharmonic operator, or bi-Laplacian, which consists of the composition of the Laplacian with itself, or $\Delta\Delta$. A simple approximation may be given as

$$\delta_{\Delta\boxplus,\Delta\boxplus} \triangleq \delta_{\Delta\boxplus}\delta_{\Delta\boxplus} = \Delta\Delta + O(h^2)$$

One could go further here and develop a family of approximations using a parameterized combination of the operators $\delta_{\Delta\boxplus}$ and $\delta_{\Delta\boxtimes}$—see [48] for more on this topic, and the text of Szilard [348], which covers difference approximations to the biharmonic operator in great detail.

The stencils or footprints of the above spatial difference operators are illustrated in Figure 10.2. The precise coefficients to be applied at the various points are not indicated, but easily determined—see Problem 10.1.

10.2.1 Interpolation in 2D and spreading operators

Interpolation, necessary for reading out a waveform from a discrete grid, and spreading, necessary when one is interested in exciting such a grid, or coupling it to another object, are direct extensions of their 1D counterparts, as described in Section 5.2.4.

For a grid function $u_{l,m}$, defined for integer l and m, with grid spacings h_x and h_y, a zeroth-order (westward/southward) interpolant $I_0(x_o, y_o)$ operating at position (x_o, y_o) is defined by

$$I_0(x_o, y_o)u = u_{l_o,m_o} \qquad \text{where} \qquad l_o = \text{floor}(x_o/h_x), \quad m_o = \text{floor}(y_o/h_y) \tag{10.11}$$

Such an interpolant corresponds to a crude "staircase" approximation, as illustrated in Figure 10.3(b). It is particularly useful in cases in which the interpolation point is static, and when there is good grid resolution.

Another choice which is appealing, due to its simplicity, is the bilinear interpolant, $I_1(x_o, y_o)$. If the grid indices l_o and m_o are as given in (10.11), and furthermore the remainders by $\alpha_{x,o} = x_o/h_x - l_o$ and $\alpha_{y,o} = y_o/h_y - m_o$, it is defined as

$$I_1(x_o, y_o)u = (1-\alpha_{x,o})(1-\alpha_{y,o})u_{l_o,m_o} + (1-\alpha_{x,o})\alpha_{y,o}u_{l_o,m_o+1}$$

$$+ \alpha_{x,o}(1-\alpha_{y,o})u_{l_o+1,m_o} + \alpha_{x,o}\alpha_{y,o}u_{l_o+1,m_o+1}$$

1
2
3
4
5
6
7
8
9
10
11
12
13
14
15
16
17
18
19
20
21
22
23
24
25
26
27
28
29
30
31
32
33
34
35
36
37
38
39
40
41
42
43
44
45
46
47
48
49
50
51

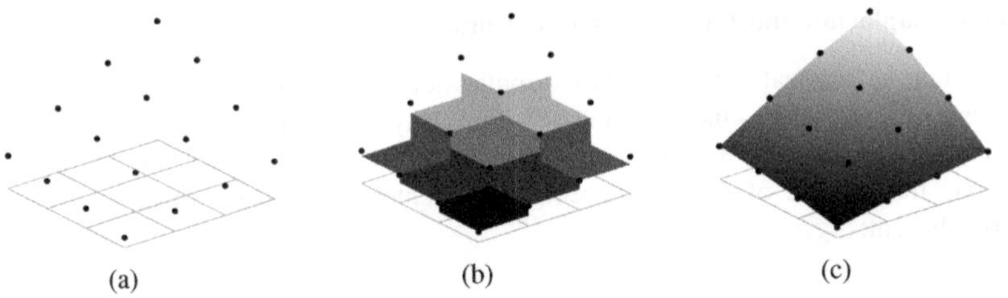

Figure 10.3   Interpolation in 2D: (a) values of a grid function; (b) the simple truncating interpolant I_0; and (c) a bilinear interpolant I_1. The interpolants are viewed as "reconstructing" a 2D function underlying the grid function shown in (a), from which interpolated values may then be drawn.

This interpolant makes use of the four grid points neighboring the interpolation point, using a bilinear function of these values—see Figure 10.3(c). It is more accurate than I_0, and the simplest interpolant one could realistically use in situations where the readout point is moving. See Programming Exercise 10.1.

Spreading grid functions $J_0(x_i, y_i)$ and $J_1(x_i, y_i)$, operating at position (x_i, y_i), may be similarly defined as the duals to these interpolants, i.e.,

$$J_{l,m,0}(x_i, y_i) = \frac{1}{h_x h_y} \begin{cases} 1, & l = l_i, m = m_i \\ 0, & \text{else} \end{cases}$$

$$J_{l,m,1}(x_i, y_i) = \frac{1}{h_x h_y} \begin{cases} (1 - \alpha_{x,i})(1 - \alpha_{y,i},) & l = l_i, m = m_i \\ (1 - \alpha_{x,i})\alpha_{y,i}, & l = l_i, m = m_i + 1 \\ \alpha_{x,i}(1 - \alpha_{y,i}), & l = l_i + 1, m = m_i \\ \alpha_{x,i}\alpha_{y,i}, & l = l_i + 1, m = m_i + 1 \\ 0, & \text{else} \end{cases}$$

where $l_i = \text{floor}(x_i/h_x)$, $m_i = \text{floor}(y_i/h_y)$, $\alpha_{x,i} = x_i/h_x - l_i$, and $\alpha_{y,i} = y_i/h_y - m_i$. Either approximates a 2D Dirac delta function $\delta(x - x_i, y - y_i)$.

One could go further here, and develop higher-order interpolants—as those with a background in image processing may know, this is a much more complex matter in 2D than in the 1D case [306], and the matter is not pursued further here. See also Programming Exercise 11.2 for some exploration of the perceptual effects of the choice of a bilinear interpolant in audio applications.

10.2.2   Frequency domain analysis

Frequency domain analysis of difference operators in the Cartesian case is a straightforward generalization from 1D. Skipping over the definition of Fourier and z transforms, the ansatz is now

$$u_{l,m}^n = z^n e^{jh(l\beta_x + m\beta_y)} \tag{10.12}$$

where, again, β_x and β_y are components of a vector wavenumber $\boldsymbol{\beta} = (\beta_x, \beta_y)$ of magnitude $|\boldsymbol{\beta}| = (\beta_x^2 + \beta_y^2)^{1/2}$. The frequency domain behavior of temporal operators is unchanged from the 1D case.

Defining the variables p_x and p_y by

$$p_x = \sin^2(\beta_x h/2) \qquad p_y = \sin^2(\beta_y h/2) \tag{10.13}$$

it is true for a single component of the form (10.12) that

$$\delta_{xx} u = -\frac{4}{h^2} p_x u \qquad\qquad \delta_{yy} u = -\frac{4}{h^2} p_y u$$

$$\delta_{\Delta\boxplus} u = -\frac{4}{h^2}\left(p_x + p_y\right) u \qquad \delta_{\Delta\boxtimes} u = -\frac{4}{h^2}\left(p_x + p_y - 2 p_x p_y\right) u \qquad \delta_{\Delta\boxplus,\Delta\boxplus} u = \frac{16}{h^4}\left(p_x + p_y\right)^2 u$$

$$\tag{10.14}$$

Notice in particular that the frequency domain multiplication factors for the approximations to the Laplacian are bilinear functions of p_x and p_y defined over the unit square—one may use properties of such functions in order to simplify stability analysis. See Problem 10.2.

Anisotropic behavior

One new facet of finite difference schemes in 2D is numerical anisotropy—waves travel at different speeds in different directions, even when the underlying problem is isotropic. This is wholly due to the directional asymmetry imposed on a problem by introducing a grid and is a phenomenon which shows itself most prominently at high frequencies (or short wavelengths)—in the long-wavelength limit, the numerical behavior of operators which approximate isotropic differential operators becomes approximately isotropic.

As a simple example of this, consider the operator $\delta_{\Delta\boxplus}$, as defined in (10.9). It is perhaps easiest to examine the anisotropy in the frequency domain representation. Expanding from (10.14) in powers of the wavenumber components β_x and β_y gives

$$\delta_{\Delta\boxplus} \Longrightarrow -\frac{4}{h^2}\left(p_x + p_y\right) = -|\beta|^2 + \frac{h^2}{12}\left(\beta_x^4 + \beta_y^4\right) + O(h^4)$$

Thus, as expected, the operator $\delta_{\Delta\boxplus}$ approximates the Laplacian Δ to second-order accuracy in the grid spacing h, but the higher-order terms cannot be grouped in terms of the wavenumber magnitude alone. Such numerical anisotropy, and ways of reducing it, will be discussed with regard to the 2D wave equation in Section 11.3. See also Problem 10.3 and Programming Exercise 10.2.

Amplification polynomials

Just as in the lumped and 1D cases, for LSI problems in 2D, in the analysis of difference schemes, one often arrives at amplification polynomials of the following form:

$$P(z) = \sum_{l=0}^{N} a_l(\beta_x, \beta_y) z^l = 0 \tag{10.15}$$

As before, a stability condition is arrived at by finding conditions such that the roots are bounded by one in magnitude, now for all values of β_x and β_y supported on the grid.

10.2.3 A discrete inner product

The discrete inner product and norm over a Cartesian grid in 2D are a direct extension of those given in Section 5.2.9, in the 1D case. For an arbitrary domain $\mathcal{D}$, the simplest definition, for two grid functions $f_{l,m}$, $g_{l,m}$ defined over a grid of uniform spacing h in the x and y directions, is

$$\langle f, g \rangle_{\mathcal{D}} = \sum_{(l,m)\in\mathcal{D}} h^2 f_{l,m} g_{l,m} \qquad\qquad \|f\|_{\mathcal{D}} = \langle f, f \rangle_{\mathcal{D}}$$

The Cauchy-Schwartz and triangle inequalities again hold, as in 1D.

Summation by parts and inequalities

Summation by parts extends naturally to 2D. Consider, in the first instance, grid functions f and g defined over the domain $\mathcal{D} = \mathbb{Z}^2$. It can be directly shown that

$$\langle f, \delta_{x-}g\rangle_{\mathbb{Z}^2} = -\langle\delta_{x+}f, g\rangle_{\mathbb{Z}^2} \qquad\qquad \langle f, \delta_{y-}g\rangle_{\mathbb{Z}^2} = -\langle\delta_{y+}f, g\rangle_{\mathbb{Z}^2} \qquad (10.16)$$

From these identities, one may go further and show, for the five-point Laplacian, that

$$\langle f, \delta_{\Delta\boxplus}g\rangle_{\mathbb{Z}^2} = -\langle\delta_{x-}f, \delta_{x-}g\rangle_{\mathbb{Z}^2} - \langle\delta_{y-}f, \delta_{y-}g\rangle_{\mathbb{Z}^2} = \langle\delta_{\Delta\boxplus}f, g\rangle_{\mathbb{Z}^2} \qquad (10.17)$$

Inequalities relating norms of grid functions under difference operators to norms of the grid functions themselves also follow:

$$\|\delta_{x+}u\|_{\mathbb{Z}^2} \leq \frac{2}{h}\|u\|_{\mathbb{Z}^2} \quad \|\delta_{y+}u\|_{\mathbb{Z}^2} \leq \frac{2}{h}\|u\|_{\mathbb{Z}^2} \quad \|\delta_{xx}u\|_{\mathbb{Z}^2} \leq \frac{4}{h^2}\|u\|_{\mathbb{Z}^2} \quad \|\delta_{yy}u\|_{\mathbb{Z}^2} \leq \frac{4}{h^2}\|u\|_{\mathbb{Z}^2}$$

$$(10.18)$$

from which it may be deduced that

$$\|\delta_{\Delta\boxplus}u\|_{\mathbb{Z}^2} = \|\left(\delta_{xx} + \delta_{yy}\right)u\|_{\mathbb{Z}^2} \leq \|\delta_{xx}u\|_{\mathbb{Z}^2} + \|\delta_{yy}u\|_{\mathbb{Z}^2} \leq \frac{8}{h^2}\|u\|_{\mathbb{Z}^2}$$

Boundary terms

When the domain has an edge, boundary terms appear in the summation by parts identities above. Consider, for example, the half plane $\mathcal{D} = \mathbb{Z}^{2,x+}$. Now, instead of the first of (10.16), one has

$$\langle f, \delta_{x-}g\rangle_{\mathbb{Z}^{2,x+}} = -\langle\delta_{x+}f, g\rangle_{\mathbb{Z}^{2,x+}} - \{f, e_{x-}g\}_{(0,\mathbb{Z})} \qquad (10.19)$$

Here, the $\{\cdot, \cdot\}$ notation indicates a 1D inner product over the boundary of the region $\mathbb{Z}^{2,x+}$, i.e.,

$$\{f, e_{x-}g\}_{(0,\mathbb{Z})} = \sum_{m=-\infty}^{\infty} hf_{0,m}g_{-1,m}$$

Notice the appearance here of values of the grid function at virtual locations with $l = -1$; such values may be set once boundary conditions have been specified.

Similarly, over the domain $\mathcal{D} = \mathbb{Z}^{2,y+}$, summation by parts becomes

$$\langle f, \delta_{y-}g\rangle_{\mathbb{Z}^{2,y+}} = -\langle\delta_{y+}f, g\rangle_{\mathbb{Z}^{2,y+}} - \{f, e_{y-}g\}_{(\mathbb{Z},0)}$$

The above identities allow the determination of numerical boundary conditions when energy methods are employed. For examples, see the case of the 2D wave equation, in Section 11.2.2, and linear plate vibration, on page 338.

10.2.4 Matrix interpretation of difference operators

As in 1D, it is sometimes useful to represent difference operators in matrix form, especially in the case of implicit schemes which require linear system solution techniques. As a first step, the grid function to be operated on should be "flattened" to a vector. For a grid function $u_{l,m}$, for instance, defined over $\mathcal{D} = \mathbb{Z}^2$, one can stack the columns to create a vector $\mathbf{u}$, as

$$\mathbf{u} = [\ldots, \mathbf{u}_{l-1}^T, \mathbf{u}_l^T, \mathbf{u}_{l+1}^T, \ldots]^T$$

where $\mathbf{u}_l = [\ldots, u_{l,m-1}, u_{l,m}, u_{l,m+1}, \ldots]^T$. (In other words, consecutive vertical strips of the 2D grid function u are lined up end to end in a single-column vector.) Matrix forms of difference operators, then, have a particularly sparse form. Consider, for example, the operators δ_{xx} and δ_{yy}, corresponding to second derivatives in the x and y directions, respectively. In matrix form, and assuming equal grid spacings $h_x = h_y = h$, these look like

$$
\mathbf{D}_{xx}^{(2)} = \frac{1}{h^2}
\begin{bmatrix}
\ddots & \ddots & & & & \mathbf{0} \\
\ddots & -2\mathbf{I} & \mathbf{I} & & & \\
& \mathbf{I} & -2\mathbf{I} & \mathbf{I} & & \\
& & \mathbf{I} & -2\mathbf{I} & \mathbf{I} & \\
\mathbf{0} & & & \mathbf{I} & -2\mathbf{I} & \ddots \\
& & & & \ddots & \ddots
\end{bmatrix}
\qquad
\mathbf{D}_{yy}^{(2)} =
\begin{bmatrix}
\ddots & & & \\
& \mathbf{D}_{yy}^{(1)} & & \\
& & \mathbf{D}_{yy}^{(1)} & \\
& & & \mathbf{D}_{yy}^{(1)} \\
& & & & \ddots
\end{bmatrix}
$$

where the superscript (2) indicates that the matrix operators are not to be confused with their 1D counterparts. Here, $\mathbf{I}$ is again the identity matrix, and $\mathbf{D}_{yy}^{(1)}$ is a 1D difference matrix, identical in form to that of $\mathbf{D}_{xx}$ given in (5.17).

Matrix forms of other difference operators follow immediately. The difference operators $\delta_{\Delta\boxplus}$ and $\delta_{\Delta\boxplus,\Delta\boxplus}$, discrete approximations to the Laplacian and biharmonic operators, have the following forms, at interior points in the domain:

$$
\mathbf{D}_{\Delta\boxplus} = \mathbf{D}_{xx}^{(2)} + \mathbf{D}_{yy}^{(2)} \qquad\qquad \mathbf{D}_{\Delta\boxplus,\Delta\boxplus} = \mathbf{D}_{\Delta\boxplus}\mathbf{D}_{\Delta\boxplus}
$$

It is probably easiest to understand the action of these operators by examining sparsity plots, indicating where non-zero entries occur, as shown in Figure 10.4.

Boundary conditions

As in 1D, when boundary conditions are taken into account, the matrices are of finite size, though values in the extreme blocks, and also in extreme rows and columns of other blocks, must be modified. From an implementation point of view, it is useful to examine the form of such modifications.

As an example, consider the operator $\delta_{\Delta\boxplus}$, operating on a grid function $u_{l,m}$ defined over the finite rectangular domain $\mathcal{D} = \mathbb{U}_{N_x,N_y}^2$, or, in other words, the set of values of $u_{l,m}$ defined for $0 \leq l \leq N_x$, $0 \leq m \leq N_y$. A particularly simple case is that of Dirichlet, or fixed termination, in which case the values of $u_{l,m}$ are set permanently to zero at the domain boundary. The total grid consists of $N_x - 1$ vertical strips of length $N_y - 1$, leaving out the values on the boundary. Thus,

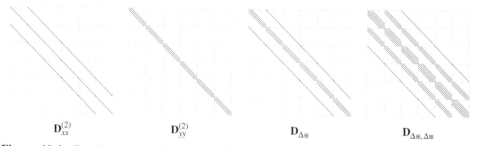

$$\mathbf{D}_{xx}^{(2)} \qquad\qquad \mathbf{D}_{yy}^{(2)} \qquad\qquad \mathbf{D}_{\Delta\boxplus} \qquad\qquad \mathbf{D}_{\Delta\boxplus,\Delta\boxplus}$$

Figure 10.4   Sparsity patterns for various 2D difference operators written in matrix form, in Cartesian coordinates.

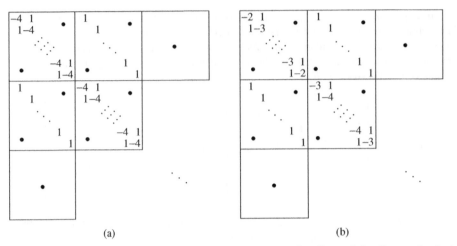

1
2
3
4
5
6
7
8
9
10
11
12
13
14
15
16

(a)   (b)

Figure 10.5   Upper left-hand corners of the matrix representation $\mathbf{D}_{\Delta\boxplus}$ of the discrete Laplacian
operator $\delta_{\Delta\boxplus}$ under (a) Dirichlet conditions and (b) Neumann conditions. Values are to be scaled
by $1/h^2$, and • indicates zero entries.

if the state vector $\mathbf{u}$ is defined as the concatenation of these vertical strips, the matrix operator $\mathbf{D}_{\Delta\boxplus}$
is as shown in Figure 10.5(a); it consists of $(N_y - 1) \times (N_y - 1)$ blocks. See also Problem 10.4.

As another example, consider the same operator acting on a grid function over the same
domain, but under Neumann, or zero normal derivative conditions on all sides:

$$\delta_{x-}u_{0,m} = 0, \qquad m = 0, \dots, N_y \qquad (10.20a)$$

$$\delta_{x+}u_{N_x,m} = 0, \qquad m = 0, \dots, N_y \qquad (10.20b)$$

$$\delta_{y-}u_{l,0} = 0, \qquad l = 0, \dots, N_x \qquad (10.20c)$$

$$\delta_{y+}u_{l,N_y} = 0, \qquad l = 0, \dots, N_x \qquad (10.20d)$$

Now, when operating at a boundary point, the operator makes use of virtual grid points outside the
domain. Consider the condition $\delta_{x-}u_{0,m} = 0$, for $0 < m < N_y$ (i.e., excluding the corner points at
$l = 0, m = 0$ and $l = 0, m = N_y$). This implies that, in terms of virtual grid points, one may write
$u_{-1,m} = u_{0,m}$. Thus in order to evaluate the discrete Laplacian $\delta_{\Delta\boxplus}$ at such a point in terms of
values over the grid interior, one has

$$\delta_{\Delta\boxplus}u_{0,m} = \frac{1}{h^2}\left(u_{0,m+1} + u_{0,m-1} + u_{-1,m} + u_{1,m} - 4u_{0,m}\right)$$

$$= \frac{1}{h^2}\left(u_{0,m+1} + u_{0,m-1} + u_{1,m} - 3u_{0,m}\right) \qquad (10.21)$$

A similar evaluation may be written for points with $0 < l < N_x$, and $m = 0$. At a domain corner,
such as $l = 0, m = 0$, when Neumann conditions are employed along both edges, one has $\delta_{x-}u_{0,0} =
\delta_{y-}u_{0,0} = 0$, and thus, for the Laplacian,

$$\delta_{\Delta\boxplus}u_{0,0} = \frac{1}{h^2}\left(u_{0,1} + u_{1,0} - 2u_{0,0}\right) \qquad (10.22)$$

The matrix operator $\mathbf{D}_{\Delta\boxplus}$ operates over the full grid, which when written as a vector consists of
$N_x + 1$ concatenated vertical strips of length $N_y + 1$ (i.e., the points on the boundary now form

part of the state). The matrix operator appears in Figure 10.5(b), where it is to be noted that the top left-hand block and the top row entries of the other central blocks have slightly modified values. For different approximations to the Neumann condition, the modifications are distinct. See Problem 10.5 and Programming Exercise 10.3. Both the Dirichlet and Neumann conditions presented here arise naturally in the analysis of finite difference schemes for the 2D wave equation—see Section 11.2.2.

As one can imagine, for operators of wider stencil, such as, for example, $D_{\Delta\boxplus,\Delta\boxplus}$, more boundary conditions are required, and thus more values in the resulting matrix form must be modified. See Problem 10.6 and Programming Exercise 10.5.

10.3   Grid functions and difference operators: radial coordinates

Problems defined over a circular geometry play a large role in musical acoustics, in particular when it comes to the modeling of percussion instruments such as drums and gongs. Though finite element models are often used under such conditions, a finite difference approach is still viable, and can lead to very efficient and easily programmed sound synthesis algorithm designs. A grid function $u_{l,m}^n$, for $(l, m) \in \mathcal{D}$, and $n \geq 0$, represents an approximation to a continuous function $u(r, \theta, t)$, at coordinates $r = lh_r$, $\theta = mh_\theta$, and $t = nk$. In general, the grid spacings h_r and h_θ will not be the same. See Figure 10.6(a). Here, the main domain of interest will be the unit area circle $\mathcal{D} = \mathbb{U}_{\circ,N_r,N_\theta}^2$, the set of points l, m with $0 \leq l \leq N_r$, and $0 \leq m \leq N_\theta - 1$, where $h_r = 1/N_r$ and $h_\theta = 2\pi/N_\theta$. Also useful is the domain $\overline{\mathbb{U}}_{\circ,N_r,N_\theta}^2$ which is the same as $\mathbb{U}_{\circ,N_r,N_\theta}^2$ without the central grid location at $l = 0$. At the central grid point, at $l = 0$, for any m, any grid function u is assumed to be single valued, and its value here will be called $u_{0,0}$. A special grid function of interest is $r_l = lh_r$.

Spatial shift operators in the r and θ directions may be defined as

$$e_{r+}u_{l,m}^n = u_{l+1,m}^n \qquad e_{r-}u_{l,m}^n = u_{l-1,m}^n \qquad e_{\theta+}u_{l,m}^n = u_{l,m+1}^n \qquad e_{\theta-}u_{l,m}^n = u_{l,m-1}^n$$

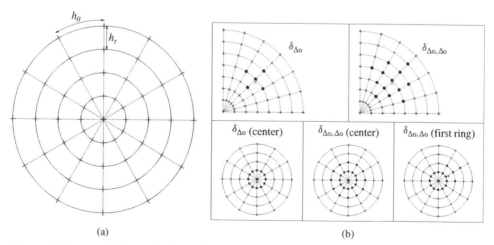

(a)   (b)

Figure 10.6   (a) Grid in radial coordinates, with radial spacing h_r and angular spacing h_θ. (b) Stencils of the discrete Laplacian $\delta_{\Delta\circ}$ and biharmonic operator $\delta_{\Delta\circ,\Delta\circ}$, with specialized forms near the grid center. In each case, the point at which the operator acts is indicated by a $\times$ symbol.

and forward, backward, and centered difference operators as

$$\delta_{r+} \triangleq \frac{1}{h_r}(e_{r+} - 1) \approx \frac{\partial}{\partial r} \qquad \delta_{r-} \triangleq \frac{1}{h_r}(1 - e_{r-}) \approx \frac{\partial}{\partial r} \qquad \delta_{r\cdot} \triangleq \frac{1}{2h_r}(e_{r+} - e_{r-}) \approx \frac{\partial}{\partial r}$$

$$\delta_{\theta+} \triangleq \frac{1}{h_\theta}(e_{\theta+} - 1) \approx \frac{\partial}{\partial \theta} \qquad \delta_{\theta-} \triangleq \frac{1}{h_\theta}(1 - e_{\theta-}) \approx \frac{\partial}{\partial \theta} \qquad \delta_{\theta\cdot} \triangleq \frac{1}{2h_\theta}(e_{\theta+} - e_{\theta-}) \approx \frac{\partial}{\partial \theta}$$

The operators e_{r-}, δ_{r-}, and $\delta_{r\cdot}$ above are only well defined at grid locations with $l \geq 1$. The operators in θ act on grid points with index m modulo N_θ, e.g., $\delta_{\theta-}u_{l,0} = (u_{l,0} - u_{l,N_\theta-1})/h_\theta$.

In analogy with the second form in (10.4), one may define a discrete inner product, over the domain $\mathcal{D} = \overline{\mathbb{U}}^2_{\circ,N_r,N_\theta}$, as

$$\langle f, g \rangle^2_{\overline{\mathbb{U}}_{\circ,N_r,N_\theta}} = \sum_{l=1}^{N_r} \sum_{m=0}^{N_\theta-1} h_\theta h_r r_l f_{l,m} g_{l,m}$$

The discrete Laplacian and biharmonic operators in radial coordinates

The main operator of interest is, as in Cartesian coordinates, the Laplacian, defined in radial coordinates in (10.2). Here is a second-order accurate approximation, as applied to a grid function u:

$$\delta_{\Delta\circ}u = \frac{1}{r}\delta_{r+}((\mu_{r-}r)\delta_{r-}u) + \frac{1}{r^2}\delta_{\theta\theta}u \tag{10.23}$$

where $\delta_{\theta\theta} = \delta_{\theta+}\delta_{\theta-}$. When expanded, this reads as

$$\delta_{\Delta\circ}u_{l,m} = \frac{1}{lh_r^2}\left((l + 1/2)u_{l+1,m} - 2lu_{l,m} + (l - 1/2)u_{l-1,m}\right) + \frac{1}{l^2h_r^2h_\theta^2}\left(u_{l,m+1} - 2u_{l,m} + u_{l,m-1}\right)$$

The above difference operation holds at grid points $u_{l,m}$ with $l > 0$. At the center point, a special form is necessary [121]:

$$\delta_{\Delta\circ}u_{0,0} = \frac{4}{N_\theta h_r^2}\sum_{m=0}^{N_\theta-1}(u_{1,m} - u_{0,0}) \tag{10.24}$$

It is not difficult to show that this operator indeed approximates the Laplacian to second-order accuracy at the domain center—see Problem 10.7. The matrix form of this operator may be constructed without much difficulty—see Programming Exercise 10.6.

The biharmonic operator in radial coordinates $\delta_{\Delta\circ,\Delta\circ}$ may be defined, at interior points in a domain, as

$$\delta_{\Delta\circ,\Delta\circ}u_{l,m} = \delta_{\Delta\circ}\delta_{\Delta\circ}u_{l,m} \qquad 2 \leq l \leq N_r - 2 \tag{10.25}$$

At grid points near the boundary, the form of the operator must be specialized to include boundary conditions. As for the case of the Laplacian, however, in the neighborhood of the center, at grid locations l, m, with $l = 0, 1$, special forms are necessary:

$$\delta_{\Delta\circ,\Delta\circ}u_{0,0} = \frac{16}{3N_\theta h_r^4}\sum_{m=0}^{N_\theta-1}(u_{2,m} - 4u_{1,m} + 3u_{0,0}) \tag{10.26a}$$

$$\delta_{\Delta\circ,\Delta\circ}u_{1,m} = \frac{4}{N_\theta h_r^2}\sum_{m=0}^{N_\theta-1}\delta_{\Delta\circ}u_{1,m} - \delta_{\Delta\circ}u_{0,0} \tag{10.26b}$$

Slightly different settings have been proposed—see [12]. See also Programming Exercise 10.7.

Summation by parts

For circular domains, identities analogous to integration by parts are available, but one must pay special attention to the definition of the Laplacian at the center point. As a practically important example, consider the inner product of a grid function f and the discrete Laplacian applied to a grid function g, over the domain $\bar{\mathbb{U}}^2_{\circ,N_r,N_\theta}$, the unit circle without its center grid point. In this case, the definition (10.23) holds at all points in the domain, and one has

$$\langle f, \delta_{\Delta\circ}g\rangle_{\bar{\mathbb{U}}^2_{\circ,N_r,N_\theta}} = -\left\langle \delta_{r-}f, \frac{\mu_{r-}r}{r}\delta_{r-}g\right\rangle_{\bar{\mathbb{U}}^2_{\circ,N_r,N_\theta}} - \left\langle \delta_\theta - f, \frac{1}{r^2}\delta_\theta - g\right\rangle_{\bar{\mathbb{U}}^2_{\circ,N_r,N_\theta}} + b_{\text{outer}} - b_{\text{inner}}$$

where

$$b_{\text{outer}} = \{f, \mu_{r+}r\delta_{r+}g\}_{(N_r,[0,N_\theta-1])} \triangleq \sum_{m=0}^{N_\theta-1} h_\theta f_{N_r,m}\mu_{r+}r_{N_r}\delta_{r+}g_{N_r,m}$$

$$b_{\text{inner}} = \{e_r - f, \mu_r - r\delta_r - g\}_{(1,[0,N_\theta-1])} \triangleq \sum_{m=0}^{N_\theta-1} h_\theta f_{0,0}\mu_r - r_1\delta_r - g_{1,m}$$

The term b_{outer} clearly corresponds to the boundary term at the domain edge in (10.8a). But the term b_{inner} results purely from the choice of the domain of summation. But it may be rewritten as follows, using single-valuedness of f and g at the grid location $l = 0$, m, and the definition of the discrete Laplacian at the central grid point, from (10.24):

$$b_{\text{inner}} = \frac{f_{0,0}h_\theta}{2}\sum_{m=0}^{N_\theta-1}(g_{1,m} - g_{0,0}) = \frac{\pi h_r^2}{4}f_{0,0}\delta_{\Delta\circ}g_{0,0}$$

Thus, finally, one has

$$\langle f, \delta_{\Delta\circ}g\rangle_{\bar{\mathbb{U}}^2_{\circ,N_r,N_\theta}} + \frac{\pi h_r^2}{4}f_{0,0}\delta_{\Delta\circ}g_{0,0} = -\left\langle \delta_{r-}f, \frac{\mu_{r-}r}{r}\delta_{r-}g\right\rangle_{\bar{\mathbb{U}}^2_{\circ,N_r,N_\theta}}$$

$$-\left\langle \delta_\theta - f, \frac{1}{r^2}\delta_\theta - g\right\rangle_{\bar{\mathbb{U}}^2_{\circ,N_r,N_\theta}} + b_{\text{outer}} \qquad (10.27)$$

Bounds

As before, bounds are available relating the norms of grid functions under difference operators to norms of the grid functions themselves. Here are two of interest in the analysis of schemes involving the discrete Laplacian:

$$\|\delta_\theta - f\|^2_{\bar{\mathbb{U}}_{\circ,N_r,N_\theta}} \leq \frac{2}{h_\theta}\|f\|^2_{\bar{\mathbb{U}}^2_{\circ,N_r,N_\theta}} \qquad \|\sqrt{\mu_{r-}r/r}\delta_{r-}f\|^2_{\bar{\mathbb{U}}^2_{\circ,N_r,N_\theta}} \leq \frac{4}{h_r^2}\|f\|^2_{\bar{\mathbb{U}}^2_{\circ,N_r,N_\theta}} + 2\pi f_{0,0}^2$$

$$(10.28)$$

10.4   Problems

Problem 10.1   *The stencils of various 2D difference operators are shown in Figure 10.2. Not shown, however, are the coefficients to be applied at each point included in the stencil. Determine these for all the operators shown in the figure, assuming equal grid spacings $h_x = h_y = h$. (For the* operator $\delta_{\Delta\boxplus}$, for example, the coefficients from left to right, and top to bottom, are: $1/h^2$, $1/h^2$, $-4/h^2$, $1/h^2$, and $1/h^2$.)

There are certain operators which appear in the figure which are not defined in the main body of the text, namely averaging and mixed derivative operators:

$$\mu_{x+} = \frac{1}{2}(e_{x+} + 1) \qquad \mu_{x-} = \frac{1}{2}(1 + e_{x-}) \qquad \mu_{y+} = \frac{1}{2}(e_{y+} + 1) \qquad \mu_{y-} = \frac{1}{2}(1 + e_{y-})$$

$$\delta_{x+y+} = \delta_{x+}\delta_{y+} \qquad \delta_{x+y-} = \delta_{x+}\delta_{y-} \qquad \delta_{x-y+} = \delta_{x-}\delta_{y+} \qquad \delta_{x-y-} = \delta_{x-}\delta_{y-}$$

Problem 10.2   Given a general bilinear function $f(p, q)$ in the variables p and q

$$f(p, q) = a + bp + cq + dpq$$

defined over the square region $0 \le p, q \le 1$, for constants a, b, c, and d, show that f takes on its maximum and minimum values at the corners of the domain.

Problem 10.3   Recalling the analysis of the anisotropy of the operator $\delta_{\Delta\boxplus}$ in Section 10.2.1, consider the nine-point Laplacian operator as given in (10.10), which depends on the free parameter α, and show that its expansion, in terms of wavenumber components β_x and β_y, is

$$\delta_{\Delta\alpha} \triangleq \alpha\delta_{\Delta\boxplus} + (1 - \alpha)\delta_{\Delta\boxtimes} \Longrightarrow -\left(\beta_x^2 + \beta_y^2\right) + \frac{h^2}{12}\left(\beta_x^4 + 6(1 - \alpha)\beta_x^2\beta_y^2 + \beta_y^4\right) + O(h^4)$$

For an arbitrary choice of α, can the $O(h^2)$ term be written in terms of the wavenumber magnitude $|\beta| = (\beta_x^2 + \beta_y^2)^{1/2}$ alone? If not, is there a value (or values) of α such that it can be? If you can find such a value of α, then the anisotropic behavior of the parameterized operator will exhibit itself only at fourth order (though the operator remains a second-order accurate approximation to the Laplacian).

Problem 10.4   Find the matrix form $\mathbf{D}_{\Delta\alpha}$ of the operator $\delta_{\Delta\alpha}$, assuming that it acts on a grid function defined over $\mathbb{U}_{N_x,N_y}$, under Dirichlet conditions.

Problem 10.5   Consider the operator $\delta_{\Delta\boxplus}$, operating over the rectangular domain $\mathbb{U}_{N_x,N_y}^2$, which is of size $(N_x + 1) \times (N_y + 1)$ points. A centered zero derivative, or Neumann condition, may be written as

$$\delta_x.u_{0,m} = 0, \qquad m = 0, \ldots, N_y$$

$$\delta_x.u_{N_x,m} = 0, \qquad m = 0, \ldots, N_y$$

$$\delta_y.u_{l,0} = 0, \qquad l = 0, \ldots, N_x$$

$$\delta_y.u_{l,N_y} = 0, \qquad l = 0, \ldots, N_x$$

Supposing that the state vector is defined as the concatenation of $N_x + 1$ vertical strips of length $N_y + 1$, write the matrix form of the operator under the conditions above. Assume that $h_x = h_y = h$. Again, as in the case of the non-centered condition discussed beginning on page 296, your matrix will consist of $(N_y + 1) \times (N_y + 1)$ blocks, each of which is Toeplitz except in the extreme rows and columns. See also Programming Exercise 10.3.

Problem 10.6   Consider the discrete biharmonic operator $\delta_{\Delta\boxplus,\Delta\boxplus}$, operating over the rectangular domain $\mathbb{U}_{N_x,N_y}^2$, which is of size $(N_x + 1) \times (N_y + 1)$ points. Consider the following two sets of boundary conditions:

Clamped:

$$\delta_{x-}u_{0,m} = 0, \qquad u_{0,m} = 0, \quad m = 0, \ldots, N_y$$
$$\delta_{x+}u_{N_x,m} = 0, \qquad u_{N_x,m} = 0, \quad m = 0, \ldots, N_y$$
$$\delta_{y-}u_{l,0} = 0, \qquad u_{l,0} = 0, \quad l = 0, \ldots, N_x$$
$$\delta_{y+}u_{l,N_y} = 0, \qquad u_{l,N_y} = 0, \quad l = 0, \ldots, N_x$$

Simply supported:

$$\delta_{xx}u_{0,m} = 0, \qquad u_{0,m} = 0, \quad m = 0, \ldots, N_y$$
$$\delta_{xx}u_{N_x,m} = 0, \qquad u_{N_x,m} = 0, \quad m = 0, \ldots, N_y$$
$$\delta_{yy}u_{l,0} = 0, \qquad u_{l,0} = 0, \quad l = 0, \ldots, N_x$$
$$\delta_{yy}u_{l,N_y} = 0, \qquad u_{l,N_y} = 0, \quad l = 0, \ldots, N_x$$

First, find the explicit form of the stencil of the operator, including all coefficients, when applied at any point directly adjacent to the boundary—take special care when near corners! Then, write the matrix form $\mathbf{D}_{\Delta\boxplus,\Delta\boxplus}$ of the operator, assuming that it acts on a vector consisting of concatenated vertical strips of the grid function $u_{l,m}$. You may leave out values on the boundary itself (which are constrained to be zero in either case), so your matrix will be square and of size $(N_x - 1)(N_y - 1) \times (N_x - 1)(N_y - 1)$.

Problem 10.7 *Consider the discrete Laplacian operator, in radial coordinates, acting on a grid function $u_{l,m}$ at the central grid point $l = 0$, $m = 0$. Given the definition of this operator, from (10.24), prove that it is indeed a second-order accurate approximation to the Laplacian. In order to do this, consider the values of the grid function $u_{1,m}$ which appear in the definition to be values of a continuous function at the location $x = h_r \cos(mh_\theta)$, $y = h_r \sin(mh_\theta)$, and perform Taylor expansions about the point $x = 0$, $y = 0$.*

10.5   Programming exercises

Programming Exercise 10.1 *Create a Matlab function which, for a given rectangular grid function, calculates an interpolated value at coordinates x_o, y_o, using either truncation or bilinear interpolation, as described in Section 10.2.1. Assume equal grid spacings in the x and y directions, and thus that the aspect ratio may be determined from the dimensions of the input grid function. Make sure that your code takes account of whether the input grid function includes values on its boundary—this must also be specified as an input parameter.*

Programming Exercise 10.2 *Consider the parameterized nine-point approximation $\delta_{\Delta\alpha}$ to the Laplacian, as defined in (10.10). When applied to a test function of the form $u_{l,m} = e^{jh(\beta_x l + \beta_y m)}$, it behaves as*

$$\delta_{\Delta\alpha}u = \frac{-4}{h^2}\left(\sin^2\left(\beta_x h/2\right) + \sin^2\left(\beta_y h/2\right) - 2(1-\alpha)\sin^2(\beta_x h/2)\sin^2(\beta_y h/2)\right)u = F_\alpha(\beta_x, \beta_y)u$$

Create a Matlab script which plots the function $-F_\alpha(\beta_x, \beta_y)/|\boldsymbol{\beta}|^2$ as a function of $\beta_x h$ and $\beta_y h$, for $-\pi \le \beta_x h, \beta_y h \le \pi$ as a surface, for various values of the free parameter α. (This function is a comparison of the dispersive behavior of the difference operator with the continuous operator Δ as a function of wavenumber.) Verify that the difference operator is approximately isotropic when $\alpha \approx 2/3$.

Programming Exercise 10.3 *Create a Matlab function which generates difference matrices $\mathbf{D}_{\Delta\boxplus}$ corresponding to the discrete Laplacian operator $\delta_{\Delta\boxplus}$, operating over the rectangular domain $U^2_{N_x,N_y}$. Suppose also that the aspect ratio is $\epsilon = N_x/N_y$, and that the grid spacing is $h = \sqrt{\epsilon}/N_x$. Your code thus depends only on N_x and N_y, and should generate matrices corresponding to fixed* *or Dirichlet conditions, non-centered Neumann conditions, and centered Neumann conditions—the first two cases are discussed in Section 10.2.4 and the third in Problem 10.5. Note that your output matrix will be square, and of size $(N_x - 1)(N_y - 1) \times (N_x - 1)(N_y - 1)$ in the first case, and $(N_x + 1)(N_y + 1) \times (N_x + 1)(N_y + 1)$ in the latter two. Be sure that the matrix is generated in sparse form—make use of the function* sparse *for this purpose.*

Programming Exercise 10.4   *Create a Matlab function which generates a difference matrix* $\mathbf{D}_{\Delta\alpha}$ *corresponding to the parameterized nine-point discrete Laplacian operator* $\delta_{\Delta\alpha}$, *operating over the rectangular domain* $\mathbb{U}^2_{N_x,N_y}$, *under Dirichlet conditions. Your code will necessarily depend on the free parameter* α.

Programming Exercise 10.5   *Create a Matlab function which generates difference matrices* $\mathbf{D}_{\Delta\boxplus,\Delta\boxplus}$ *corresponding to the discrete biharmonic operator* $\delta_{\Delta\boxplus,\Delta\boxplus}$, *operating over the rectangular domain* $\mathbb{U}^2_{N_x,N_y}$. *As above, suppose also that the aspect ratio is* $\epsilon = N_x/N_y$, *and that the grid spacing is* $h = \sqrt{\epsilon}/N_x$. *Your code should generate matrices corresponding to clamped and simply supported conditions, as described in Problem 10.6. Your output matrix will be square and of size* $(N_x - 1)(N_y - 1) \times (N_x - 1)(N_y - 1)$.

Programming Exercise 10.6   *Consider the discrete Laplacian operator* $\delta_{\Delta\circ}$ *in radial coordinates, operating over the domain* $\mathbb{U}^2_{\circ,N_r,N_\theta}$, *which is defined by (10.23) at grid points* $l > 0$ *and by (10.24) at* $l = 0$. *Create a Matlab function which generates, for a given* N_r *and* N_θ, *the matrix form* $\mathbf{D}_\circ$ *of the operator, under fixed conditions at the outer edge of the domain, at* $l = N_r$.

In preparation for this, suppose that the values of the grid function $u_{l,m}$ *on which* $\mathbf{D}_{\Delta\circ}$ *operates are written as a vector* $\mathbf{u}$ *consisting of the central value* $u_{0,0}$, *followed by concatenated concentric rings of the grid function, or as*

$$\mathbf{u} = [u_{0,0}, u_{1,0}, \dots, u_{1,N_\theta-1}, \dots, u_{N_r-1,0}, \dots, u_{N_r-1,N_\theta-1}]^T$$

As such, the matrix $\mathbf{D}_{\Delta\circ}$ *will be of size* $(N_\theta(N_r - 1) + 1) \times (N_\theta(N_r - 1) + 1)$.

Programming Exercise 10.7   *Consider the discrete biharmonic operator* $\delta_{\Delta\circ,\Delta\circ}$ *in radial coordinates, operating over the domain* $\mathbb{U}^2_{\circ,N_r,N_\theta}$, *which is defined by (10.25) at grid points* $l > 1$ *and by (10.26) at* $l = 0$ *and* $l = 1$. *Create a Matlab function which generates, for a given* N_r *and* N_θ, *the matrix form* $\mathbf{D}_{\Delta\circ,\Delta\circ}$ *of the operator.*

Assume clamped boundary conditions at the domain edge, i.e., $u_{N_r,m} = \delta_{r+}u_{N_r,m} = 0$, *so that as in the case of the Laplacian in the previous exercise, the matrix operates only over values of the grid function for* $l < N_r$.

11

The 2D wave equation

A good starting point in the investigation of 2D synthesis is, as in 1D, the wave equation, introduced in Section 11.1, which serves as a useful test problem for the vibration of membranes as well as room acoustics, and also as another good point of comparison for the various physical modeling synthesis techniques, including finite difference schemes (Section 11.2 and Section 11.3), digital waveguide meshes (Section 11.4), lumped networks (Section 11.5), and modal methods (Section 11.6). Finally, finite difference schemes are developed in radial coordinates in Section 11.7. The previous chapter serves as a reference for the techniques to be discussed here and in the following two chapters.

11.1 Definition and properties

The wave equation in one spatial dimension (6.1) may be directly generalized to 2D as

$$u_{tt} = c^2 \Delta u \tag{11.1}$$

Here, u is the dependent variable of interest, c is a wave speed, and Δ is the 2D Laplacian operator as discussed in Chapter 10. The problem is assumed defined over some 2D domain $\mathcal{D}$. When the spatial coordinates are scaled using a characteristic length L, the 2D wave equation is of the form

$$u_{tt} = \gamma^2 \Delta u \tag{11.2}$$

where, again, $\gamma = c/L$ is a parameter with units of frequency. In some cases, a good choice of the scaling parameter L for problems defined over a finite region $\mathcal{D}$ is $L = \sqrt{|\mathcal{D}|}$, so that (11.2) is then defined over a region of unit area. For other domains, such as the circle of radius R, it may be more convenient to choose $L = R$, so that the problem is then defined over a unit circle.

The 2D wave equation, as given above, is a simple approximation to the behavior of a vibrating membrane; indeed, a lumped model of membrane is often employed in order to derive the 2D wave equation itself—see Section 11.5. It also can serve as a preliminary step toward the treatment of room acoustics problems (where, in general, a 3D wave equation would be employed); direct solution of the 2D and 3D wave equations for room modeling has been employed for some time [56], and artificial reverberation applications are currently an active research topic [249, 250, 28, 208]. Other applications include articulatory vocal tract modeling [246, 247], and detailed studies of wind

Numerical Sound Synthesis: Finite Difference Schemes and Simulation in Musical Acoustics   Stefan Bilbao
© 2009 John Wiley & Sons, Ltd

instrument bores [258, 254, 255]. It will be assumed, for the moment, that the 2D wave equation is defined over $\mathbb{R}^2$, so that a discussion of boundary conditions may be postponed.

The wave equation, like all PDEs of second order in time, must be initialized with two functions (see Section 6.1.3); in Cartesian coordinates, for example, one would set, normally, $u(x, y, 0) = u_0(x, y)$ and $(\partial u/\partial t)(x, y, 0) = v_0(x, y)$. In the case of a membrane, as for the string, the first condition corresponds to a pluck and the second to a strike. A useful all-purpose initializing distribution is a 2D raised cosine, of the form

$$c_{\mathrm{rc}}(x, y) = \begin{cases} \frac{c_0}{2}\left(1 + \cos\left(\pi \sqrt{(x - x_0)^2 + (y - y_0)^2}/r_{\mathrm{hw}}\right)\right), & \sqrt{(x - x_0)^2 + (y - y_0)^2} \leq r_{\mathrm{hw}} \\ 0, & \sqrt{(x - x_0)^2 + (y - y_0)^2} > r_{\mathrm{hw}} \end{cases}$$

(11.3)

which has amplitude c_0, half-width r_{hw}, and is centered at coordinates (x_0, y_0). Such a distribution can be used in order to model both plucks and strikes. Of course, in full models of percussion instruments, a model of the excitation mechanism, such as a mallet, should be included as well—see Section 12.3 where this topic is taken up in the more musically interesting setting of plate vibration.

A pair of simulation results, under plucked and struck conditions, is illustrated in Figure 11.1. The main feature which distinguishes the behavior of solutions to the 2D wave equation from the 1D case is the reduction in amplitude of the wave as it evolves, due to spreading effects. Related to this is the presence of a "wake" behind the wavefront, which is absent in the 1D case, as well as the fact that, even when simple boundary conditions are employed, the solution is not periodic—reflections from domain boundaries occur with increasing frequency, as illustrated in Figure 11.2(a). One might guess, from these observations alone, that the efficiency of the digital waveguide formulation for the 1D case, built around waves which travel without distortion, will disappear in this case—this is in fact true, as will be discussed in Section 11.4.

11.1.1   Phase and group velocity

Assuming, in Cartesian coordinates, a plane-wave solution of the form

$$u(x, y, t) = e^{st + j(\beta_x x + \beta_y y)}$$

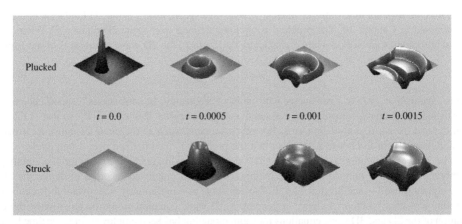

Figure 11.1   Time evolution of solutions to the 2D wave equation, defined over a unit square, with fixed boundary conditions. In this case, $\gamma = 400$, and snapshots of the displacement are shown at times as indicated, under plucked conditions (top row) and struck conditions (bottom row). In the first case, the initial displacement condition is a raised cosine of half-width 0.15, centered at coordinates $x = 0.3$, $y = 0.5$, and, in the second, the initial velocity profile is a raised cosine of half-width 0.15, centered at the same location.

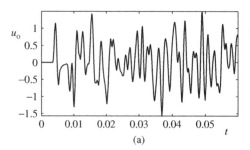
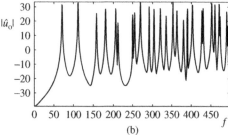

(a)   (b)

Figure 11.2 Solution of the 2D wave equation, with $\gamma = 100$, defined over a unit square, in response to a plucked excitation, in the form of a raised cosine, centered at $x = 0.7$, $y = 0.5$, of amplitude 10 and half-width 0.2. (a) Time response, at location $x = 0.3$, $y = 0.7$. (b) Its frequency spectrum.

leads to the characteristic equation and dispersion relation

$$s^2 = -\gamma^2 |\boldsymbol{\beta}|^2 \qquad \longrightarrow \qquad \omega = \pm \gamma |\boldsymbol{\beta}|$$

and, thus, to expressions for the phase and group velocity,

$$v_\phi = \gamma \qquad\qquad v_g = \gamma$$

Thus, just as in 1D, all wavelike components travel at the same speed. Note that as the Laplacian operator is isotropic, wave speed is independent not only of frequency or wavenumber, but also of direction.

In 1D, for LSI systems, it is often possible to rewrite the phase and group velocities as functions of frequency alone. While this continues to be possible for isotropic systems in 2D, it is not possible when the system exhibits anisotropy. Furthermore, most numerical methods exhibit spurious anisotropy, and thus the only way to analyze such behavior is through expressions of wavenumber.

11.1.2 Energy and boundary conditions

The 2D wave equation, like its 1D counterpart, is lossless. This can be seen, as usual, by writing the energy for the system, which is conserved. Assuming (11.2) to be defined over the infinite plane $\mathcal{D} = \mathbb{R}^2$, taking an inner product with u_t in Cartesian coordinates followed by integration by parts leads to

$$\langle u_t, u_{tt}\rangle_{\mathcal{D}} = \gamma^2 \langle u_t, \Delta u\rangle_{\mathcal{D}} = \gamma^2 \langle u_t, u_{xx}\rangle_{\mathcal{D}} + \gamma^2 \langle u_t, u_{yy}\rangle_{\mathcal{D}} = -\gamma^2 \langle u_{xt}, u_x\rangle_{\mathcal{D}} - \gamma^2 \langle u_{yt}, u_y\rangle_{\mathcal{D}}$$

or

$$\frac{d\mathfrak{H}}{dt} = 0 \qquad \text{with} \qquad \mathfrak{H} = \mathfrak{T} + \mathfrak{V}$$

and

$$\mathfrak{T} = \frac{1}{2}\|u_t\|_{\mathcal{D}}^2 \qquad \mathfrak{V} = \frac{\gamma^2}{2}\left(\|u_x\|_{\mathcal{D}}^2 + \|u_y\|_{\mathcal{D}}^2\right) = \frac{\gamma^2}{2}\||\nabla u\||_{\mathcal{D}}^2 \tag{11.4}$$

where ∇ signifies the gradient operation. Such a result is obviously independent of the chosen coordinate system. The expression is, again, non-negative, and leads immediately to bounds on the growth of the norm of the solution, by exactly the same methods as discussed in Section 6.1.8.

Edges

In order to examine boundary conditions at, for instance, a straight edge, consider (11.1) defined over the semi-infinite region $\mathcal{D} = \mathbb{R}^{2,x+}$, as discussed in Section 10.1.2. Through the same manipulations above, one arrives at the energy balance

$$\frac{d\mathfrak{H}}{dt} = \mathfrak{B} \quad \text{with} \quad \mathfrak{H} = \mathfrak{T} + \mathfrak{V} \tag{11.5}$$

where $\mathfrak{T}$ and $\mathfrak{V}$ are as defined in (11.4) above. The boundary term $\mathfrak{B}$, depending only on values of the solution at $x = 0$, is

$$\mathfrak{B} = -\gamma^2 \{u_x, u_t\}_{(0,\mathbb{R})} \triangleq -\gamma^2 \int_{-\infty}^{\infty} u_x(0, y', t) u_t(0, y', t) dy' \tag{11.6}$$

Thus, the natural extensions of the lossless Dirichlet and Neumann conditions (6.18) and (6.19) for the 1D wave equation are

$$u(0, y, t) = 0 \quad \text{or} \quad u_x(0, y, t) = 0 \quad \text{at} \quad x = 0$$

in which case $\mathfrak{B}$ vanishes. In the case of the membrane, where u is a displacement, these correspond to fixed and free conditions, respectively. For room acoustics problems, in which case u is a pressure, the Neumann condition corresponds to a rigid wall termination. As in the case of the 1D wave equation, it should be obvious that many other terminations, including those of lossless energy-storing type and lossy conditions, possibly nonlinear, and combinations of these can be arrived at through the above analysis. One particularly interesting family of conditions, useful in modeling terminations in this setting of room acoustics [208], appears in Problem 11.1.

Corners

An extra concern, especially when working in Cartesian coordinates in 2D, is the domain corner. Though it is not particularly problematic in the case of the wave equation, for more complex systems, such as the stiff plate, one must be very careful with such points, especially in the discrete setting. To this end, consider the wave equation defined over the quarter plane $\mathcal{D} = \mathbb{R}^{2,x+y+}$. The energy balance is again as in (11.5), but the boundary term is now

$$\mathfrak{B} = -\gamma^2 \int_0^{\infty} u_x(0, y', t) u_t(0, y', t) dy' - \gamma^2 \int_0^{\infty} u_y(x', 0, t) u_t(x', 0, t) dx'$$

$$= -\gamma^2 \{u_x, u_t\}_{(0,\mathbb{R}+)} - \gamma^2 \{u_y, u_t\}_{(\mathbb{R}+,0)}$$

The system is lossless under a combination of the conditions

$$u_x(0, y, t) = 0 \quad \text{or} \quad u_t(0, y, t) = 0 \quad \text{at} \quad x = 0 \tag{11.7a}$$

$$u_y(x, 0, t) = 0 \quad \text{or} \quad u_t(x, 0, t) = 0 \quad \text{at} \quad y = 0 \tag{11.7b}$$

It is thus possible to choose distinct conditions over each edge of the domain; notice, however, that if free or Neumann conditions are chosen on both edges, then at the domain corner $x = y = 0$, both such conditions must be enforced.

Though only a quarter plane has been analyzed here, it should be clear that such results extend to the case of a rectangular domain—see Problem 11.2.

1
2
3
4
5
6
7
8
9
10
11
12
13
14
15
16
17
18
19
20
21
22
23
24
25
26
27
28
29
30
31
32
33
34
35
36
37
38
39
40
41
42
43
44
45
46
47
48
49
50
51

11.1.3 Modes

The modal decomposition of solutions to the 2D wave equation under certain simple geometries and boundary conditions is heavily covered in the musical acoustics literature—see, e.g., standard texts such as [136, 244]. It is useful, however, to at least briefly review such a decomposition in the case of the rectangular domain.

As in the case of the 1D wave equation (see Section 6.1.11) and the ideal bar equation (see Section 7.1.3), one may assume an oscillatory solution to the 2D wave equation of the form $u(x, y, t) = e^{j\omega t} U(x, y)$, leading to

$$-\omega^2 U = \gamma^2 \Delta U$$

The wave equation defined over a unit area rectangle $\mathbb{U}_\epsilon^2$ of aspect ratio ϵ and under fixed boundary conditions is separable, and the Fourier series solution to the above equation is

$$U_{p,q}(x, y) = \sin(p\pi x/\sqrt{\epsilon}) \sin(q\pi \sqrt{\epsilon} y) \qquad \omega_{p,q} = \pi\gamma\sqrt{p^2/\epsilon + \epsilon q^2} \qquad (11.8)$$

The modal functions are illustrated in Figure 11.3, in the case of a square domain. (It is worth pointing out that, under some choices of the aspect ratio ϵ, it is possible for modal frequencies corresponding to distinct modes to coincide or become degenerate.)

Given the above expression for the modal frequencies $\omega_{p,q} = 2\pi f_{p,q}$, it is not difficult to show that the number of degrees of freedom, for frequencies less than or equal to $f_s/2$, will be[1]

$$N_m(f_s/2) = \frac{\pi f_s^2}{2\gamma^2} \qquad (11.9)$$

See Problem 11.3. Twice this number is, as before, the number of degrees of freedom of the system when it is simulated at a sample rate f_s. This indicates that the density of modes increases

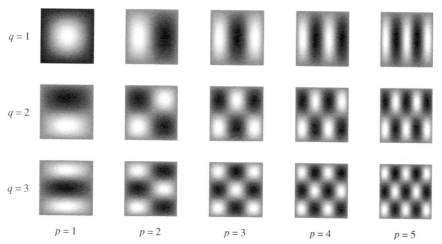

Figure 11.3 Modal shapes $U_{p,q}(x, y)$ for a square membrane, under fixed boundary conditions. In all cases, dark and light areas correspond to modal maxima and minima.

---

[1] This expression is approximate, and does not take into account modal degeneracy. It is correct in the limit of high f_s. See [243] for exact expressions for the numbers of modes in 3D.

strongly with frequency, which is easily visible in a spectral plot of output taken from the solution to the 2D wave equation, as shown in Figure 11.2(b). This is to be compared to the situation for the 1D wave equation, where modal density is roughly constant—see Section 6.1.11. Serious (and not unexpected) ramifications in terms of computational complexity result, as will be discussed shortly. For more on synthesis for the 2D wave equation using modal methods, see Section 11.6.

This modal analysis can be directly extended to the case of the wave equation in 3D, defined over a suitable region such as a cube; such analysis yields useful information about modal densities in the context of room acoustics. See Problem 11.4. Another system which may be analyzed in this way is the membrane coupled to a cavity, which serves as a simple model of a drum-like instrument—see Problem 11.5.

11.2   A simple finite difference scheme

Consider the wave equation in Cartesian coordinates. The simplest possible finite difference scheme employs a second difference in time, and a five-point Laplacian approximation $\delta_{\Delta\boxplus}$, as defined in Section 10.2:

$$\delta_{tt}u = \gamma^2 \delta_{\Delta\boxplus}u \tag{11.10}$$

where $u = u_{l,m}^n$ is a 2D grid function representing an approximation to the continuous solution $u(x, y, t)$ at $x = lh_x$, $y = mh_y$, $t = nk$, for integer l, m, and n.

The case of equal grid spacings $h_x = h_y = h$ is the most straightforward in terms of analysis and implementation; expanding out the operator notation above leads to

$$u_{l,m}^{n+1} = \lambda^2 \left(u_{l+1,m}^n + u_{l-1,m}^n + u_{l,m+1}^n + u_{l,m-1}^n\right) + 2\left(1 - 2\lambda^2\right)u_{l,m}^n - u_{l,m}^{n-1} \tag{11.11}$$

where again, as in 1D, the Courant number λ is defined as

$$\lambda = \frac{k\gamma}{h}$$

Notice that under the special choice of $\lambda = 1/\sqrt{2}$ (this case is of particular relevance to the so-called digital waveguide mesh, to be discussed in Section 11.4), the recursion above may be simplified to

$$u_{l,m}^{n+1} = \frac{1}{2}\left(u_{l+1,m}^n + u_{l-1,m}^n + u_{l,m+1}^n + u_{l,m-1}^n\right) - u_{l,m}^{n-1} \tag{11.12}$$

which requires only a single multiplication by the factor $1/2$, and one fewer addition than the general form (11.11). Again, as in the case of the special difference scheme for the 1D wave equation (6.54), the value at the central grid point at l, n is no longer employed. Related to this is the interesting observation that the scheme may be decomposed into two independent schemes operating over the black and white squares on a "checkerboard" grid. See Problem 11.6.

Scheme (11.10) continues to hold if the grid spacings are not the same, though the stability condition (discussed below) must be altered, and computational complexity increases. See Problem 11.7. There is a slight advantage if such a scheme is to be used for non-square regions, but perhaps not enough to warrant its use in synthesis applications, except for high values of γ, where the grid is necessarily coarse, and truncation becomes an issue. See Programming Exercise 11.1.

Output may be drawn from the scheme using 2D interpolation operators—see Section 10.2.1. For example, one may take output from a position x_0, y_0 as $u_o = I(x_0, y_0)u$. For a static output location, a simple truncated interpolant is probably sufficient, but for moving output locations, a bilinear interpolant is a better choice—see Programming Exercise 11.2.

Beyond being a synthesis algorithm for a simple percussion instrument, such a scheme can be modified to behave as an artificial reverberation algorithm through the insertion of an input signal—see Programming Exercise 11.4.

It is direct to develop schemes for the 3D wave equation in a similar manner (see Problem 11.8), as well as for the case of the membrane coupled to a cavity (see Problem 11.9 and Programming Exercise 11.5).

11.2.1   von Neumann analysis

Use of the ansatz $u^n_{l,m} = z^n e^{jh(l\beta_x + m\beta_y)}$ leads to the characteristic equation

$$z - 2 + 4\lambda^2 \left(p_x + p_y \right) + z^{-1} = 0$$

in the two variables $p_x = \sin^2 \left(\beta_x h/2 \right)$ and $p_y = \sin^2 \left(\beta_y h/2 \right)$, as defined in Section 10.2.2. This equation is again of the form (2.13), and the solutions in z will be of unit modulus when

$$0 \le \lambda^2 \left(p_x + p_y \right) \le 1$$

The left-hand inequality is clearly satisfied. Given that the variables p_x and p_y take on values between 0 and 1, the right-hand inequality is satisfied for

$$\lambda \le \frac{1}{\sqrt{2}} \tag{11.13}$$

which is the stability condition for scheme (11.10). Notice that just as in the case of scheme (6.34) for the 1D wave equation, at the stability limit (i.e., when $\lambda = 1/\sqrt{2}$), a simplified scheme results, namely (11.12).

11.2.2   Energy analysis and numerical boundary conditions

In order to arrive at stable numerical boundary conditions for scheme (11.10), it is again of great use to derive an expression for the numerical energy. Considering first the case of the scheme defined over the infinite region $\mathcal{D} = \mathbb{Z}^2$, taking an inner product with $\delta_t.u$ and using summation by parts (10.17) leads to

$$\langle \delta_t.u, \delta_{tt}u \rangle_{\mathbb{Z}^2} = \gamma^2 \langle \delta_t.u, \delta_{\Delta\boxplus}u \rangle_{\mathbb{Z}^2} = \gamma^2 \left(\langle \delta_t.u, \delta_{xx}u \rangle_{\mathbb{Z}^2} + \langle \delta_t.u, \delta_{yy}u \rangle_{\mathbb{Z}^2} \right)$$

$$= -\gamma^2 \left(\langle \delta_t.\delta_{x+}u, \delta_{x+}u \rangle_{\mathbb{Z}^2} + \langle \delta_t.\delta_{y+}u, \delta_{y+}u \rangle_{\mathbb{Z}^2} \right)$$

and, finally, to energy conservation

$$\delta_{t+}\mathfrak{h} = 0 \qquad \text{with} \qquad \mathfrak{h} = \mathfrak{t} + \mathfrak{v}$$

and

$$\mathfrak{t} = \frac{1}{2} \|\delta_{t-}u\|^2_{\mathbb{Z}^2} \qquad \mathfrak{v} = \frac{\gamma^2}{2} \left(\langle \delta_{x+}u, e_{t-}\delta_{x+}u \rangle_{\mathbb{Z}^2} + \langle \delta_{y+}u, e_{t-}\delta_{y+}u \rangle_{\mathbb{Z}^2} \right) \tag{11.14}$$

The basic steps in the stability analysis are the same as in the 1D case: Beginning from the expression above for the numerical potential energy $\mathfrak{v}$, and assuming, for simplicity, $h_x = h_y = h$, one may bound it, using inequalities of the form (10.18), as

$$\mathfrak{v} \ge -\frac{\gamma^2 k^2}{8} \left(\|\delta_{x+}\delta_{t-}u\|^2_{\mathbb{Z}^2} + \|\delta_{y+}\delta_{t-}u\|^2_{\mathbb{Z}^2} \right) \ge -\frac{\gamma^2 k^2}{2h^2} \left(\|\delta_{t-}u\|^2_{\mathbb{Z}^2} + \|\delta_{t-}u\|^2_{\mathbb{Z}^2} \right)$$

and thus

$$\mathfrak{h} \geq \frac{1}{2}\left(1 - \frac{2\gamma^2 k^2}{h^2}\right)\|\delta_{t-}u\|_{\mathbb{Z}^2}^2$$

so the energy is non-negative under condition (11.13), obtained through von Neumann analysis.

To arrive at stable numerical boundary conditions, one may proceed as in the continuous case. Jumping directly to the case of a discrete quarter plane $\mathcal{D} = \mathbb{Z}^{2,x+y+}$, the energy balance above becomes

$$\delta_{t+}\mathfrak{h} = \mathfrak{b}$$

where

$$\mathfrak{b} = -\gamma^2\left(\sum_{m=0}^{\infty} h\delta_t.u_{0,m}\delta_{x-}u_{0,m} + \sum_{l=0}^{\infty} h\delta_t.u_{l,0}\delta_{y-}u_{l,0}\right)$$

$$= -\gamma^2\left(\{\delta_t.u, \delta_{x-}u\}_{(0,\mathbb{Z}^+)} + \{\delta_t.u, \delta_{y-}u\}_{(\mathbb{Z}^+,0)}\right)$$

For more on these boundary terms, see the discussion on page 296. The lossless numerical conditions which then follow are

$$u_{0,m\geq0} = 0 \quad \text{or} \quad \delta_{x-}u_{0,m\geq0} = 0 \qquad \text{and} \qquad u_{l\geq0,0} = 0 \quad \text{or} \quad \delta_{y-}u_{l\geq0,0} = 0 \qquad (11.15)$$

The first in each pair corresponds, naturally, to a Dirichlet condition, and the second to a Neumann condition, as in the continuous case as per (11.7). Given losslessness of the boundary condition (i.e., $\mathfrak{b} = 0$), stability analysis follows as for the case of the scheme defined over $\mathbb{Z}^2$. Implementation details of these conditions, as well as the matrix form of the discrete Laplacian, have been discussed in Section 10.2.4. Such conditions are first-order accurate, so there will be some distorting effect on modal frequencies; through the use of a different inner product, it is possible to arrive at second-order (or centered) boundary conditions which are provably stable—see Problem 11.10 and Programming Exercise 11.6 for some investigation of this.

11.3   Other finite difference schemes

In the case of the 1D wave equation, certain parameterized finite difference schemes have been examined in Section 6.3, but given the good behavior of the simplest explicit scheme, these variations are of virtually no use—the power of such parameterized methods has been seen to some extent in the case of bar and stiff string simulation, in Section 7.1.5 and Section 7.2.3, and is even more useful in the present case of multidimensional systems such as the 2D wave equation (among others). The chief interest is in reducing numerical dispersion. The 2D wave equation, like its 1D counterpart, is a standard numerical test problem, and, as such, finite difference schemes have seen extensive investigation—see, e.g., [366, 49, 40].

11.3.1   A parameterized explicit scheme

Instead of a five-point Laplacian approximation, as employed in scheme (11.10), one might try a nine-point approximation, of the type discussed in Section 10.2. This leads to

$$\delta_{tt}u = \gamma^2\delta_{\Delta\alpha}u = \gamma^2\left(\alpha\delta_{\Delta\boxplus}u + (1-\alpha)\delta_{\Delta\boxtimes}\right)u \qquad (11.16)$$

which reduces to scheme (11.10) when $\alpha = 1$. The computational stencil is, obviously, more dense in this case than for the simple scheme (11.10)—see Figure 11.4(b). Simplified forms are possible involving less computation, as in the case of scheme (11.10), as has been observed in relation to the so-called interpolated waveguide mesh [312, 41]. See Problem 11.11.

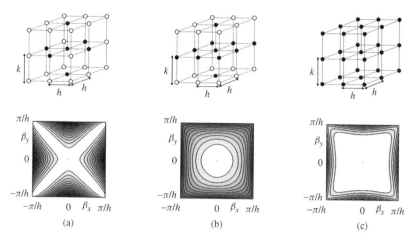

Figure 11.4 Computational stencil (top) and relative numerical phase velocity v_ϕ/γ (bottom) for: (a) the explicit scheme (11.10), with $\lambda = 1/\sqrt{2}$; (b) the parameterized scheme (11.16) with the special choice of $\alpha = 2/\pi$, and λ chosen to satisfy bound (11.17) with equality; and (c) the implicit scheme (11.18), with $\alpha = 2/\pi$, $\theta = 1.2$, and λ chosen to satisfy bound (11.19) with equality. Relative phase velocity deviations of 2% are plotted as contours in the wavenumber plane $-\pi/h \leq \beta_x, \beta_y \leq \pi/h$.

Using von Neumann analysis, it is straightforward to show that the stability conditions for this scheme are

$$\alpha \geq 0 \qquad \lambda \leq \min(1, 1/\sqrt{2\alpha}) \tag{11.17}$$

See Problem 11.12. The dispersion characteristics of this scheme depend quite heavily on the choice of α, and, as one might expect, for intermediate values of this parameter over the allowable range $\alpha \in [0, 1]$, the dispersion is far closer to isotropic—a desirable characteristic, given that the wave equation itself exhibits such behavior. Through trial and error, optimization strategies, or Taylor series analysis (see Problem 10.3) one may find particularly good behavior when α is between 0.6 and 0.8, as illustrated in the plot of relative phase velocity in Figure 11.4(b). The behavior of this scheme is clearly more isotropic than that of (11.10), but numerical dispersion still persists. See also the comparison among modal frequencies generated by the various schemes discussed here in Table 11.1.

Table 11.1 Comparison among modal frequencies of the 2D wave equation defined over a square, under fixed conditions, with $\gamma = 1000$ and modal frequencies (as well as their cent deviations from the exact frequencies) of the simple explicit scheme (11.10), the parameterized explicit scheme (11.16) with $\alpha = 2/\pi$, and the implicit scheme (11.18) with $\alpha = 2/\pi$ and $\theta = 1.2$, with a sample rate $f_s = 16\,000$ Hz, and where λ is chosen so as to satisfy the stability condition in each case as close to equality as possible.

Mode number	Exact freq.	Explicit		Nine-pt. explicit		Implicit	
		Freq.	Cent dev.	Freq.	Cent dev.	Freq.	Cent dev.
(1,1)	707.1	707.0	−0.3	706.3	−2.0	707.1	−0.1
(1,2)	1118.0	1114.0	−6.2	1114.9	−4.8	1118.0	0.0
(2,2)	1414.2	1413.1	−1.3	1407.6	−8.1	1413.4	−1.0
(1,4)	2061.6	2009.2	−44.5	2042.7	−15.9	2058.8	−2.2
(3,3)	2121.3	2117.5	−3.1	2098.7	−18.5	2115.7	−4.6

Such a choice may be justified, again, by looking at computational complexity (see Section 7.1.5 for similar analysis in the case of the ideal bar). For a surface of unit area, and when the stability bound above is satisfied with equality, the number of degrees of freedom will be

$$N_{\text{fd}} = \frac{2}{h^2} = \frac{2 f_s^2 \min(1, 1/2\alpha)}{\gamma^2}$$

and equating this with the number of degrees of freedom in a modal representation, one arrives at a choice of $\alpha = 2/\pi = 0.637$.

11.3.2   A compact implicit scheme

A family of compact implicit schemes for the 2D wave equation is given by

$$\delta_{tt} u = \gamma^2 \left(1 + \frac{k^2(1-\theta)}{2} \delta_{tt} \right) \delta_{\Delta\alpha} u \tag{11.18}$$

This scheme depends on the free parameters θ, as well as α through the use of the nine-point discrete Laplacian operator $\delta_{\Delta\alpha}$.

von Neumann analysis, though now somewhat more involved, again allows fairly simple stability conditions on the free parameters and λ:

$$\alpha \geq 0 \qquad \theta \quad \text{unconstrained} \qquad \begin{cases} \lambda \leq \sqrt{\dfrac{\min(1, 1/2\alpha)}{\sqrt{(2\theta-1)}}}, & \theta > \dfrac{1}{2} \\[2mm] \lambda \text{ unconstrained}, & \theta \leq \dfrac{1}{2} \end{cases} \tag{11.19}$$

See Problem 11.13. Under judicious choices of α and θ, an excellent match to the ideal phase velocity may be obtained over nearly the entire range of wavenumbers—see Figure 11.4(c). This good behavior can also be seen in the numerical modal frequencies of this scheme, which are very close to exact values—see Table 11.1. Such is the interest in compact implicit schemes: very good overall behavior, at the additional cost of sparse linear system solutions, without unpleasant side effects such as complex boundary termination. An even more general compact family of schemes is possible—see Problem 11.14.

In this case, as in 1D, a vector–matrix representation is necessary. Supposing that the problem is defined over the finite rectangular domain $\mathcal{D} = \mathbb{U}_{N_x, N_y}^2$, and, referring to the discussion in Section 10.2.4, scheme (11.18) may be written as

$$\mathbf{A}\mathbf{u}^{n+1} + \mathbf{B}\mathbf{u}^n + \mathbf{A}\mathbf{u}^{n-1} = 0 \tag{11.20}$$

where, here, $\mathbf{u}^n$ is a vector consisting of the consecutive vertical strips of the 2D grid function $u_{l,m}^n$ laid end to end (each such strip will consist of $N_y - 1$ values in the case of Dirichlet conditions, and $N_y + 1$ values for Neumann conditions). The matrices $\mathbf{A}$ and $\mathbf{B}$ may be written as

$$\mathbf{A} = \mathbf{I} - \frac{\gamma^2 k^2 (1-\theta)}{2} \mathbf{D}_{\Delta\alpha} \qquad \mathbf{B} = -2\mathbf{I} - \gamma^2 k^2 \theta \mathbf{D}_{\Delta\alpha}$$

where $\mathbf{D}_{\Delta\alpha}$ is a matrix operator corresponding to $\delta_{\Delta\alpha}$. See Programming Exercise 11.7.

11.3.3   Further varieties

Beyond the two families of schemes presented here, there are of course many other varieties—further properties of parameterized schemes for the 2D wave equation are detailed elsewhere [40, 208], and other schemes are discussed in standard texts [342]. In musical acoustics, finite difference schemes for the wave equation in 2D and 3D have also been employed in detailed studies of wind instrument bores, sometimes involving more complex coordinate systems—see, e.g., [254, 255, 258].

11.4   Digital waveguide meshes

The extension of digital waveguides to multiple dimensions for sound synthesis applications was first undertaken by van Duyne and Smith in the mid 1990s [384–386]. It has continued to see a fair amount of activity in sound synthesis and artificial reverberation applications—see the comments and references in Section 1.2.3. Most interesting was the realization by van Duyne and others of the association with finite difference schemes [384, 41]. Waveguide meshes may be viewed as acoustic analogues to similar scattering structures which appear in electromagnetic simulation, such as the transmission line matrix method (TLM) [182, 83, 174].

A regular Cartesian mesh is shown in Figure 11.5(a). Here, each box labeled **S** represents a four-port parallel scattering junction. A scattering junction at location $x = lh$, $y = mh$ is connected to its four neighbors on the grid by four bidirectional delay lines, or waveguides, each of a single sample delay (of k seconds, where $f_s = 1/k$ is the sample rate). The signals or wave variables impinging on a given scattering junction at grid location l, m at time step n from a waveguide from the north, south, east, and west are written as $u_{l,m}^{n,(+),N}$, $u_{l,m}^{n,(+),S}$, $u_{l,m}^{n,(+),E}$, and $u_{l,m}^{n,(+),W}$, respectively, and those exiting as $u_{l,m}^{n,(-),N}$, $u_{l,m}^{n,(-),S}$, $u_{l,m}^{n,(-),E}$, and $u_{l,m}^{n,(-),W}$. The scattering operation at a given junction may be written as

$$u_{l,m}^n = \frac{1}{2}\left(u_{l,m}^{n,(+),N} + u_{l,m}^{n,(+),S} + u_{l,m}^{n,(+),E} + u_{l,m}^{n,(+),W}\right) \tag{11.21}$$

$$u_{l,m}^{n,(-),\bullet} = -u_{l,m}^{n,(+),\bullet} + u_{l,m}^n \tag{11.22}$$

Here, $u_{l,m}^n$ is the junction variable (often referred to as a junction pressure, and written as p in room acoustics applications). Shifting in digital waveguides themselves can be written as

$$u_{l,m}^{n,(+),N} = u_{l,m+1}^{n-1,(-),S} \qquad u_{l,m}^{n,(+),S} = u_{l,m-1}^{n-1,(-),N} \qquad u_{l,m}^{n,(+),E} = u_{l+1,m}^{n-1,(-),W} \qquad u_{l,m}^{n,(+),W} = u_{l-1,m}^{n-1,(-),E}$$

$$\tag{11.23}$$

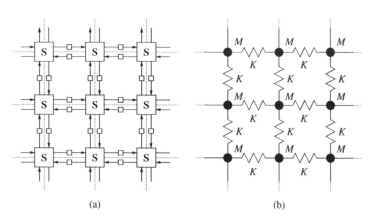

(a)   (b)

Figure 11.5   (a) A digital waveguide network corresponding to scheme (11.10) for the wave equation, under the special choice of $\lambda = 1/\sqrt{2}$. (b) A lumped network corresponding to the same scheme, for any value of λ.

The scattering and shifting operations are the basis of all wave-based numerical methods, including, in addition to digital waveguides, wave digital filter methods, as well as the transmission line matrix method mentioned above. Numerical stability for an algorithm such as the above is obvious: the shifting operations clearly cannot increase any norm of the state, in terms of wave variables, and the scattering operation corresponds to an orthogonal (i.e., l_2 norm-preserving) matrix multiplication.

On the other hand, by applying the scattering and shifting rules above, one may arrive at a recursion in the junction variables $u_{l,m}^n$, which is none other than scheme (11.10), with $\lambda = \gamma k/h = 1/\sqrt{2}$—see Problem 11.15. Notice, however, that the finite difference scheme requires two units of memory per grid point, whereas in the wave implementation, five are necessary (i.e., in order to hold the waves impinging on a junction at a given time step, as well as the junction variable itself). Furthermore, the mesh requires eight arithmetic operations (four in order to form the junction variable and four in order to perform scattering), whereas the finite difference scheme requires five. Thus the efficiency advantage of the waveguide in 1D, based around the use of delay lines, does not carry over to the multidimensional case. Indeed, the finite difference scheme computes an identical solution, at roughly half the cost. Still, the structural robustness of the waveguide mesh is a very desirable property—termination of a mesh structure using passive filtering blocks (thus ensuring stability) can be a nice alternative to the more involved energy analysis tools described here, though one must beware the temptation to extend such results to more complex systems. This mesh structure may be extended, through the addition of an extra "self-loop" at each junction, in order to correspond directly to scheme (11.10), for any allowable value of λ [41]. Other more commonly seen extensions include different tilings of 2D and 3D space, involving, for example, hexagonal, triangular, or tetrahedral grids [386, 28], which also correspond to well-known finite difference schemes [41]. Such non-Cartesian grids have also, of course, been examined in the mainstream simulation literature [420, 363].

11.5   Lumped mass–spring networks

A regular lumped network of masses and springs also, not surprisingly, may be viewed in terms of the same underlying finite difference scheme; the manipulations are very similar to those used in the case of the 1D wave equation, as discussed in Section 6.1.1. It may also, of course, be used as a starting point for a derivation of the 2D wave equation (see, e.g., [115]); 2D lumped structures simulating membranes appear as components in, for example, the TAO synth environment [267]. Suppose that, as shown in Figure 11.5(b), the network consists of a regularly spaced array of masses M, located at positions $x = lh$, $y = mh$, and constrained to move vertically (i.e., in and out of the plane array), with displacement indicated by $u_{l,m}(t)$. Each is connected to neighboring masses by springs of stiffness K, and the force exerted on the mass l, m by its neighbors to the north and east are indicated by $f_{l,m+1/2}$ and $f_{l+1/2,m}$, respectively.

The equation of motion for a single mass will be

$$M\frac{d^2u_{l,m}}{dt^2} = f_{l,m+1/2} - f_{l,m-1/2} + f_{l+1/2,m} - f_{l-1/2,m}$$

with

$$f_{l,m+1/2} \cong K(u_{l,m+1} - u_{l,m}) \qquad f_{l+1/2,m} \cong K(u_{l+1,m} - u_{l,m})$$

Just as in 1D, these two definitions coalesce as

$$M\frac{d^2u_{l,m}}{dt^2} = K\left(u_{l,m+1} + u_{l,m-1} + u_{l+1,m} + u_{l-1,m} - 4u_{l,m}\right)$$

Discretizing the above system of ODEs with a second time difference δ_{tt} leads immediately to scheme (11.10) for the 2D wave equation, with $\gamma = h\sqrt{K/M}$.

11.6 Modal synthesis

One of the interesting (and attractive) things about modal synthesis is that, once one has determined the modal frequencies, and the weighting coefficients, the form of the algorithm is completely insensitive to problem dimensionality—all one is doing is summing sine waves or, more generally, damped sine waves. Modal synthesis for 2D objects such as plates has been developed by various researchers, and membrane- and plate-like objects are components within the Modalys/MOSAIC synthesis environment developed at IRCAM [242].

Consider the case of the 2D wave equation, defined over the unit area rectangle of aspect ratio ϵ, $\mathcal{D} = \mathbb{U}_\epsilon^2$. Again, just as in 1D (see Section 6.1.11), once one has derived a set of modal functions $U_m(x, y)$ ordered according to some index m, where the mth modal frequency is ω_m, the modal decomposition is of the form

$$u(x, y, t) = \sum_m U_m(x, y)\Phi_m(t) \qquad \text{with} \qquad \frac{d^2\Phi_m(t)}{dt^2} = -\omega_m^2\Phi_m(t)$$

It is useful to order the modes such that $\omega_m \geq \omega_{m'}$ when $m \geq m'$. (In general, the 2D modal functions cannot be consistently ordered according to two indices except in regular geometries such as the rectangle and circle, and under particular boundary conditions; for the rectangle, Dirichlet or Neumann conditions at all edges are among these, and one may instead use functions $U_{p,q}(x, y)$ indexed according to p and q as described in Section 11.1.3.)

This form is now suitable for discretization along the lines presented in Chapter 3. For each SHO in the set above, one could use a simple scheme such as (3.12), but there is no reason not to use the exact scheme (3.39) at sample rate $f_s = 1/k$, for some time step k:

$$u^n(x_0, y_0) = \sum_{m=1}^{N_m/2} U_m(x_0, y_0)\Phi_m^n \qquad \Phi_m^{n+1} = 2\cos(\omega_m k)\Phi_m^n - \Phi_m^{n-1} \quad \text{for} \quad m = 1, \dots, N_m/2$$

$$(11.24)$$

Here x_0, y_0 are the readout coordinates, and N_m, the number of degrees of freedom, should be chosen such that $\omega_{N_m/2} \leq \pi f_s$, to avoid aliasing. For an initial value problem, the variables Φ_m must be initialized using Fourier expansion coefficients of the initializing distribution—see Programming Exercise 11.8 for more details.

It is instructive to compare the output of this modal method to that of a finite difference scheme, such as (11.10)—see Figure 11.6, in which time responses for the two methods are plotted together,

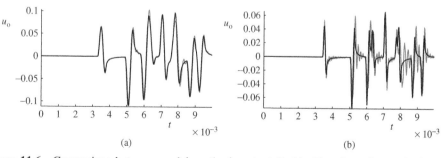

(a)   (b)

Figure 11.6 Comparison between modal synthesis output (in black), using scheme (11.24), and that of finite difference scheme (11.10) (in grey), for the 2D wave equation, with $\gamma = 200$ and aspect ratio $\epsilon = 1$. The system is subjected to a "plucked" initial condition in the form of a raised 2D cosine, of amplitude 1, centered at $x = 0.3$, $y = 0.3$, of half-width 0.1 in (a), and a narrower distribution of half-width 0.05 in (b). In both cases, output is produced at 44.1 kHz, and read from the position $x_0 = 0.8$, $y_0 = 0.8$.

in the cases of plucked initial conditions of (a) wide and (b) narrow spatial extent. For the wide excitation, which excites mainly the lower modes, the two responses are nearly identical; but in the case of the narrow excitation, numerical dispersion effects of the finite difference scheme, leading to "ringing" of sharp transients (due to reflections) in the signal, are clearly in evidence. For the modal method, no such dispersion is evident, and transients remain well localized. On the other hand, as this dispersion is only an issue at high frequencies, it is questionable whether it is in fact audible—to this end, the reader may wish to experiment with the two methods.

11.7   Finite difference schemes in radial coordinates

The 2D wave equation defined over a circular region is a good starting point for drum models. Here, due to the geometry, if one is interested in pursuing a finite difference synthesis approach, radial coordinates are convenient. The wave equation in radial coordinates, using the form of the Laplacian given on the right in (10.2), is as follows:

$$u_{tt} = \gamma^2 \left(\frac{1}{r}(ru_r)_r + \frac{1}{r^2}u_{\theta\theta} \right)$$

The equation is assumed defined over the unit circle $\mathcal{D} = \mathbb{U}_\circ^2$, and scaled such that, if the physical wave speed is c, and the radius is R, $\gamma = c/R$. Energy analysis leads to the usual expression for energy conservation, i.e.,

$$\frac{d\mathfrak{H}}{dt} = \mathfrak{B}$$

with

$$\mathfrak{T} = \frac{1}{2}\|u_t\|_{\mathbb{U}_\circ^2}^2 \qquad \mathfrak{V} = \frac{\gamma^2}{2}\left(\|u_r\|_{\mathbb{U}_\circ^2}^2 + \|u_\theta/r\|_{\mathbb{U}_\circ^2}^2 \right) \qquad \mathfrak{B} = \gamma^2\{u_t, u_r\}_{(1,[0,2\pi))}$$

(See Section 10.1.5 for information on integration by parts in radial coordinates.) Clearly, the conditions $u = 0$ or $u_r = 0$ at the outer rim of the circle lead to losslessness.

11.7.1   An explicit finite difference scheme

An obvious choice of explicit difference scheme (and one the reader is advised against using—read on) is the following:

$$\delta_{tt}u = \gamma^2\delta_{\Delta\circ}u \tag{11.25}$$

where the discrete Laplacian $\delta_{\Delta\circ}$ is as defined in (10.23), with the exception of at the center point, where the definition (10.24) is used. The update form of this scheme, when $l > 0$, is

$$u_{l,m}^{n+1} = 2u_{l,m}^n - u_{l,m}^{n-1} + \frac{\gamma^2 k^2 \mu_{r+} r_l}{r_l h_r^2}u_{l+1,m}^n - \frac{2\gamma^2 k^2}{h_r^2}u_{l,m}^n + \frac{\gamma^2 k^2 \mu_{r-} r_l}{r_l h_r^2}u_{l-1,m}^n$$

$$+ \frac{\gamma^2 k^2}{r_l^2 h_\theta^2}\left(u_{l,m+1}^n - 2u_{l,m}^n + u_{l,m-1}^n \right)$$

Here, the subscripts l and m refer to grid points, of spacing h_r and h_θ, in the radial and angular coordinate, respectively; the index m is taken modulo N_θ, where $h_\theta = 2\pi/N_\theta$. At the central grid point $l = 0$, the update is

$$u_{0,0}^{n+1} = 2u_{0,0}^n - u_{0,0}^{n-1} + \frac{4\gamma^2 k^2}{N_\theta h_r^2}\sum_{m=0}^{N_\theta-1}\left(u_{1,m}^n - u_{0,0}^n \right)$$

Energy analysis and numerical boundary conditions

von Neumann analysis is not available in a direct form in order to determine stability conditions in radial coordinates, but energy methods remain viable. One must, however, take special care with regard to the center point. To this end, take the inner product with $\delta_t . u$ over the region $\overline{\mathbb{U}}^2_{\circ,N_r,N_\theta}$, consisting of the grid locations $l = 1, \ldots, N_r$, $m = 0, \ldots, N_\theta - 1$, and employ the summation by parts identity (10.27):

$$\langle \delta_t . u, \delta_{tt} u \rangle_{\overline{\mathbb{U}}^2_{\circ,N_r,N_\theta}} = \gamma^2 \langle \delta_t . u, \delta_{\Delta\circ} u \rangle_{\overline{\mathbb{U}}^2_{\circ,N_r,N_\theta}}$$

$$= -\gamma^2 \left\langle \delta_t . \delta_{r-} u, \frac{\mu_{r-} r}{r} \delta_{r-} u \right\rangle_{\overline{\mathbb{U}}^2_{\circ,N_r,N_\theta}} - \gamma^2 \left\langle \delta_t . \delta_{\theta-} u, \frac{1}{r^2} \delta_{\theta-} u \right\rangle_{\overline{\mathbb{U}}^2_{\circ,N_r,N_\theta}}$$

$$+ \mathfrak{b} - \frac{\gamma^2 \pi h_r^2}{4} \delta_t . u_{0,0} \delta_{\Delta\circ} u_{0,0}$$

This may be written, as usual, as $\delta_{t+} \mathfrak{h} = \mathfrak{b}$, where $\mathfrak{h} = \mathfrak{t} + \mathfrak{v}$, and

$$\mathfrak{t} = \frac{1}{2} \| \delta_{t-} u \|^2_{\overline{\mathbb{U}}^2_{\circ,N_r,N_\theta}} + \frac{\pi h_r^2}{8} \left(\delta_{t-} u_{0,0} \right)^2$$

$$\mathfrak{v} = \frac{\gamma^2}{2} \left\langle \delta_{r-} u, \frac{\mu_{r-} r}{r} e_{t-} \delta_{r-} u \right\rangle_{\overline{\mathbb{U}}^2_{\circ,N_r,N_\theta}} + \frac{\gamma^2}{2} \left\langle \delta_{\theta-} u, \frac{1}{r^2} e_{t-} \delta_{\theta-} u \right\rangle_{\overline{\mathbb{U}}^2_{\circ,N_r,N_\theta}}$$

$$\mathfrak{b} = \gamma^2 \{ \delta_t . u, \mu_{r+} r \delta_{r+} u \}_{(N_r, [0, N_\theta - 1])}$$

Notice in particular the appearance of a component of the kinetic energy at the central grid location. Clearly, $\mathfrak{t}$ is non-negative, and for stability it suffices to bound $\mathfrak{v}$ in terms of it. To this end, one may write, using the bounds (10.28),

$$\mathfrak{v} \geq -\frac{\gamma^2 k^2}{8} \| \sqrt{\mu_{r-} r / r} \delta_{r-} \delta_{t-} u \|^2_{\overline{\mathbb{U}}^2_{\circ,N_r,N_\theta}} - \frac{\gamma^2 k^2}{8} \| (1/r) \delta_{\theta-} \delta_{t-} u \|^2_{\overline{\mathbb{U}}^2_{\circ,N_r,N_\theta}}$$

$$\geq -\frac{\gamma^2 k^2}{2h_r^2} \| \delta_{t-} u \|^2_{\overline{\mathbb{U}}^2_{\circ,N_r,N_\theta}} - \frac{\pi \gamma^2 k^2}{4} \left(\delta_{t-} u_{0,0} \right)^2 - \frac{\gamma^2 k^2}{2h_\theta^2} \| (1/r) \delta_{t-} u \|^2_{\overline{\mathbb{U}}^2_{\circ,N_r,N_\theta}}$$

Now that $\mathfrak{v}$ has been bounded in terms of the grid function $\delta_{t-} u$, it is possible to extract the following conditions for non-negativity of $\mathfrak{h}$:

$$\frac{\gamma^2 k^2}{h_r^2} \left(1 + \frac{1}{h_\theta^2} \right) \leq 1 \qquad\qquad h_r \geq \sqrt{2} \gamma k \qquad\qquad (11.26)$$

The first condition arises from examination of the grid function over interior points, and the second for the central point; normally, the first condition above is much stronger than the second. These serve as stability conditions for scheme (11.25), as long as lossless or dissipative boundary conditions are applied; notice that $\mathfrak{b}$ vanishes when

$$u_{N_r, m} = 0 \qquad \text{or} \qquad \delta_{r+} u_{N_r, m} = 0$$

These conditions correspond to Dirichlet and Neumann conditions at the outer edge of the circle.

In general, h_r and h_θ are independent in the above scheme, and there is thus an extra degree of freedom when these quantities are subject to the stability condition (11.26). For some guidance as to how to proceed in choosing these, see Problem 11.16.

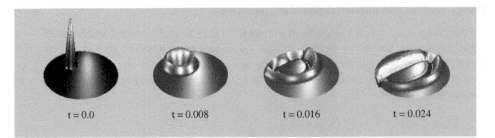

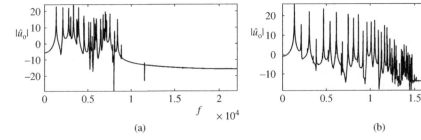

Figure 11.7 Snapshots of the time evolution of the solution to the 2D wave equation, with $\gamma = 40$, defined over a unit circle with fixed boundary conditions, at times as indicated. Scheme (11.25) is employed, at a sample rate of 44 100 Hz, and is initialized with a raised cosine distribution.

Numerical bandwidth

The behavior of this scheme is, at first sight, as expected—see Figure 11.7, which illustrates the time evolution of a plucked initial condition. Upon inspection of a typical spectral output, however, it is clear that all is not well, as in Figure 11.8(a). The output is severely band-limited, in some cases to as low as one-eighth the sample rate. Furthermore, the components which do appear suffer from extreme numerical dispersion. This scheme, though it has been employed by various authors in an analysis setting, is probably not suitable for synthesis, except at extremely high sample rates—clearly, more work at the stage of scheme design is necessary.

11.7.2   A parameterized scheme

Given the difficulties mentioned above, one might wonder whether one can do better with a parameterized implicit scheme—and indeed one can. Here is a simple form:

$$\left(1 + \gamma^2 k^2 \alpha \delta_{\Delta\circ}\right) \delta_{tt} u = \gamma^2 \delta_{\Delta\circ} u \tag{11.27}$$

The new free parameter is α, and the scheme reduces to (11.25) when $\alpha = 0$. In vector–matrix form, the scheme update looks like

$$\mathbf{A}\mathbf{u}^{n+1} + \mathbf{B}\mathbf{u}^n + \mathbf{A}\mathbf{u}^{n-1} = \mathbf{0}$$

where

$$\mathbf{A} = \mathbf{I} + \gamma^2 k^2 \alpha \mathbf{D}_{\Delta\circ} \qquad \mathbf{B} = -2\mathbf{I} - (2\alpha + 1)\gamma^2 k^2 \mathbf{D}_{\Delta\circ}$$

Figure 11.8 Typical output spectra for radial finite difference schemes for the 2D wave equation defined over the unit area circle, with $\gamma = 2000$, under fixed boundary conditions at the outer edge. In (a), scheme (11.25) is employed, and in (b), the parameterized scheme (11.27), with $\alpha = -0.248$. In both cases, the sample rate is 44 100 Hz and $h_\theta / h_r \approx 6$.

Here, $\mathbf{u}^n$ is a vector consisting of the value $u_{0,0}^n$ followed by a concatenation of the successive concentric rings of the grid function $u_{l,m}^n$ for $l = 1, 2, \ldots$ and $\mathbf{D}_{\Delta\circ}$ is the Laplacian operator in matrix form.

The stability condition for scheme (11.27) must be adjusted from (11.26) to

$$\frac{4(\alpha + 1/4)\gamma^2 k^2}{h_r^2}\left(1 + \frac{1}{h_\theta^2}\right) \leq 1 \tag{11.28}$$

when $\alpha \geq -1/4$ (otherwise the scheme is unconditionally stable).

For certain ranges of the parameter α, particularly when α is slightly above $-1/4$, this scheme exhibits markedly better performance, in terms of bandwidth, and numerical dispersion, though even under optimal conditions it performs less well than schemes in Cartesian coordinates—see Figure 11.8(b). For some exploration of this family of difference schemes, see Programming Exercise 11.9.

11.8 Comparative study II

The case of the 2D wave equation is somewhat more representative of the relative merits of the various synthesis methods than its counterpart in 1D. This section continues the previous discussion of computational issues associated with various different synthesis methods with regard to the 1D wave equation in Section 6.6.

The most important observation that one can make is that the efficiency advantage of digital waveguides does not extend to 2D—indeed, any solution produced by a digital waveguide mesh structure can always be more efficiently calculated using an associated finite difference scheme. Similarly, lumped network representations also can be viewed, as in 1D, as finite difference schemes.[2] Thus the main comparison here will be between difference schemes and modal methods, which remain distinct in the 2D case.

With regard to accuracy, modal methods are, under fairly strict conditions on problem geometry and boundary conditions, and if properly employed, extremely accurate. Finite difference methods suffer from a greater degree of numerical dispersion (and thus mode detuning) than in the 1D case, where an exact finite difference (FD) solution is available. In addition, there is the added issue of numerical anisotropy. A more interesting question, and one which is too involved to address here, is the perceptual relevance of such dispersion effects. More elaborate schemes may be designed which minimize such dispersive effects, at the expense of higher computational cost and algorithm complexity.

In terms of memory use, modal methods and difference schemes are roughly comparable. For a unit area domain, and for a given wave speed γ and sampling rate f_s, the number of memory locations necessary to store state in a modal method will be twice the number of modes in the range $[0, f_s/2]$, or, from (11.9), $\pi f_s^2/2\gamma^2$. For a typical difference scheme, the stability condition leads to a minimum grid spacing which again determines the number of memory locations. For scheme (11.10), for example, which is a two-step scheme, the memory requirement will be f_s^2/γ^2, which is on the same order as for a modal method (less, in fact, though this apparent advantage is illusory once numerical dispersion effects are taken into account). As in 1D, however, if the modal shapes are not expressible in closed form, then one is again faced with the extra tasks of (1) computing the mode shapes, through the solution of a potentially large eigenvalue problem and reintroducing numerical inaccuracy, and possibly (2) storing them. For even moderately low

---

[2] In fact, it is generally only easy to associate mesh structures and lumped networks with simple explicit schemes such as (11.10); making this association with more refined designs, such as implicit schemes, is very strenuous, and thus there is a real advantage to a finite difference framework, from a design perspective.

values of γ, and at audio sample rates, this is, in 2D, a daunting task, as full storage of $\pi f_s^2 / 2\gamma^2$
modal shapes with sufficient spatial resolution amounts to storage on the order of f_s^4 / γ^4 units,
which can be very large indeed. On the other hand, in a modal approach, it is relatively easy
to discard higher modal frequencies and thus reduce computational cost; in an FD scheme, this
can be done by increasing the grid spacing away from that prescribed by the stability bound, at
the expense of introducing serious dispersion effects. In either case, however, the best way to
reduce computational complexity is to simply work at a reduced sample rate, in which case the
two methods are again on an equal footing in terms of computational cost.

The operation count/time step scales, as in 1D, with the number of degrees of freedom for a
given γ and f_s. Calling this number N (as mentioned above, it is comparable for FD schemes and
modal methods). A modal method requires, in the lossless case, $2N$ additions/multiplications/time
step, whereas for an FD scheme, the number of operations depends on the sparsity of the scheme,
as αN, for some (low) scheme-dependent parameter α. For the scheme (11.10), $\alpha = 7$, but it will
be larger for interpolated explicit schemes such as (11.16), and even larger if an implicit method
such as (11.18) is used.

The issues of precomputation, stability, and generating output may be addressed in a manner
similar to those of the 1D case.

For more general comments on the relative merits of these methods, see the closing remarks
in Section 14.1.

11.9   Problems

Problem 11.1   *Consider the 2D wave equation, defined over the half plane $\mathbb{R}^{2,x+}$, and recall the
expression for the energy balance given in (11.5) and (11.6):*

$$\frac{d\mathfrak{H}}{dt} = -\gamma^2 \{u_x, u_t\}_{(0,\mathbb{R})}$$

Suppose the boundary condition, at $x = 0$, is given as follows:

$$u_t = \alpha u_x + \phi u_{xt} + \epsilon m \qquad \text{with} \qquad m_t = u_x(0, y, t)$$

*and where the constants α, ϕ, and ϵ are non-negative. Such an energy-storing condition may be
used in order to model effects of mass, stiffness, and loss at a wall in the context of room acoustics
[208]. Show that the above condition implies that the energy balance becomes*

$$\frac{d}{dt}(\mathfrak{H} + \mathfrak{H}_b) = -\mathfrak{Q}$$

*where $\mathfrak{H}_b \geq 0$ and $\mathfrak{Q} \geq 0$. Thus the total energy $\mathfrak{H} + \mathfrak{H}_b$ remains non-negative and monotonically
decreasing.*

Problem 11.2   *Extend the energy analysis of the 2D wave equation to the case for which the
domain $\mathcal{D}$ is a unit area rectangle $\mathbb{U}_\epsilon^2 = [0, \sqrt{\epsilon}] \times [0, 1/\sqrt{\epsilon}]$. Show that the energy balance (11.5)
holds as before, where the boundary term $\mathfrak{B}$ is given by*

$$\mathfrak{B} = \gamma^2 \left(\{u_x, u_t\}_{(\sqrt{\epsilon},[0,1/\sqrt{\epsilon}])} - \{u_x, u_t\}_{(0,[0,1/\sqrt{\epsilon}])} + \{u_y, u_t\}_{([0,\sqrt{\epsilon}],1/\sqrt{\epsilon})} - \{u_y, u_t\}_{([0,\sqrt{\epsilon}],0)} \right)$$

Problem 11.3   *Considering the 2D wave equation defined over a square of unit area, under fixed
boundary conditions, the frequency of mode (p, q) is given by (11.8) or, in Hertz,*

$$f_{p,q} = \frac{\gamma}{2}\sqrt{p^2 + q^2}$$

for $p, q > 0$.

(a) Show that $f_{p,q}$ corresponds to the distance between the origin and the point of coordinates $(p\gamma/2, q\gamma/2)$ in a plane.

(b) Find the density (per unit area) of such points in the plane.

(c) The total number of modes of frequency less than or equal to $f_s/2$ may be represented as the number of modal points contained within a quarter circle of radius $f_s/2$ in the plane. Given the expression obtained above for the density of such points, find the approximate value for $N_m(f_s/2)$ given in (11.9). (N_m is twice the number of modes over this band.)

(d) Show that this expression remains unchanged, in the limit of high f_s, if the 2D wave equation is defined instead over a arbitrary rectangle of unit area, i.e., over $\mathbb{U}_\epsilon^2$.

(e) Show that this expression remains unchanged, in the limit of high f_s, in the case of free boundary conditions at all edges of the rectangular domain.

Problem 11.4   (The 3D wave equation I) *Most key components of musical instruments, such as strings, bars, plates, membranes, and acoustic tubes, are well modeled in 1D or 2D. There are, however, occasions when one might be interested in full 3D modeling—this comes up when one is faced with, say, the interior of an instrument body, such as an acoustic guitar or kettledrum, whose dimensions are not small in any coordinate direction. Another application, slightly removed from synthesis, is room acoustics simulation, of interest in developing physical artificial reverberation algorithms. The equation to be solved in these cases is invariably the 3D wave equation, written in terms of time t, coordinates x, y, and z, and wave speed c as*

$$u_{tt} = c^2 \Delta u = c^2\left(u_{xx} + u_{yy} + u_{zz}\right)$$

or, when spatially scaled with reference to a characteristic length L,

$$u_{tt} = \gamma^2 \Delta u \qquad\qquad (11.29)$$

with $\gamma = c/L$.

(a) Supposing that the 3D wave equation is defined over a unit cube, under fixed boundary conditions, show that the modal frequencies $\omega_{p,q,r}$ are given by

$$\omega_{p,q,r} = \pi\gamma\sqrt{p^2 + q^2 + r^2}$$

(b) Extend the analysis of Problem 11.3, and show that an expression for the number of degrees of freedom (or twice the number of modes of frequency less than $f_s/2$) is given by

$$N_m(f_s/2) = \frac{\pi f_s^3}{3\gamma^3}$$

(c) Given a typical audio range (i.e., choose $f_s = 44\,100$ Hz), and for a wave speed $c = 340$ m/s, determine the number of modes necessary to describe the behavior of an object such as a violin, a kettledrum, or a large concert hall. (For each, estimate a characteristic length as $L = V^{1/3}$, where V is the total volume enclosed, and thus obtain a rough estimate of $\gamma = c/L$.) Comment on the feasibility of performing simulations using modal methods for each of these cases, keeping in mind the memory available in RAM on typical computers (look this up for your own machine).

Problem 11.5   (Kettledrum I) *Drum modeling always takes as its starting point a membrane model, described by a variant of the 2D wave equation (perhaps involving stiffness—see the next chapter), coupled to a resonator, which is effectively a closed cavity. A detailed model necessarily requires the solution of the 3D wave equation in the body of the resonator, through either a time domain method, or a modal decomposition. (One such study has been carried out, in the case of the kettledrum, by Rhaouti et al. [283].)*

1
2
3
4
5
6
7
8
9
10
11
12
13
14
15
16
17
18
19
20
21
22
23
24
25
26
27
28
29
30
31
32
33
34
35
36
37
38
39
40
41
42
43
44
45
46
47
48
49
50
51

Here is a very crude model, proposed early on by Morse [243]. For simplicity, assume an $L \times L$ square membrane, with wave speed c_M, under fixed boundary conditions, coupled to an enclosed volume of air, of density ρ, volume V_0, with wave speed c_0, and under tension T_0 per unit length applied at the edge. In scaled form, the equation of motion of the membrane is

$$u_{tt} = \gamma^2 \Delta u - \gamma^2 d^2 \int_0^1 \int_0^1 u \, dx \, dy \qquad for \quad (x, y) \in \mathbb{U}^2$$

where $\gamma = c_M/L$, and where $d^2 = \rho c_0^2 L^4/(T_0 V_0)$ is a dimensionless parameter. Such a model, in that the effect of the cavity is averaged over the membrane, is reminiscent of the Kirchhoff–Carrier string model (see Section 8.1), though here the averaging is linear. One should only expect it to hold for low frequencies.

(a) Assuming a modal solution of the form $u(x, y, t) = e^{j\omega t} \sin(p\pi x) \sin(q\pi y)$, show that the modal frequencies $\omega_{p,q}$ are given by

$$\omega_{p,q}^2 = \gamma^2 \pi^2 \left(p^2 + q^2\right) + \frac{\gamma^2 d^2}{pq\pi^2} \left((-1)^p - 1\right)\left((-1)^q - 1\right), \qquad p, q \geq 1 \qquad (11.30)$$

Which modal frequencies are altered with respect to those of the uncoupled wave equation (i.e., when $d = 0$)? Are they raised or lowered?

(b) Show that an expression for the total energy of the membrane coupled to the cavity is given by

$$\mathfrak{H} = \frac{1}{2} \|u_t\|_{\mathbb{U}^2}^2 + \frac{\gamma^2}{2} \left(\|u_x\|_{\mathbb{U}^2}^2 + \|u_y\|_{\mathbb{U}^2}^2\right) + \frac{\gamma^2 d^2}{2} \left(\langle u, 1\rangle_{\mathbb{U}^2}\right)^2 \qquad (11.31)$$

which remains non-negative.

Problem 11.6 *Show that scheme (11.10), operating over the infinite domain $\mathcal{D} = \mathbb{Z}^2$, and at the stability limit $\lambda = 1/\sqrt{2}$, may be decomposed into two separate schemes, one operating over values of the grid function $u_{l,m}^n$ for even values of $n + l + m$, and one for odd values. If the scheme is restricted to operate over a finite domain, discuss the effects of various boundary conditions on the ability to obtain such a decomposition.*

Problem 11.7 *Consider scheme (11.10), but with h_x and h_y not, in general, equal.*
(a) Show, from von Neumann analysis, that the stability condition relating k, h_x, and h_y becomes

$$\gamma^2 k^2 \leq \frac{h_x^2 h_y^2}{h_x^2 + h_y^2} \qquad (11.32)$$

(b) Write the update explicitly in terms of the grid function $u_{l,m}^n$, in a manner similar to that shown in (11.11). How many additions/multiplications are necessary in order to perform the update at a given grid point? Is there a particular choice of k, h_x, and h_y such that computational complexity may be reduced?

Problem 11.8 **(The 3D wave equation II)** *The direct extension of scheme (11.10) for the 2D wave equation to the 3D wave equation (11.29) is of the following form:*

$$\delta_{tt} u = \gamma^2 \left(\delta_{xx} u + \delta_{yy} u + \delta_{zz} u\right)$$

Here, $u = u_{l,m,p}^n$ is a 3D grid function representing an approximation to $u(x, y, z, t)$ at $x = lh$, $y = mh$, $z = ph$, $t = nk$. for a time step t and a grid spacing h (assumed uniform in all directions).

The spatial difference operators δ_{xx} and δ_{yy} are as in the 2D case, and δ_{zz} is defined, in terms of its action on the grid function u, as

$$\delta_{zz} u_{l,m,p}^n = \frac{1}{h^2} \left(u_{l,m,p+1}^n - 2u_{l,m,p}^n + u_{l,m,p-1}^n \right) \tag{11.33}$$

(a) Using an extension of either von Neumann analysis or energy methods, show that the stability condition for the scheme will be

$$\frac{\gamma k}{h} \leq \frac{1}{\sqrt{3}}$$

(b) Assuming that the 3D wave equation is defined over a unit volume, and that the stability condition above is satisfied with equality, how does the number of degrees of freedom (twice the number of grid points necessary to fill the domain) depend on γ and the sample rate $f_s = 1/k$? Compare your answer to your calculation of the number of modes in Problem 11.4.

Problem 11.9   (Kettledrum II) *Consider the following explicit finite difference scheme for the coupled membrane/cavity system given in Problem 11.5:*

$$\delta_{tt} u = \gamma^2 \delta_{\Delta\boxplus} u - \gamma^2 d^2 \langle u, 1 \rangle_{\mathbb{U}_{N,N}^2} \qquad \text{over} \qquad \mathbb{U}_{N,N}^2$$

where "1" refers to a grid function taking the value unity over the entire domain. Assume fixed boundary conditions, i.e., the grid function u takes on the value zero at the edges of the domain $\mathbb{U}_{N,N}^2$.
(a) Find an expression for the conserved energy of this scheme, by taking an inner product of the scheme with $\delta_t.u$ over $\mathbb{U}_{N,N}^2$. It should correspond to (11.31) for the model system.
(b) By ensuring non-negativity of this expression, show that the CFL condition becomes

$$h \geq \gamma k \sqrt{\frac{2}{1 - d^2 \gamma^2 k^2 / 4}} \tag{11.34}$$

For what values of d will this scheme allow such a stability condition? How does the number of degrees of freedom (i.e., the grid size for a given γ and time step k) change with d? Does this coincide with your analysis of the deviation in modal frequencies with d, in Problem 11.5?

Problem 11.10   *Consider scheme (11.10) for the 2D wave equation, defined over the quarter space $\mathcal{D} = \mathbb{Z}^{2,x+y+}$. Assume $h_x = h_y = h$. Instead of the first-order Neumann boundary conditions given as the second of each pair in (11.15), consider the following centered (second-order) conditions:*

$$\delta_x.u_{0,m\geq0} = 0 \qquad \delta_y.u_{l\geq0,0} = 0$$

Such conditions have been introduced earlier in Problem 10.5. Show numerical stability, using energy methods. Recall the use of the primed inner product in the analogous case in 1D, as described on page 138. Here, consider an inner product of the form

$$\langle f, g \rangle'_{\mathbb{Z}^{2,x+y+}} = \sum_{l=1}^{\infty}\sum_{m=1}^{\infty} h^2 f_{l,m} g_{l,m} + \frac{h^2}{2} \sum_{l=1}^{\infty} f_{l,0} g_{l,0} + \frac{h^2}{2} \sum_{m=1}^{\infty} f_{0,m} g_{0,m} + \frac{h^2}{4} f_{0,0} g_{0,0}$$

Problem 11.11   *For the parameterized explicit scheme (11.16) for the 2D wave equation:*
(a) Write the update explicitly in terms of the grid function $u_{l,m}^n$, in a manner similar to that shown in (11.11).

(b) For a given value of α, the scheme free parameter, what is the condition on λ such that the scheme update no longer depends on the value of the grid function $u_{l,m}^n$ at the "center point?" Does this condition conflict with the stability condition (11.17) for the scheme? (This case has received some attention in the literature, as it corresponds to the so-called "interpolated digital waveguide mesh" [312].)

(c) Discuss the significance and ramifications of a choice of λ away from the stability condition, with reference to Rule of Thumb #1, given on page 136.

Problem 11.12 *Show that the characteristic polynomial corresponding to the "nine-point" explicit scheme (11.16) is given by*

$$z - 2 + 4\lambda^2 \left(p_x + p_y - 2(1 - \alpha)p_x p_y \right) + z^{-1}$$

where p_x and p_y are as defined in terms of wavenumber components as in (10.13), and take on values between 0 and 1. The stability condition is thus

$$0 \le \lambda^2 \left(p_x + p_y - 2(1 - \alpha)p_x p_y \right) \le 1$$

Show that these conditions lead immediately to the stability conditions given in (11.17).

Hint: Begin with the left inequality, and derive a condition on α alone, then use the right inequality to find the condition on λ. (Your result from Problem 10.2 will be of great use here.)

Problem 11.13 *Show that the characteristic polynomial corresponding to the compact implicit scheme (11.18) is given by*

$$z - 2 + \frac{4\lambda^2 \left(p_x + p_y - 2(1 - \alpha)p_x p_y \right)}{1 + 2(1 - \theta)\lambda^2 \left(p_x + p_y - 2(1 - \alpha)p_x p_y \right)} + z^{-1} = 0$$

where p_x and p_y are again as defined in (10.13), and take on values between 0 and 1. The stability condition is thus

$$0 \le \frac{\lambda^2 \left(p_x + p_y - 2(1 - \alpha)p_x p_y \right)}{1 + 2(1 - \theta)\lambda^2 \left(p_x + p_y - 2(1 - \alpha)p_x p_y \right)} \le 1$$

Show that these conditions lead immediately to the stability conditions given in (11.19).

This is much trickier than the above problem, in that now the function to be bounded is rational rather than polynomial. There are essentially three steps: (1) Find conditions under which the numerator of the expression above is non-negative. (2) Given this condition, find conditions under which the denominator is non-negative. (3) Given the conditions derived in (1) and (2) here, find conditions under which the numerator is less than or equal to the denominator. Your bounds on λ may overlap, depending on the choice of θ and α.

Problem 11.14 *Consider the following family of implicit finite difference schemes for the 2D wave equation, generalizing scheme (11.18):*

$$\left(1 + \theta \gamma^2 k^2 \delta_{\Delta\alpha_1} \right) \delta_{tt} u = \gamma^2 \delta_{\Delta\alpha_2} u$$

This scheme now depends on the parameters θ, α_1, and α_2—the two nine-point approximations to the Laplacian are distinct. Using von Neumann analysis, find a stability condition for this scheme of the form $\lambda \le \lambda^*(\theta, \alpha_1, \alpha_2)$.

Problem 11.15 *Beginning from the definition of the grid variable $u_{l,m}^{n+1}$ in terms of wave variables, from (11.21), use the scattering operation (11.22) and the shifting operation (11.23) in order to* show that the waveguide mesh calculates solutions to the finite difference scheme (11.10), under the special choice of $\lambda = \gamma k/h = 1/\sqrt{2}$.

Problem 11.16   The stability condition for scheme (11.25) for the wave equation in radial coordinates, relating the radial and angular grid spacings h_r and h_θ to the time step k, is given in (11.26). In order to set the grid spacings for a given sample rate, it is useful to set, beforehand, a parameter $q = h_\theta/h_r$. Show that for a given q, a bound on h_r is then

$$h_r^2 \geq \frac{\gamma^2 k^2}{2} \left(1 + \sqrt{1 + \frac{4}{q^2\gamma^2 k^2}} \right)$$

Given that, in an implementation, the grid spacings must be quantized as $h_r = 1/N_r$ and $h_\theta = 2\pi/N_\theta$, for integer N_r and N_θ, can you find a stability condition in terms of N_θ and N_r?

11.10   Programming exercises

Programming Exercise 11.1   Modify the code implementation of scheme (11.10) for the 2D wave equation given in Section A.11, such that the grid spacings h_x and h_y are not the same. Again, the problem is assumed defined over the unit area rectangle $\mathbb{U}_\epsilon^2$, and with Dirichlet conditions on all four sides. The main question here is the following: given a sample rate $f_s = 1/k$, how are h_x and h_y to be chosen such that the bound (11.32) is satisfied as close to equality as possible, given the further restriction that $h_x = \sqrt{\epsilon}/N_x$, $h_y = 1/\sqrt{\epsilon}N_y$, for a given ϵ, and for integer N_x and N_y? Once you have found a solution to this problem, and made the necessary changes to the rest of the code, try comparing the output of your new scheme to that of the scheme with equal grid spacing, for a variety of different choices of the aspect ratio ϵ and the wave speed γ. Under what conditions are these perceptually distinct?

Programming Exercise 11.2   Modify the code implementation of scheme (11.10) for the 2D wave equation given in Section A.11, such that the output interpolation location is time varying (i.e., moving). One simple way of specifying a trajectory is as follows: for a rectangular domain of aspect ratio ϵ, and thus side lengths $\sqrt{\epsilon}$ and $1/\sqrt{\epsilon}$, let the continuous output coordinates x_o and y_o be defined as

$$x_o(t) = \frac{\sqrt{\epsilon}}{2} + A\cos(2\pi f_o t) \qquad y_o(t) = \frac{1}{2\sqrt{\epsilon}} + A\sin(2\pi f_o t)$$

Here, f_o is a scan frequency, typically on the order of 1 Hz or less, and A specifies the radius of a circle along which the output location travels (how large can A be?). (This means of obtaining output is similar to so-called scanned synthesis [401]—see also Programming Exercise 6.6, which deals with the 1D case.)

Employ bilinear interpolation at each sampling instant (see Section 10.2.1 and Programming Exercise 10.1). For which range of values of γ and f_s do you hear truncation effects? Extend your code such that the output is stereo, with each channel drawn from a separate output location, each specified by a given scan frequency and circle radius.

Programming Exercise 11.3   Modify the code implementation in Section A.11 such that Neumann conditions are enforced—try both the first-order accurate conditions given in (10.20) and the second-order accurate conditions given in Problem 10.5. Because the solution is now free to drift, you will need to apply some sort of DC blocking filter to your output signal u_o^n, if it is drawn directly from values computed on the grid. A simple one–zero filter output v_o^n is given by

$v_0^n = (u_0^n - u_0^{n-1})/k$, and is equivalent to reading a velocity. Can you hear the difference in the resulting sound between the two types of boundary condition?

Programming Exercise 11.4 (Artificial reverberation in 2D) *Now that you have a code implementation of the 2D wave equation under Neumann boundary conditions, it is possible to use it as a crude physical model of a 2D "room," in order to apply artificial reverberation to an input audio signal. The finite difference scheme will be of the form*

$$\delta_{tt} u = \gamma^2 \delta_{\Delta\boxplus} u + J(x_i, y_i) F$$

where $J(x_i, y_i)$ is an input spreading operator acting at the desired source position (x_i, y_i), as described in Section 10.2.1. Be careful to take these coordinates relative to the side lengths of the domain. In order to do this, first remove the initial condition from the code. Then, read in a mono soundfile (read about Matlab functions for doing this, such as, for example, wavread*), which will become $F = F^n$ in the above recursion.*

The parameter $\gamma = c/L$ may be used in order to scale the "size" of the virtual reverberant room—do not be surprised if, for particularly low values of γ, the calculation takes quite a while, or if you run into an "out of memory" error. This is a big calculation! In fact, it will be essential for you to use a relatively low audio sample rate (such as 8000 Hz) in order to get the effect of a reasonably sized room in a short calculation. Make sure that your input soundfile is thus properly downsampled before beginning! Also, make sure that the input signal has a zero DC offset before processing—otherwise, your "room" will drift away (think of it as a membrane under free conditions).

You might also wish to generalize the code such that it generates stereo output, by reading from separate locations over the grid.

Programming Exercise 11.5 *Modify the code implementation of scheme (11.10) for the 2D wave equation given in Section A.11, such that it simulates a membrane coupled to a cavity, as described in Problems 11.5 and 11.9. (This should be a very minor operation!) Make sure that for a given k, γ, and d, h is chosen according to the more general stability condition (11.34). Verify, by taking the Fourier transform of the response of the membrane to an impulsive excitation, that the modal frequencies deviate from those of the uncoupled case according to (11.30).*

Programming Exercise 11.6 *For the scheme (11.10) with $h_x = h_y$, defined over the square $U_{N,N}^2$, calculate numerical modal frequencies using the first-order accurate Neumann conditions given as the second of each pair in (11.15), applied at all four edges of the domain, and the second-order accurate conditions given in Problem 11.10. In either case, the scheme, in vector–matrix form, will look like*

$$\mathbf{u}^{n+1} = 2\mathbf{u}^n - \mathbf{u}^{n-1} + \gamma^2 k^2 \mathbf{D}_{\Delta\boxplus} \mathbf{u}^n$$

where $\mathbf{u}^n$ is the grid function $u_{l,m}^n$ rewritten as a vector (see Section 10.2.4), and where $\mathbf{D}_{\Delta\boxplus}$ is the matrix form of the Laplacian operator, incorporating the particular boundary conditions. The modal frequencies, in Hertz, will be given by $f = (1/\pi k) \sin^{-1}(\gamma k \sqrt{-\mathrm{eig}(\mathbf{D}_{\Delta\boxplus})}/2)$. Assume the sample rate to be $f_s = 44\,100$ Hz and $\gamma = 1000$. Produce a sorted list of these frequencies for both types of boundary condition, and compare the first few (say, 20) to the exact frequencies, which are given by

$$f_{p,q} = \frac{\gamma}{2} \sqrt{p^2 + q^2} \qquad \text{for} \qquad p, q = 0, \dots$$

Programming Exercise 11.7 *Implement the two-parameter scheme (11.18) for the 2D wave equation, defined over a rectangular region U_ϵ^2, according to the vector–matrix update form (11.20). Assume Dirichlet boundary conditions. In order to do this, you will need a matrix form* *of the operator* $\mathbf{D}_{\Delta\alpha}$—*see Problem 10.4 and Programming Exercise 10.4. In order to perform the update, make use of the standard linear system updating package in Matlab. Compare the computing time required to that of the explicit scheme, which is a special case of scheme* (11.18) *with* $\alpha = \theta = 1$.

In addition, compute the numerical modal frequencies of scheme (11.18) *directly as*

$$f = \frac{1}{2\pi k}\cos^{-1}\left(-\mathrm{eig}(\mathbf{A}^{-1}\mathbf{B})\right)$$

Programming Exercise 11.8   *Create a Matlab implementation of modal synthesis for the 2D wave equation, defined over the unit square* $\mathbb{U}^2$, *under fixed or Dirichlet boundary conditions, and for a plucked initial condition of the form of a 2D raised cosine. Here, the update is as in* (11.24), *with frequencies* ω *as given in* (11.8). *In fact, the update is very straightforward; the determination of the initializing values for the state* Φ_m *is more difficult (read about the 2D FFT function* fft2 *in Matlab).*

Programming Exercise 11.9   *Create a Matlab script which calculates a finite difference solution to the 2D wave equation, defined over the unit circle, using the family of schemes* (11.27). *Make use of a fixed (Dirichlet) condition at the outer edge of the circle. As this is an implicit scheme, a vector–matrix form, requiring linear system solutions, is essential—you will need to arrange the grid function as a vector* $\mathbf{u}$, *and generate the matrix form of the operator* $\delta_{\Delta\circ}$ *(see Programming Exercise 10.6). You will also need to ensure that you have satisfied the stability condition* (11.28) *as close to equality as possible. In order to do this, rewrite this condition in terms of* h_r *and* $q = h_\theta/h_r$, *as in Problem 11.16.*

For a given value of γ, *such as* $\gamma = 2000$, *perform a study of output bandwidth as a function of the free parameter* α, *as well as the ratio* $q = h_\theta/h_r$. *Initialize the scheme with a sharply peaked pluck-like distribution, so that you will excite all the modes sufficiently, and plot an output spectrum, from which the bandwidth should be easily observable—ignore any isolated spurious modes which appear high in the audio spectrum.*

1
2
3
4
5
6
7
8
9
10
11
12
13
14
15
16
17
18
19
20
21
22
23
24
25
26
27
28
29
30
31
32
33
34
35
36
37
38
39
40
41
42
43
44
45
46
47
48
49
50
51

12

Linear plate vibration

The 2D wave equation has been treated in the previous chapter as a test case for sound synthesis methods. But, aside from the case of the vibrating membrane, it is often materials with an inherent stiffness which are of interest in musical acoustics. When these are flat, they are referred to as plates, and when curved, as shells. The physics of vibrating plates is far more complex than that of the membrane, described by the 2D wave equation, and this complexity shows itself in the resulting equations of motion, even in the simplest case of thin linear plate vibration.

Because the 2D wave equation is so simply expressed, it is often assumed that the increased model complexity for systems such as plates must translate to more computational work. But, as seen in Chapter 7, stiffness tends to *reduce* computational costs. The same is true of plates—whereas simulation of membrane vibration in real time is, even now, quite daunting, plate synthesis is not. This is good news, as the world of sounds produced by plates is a very rich one indeed. The lossless Kirchhoff thin plate model, as well as modal analysis and finite difference schemes, is introduced in Section 12.1 and frequency-dependent loss in Section 12.2. Coupling to various excitation mechanisms such as the mallet and bow, as well as the related case of plate reverberation, is treated in Section 12.3 and coupling to strings in Section 12.4. Anisotropic plate vibration is briefly discussed in Section 12.5, and, finally, schemes for the thin plate equation are developed in radial coordinates in Section 12.6.

12.1   The Kirchhoff thin plate model

The Kirchhoff model of a uniform thin isotropic plate [244] is defined as

$$\rho H u_{tt} = -D\Delta\Delta u \qquad (12.1)$$

Here, u is the plate deflection in a transverse direction, ρ is a material density, H is the plate thickness, and the constant D defined by

$$D = \frac{EH^3}{12(1 - \nu^2)}$$

is sometimes known as the plate flexural rigidity, and depends on Young's modulus E and Poisson's ratio $\nu < 1/2$. When spatially scaled with respect to a length parameter L, the Kirchhoff model

Numerical Sound Synthesis: Finite Difference Schemes and Simulation in Musical Acoustics   Stefan Bilbao
© 2009 John Wiley & Sons, Ltd

may be written as

$$u_{tt} = -\kappa^2 \Delta \Delta u \tag{12.2}$$

where

$$\kappa^2 = \frac{D}{\rho H L^4} \tag{12.3}$$

As usual for problems which are second order in time, two initial conditions must be supplied (normally displacement and velocity). Boundary termination is a much more complex matter than in the case of the 2D wave equation; conditions will be given shortly, in Section 12.1.2.

The model above is but the simplest representation of plate dynamics. It does not take into account effects that occur at high amplitudes, which will be covered in the next chapter, nor does it hold when the plate becomes thick (i.e., when H/L becomes large in some sense), in which case a thick plate model (some examples of which are very well covered in the text by Graff [156]) is perhaps more appropriate. Most plates which occur in a musical setting, however, are quite thin, and the above model is sufficient for a preliminary foray into physical modeling synthesis. For a quantitative look at the range of applicability of the thin plate hypothesis in musical acoustics, through a comparison with the Mindlin–Reissner thick plate theory, see the next section.

12.1.1 Phase and group velocity

The characteristic equation or dispersion relation for the thin plate equation (12.2) is

$$s^2 = -\kappa^2 |\boldsymbol{\beta}|^2 \qquad \longrightarrow \qquad \omega = \pm \kappa |\boldsymbol{\beta}|^2$$

and expressions for the phase and group velocity follow as

$$v_\phi = \kappa |\boldsymbol{\beta}| \qquad\qquad v_g = 2\kappa |\boldsymbol{\beta}|$$

Again, just as in the case of the ideal bar in 1D, wave propagation is dispersive, with short wavelength components traveling faster than those of long wavelength. See Figure 12.1, which shows the time evolution of an initial displacement—the dispersive behavior may again be seen in the high-frequency ripples preceding the main body of the disturbance.

This system, like the wave equation, is isotropic—again, though it would be possible to write the expressions for phase and group velocity in terms of frequency ω alone, the associated difference schemes lose this isotropic property, and the easiest comparison is through the expressions above, in terms of wavenumber $\boldsymbol{\beta}$. An extension of the thin plate model to the anisotropic case is indeed of interest in musical acoustics as well, and will be described more fully in Section 12.5.

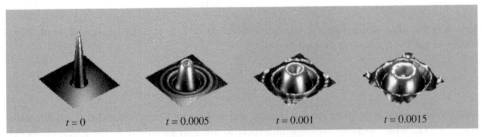

$t = 0$ $\qquad\qquad\qquad$ $t = 0.0005$ $\qquad\qquad$ $t = 0.001$ $\qquad\qquad$ $t = 0.0015$

Figure 12.1 Time evolution of the displacement of a plate. Here, the plate has stiffness parameter $\kappa = 5$, an aspect ratio of $\epsilon = 1$, and free boundary conditions are applied at the edges. The initial condition is of plucked type, in the form of a raised cosine at the domain center.

Thick vs. thin plate models

Plates which occur as components of musical instruments are thin. One question which then arises is: are thin plate models sufficient to describe the behavior of such objects subject to the constraints of human audition? One way of answering this question is through a comparison to certain thick plate models, via dispersion relations. For the sake of this comparison, consider the thin Kirchhoff plate model, and what is perhaps the simplest possible model of thick plate vibration (taking into account shear and rotatory inertia effects) due to Mindlin and Reissner [239, 156]; this model will not be presented here, but may be viewed as the direct extension of the Timoshenko beam theory to 2D. (The Timoshenko model is presented briefly in Problem 7.1.)

From the plots in Figure 12.2, it should be clear that the deviation of the dispersion relation of the Kirchhoff model (and thus modal frequencies) from that of the thick plate model is pronounced at high frequencies—the thinner the plate, the less influence over frequencies in the audio range. For metal plates of roughly 1 mm thickness, the effect is minimal, though for other materials, such as glass, the effect may be more pronounced. Not shown in the dispersion plots are an additional family of frequencies, which lie well above the audio range for the two example thicknesses considered here.

Thick plate models are heavily used in finite element calculations, but may well be overkill when it comes to plates such as those which occur in musical acoustics; given that simulating the thick model involves a good deal more computational work, one should consider very carefully the use of standard finite element packages, designed for industrial applications, in physical modeling sound synthesis.

12.1.2 Energy and boundary conditions

For the Kirchhoff plate defined over a domain $\mathcal{D}$, the energy may be found, using the usual manipulations, as

$$\frac{d\mathfrak{H}_0}{dt} = \mathfrak{B}_0 \qquad \text{with} \qquad \mathfrak{H}_0 = \mathfrak{T} + \mathfrak{V}_0 \tag{12.4}$$

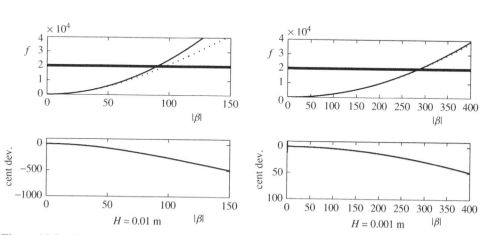

Figure 12.2 Comparison between thick and thin plate models, for a steel plate of thickness 1 cm (left) and 1 mm (right). Top: dispersion relation with frequency $f = f(\beta)$ (dimensional form) for the Kirchhoff thin plate model (solid line) and the Mindlin–Reissner thick plate model (dotted line). The upper limit of human hearing, at $f = 20$ kHz, is plotted as a thick black line. Bottom: the deviation, in cents, between the two profiles as a function of wavenumber.

where $\mathfrak{B}_0$ is a term resolved on the boundary of $\mathcal{D}$, and

$$\mathfrak{T} = \frac{1}{2}\|u_t\|_{\mathcal{D}}^2 \qquad \mathfrak{V}_0 = \frac{\kappa^2}{2}\|\Delta u\|_{\mathcal{D}}^2$$

which are similar to the expressions for the ideal bar, from (7.5). The expression $\mathfrak{V}_0$ (and thus $\mathfrak{H}_0$), however, though valid in the case of the infinite plate, may need to be modified under certain boundary conditions—see below.

Edges and fixed boundary conditions

At an edge of a Cartesian domain, say at $x = 0$ for $\mathcal{D} = \mathbb{R}^{2,x+}$, integration by parts leads, from (10.5), to the following expression for the boundary term $\mathfrak{B}_0$ in (12.4):

$$\mathfrak{B}_0 = \kappa^2 \left(\{u_t, (\Delta u)_x\}_{(0,\mathbb{R})} - \{u_{tx}, \Delta u\}_{(0,\mathbb{R})} \right)$$

(Recall the use of the $\{\cdot, \cdot\}$ notation to indicate a 1D inner product over a boundary, from (10.7).) One may immediately extract the following two sets of boundary conditions:

$$u = u_x = 0 \qquad \text{clamped} \qquad\qquad (12.5a)$$

$$u = u_{xx} = 0 \qquad \text{simply supported} \qquad\qquad (12.5b)$$

(In fact, the simply supported condition is normally written in a slightly different form—see the following discussion of free boundary conditions.) These conditions are directly analogous to those for the ideal bar, from (7.7a) and (7.7b). One might also suppose, by analogy, that the conditions $u_{xx} = u_{xxx} = 0$ correspond to a free edge condition; in fact, they do not. The difficulty is that $\mathfrak{V}_0$ may be interpreted as a potential energy only under a fixed termination. It may be modified in the following way.

The operator $\mathcal{L}(\cdot, \cdot)$ and free boundary conditions

In order to address the issue of free boundary conditions in a thin plate, it turns out to be useful to introduce an operator which appears with great frequency in problems in thin plate vibration [286]. The operator $\mathcal{L}(\cdot, \cdot)$ is defined, in Cartesian coordinates, with respect to two functions $\alpha(x, y)$ and $\beta(x, y)$, as

$$\mathcal{L}(\alpha, \beta) = \alpha_{xx}\beta_{yy} + \alpha_{yy}\beta_{xx} - 2\alpha_{xy}\beta_{xy} \qquad\qquad (12.6)$$

Though this operator will crop up in a more central way in the study of nonlinear plate vibration in Chapter 13, it possesses several properties which are useful in arriving at free boundary conditions even in the linear case. First, it is bilinear, and also symmetric, so that $\mathcal{L}(\alpha, \beta) = \mathcal{L}(\beta, \alpha)$, implying further that, if α and β also depend on t,

$$(\mathcal{L}(\alpha, \beta))_t = \mathcal{L}(\alpha_t, \beta) + \mathcal{L}(\alpha, \beta_t) \qquad\qquad (12.7)$$

Next, assuming for the moment that $\mathcal{L}(\alpha, \beta)$ is defined over the half plane domain $\mathcal{D} = \mathbb{R}^{2,x+}$,

$$\langle \mathcal{L}(\alpha, \beta), 1 \rangle_{\mathbb{R}^{2,x+}} = \int_{-\infty}^{\infty} \int_0^{\infty} \mathcal{L}(\alpha, \beta) dx dy = -\int_{-\infty}^{\infty} \alpha_x \beta_{yy} + \alpha \beta_{xyy} dy$$

$$= -\{\alpha_x, \beta_{yy}\}_{(0,\mathbb{R})} - \{\alpha, \beta_{xyy}\}_{(0,\mathbb{R})} \qquad (12.8)$$

Thus $\mathcal{L}(\alpha, \beta)$, when integrated over the spatial domain, may be resolved into terms which act over the boundary alone—note in particular that if α and β are constrained to be zero over this boundary, then the integral vanishes.

With this in mind, one may now return to the problem of the free boundary condition over the half plane $\mathcal{D} = \mathbb{R}^{2,x+}$. Set $\alpha = \beta = u$, and define the quantity $\mathfrak{V}_{\text{free}}$ by

$$\mathfrak{V}_{\text{free}} = \frac{\kappa^2(\nu - 1)}{2}\langle\mathcal{L}(u, u), 1\rangle_{\mathbb{R}^{2,x+}}$$

Then, using properties (12.7) and (12.8) above,

$$\frac{d\mathfrak{V}_{\text{free}}}{dt} = \mathfrak{B}_{\text{free}} = \kappa^2(1 - \nu)\left(\{u_{xt}, u_{yy}\}_{(0,\mathbb{R})} + \{u_t, u_{xyy}\}_{(0,\mathbb{R})}\right)$$

and, interpreting $\mathfrak{V}_{\text{free}}$ as a contribution to the potential energy of the plate, one has finally

$$\frac{d\mathfrak{H}}{dt} = \mathfrak{B} \qquad \text{where} \qquad \mathfrak{H} = \mathfrak{H}_0 + \mathfrak{V}_{\text{free}} \tag{12.9}$$

and where the boundary term is

$$\mathfrak{B} = \mathfrak{B}_0 + \mathfrak{B}_{\text{free}} = \kappa^2\left(\{u_t, u_{xxx} + (2 - \nu)u_{xyy}\}_{(0,\mathbb{R})} - \{u_{tx}, u_{xx} + \nu u_{yy}\}_{(0,\mathbb{R})}\right) \tag{12.10}$$

Though $\mathfrak{H}_0$ is obviously non-negative, it is not immediately clear that $\mathfrak{H} = \mathfrak{H}_0 + \mathfrak{V}_{\text{free}}$ will be, given that $\mathcal{L}(u, u)$ is of indeterminate sign. With a little additional effort, one may show non-negativity of $\mathfrak{H}$—see Problem 12.1.

Upon inspection of the new boundary term $\mathfrak{B}$, the conventional lossless free boundary condition may be extracted:

$$u_{xx} + \nu u_{yy} = u_{xxx} + (2 - \nu)u_{xyy} = 0 \qquad \text{free} \tag{12.11}$$

Notice that the boundary conditions now depend on ν and, as such, it is an extra parameter which must appear in any simulation, and which cannot be eliminated through scaling techniques.[1] For steel, which is a common choice of material in musical instruments, ν is approximately 0.3. The more conventional form of the simply supported condition, equivalent to that given in (12.5b), also emerges—see Problem 12.2.

Though fixed and free conditions have been shown here for a domain with a single edge, it should be clear that, at least over a rectangular domain, they may be used at any edge, where x may be interpreted as a coordinate normal to the plate edge, and y to a tangential coordinate.

Corners

Corners pose slightly more difficulty in the case of the plate than for the 2D wave equation. Consider a thin Kirchhoff plate defined over the quarter plane $\mathcal{D} = \mathbb{R}^{2,x+y+}$. Through energy analysis (see Problem 12.3), one may show that under fixed conditions, no further condition at $x = 0$, $y = 0$ need be supplied other than $u = 0$. Under free conditions, however, a new condition intervenes:

$$u_{xy}|_{x=0,y=0} = 0 \qquad \text{free at corner} \tag{12.12}$$

which must be enforced in addition to the edge conditions.

[1] In the simulation setting, this is a consideration which strongly affects modal algorithms—the modal shapes and frequencies will be dependent not just on geometry, but also on ν, and must be recalculated as the material is changed. Time domain methods, once the proper boundary conditions are inserted into the algorithm, are insensitive to this choice.

12.1.3 Modes

Modal analysis for thin plates is similar to that applied to the 2D wave equation, in Section 11.1.3. As for the case of the ideal bar, however (see Section 7.1.3), closed-form expressions for modal frequencies and shapes are rare—for a rectangular plate of aspect ratio ϵ, defined over the unit area rectangle $\mathcal{D} = \mathbb{U}_\epsilon^2$, only simply supported conditions such as (12.5b) applied on all edges lead to a simple expression:

$$U_{p,q}(x, y) = \sin(p\pi x/\sqrt{\epsilon})\sin(q\pi\sqrt{\epsilon}y) \qquad \omega_{p,q} = \pi^2\kappa\left(p^2/\epsilon + \epsilon q^2\right) \qquad (12.13)$$

In all other cases of interest (and in particular, that of free termination, which plays a large role in models of percussion instruments), the shapes and frequencies must be computed numerically. See Figure 12.3 for an illustration of the modal shapes. Under free conditions at all edges of a rectangular plate, there will be three additional zero-frequency modes corresponding to "rigid body" motion—see Programming Exercise 12.1 for some exploration of this.

Just as in the case of the ideal bar, it should be apparent that the frequencies increase more quickly with mode number for this stiff 2D system, with respect to those of the analogous non-stiff system, the 2D wave equation. From the above expression for the modal frequencies, one may arrive at the following count for the number of degrees of freedom $N_m(f_s/2)$ (twice the number of modal frequencies less than $f_s/2$):

$$N_m(f_s/2) = \frac{f_s}{2\kappa}$$

In comparison with the analogous expression for the 2D wave equation (or for a membrane) from (11.9), note that the number of modes depends linearly on f_s, implying a uniform density of modes. In fact, one has an average spacing between modes of 2κ Hz. See Figure 12.4. This implies,

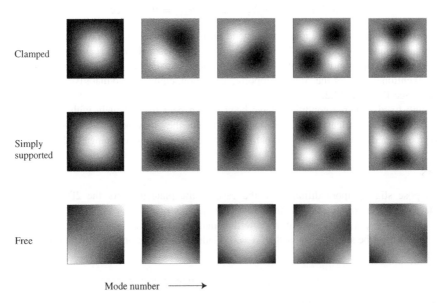

Clamped

Simply supported

Free

Mode number ⟶

Figure 12.3 The first five modes of vibration for a thin square plate, under clamped (top), simply supported (middle), and free (bottom) boundary conditions. In all cases, dark and light areas correspond to modal maxima and minima. In the case of the free condition, the first five modes of non-zero frequency are shown (i.e., three modes corresponding to rigid body motion are not shown here).

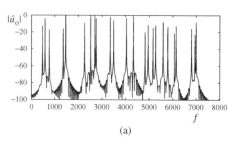
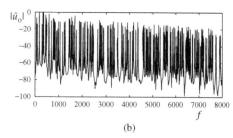

Figure 12.4 Output spectra, showing an even distribution of modes, for a thin plate model. In this case, the plate is square, under free boundary conditions; in (a), the stiffness parameter $\kappa = 200$, and in (b), $\kappa = 20$.

furthermore, a reduction in the number of degrees of freedom necessary to describe the plate up to a given frequency. As a result, the simulation of plate vibration is far less computationally intensive than membrane vibration[2]—which is perhaps surprising! As usual, the same reduction in computational expense follows through to the case of finite difference schemes, which are covered next.

12.1.4 A simple finite difference scheme

Probably the most straightforward finite difference method for the Kirchhoff plate employs the five-point approximation to the Laplacian, twice, as discussed in Section 10.2:

$$\delta_{tt}u = -\kappa^2\delta_{\Delta\boxplus,\Delta\boxplus}u \tag{12.14}$$

When written out in full in terms of the grid function $u^n_{l,m}$, assuming that the grid spacing is equal to h in both the x and y directions, the scheme is of the form

$$u^{n+1}_{l,m} = \left(2 - 20\mu^2\right)u^n_{l,m} + 8\mu^2\left(u^n_{l,m+1} + u^n_{l,m-1} + u^n_{l+1,m} + u^n_{l-1,m}\right)$$
$$- 2\mu^2\left(u^n_{l+1,m+1} + u^n_{l+1,m-1} + u^n_{l-1,m+1} + u^n_{l-1,m-1}\right)$$
$$- \mu^2\left(u^n_{l,m+2} + u^n_{l,m-2} + u^n_{l+2,m} + u^n_{l-2,m}\right) - u^{n-1}_{l,m}$$

and depends on the scheme parameter μ, defined as

$$\mu = \frac{\kappa k}{h^2}$$

As one might gather, there are many possibilities for the generalization of scheme (12.14), through parameterized approximations to $\Delta\Delta$ [48], and perhaps implicit constructions—one such parameterized family of schemes will be explored in Section 12.1.5, and other schemes used in investigations in musical acoustics appear in [316], for a system equivalent to (12.1). Finite difference schemes for rectangular plates are examined in much more detail in the book by Szilard [348].

---

[2] This is true for a thin plate model, but, when a full thick plate model is employed, one may expect an avalanche of modes in the high-frequency range. Given the discussion of the applicability of the thick plate model in musical acoustics, on page 333, the increased modal density will not exhibit itself, at least for reasonably thin plates, until well beyond the upper reaches of the audio frequency range.

von Neumann analysis and stability

The characteristic polynomial for scheme (12.14) is

$$z + \left(16\mu^2(p_x + p_y)^2 - 2\right) + z^{-1} = 0$$

in terms of the variables $p_x = \sin^2(\beta_x h/2)$ and $p_y = \sin^2(\beta_y h/2)$. The roots are of unit magnitude under the conditions

$$0 \leq 4\mu^2(p_x + p_y)^2 \leq 1$$

which is satisfied when

$$\mu \leq \frac{1}{4} \qquad \longrightarrow \qquad h \geq 2\sqrt{\kappa k} \qquad (12.15)$$

Energy and numerical boundary conditions

Finding numerical boundary conditions which correspond to typical lossless conditions of the type discussed in Section 12.1.2 is straightforward, but proving stability for a choice of such conditions can be a very delicate and involved matter. It is worth showing how this may be done, using energy methods, for one such set.

Consider the scheme (12.14), defined over the half plane $\mathbb{Z}^{2,x+}$. Taking an inner product with $\delta_t.u$ leads directly, using summation by parts from (10.19), to

$$\delta_{t+}\mathfrak{t} = -\kappa^2 \langle \delta_{\Delta\boxplus}\delta_t.u, \delta_{\Delta\boxplus}u \rangle_{\mathbb{Z}^{2,x+}} + \mathfrak{b}_0 = -\delta_{t+}\mathfrak{v}_0 + \mathfrak{b}_0 \qquad \longrightarrow \qquad \delta_{t+}\mathfrak{h}_0 = \mathfrak{b}_0 \qquad (12.16)$$

where $\mathfrak{h}_0 = \mathfrak{t} + \mathfrak{v}_0$, and

$$\mathfrak{t} = \frac{1}{2}\|\delta_{t-}u\|^2_{\mathbb{Z}^{2,x+}} \qquad \mathfrak{v}_0 = \frac{\kappa^2}{2}\langle \delta_{\Delta\boxplus}u, e_{t-}\delta_{\Delta\boxplus}u \rangle_{\mathbb{Z}^{2,x+}} \qquad (12.17a)$$

$$\mathfrak{b}_0 = \kappa^2\{\delta_t.u, \delta_x - \delta_{\Delta\boxplus}u\}_{(0,\mathbb{Z})} - \kappa^2\{\delta_x - \delta_t.u, \delta_{\Delta\boxplus}u\}_{(0,\mathbb{Z})} \qquad (12.17b)$$

One may immediately extract numerical clamped and simply supported conditions as

$$u = \delta_{x-}u = 0 \qquad \text{clamped} \qquad (12.18a)$$

$$u = \delta_{xx}u = 0 \qquad \text{simply supported} \qquad (12.18b)$$

In either case the scheme conserves numerical energy. Stability follows, as usual, by finding conditions under which the energy remains non-negative.

The case of the free boundary condition is more complex. One may write, for the potential energy $\mathfrak{v}_0$, and defining $v \triangleq \delta_t.u$,

$$\delta_{t+}\mathfrak{v}_0 = \kappa^2 \langle \delta_{\Delta\boxplus}v, \delta_{\Delta\boxplus}u \rangle_{\mathbb{Z}^{2,x+}}$$

$$= \kappa^2 v \langle \delta_{\Delta\boxplus}v, \delta_{\Delta\boxplus}u \rangle_{\mathbb{Z}^{2,x+}} + \kappa^2(1-v)\langle \delta_{\Delta\boxplus}v, \delta_{\Delta\boxplus}u \rangle_{\mathbb{Z}^{2,x+}}$$

$$= \kappa^2 v \langle \delta_{\Delta\boxplus}v, \delta_{\Delta\boxplus}u \rangle_{\mathbb{Z}^{2,x+}} + \kappa^2(1-v)\left(\langle \delta_{xx}v, \delta_{xx}u \rangle_{\mathbb{Z}^{2,x+}} + \langle \delta_{yy}v, \delta_{yy}u \rangle_{\mathbb{Z}^{2,x+}}\right)$$

$$+ \kappa^2(1-v)\left(\langle \delta_{xx}v, \delta_{yy}u \rangle_{\mathbb{Z}^{2,x+}} + \langle \delta_{yy}v, \delta_{xx}u \rangle_{\mathbb{Z}^{2,x+}}\right)$$

Finally, using summation by parts on the final two terms in the above expression leads to

$$\delta_{t+}\mathfrak{v}_0 = \kappa^2 v \langle \delta_{\Delta\boxplus}v, \delta_{\Delta\boxplus}u \rangle_{\mathbb{Z}^{2,x+}} + \kappa^2(1-v)\left(\langle \delta_{xx}v, \delta_{xx}u \rangle_{\mathbb{Z}^{2,x+}} + \langle \delta_{yy}v, \delta_{yy}u \rangle_{\mathbb{Z}^{2,x+}}\right)$$

$$+ 2\kappa^2(1-v)\langle \delta_{x+y+}v, \delta_{x+y+}u \rangle_{\mathbb{Z}^{2,x+}} - \mathfrak{b}'$$

$$= \delta_{t+}\mathfrak{v} - \mathfrak{b}'$$

where

$$\mathfrak{v} = \frac{\kappa^2 \nu}{2} \langle \delta_{\Delta\boxplus} u, e_{t-}\delta_{\Delta\boxplus} u \rangle_{\mathbb{Z}^{2,x+}} + \frac{\kappa^2(1-\nu)}{2} \left(\langle \delta_{xx} u, e_{t-}\delta_{xx} u \rangle_{\mathbb{Z}^{2,x+}} + \langle \delta_{yy} u, e_{t-}\delta_{yy} u \rangle_{\mathbb{Z}^{2,x+}} \right)$$

$$+ \kappa^2(1-\nu)\langle \delta_{x+y+} u, e_{t-}\delta_{x+y+} u \rangle_{\mathbb{Z}^{2,x+}} \tag{12.19a}$$

$$\mathfrak{v}' = \kappa^2(1-\nu)\{\delta_{t\cdot} u, \delta_{x-}\delta_{yy} u\}_{(0,\mathbb{Z})} + \kappa^2(1-\nu)\{\delta_{x-}\delta_{t\cdot} u, \delta_{yy} u\}_{(0,\mathbb{Z})} \tag{12.19b}$$

and finally, from (12.16), to

$$\delta_{t+}\mathfrak{h} = \mathfrak{b} \tag{12.20}$$

where $\mathfrak{h} = \mathfrak{t} + \mathfrak{v}$, and where $\mathfrak{b} = \mathfrak{b}_0 + \mathfrak{b}'$ is of the form

$$\mathfrak{b} = \kappa^2\{\delta_{t\cdot} u, \delta_{x-}\left(\delta_{xx} + (2-\nu)\delta_{yy}\right) u\}_{(0,\mathbb{Z})} - \kappa^2\{\delta_{x-}\delta_{t\cdot} u, \left(\delta_{xx} + \nu\delta_{yy}\right) u\}_{(0,\mathbb{Z})}$$

Clearly, the boundary term vanishes when

$$\left(\delta_{xx} + \nu\delta_{yy}\right) u = \delta_{x-}\left(\delta_{xx} + (2-\nu)\delta_{yy}\right) u = 0 \qquad \text{free} \tag{12.21}$$

which corresponds directly to the boundary condition (12.11). Still, however, the above analysis is not sufficient to show stable behavior of the scheme. As usual, one must show that the conserved energy is a non-negative function of the state defined over the grid. Even in this simple case of the scheme defined over the half plane, this is complicated by the fact that the expressions for the energy now include values outside the domain, at virtual grid locations. This analysis is performed in [46], and in a step-by-step fashion in Problem 12.4.

Scheme (12.14), under the above conditions (12.18a), (12.18b), or (12.21), is conservative over the half plane. This analysis can be extended directly to the quarter plane; if the scheme (12.14) is defined over the region $\mathcal{D} = \mathbb{Z}^{2,x+y+}$, the numerical boundary conditions above continue to hold at the boundary at $x = 0$, and the same conditions hold, with x and y reversed, at the boundary at $y = 0$. For free boundary conditions on both edges, the corner condition corresponding to (12.12) will be

$$\delta_{x-y-}u_{0,0} = 0 \tag{12.22}$$

See Problem 12.5. These conditions may be extended, by symmetry, to a rectangular region. For more on the construction of the related operator $\delta_{\Delta\boxplus,\Delta\boxplus}$, see Problem 12.6 and Programming Exercise 12.2.

12.1.5   An implicit family of schemes

Just as in the case of the ideal bar, the dispersive behavior of scheme (12.14) leads to an audible mistuning of modes—see Figure 12.5(b), showing the numerical phase velocity for this scheme relative to the phase velocity of the model system, as a function of wavenumber, and Table 12.1, which compares numerical modal frequencies to exact values for a particular instance of a plate under simply supported boundary conditions.

As before, for very fine modeling, particularly for high-pitched plates (i.e., for high values of κ), an implicit generalization of scheme (12.14) may be of use. Consider, thus, the two-parameter family of schemes given by

$$\left(1 + \alpha\kappa\kappa\delta_{\Delta\boxplus} + \phi k^2\kappa^2\delta_{\Delta\boxplus,\Delta\boxplus}\right)\delta_{tt} u = -\kappa^2\delta_{\Delta\boxplus,\Delta\boxplus} u \tag{12.23}$$

where α and ϕ are the free parameters. When $\alpha = \phi = 0$, the scheme reduces to (12.14).

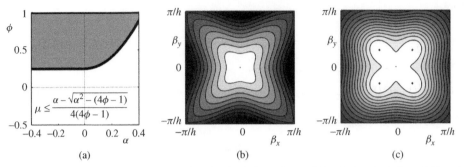

(a)   (b)   (c)

Figure 12.5 (a) Regions of unconditional (shaded) and conditional (unshaded) stability for scheme (12.23), in the (α, ϕ) parameter space. Over the region of conditional stability, the bound $\mu \leq \mu_{max}(\alpha, \phi)$ is as indicated. (b) A contour plot of numerical phase velocity relative to the exact phase velocity for the plate equation, as a function of the wavenumber components β_x and β_y, for the explicit scheme (12.14). (c) A similar plot for the implicit scheme (12.23) with $\alpha = 0.47$ and $\phi = 0.3$. Contours indicate deviations of 5% from the exact value of one.

Stability analysis, though now more complex, yields the bounds $\mu \leq \mu_{max}(\alpha, \phi)$, as given over regions of the (α, ϕ) plane in Figure 12.5(a); notice that, as in the case of schemes mentioned earlier for the wave equation and the ideal bar, there are choices of the parameters such that the scheme is unconditionally stable. See Problem 12.7.

As expected, it is possible to choose the parameters such that dispersion is minimized, particularly in the low-frequency limit, and the accuracy of the numerical modal frequencies is much greater. See Figure 12.5(c) and Table 12.1. The poor performance of the explicit scheme is clearly in evidence in the table; deviations of a semitone or more are possible even for relatively low frequencies. The parameters α and ϕ have been chosen here in an ad hoc manner—computer optimization techniques are advisable, perhaps with a goal of minimizing the variation in relative phase velocity over the entire range of wavenumbers, though one must bear in mind that the choice of μ, which is dependent on α and ϕ, will have great bearing on computational cost, and such an attribute must be accounted for in any optimization procedure.

Table 12.1 Comparison among modal frequencies for the plate equation defined over a square, under simply supported conditions, with $\kappa = 100$, and modal frequencies (as well as their cent deviations from the exact frequencies) of the simple explicit scheme (12.14), and the implicit scheme (12.23), with $\alpha = 0.47$ and $\phi = 0.3$, with a sample rate $f_s = 44\,100\,Hz$. μ is chosen so as to satisfy the stability condition given in Figure 12.5(a) in each case as close to equality as possible.

Mode number	Exact freq.	Explicit		Implicit	
		Freq.	Cent dev.	Freq.	Cent dev.
(1,1)	314.2	311.6	−14.1	315.9	9.5
(1,2)	785.4	764.1	−47.6	792.2	14.9
(2,2)	1256.6	1217.4	−54.9	1281.9	34.5
(1,3)	1570.8	1470.6	−114.1	1583.0	13.4
(2,3)	2042.0	1926.1	−101.2	2092.9	42.6
(1,4)	2670.4	2366.5	−209.2	2672.7	1.5
(2,5)	4555.3	3838.7	−296.3	4573.0	6.7

12.2 Loss and tension

As in the case of the ideal bar, loss modeling in plates is a very involved matter—there are various sources of such loss, including thermoelasticity, viscoelasticity, and radiation; see [79] for a complete picture of such effects. Tension may also be added, as in the case of the stiff string, in order to yield a general model for a stiff membrane [136]. A simple, perceptually correct plate model is a direct extension of the case of the bar:

$$u_{tt} = -\kappa^2 \Delta\Delta u + \gamma^2 \Delta u - 2\sigma_0 u_t + 2\sigma_1 \Delta u_t$$

As before, σ_0, in the absence of the term with coefficient σ_1 gives rise to frequency-independent damping, and when this other term is added, increasing damping at higher frequencies is modeled. As before, it is possible to rewrite σ_0 and σ_1 in terms of two chosen values of decay constant T_{60} at specified frequencies—the expressions are identical to those given in (7.29). The obvious explicit extension of scheme (12.14) is

$$\delta_{tt} u = -\kappa^2 \delta_{\Delta\boxplus,\Delta\boxplus} u + \gamma^2 \delta_{\Delta\boxplus} u - 2\sigma_0 \delta_{t\cdot} u + 2\sigma_1 \delta_{t-} \delta_{\Delta\boxplus} u \tag{12.24}$$

Implicit versions are of course available, useful both in reducing numerical dispersion and in improved (centered) modeling of the frequency-dependent damping term. See Programming Exercise 12.3.

12.3 Plate excitation

Excitation, using physical models of a hammer-like object and a bow, has been covered in the lumped context in Section 4.2.3 and Section 4.3.1, and in the case of 1D systems such as strings and bars in Section 7.5 and Section 7.4. From a functional point of view, the situation is not extremely different in the case of 2D systems such as plates, though, of course, the sound output is of an entirely different character.

In both cases, one may connect the plate to the excitation by using a distribution $e_{exc}(x, y)$ representing the spatial extent of the excitation. In the case of an ideal thin plate with loss, but without tension, for example, the combined system is of the following form:

$$u_{tt} = -\kappa^2 \Delta\Delta u - 2\sigma_0 u_t + 2\sigma_1 \Delta u_t + e_{exc}(x, y)F \tag{12.25}$$

where $F(t)$ is a force divided by the total plate mass. Usually it is simplest to use a localized distribution of the form of a 2D Dirac delta function $e_{exc}(x, y) = \delta(x - x_i, y - y_i)$; this is certainly sufficient for bowing, though for large mallets (or small plates) a more general distribution (e.g., a 2D raised cosine, as per (11.3)) may be advisable. The excitation point $x = x_i$, $y = y_i$ has been left fully general here. In the case of the bow, however, it is only physically reasonable to bow at an edge, though in simulation, of course, one can bow wherever one likes!

F may derive from a physical model of an excitation mechanism, generally driven by gestural data at a control rate. On the other hand, in one very interesting application of physical modeling, namely plate reverberation, F is an audio signal, and is "processed" by a plate—see Section 7.9 for more on the use of physical modeling principles in the emulation of analog audio effects.

A simple scheme, assuming that the excitation acts at a point with coordinates x_i, y_i, then, is the following:

$$\delta_{tt} u = -\kappa^2 \delta_{\Delta\boxplus,\Delta\boxplus} u - 2\sigma_0 \delta_{t\cdot} u + 2\sigma_1 \delta_{t-} \delta_{\Delta\boxplus} u + J_p(x_i, y_i)F \tag{12.26}$$

where $J_p(x_i, y_i)$ is a pth-order spreading function, as described in Section 10.2.1. Notice that as in the case of the bar, a backward difference has been employed to approximate the frequency-dependent loss term—this could be adjusted to a centered difference, at the expense of requiring an implicit update.

12.3.1   Coupling to a mallet model

The interaction with a mallet-like object may be generalized directly from the case of the hammer–string interaction in 1D, as described in Section 7.5. In this case, if the vertical position of the mallet is $u_H(t)$, the force term F is given by

$$F = -\mathcal{M}\frac{d^2 u_H}{dt^2} = \omega_H^{1+\alpha} \left([u_H - \langle e_{exc}, u \rangle_\mathcal{D}]^+ \right)^\alpha$$

As before, the interaction is modeled using a one-sided power law nonlinearity. $\mathcal{M}$ is the ratio of the mass of the mallet to that of the plate, ω_H is a stiffness parameter, and α the stiffness exponent. Again, the operation $[\cdot]^+$ indicates the "positive part of," and thus the interaction is active only when the mallet and plate are in contact. Such a model, when coupled to a membrane rather than a plate, has been employed in time domain simulations of drums [283, 216] as well as anisotropic plates [217].

Given the previous encounters with this type of nonlinearity in Section 4.2.2 and Section 7.5, a well-behaved difference approximation to the force equations above is of semi-implicit type:

$$F = -\mathcal{M}\delta_{tt} u_H = \omega_H^{1+\alpha} \mu_{t\cdot} \left(u_H - I_p(x_i, y_i) u \right) \left([u_H - I_p(x_i, y_i) u]^+ \right)^{\alpha-1} \tag{12.27}$$

where $I_p(x_i, y_i)$ is a pth-order interpolation operator, as described in Section 10.2.1. As expected, such an approximation allows for a unique update, when coupled with (12.26). The major effect of the nonlinearity can be seen to be a reduction in the total contact duration and increase in brightness with increasing strike velocity—see Figure 12.6. Notice also the characteristic deformation of the force curves, resulting from reflections from the plate boundaries—recontact phenomena are also possible.

A synthesis shortcut

Given that the total contact time between a mallet or hammer and a plate (or a string for that matter) is often quite short (usually on the order of 1–5 ms), one might remark that, to a first approximation, the precise details of the force interaction may not be of great psychoacoustic importance. On the other hand, as mentioned above, the nonlinearity of the mallet interaction does lead to a change in the contact duration, which will indeed affect the brightness of the resulting sound.

One convenient way of avoiding explicitly integrating the nonlinear coupled system, then, is to simply specify an excitation function $F(t)$ in system (12.25) and subsequently in scheme (12.26). Because the system is linear, stability concerns are eased considerably. Here is a simple pulse-like choice of excitation function:

$$F = F_{exc}(t) = \begin{cases} \dfrac{F_{max}}{2}\left(1 - \cos\left(\dfrac{2\pi(t - t_0)}{T_{exc}}\right)\right), & t_0 \le t \le t_0 + T_{exc} \\ 0, & \text{otherwise} \end{cases} \tag{12.28}$$

which is parameterized by F_{max}, the maximum force, T_{exc}, the pulse duration, and t_0, the time at which the pulse occurs. For curves of relatively simple form, the difference in sound output compared to that generated using a full mallet model is minimal. See Figure 12.7.

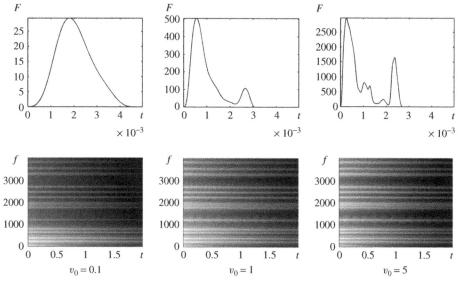

Figure 12.6   Force profiles (top), and output spectra (bottom), for a mallet striking a plate. Here, the plate has $\kappa = 100$, aspect ratio 1.3, a uniform decay time of $T_{60} = 2$ s, and is under free boundary conditions. The mallet/plate mass ratio is $\mathcal{M} = 0.4$, and the stiffness parameters are $\omega_{\mathrm{H}} = 1000$ and $\alpha = 3$. The plate is struck at the plate center, and readout is taken at coordinates $x_{\mathrm{o}} = 0.8$, $y_{\mathrm{o}} = 0.6$. Striking velocities v_0 are as indicated. Scheme (12.26) is employed, accompanied by (12.27), running at a sample rate of 44.1 kHz.

The main difficulty here is that due to the departure from a strict physical model, one must have a convenient means of parameterizing the curve $F(t)$ in terms of initial strike velocity, which will involve additional experimentation. Still, it is a relatively safe way of generating sound in a first attempt. See Section 13.2.6 for an application to synthesis using a nonlinear plate vibration model.

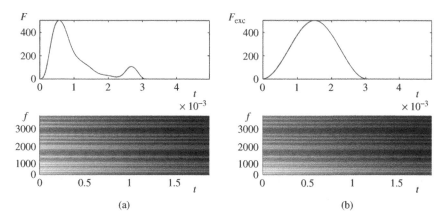

Figure 12.7   Comparison between outputs for (a) the mallet–plate interaction, using the parameters and scheme as described in the caption to Figure 12.6, with $v_0 = 1$, and (b) output using a synthetic excitation function $F_{\mathrm{exc}}(t)$.

12.3.2   Coupling to a bow model

The bow model, presented earlier in Section 4.3.1 and Section 7.4, may also be used for an excitation to a vibrating plate. Now, assuming an excitation distribution of the form of a Dirac delta function, F in (12.25) is of the form

$$F = -F_B \phi(v_{rel}) \qquad \text{where} \qquad v_{rel} = u_t(x_i, y_i) - v_B \tag{12.29}$$

Here, $F_B = F_B(t)$ is interpreted as a bowing force/total plate mass, and $v_B = v_B(t)$ is the bow velocity. The function ϕ is a friction characteristic of the form discussed in Section 4.3.1. Using scheme (12.26) with

$$v_{rel} = I_p(x_i, y_i)\delta_t.u - v_B \tag{12.30}$$

leads to a scheme which may be updated explicitly, using Newton's method; as in the case of the string interaction, an additional condition on μ arises which must be satisfied for uniqueness—see Problem 12.8. The variety of sounds which may be produced using such a bow model is enormous; some configurations produce quasi-harmonic tones, others produce more noise-like outputs. A good choice of boundary condition for the plate under bowing conditions is to leave one edge free, where the bow is applied, and to use simply supported or clamped conditions at all other edges—see Figure 12.8.

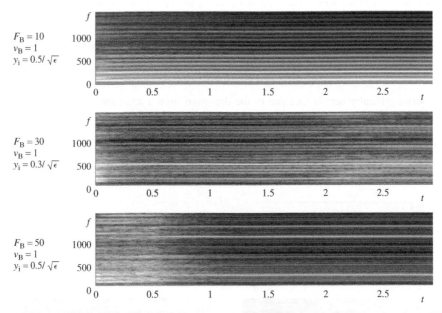

Figure 12.8   Spectrograms of output from a bowed plate model. In this case, the plate has stiffness parameter $\kappa = 20$, aspect ratio $\epsilon = 1$, and $T_{60} = 4$ s, and is under free conditions at $x = 0$ and clamped conditions on all other sides. The bow force/total plate mass F_B, bow velocity v_B, and bowing position $(0, y_i)$ are as given above, in three cases. Scheme (12.26) is used, accompanied by (12.29) and (12.30), at a sample rate of 44.1 kHz, and output is read at $x_o = 0.7$, $y_o = 0.7$. At top, a quasi-harmonic tone is produced, at a low pitch. As the bowing point is varied, various harmonics of the plate may be singled out, as shown in the middle panel. Finally, at high bow forces, a dramatic scraping or noise-like sound may be generated initially, before settling down to a pitched tone.

12.3.3   Plate reverberation

Plate reverberation, the granddaddy of all analog audio effects, developed in the 1950s [212] and subsequently became the high-end artificial reverberation device of choice for decades, until the advent of digital reverberation decades later. Operation is relatively straightforward—a large metal plate, of varying dimensions, but sometimes as long as 2 meters, is fed with a dry input signal, and a pickup reads an output signal at a given position on the plate. The typical plate reverberation characteristic is very different from that of a room, mainly due to the absence of strong early reflections, and to the modal distribution, which is nearly uniform—both attributes result from the inherently dispersive nature of wave propagation in a plate, as discussed in Section 12.1.1. In spite of this, the plate reverb sound has become one of the most sought-after effects in digital audio. Simulation, as in the case of the helical spring (see Section 7.9), is another interesting application of physical modeling principles, not to a musical instrument, but a processing unit.

Finite difference schemes are an excellent match to this problem, as the geometry of typical units is rectangular; some recent studies have been carried out by this author [44, 47] and others, primarily Arcas [12]. The basic system is of the form of (12.25), and the associated difference scheme is (12.26), where for a typical plate reverb unit, κ is on the order of approximately two, or less. The function F, in this case, is an input waveform, perhaps after having undergone equalization—the precise form of such equalization is not important for the present purposes, but is described in detail in [12]. A single output $m(t)$ is normally drawn from the plate through an accelerometer placed at given coordinates x_0, y_0 relative to the plate corner; in terms of the finite difference scheme (12.26), a sequence m^n may be obtained as

$$m^n = \delta_{tt} I(x_0, y_0) u^n$$

where $I(x_0, y_0)$ is an interpolation operator. This operation eliminates the need to consider rigid body motion of the plate, essentially filtering out any DC drift. (A more physical approach would be to model the means by which the plate is supported.) On the other hand, it does impose a high-pass character to the output, which must be rectified through filtering operations (or, again, through a model of equalization at the input stage). See Figure 12.9 for a typical example of an impulse response generated using such a scheme. The character of the response, as shown in (a), is nearly noise-like—notice in particular the uniform spacing of modal frequencies, as shown over different frequency ranges in (b) and (c).

A finite difference implementation has many desirable features, not least of which are: the ability to obtain multiple outputs cheaply, at distinct and possibly time-varying locations (thus

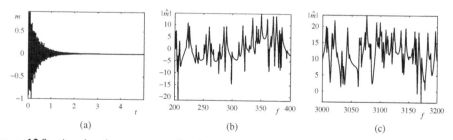

(a)   (b)   (c)

Figure 12.9   Acceleration response of a plate model to a force impulse. Here, the plate model is of the form of (12.25), with $\kappa = 2$, aspect ratio $\epsilon = 2$, under free boundary conditions, and with T_{60} decay times of 10 s at 500 Hz and 8 s at 2000 Hz. The impulse is inserted at the location $x_i = 0.807$, $y = 0.353$, and output acceleration m is read from $x_0 = 0.607$, $y_0 = 0.303$. The difference scheme (12.26) is used, at a sample rate 44.1 kHz. (a) Time response, (b) frequency response over a low-frequency range, and (c) frequency response over a mid-frequency range.

generalizing the functionality of the physical plate reverberation unit); the possibility of introducing
other features such as pointwise clamping (for the sake of tuning) along the boundary; and possibly the clamping of regions of the boundary along the corners. Such features are discussed
in [44]. Note that, even in the simple case of a rectangular plate with free edges, there is not,
in general, a closed-form expression for the modal shapes and frequencies, and thus a modal
implementation, while possible, may require an enormous amount of precomputation for each new
input/output/boundary condition configuration—there can be upward of 10 000 modes in the audio
range for a typical plate reverberation unit.

12.4   Plate–string connections

Another use of the plate-like structure in musical acoustics is as a soundboard, particularly in the
piano and other keyboard instruments. Here, it functions as an auxiliary element connected to
the main resonator (usually a string), and is employed so as to increase the radiation efficiency of the
resonator. For an overview, see [136] and the references therein. Simulation routines, typically for
use in comparing measurement with theory, have been developed by various authors—given the
geometrical complexity of real-world soundboards, this may involve finite element methods (a wise
choice) [347]. For applications closer to synthesis, finite difference schemes have been employed
[154], and are a good choice, especially if one is interested in programming simplicity, efficiency,
as well as exploring situations which are more than a little removed from strict acoustical modeling of real-world instruments! When digital waveguides are employed for the strings, a common
technique for the emulation of the soundboard effect on the resulting sound is known as "commuted synthesis" [338, 375]—the waveguides are terminated with filters derived from measured
soundboard responses. While allowing for very realistic sound output, the interest here is in design
flexibility, rather than high-fidelity sound synthesis based on a fixed instrument configuration.

Real soundboards, as mentioned above, are enormously complicated objects [153]. Not only
is there the geometrical complexity of the board, which is often of an irregular shape, of variable
thickness, strongly anisotropic, and perhaps accompanied by struts, but there is the also the nature
of the coupling to the strings, through the bridge. Such an object responds to longitudinal string
vibrations as well as transverse—indeed, phenomena such as phantom partials in piano and guitar
strings are audible precisely because of the transfer of longitudinal motion through the bridge [86].
As a first stab, however, it is worth spending some time examining the most rudimentary possible
connection between a string and a plate, and how it may be implemented using time domain
methods. The situation is not enormously different from the case of coupled bars, as discussed in
Section 7.8, with the exception that one must now pay special attention to the string boundary
conditions.

Consider the following system, in dimensional form:

$$\rho_P H u_{tt} = -D\Delta\Delta u + \delta(x - x_{S1}, y - y_{S1})f_1 + \delta(x - x_{S2}, y - y_{S2})f_2 \qquad \rho_S A w_{tt} = T_0 w_{\eta\eta} \tag{12.31}$$

Here, $u(x, y, t)$ is the transverse displacement of a thin, linear, lossless and isotropic plate, of
material density ρ_P, thickness H, and flexural rigidity D, defined over a rectangle of side lengths
L_x and L_y, and $w(\eta, t)$ is the transverse displacement of an ideal string, of material density ρ_S,
cross-sectional area A, under tension T_0, and of length L. Notice that the spatial coordinate η is
used in the case of the string so as not to confuse it with the coordinates describing the plate. The
string is connected to the plate at coordinates (x_{S1}, y_{S1}) at one end, and (x_{S2}, y_{S2}) at the other
end, exerting pointwise transverse forces f_1 and f_2. Note the use of 2D Dirac delta functions here
(these could be generalized to forces operating over a region of the plate without much difficulty).

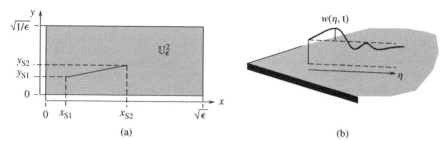

Figure 12.10 Geometry of the plate–string connection described by (12.32): (a) top view; (b) side view.

When the coordinates x, y, and η are spatially scaled, with respect to a characteristic length $\sqrt{L_x L_y}$ in the case of the plate, and L in the case of the string, the following system results:

$$u_{tt} = -\kappa^2 \Delta\Delta u + \delta(x - x_{S1}, y - y_{S1})F_1 + \delta(x - x_{S2}, y - y_{S2})F_2 \qquad \mathcal{M}w_{tt} = \mathcal{M}\gamma^2 w_{\eta\eta}$$

$$\text{(12.32)}$$

where $F_1 = f_1/\rho_P H L_x L_y$, $F_2 = f_2/\rho_P H L_x L_y$, and the string/plate mass ratio $\mathcal{M}$ is $\rho_S A L/\rho_P H L_x L_y$. See Figure 12.10.

The one missing piece, here, is the relationship between the pointwise forces F_1 and F_2 and the string displacement. Energy analysis deals with this nicely.

Energy analysis

First, for simplicity, assume that the plate boundary is fixed (in the case of the soundboard, it is often assumed clamped [347]). Taking inner products with u_t over $\mathbb{U}_\epsilon^2$, in the case of the plate equation, and with w_t over $\mathbb{U}$ in the case of the ideal string equation, leads to the following energy balance:

$$\frac{d}{dt}\left(\mathfrak{H}_P + \mathfrak{H}_S\right) = \mathfrak{B} + F_1 u_t(x_{S1}, y_{S1}, t) + F_2 u_t(x_{S2}, y_{S2}, t)$$

where

$$\mathfrak{H}_P = \frac{1}{2}\|u_t\|_{\mathbb{U}_\epsilon^2}^2 + \frac{\kappa^2}{2}\|\Delta u\|_{\mathbb{U}_\epsilon^2}^2 \qquad \mathfrak{H}_S = \frac{\mathcal{M}}{2}\|w_t\|_{\mathbb{U}}^2 + \frac{\gamma^2\mathcal{M}}{2}\|w_\eta\|_{\mathbb{U}}^2$$

$$\mathfrak{B} = -\gamma^2\mathcal{M}\left(w_\eta(0, t)w_t(0, t) - w_\eta(1, t)w_t(1, t)\right)$$

The system is lossless when

$$F_1 u_t(x_{S1}, y_{S1}) + F_2 u_t(x_{S2}, y_{S2}) - \gamma^2\mathcal{M}\left(w_\eta(0, t)w_t(0, t) - w_\eta(1, t)w_t(1, t)\right) = 0$$

from which the following conditions for a rigid connection may be extracted:

$$w(0, t) = u(x_{S1}, y_{S1}, t) \quad w(1, t) = u(x_{S2}, y_{S2}, t) \quad F_1 = \mathcal{M}\gamma^2 w_\eta(0, t) \quad F_2 = -\mathcal{M}\gamma^2 w_\eta(1, t)$$

$$\text{(12.33)}$$

The first two conditions specify that the displacements of the string and plate should be the same at the connection points, and the second two that the forces acting on the plate are proportional to the string slopes at its endpoints. Such conclusions are, of course, obvious from simple dynamic considerations, but, as usual, the explicit relation to energy principles allows one to deduce similar conditions in the discrete case. One could, of course, go much further in specifying more complex connection conditions, involving lumped masses, springs, dampers, etc., exactly along the lines of the coupled bar system in Section 7.8. Such conditions could be of use in describing, say, the effects of ribs often attached to real soundboards, which serve to alter the frequency response considerably.

A finite difference scheme

The obvious discretization for system (12.32) is as follows:

$$\delta_{tt}u = -\kappa^2\delta_{\Delta\boxplus,\Delta\boxplus}u + J(x_{S1}, y_{S1})F_1 + J(x_{S2}, y_{S2})F_2 \tag{12.34a}$$

$$\mathcal{M}\delta_{tt}w = \mathcal{M}\gamma^2\delta_{\eta\eta}w \tag{12.34b}$$

Note the use, now, of the 2D spreading function J, as described in Section 10.2.1; any interpolant may be used, but in practice, for a static connection, simple truncation (i.e., using J_0) is probably sufficient. In the simulations which follow, the grid spacing is chosen as $h_x = h_y = h_P$ for the plate and h_S for the string. For stability, in addition to the stability condition (12.15) for the plate relating h_P and k, a CFL-type condition $h_S \geq \gamma k$ must also hold. The numerical boundary conditions corresponding to (12.33) are

$$w_0 = I(x_{S1}, y_{S1})u \qquad w_N = I(x_{S2}, y_{S2})u \qquad F_1 = \mathcal{M}\gamma^2\delta_{\eta-}w_0 \qquad F_2 = -\mathcal{M}\gamma^2\delta_{\eta+}w_N$$
$$\tag{12.35}$$

which are provably numerically stable, and which lead to a unique update—see Problem 12.9.

Variation of the string/plate mass ratio

Though the string/plate mass ratio in most instrument configurations is rather small, it is interesting to examine the effects of varying this ratio. See Figure 12.11, which shows temporal vibration envelopes for such a string, as well as spectra, under different choices of this ratio. When the string and plate are of widely differing material properties (e.g., when $\mathcal{M}$ is very small), the modal

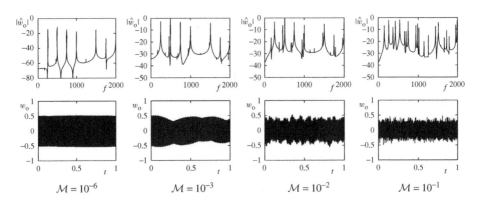

Figure 12.11   Plate–string connection. Referring to system (12.32), a string, with $\gamma = 500$, is connected to a plate, of aspect ratio 1.3, under simply supported boundary conditions, and of stiffness $\kappa = 50$, at coordinates $(0.3, 0.5)$ and $(0.7, 0.8)$. The string is initialized with a narrow raised cosine distribution. The output spectrum $|\hat{w}_o|$ in decibels and the temporal envelope w_o of the string vibration, taken at position $\eta = 0.2$ on the string, are plotted for a variety of choices of the string/plate mass ratio, as indicated.

frequencies of the plate appear as a form of coloration—as the ratio is increased, one begins to
see such components featuring strongly in the string's vibration spectrum, as well as interesting
modulation of the temporal envelope, reflecting the gradual trade of energy between plate and string.

It is important to point out, however, that even though for small mass ratios the modal frequencies of the plate and string remain generally uninfluenced by one another, in general the concept
of a "modal frequency" for a part of a coupled system is not well defined. In fact, there is no
simple way of determining the frequencies of the combined system without some sort of eigenvalue
analysis for the combined global system. In the case of the piano, a very useful simplification,
proposed by Smith and van Duyne [338] involves prefiltering an impulse (such as a hammer strike
excitation function) by a measured response for the soundboard—such a technique is known as
commuted synthesis, as mentioned earlier. One must beware the temptation to conclude that such
an operation is generally valid, even in the linear case, although it is beyond question a good idea
in the case of fixed instrument configurations such as the piano.

Sympathetic vibration

It is not a huge step to move from the case of one string connected to a plate to several. The model
described by system (12.32) may be generalized directly to the case of M strings as follows:

$$u_{tt} = -\kappa^2 \Delta\Delta u + \sum_{q=1}^{M} \delta(x - x_{S1}^{(q)}, y - y_{S1}^{(q)})F_1^{(q)} + \delta(x - x_{S2}^{(q)}, y - y_{S2}^{(q)})F_2^{(q)} \quad (12.36a)$$

$$\mathcal{M}^{(q)} w_{tt}^{(q)} = \mathcal{M}^{(q)} (\gamma^{(q)})^2 w_{\eta^{(q)}\eta^{(q)}}^{(q)} \qquad q = 1, \ldots, M \quad (12.36b)$$

where, now, the displacement of the qth string, of wave speed $\gamma^{(q)}$ and string/plate mass ratio
$\mathcal{M}^{(q)}$, and defined over spatial coordinate $\eta^{(q)}$, is $w^{(q)}$. The qth string is connected to the plate
at coordinates $(x_{S1}^{(q)}, y_{S1}^{(q)})$ at one end and $(x_{S2}^{(q)}, y_{S2}^{(q)})$ at the other. Needless to say, there is almost
no additional "intellectual overhead" associated with generalizing finite difference scheme (12.34);
each term in the sum in (12.36a) may be treated exactly as in (12.34a), and each of (12.36b) as
(12.34b).

This is now a rather complex object, musically speaking, and a full exploration of this system
could occupy an entire volume, but the main feature is the transfer of energy between the strings
and the soundboard, a phenomenon known as sympathetic vibration. As a simple example, consider
the case of two strings attached to a plate, as illustrated in Figure 12.12, which shows the time
evolution of the displacements of the plate and strings, when one of the strings is subjected to a
plucked excitation.

All properties of numerical conservation and stability carry over directly to the discrete
case—see Figure 12.13.

12.5   Anisotropic plates

The model presented above for a connection between a string and a plate is extremely crude, but the
basic idea can be significantly extended, by introducing effects of stiffness and frequency-dependent
loss in the string, as described in Section 7.3, as well as loss in the plate itself, as per Section 12.2.
There is one feature of plate vibration, however, which is peculiar to 2D systems, and which
is rather important with regard to typical soundboards, namely anisotropy, or variation in the
properties of a plate with the direction of propagation of a wave.[3] Anisotropic plate vibration

---

[3] Note that the concept of anisotropy is distinct from that of point-to-point spatial variation in a system.
A spatially uniform anisotropic system behaves in the same way at every point, and is thus LSI, and amenable to
spatial Fourier analysis, whereas a spatially varying, but isotropic system will not be.

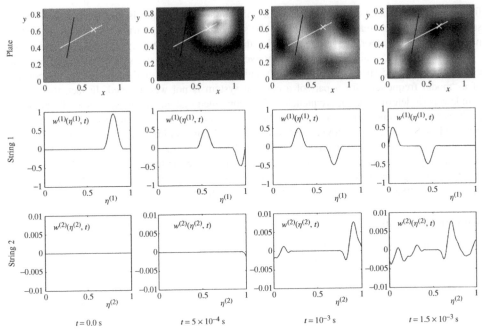

$t = 0.0$ s $t = 5 \times 10^{-4}$ s $t = 10^{-3}$ s $t = 1.5 \times 10^{-3}$ s

Figure 12.12 Simulation of a plate connected with two strings; the white and black lines in the upper row of plots indicate the first and second strings, and the first string is initialized with a narrow raised cosine distribution (pluck) at time $t = 0$, at the location marked with a white cross. From left to right, snapshots of the time evolution of the plate displacement (top row), the first string (middle row), and second string (bottom row) are plotted. Referring to system (12.36), the plate is of aspect ratio 0.8 and stiffness $\kappa = 50$, and the strings have $\gamma^{(1)} = 500$ and $\gamma^{(2)} = 400$, respectively, with mass ratios $\mathcal{M}^{(1)} = \mathcal{M}^{(2)} = 0.01$ with respect to the plate. A scheme generalizing (12.34) is used, at sample rate 44 100 Hz.

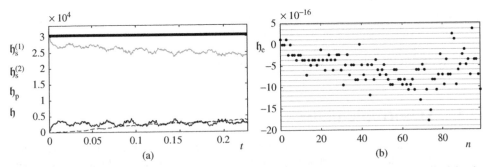

Figure 12.13 Variation in numerical energy for the two string–plate system described in the caption to Figure 12.12. (a) The energy of the first (struck) string $\mathfrak{h}_S^{(1)}$, in grey, the second string $\mathfrak{h}_S^{(2)}$, in dashed black, the plate $\mathfrak{h}_P$, in black, and the total energy $\mathfrak{h}$, as a thick black line. (b) Relative variation in error, $\mathfrak{h}_e^n = (\mathfrak{h}^n - \mathfrak{h}^0)/\mathfrak{h}^0$, as a function of time step. Multiples of machine epsilon are indicated by solid grey lines.

has been studied with regard to loss models by Chaigne and Lambourg [79], and finite difference schemes for use in simulation by the same authors [217], as well as Giordano and his group [152, 154], in the context of piano soundboard modeling.

The simplest type of anisotropic thin plate model is referred to as orthotropic, and may be described by the following equation [55]:

$$\rho H u_{tt} = -D_x u_{xxxx} - D_y u_{yyyy} - D_{xy} u_{xxyy} \tag{12.37}$$

where the density ρ and thickness H are as for the isotropic model given in (12.1), but where the stiffness constants D_x, D_y, and D_{xy} are defined as

$$D_x = \frac{E_x H^3}{12(1 - \nu_{xy}\nu_{yx})} \qquad D_y = \frac{E_y H^3}{12(1 - \nu_{xy}\nu_{yx})} \qquad D_{xy} = \nu_{yx} D_x + \nu_{xy} D_y + \frac{G_{xy} H^3}{3}$$

for material constants E_x and E_y (Young's modulus in the coordinate directions), ν_{xy} and ν_{yx} (Poisson's ratios), and G_{xy} (a shear coefficient). When $E_x = E_y = E$, $\nu_{xy} = \nu_{yx} = \nu$, and $G_{xy} = E/2(1 + \nu)$, (12.37) reduces to the isotropic plate equation (12.1). For certain materials, in particular wooden soundboards with an anisotropic character due to grain and ribbing, the ratio of Young's moduli may be as high as 10:1 or 20:1 [152, 217]. The equation above is often written as a system of second-order equations in displacement and moments [217].

When spatially scaled with respect to a length L, (12.37) may be written as

$$u_{tt} = -\kappa_x^2 u_{xxxx} - \kappa_y^2 u_{yyyy} - \kappa_{xy}^2 u_{xxyy} \tag{12.38}$$

where $\kappa_x^2 = D_x/\rho H L^4$, $\kappa_y^2 = D_y/\rho H L^4$, and $\kappa_{xy}^2 = D_{xy}/\rho H L^4$.

Dispersion relation

The dispersion relation for (12.38) is given by

$$\omega^2 = \kappa_x^2 \beta_x^4 + \kappa_y^2 \beta_y^4 + \kappa_{xy}^2 \beta_x^2 \beta_y^2$$

in terms of components of the wavenumber $\beta = [\beta_x, \beta_y]$. Without resorting to the definition of a directional phase or group velocity, it should be clear that propagation speed, for a given wavenumber magnitude, will be different by a factor of κ_x/κ_y in direction x with respect to direction y.

Finite difference schemes

Time domain finite difference schemes of various types have been proposed—see the references at the beginning of this section. A simple explicit scheme, equivalent to one of those presented in [217], is of the following form:

$$\delta_{tt} u = -\kappa_x^2 \delta_{xxxx} u - \kappa_y^2 \delta_{yyyy} u - \kappa_{xy}^2 \delta_{xx} \delta_{yy} u \tag{12.39}$$

Due to the anisotropy of the system, one can perhaps foresee problems in the choice of the grid spacing; here, the grid spacings h_x and h_y will remain, generally, independent of one another. The reasoning against the use of a uniform grid is straightforward, and may be related to Rule of Thumb #1, on page 136—a uniform grid means that, in at least one of the coordinate directions, the grid spacing will not be optimal, and thus one will observe mistuning of modal frequencies, which can potentially be very severe for great differences in the directional stiffnesses.

Table 12.2 Simulation results for an anisotropic wooden plate, corresponding to that investigated in [217], under simply supported conditions. The plate is of aspect ratio 1.248, and the stiffness parameters (referring to (12.38)) are $\kappa_x = 36.5$, $\kappa_y = 8.41$, and $\kappa_{xy} = 18.1$. Scheme (12.39) is used, with a sample rate of 44 100 Hz. Exact modal frequencies are given, as well as numerical frequencies for a scheme employing an equal grid spacing $h_x = h_y$, and an unequal spacing given by (12.41), as well as deviations in cents.

Mode number	Exact freq.	$r = 1$		$r = \sqrt{\kappa_y/\kappa_x}$	
		Freq.	Cent dev.	Freq.	Cent dev.
(1,1)	56.5	56.4	−2.5	56.4	−3.1
(1,2)	98.4	97.9	−9.6	98.2	−4.4
(2,2)	225.9	224.5	−10.1	224.3	−12.2
(1,3)	177.1	174.4	−26.5	176.1	−9.7
(2,3)	291.2	288.1	−18.9	289.1	−12.8
(1,4)	290.7	282.2	−51.3	287.8	−18.0
(2,5)	533.1	512.6	−67.7	525.1	−26.1

Given this choice, and writing $r = h_y/h_x$ for what might be called the grid aspect ratio, the stability condition for scheme (12.39) may be arrived at using the usual von Neumann techniques (see Problem 12.10):

$$h_x \geq \left(4k^2 \left(\kappa_x^2 + \kappa_y^2/r^4 + \kappa_{xy}^2/r^2\right)\right)^{1/4} \tag{12.40}$$

A good guess at a useful setting for r is the following:

$$r = \sqrt{\frac{\kappa_y}{\kappa_x}} \tag{12.41}$$

which symmetrizes the effects of stiffness in the two coordinate directions. As an example, consider the case of a wooden plate of parameters as given in Table 12.2, which exhibits a strong anisotropy. Under simply supported conditions, one may compare numerically computed frequencies to exact values—clearly the choice (12.41) allows for a greater degree of accuracy than a choice of equal grid spacings (or $r = 1$), at virtually no added computational expense.

12.6   The thin plate in radial coordinates

As some percussion instruments (such as the cymbal) may be modeled, to a first approximation, as circular plates, it is worth examining finite difference schemes in radial coordinates. The discussion in this section is a continuation of that of Section 10.3 and Section 11.7, and will be extended to the case of nonlinear shell vibration in Section 13.3.

In radial coordinates, the thin plate equation is as in (12.2), but the Laplacian operator is as defined in the second of (10.2). The problem, when spatially scaled, is defined over the unit circle $\mathcal{D} = \mathbb{U}_\circ$, and thus the constant κ is defined by $\kappa = \sqrt{D/\rho H R^4}$, where R is the physical radius of the plate.

In radial coordinates, the clamped and simply supported conditions at $r = 1$ take on a relatively simple form:

$$u = u_r = 0 \qquad\qquad \text{clamped} \tag{12.42a}$$

$$u = u_{rr} + \nu u_r + \nu u_{\theta\theta} = 0 \quad \text{simply supported} \tag{12.42b}$$

In general, however, it is the free edge condition which is of most interest in musical acoustics:

$$u_{rr} + \nu u_r + \nu u_{\theta\theta} = u_{rrr} + u_{rr} - u_r + (\nu - 3)u_{\theta\theta} + (2 - \nu)u_{r\theta\theta} = 0 \qquad \text{free} \qquad (12.43)$$

If the plate is free to vibrate at its center, then no further condition is required. In the case of some instruments, such as cymbals, however, this is clearly not the case. Here, as a first stab, is a crude clamped condition, when the plate is assumed defined over the annular region $\epsilon \leq r \leq 1$:

$$u = u_r = 0 \qquad \text{at} \qquad r = \epsilon \qquad (12.44)$$

For small ϵ, this is a good starting point for, say, a high-hat model. See Figure 12.14 for a comparison of the behavior of a free edge plate under this condition and with no condition applied—from the figure, the behavior is not noticeably different, but there will be a slight shifting of the lower modal frequencies. Needless to say, rigid body motion is ruled out under condition (12.44).

12.6.1   Finite difference schemes

Given that explicit schemes for the 2D wave equation in radial coordinates behave poorly, with regard to numerical dispersion and output bandwidth, it is perhaps useful to begin from a parameterized implicit scheme:

$$\left(1 + \alpha \kappa^2 k^2 \delta_{\Delta\circ,\Delta\circ}\right) \delta_{tt} u = -\kappa^2 \delta_{\Delta\circ,\Delta\circ} u \qquad (12.45)$$

Here, $\delta_{\Delta\circ,\Delta\circ}$ is an approximation to the biharmonic operator as discussed on page 300.

Numerical boundary conditions corresponding to the clamped edge have been addressed in Programming Exercise 10.7. For the free edge, conservative boundary conditions analogous to (12.43) may be arrived at through analysis similar to the case of Cartesian coordinates. There are many possibilities; here is a set of first-order accurate conditions:

$$((\mu_{r+}r)\delta_{\Delta\circ} - (1 - \nu)\delta_{r+} - (1 - \nu)\delta_{\theta\theta}) u_{N_r,m} = 0 \qquad (12.46a)$$

$$((\mu_{r+}r)\delta_{r+}\delta_{\Delta\circ} + (1 - \nu)\delta_{r+}\delta_{\theta\theta} - (1 - \nu)\delta_{\theta\theta}) u_{N_r,m} = 0 \qquad (12.46b)$$

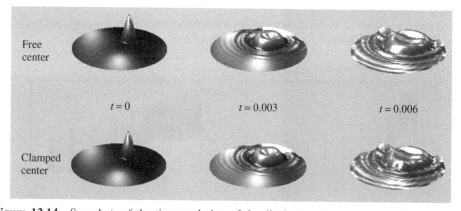

Figure 12.14   Snapshots of the time evolution of the displacement of a thin circular plate, with $\kappa = 3$, at times as indicated, under free edge conditions, and with no condition at the plate center (at top) and with a clamped center condition (at bottom). The plate is initialized using a raised cosine distribution.

These are relatively easy to implement, and suitable when the grid is dense (i.e., when κ is low, as in the case of large gongs). Second-order accurate conditions may be employed as well:

$$(\delta_{A\circ} - (1 - \nu)\delta_{r\cdot} - (1 - \nu)\delta_{\theta\theta}) u_{N_r,m} = 0 \tag{12.47a}$$

$$(\mu_{r-} ((\mu_{r+}r)\delta_{r+}\delta_{A\circ}) + (1 - \nu)\delta_{r\cdot}\delta_{\theta\theta} - (1 - \nu)\delta_{\theta\theta}) u_{N_r,m} = 0 \tag{12.47b}$$

The free center condition has been discussed on page 300. For the clamped center condition (12.44), assuming that the clamping radius is small, one may set

$$u_{0,0} = u_{1,m} = 0 \qquad \text{for all } m \tag{12.48}$$

See also Programming Exercise 12.5.

Stability conditions for this scheme may be arrived at, through extensive analysis—when $\alpha > 1/4$, the scheme is unconditionally stable, but for $\alpha \le 1/4$, the scheme update at the center point has an influence on the form of the condition. Here are two conditions of interest:

$$\frac{2\sqrt{1 - 4\alpha\kappa k}}{h_r^2}\left(1 + \frac{1}{h_\theta^2}\right) \le 1 \qquad \text{free center} \tag{12.49a}$$

$$\frac{2\sqrt{1 - 4\alpha\kappa k}}{h_r^2}\left(1 + \frac{1}{4h_\theta^2}\right) \le 1 \qquad \text{clamped center (12.48)} \tag{12.49b}$$

The stability condition under clamped conditions allows for a smaller choice of h_r, for a given sample rate, than the free center stability condition. As it turns out, good results are obtained when α is chosen slightly below $1/4$.

Figure 12.15 shows a comparison of output spectra for this scheme under the choice $\alpha = 0$, corresponding to an explicit scheme, and for a value of $\alpha = 0.2495$. As expected, the bandwidth of the explicit scheme, except for various spurious modes, is limited to approximately 2 kHz, which is useless for synthesis purposes. The implicit scheme does somewhat better in that the overall distribution of modal frequencies is correct for a large part of the spectrum, but nevertheless, only the lowest frequencies are reasonably accurate. See also Programming Exercise 12.6.

Given the previous discussion in Section 11.7.1, one may infer the following:

Rule of Thumb #5

Finite difference schemes in radial coordinates exhibit heavy numerical dispersion, and explicit schemes in particular produce a severely band-limited result.

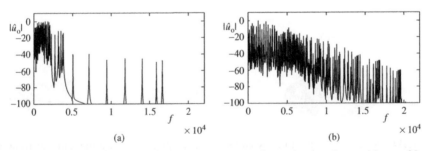

(a)   (b)

Figure 12.15 Typical difference scheme output spectra for a circular plate, with $\kappa = 30$, under free edge and clamped center conditions. The family of schemes (12.45) is used, at 44.1 kHz, with (a) $\alpha = 0$ and (b) $\alpha = 0.2495$.

12.7   Problems

Problem 12.1   *For the plate defined over the half plane $\mathcal{D} = \mathbb{R}^{2,x+}$, show that the total energy $\mathfrak{H}$, as given in (12.9), may be rewritten, using the definition of $\mathcal{L}[\cdot, \cdot]$, as*

$$\mathfrak{H} = \frac{1}{2}\|u_t\|^2_{\mathbb{R}^{2,x+}} + \frac{\nu\kappa^2}{2}\|\Delta u\|^2_{\mathbb{R}^{2,x+}} + \frac{(1-\nu)\kappa^2}{2}\left(\|u_{xx}\|^2_{\mathbb{R}^{2,x+}} + \|u_{yy}\|^2_{\mathbb{R}^{2,x+}} + 2\|u_{xy}\|^2_{\mathbb{R}^{2,x+}}\right)$$

and conclude that $\mathfrak{H} \geq 0$, because every term is non-negative.

Problem 12.2   *Show that the simply supported condition at the edge of a free plate at $x = 0$,*

$$u = 0 \qquad u_{xx} + \nu u_{yy} = 0$$

which may be arrived at through inspection of the boundary term $\mathfrak{B}$ in the energy balance (12.10), is equivalent to the condition (12.5b).

Problem 12.3   *Consider a plate defined over the quarter plane $\mathcal{D} = \mathbb{R}^{2,x+y+}$. Show that an energy balance of the form $d\mathfrak{H}/dt = \mathfrak{B}$ holds as before, where $\mathfrak{H}$ is as defined as in (12.9), but over $\mathbb{R}^{2,x+y+}$, and where the boundary term is now*

$$\mathfrak{B} = \kappa^2 \left(\{u_t, u_{xxx} + (2-\nu)u_{xyy}\}_{(0,\mathbb{R}^+)} - \{u_{tx}, u_{xx} + \nu u_{yy}\}_{(0,\mathbb{R}^+)}\right)$$

$$+ \kappa^2 \left(\{u_t, u_{yyy} + (2-\nu)u_{yxx}\}_{(\mathbb{R}^+,0)} - \{u_{ty}, u_{yy} + \nu u_{xx}\}_{(\mathbb{R}^+,0)}\right)$$

$$+ 2\kappa^2(1-\nu)u_t u_{xy}|_{x=0,y=0}$$

Thus, if a free boundary condition such as (12.11) is satisfied along both edges, and if the corner condition (12.12) holds, the plate is lossless.

Problem 12.4   *Consider the scheme (12.14) for the Kirchhoff thin plate equation, defined over the half plane $\mathcal{D} = \mathbb{Z}^{2,x+}$. It has been shown, in the analysis beginning on page 338, that the boundary conditions (12.18a), (12.18b), and (12.21) lead to exact numerical energy conservation, for a function $\mathfrak{h} = \mathfrak{t} + \mathfrak{v}$, where $\mathfrak{t}$ and $\mathfrak{v}$ are as defined in (12.17a) and (12.19a), respectively. It remains to show that this energy function is a non-negative function of the state u defined over $\mathbb{Z}^{2,x+}$.*

(a) Show, using identity (2.22f), that $\mathfrak{v}$ may be bounded from below as

$$\mathfrak{v} \geq -\frac{\kappa^2 k^2 \nu}{8}\|\delta_{\Delta\boxplus}\delta_{t-}u\|^2_{\mathbb{Z}^{2,x+}} - \frac{\kappa^2 k^2(1-\nu)}{8}$$

$$\times \left(\|\delta_{xx}\delta_{t-}u\|^2_{\mathbb{Z}^{2,x+}} + \|\delta_{yy}\delta_{t-}u\|^2_{\mathbb{Z}^{2,x+}} + 2\|\delta_{x+y+}\delta_{t-}u\|^2_{\mathbb{Z}^{2,x+}}\right)$$

and, using the definition of $\delta_{\Delta\boxplus}$, from (10.9), as

$$\mathfrak{v} \geq -\frac{\kappa^2 k^2}{8}\left(\|\delta_{xx}\delta_{t-}u\|^2_{\mathbb{Z}^{2,x+}} + \|\delta_{yy}\delta_{t-}u\|^2_{\mathbb{Z}^{2,x+}} + 2\nu\langle\delta_{xx}u, \delta_{yy}u\rangle_{\mathbb{Z}^{2,x+}} + 2(1-\nu)\|\delta_{x+y+}\delta_{t-}u\|^2_{\mathbb{Z}^{2,x+}}\right)$$

(b) Using summation by parts of the term involving the inner product above, show that

$$\mathfrak{v} \geq -\frac{\kappa^2 k^2}{8}\left(\|\delta_{xx}\delta_{t-}u\|^2_{\mathbb{Z}^{2,x+}} + \|\delta_{yy}\delta_{t-}u\|^2_{\mathbb{Z}^{2,x+}} + 2\|\delta_{x+y+}\delta_{t-}u\|^2_{\mathbb{Z}^{2,x+}}\right) + \frac{\kappa^2 k^2 \nu}{4}\{\delta_{yy}u, \delta_{x-}u\}_{(0,\mathbb{Z})}$$

Besides the boundary term, the only term in the above expression that depends on values of the grid function u outside $\mathbb{Z}^{2,x+}$ is the first in parentheses above.

(c) *Show that, for any grid function* f *defined over* $\mathbb{Z}^{2,x+}$,

$$\|\delta_{yy} f\|^2_{\mathbb{Z}^{2,x+}} \leq \frac{16}{h^4} \|f\|_{\mathbb{Z}^{2,x+}}$$

$$\|\delta_{x+y+} f\|^2_{\mathbb{Z}^{2,x+}} \leq \frac{16}{h^4} \|f\|_{\mathbb{Z}^{2,x+}}$$

$$\|\delta_{xx} f\|^2_{\mathbb{Z}^{2,x+}} \leq \frac{16}{h^4} \|f\|_{\mathbb{Z}^{2,x+}} - 2\{\delta_{x-} f, \delta_{xx} f\}_{(0,\mathbb{Z})}$$

and thus that

$$\mathfrak{v} \geq -\frac{8\kappa^2 k^2}{h^4} \|\delta_t - u\|^2_{\mathbb{Z}^{2,x+}} + \frac{\kappa^2 k^2}{4} \{(\delta_{xx} + v\delta_{yy}) u, \delta_{x-} u\}_{(0,\mathbb{Z})}$$

(d) *Finally, show that when any of the boundary conditions (12.18a), (12.18b), or (12.21) holds, the boundary term in the above inequality vanishes, and it is true that*

$$\mathfrak{h} = \mathfrak{t} + \mathfrak{v} \geq \left(\frac{1}{2} - \frac{8\kappa^2 k^2}{h^4} \right) \|\delta_t - u\|^2_{\mathbb{Z}^{2,x+}}$$

The above expression is non-negative under condition (12.15), obtained using von Neumann analysis.

Problem 12.5   *Consider the scheme (12.14), defined now over the quarter plane* $\mathcal{D} = \mathbb{Z}^{2,x+y+}$. *Using an analysis similar to that carried out beginning on page 338, show that an energy balance is of the form* $\delta_{t+}\mathfrak{h} = \mathfrak{b}$, *where* $\mathfrak{h} = \mathfrak{t} + \mathfrak{v}$, *for* $\mathfrak{t}$ *and* $\mathfrak{v}$ *as defined in (12.17a) and (12.19a), respectively, but over the quarter plane, and where* $\mathfrak{b}$ *is now given by*

$$\mathfrak{b} = \kappa^2 \{\delta_t . u, \delta_{x-} \left(\delta_{xx} + (2-v)\delta_{yy} \right) u\}_{(0,\mathbb{Z})} - \kappa^2 \{\delta_{x-}\delta_t . u, \left(\delta_{xx} + v\delta_{yy} \right) u\}_{(0,\mathbb{Z})}$$

$$+ \kappa^2 \{\delta_t . u, \delta_{y-} \left(\delta_{yy} + (2-v)\delta_{xx} \right) u\}_{(\mathbb{Z},0)} - \kappa^2 \{\delta_{y-}\delta_t . u, \left(\delta_{yy} + v\delta_{xx} \right) u\}_{(\mathbb{Z},0)}$$

$$+ 2\kappa^2 (1-v)\delta_t . u_{0,0}\delta_{x-y-}u_{0,0}$$

and deduce clamped, simply supported, and free numerical boundary conditions.

Problem 12.6   *Consider the operator* $\delta_{\Delta\boxplus,\Delta\boxplus}$, *defined over the quarter plane* $\mathbb{Z}^{2,x+y+}$, *assuming equal grid spacings* $h_x = h_y = h$, *free boundary conditions (12.21), and the corner condition (12.22). Use these conditions, and the definition of* $\delta_{\Delta\boxplus,\Delta\boxplus}$, *in order to find an explicit expression for* $\delta_{\Delta\boxplus,\Delta\boxplus}u_{l,m}$ *at any point* $l \geq 0$, $m \geq 0$ *in the interior of the domain. You need only construct the operator at six representative locations* (l, m): $(0, 0)$, $(1, 0)$, $(1, 1)$, $(2, 0)$, $(2, 1)$, $(2, 2)$; *the operator will take one of these forms at all other points in the domain. Hint: As an example, consider the explicit form of the operation at* $l = 2$, $m = 0$:

$$h^4\delta_{\Delta\boxplus,\Delta\boxplus}u_{2,0} = (11 - 4v - 6v^2)u_{2,0} + (-6 + 2v + 4v^2)(u_{3,0} + u_{1,0}) + (-6 + 2v)u_{2,1}$$

$$+ (2-v)(u_{3,1} + u_{1,1}) + (1 - v^2)\left(u_{4,0} + u_{0,0} \right) + u_{2,2}$$

Continue, and consider the case of the operator $\delta_{\Delta\boxplus,\Delta\boxplus}$ *defined over the rectangular domain* $\mathbb{U}^2_{N_x,N_y}$, *with free boundary conditions on all four sides, and corner conditions analogous to (12.22) at the four corners. Construct the matrix form* $\mathbf{D}_{\Delta\boxplus,\Delta\boxplus}$, *which will be an* $(N_x + 1)(N_y + 1) \times (N_x + 1)(N_y + 1)$ *sparse matrix. See also Programming Exercise 12.2.*

Problem 12.7   *For the family of schemes given in (12.23), which depends on the free parameters α and ϕ, use von Neumann analysis to prove the stability bound given in Figure 12.5(a), i.e.,*

$$\begin{cases} \mu \leq \dfrac{\alpha - \sqrt{\alpha^2 - (4\phi - 1)}}{4(4\phi - 1)}, & \phi \leq \dfrac{1}{4} \quad or \quad \alpha \geq 0 \quad and \quad \phi \leq \dfrac{1 + \alpha^2}{4} \\ \mu \text{ unconstrained}, & \text{otherwise} \end{cases} \tag{12.50}$$

Problem 12.8   *Consider the case of the scheme (12.26) simulating plate vibration, with equal grid spacings $h_x = h_y = h$, coupled with a bow model of bow force $F_B(t)$ and velocity $v_B(t)$, through (12.29) and (12.30), and suppose that the plate is lossless (i.e., $\sigma_0 = \sigma_1 = 0$). The scheme is stable when $\mu \leq 1/4$, where $\mu = k\kappa/h^2$. Show that the condition for uniqueness of numerical solutions is that*

$$\mu \leq -\frac{2\kappa}{\max(F_B)\min(\phi')}$$

when $\min(\phi') \leq 0$, and when the interpolant J_p satisfies $\|J_p\|_{\mathcal{D}} \leq 1/h$. Hint: Proceed as in the case of the bow–string interaction, as outlined in Section 7.4, by taking the inner product of (12.26) with $J_p(x_i, y_i)$.

Problem 12.9   *Consider scheme (12.34) for the plate–string connection.*

(a) Show that, if the numerical boundary conditions (12.35) for the string are employed, and the plate has lossless boundary conditions, the scheme conserves a numerical energy $\mathfrak{h} = \mathfrak{h}_P + \mathfrak{h}_S$, where $\mathfrak{h}_P$ is a numerical energy corresponding to the plate (see page 338) and $\mathfrak{h}_S$ an energy corresponding to a scheme for the 1D wave equation (see Section 6.2.6). Show that each term is individually non-negative if the conditions $h_P \geq 2\sqrt{\kappa k}$ and $h_S \geq \gamma k$ are respected, and that the combination is thus stable.

(b) By applying the interpolation operators $I(x_{S1}, y_{S1})$ and $I(x_{S2}, y_{S2})$ to the finite difference scheme (12.34a), and assuming that the two endpoints of the string are sufficiently separated, show, by combination with (12.34a) and the numerical boundary conditions (12.35), that the forces F_1 and F_2 may be determined, at each time step, in terms of previously computed values of the string and plate states, and thus the scheme may be updated explicitly.

Problem 12.10   *Using von Neumann analysis, prove the stability condition (12.40) for scheme (12.39) for the linear lossless orthotropic plate.*

12.8   Programming exercises

Programming Exercise 12.1   *Consider the thin plate equation (12.2), defined over the rectangular region $\mathbb{U}_\epsilon^2$. A modal function $U(x, y)$, at frequency ω, satisfies*

$$\omega^2 U = \kappa^2 \Delta\Delta U$$

In order to approximate these modal functions, one might employ a finite difference operator $\delta_{\Delta\boxplus, \Delta\boxplus}$ applied to a grid function $\phi = \phi_{l,m}$, defined over $\mathbb{U}_{N_x, N_y}^2$, and approximate the modal equation above as

$$\omega^2 \phi = \kappa^2 \delta_{\Delta\boxplus, \Delta\boxplus}\phi$$

In matrix form, when ϕ is reconstituted as a vector $\boldsymbol{\phi}$ consisting of concatenated vertical strips of ϕ, and $\delta_{\Delta\boxplus, \Delta\boxplus}$ is written as a sparse matrix $\mathbf{D}_{\Delta\boxplus, \Delta\boxplus}$, incorporating boundary conditions, the mth modal frequency and shape may be found as

$$\omega_m = \kappa\sqrt{\text{eig}_m(\mathbf{D}_{\Delta\boxplus, \Delta\boxplus})} \qquad \boldsymbol{\phi}_m = \text{eigenvector}_m(\mathbf{D}_{\Delta\boxplus, \Delta\boxplus})$$

where eig_m *and* $eigenvector_m$ *signify the "mth eigenvalue, and associated eigenvector of." Write a Matlab script which generates, for such a rectangular plate, plots of the first 25 modal functions, under simply supported or clamped conditions at all four sides of the domain. In order to do this, you will need to have generated the matrix* $\mathbf{D}_{\triangle\boxplus,\triangle\boxplus}$—*see Programming Exercise 10.5. Also, in the case of simply supported conditions, perform a study of the accuracy of these numerical modal frequencies through comparison with exact values, from (12.13), and under different choices of the grid spacing. (You may find, however, that, even for relatively small choices of the grid dimensions* N_x *and* N_y, *the calculation of eigenvalues can take a very long time, so be sure to keep these numbers small.)*

Programming Exercise 12.2   *Extend the code you have written in Programming Exercise 10.5, which generates a sparse matrix form* $\mathbf{D}_{\triangle\boxplus,\triangle\boxplus}$ *corresponding to the discrete biharmonic operator* $\delta_{\triangle\boxplus,\triangle\boxplus}$, *operating over the rectangular domain* $\mathbb{U}^2_{N_x,N_y}$, *to the case of the free boundary conditions (12.21) at the edge with* $x = 0$, *and conditions (12.22) at the corner at* $x = 0$, $y = 0$, *and equivalent conditions, obtained by interchanging* x *and* y, *at the other three edges and corners. The results of Problem 12.6 will be of use here.*

Programming Exercise 12.3   *Create a Matlab script which calculates the response of a rectangular plate to a given initial condition, using the finite difference scheme (12.24) for a plate with frequency-dependent loss. Assume that the applied tension is zero, and that the excitation is an initial velocity with a 2D raised cosine distribution, according to (11.3). Your code will depend on a number of parameters:*

- *sample rate* f_s;

- *simulation duration* T_f;

- *plate stiffness parameter* κ;

- *plate aspect ratio* ϵ;

- *loss parameters* σ_0 *and* σ_1, *or, equivalently, two values of* T_{60} *specified at distinct frequencies* f_1 *and* f_2;

- *excitation center coordinates* x_i, y_i, *excitation radius* r_{hw}, *and amplitude* c_0;

- *readout coordinates* x_o, y_o;

- *boundary condition type (clamped, simply supported, or free).*

    It is probably easiest to program this algorithm by making use of the sparse matrix form $\mathbf{D}_{\triangle\boxplus,\triangle\boxplus}$ *of the discrete biharmonic operator—see Programming Exercise 12.2.*

Programming Exercise 12.4   *Extend the plate synthesis algorithm from Programming Exercise 12.3 to allow, simultaneously:*

- *Mallet strikes, as described in Section 12.3.1. Control data, in this case, should consist of times, velocities, and locations of strikes, and extra necessary parameters will be the mallet/plate mass ratio* M, *a stiffness parameter* ω_H, *and a nonlinearity exponent* α.

- *Bowing gestures, as described in Section 12.3.2. Control data should consist of bow force and velocity curves, and a bowing location, and you will need to specify a friction characteristic* ϕ *as well.*

- *Input from an external audio source, as described in Section 12.3.3, where control data will consist of a readin location (or perhaps trajectory).*

- *The connection to multiple strings, as described in Section 12.4. You will need to specify, for each string, the string/plate mass ratio $\mathcal{M}$, wave speed γ, and connection coordinates (x_{S1}, y_{S1}) and (x_{S2}, y_{S2}) for the two string ends. You may wish to allow for readout from the strings themselves.*

   The main programming work here will be managing (a) the control data and (b) the connection points. Use bilinear interpolation for these connections, and make sure that your code does not allow more than a single connection at a given location (though there is no reason why this cannot be done, at least in a virtual environment).

Programming Exercise 12.5   *Extend the code you have written in Programming Exercise 10.7, which generates a sparse matrix form $\mathbf{D}_{\Delta\circ,\Delta\circ}$ of the biharmonic operator in radial coordinates, in the following way:*

- *Implement the free edge conditions given in (12.46) and (12.47).*

- *Implement the clamped center condition, according to conditions (12.48).*

The user should be able to decide between clamped/free conditions at the center or edge through the specification of an input flag. Note that the size of the output matrix will depend on these conditions. For example, under clamped edge and center conditions, the matrix will be of size $(N_\theta(N_r - 2)) \times (N_\theta(N_r - 2))$, but under clamped edge/free center conditions, it will be of size $(N_\theta(N_r - 1) + 1) \times (N_\theta(N_r - 1) + 1)$.

Programming Exercise 12.6   *Implement the implicit scheme (12.45) for the plate defined over a circular geometry; here, you will need to rewrite the scheme in a vector–matrix update form, and determine the update matrices, which will depend on $\mathbf{D}_{\Delta\circ,\Delta\circ}$, which you have generated, under a variety of edge and center conditions, in the previous exercise. Make sure that you choose the grid spacings such that the appropriate stability condition from (12.49) is satisfied. Use, as an initial condition, a plucked raised cosine distribution of the form given in (11.3).*

   Perform a study of output bandwidth, as a function of α and the parameter $q = h_\theta / h_r$, and for a given value of κ, such as $\kappa = 20$. How does computational complexity depend on α?

1
2
3
4
5
6
7
8
9
10
11
12
13
14
15
16
17
18
19
20
21
22
23
24
25
26
27
28
29
30
31
32
33
34
35
36
37
38
39
40
41
42
43
44
45
46
47
48
49
50
51

13

Nonlinear plate vibration

Perhaps the most dramatic example of nonlinear behavior in all of musical acoustics is afforded by the vibration of a metal plate at high amplitudes. Various percussion instruments, and especially gongs and cymbals, owe their characteristic sound almost entirely to this behavior [300]. To the listener, the perceptual results of the nonlinearity are dominant, and include effects such as the rapid buildup of high-frequency energy as heard in cymbal crashes, subharmonic generation, as well as pitch glides, which have been discussed in some detail in the case of the string in Chapter 8. For sound synthesis purposes, a linear model does not even begin to approximate the sound of these instruments.

There are a variety of models of nonlinear plate vibration; when the plate is thin, and vibration amplitudes are low, all of these reduce to the Kirchhoff model discussed in Section 12.1. (Plates which appear in a musical setting are generally thin, and so there is little reason to delve into the much more involved topic of thick plate vibration, which, even in the linear case, is orders of magnitude more involved than dealing with simple thin plate models—see the comments on page 333.) Perhaps the simplest nonlinear thin plate model is that of Berger [37], which is discussed in Section 13.1; this system is a 2D analogue of the Kirchhoff–Carrier or "tension-modulated" string discussed in Section 8.1, and the predominant perceptual result of employing such a model is the pitch glide. Though this model leads to computationally attractive finite difference schemes, it is not capable of rendering the more interesting effects mentioned above, which are defining characteristics of some percussion instruments. To this end, the more complex model of von Kármán [252, 348] is introduced in Section 13.2, as are various finite difference schemes. Extensions to the nonlinear vibration of spherical shells appear in Section 13.3. For the sake of brevity, only simple rectangular and circular structures are covered in this chapter.

13.1 The Berger plate model

The simplest model of nonlinear plate vibration is due to Berger [37, 281]; as mentioned above, it is a direct generalization of the Kirchhoff–Carrier system (12.1) to 2D (or rather, the nonlinear bar vibration model presented in Section 8.1.4, which includes the effects of stiffness). Because of the earlier extended discussion of the string model, the treatment here will be brief; 2D models similar to that of Berger have recently been explored in the context of sound synthesis [271].

Numerical Sound Synthesis: Finite Difference Schemes and Simulation in Musical Acoustics   Stefan Bilbao
© 2009 John Wiley & Sons, Ltd

When defined over a domain $\mathcal{D}$, Berger's equation takes the following form:

$$\rho H u_{tt} = -D\Delta\Delta u + \left(\frac{6D}{|\mathcal{D}|H^2}\int_{\mathcal{D}}|\nabla u|^2 dA\right)\Delta u - 2\rho H\sigma_0 u_t$$

Here, the parameters D, H, and ρ are as for the case of linear plate vibration, $|\mathcal{D}|$ is the surface area of the plate, and ∇u is the gradient of u. A linear loss term has been included. Clearly, the equation above reduces to the linear model (12.1) at low vibration amplitudes and under lossless conditions.

When scaled, using (in Cartesian coordinates, for example) $x' = x/\sqrt{|\mathcal{D}|}$, $y' = y/\sqrt{|\mathcal{D}|}$, and $u' = u/u_0$, with $u_0 = H/\sqrt{6}$, after removing primes the equation is of the form

$$u_{tt} = -\kappa^2\left(\Delta\Delta u - \mathfrak{M}\Delta u\right) - 2\sigma_0 u_t \qquad \mathfrak{M} = \int_{\mathcal{D}}|\nabla u|^2 dA \qquad (13.1)$$

where the integral $\mathfrak{M}$ above is defined over a unit area region $\mathcal{D}$. As in the case of the string, the most obvious effect of the nonlinear term is to allow for a change in pitch with vibration amplitude—the loss term leads to pitch glide effects. In Cartesian coordinates, fixed boundary conditions such as (12.5) may be shown to be lossless, but the free conditions must be altered slightly—see Problem 13.1.

It is rather simple to arrive at a difference scheme simulating the Berger model. Consider (13.1) defined over the unit area rectangle $\mathbb{U}_\epsilon^2$, of aspect ratio ϵ in Cartesian coordinates. A general choice of scheme for (13.1) is

$$\delta_{tt}u = -\kappa^2\left(\delta_{\Delta\boxplus,\Delta\boxplus}u - [m]\delta_{\Delta\boxplus}u\right) - 2\sigma_0\delta_{t\cdot}u \qquad (13.2)$$

where $[m]$ is some discrete approximation to $\mathfrak{M}$ as given in (13.1). The scheme above is defined over the rectangular region $\mathbb{U}_{N_x,N_y}^2$. There are, as before, many approximations available for the nonlinear term—given the extended discussion in Section 8.1.2, here is a good choice:

$$[m] = \mu_{t+}\left(\sum_{l=1}^{N_x}\sum_{m=0}^{N_y}h^2\delta_{x-}u_{l,m}e_{t-}\delta_{x-}u_{l,m} + \sum_{l=0}^{N_x}\sum_{m=1}^{N_y}h^2\delta_{y-}u_{l,m}e_{t-}\delta_{y-}u_{l,m}\right)$$

which leads to stable behavior under the condition (12.15), under conservative or lossy boundary conditions. Like scheme (8.7) for the Kirchhoff–Carrier equation, with the nonlinearity discretized as in (8.9), though this scheme is apparently implicit, it may be rewritten in a fully explicit form.

Some typical pitch glides are shown in Figure 13.1; as before, the precise details of the loss model will be of great importance in determining the pitch trajectory. As one might expect, though stable, this scheme exhibits many of the same deficiencies as the related scheme for the Kirchhoff–Carrier string, as discussed on page 225. In particular, numerical oscillations can appear when the stability condition is satisfied near equality, accompanied by a suppression of the pitch glide effect. Improved θ schemes are a good remedy. A modal approach, such as that outlined in Section 8.1.3, is again a possibility, but with the added complication that now, in general, the modal shapes and frequencies for the plate are not available in closed form, except under simply supported conditions at all edges, and thus must be precomputed.

Instead of dwelling on the details of algorithms for the Berger model, however, it is probably best to turn to a more detailed approximation which better captures the important perceptual effects of nonlinear plate vibration.

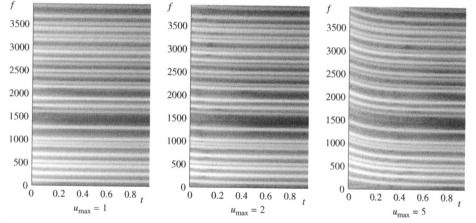

Figure 13.1 Spectrograms of output from scheme (13.2) for the Berger system, for a square plate with $\kappa = 34$, under simply supported boundary conditions, and with $\sigma_0 = 3.18$. The excitation is of the form of a narrow raised cosine distribution, of amplitude u_{max} centered at the plate center. Pitch glides become apparent as u_{max} is raised. The sample rate is 44.1 kHz.

13.2   The von Kármán plate model

A widely used model of the nonlinear vibration of plates at moderate amplitudes is the so-called dynamic analog of the system of von Kármán [348, 252]. Its form is quite compact:

$$\rho H u_{tt} = -D\Delta\Delta u + \mathcal{L}(\Phi, u) \tag{13.3a}$$

$$\Delta\Delta\Phi = -\frac{EH}{2}\mathcal{L}(u, u) \tag{13.3b}$$

Here, as in the linear case, $u(x, y, t)$ is the transverse plate deflection and the new variable $\Phi(x, y, t)$ is often referred to as the Airy stress function. Both are defined over a region $(x, y) \in \mathcal{D} \subset \mathbb{R}^2$. E, H, ρ as well as D are as defined for the linear thin plate system in Section 12.3, and the nonlinear operator $\mathcal{L}(\cdot, \cdot)$ is defined (in Cartesian coordinates) in (12.6). The system is initialized using the functions $u(x, y, 0)$ and $u_t(x, y, 0)$—note that no initial condition is required for Φ, which may be set from the initial condition for u from (13.3b). Clearly, system (13.3) reduces to the linear thin plate equation (12.1) in the limit of small amplitudes (note that the terms involving the operator $\mathcal{L}$ are second order in u and Φ).

It is worth noting that there are several variants of the von Kármán system: that given above is simplified from the so-called "full" or "complete" system, in which in-plane displacements appear explicitly [205, 252, 204]; all such systems may themselves be derived from even more general forms [417]. The Berger model, described in Section 13.1, may be derived from this form, under somewhat subtle assumptions. Interestingly, it is possible to arrive at a nonlinear modal description of the von Kármán system, especially useful in the study of mode couplings and bifurcations in the case of plates defined over a circular geometry—see, e.g., [360, 356].

13.2.1   More on the operator $\mathcal{L}(\cdot, \cdot)$

The operator $\mathcal{L}(\cdot, \cdot)$ is defined in (12.6), in Cartesian coordinates, as a means of analyzing boundary conditions in the case of thin linear plate vibration. It plays, obviously, a much greater role in the nonlinear case, and possesses a useful symmetry property beyond those described in the earlier

section. This symmetry property, first noted in [46], and also described recently in [355], will be
called, for lack of a better term, "triple self-adjointness." For any three smooth functions α, β, and
γ defined over $\mathcal{D}$,

$$\iint_{\mathcal{D}} \alpha \mathcal{L}(\beta, \gamma) d\sigma = \iint_{\mathcal{D}} \mathcal{L}(\alpha, \beta) \gamma d\sigma + \mathcal{J} \tag{13.4}$$

In other words, variables may be interchanged in the above integral, leading only to terms $\mathcal{J}$ which
are resolved on the boundary of the region $\mathcal{D}$. In the case of, for instance, the half plane $\mathcal{D} = \mathbb{R}^{2,x+}$,
$\mathcal{J}$ is of the form

$$\mathcal{J} = \int_{-\infty}^{\infty} \alpha_x \beta_{yy} \gamma - \alpha \left(\beta_{yy}\gamma\right)_x - \alpha_y \beta_{xy} \gamma + \alpha \left(\beta_{xy}\gamma\right)_y dy$$

In designing a stable numerical scheme for (13.3), it is crucial that a discrete analogue of the
property (13.4) be maintained—see Section 13.2.7.

13.2.2   Scaled form

As in the case of nonlinear string vibration, it is of interest to scale not only the spatial coordinates
(in Cartesian coordinates, one may choose $x' = x/L$, $y' = y/L$, for some constant L of dimensions
of length, such as $L = \sqrt{|\mathcal{D}|}$ in a problems defined over a rectangular region), but also the dependent
variables u and Φ, by introducing dimensionless variables $u' = u/u_0$, $\Phi' = \Phi/\Phi_0$. The particular
choice of the scaling constants u_0 and Φ_0 is important in an analysis setting, but numerically the
problem is insensitive to the choice, and it is thus best to choose them such that the problem is
expressible in terms of the fewest number of parameters. Under the choices

$$\Phi_0 = D \qquad\qquad u_0 = H/\sqrt{6(1 - v^2)} \tag{13.5}$$

and after substitution in system (13.3), the following system results:

$$u_{tt} = -\kappa^2 \Delta\Delta u + \kappa^2 \mathcal{L}(\Phi, u) \tag{13.6a}$$

$$\Delta\Delta\Phi = -\mathcal{L}(u, u) \tag{13.6b}$$

where the sole parameter is κ is as defined in (12.3).

13.2.3   Energy analysis

The energy analysis of system (13.6) is a simple extension of that carried out in Section 12.1.2 in
the case of linear plate vibration. In this case, an inner product of (13.6a) with u_t over the domain
$\mathcal{D}$ leads directly to

$$\frac{d\mathfrak{H}_{\text{lin}}}{dt} = \kappa^2 \langle u_t, \mathcal{L}(\Phi, u)\rangle_{\mathcal{D}} + \mathfrak{B}_{\text{lin}}$$

where $\mathfrak{H}_{\text{lin}}$ is the total energy of the plate due to linear effects, and $\mathfrak{B}_{\text{lin}}$ is the accompanying
boundary term (particular forms of these expressions are given in the case of the quarter plane in
Section 12.1.2). Now, employing various properties of the operator $\mathcal{L}$, and integration by parts,
beginning with the triple self-adjointness property (13.4) leads to

$$\frac{d\mathfrak{H}_{\text{lin}}}{dt} \overset{(13.4)}{=} \kappa^2 \langle \Phi, \mathcal{L}(u_t, u)\rangle_{\mathcal{D}} + \mathfrak{B}_{\text{lin}} + \mathfrak{B}_{\text{nonlin}} \tag{13.7a}$$

$$\overset{(12.7)}{=} \frac{\kappa^2}{2} \langle \Phi, (\mathcal{L}(u, u))_t\rangle_{\mathcal{D}} + \mathfrak{B}_{\text{lin}} + \mathfrak{B}_{\text{nonlin}} \tag{13.7b}$$

$$\stackrel{(13.6b)}{=} -\frac{\kappa^2}{2}\langle\Phi, \Delta\Delta\Phi_t\rangle_{\mathcal{D}} + \mathfrak{B}_{\text{lin}} + \mathfrak{B}_{\text{nonlin}} \tag{13.7c}$$

$$\stackrel{(10.6)}{=} -\frac{\kappa^2}{2}\langle\Delta\Phi, \Delta\Phi_t\rangle_{\mathcal{D}} + \mathfrak{B}_{\text{lin}} + \mathfrak{B}_{\text{nonlin}} + \mathfrak{B}'_{\text{nonlin}} \tag{13.7d}$$

$$= -\frac{\kappa^2}{4}\frac{d}{dt}\|\Delta\Phi\|_{\mathcal{D}}^2 + \mathfrak{B}_{\text{lin}} + \mathfrak{B}_{\text{nonlin}} + \mathfrak{B}'_{\text{nonlin}} \tag{13.7e}$$

and thus

$$\frac{d\mathfrak{H}}{dt} = \mathfrak{B} \qquad \text{with} \qquad \mathfrak{H} = \mathfrak{H}_{\text{lin}} + \frac{\kappa^2}{4}\|\Delta\Phi\|_{\mathcal{D}}^2$$

and where $\mathfrak{B} = \mathfrak{B}_{\text{lin}} + \mathfrak{B}_{\text{nonlin}} + \mathfrak{B}'_{\text{nonlin}}$ are boundary terms. $\mathfrak{H}$ is again non-negative, and conserved when the boundary terms vanish.

Boundary conditions

In order to examine boundary conditions, consider the system defined over the half plane $\mathcal{D} = \mathbb{R}^{2,x+}$. For losslessness, the boundary terms $\mathfrak{B}_{\text{lin}}$, $\mathfrak{B}_{\text{nonlin}}$, and $\mathfrak{B}'_{\text{nonlin}}$ should vanish. $\mathfrak{B}_{\text{lin}}$ is the term which appears in the case of linear plate vibration, in (12.10). As such, the boundary conditions (12.5a), (12.5b), and (12.11), corresponding to clamped, simply supported, and free termination, should continue to hold in the nonlinear case.

There is not a consensus in the literature as to how to set boundary conditions for Φ (two required at an edge) in the three cases mentioned above—for a simply supported condition, for example, a variety of settings are considered by different authors [248, 177, 81]. See [149] for some general comments on this topic. An examination of the boundary terms $\mathfrak{B}_{\text{nonlin}}$ and $\mathfrak{B}'_{\text{nonlin}}$, which involve the function Φ over the boundary, is revealing:

$$\mathfrak{B}_{\text{nonlin}} = -\kappa^2\{u_t u_{yy}, \Phi_x\}_{(0,\mathbb{R})} - 2\kappa^2\{u_{ty}u_{xy}, \Phi\}_{(0,\mathbb{R})} - \kappa^2\{u_t u_{xyy}, \Phi\}_{(0,\mathbb{R})} + \kappa^2\{u_{tx}u_{yy}, \Phi\}_{(0,\mathbb{R})}$$

$$\mathfrak{B}'_{\text{nonlin}} = \frac{\kappa^2}{2}\{\Phi, (\Delta\Phi)_x\}_{(0,\mathbb{R})} - \frac{\kappa^2}{2}\{\Phi_x, \Delta\Phi\}_{(0,\mathbb{R})}$$

(Note that $\mathfrak{B}_{\text{nonlin}}$ results from the triple self-adjointness property (13.4).) Consider the following pair of conditions on Φ, for which the boundary terms above vanish:

$$\Phi = \Phi_x = 0 \tag{13.8}$$

The conditions (13.8), when combined with conditions (12.5a), correspond to a clamped condition [175] and are also sometimes argued to correspond to a simply supported condition [315, 81], in conjunction with (12.5b). For the free boundary, a condition is often given in terms of higher derivatives of Φ, but conditions (13.8) can be shown to be equivalent (see Problem 13.2). For this reason, in the remainder of this chapter, it will be assumed that conditions (13.8) are satisfied at any edge of the domain (where x is interpreted as an outward normal coordinate). Note, however, that other conditions, such as $\Phi = \Delta\Phi = 0$ in conjunction with any fixed condition with $u = 0$, also lead to lossless behavior.

13.2.4   Nonlinear behavior in the frequency domain

Just as for the system describing large-amplitude vibration of strings, described in Section 8.2, one of the main perceptual effects of the nonlinearity in the von Kármán model is in the complexity of the resulting response, especially when viewed in the frequency domain. The big distinction between the case of the plate and that of the string, though, under musical playing conditions, is in

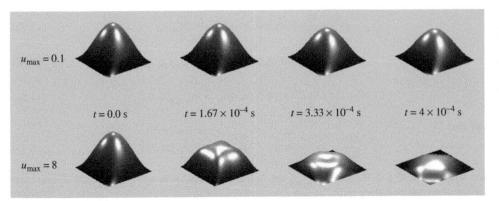

Figure 13.2   Snapshots of the solution to the von Kármán system, at times as indicated. The plate is square, with $\kappa = 114.4$, and is under simply supported conditions. The plate is initialized with a distribution corresponding to the lowest-frequency mode of the plate under linear conditions, with maximum amplitude u_{max}. At top, under low-amplitude conditions, for $u_{\text{max}} = 0.1$ the plate remains in the modal configuration, but at a higher amplitude of $u_{\text{max}} = 8$, the evolution is more complex, with a generation of higher-frequency modes.

the relative importance of these effects—for the string, it is possible to generate phantom partials, which lend an extra coloration to the resulting sound, but for plates at high amplitudes the effects are perceptually dominant.

As the system is nonlinear, one should expect that the modes which describe linear vibration of a plate will interact in the nonlinear case—see Figure 13.2, which illustrates the time evolution of the state of a rectangular plate initialized in a configuration corresponding to the lowest mode, under both low-amplitude and high-amplitude conditions. At high amplitudes, higher modal components are spontaneously generated—this is also visible in a plot of the spectrum of plate displacement, where new harmonics (as well as subharmonics) show an increasing presence at higher amplitudes—see Figure 13.3. Coupling between modes in the von Kármán system is an extremely complex matter, but has been studied extensively, especially for circular plates, in which case closed-form expressions for the modal shapes are sometimes available—see, e.g., [360, 355, 356].

Other important perceptual effects, such as pitch glides and crashes, are intimately related to loss modeling; more examples will be shown in Section 13.2.6.

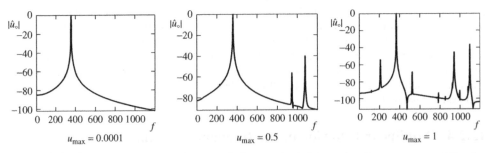

Figure 13.3   Frequency spectrum of output displacement, at plate center, for a square von Kármán plate, with $\kappa = 114.4$, under simply supported conditions. In all cases, the plate is initialized with a distribution corresponding to the lowest-frequency mode of the plate under linear conditions, with maximum amplitude u_{max} as given.

13.2.5   Loss and excitation

It is convenient to make use of a simple model of frequency-dependent loss, which is a simple extension of that applied to the case of the linear plate, in Section 12.2:

$$u_{tt} = -\kappa^2 \Delta\Delta u + \kappa^2 \mathcal{L}(\Phi, u) - 2\sigma_0 u_t + 2\sigma_1 \Delta u_t + e_{\mathrm{exc}} F(t) \tag{13.9a}$$

$$\Delta\Delta\Phi = -\mathcal{L}(u, u) \tag{13.9b}$$

As before, the term with coefficient $2\sigma_0$ gives rise to frequency-independent loss, and, when the term with coefficient $2\sigma_1$ is included, frequency-dependent loss is modeled. This is, of course, an enormously oversimplified loss model—see [79] for a more complete treatment of the various sources of loss in the case of linear plate vibration.

The term $e_{\mathrm{exc}} F(t)$ represents a possible excitation, where e_{exc} is a spatial distribution (perhaps localized, so as to correspond to a strike), and where $F(t)$ results from coupling to a model of an excitation element, or is perhaps given as a function of time—see Section 12.3.

13.2.6   Finite difference schemes

Simulation of different varieties of the von Kármán system has seen a rather large amount of activity. The dynamic case has been much less investigated than the static, and many different techniques have been employed—see, e.g., [205, 223] as representative recent examples in the literature. So as not to stray too far from basic principles, it is worth taking a look at some very simple (and perhaps not extremely accurate!) difference schemes—there are a wide variety of possibilities, due to the number of possible discretization choices for the nonlinearities, represented by the terms involving the operator $\mathcal{L}$. Here is one family, simulating the lossy system (13.9):

$$\delta_{tt} u = -\kappa^2 \delta_{\Delta\boxplus,\Delta\boxplus} u + \kappa^2 [\mathcal{L}(\Phi, u)] - 2\sigma_0 \delta_t . u + 2\sigma_1 \delta_{\Delta\boxplus} \delta_{t-} u + e_{\mathrm{exc}} F \tag{13.10a}$$

$$\delta_{\Delta\boxplus,\Delta\boxplus} \Phi = -[\mathcal{L}(u, u)] \tag{13.10b}$$

Here, the two instances of $[\mathcal{L}]$ indicate some unspecified (possibly distinct) second-order accurate approximations to the nonlinear terms. As in the case of nonlinear string vibration, one may observe that, because the scheme reduces to scheme (12.14) for the Kirchhoff plate at low amplitudes, a necessary condition for stability will be (12.15) (which should be slightly modified when σ_1 is non-zero). A complication results from the second difference equation (13.10b), which is not time dependent—it will be necessary to solve a linear system involving the operator $\delta_{\Delta\boxplus,\Delta\boxplus}$ at each time step in order to obtain values of the grid function Φ. Thus, all such schemes have an implicit character. This feature is peculiar to the assumptions underlying this particular model of plate vibration, in which the effects of in-plane displacements are condensed into a single potential function Φ. If the in-plane displacements are explicitly modeled, as is the case for the full von Kármán system [205], then the resulting system becomes similar to the model of nonlinear string vibration covered in Section 8.2, which can be integrated explicitly—but new in-plane wave speeds will appear, and simulating the resulting system will again require specialized numerical techniques, such as interpolation or θ schemes. In this light, the system (13.9), despite the required implicit update in scheme (13.10), is a simple and elegant choice of model.

The discretization of the nonlinear bracket operator $\mathcal{L}$ is an important first step—here is one choice, defined for any two grid functions α and β:

$$l(\alpha, \beta) = \delta_{xx}\alpha\delta_{yy}\beta + \delta_{yy}\alpha\delta_{xx}\beta - 2\mu_{x-}\mu_{y-}\left(\delta_{x+y+}\alpha\delta_{x+y+}\beta\right) \tag{13.11}$$

This is perhaps not the simplest possible choice, but it is one which possesses properties which are of great use in proving stability in conservative schemes—see [46] and the analysis in Section 13.2.7. See also Programming Exercise 13.1.

Once one has made a choice of the particular discrete form $\mathfrak{l}$, a simple scheme then follows from (13.10) under the choice

$$[\mathcal{L}] = \mathfrak{l} \qquad\qquad (13.12)$$

In this case, it is only (13.10b) which requires a linear system solution; (13.10a) may be updated explicitly. The same is not true of other types of schemes, and in particular those with superior stability properties—see Section 13.2.7, as well as Problem 13.5.

Simulation results: pitch glides and crashes

Scheme (13.10) is a good ad hoc means of generating synthetic sound, and the results are surprisingly rich. Consider the case of a struck excitation, in which case the excitation function F would result from coupling to a mallet model, as described in Section 12.3.1. As a simple alternative, consider using a pulse-like function $F = F_{exc}(t)$ of the form given in (12.28); the spatial distribution e_{exc} is taken to be a 2D Dirac delta function. As the strength of the excitation increases, beyond the pitch glide effect exhibited by the Berger model, there is the generation of new partials and a noise-like component to the output—see Figure 13.4 and, for comparison, Figure 13.1. For low values of κ, crash-like sounds can be produced—at high striking amplitudes, there is a slow buildup of high-frequency energy—see Figure 13.5. These sounds need to be heard to be appreciated, and are excellent examples of synthetic sounds with a dense character which could almost certainly not be generated using anything other than a physical model. See Programming Exercise 13.2.

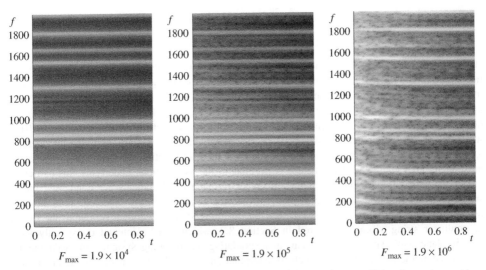

Figure 13.4 Spectrograms of output from scheme (13.10) for the von Kármán system, using discretization (13.12) for the nonlinearity, for a square plate with $\kappa = 20$, under free boundary conditions, and with $\sigma_0 = 1.38$ and $\sigma_1 = 0.001$. Excitation is applied at the plate center, using a spatial distribution e_{exc} of the form of a Dirac delta function, and with a forcing pulse of the form $F = F_{exc}(t)$ as given in (12.28), with a duration of 3 ms, and with varying amplitudes F_{max} as given in the panels above. The sample rate is 44.1 kHz.

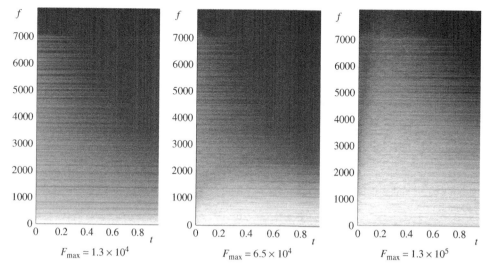

Figure 13.5 Spectrograms of crash-like output from scheme (13.10) for the von Kármán system, using discretization (13.12) for the nonlinearity, for a square plate with $\kappa = 5$, under free boundary conditions, and with $\sigma_0 = 1.38$ and $\sigma_1 = 0.005$. Excitation is applied at coordinates $x_i = 0.2$, $y_i = 0.3$ relative to the plate corner, using a spatial distribution e_{exc} of the form of a Dirac delta function, and with a forcing pulse of the form $F = F_{exc}(t)$ as given in (12.28), with a duration of 16 ms, and with varying amplitudes F_{max} as given in the panels above. The sample rate is 16 kHz.

Numerical instability

Scheme (13.10), with the nonlinearity discretized as in (13.12) is, unfortunately, unstable at high excitation amplitudes—see Figure 13.6. As is common in nonlinear simulation (see the rudimentary case of the cubic nonlinear oscillator in Figure 4.3), this instability can occur without warning after many time steps of apparently stable behavior. Though it is very difficult to analyze the properties of this scheme in a rigorous way, as a general rule instability occurs when vibration amplitudes approach the limit of validity of the von Kármán model itself (i.e., when the amplitude u takes on values approaching five or higher, corresponding, in the case of dimensional variables, to plate displacements on the order of several times the thickness). This is not unexpected, but there is an additional dependence on the exact form of the initial conditions and/or the excitation function

$t = 0$ $t = 0.0046$

Figure 13.6 Unstable behavior in scheme (13.10) for the von Kármán system. In this case, the plate is square, with $\kappa = 11.44$, lossless, and under simply supported boundary conditions. The scheme, running at 44.1 kHz, is initialized with the first modal shape for the linear problem, with a peak amplitude of 14. Generally, in the unstable regime, the larger the amplitude of the initial condition, the shorter the time to the explosion of the solution.

$F(t)$ and distribution e_{exc}, making such a scheme somewhat unwieldy in practice—often the most interesting sounds are generated quite near the stability limit, when nonlinear effects are strongest.

13.2.7 Conservation and numerical stability

Scheme (13.10), with the nonlinearity discretized as in (13.12), has somewhat obscure stability properties. As one might guess, it is indeed possible to go further and find schemes with more robust behavior. As might be expected from the sequence of steps in (13.7), energy techniques provide a means of showing stable behavior. In this section, for the sake of clarity, only the lossless unforced problem (13.6) is considered.

A preliminary consideration is that the operator $\mathfrak{l}$ satisfy a self-adjointness property analogous to (13.4). For the particular choice of $\mathfrak{l}$ from (13.11), this is indeed true—for any three grid functions α, β, and γ defined over a domain $\mathcal{D}$ which is a subset of $\mathbb{Z}^2$,

$$\langle \alpha, \mathfrak{l}(\beta, \gamma) \rangle_{\mathcal{D}} = \langle \mathfrak{l}(\alpha, \beta), \gamma \rangle_{\mathcal{D}} + \mathfrak{j} \tag{13.13}$$

where $\mathfrak{j}$ is a boundary term. This property does not hold for all possible discretizations of $\mathfrak{l}$. See Problem 13.3.

Because the operator $\mathfrak{l}$ is, like its continuous counterpart, bilinear, an identity corresponding to (12.7) follows:

$$\delta_{t+}\mathfrak{l}(\alpha, e_{t-}\alpha) = 2\mathfrak{l}(\delta_{t\cdot}\alpha, \alpha) \tag{13.14}$$

A stable scheme

Consider now the following scheme:

$$\delta_{tt}u = -\kappa^2 \delta_{\Delta\boxplus, \Delta\boxplus}u + \kappa^2 \mathfrak{l}(\mu_{t\cdot}\Phi, u) \tag{13.15a}$$

$$\mu_{t-}\delta_{\Delta\boxplus, \Delta\boxplus}\Phi = -\mathfrak{l}(u, e_{t-}u) \tag{13.15b}$$

Notice that this scheme has an implicit character beyond that of scheme (13.10), in that time averaging is applied inside the first instance of the bracket operator—see Problem 13.5 for more on implementation details for this scheme. To analyze this scheme, assume, for simplicity, that it is defined over the plane $\mathcal{D} = \mathbb{Z}^2$. Following a similar series of steps to the continuous case, as outlined in Section 13.2.3, one has

$$\delta_{t+}\mathfrak{h}_{\text{lin}} = \kappa^2 \langle \delta_{t\cdot}u, \mathfrak{l}(\mu_{t\cdot}\Phi, u) \rangle_{\mathbb{Z}^2}$$

where $\mathfrak{h}_{\text{lin}}$ is the discrete energy corresponding to the linear scheme (12.14), as given in (12.20) (with boundary terms ignored here).

The following series of manipulations exactly mirrors that of the continuous case, from (13.7):

$$\delta_{t+}\mathfrak{h}_{\text{lin}} \overset{(13.13)}{=} \kappa^2 \langle \mu_{t\cdot}\Phi, \mathfrak{l}(\delta_{t\cdot}u, u) \rangle_{\mathbb{Z}^2}$$

$$\overset{(13.14)}{=} \frac{\kappa^2}{2} \langle \mu_{t\cdot}\Phi, \delta_{t+}\mathfrak{l}(u, e_{t-}u) \rangle_{\mathbb{Z}^2}$$

$$\overset{(13.15b)}{=} -\frac{\kappa^2}{2} \langle \mu_{t\cdot}\Phi, \delta_{t\cdot}\delta_{\Delta\boxplus, \Delta\boxplus}\Phi \rangle_{\mathbb{Z}^2}$$

$$\overset{(10.17)}{=} -\frac{\kappa^2}{2} \langle \mu_{t\cdot}\delta_{\Delta\boxplus}\Phi, \delta_{t\cdot}\delta_{\Delta\boxplus}\Phi \rangle_{\mathbb{Z}^2}$$

$$= -\frac{\kappa^2}{4}\delta_{t+}\mu_{t-}\|\delta_{\Delta\boxplus}\Phi\|_{\mathbb{Z}^2}^2 = -\delta_{t+}\mathfrak{v}_{\text{nonlin}}$$

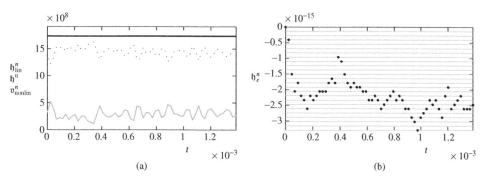

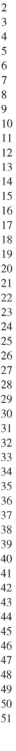

Figure 13.7 (a) Variation of the discrete potential energy due to nonlinear effects $\mathfrak{v}^n_{\mathrm{nonlin}}$ (solid grey line), that due to linear effects $\mathfrak{h}^n_{\mathrm{lin}}$ (dotted black line), and total discrete energy $\mathfrak{h}^n$ (solid black line), plotted against time t, for the output of scheme (13.15) for the von Kármán system. In this case, $\kappa = 127$, the plate aspect ratio is 1.5, and boundary conditions are of free type. The scheme is run at 44.1 kHz, and is initialized with a raised cosine distribution centered at the plate center, of amplitude 10. (b) Variation of the error in energy $\mathfrak{h}^n_e$, defined, at time step n, as $\mathfrak{h}^n_e = \left(\mathfrak{h}^n - \mathfrak{h}^0\right)/\mathfrak{h}^0$, plotted as black points. Multiples of single-bit variation are plotted as grey lines.

where

$$\mathfrak{v}_{\mathrm{nonlin}} = \frac{\kappa^2}{4}\mu_{t-}\|\delta_{\Delta\boxplus}\Phi\|^2_{\overline{\mathbb{Z}^2}}$$

is the contribution to potential energy due to nonlinear effects. As a result, the scheme is conservative, i.e., $\delta_{t+}\mathfrak{h} = 0$, with $\mathfrak{h} = \mathfrak{h}_{\mathrm{lin}} + \mathfrak{v}_{\mathrm{nonlin}}$. In this case, the added energy is non-negative, so numerical stability is ensured under condition (12.15) which applies to the linear case.

Though boundary conditions are not treated here, conditions analogous to (13.8) may be extracted. At a plate edge at $x = 0$, for example, the conditions

$$\Phi = \delta_{x-}\Phi = 0$$

may easily be shown to be conservative. See [46] for full details. Boundary conditions for u are exactly as in the linear case—see page 338. As for all conservative methods, numerical energy is conserved to machine accuracy—see Figure 13.7.

Scheme (13.15) is but one member of a larger family of conservative methods for the von Kármán system [46]; the members of this family vary considerably in terms of properties such as stability, as well as computability—see Problem 13.4.

13.3 Spherical shell vibration

Real plates, when used as percussion instruments, are often curved—the models described in the previous sections must be extended considerably to account for the effects of this curvature (which are not necessarily small, even for very mildly curved structures!). Shell models, for general curved geometries, are highly complex objects, and there is no possibility of doing justice to this topic in the twilight sections of this book. See [221] for an overview of this vast topic. Indeed, in simulating such a general shell structure, a finite difference scheme is probably not the best choice of method, given that the curvature may make the use of a regular set of coordinates impossible; finite element methods are really the only option under such conditions.

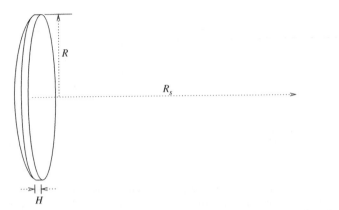

Figure 13.8   Geometry of a spherical cap, with radius R, thickness H, and radius of curvature R_s.

On the other hand, shells as they occur in musical acoustics (such as the cymbal or gong) often have a particularly simple form. If, as a first approximation, the shell is modeled as a spherical cap, a particularly compact extension of the von Kármán system is available [357]:

$$\rho H u_{tt} = -D\Delta\Delta u + \mathcal{L}(\Phi, u) - \frac{1}{R_s}\Delta\Phi \tag{13.16a}$$

$$\Delta\Delta\Phi = -\frac{EH}{2}\mathcal{L}(u, u) + \frac{EH}{R_s}\Delta u \tag{13.16b}$$

Here, the constants D, ρ, H are as for the von Kármán system, and E is Young's modulus. The new parameter R_s is the radius of curvature of the spherical cap—notice that the system reduces to the von Kármán system (13.3) as the radius of curvature becomes large. The system is defined over a circle of radius R, and is obviously best dealt with in radial coordinates. See Figure 13.8.

A necessary component in the above description is a form of the bracket operator $\mathcal{L}$ in radial coordinates:

$$\mathcal{L}(\alpha, \beta) = \frac{\alpha_{rr}}{r}\left(\beta_r + \frac{\beta_{\theta\theta}}{r}\right) + \frac{\beta_{rr}}{r}\left(\alpha_r + \frac{\alpha_{\theta\theta}}{r}\right) - \frac{2}{r^2}\left(\alpha_{r\theta} - \frac{\alpha_\theta}{r}\right)\left(\beta_{r\theta} - \frac{\beta_\theta}{r}\right) \tag{13.17}$$

Scaled form, loss, and excitation

In scaled form, for coordinates $r' = r/R$, and using the scaling of variables $u' = u/u_0$ and $\Phi' = \Phi/\Phi_0$, where u_0 and Φ_0 are as given for the von Kármán system in (13.5), the form of the system is, after removing primed variables and introducing frequency-dependent loss terms and an excitation,

$$u_{tt} = -\kappa^2\left(\Delta\Delta u - \mathcal{L}(\Phi, u) + q\Delta\Phi\right) - 2\sigma_0 u_t + 2\sigma_1\Delta u_t + F_{exc}(t)e_{exc} \tag{13.18a}$$

$$\Delta\Delta\Phi = -\mathcal{L}(u, u) + q\Delta u \tag{13.18b}$$

so that the problem is now defined over the unit circle $\mathcal{D} = \mathbb{U}_\circ^2$, and where the parameters κ and q are given by

$$\kappa = \sqrt{\frac{D}{\rho H R^4}} \qquad q = \frac{R^2\sqrt{6(1 - \nu^2)}}{HR_s}$$

The terms involving σ_0 and σ_1 are the usual loss terms, and the excitation is modeled here in terms of a force-like excitation function F_{exc} and spatial distribution $e_{exc}(r, \theta)$. As discussed earlier, F_{exc} can result from coupling to a mallet model, or, in the simplest case, is supplied externally.

Boundary and center conditions

Boundary conditions at the shell rim at $r = 1$ will be assumed here to be of free type—for the variable u, the conditions (12.43) should be used, and for Φ, the conditions

$$\Phi = \Phi_r = 0$$

though free conditions are often given in terms of higher derivatives of Φ—see [357]. Special care is necessary at the center of the domain. In some cases, there may be no support at the center (as in the case of the gong, but one should also be alert to the need for modeling the raised central dome which is often seen in such instruments), in which case no further condition is necessary. In other cases, such as some types of cymbals, the shell is fixed to a support. There are obviously many modeling issues—clearly the center should be fixed, but the support may allow the shell to tilt, and may also involve a distributed connection to an annular support structure, which will have its own physical properties. As a simple first approximation to such a support, and one which is not necessarily realistic but rather easy to work with, it is supposed here that the shell is clamped over an inner circumference of radius $\epsilon \ll 1$:

$$u = u_r = 0 \qquad \text{and} \qquad \Phi = \Phi_r = 0 \qquad \text{at} \quad r = \epsilon \tag{13.19}$$

which generalizes condition (12.44) applied to the case of the flat circular plate.

13.3.1 Difference schemes

Without further delay, one may move directly to a difference scheme for system (13.18), which is an extension of scheme (13.10) for the von Kármán system, now in radial coordinates:

$$\left(1 + \alpha\kappa^2 k^2 \delta_{\Delta\circ,\Delta\circ}\right)\delta_{tt}u = -\kappa^2\left(\delta_{\Delta\circ,\Delta\circ}u - [\mathcal{L}(\Phi, u)] + q\delta_{\Delta\circ}\Phi\right)$$

$$-2\sigma_0\delta_{t\cdot}u_t + 2\sigma_1\delta_{\Delta\circ}\delta_{t-}u + F_{exc}e_{exc} \tag{13.20a}$$

$$\delta_{\Delta\circ,\Delta\circ}\Phi = -[\mathcal{L}(u, u)] + q\delta_{\Delta\circ}u \tag{13.20b}$$

The scheme is defined over the circular region $\mathbb{U}^2_{\circ,N_r,N_\theta}$, with grid spacings h_r and h_θ, and the discrete Laplacian and biharmonic operators $\delta_{\Delta\circ}$ and $\delta_{\Delta\circ,\Delta\circ}$ are as described beginning on page 300. Taking a cue from the discussion of schemes for the circular plate, in Section 12.6.1, the scheme has a free parameter α, useful in maximizing output bandwidth.

One form of the discrete operator $[\mathcal{L}]$ approximating (13.17) is

$$[\mathcal{L}] = \mathfrak{l} = \frac{\delta_{rr}\alpha}{r}\left(\delta_r.\beta + \frac{\delta_{\theta\theta}\beta}{r}\right) + \frac{\delta_{rr}\beta}{r}\left(\delta_r.\alpha + \frac{\delta_{\theta\theta}\alpha}{r}\right) - \frac{2}{r^2}\left(\delta_r.\delta_\theta.\alpha - \frac{\delta_\theta.\alpha}{r}\right)\left(\delta_r.\delta_\theta.\beta - \frac{\delta_\theta.\beta}{r}\right)$$

$$\tag{13.21}$$

As in the case of the discrete Laplacian (see (10.24)), a special form of $\mathfrak{l}$ is necessary if the center of the shell is unconstrained. Here is the simplest possible second-order accurate form, for radial grid functions $\alpha_{l,m}$ and $\beta_{l,m}$:

$$\mathfrak{l}_{0,0}(\alpha, \beta) = \frac{4}{N_\theta^2 h_r^4}\sum_{p=0}^{N_\theta-1}\sum_{q=0}^{N_\theta-1}\left(1 - 4c_pc_q - 4s_ps_q\right)\alpha_{1,p}\beta_{1,q} - 2\alpha_{1,p}\beta_{0,0} - 2\alpha_{0,0}\beta_{1,q} + 2\alpha_{0,0}\beta_{0,0}$$

$$\tag{13.22}$$

where $c_l = \cos(4\pi l/N_\theta)$ and $s_l = \sin(4\pi l/N_\theta)$. See Programming Exercise 13.1.

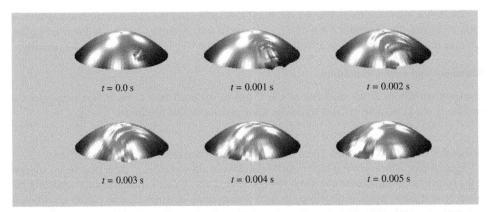

$t = 0.0$ s $t = 0.001$ s $t = 0.002$ s

$t = 0.003$ s $t = 0.004$ s $t = 0.005$ s

Figure 13.9 Snapshots of the time evolution of a spherical shell, according to (13.18), at times as indicated. Here, the shell is lossless, with $\kappa = 5$ and $q = 60$, and is under free edge conditions, with a clamped center condition. Scheme (13.20) is used under unforced conditions $F_{\text{exc}} = 0$, and the initial condition is a displacement of the form of a raised cosine distribution.

Necessary stability conditions for this scheme, distinct for clamped and free center conditions, are

$$\frac{2\kappa k \sqrt{1 - 4\alpha}}{h_r^2 \sqrt{1 - k^2 \kappa^2 q^2 / 4}} \left(1 + \frac{1}{h_\theta^2} \right) \leq 1 \qquad \text{free center}$$

$$\frac{2\kappa k \sqrt{1 - 4\alpha}}{h_r^2 \sqrt{1 - k^2 \kappa^2 q^2 / 4}} \left(1 + \frac{1}{4h_\theta^2} \right) \leq 1 \qquad \text{clamped center} \quad (13.19)$$

for $\alpha < 1/4$—especially good (i.e., wide-band) behavior is observed when α is slightly less than $1/4$. See Programming Exercise 13.3.

See Figure 13.9 for plots of output generated using this scheme.

13.3.2 Shifting of mode locations

For even a very light degree of curvature in a shell, the spectral characteristics can be dramatically changed with respect to the case of the flat plate. In the absence of nonlinear effects (i.e., when the bracket terms in system (13.18) are neglected), it is useful to examine some plots of typical output spectra for a shell under free boundary and center conditions, under different choices of the curvature parameter q, as shown in Figure 13.10. As pointed out in [357], there are essentially two families of modes: the series of asymmetric modes without nodal circles, the frequencies of which are affected only very slightly by an increase in curvature; and the remaining modes, the frequencies of which exhibit a strong upward shift with increased curvature. As such, for strongly curved shells, the majority of the spectrum is shifted upward, leaving a very sparse distribution of modes in the lower end of the spectrum. Perceptually, the resulting sound is brighter, with an extra degree of dissonance due to the increased density of modes in the mid range of the spectrum. This overall trend is roughly similar for free edge shells under a clamped center condition.

13.3.3 Crashes

The variety of crash-like sounds which can be produced using a shell model is quite large—there is a dependence on amplitude of excitation as well as the curvature parameter q. See Figure 13.11 for

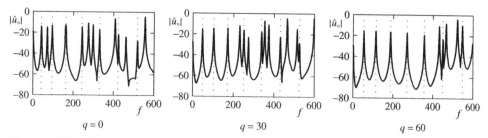

Figure 13.10 Typical output spectra for a spherical shell, according to (13.18), under low-amplitude conditions. Here, $\kappa = 50$, and the curvature parameter q is as indicated in the panels above; boundary and center conditions are of free type. The vertical dotted lines indicate frequencies corresponding to the series of asymmetric modes without a nodal circle.

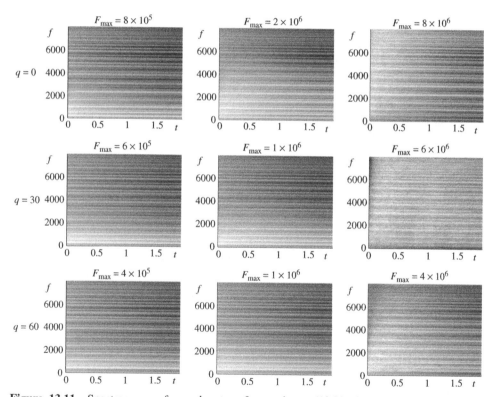

Figure 13.11 Spectrograms of sound output from scheme (13.20) for a spherical shell, with $\kappa = 50$, $\sigma_0 = 1.34$, and $\sigma_1 = 0.003$, and under conditions of zero curvature ($q = 0$) at top, moderate curvature ($q = 30$) in the middle row, and high curvature ($q = 60$) at bottom. In all cases, the shell is excited using a forcing function $F_{\text{exc}}(t)$, of the form given in (12.28), applied at time $t = 0$, of duration 3 ms, at a point half-way from the center to the rim, and of maximum value F_{max} as indicated in the panels above. The center point of the shell is clamped, and the sample rate is 32 kHz.

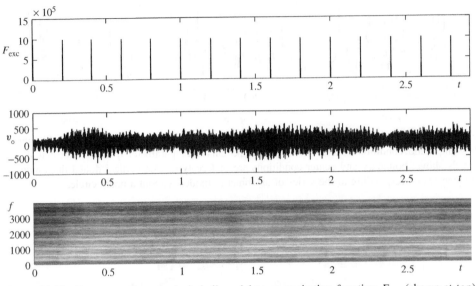

Figure 13.12 Response of a spherical shell model to an excitation function F_{exc} (shown at top) consisting of a series of sharp pulses, approximating a percussionist's gesture. Here, the shell has $q = 30$, with all other parameters as in the caption to Figure 13.11, and is clamped at the center; the excitation is applied at a point midway between the center and edge. The output velocity at a point on the shell's surface is shown in the middle panel, and its spectrogram at bottom. Scheme (13.20) is used, at 32 kHz.

some exploration of this. (There is also, of course, a strong additional dependence on the striking location.)

As the closing example in this book, and one which is an excellent example of the power of physical modeling at its best, consider the shell model subject to a periodic striking gesture, as illustrated in Figure 13.12. The resulting sound possesses a metallic pitched quality, superimposed on a bed of noise, which grows in amplitude as more energy is injected into the system; very uneven fluctuations in the output amplitude result, and it is clear that a linear model would be unable to react in such a manner. Furthermore, it is difficult to imagine how to construct an abstract synthesis method that would give such interesting unpredictability, given such a basic input gesture—see the comments on page 23.

13.4 Problems

Problem 13.1 *For Berger's equation, in Cartesian coordinates, and defined over a rectangular region $\mathbb{U}_e^2$, show an energy balance of the form $d\mathfrak{H}/dt = -\mathfrak{Q} + \mathfrak{B}$, and determine $\mathfrak{H}$, $\mathfrak{Q}$, and $\mathfrak{B}$. Show that under clamped or simply supported conditions (12.5) at any edge, the system remains lossless, but free boundary conditions (12.11) should be altered to*

$$u_{nn} + v u_{ss} = 0 \qquad u_{nnn} + (2 - v)u_{nss} - \mathfrak{M}u_n = 0$$

at an edge with outward normal coordinate n and tangential coordinate s. Do you anticipate any difficulties in implementing these conditions in a finite difference scheme? Discuss.

Problem 13.2   *Consider the von Kármán system, defined over the half plane $\mathcal{D} = \mathbb{R}^{2,x+}$. The free boundary condition for Φ at $x = 0$ is often given not as (13.8) but as*

$$\Phi_{yy} = \Phi_{xy} = 0 \qquad (13.23)$$

Argue that these conditions are equivalent to those given in (13.8) using the following reasoning.
   (a) Assume that conditions (13.8) hold at $x = 0$, and that these imply the conditions (13.23).
   (b) Now, assume that conditions (13.23) hold at $x = 0$. At any point $x = 0$, $y = y_0$ along the boundary, $\Phi(x, y, t)$ may be expanded in a Taylor series as follows, assuming that it is smooth:

$$\Phi(x, y, t) = \sum_{l=0}^{\infty} \sum_{m=0}^{\infty} q_{l,m}(y_0, t) x^l (y - y_0)^m$$

Show that if conditions (13.23) hold, then the coefficients $q_{l,m}(y_0, t)$ must vanish for $l = 0$, $m \geq 2$, and for $l = 1$, $m \geq 1$.
   (c) Following from the above reasoning, the expansion for Φ is now of the form

$$\Phi(x, y, t) = q_{0,0}(y_0, t) + q_{1,0}(y_0, t)x + q_{0,1}(y_0, t)(y - y_0) + Q(x, y, t)$$

where $Q(x, y, t)$ is an expansion possessing only terms in the second power of x or higher. Evaluate this expression, as well as Φ_x at $x = 0$, and from the uniqueness of Φ at the boundary, argue that the expression for $\Phi(x, y, t)$ must be independent of the expansion point, i.e., $\Phi = a(t) + b(t)x + c(t)y + Q(x, y, t)$.
   (d) From the definition of the von Kármán system in (13.6), argue that if $\Phi(x, y, t)$ is a solution, so is any function $\Phi'(x, y, t) = \Phi(x, y, t) - a(t) - b(t)x - c(t)y$. (In other words, it is only second and higher spatial derivatives of Φ which appear in the system.)
   (e) Show that if Φ satisfies boundary conditions (13.23), then there is a function Φ' which satisfies conditions (13.8) and which is also a solution to the von Kármán system.

Problem 13.3   *Show condition (13.11) for the discrete operator $\mathfrak{l}$.*

Problem 13.4   *Scheme (13.15) for the von Kármán system is one member of a larger family of second-order accurate conservative numerical methods:*

$$\delta_{tt}u = -\kappa^2 \delta_{\Delta\boxplus,\Delta\boxplus}u + \kappa^2 \mathfrak{l}(\bar{\Phi}, \bar{u})$$

$$\mu_{t-}\delta_{\Delta\boxplus,\Delta\boxplus}\Phi = -\left(\alpha\mathfrak{l}(u, e_{t-}u) + (1 - \alpha)\mu_{t-}\mathfrak{l}(u, u)\right)$$

where

$$\bar{u} = \alpha u + (1 - \alpha)\mu_{t\cdot}u \qquad \bar{\Phi} = \beta\Phi + (1 - \beta)\mu_{t\cdot}\Phi$$

This family depends on two free parameters, α and β.
   (a) Generalize the analysis of Section 13.2.7, and find the form $\mathfrak{v}_{\text{nonlin}}$ of the additional energy due to nonlinear effects. Under what conditions on α and β is it guaranteed to be non-negative?
   (b) For which values of α and β does this set of schemes admit a unique update?

Problem 13.5   *Consider the conservative scheme (13.15) for the von Kármán system. Because of the time-averaging operators applied within the first instance of the nonlinear bracket operator $\mathfrak{l}$, u cannot be updated explicitly. On the other hand, recall that the operator $\mathfrak{l}$ is bilinear—thus unknowns u^{n+1} in the resulting recursion appear linearly. Find a vector–matrix update form of the scheme suitable for implementation.*

As a starting point, it is useful to rewrite the scheme as

$$\mathbf{u}^{n+1} - 2\mathbf{u}^n + \mathbf{u}^{n-1} = -\kappa^2 k^2 \mathbf{D}^{(1)}_{\Delta\boxplus,\Delta\boxplus}\mathbf{u}^n + \frac{\kappa^2 k^2}{2}\left(\mathfrak{l}(\boldsymbol{\Phi}^{n+1}, \mathbf{u}^n) + \mathfrak{l}(\boldsymbol{\Phi}^{n-1}, \mathbf{u}^n)\right)$$

$$\frac{1}{2}\mathbf{D}^{(2)}_{\Delta\boxplus,\Delta\boxplus}\left(\boldsymbol{\Phi}^{n+1} + \boldsymbol{\Phi}^n\right) = -\mathfrak{l}(\mathbf{u}^{n+1}, \mathbf{u}^n)$$

where here, $\mathbf{u}^n$ and $\boldsymbol{\Phi}^n$ are the grid functions u and Φ arranged as vectors, and where $\mathbf{D}^{(1)}_{\Delta\boxplus,\Delta\boxplus}$ and $\mathbf{D}^{(2)}_{\Delta\boxplus,\Delta\boxplus}$ are two distinct matrix forms of the discrete biharmonic operator $\delta_{\Delta\boxplus,\Delta\boxplus}$, with boundary conditions appropriate to u and Φ, respectively. You must now find a linear system which, when solved, yields the unknowns $\mathbf{u}^{n+1}$ and $\boldsymbol{\Phi}^{n+1}$. For more details, see [46].

13.5 Programming exercises

Programming Exercise 13.1   *Create a Matlab script which calculates, for two given grid functions α and β, the value of the discrete bracket operator $\mathfrak{l}$, in both Cartesian coordinates (according to (13.11)) and radial coordinates (according to (13.21) and (13.22)). In the former case, assume that the grid functions α and β are defined over the rectangular region $\mathbb{U}^2_{N_r,N_\theta}$, under any choice of clamped or free conditions for either of α or β. In the latter, assume that α and β are defined over $\mathbb{U}^2_{\circ,N_r,N_\theta}$, and that boundary conditions at the edge are of free or clamped type. Allow the user to specify a clamped or free center condition.*

Programming Exercise 13.2   *Program the difference scheme (13.10) for the von Kármán system, defined over the unit area rectangle $\mathbb{U}^2_\epsilon$. In order to do this, you will need to have generated a matrix form $\mathbf{D}_{\Delta\boxplus,\Delta\boxplus}$ of the operator $\delta_{\Delta\boxplus,\Delta\boxplus}$, so as to perform the required linear system solution in (13.10b). (See Programming Exercise 12.2.) Beyond allowing the specification of the plate parameters κ, ϵ, σ_0, and σ_1, and readout locations x_0 and y_0, allow an excitation function F_{exc} of the form (12.28), and assume that it is applied at a single point.*

Programming Exercise 13.3   *Program the difference scheme (13.20) for the spherical shell system, defined over the unit circle $\mathbb{U}^2_\circ$. In order to do this, you will need to have generated a matrix form $\mathbf{D}_{\Delta\circ,\Delta\circ}$ of the operator $\delta_{\Delta\circ,\Delta\circ}$, so as to perform the required linear system solutions. (See Programming Exercise 12.5.) Assume that boundary conditions are of free type at the edge and of either free or clamped type at the center. As above, allow an excitation function F_{exc} of the form (12.28), and assume that it is applied at a single point. You may wish to make use of the results of Programming Exercise 12.6 as a starting point.*

14

Conclusion and perspectives

Many systems of interest in musical acoustics have been examined in this book, from a numerical perspective, and with an eye toward applications in sound synthesis. In closing, it is perhaps useful to return to some of the underlying issues. The question of computational complexity has arisen frequently, and some general bounds on performance, for a given system, appear in Section 14.1. But such bounds, though they apply to any numerical method, are too crude to reveal the distinctions among the various physical modeling sound synthesis paradigms—some final words on this subject appear in Section 14.2. And then, in Section 14.3, just a little bit more—there are many methods which do not appear in this book (and which perhaps should!).

14.1 A family of musical systems

Members of a rather large class of musical systems can be described by an equation of the form

$$u_{tt} + b^2 (-\Delta_d)^p u = 0 \qquad (14.1)$$

Here, Δ_d is the d-dimensional Laplacian operator, and p is a constant equal to one for non-stiff systems and equal to two for stiff systems. Equation (14.1) is assumed spatially scaled such that it is defined over a region of unit d-dimensional volume. When $p = 1$, (14.1) is the wave equation, and when $p = 2$, it is the equation of motion of an ideal bar (in 1D) or a thin plate (in 2D). In either case, b is a parameter with dimensions of frequency. Under different choices of d and p, the systems which are described to a very rough approximation are as given below:

$p\backslash d$	1	2	3
1	Strings, acoustic tubes	Membranes	Room acoustics
2	Thin bars	Thin plates	

Equation (14.1) is studied here primarily because of simplicity of analysis, but strictly speaking, it only describes systems which are linear, shift-invariant, lossless, and isotropic. Most of the analysis which follows on computational complexity is affected relatively little by the addition of loss (which is normally quite small in most musical systems), spatial variation, and anisotropy.

Numerical Sound Synthesis: Finite Difference Schemes and Simulation in Musical Acoustics   Stefan Bilbao
© 2009 John Wiley & Sons, Ltd

There are also, of course, other LSI systems which have been described in this book, such as strings with stiffness, and helical springs, which are not described by (14.1), but again the analysis may be extended to cover these cases.

A starting point for analysis of complexity in both the case of modal methods and those based on direct time–space integration methods is the dispersion relation for (14.1), which is

$$\omega = b|\boldsymbol{\beta}_d|^p \qquad \longrightarrow \qquad f = \frac{b\,(2\pi)^{p-1}}{\Lambda^p} \tag{14.2}$$

where $\boldsymbol{\beta}_d$ is a d-dimensional wavenumber, ω is angular frequency, $f = \omega/2\pi$ is frequency in Hertz, and wavelength $\Lambda = 2\pi/|\boldsymbol{\beta}_d|$.

14.1.1   Sampling theorems and complexity bounds

It is possible to arrive at estimates of complexity for direct numerical simulation methods for (14.1), through a dual application of Shannon's sampling theorem in time and space. Beginning from a choice f_s for the audio sample rate, it should be clear that one would expect that, at best, any numerical method operating as a recursion (this includes nearly all numerical methods for time-dependent systems) should be capable of simulating frequencies up to the Nyquist, or $f_s/2$—one might argue that one could perhaps save on computation by computing results over a smaller bandwidth, but, as has been shown at various points in this book, this is really a waste of audio bandwidth, and one could save far more work by simply reducing the sample rate, and then perhaps upsampling the resulting sound output in a postprocessing step.

The question then turns to the range of wavelengths which must be resolved by the numerical method. At sampling frequency f_s, the shortest such wavelength[1] will be given by the dispersion relation (14.2) as

$$\Lambda_{\min} = 2\pi^{1-1/p}\left(\frac{b}{f_s}\right)^{1/p} \tag{14.3}$$

For a numerical method operating over a grid, it should be clear that the spacing between adjacent points must be on the order of less than half the smallest wavelength to be rendered, or $\Lambda_{\min}/2$—there will be slight variations in the required density depending on the type of grid to be used, especially in the multidimensional case. For a unit volume, and given the requirement above on the spacing between grid points, the number of grid points needed to fill the space will be approximately $1/(\Lambda_{\min}/2)^d$, and, for a two-step difference scheme, the total number of memory locations required will be twice this, or approximately

$$N_{\mathrm{fd}} \cong 2\pi^{d/p-d}\left(\frac{f_s}{b}\right)^{d/p} \tag{14.4}$$

For a sparse finite difference scheme, the number of operations O_{fd} per second required will be approximately

$$O_{\mathrm{fd}} = \alpha f_s N_{\mathrm{fd}} \cong 2\alpha f_s \pi^{d/p-d}\left(\frac{f_s}{b}\right)^{d/p} \tag{14.5}$$

where α is a parameter which depends on the type of scheme—generally, it will lie in the range of between 1 and 10 for most of the systems encountered in musical acoustics and for reasonably simple schemes.

---

[1] This holds for any dispersion relation for which the $\omega - \beta$ dispersion relation is monotonically increasing—which is not always the case! See, e.g., Section 7.9, which deals with the case of helical springs.

It is worth noting the dependence on the parameters d and p, which behave in opposite respects with regard to complexity: memory and the operation count increase severely with the dimension, but are reduced with increasing stiffness; this is the reason that, say, full room acoustics simulation for artificial reverberation is a massive task—probably decades away from real time—whereas a model of plate reverberation is manageable and even possible in real time—see Section 12.3.3.

14.1.2   Modal representations and complexity bounds

Beginning from a choice f_s for the audio sampling rate, one may again make use of the dispersion relation (14.2) in order to arrive at a bound on computational complexity, this time using principles of modal density—see, e.g., the chapter by Weinreich for more information [408].

Suppose, for simplicity, that (14.1) is defined over a unit hypercube in d dimensions, and that the boundary conditions are of fixed/simply supported type (i.e., $u = 0$ on the boundary, and additionally $\Delta_d u = 0$ on the boundary if $p = 2$). The wavenumber $\boldsymbol{\beta}_d$ must then be of the form $\boldsymbol{\beta}_d = \pi \mathbf{n}_d$, where $\mathbf{n}_d = [n_1, n_2, \ldots, n_d]$ for (non-negative) integers $n_1, n_2, \ldots, n_d$. The dispersion relation may then be rewritten as

$$|\mathbf{n}_d| = \pi^{1/p-1} \left(\frac{2 f_\mathbf{n}}{b}\right)^{1/p} \tag{14.6}$$

where the frequencies $f = f_\mathbf{n}$ are now limited to a countably infinite set indexed by the vector $\mathbf{n}$. It now remains to determine the number of frequencies $f_\mathbf{n}$ which lie below the Nyquist frequency $f_s/2$. As $|\mathbf{n}_d|$ is the Euclidean length of the vector $\mathbf{n}_d$ in a d-dimensional space, the number of modes will then be that number which lies within the positive d-dimensional quadrant of the sphere of radius $\pi^{1/p-1}(f_s/b)^{1/p}$. Given that each mode possesses two degrees of freedom, the total number of degrees of freedom (or number of units of memory required) will be approximately

$$N_\mathrm{m} \cong 2\pi^{d/p-d} \left(\frac{f_s}{b}\right)^{d/p} \tag{14.7}$$

for small values of d (note that there will be an additional weak dependence on dimension d due to geometric considerations). This is the same as the bound obtained using principles of sampling theory in the previous section.

Though the above steps depend on several restrictive conditions (i.e., degeneracy of modes is ignored, and a simple geometry and boundary conditions are chosen), the analysis is in fact more general than it appears to be. Addressing each condition in turn, the issue of degeneracy of modes is minor, in that (1) the proportion of such modes which are degenerate under the conditions above vanishes in the limit of large $|\mathbf{n}|$, leading to the same expression for the number of modes; and (2) furthermore, degeneracy only occurs under very precise geometrical conditions which occur rarely if at all in practice. The issue of the special choice of geometry (i.e., a unit hypercube) in order to obtain a set of modes which may be easily ordered (and thus counted) is also minor: any unit volume will possess the same distribution of modes in the limit of high frequencies. Similarly, different choices of boundary conditions will affect only the frequencies of the lowest modes and not the distribution in the limit of high frequencies.

14.1.3   Nonlinear systems

The notion of a number of degrees of freedom for a nonlinear system is an unwieldy one—one can, however, make a few observations. First, consider an extension of system (14.1) of the form

$$u_{tt} + b^2 (-\Delta_d)^p u = f(u) \tag{14.8}$$

where $f(u)$ is some nonlinear function of the dependent variable u and its derivatives, which has
the property that it vanishes relative to the terms on the left-hand side of the equation in the limit
as u becomes small. The systems describing nonlinear string vibration in Chapter 8, and nonlinear
plate and shell vibration in Chapter 13, are of this form. One may immediately see that, if the
number of degrees of freedom necessary to represent the solution to (14.8) is $N_{nonlinear}$ at a given
sample rate, and that for system (14.1) is N_{linear}, then

$$N_{nonlinear} \geq N_{linear}$$

for the simple reason that the number of degrees of freedom $N_{nonlinear}$ must be sufficient to resolve
solutions to the underlying linear system.

Can one go any further? Clearly the analysis methods of the preceding sections, which rely on
concepts such as frequency and wavenumber, cannot be easily extended—but, if one is willing to
accept stability conditions for numerical schemes as a measure of complexity (and it is not obvious
that one should!), it is worth noting that for some systems (such as the nonlinear strings and plates
mentioned above), it is possible to find schemes such that

$$N_{nonlinear} = N_{linear}$$

The key feature of such systems is that the nonlinear terms always serve to increase the system
potential energy, for a given state—and as a result "stiffen" it, increasing wave speeds and also, if
one can use the term, frequencies. Tension modulation of strings (see Section 8.1.1) is an elementary
example of such behavior. As has been seen repeatedly throughout this book, increased wave
speeds lead to more coarse grid approximations (one can invoke CFL criteria here), and increased
frequencies to a smaller total number of modes for a given sample rate—regardless of the point of
view taken (neither of which is rigorous), such nonlinearities do not tend to increase the number of
degrees of freedom necessary in simulation. Swept under the rug here is the issue of aliasing—for
some nonlinear systems, operation very near a CFL-like bound must be approached with great
caution in musical sound synthesis applications, because crucial audible phenomena (such as, for
example, pitch glides) may be suppressed. But operation away from a stability limit again tends to
reduce complexity (i.e., one increases the grid spacing for a scheme operating at a given sample
rate)—now, however, at the expense of decreased bandwidth.

14.2   Comparative study III

Though this book is mainly concerned with synthesis applications of time domain finite difference
methods, other techniques have been touched upon at various points; the wave equation in 1D and
2D has been used as a point of comparison among these methods, over a range of computational
issues, in Section 6.6 and Section 11.8, respectively.

14.2.1   Lumped mass–spring networks

Lumped networks of masses and springs have been very briefly discussed, with regard to the
wave equation in 1D and 2D, in Section 6.1.1 and Section 11.5, respectively. It has been shown
in both cases that such networks yield numerical methods which are equivalent to simple finite
difference schemes—but these cases are not really representative of the way in which such models
are employed in synthesis environments (such as CORDIS [68]). In fact, the interest is rather
in allowing the user (composer) the ability to construct abstract networks of lumped elements,
regardless of whether there is an underlying distributed model. Indeed, if this is the goal, a large
ODE solver, which is under the hood in such environments, is really the only way of proceeding.

If, on the other hand, the system to be represented is indeed distributed, then working with lumped elements is somewhat cumbersome, especially when an elegant mathematical representation of the distributed system is available (this is often the case in musical acoustics). The distinction between the use of lumped and distributed modeling can be described as *physical*, in the former case, and *mathematical* in the latter. The relative advantages of the two approaches was well expressed many years ago by Ames [8]:

> The specialist sometimes finds the physical approach useful in motivating further analyses. In such a modus operandi the discrete (physical) model is given the lumped physical characteristics of the continuous system. For example, a heat conducting slab could be replaced by a network of heat conducting rods. The governing equations are then developed by direct application of the physical laws to the discrete system. On the other hand, in the mathematical approach the continuous formulation is transformed to a discrete formulation by replacing derivatives by, say, finite difference approximations. When the continuous problem formulation is already available this procedure is more flexible.

Ames was not speaking about musical systems, but by replacing "heat conducting slab" and "heat conducting rods" above by "membrane" and "masses and springs," one can translate his point to the musical sound synthesis setting. Furthermore, no less a figure than Philip Morse himself gave the following rationale for abandoning the lumped approach in the analysis of the 1D wave equation [243]:

> But this is a very awkward way of solving a problem that is essentially simple. What is needed is a new point of view, a new method of attack.

> The new point of view can be summarized as follows: We must not concern ourselves with the motion of each of the infinite number of points of the string, considered as separate points, but we must consider the string shape as a whole.

As mentioned above, when a lumped network is intended to behave as a distributed object, an equivalent finite difference scheme can be shown to exist. But the converse is not necessarily true. It quickly becomes difficult to deal with important numerical issues such as accuracy, or global approximations to derivatives, complex boundary conditions, or highly nonlinear systems; a fully distributed model is indispensable in such cases. An excellent example of such a system presented in this book is the helical spring (see Section 7.9)—designing a scheme which operates even passably well at an audio sample rate would be impossible if one were to begin from a lumped representation. And the helical spring is linear—when nonlinearities intervene, the situation becomes far more involved.

In short, the entire apparatus of network theory, necessary in order to manage the connection of a large number of elements, may be abandoned when a PDE formulation is available—and one may say the same thing of a scattering network based on lumped elements.

14.2.2 Modal synthesis

One of the most attractive features of modal synthesis is that, for a given problem, once one has a set of modal data (i.e., natural frequencies, and modal shapes, or, alternatively, expansion coefficients at input and output locations), the programming task is extremely simple—all the modes are uncoupled, and may thus be treated exactly like damped harmonic oscillators, as per Section 3.5. Ensuring stability is almost trivial in such an uncoupled setting, and, even better, an exact solution may be calculated, at least up to a given sample rate (provided that the modal data are exact). What is more, the run-time loop in a modal simulation routine depends in no way on problem geometry or even on dimensionality. One particular example of a system which is very cleanly dealt with in this case is the ideal bar, under simply supported conditions at both ends. The modal frequencies and shapes are known exactly in closed form, and a modal solution almost certainly is ideal—difference schemes will introduce undesirable numerical dispersion which must be reduced through more involved design procedures, and waveguide methods are a very poor match for stiff systems, due to large-order terminating filters which will be necessary in order to correct for the unphysical use of a dispersionless delay-line structure. Another example is the 2D wave equation, defined over a rectangular domain, and under fixed or free boundary conditions.

All is well in the run-time loop in a modal algorithm—indeed, a modal algorithm, requiring only two or three arithmetic operations per degree of freedom, will be more efficient than, say, a finite difference scheme, though generally not by a factor of more than four or five. The difficulties arise in obtaining the modal data at the outset, before run time—a potentially serious concern which is not often addressed in the literature [416]. With few exceptions (two of which are noted in the paragraph above), the modal shapes and frequencies must be determined numerically, through the solution of an eigenvalue problem. There are numerous downsides to such a requirement:

- **Precomputation**: Though for systems with a small number of degrees of freedom such a calculation is reasonable, and will not cause any latency, for larger systems it can be very large indeed, and will cause a noticeable delay before sound can be generated in the run-time loop. (A model of plate reverberation, for example, will require the calculation of approximately 10 000 modal frequencies and shapes.)

- **Storage**: Storage of the modal shapes themselves, which is on the order of N^2 for a system with N degrees of freedom, can dwarf that required in, for example, a time domain method. If one is really interested in accessing the underlying system at fixed locations, however, one need only store the expansion coefficients at these locations, but changes in the input/output locations will require the storage of separate sets of such coefficients.

- **Numerical inaccuracy**: In general, any numerical computation of the modal frequencies and shapes (say, using finite element methods or finite differences) will yield only approximate results, thus eliminating the possibility of an exact solution mentioned in the previous paragraph.

- **Modularity**: Each change in the problem geometry, boundary conditions, or, if in a modular setting, the location or nature of a connection between components, will require a complete recalculation of the entire set of modal data.

A deeper issue is that of the range of systems to which modal techniques may be usefully applied. While all LTI systems may be dealt with rigorously using modal analysis, the extension to nonlinear systems is problematic—while one may indeed develop a modal representation for a nonlinear distributed system, which is essentially a system of ODEs (for such analysis applied to the Kirchhoff–Carrier equation for nonlinear string vibration, see [105], and to the von Kármán system, see [360], and to nonlinear spherical shell vibration, see [357]), the ODEs are no longer uncoupled. Programming and computational complexity then rises to approximately the level of a time–space method such as a finite difference scheme, but with the additional precomputational load and other issues mentioned above to contend with; stability concerns also reappear.

14.2.3 Digital waveguides and scattering methods

If one has compared computation time for a difference scheme to that of a digital waveguide, in certain cases it should be clear that the waveguide formulation is far more efficient. These

cases are all based on variants of the 1D wave equation, when (very mild!) effects of loss and
dispersion are included. This covers most musically interesting cases of linear string vibration and
cylindrical and conical tubes. That they are also very easily programmed, and readily connected
to lumped excitation mechanisms, makes them, clearly, the best approach in such scenarios, by
almost any measure. This is something which can rarely be said about any numerical technique.
Simple conditions for stability are an extra advantage to a scattering formulation.

Any numerical method which is targeted toward simulation of a particular phenomenon (in the
case of waveguides, the propagation of distortionless traveling waves) must suffer a lack of exten-
sibility when the phenomenon is no longer a good model of the underlying dynamics. Waveguides
may be extended to incorporate some deviations from the strict 1D traveling wave decomposition,
particularly through "lumping" of such effects at terminations, but such consolidation obscures the
underlying dynamics, and can make modular interconnection (through connection to wave digital
elements, or perhaps hybrid finite difference modules) difficult. If the order of the lumped terminating filter becomes large, waveguides can lose a lot of their computational advantage, as is the
case for stiff bars, for which a direct solution by, say, finite differences is already quite cheap.
The extension of waveguides to highly nonlinear, spatially varying, or multidimensional systems
is very strenuous, and, provided one can even do it rigorously, almost certainly leads to a less
efficient implementation than what one could obtain by more direct means.

14.2.4   Finite difference methods

Perhaps the greatest strength of direct techniques such as finite difference methods is
generality—the number of a priori assumptions made about the form of the solution is notably
fewer than in the case of, for example, waveguides, modal synthesis, or lumped methods. Indeed,
there is only one assumption—that it is possible to represent the behavior of a continuous system
over a grid—which is indeed not very restrictive. Other strengths include ease of programming,
minimal precomputation, simplified input/output, and modularity—all of which result from the
direct availability of the entire physical state of the virtual object. For a difference scheme, at the
level of programming, there is little or no distinction among the various types of system (LTI,
LSI, nonlinear, etc.) which occur frequently in musical acoustics.

The main difficulties are at the level of analysis and design of schemes:

- **Stability**: Necessary conditions for stability may be ensured by frequency domain analysis,
  and, in order to determine stable numerical boundary conditions and for nonlinear systems,
  more involved energy analysis techniques must be invoked.

- **Numerical dispersion**: Numerical dispersion leads, in the audio context, to a deviation
  of computed frequencies from those of the model system—such deviations range from
  inaudible to very large (in the case of, say, explicit schemes in radial coordinates).

Strategies for dealing with both such difficulties, geared toward audio and synthesis applications,
have been indicated at many points in this book. But the important point, and the reason that
such methods have been given center stage here, is that the problems inherent in the use of such
schemes are of a different nature from those of the other physical modeling synthesis techniques.
Certainly, the difficulties noted above pose analytical challenges—which can be surmounted. But,
once surmounted, the analytical difficulties are not reflected in an adverse way in the resulting
implementation, which can be exceedingly simple. Another important point is that such difficulties
only occur in a serious way when dealing with systems which are not easily approached using
other physical modeling techniques, and so cannot really be viewed as a disadvantage.

More profound weaknesses are, of course, that difference schemes as presented in this book
are not well adapted to general problems of arbitrary geometry, and, in some cases (such as over

circular geometries), can compute solutions of acceptable audio quality only with a good deal of tricky design intervention.

14.3   Beyond finite difference methods

Finite difference methods are well suited to problems defined either in one spatial dimension, or over a simple geometry in 2D (such as rectangular or circular). This covers all string models, 1D tube models, bars, and rectangular or circular percussion instruments. In general, finite difference methods rely on the use of regular grids, and, for finer modeling in irregular geometries (perhaps geared toward musical instrument design rather than sound synthesis), are not always the best choice. There are certain strategies which may be employed: the use of form-fitting coordinates is one, and domain decomposition [71] is another. On the other hand, for extremely complex geometries, such approaches become unwieldy. Another concern is accuracy—though finite difference methods perform well in some settings, in others they do not, and require a fair amount of work at the design stage (the various implicit methods presented in this book serve as examples).

Finite difference methods are based on approximations to derivatives using neighboring points on a grid. A more modern approach is to approximate the underlying unknown solution using a function expansion, and then solve for a set of coefficients which minimizes some measure of error with respect to the true solution. In 1D, for example, one might write such an expansion for a function $u(x)$ as

$$u(x) = \sum_{p=1}^{N} a_p u_p(x) \tag{14.9}$$

One example of such a representation which has appeared in this book is the Fourier expansion, used in the case of the 1D wave equation in Section 6.1.11, and the ideal bar Section 7.1.3, and which has been extended to 2D in the case of the wave equation in Section 11.1.3. But there are others types of expansions—finite element methods, for example, are based around the use of simple functions defined locally over small regions, and spectral methods make use of functions defined globally, over the whole problem domain. For an excellent unified view of such techniques, see the text by Quarteroni and Valli [278].

14.3.1   Finite element methods

Finite element methods are designed to deal with such problems in irregular geometries. As mentioned above, they are based on a distinct point of view; instead of approximating an underlying differential equation, pointwise, over a grid, the solution is approximated using a collection of so-called shape or basis functions, which may or may not lie in a regular arrangement. These functions are usually of a relatively simple form, e.g., low-order polynomial or multinomial functions, and are defined locally—see Figure 14.1(a) for a representation of very simple hat-shaped functions, useful as a conceptual point of departure for 1D systems. This is not to say that there is no grid at all—it is rather that the grid may be unstructured, a great advantage in problems in 2D or 3D—see Figure 14.2(b). The construction of finite element simulation routines is often approached using integral and variational methods, rather than differential approximations—as such, energy methods and inner product formulations very similar to those presented in this book play a large role [278]. In practice, the finite element procedure is usually applied to spatial differential operators, reducing the problem to a system of time-dependent ODEs. For the solution to a dynamic problem, the solution may be advanced using one of a number of well-known time-integration

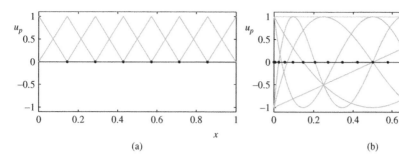

(a)   (b)

Figure 14.1 Basis functions over a 1D unit interval: (a) simple hat-shaped finite element basis functions, defined locally, with nodes indicated by black points; and (b) a globally defined set of Chebyshev polynomials; also indicated are a set of collocation points.

strategies,[2] such as, for example, Runge–Kutta methods [65]. In the end, finite element methods employed in this way for problems in dynamics operate much as finite difference methods do, through matrix recursions at a given (or perhaps variable) sample rate. Another approach, given a system of coupled ODEs, resulting from a finite element approximation to the spatial part of a problem, is to diagonalize it, leading to what is essentially a modal form. Needless to say, the literature on finite element methods is vast—see [93] for an overview.

If the goal of a simulation is to elucidate the behavior and functioning of a real-world musical instrument, necessarily an interconnection of components of irregular geometry, rather than to synthesize sound, then finite element methods are a natural choice. As is to be expected, they have been applied to nearly all families of acoustic instruments: pianos [229], guitars [114, 103, 20], stringed instruments such as violins [318, 62], the vocal tract [164] including modeling of the vocal folds themselves [353], organ pipes [207], the clarinet [122], xylophone and marimba bars [61], and timpani [283], and various more exotic percussive instruments, such as crotales [104],

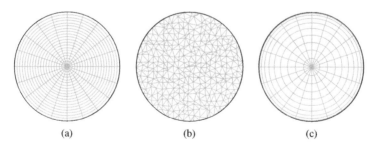

(a)   (b)   (c)

Figure 14.2 Computational grids for a problem defined over a circular geometry: (a) a typical uniform finite difference grid; (b) an unstructured mesh of triangular elements; and (c) a grid suitable for spectral collocation, employing a uniform grid in the angular direction and a Chebyshev grid in the radial direction.

---

[2] This separation of the space and time discretization is a nice conceptual simplification, but constitutes a significant distinction with finite difference methods as presented here, in which, in some cases, the time and space discretizations are carried out together. Indeed, a simultaneous time–space discretization can lead to cancellation between errors produced in the two discretizations alone, and to very good accuracy over the entire spectrum. In the case of, for instance, the ideal bar, even if one were to employ a highly accurate finite element or spectral method to the spatial part of the problem, the errors introduced using a high-order time-stepping algorithm could be larger than those of an implicit scheme such as that given in Section 7.1.5.

Korean chimes [414], and the thumb piano [238]. Nearly always, such simulations are concerned
with linear behavior and, in particular, with determining modal frequencies (some exceptions are
to be noted in [103, 283] above). In most of the musical acoustics literature, software packages
are liberally employed, and the proper functioning of a finite element method is taken for granted,
and its inner workings not often described. Finite element methods are also beginning to appear
in pure sound synthesis applications—see, e.g., [64, 36].

In the run-time loop, as mentioned above, a finite element solver for a time-dependent system
behaves in a manner very much like the finite difference schemes described here—if the finite
element discretization has been diagonalized, it may be time integrated as a modal method. In terms
of a raw operation count, there is no disadvantage to using finite element methods; update matrices
are sparse, because of the essentially local nature of the finite element approximation, and should
have approximately the same number of degrees of freedom as a finite difference method. The
downside, with respect to a difference scheme, is that writing finite element code is considerably
more involved, partly because of the many new choices available to the designer: one needs
to choose an appropriate grid, decide on a set of approximating functions (the finite elements),
of which there are many varieties, and finally determine the forms of the update matrices. The
upshot is that finite element code will inevitably be many times longer than its finite difference
counterpart, in cases for which the two methods may be employed—indeed, nearly the entirety of
the implementation will be devoted to set-up procedures, before the run-time loop. Generally, then,
one must rely on software packages to perform this set-up, which can be good or bad, depending
on one's point of view. In the context of sound synthesis, it is good in the sense that the user (i.e., a
composer or sound designer in this case) may handle relatively complex objects while being freed
from concerns about the inner workings of the algorithms, and bad in the sense that there is a great
loss of control, and the ability to make adjustments to the code if results are not as expected. It
is probably unwise to use an industrial finite element package directly as a front-end for physical
modeling synthesis, as the peculiarities of audio (such as those mentioned in Section 2.1, as well as
concerns having to do with bandwidth and numerical inharmonicity) will certainly not have been
taken into account. Finite element solvers specialized to physical modeling synthesis are currently
under development as an extension of Modalys [36].

14.3.2   Spectral methods

One of the most serious drawbacks to the use of time domain methods relates to the effect of
numerical dispersion, which leads, at least in the linear case, to mistuning of modal frequencies;
numerical dispersion itself results from insufficient accuracy in a numerical method. While the
perceptual importance of numerical dispersion in musical sound synthesis applications, which is
generally limited to the upper end of the human hearing range, is a matter of debate, this is a good
point to introduce other numerical techniques which can have much better accuracy.

Finite difference methods and finite element methods are based on essentially local discretizations of a model system; generally, one models the system either through combinations of values
at neighboring points over a grid, or through relationships between shape functions defined over
neighboring elements. Better accuracy may be achieved as more neighboring points or nodes are
used in the calculation; this renders the calculations less local. In the most well-known mani-
festations of spectral methods[3] [71, 364, 141, 278] approximations are global; an approximation
to a PDE system calculated at a given location will make use of information from the entire
spatial domain of the problem. The solution itself is considered to be decomposed into a set of

---

[3] It is worth being quite clear on the use of the word "spectral," in this case, which is not used in the sense
of spectral modeling or spectral analysis, common techniques in audio and sound synthesis. The word "spectral"
refers to extremely high accuracy of numerical methods—though such methods can be based on the use of Fourier
series, in most cases of interest they are based on more general polynomial series approximations.

1
2
3
4
5
6
7
8
9
10
11
12
13
14
15
16
17
18
19
20
21
22
23
24
25
26
27
28
29
30
31
32
33
34
35
36
37
38
39
40
41
42
43
44
45
46
47
48
49
50
51

basis functions—see Figure 14.1(b). These often take the form of Chebyshev polynomials, but Fourier decomposition is also a possibility—indeed, modal synthesis in its simplest form, and other Fourier-based forms seen in synthesis [147, 396], are examples of spectral methods.

A particularly well-known form of the spectral method ("pseudospectral") results from the particular choice of error between the model expansion (of the form of, for example, (14.9), in 1D, where the functions $u_p(x)$ are Chebyshev polynomials) and the exact solution—if the error is to be minimized at a finite collection of points in the spatial domain, one speaks of a collocation method (if the error is minimized over the entire domain, Galerkin-type methods result). Shown in Figure 14.1(b), along with a set of Chebyshev polynomials, is a particular choice in 1D, known as the Gauss–Lobatto collocation points—notice that they are not uniformly spaced over the domain, with a higher density nearer the endpoints. The same holds true of extensions to 2D problems—see Figure 14.2(c). As should be expected, matrix representations of differential operators, in contrast to the case of methods based on local representations such as finite difference methods or finite element methods, are not sparse—they are, however, structured, and fast algorithms (such as the FFT) may be used in order to compute spectral derivatives efficiently [364].

As a very simple example of spectral accuracy, consider the eigenvalue problem $\Delta u = -\lambda u$, defined over the unit square region $\mathbb{U}^2$, with boundary conditions fixed at zero. Using a simple five-point finite difference approximation to the Laplacian, of the type described in (10.9), one could construct a matrix approximation $\mathbf{D}_{\Delta\boxplus}$, and solve the eigenvalue problem $\mathbf{D}_{\Delta\boxplus}u = \lambda u$, where u is some grid function defined over the usual Cartesian grid. Using a pseudospectral method, one could generate a spectral differentiation matrix $\mathbf{D}_{\Delta,\text{spectral}}$, operating over the collocation points, and solve a similar eigenvalue problem. In Figure 14.3, results are compared to exact values, for the case of a matrix operator of size 24×24. The most striking thing is that even on a relatively coarse grid such as this, the spectral method generates results that are nearly of machine accuracy, while the usual error is seen for the finite difference approximation.

There are a few things worth noting here—first, though it is possible to obtain such accuracy for the eigenvalue problem, when it comes to a time-dependent simulation (referring to the above example, if one were to solve the 2D wave equation over the unit square), dispersion will be reintroduced by the time differencing. Usually, then, spectral methods are coupled with high-order time differencing methods, such as, for example, Adams, Runge–Kutta, etc. [65]. One issue of importance in sound synthesis, however, given that one is interested in not just the lowest modes, is that although spectral methods calculate the lower eigenvalues (or modes) with high accuracy,

Mode	Exact	FD	Spectral
1	19.73920880217	19.71103939474	19.73920880219
2	49.34802200544	49.10896781236	49.34802200544
3	49.34802200544	49.10896781236	49.34802200545
4	78.95683520871	78.50689622998	78.95683520872
5	98.69604401089	97.54629824436	98.69604401089
6	98.69604401089	97.54629824436	98.69604401089
7	128.30485721416	126.94422666198	128.30485721415

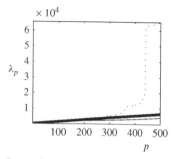

Figure 14.3 Eigenvalues of difference approximations to the Laplacian over a unit square, with fixed boundary conditions. Left, a table showing a comparison among exact values, those calculated by a five-point finite difference (FD) operator, and a spectral operator, for the first seven modes; and right, the eigenvalues λ_p plotted against p, with exact values represented by a thick black line, those calculated through a finite difference approximation by a solid black line, and through a spectral approximation by a dashed line. In either case, the matrix operator is of size 24×24.

there is a notable drop-off in accuracy for the high modes—see the plot in Figure 14.3. Indeed, in the upper reaches, the computed values are entirely spurious. A finite difference calculation produces poorer results for the low modes, but without a dramatic loss of accuracy for the higher modes. Because, for a spectral method, the spurious eigenvalues are generally quite high, one should expect that when coupled with a time domain method, problems in obtaining reasonable audio bandwidth will arise, and even more severely than in the case of finite difference methods.

Like finite difference methods, spectral methods are not particularly well adapted to problems defined over irregular geometries—but newer hybrid developments such as *hp* spectral elements are formulations similar to spectral methods, but on a local basis, like finite element methods, using local polynomial interpolants of very high order—see the many references in [59].

To date, the use of spectral methods in musical acoustics problems remains almost entirely unexplored (after an extensive literature search, the author could find only a single isolated example [311]). On the other hand, as mentioned above, spectral representations of spatial derivatives, particularly through the use of Fourier series representations, have indeed appeared from time to time in the musical acoustics literature—see [396, 147]. It is worth noting, however, that outside of musical acoustics, many systems which appear in this book have been approached using spectral methods—see, e.g., [205, 204], in which spectral methods are used to solve a von Kármán nonlinear plate vibration problem.

14.3.3   Other methods

Finite element and spectral methods are the most natural generalizations of finite difference methods, and probably the most suitable for sound synthesis applications. There are, of course, many other techniques which could also play a role, in certain limited contexts.

For certain systems, it is possible to reformulate a PDE system in terms of boundary integrals—generally, this is true for linear systems. The boundary element method refers to the numerical solution of such boundary integrals, with the solution at an interior point in the domain then computed through Green's function expansions. Boundary elements have been used fleetingly in investigations in musical acoustics [265], and perhaps more frequently in room acoustics problems, described by the wave equation, to which the boundary element method is a good match [142]. For an overview of the use of boundary element methods in acoustics, see [60].

One area of musical acoustics which is ripe for the application of modern numerical techniques is wind instrument modeling. The acoustics of such instruments are often modeled as linear, but, as mentioned in Section 9.4, nonlinear effects can appear at high blowing pressures for members of the brass family. For nonlinear problems in fluid mechanics, a method which has developed relatively recently is the so-called lattice–Boltzmann method, which has seen some use in the acoustics of wind instruments [97]. Such methods are rather different from conventional numerical methods, in that a PDE model (in this case, the Navier–Stokes equations) is not used as a starting point—instead, the dynamics are modeled at the level of interaction of individual "particles." In the end, however, such methods operate over grids, and have been shown to be equivalent to finite difference schemes in some cases [185], and are increasingly viewed as such. More closely related to the techniques described in this book are finite volume methods, which are also geared toward nonlinear problems in fluid dynamics, and especially shock capturing—there is a heavy reliance on discrete conservation properties, often over unstructured grids, though there is a much stronger link with finite difference methods than in the case of finite element methods. See the text by Leveque [224] for an introduction.

Appendix A

Matlab code examples

In this appendix, various simple code fragments are provided. All can be viewed as prototypes for physical modeling sound synthesis. The coding style reflects something of a compromise between efficiency, on the one hand, and brevity and intelligibility, on the other. The choice of Matlab as a programming environment definitely reflects the latter sensibility, though the use of Matlab as an actual synthesis engine is not recommended. Some of these examples make use of constructs and features which need not appear in a code fragment intended for synthesis, including various calls to plotting functions, as well as the demonstration of energy conservation in some cases. It should be clear, in all cases, which elements of these examples may be neglected in an actual implementation. For the sake of brevity, these examples are too crude for actual synthesis purposes, but many features, discussed at various points in the texts and exercises, may be added.

A.1   The simple harmonic oscillator

```
% matlab script sho.m
% finite difference scheme for simple harmonic oscillator

%%%%%% begin global parameters

SR = 44100;                       % sample rate (Hz)
f0 = 1000;                        % fundamental frequency (Hz)
TF = 1.0;                         % duration of simulation (s)
u0 = 0.3;                         % initial displacement
v0 = 0.0;                         % initial velocity

%%%%%% end global parameters

% check that stability condition is satisfied

if(SR<=pi*f0)
    error('Stability condition violated');
end
```

```
% derived parameters

k = 1/SR;                          % time step
coef = 2-k^2*(2*pi*f0)^2;          % scheme update coefficient
NF = floor(TF*SR);                 % duration of simulation (samples)

% initialize state of scheme

u1 = u0+k*v0;                      % last value of time series
u2 = u0;                           % one before last value of time series

% initialize readout

out = zeros(NF,1); out(1) = u2; out(2) = u1;

%%%%%% start main loop

for n=3:NF
    u=coef*u1-u2;                  % difference scheme calculation
    out(n) = u;                    % read value to output vector
    u2 = u1; u1 = u;               % update state of difference scheme
end

%%%%%% end main loop

% play sound

soundsc(out,SR);

% plot output waveform

plot([0:NF-1]*k, out, 'k');
xlabel('t'); ylabel('u'); title('SHO: Scheme Output'); axis tight
```

A.2   Hammer collision with mass–spring system

```
% matlab script hammermass.m
% hammer collision with a mass-spring system

%%%%%% begin global parameters

SR = 44100;                        % sample rate (Hz)
xH0 = -0.001; vH0 = 2;             % initial conditions of hammer
TF = 0.05;                         % duration of simulation (s)
w0 = 2000;                         % angular frequency of mass-spring system
MR = 10;                           % hammer/target mass ratio
wH = 1000;                         % stiffness parameter for hammer
alpha = 2;                         % hammer stiffness nonlinearity exponent

%%%%%% end global parameters

% derived parameters

k = 1/SR;
NF = floor(TF*SR);
```

```
% initialization                                                          1
                                                                          2
uH2 = xH0; uH1 = xH0+k*vH0;              % hammer                         3
u2 = 0; u1 = 0;                          % mass-spring system             4
out = zeros(NF,1); f = zeros(NF,1);                                       5
out(1) = u2; out(2) = u1;                                                 6
                                                                          7
%%%%%% start main loop                                                    8
                                                                          9
for n=3:NF                                                               10
    if(uH1>u1)                                                           11
        f(n-1) = wH^(1+alpha)*(uH1-u1)^alpha;                            12
    else f(n-1) = 0;                                                     13
    end                                                                  14
    uH = 2*uH1-uH2-k^2*f(n-1);                                           15
    u = 2*u1-u2-w0^2*k^2*u1+MR*k^2*f(n-1);                               16
    out(n) = u;                                                          17
    u2 = u1; u1 = u;                                                     18
    uH2 = uH1; uH1 = uH;                                                 19
end                                                                      20
                                                                         21
%%%%%% end main loop                                                     22
                                                                         23
% plots of displacement of target mass and force                        24
                                                                         25
subplot(2,1,1)                                                           26
plot([0:NF-1]*k, out, 'k'); title('Position of Target Mass'); xlabel('t'); 27
axis tight                                                               28
subplot(2,1,2)                                                           29
plot([0:NF-1]*k, f, 'k'); title('Hammer Force/Mass'); xlabel('t');       30
axis tight                                                               31
```

A.3   Bowed mass–spring system

```
% matlab script bowmass.m                                               33
% finite difference scheme for a bowed mass-spring system               34
% soft friction characteristic w/iterative Newton-Raphson method        35
                                                                        36
%%%%%% begin global parameters                                          37
                                                                        38
SR = 44100;              % sample rate (Hz)                             39
f0 = 200;                % oscillator frequency (Hz)                    40
FB = 500;                % bow force/mass (m/s^2)                       41
TF = 0.1;                % simulation duration (s)                      42
vB = 0.2;                % bow velocity (m/s)                           43
sig = 100;               % friction law free parameter (1/m^2)          44
tol = 1e-4;              % tolerance for Newton-Raphson method           45
                                                                        46
%%%%%% end global parameters                                            47
                                                                        48
% derived parameters                                                    49
                                                                        50
NF = floor(TF*SR);                                                      51
k = 1/SR;
A = exp(1/2)*sqrt(2*sig);
```

```
% initialize time series/iterative method

u = zeros(NF,1); f = zeros(NF,1); vr = zeros(NF,1);
qlast = 0;

% time step restrictions

if(k>min(1/(pi*f0),exp(1)/(FB*sqrt(2*sig))))
    error('Time step too large');
end

%%%%%% start main loop

for n=3:NF
    % Newton-Raphson method to determine relative velocity
    b = (2*pi*f0)^2*u(n-1)-(2/k^2)*(u(n-1)-u(n-2))+(2/k)*vB;
    eps = 1;
    while eps>tol
        q=qlast-(FB*A*qlast*exp(-sig*qlast^2)+2*qlast/k+b)/...
        (FB*A*(1-2*sig*qlast^2)*exp(-sig*qlast^2)+2/k);
        eps = abs(q-qlast);
        qlast = q;
    end
    % update position of mass and relative bow velocity
    u(n) = 2*k*(q+vB)+u(n-2); vr(n-1) = q;
end

%%%%%% end main loop

% plot mass displacement and relative bow velocity

tax = [0:NF-1]*k;
subplot(2,1,1); plot(tax, u, 'k');
title('Displacement of Mass'); xlabel('time (s)');
subplot(2,1,2); plot(tax, vr, 'k');
title('Relative Bow Velocity'); xlabel('time (s)');
```

A.4   The 1D wave equation: finite difference scheme

```
% matlab script waveeq1dfd.m
% finite difference scheme for the 1D wave equation
% fixed boundary conditions
% raised cosine initial conditions

%%%%%% begin global parameters

SR = 44100;                      % sample rate (Hz)
f0 = 330;                        % fundamental frequency (Hz)
TF = 1;                          % duration of simulation (s)
ctr = 0.7; wid = 0.1;            % center location/width of excitation
u0 = 1; v0 = 0;                  % maximum initial displacement/velocity
rp = 0.3;                        % position of readout (0-1)
lambda = 1;                      % Courant number

%%%%%% end global parameters
```

1
2
3
4
5
6
7
8
9
10
11
12
13
14
15
16
17
18
19
20
21
22
23
24
25
26
27
28
29
30
31
32
33
34
35
36
37
38
39
40
41
42
43
44
45
46
47
48
49
50
51

```
% begin derived parameters                                                     1
                                                                               2
gamma = 2*f0;                    % wave equation free parameter                3
k = 1/SR;                        % time step                                   4
NF = floor(SR*TF);               % duration of simulation (samples)            5
                                                                               6
% stability condition/scheme parameters                                        7
                                                                               8
h = gamma*k/lambda; N = floor(1/h); h = 1/N; lambda = gamma*k/h;               9
s0 = 2*(1-lambda^2); s1 = lambda^2;                                            10
                                                                              11
% readout interpolation parameters                                            12
                                                                              13
rp_int = 1+floor(N*rp);          % rounded grid index for readout             14
rp_frac = 1+rp/h-rp_int;         % fractional part of readout location        15
                                                                              16
% create raised cosine                                                        17
                                                                              18
xax = [0:N]'*h;                                                               19
ind = sign(max(-(xax-ctr-wid/2).*(xax-ctr+wid/2),0));                         20
rc = 0.5*ind.*(1+cos(2*pi*(xax-ctr)/wid));                                    21
                                                                              22
% initialize grid functions and output                                       23
                                                                              24
u2 = u0*rc; u1 = (u0+k*v0)*rc; u = zeros(N+1,1); out = zeros(NF,1);           25
                                                                              26
%%%%%% start main loop                                                        27
                                                                              28
for n=3:NF                                                                    29
  u(2:N) = -u2(2:N)+s0*u1(2:N)+s1*(u1(1:N-1)+u1(3:N+1)); % scheme calculation 30
  out(n) = (1-rp_frac)*u(rp_int)+rp_frac*u(rp_int+1);      % readout          31
  u2 = u1; u1 = u; % update of grid variables                                 32
end                                                                           33
                                                                              34
%%%%%% end main loop                                                          35
                                                                              36
% plot output waveform                                                        37
                                                                              38
plot([0:NF-1]*k, out, 'k');                                                   39
xlabel('t'); ylabel('u'); title('1D Wave Equation: FD Output'); axis tight    40
                                                                              41
% play sound                                                                  42
                                                                              43
soundsc(out,SR);                                                              44
```

A.5 The 1D wave equation: digital waveguide synthesis

```
% matlab script waveeq1ddw.m                                                  45
% digital waveguide method for the 1D wave equation                          46
% fixed boundary conditions                                                   47
% raised cosine initial conditions                                           48
                                                                              49
%%%%%% begin global parameters                                               50
                                                                              51
SR = 44100;                      % sample rate (Hz)
f0 = 441;                        % fundamental frequency (Hz)
```

```
TF = 1;                          % duration of simulation (s)                    1
ctr = 0.7; wid = 0.1;            % center location/width of excitation           2
u0 = 1; v0 = 0;                  % maximum initial displacement/velocity         3
rp = 0.3;                        % position of readout (0-1)                     4
                                                                                 5
%%%%%% end global parameters                                                     6
                                                                                 7
% begin derived parameters                                                       8
                                                                                 9
k = 1/SR;                        % time step                                     9
NF = floor(SR*TF);               % duration of simulation (samples)            10
N = floor(0.5*SR/f0);            % length of delay lines                       11
rp_int = 1+floor(N*rp);          % rounded grid index for readout              12
rp_frac = 1+rp*N-rp_int;         % fractional part of readout location         13
                                                                               14
% initialize delay lines and output                                            15
                                                                               16
wleft = zeros(N,1); wright = zeros(N,1);                                        17
out = zeros(NF,1);                                                             18
                                                                               19
% create raised cosine and integral                                            20
                                                                               21
xax = ([1:N]'-1/2)/N;                                                          21
ind = sign(max(-(xax-ctr-wid/2).*(xax-ctr+wid/2),0));                          22
rc = 0.5*ind.*(1+cos(2*pi*(xax-ctr)/wid));                                     23
rcint = zeros(N,1);                                                           24
for qq=2:N                                                                     25
   rcint(qq) = rcint(qq-1)+rc(qq)/N;                                           26
end                                                                           27
                                                                               28
% set initial conditions                                                       29
                                                                               30
wleft = 0.5*(u0*rc+v0*rcint/(2*f0));                                           30
wright = 0.5*(u0*rc-v0*rcint/(2*f0));                                          31
                                                                               32
%%%%%% start main loop                                                         33
                                                                               34
for n=3:NF                                                                     35
   temp1 = wright(N); temp2 = wleft(1);                                        36
   wright(2:N) = wright(1:N-1); wleft(1:N-1) = wleft(2:N);                     37
   wright(1) = -temp2; wleft(N) = -temp1;                                      38
   % readout                                                                   
   out(n) = (1-rp_frac)*(wleft(rp_int)+wright(rp_int))...                      39
     +rp_frac*(wleft(rp_int+1)+wright(rp_int+1));                             40
end                                                                           41
                                                                               42
%%%%%% end main loop                                                           43
                                                                               44
% plot output waveform                                                         45
                                                                               46
plot([0:NF-1]*k, out, 'k');                                                    47
xlabel('t'); ylabel('u');                                                      48
                                                                               49
title('1D Wave Equation: Digital Waveguide Synthesis Output');                 49
axis tight                                                                     50
                                                                               51
% play sound

soundsc(out,SR);
```

A.6   The 1D wave equation: modal synthesis

```
% matlab script waveeq1dmod.m
% modal synthesis method for the 1D wave equation
% fixed boundary conditions
% raised cosine initial conditions


%%%%%% begin global parameters

SR = 44100;                        % sample rate (Hz)
f0 = 441;                          % fundamental frequency (Hz)
TF = 1;                            % duration of simulation (s)
ctr = 0.7; wid = 0.1;              % center location/width of excitation
u0 = 1; v0 = 0;                    % maximum initial displacement/velocity
rp = 0.3;                          % position of readout (0-1)

%%%%%% end global parameters

% begin derived parameters/temporary storage

k = 1/SR;                          % time step
NF = floor(SR*TF);                 % duration of simulation (samples)
N = floor(0.5*SR/f0);              % number of modes
temp = 2*pi*[1:N]'*f0/SR; coeff = 2*cos(temp); outexp = sin([1:N]*pi*rp);

% initialize grid functions and output

U = zeros(N,1); U1 = zeros(N,1); U2 = zeros(N,1);
out2 = zeros(NF,1);

% create raised cosine and find Fourier coefficients

xax = [0:N-1]'/N;
ind = sign(max(-(xax-ctr-wid/2).*(xax-ctr+wid/2),0));
rc = 0.5*ind.*(1+cos(2*pi*(xax-ctr)/wid));
rcfs = -imag(fft([rc; zeros(N,1)])); rcfs = 2*rcfs(2:N+1)/N;

% set initial conditions

U2(1:N) = u0*rcfs;
U1(1:N) = (u0*cos(temp)+v0*sin(temp)./(2*pi*[1:N]'*f0)).*rcfs;

%%%%%% start main loop

for n=3:NF
    U = -U2+coeff.*U1;             % scheme calculation
    out(n) = outexp*U;             % readout
    U2 = U1; U1 = U;               % update of modal weights
end

%%%%%% end main loop

% plot output waveform

plot([0:NF-1]*k, out, 'k');
xlabel('t'); ylabel('u'); title('1D Wave Equation: Modal Synthesis Output');
axis tight
```

```
% play sound
```
```
soundsc(out,SR);
```

A.7   The ideal bar

```
% matlab script idealbarfd.m
% finite difference scheme for the ideal bar equation
% clamped/pivoting boundary conditions
% raised cosine initial conditions


%%%%%% begin global parameters

SR = 44100;                     % sample rate (Hz)
K = 10;                         % stiffness parameter
TF = 1;                         % duration of simulation (s)
ctr = 0.7; wid = 0.1;           % center location/width of excitation
u0 = 1; v0 = 0;                 % maximum initial displacement/velocity
mu = 0.5;                       % scheme free parameter
rp = 0.85;                      % position of readout (0-1)
bc = [2 2];                     % boundary condition type,
                                  [left right] with
                                % 1: clamped, 2: pivoting

%%%%%% end global parameters

% begin derived parameters

k = 1/SR;                       % time step
NF = floor(SR*TF);              % duration of simulation (samples)

% stability condition/scheme parameters

h = sqrt(K*k/mu); N = floor(1/h); h = 1/N; mu = K*k/h^2;
s0 = 2*(1-3*mu^2); s1 = 4*mu^2; s2 = -mu^2;

% readout interpolation parameters

rp_int = 1+floor(N*rp);         % rounded grid index for readout
rp_frac = 1+rp/h-rp_int;        % fractional part of readout location

% create raised cosine

xax = [0:N]'*h;
ind = sign(max(-(xax-ctr-wid/2).*(xax-ctr+wid/2),0));
rc = 0.5*ind.*(1+cos(2*pi*(xax-ctr)/wid));

% initialize grid functions and output

u2 = u0*rc; u1 = (u0+k*v0)*rc; u = zeros(N+1,1); out = zeros(NF,1);

%%%%%% start main loop

for n=3:NF
    % scheme calculation (interior)
    u(3:N-1) = -u2(3:N-1)+s0*u1(3:N-1)+s1*(u1(2:N-2)+u1(4:N))...
```

```
      +s2*(u1(1:N-3)+u1(5:N+1));
    % calculations at boundary points
    if(bc(1)==2)
        u(2)  = -u2(2)+(s0-s2)*u1(2)+s1*u1(3)+s2*u1(4);
    end
    if(bc(2)==2)
        u(N)  = -u2(N)+(s0-s2)*u1(N)+s1*u1(N-1)+s2*u1(N-2);
    end
    out(n) = (1-rp_frac)*u(rp_int)+rp_frac*u(rp_int+1);      % readout
    u2 = u1; u1 = u;                                         % update
end

%%%%% end main loop

% plot output waveform

plot([0:NF-1]*k, out, 'k');
xlabel('t'); ylabel('u'); title('Ideal Bar Equation: FD Output');
axis tight

% play sound

soundsc(out,SR);
```

A.8   The stiff string

```
% matlab script ssfd.m
% finite difference scheme for the stiff string
% clamped boundary conditions
% raised cosine initial conditions
% stereo output
% implicit scheme: matrix update form
% two-parameter frequency-dependent loss

%%%%%% begin global parameters

SR = 44100;                      % sample rate(Hz)
B = 0.001;                       % inharmonicity parameter (>0)
f0 = 100;                        % fundamental(Hz)
TF = 2;                          % duration of simulation(s)
ctr = 0.1; wid = 0.05;           % center location/width of excitation
u0 = 1; v0 = 0;                  % maximum initial displacement/velocity
rp = [0.3 0.7];                  % positions of readout(0-1)
loss = [100, 10; 1000, 8];       % loss [freq.(Hz), T60(s), freq.(Hz), T60(s)]
theta = 1.0;                     % implicit scheme free parameter (>0.5)

%%%%%% end global parameters

% begin derived parameters

k = 1/SR;                        % time step
NF = floor(SR*TF);               % duration of simulation (samples)
gamma = 2*f0; K = sqrt(B)*(gamma/pi); % set parameters

% stability conditions
```

1
2
3
4
5
6
7
8
9
10
11
12
13
14
15
16
17
18
19
20
21
22
23
24
25
26
27
28
29
30
31
32
33
34
35
36
37
38
39
40
41
42
43
44
45
46
47
48
49
50
51

```
h = sqrt((gamma^2*k^2+sqrt(gamma^4*k^4+16*K^2*k^2*(2*theta-1)))/          1
    (2*(2*theta-1)));                                                     2
N = floor(1/h); h = 1/N; mu = K*k/h^2; lambda = gamma*k/h;               3
                                                                          4
% readout interpolation parameters                                        5
                                                                          6
rp_int = 1+floor(N*rp);              % rounded grid index for readout      7
rp_frac = 1+rp/h-rp_int;             % fractional part of readout location  8
                                                                          9
% set scheme loss parameters                                             10
                                                                         11
zeta1 = (-gamma^2+sqrt(gamma^4+4*K^2*(2*pi*loss(1,1))^2))/(2*K^2);       11
zeta2 = (-gamma^2+sqrt(gamma^4+4*K^2*(2*pi*loss(2,1))^2))/(2*K^2);       12
sig0 = 6*log(10)*(-zeta2/loss(1,2)+zeta1/loss(2,2))/(zeta1-zeta2);       13
sig1 = 6*log(10)*(1/loss(1,2)-1/loss(2,2))/(zeta1-zeta2);                14
                                                                         15
% create update matrices                                                 16
                                                                         17
M = sparse(toeplitz([theta (1-theta)/2 zeros(1,N-3)]));                  18
A = M+sparse(toeplitz([sig1*k/(h^2)+sig0*k/2 -sig1*k/(2*h^2) zeros(1,N-3)]));  19
C = M+sparse(toeplitz([-sig1*k/(h^2)-sig0*k/2 sig1*k/(2*h^2) zeros(1,N-3)]));  20
B = 2*M+sparse(toeplitz([-2*lambda^2-6*mu^2 lambda^2+4*mu^2 -mu^2...     21
    zeros(1,N-4)]));                                                     22
                                                                         23
% create raised cosine                                                   24
                                                                         25
xax = [1:N-1]'*h;                                                        25
ind = sign(max(-(xax-ctr-wid/2).*(xax-ctr+wid/2),0));                    26
rc = 0.5*ind.*(1+cos(2*pi*(xax-ctr)/wid));                               27
                                                                         28
% set initial conditions                                                 29
                                                                         30
u2 = u0*rc; u1 = (u0+k*v0)*rc; u = zeros(N+1,1); out = zeros(NF,2);      31
                                                                         32
%%%%% start main loop                                                    33
                                                                         34
for n=3:NF                                                               35
    u = A\(B*u1-C*u2);                                                   35
    out(n,:) = (1-rp_frac).*u(rp_int)'+rp_frac.*u(rp_int+1)'; % readout  36
    u2 = u1; u1 = u;                                          % update   37
end                                                                      38
                                                                         39
%%%%% end main loop                                                      40
                                                                         41
% plot output waveform                                                   42
                                                                         43
subplot(2,1,1); plot([0:NF-1]*k, out(:,1), 'k');                        44
xlabel('t'); ylabel('u'); title('Stiff String Equation: FD Output (left)');   45
subplot(2,1,2); plot([0:NF-1]*k, out(:,2), 'k');                        46
xlabel('t'); ylabel('u'); title('Stiff String Equation: FD Output (right)');  47
axis tight                                                               48
                                                                         49
% play sound                                                             50
                                                                         51
soundsc(out,SR);                                                         51
```

A.9   The Kirchhoff–Carrier equation

```
% matlab script kcfd.m
% finite difference scheme for the Kirchhoff-Carrier equation
% fixed boundary conditions
% triangular initial conditions


%%%%%% begin global parameters

SR = 44100;                          % sample rate (Hz)
f0 = 200;                            % fundamental frequency (Hz)
alpha = 10;                          % nonlinear string parameter
TF = 0.03;                           % duration of simulation (s)
ctr = 0.5;                           % center location of
                                     %   excitation (0-1)
u0 = 0.05;                           % maximum initial displacement
rp = 0.5;                            % position of readout (0-1)
lambda = 0.7;                        % Courant number


%%%%%% end global parameters

% begin derived parameters

gamma = 2*f0;                        % wave equation free parameter
k = 1/SR;                            % time step
NF = floor(SR*TF);                   % duration of simulation (samples)


% stability condition

h = gamma*k/lambda; N = floor(1/h); h = 1/N; lambda = gamma*k/h;

% readout interpolation parameters

rp_int = 1+floor(N*rp);              % rounded grid index for readout
rp_frac = 1+rp/h-rp_int;             % fractional part of readout location

% create triangular function

xax = [0:N]'*h;
tri = min(xax/ctr-1,0)+1+min((1-xax)/(1-ctr)-1,0);

% initialize grid functions and output

u2 = u0*tri; u1 = u2; u = zeros(N+1,1); out = zeros(NF,1);

%%%%%% start main loop

for n=1:NF
    % calculate nonlinearity g
    u1x = (u1(2:N+1)-u1(1:N))/h; u1xx = (u1x(2:N)-u1x(1:N-1))/h;
    g = (1+0.5*alpha^2*h*sum(u1x.*u1x))/...
(1+0.25*alpha^2*k^2*gamma^2*h*sum(u1xx.*u1xx));
    % scheme update
    u(2:N) = 2*u1(2:N)-u2(2:N)+g*gamma^2*k^2*u1xx(1:N-1);     % calculation
    out(n) = (1-rp_frac)*u(rp_int)+rp_frac*u(rp_int+1);      % readout
```

```
    u2 = u1; u1 = u;                                        % update          1
end                                                                           2
                                                                              3
%%%%% end main loop                                                           4
                                                                              5
% plot output waveform                                                        6
                                                                              7
plot([0:NF-1]*k, out, 'k');                                                   8
xlabel('t'); ylabel('u'); title('Kirchhoff-Carrier Equation: FD Output');     9
axis tight                                                                     10
```

A.10   Vocal synthesis

```
% matlab script vocalfd.m
% finite difference vocal tract simulation
% radiation loss included
% simple glottal source waveform
% static pitch

%%%%%% begin global parameters

SR = 44100;                  % sample rate (Hz)
L = 0.17;                    % tract length (m)
S0 = 0.00025;               % vocal tract surface area, left end (m^2)
c = 340;                     % wave speed (m/s)
f0 = 120;                    % fundamental frequency (Hz)
TF = 1;                      % simulation duration (s)
% vocal tract profile, non-dimensional [pos S] pairs
    % /E/
      S = [0 1;0.09 0.4;0.11 2.4;0.24 2.4;0.26 3.2;0.29 3.2;0.32 4.2;...
      0.41 4.2;0.47 3.2;0.59 1.8;0.65 1.6;0.71 1.6;0.74 1;0.76 0.8;...
      0.82 0.8;0.88 2;0.91 2;0.94 3.2;1 3.2];
    % /A/
    % S = [0 1;0.03 0.60;0.09 0.4;0.12 1.6;0.18 0.6;0.29 0.2;0.35 0.4;...
    % 0.41 0.8;0.47 1;0.50 0.6;0.59 2;0.65 3.2;0.85 3.2;0.94 2;1 2];

%%%%% end global parameters

% begin derived parameters

k = 1/SR;                          % time step
NF = floor(TF*SR);                 % sample duration
gamma = c/L;

% stability condition/scheme parameters

h = gamma*k; N = floor(1/h); h = 1/N; lambda = gamma*k/h;
S = interp1(S(:,1),S(:,2),[0:h:1])';        % interpolate vocal tract profile
alf = 2.0881*L*sqrt(1/(S0*S(N+1)));         % radiation parameter
bet = 0.7407/gamma;                         % radiation parameter
Sav = [S(1); 0.25*(S(3:N+1)+2*S(2:N)+S(1:N-1)); S(N+1)];
Sr = 1.5*S(N+1)-0.5*S(N);
sr = 0.5*lambda^2*((S(2:N)+S(3:N+1))./Sav(2:N));
sl = 0.5*lambda^2*((S(2:N)+S(1:N-1))./Sav(2:N));
s0 = 2*(1-lambda^2);
```

```
1
2
3
4
5
6
7
8
9
10
11
12
13
14
15
16
17
18
19
20
21
22
23
24
25
26
27
28
29
30
31
32
33
34
35
36
37
38
39
40
41
42
43
44
45
46
47
48
49
50
51
```

```
q1 = alf*gamma^2*k^2*Sr/(Sav(N+1)*h); q2 = bet*gamma^2*k*Sr/(Sav(N+1)*h);
r1 = 2*lambda^2/(1+q1+q2); r2 = -(1+q1-q2)/(1+q1+q2);
g1 = -(k^2*gamma^2/h/S(1))*(3*S(1)-S(2));

% initialize grid functions and output, generate glottal waveform

Psi = zeros(N+1,1); Psi1 = zeros(N+1,1); Psi2 = zeros(N+1,1);
uin = sin(2*pi*[0:NF-1]*k*f0); uin = 0.5*(uin+abs(uin));
out = zeros(NF,1);

%%%%%% begin main loop

for n=1:NF;
    Psi(2:N) = s0*Psi1(2:N)+sl.*Psi1(1:N-1)+sr.*Psi1(3:N+1)-Psi2(2:N);
    Psi(N+1) = r1*Psi1(N)+r2*Psi2(N+1);
    Psi(1) = s0*Psi1(1)+2*lambda^2*Psi1(2)-Psi2(1)+g1*uin(n);
    out(n) = SR*(Psi(N+1)-Psi1(N+1));
    Psi2 = Psi1; Psi1 = Psi;
end

%%%%%% end main loop

% plot vocal tract profile and output spectrum

subplot(2,1,1); plot([0:h:1], sqrt(S),'k', [0:h:1], -sqrt(S),'k')
title('Vocal Tract Profile'); xlabel('x'); ylabel('sqrt(S)');
subplot(2,1,2); plot([0:NF-1]*SR/NF, 10*log10(abs(fft(out))), 'k');
title('Output Spectrum'); xlabel('f');ylabel('pressure (dB)');

% play sound

soundsc(out, SR);
```

A.11   The 2D wave equation

```
% matlab script waveeq2dloss.m
% finite difference scheme for the 2D wave equation with loss
% fixed boundary conditions
% raised cosine initial conditions
% bilinear interpolation

%%%%%% begin global parameters

SR = 16000;                    % sample rate(Hz)
gamma = 200                    % wave speed (1/s)
T60 = 8;                       % 60 dB decay time (s)
epsilon = 1.3;                 % domain aspect ratio
TF = 2;                        % duration of simulation(s)
ctr = [0.3 0.5]; wid = 0.15;   % center location/width of excitation
u0 = 0; v0 = 1;                % maximum initial displacement/velocity
rp = [0.5 0.6];                % position of readout([0-1,0-1])
lambda = 1/sqrt(2);            % Courant number

%%%%%% end global parameters
```

```
% begin derived parameters                                                    1
                                                                              2
k = 1/SR;                            % time step                             3
NF = floor(SR*TF);                   % duration of simulation (samples)      4
sig0 = 6*log(10)/T60;                % loss parameter                        5
                                                                              6
% stability condition/scheme parameters                                       7
                                                                              8
h = gamma*k/lambda;                  % find grid spacing                     9
Nx = floor(sqrt(epsilon)/h);         % number of x-subdivisions of          10
                                       spatial domain                        11
Ny = floor(1/(sqrt(epsilon)*h));     % number of y-subdivisions of          12
                                       spatial domain                        13
h = sqrt(epsilon)/Nx; lambda = gamma*k/h;  % reset Courant number           14
s0 = (2-4*lambda^2)/(1+sig0*k); s1 = lambda^2/(1+sig0*k);                   15
t0 = -(1-sig0*k)/(1+sig0*k);                                                16
                                                                             17
% readout interpolation parameters                                           18
                                                                             19
rp_int = 1+floor([Nx Ny].*rp); rp_frac = 1+rp/h-rp_int;                     20
                                                                             21
% create 2D raised cosine                                                    22
                                                                             23
[X, Y] = meshgrid([0:Nx]*h, [0:Ny]*h); dist = sqrt((X-ctr(1)).^2            24
        +(Y-ctr(2)).^2);                                                     25
ind = sign(max(-dist+wid/2,0)); rc = 0.5*ind'.*(1+cos(2*pi*dist'/wid));      26
                                                                             27
% set initial conditions                                                     28
                                                                             29
u2 = u0*rc; u1 = (u0+k*v0)*rc; u = zeros(Nx+1,Ny+1); out = zeros(NF,2);      30
                                                                             31
%%%%%% start main loop                                                       32
                                                                             33
for n=3:NF                                                                   34
    u(2:Nx,2:Ny) = s1*(u1(3:Nx+1,2:Ny)+u1(1:Nx-1,2:Ny)+u1(2:Nx,3:Ny+1)+... 35
        u1(2:Nx,1:Ny-1))+s0*u1(2:Nx,2:Ny)+t0*u2(2:Nx,2:Ny);                 36
    out(n,:) = (1-rp_frac(1))*(1-rp_frac(2))*u(rp_int(1),rp_int(2))+...     37
        (1-rp_frac(1))*rp_frac(2)*u(rp_int(1),rp_int(2)+1)+...              38
        rp_frac(1)*(1-rp_frac(2))*u(rp_int(1)+1,rp_int(2))+...             39
        rp_frac(1)*rp_frac(2)*u(rp_int(1)+1,rp_int(2)+1);                  40
    u2 = u1; u1 = u;                                                        41
end                                                                         42
                                                                            43
%%%%% end main loop                                                         44
                                                                            45
% plot output waveform                                                      46
                                                                            47
plot([0:NF-1]*k, out, 'k'); xlabel('t'); ylabel('u');                      48
title('2D Wave Equation with Loss: FD Output'); axis tight                 49
                                                                            50
% play sound                                                               51
                                                                           
soundsc(out,SR);
```

A.12   Thin plate

```
% matlab script plateloss.m
% finite difference scheme for the thin plate equation with loss
% simply supported boundary conditions
% raised cosine initial conditions
% vector/matrix update form
% zeroth-order interpolation


%%%%%% begin global parameters


SR = 44100;                     % sample rate(Hz)
K = 20;                         % plate stiffness parameter (1/s)
T60 = 8;                        % 60 dB decay time (s)
epsilon = 1.2;                  % domain aspect ratio
TF = 2;                         % duration of simulation(s)
ctr = [0.8 0.9]; wid = 0.3;     % center location/width of excitation
u0 = 0; v0 = 1;                 % maximum initial displacement/velocity
rp = [0.05 0.7];                % position of readout([0-1,0-1])
mu = 0.25;                      % scheme free parameter


%%%%%% end global parameters


% begin derived parameters


k = 1/SR;                       % time step
NF = floor(SR*TF);              % duration of simulation (samples)
sig0 = 6*log(10)/T60;           % loss parameter


% stability condition/scheme parameters


h = sqrt(K*k/mu);               % find grid spacing
Nx = floor(sqrt(epsilon)/h);    % number of x-subdivisions of spatial domain
Ny = floor(1/(sqrt(epsilon)*h)); % number of y-subdivisions of spatial domain
h = sqrt(epsilon)/Nx;
ss = (Nx-1)*(Ny-1);             % total grid size


% generate difference matrix/scheme matrices


Dxx = sparse(toeplitz([-2/h^2;1/h^2;zeros(Nx-3,1)]));
Dyy = sparse(toeplitz([-2/h^2;1/h^2;zeros(Ny-3,1)]));
D = kron(eye(Nx-1), Dyy)+kron(Dxx, eye(Ny-1)); DD = D*D;
B = sparse((2*eye(ss)-K^2*k^2*DD)/(1+sig0*k));
C = ((1-sig0*k)/(1+sig0*k))*sparse(eye(ss));


% readout interpolation parameters


rp_index = (Ny-1)*floor(rp(1)*Nx)+floor(rp(2)*Ny);


% create 2D raised cosine


[X, Y] = meshgrid([1:Nx-1]*h, [1:Ny-1]*h);
dist = sqrt((X-ctr(1)*sqrt(epsilon)).^2+(Y-ctr(2)/sqrt(epsilon)).^2);
ind = sign(max(-dist+wid/2,0)); rc = 0.5*ind.*(1+cos(2*pi*dist/wid));
rc = reshape(rc, ss,1);
```

```
% set initial conditions/initialize output

u2 = u0*rc; u1 = (u0+k*v0)*rc; u = zeros(ss,1);out = zeros(NF,1);

%%%%%% start main loop

for n=3:NF
    u = B*u1-C*u2;
    u2 = u1; u1 = u;
    out(n) = u(rp_index);
end

%%%%%% end main loop

% plot output waveform

plot([0:NF-1]*k, out, 'k'); xlabel('t'); ylabel('u');
title('Thin Plate Equation with Loss: FD Output'); axis tight

% play sound

soundsc(out,SR);
```

Appendix B

List of symbols

Symbol	Meaning	Principal instance
A	string/bar cross-sectional area (m^2)	118
$\mathfrak{b}$	boundary term (discrete)	137
$\mathfrak{B}$	boundary term (continuous)	125
c	wave speed (m/s)	118
c_{rc}	raised cosine distribution	121
c_{tri}	triangular distribution	121
D	plate flexural rigidity $= EH^3/12(1-\nu^2)$	331
$\mathbf{D}_\bullet$	spatial differentiation matrix (various)	107
$\mathcal{D}$	spatial domain (continuous or discrete)	94
$\underline{\mathcal{D}}$	discrete 1D spatial domain without right endpoint	110
$\overline{\mathcal{D}}$	discrete 1D spatial domain without left endpoint	110
e_{t+}, e_{t-}	forward and backward time shift operators	27
e_{d+}, e_{d-}	forward and backward shift operators in spatial coordinate d	100
E	Young's modulus (kg/s^2 m)	118
f	frequency (1/s)	31
f_s	sample rate (1/s)	26
f_0	fundamental frequency (1/s)	46
F	force/mass (m/s^2)	67
h	grid spacing	98
h_r, h_θ	grid spacings, radial coordinates	299
$\mathfrak{h}$	total system energy (discrete)	53
H	plate thickness (m)	331
$\mathfrak{H}$	total system energy (continuous)	48
I_p	pth-order interpolation operator	102
I	bar moment of inertia	163
$\mathbf{I}$	identity matrix	142
$\mathcal{I}_{h^{(1)} \rightarrow h^{(2)}, p}$	pth-order upsampling grid interpolant	103
$\mathcal{I}^*_{h^{(2)} \rightarrow h^{(1)}, p}$	pth-order conjugate downsampling grid interpolant	104

Numerical Sound Synthesis: Finite Difference Schemes and Simulation in Musical Acoustics   Stefan Bilbao
© 2009 John Wiley & Sons, Ltd

j	$\sqrt{-1}$	31	1
J_p	pth-order spreading operator	103	2
k	time step (s)	26	3
K	stiffness (kg/s^2)	46	4
l	spatial index to grid function	98	5
L	characteristic length (m)	120	6
m	spatial index to grid function	291	7
M	mass (kg)	46	8
$\mathcal{M}$	mass ratio	80	9
$\mathbf{M_{\bullet}}$	averaging matrix (various)	107	10
n	time index	26	11
N_m	degrees of freedom (modal)	130	12
N_{fd}	degrees of freedom (difference scheme)	133	13
O	big oh, order of	30	14
$\mathfrak{Q}$	loss term (continuous)	126	15
r	radial coordinate (non-dimensional unless otherwise indicated)	288	16
$\mathbb{R}$	set of real numbers $[-\infty, \infty]$	94	17
$\mathbb{R}^+$	set of non-negative real numbers $[0, \infty]$	94	18
$\mathbb{R}^2$	set of pairs of real numbers (x, y)	288	19
$\mathbb{R}^{2,x+}$	half plane: set of pairs of real numbers (x, y), with $x \geq 0$	289	20
$\mathbb{R}^{2,x+y+}$	quarter plane: set of pairs of real numbers (x, y), with $x, y \geq 0$	289	21
s	complex frequency variable (1/s)	31	22
S	tube cross-sectional area (non-dimensional unless otherwise indicated)	251	23, 24
t	time variable (s)	26	25
$\mathfrak{t}$	kinetic energy (discrete)	53	26
$\mathfrak{T}$	kinetic energy (continuous)	48	27
T_0	nominal string tension (kg m/s^2)	118	28
T_{60}	60 dB decay time (s)	65	29
$T_{d,60}$	numerical 60 dB decay time (s)	66	30
u	dependent variable, time series, or grid function	26	31
$\hat{u}$	Laplace or Fourier transform of time series, dependent variable, or grid function u	31	32, 33
$\tilde{u}$	spatial Fourier transform of dependent variable or grid function u	96	34
$u^{(+)}, u^{(-)}$	traveling wave components	123	35
U	modal function	128	36
$\mathbb{U}$	spatial unit interval $[0,1]$	94	37
$\mathbb{U}_{\circ}^2$	unit circle	289	38
$\mathbb{U}_{\epsilon}^2$	unit area rectangle of aspect ratio ϵ	289	39
$\mathbb{U}_N$	discrete $(N+1)$-point spatial unit interval $[0, \ldots, N]$	98	40
$\mathbb{U}_{N_x,N_y}^2$	discrete rectangular region $[0, \ldots, N_x] \times [0, \ldots, N_y]$	291	41
$\mathbb{U}_{\circ,N_r,N_\theta}^2$	discrete circular region $[0, \ldots, N_r] \times [0, \ldots, N_\theta - 1]$	299	42, 43
v_g	group velocity	97	44
v_ϕ	phase velocity	97	45
$\mathfrak{v}$	potential energy (discrete)	53	46
$\mathfrak{V}$	potential energy (continuous)	48	47
x	spatial independent variable (non-dimensional unless otherwise indicated)	93	48, 49

y	spatial independent variable (non-dimensional unless otherwise indicated)	288	1
			2
z	complex frequency variable	32	3
$\mathbb{Z}$	set of all integers $[-\infty, \ldots, \infty]$	98	4
$\mathbb{Z}^+$	set of non-negative integers $[0, \ldots, \infty]$	98	5
$\mathbb{Z}^2$	set of pairs of integers, $\mathbb{Z} \times \mathbb{Z}$	291	6
β	1D wavenumber	96	7
β_p	2D wavenumber component, coordinate direction p	290	8
γ	wave speed (1/s, spatially non-dimensional)	120	9
$\delta_{t+}, \delta_{t-}, \delta_{t\cdot}$	forward, backward, and centered time difference operators	27	10
$\delta_{d+}, \delta_{d-}, \delta_{d\cdot}$	forward, backward, and centered difference operators in coordinate d		11
		100	12
δ_{tt}	second time difference operator, $= \delta_{t+}\delta_{t-}$	28	13
δ_{dd}	second difference operator in coordinate d, $= \delta_{d+}\delta_{d-}$	100	14
δ_{dddd}	fourth difference operator in coordinate d, $= \delta_{dd}\delta_{dd}$	100	15
$\delta_{\Delta\boxplus}$	five-point adjacent Laplacian difference operator	293	16
$\delta_{\Delta\boxtimes}$	five-point diagonally adjacent Laplacian difference operator	293	17
$\delta_{\Delta\alpha}$	nine-point parameterized Laplacian difference operator	293	18
$\delta_{\Delta\boxplus,\Delta\boxplus}$	biharmonic difference operator	293	19
$\delta_{\Delta\circ}$	discrete Laplacian, radial coordinates	300	20
$\delta_{\Delta\circ,\Delta\circ}$	discrete biharmonic operator, radial coordinates	300	21
$\delta(\cdot)$	Dirac delta function	180	22
Δ	Laplacian operator	289	23
$\Delta\Delta$	biharmonic operator	289	24
ϵ	aspect ratio, rectangular domain	289	25
θ	angular coordinate (rad)	288	26
θ	implicit scheme free parameter	150	27
κ	stiffness parameter, bars (plates)	164 (332)	28
λ	Courant number, for the wave equation	131	29
μ	difference scheme free parameter, bars (plates)	169 (337)	30
$\mu_{t+}, \mu_{t-}, \mu_{t\cdot}$	forward, backward, and centered time-averaging operators	27	31
$\mu_{d+}, \mu_{d-}, \mu_{d\cdot}$	forward, backward, and centered averaging operators in spatial coordinate d		32
		100	33
μ_{tt}	centered averaging operator, $= \mu_{t+}\mu_{t-}$	29	34
μ_{dd}	centered averaging operator in spatial coordinate d, $= \mu_{d+}\mu_{d-}$	100	35
ν	Poisson's ratio	331	36
ρ	material density (kg/m^3)	118	37
σ	loss (1/s)	31	38
σ_0	frequency-independent loss parameter (1/s)	63	39
σ_1	frequency-dependent loss parameter (1/s)	178	40
ω	angular frequency (rad/s)	31	41
ω_0	fundamental or oscillator angular frequency (rad/s)	46	42
1	one, or identity operation	27	43
			44
			45
			46
			47
			48
			49
			50
			51

Bibliography

[1] J. Abel, D. Berners, S. Costello, and J. O. Smith III. Spring reverb emulation using dispersive all-pass filters in a waveguide structure. Presented at the 121st Audio Engineering Society Convention, San Francisco, California, October, 2006. Preprint 6954.

[2] J. Abel, T. Smyth, and J. O. Smith III. A simple, accurate wall loss filter for acoustic tubes. In *Proceedings of the 6th International Digital Audio Effects Conference*, pages 254–258, London, UK, September 2003.

[3] S. Adachi and M. Sato. Time-domain simulation of sound production in the brass instrument. *Journal of the Acoustical Society of America*, 97(6):3850–3861, 1995.

[4] J.-M. Adrien. The missing link: Modal synthesis. In G. DePoli, A. Picialli, and C. Roads, editors, *Representations of Musical Signals*, pages 269–297. MIT Press, Cambridge, Massachusetts, 1991.

[5] J.-M. Adrien and X. Rodet. Physical models of instruments, a modular approach, application to strings. In *Proceedings of the International Computer Music Conference*, pages 85–89, Vancouver, Canada, September, 1985.

[6] A. Almeida, C. Vergez, and R. Caussé. Quasi-static non-linear characteristics of double-reed instruments. *Journal of the Acoustical Society of America*, 121(1):536–546, 2007.

[7] A. Almeida, C. Vergez, R. Caussé, and X. Rodet. Physical study of double-reed instruments for application to sound synthesis. In *Proceedings of the International Symposium on Musical Acoustics*, pages 221–226, Cancun, Mexico, December 2002.

[8] W. Ames. *Numerical Methods for Partial Differential Equations*. Thomas Nelson and Sons, London, UK, 1969.

[9] G. Anand. Large-amplitude damped free vibration of a stretched string. *Journal of the Acoustical Society of America*, 45(5):1089–1096, 1969.

[10] M. Aramaki. *Analyse-synthèse de sons impulsifs: Approches physiques et perceptives*. PhD thesis, Universite de la Mediterrannée-Aix Marseille II, 2002.

[11] M. Aramaki and R. Kronland-Martinet. Analysis-synthesis of impact sounds by real-time dynamic filtering. *IEEE Transactions on Audio Speech and Language Processing*, 14(2):695–705, 2006.

[12] K. Arcas. *Simulation numérique d'un réverbérateur à plaque*. PhD thesis, Ecole Nationale Supérieure de Techniques Avancées, Palaiseau, France, 2008.

[13] D. Arfib. Digital synthesis of complex spectra by means of multiplication of nonlinear distorted sine waves. *Journal of the Audio Engineering Society*, 27(10):757–768, 1979.

[14] M. Atig, J.-P. Dalmont, and J. Gilbert. Termination impedance of open-ended cylindrical tubes at high sound pressure level. *Comptes Rendus Mécanique*, 332:299–304, 2004.

[15] F. Avanzini and D. Rocchesso. Efficiency, accuracy, and stability issues in discrete time simulations of single reed instruments. *Journal of the Acoustical Society of America*, 111(5):2293–2301, 2002.

[16] F. Avanzini and M. van Walstijn. Modeling the mechanical response of the reed-mouthpiece-lip system of a clarinet. Part I. A one-dimensional distributed model. *Acta Acustica united with Acustica*, 90(3):537–547, 2004.

[17] J. Backus. Small vibration theory of the clarinet. *Journal of the Acoustical Society of America*, 35:305–313, 1963.

[18] J. Backus. Multiphonic tones in the woodwind instruments. *Journal of the Acoustical Society of America*, 63(2):591–599, 1978.

[19] R. Bacon and J. Bowsher. A discrete model of a struck string. *Acustica*, 41:21–27, 1978.

[20] R. Bader. *Computational Mechanics of the Classical Guitar*. Springer-Verlag, Berlin Heidelberg, 2005.

[21] B. Bank. *Physics-based Sound Synthesis of String Instruments Including Geometric Nonlinearities*. PhD thesis, Budapest University of Technology and Economics, 2006.

[22] B. Bank and L. Sujbert. Modeling the longitudinal vibration of piano strings. In *Proceedings of the Stockholm Musical Acoustics Conference*, pages 143–146, Stockholm, Sweden, August 2003.

[23] B. Bank and L. Sujbert. A piano model including longitudinal string vibration. In *Proceedings of the 7th International Digital Audio Effects Conference*, pages 89–94, Naples, Italy, October 2004.

[24] B. Bank and L. Sujbert. Generation of longitudinal vibrations in piano strings: From physics to sound synthesis. *Journal of the Acoustical Society of America*, 117(4):2268–2278, 2005.

[25] A. Barjau, V. Gibiat, and N. Grand. Study of woodwind-like systems through nonlinear differential equations. Part I. Simple geometry. *Journal of the Acoustical Society of America*, 102(5):3023–3031, 1997.

[26] A. Barjau, D. Keefe, and S. Cardona. Time-domain simulation of acoustical waveguides with arbitrarily spaced discontinuities. *Journal of the Acoustical Society of America*, 105(3):1951–1964, 1999.

[27] E. Bavu, J. Smith, and J. Wolfe. Torsional waves in a bowed string. *Acta Acustica united with Acustica*, 91(2):241–246, 2005.

[28] M. Beeson and D. Murphy. Roomweaver: A digital waveguide mesh based room acoustics research tool. In *Proceedings of the 7th International Digital Audio Effects Conference*, pages 268–273, Naples, Italy, October 2004.

[29] V. Belevitch. Summary of the history of circuit theory. *Proceedings of the IRE*, 50:848–855, 1962.

[30] V. Belevitch. *Classical Network Theory*. Holden Day, San Francisco, California, 1968.

[31] A. Benade and E. Jansson. On the mathematical theory of woodwind finger holes. *Journal of the Acoustical Society of America*, 32(12):1591–1608, 1960.

[32] A. Benade and E. Jansson. On plane and spherical waves in horns with nonuniform flare I. Theory of radiation, resonance frequencies, and mode conversion. *Acustica*, 31(2):79–98, 1974.

[33] J. Bensa, S. Bilbao, R. Kronland-Martinet, and J. O. Smith III. The simulation of piano string vibration: From physical models to finite difference schemes and digital waveguides. *Journal of the Acoustical Society of America*, 114(2):1095–1107, 2003.

[34] J. Bensa, S. Bilbao, R. Kronland-Martinet, J.O. Smith III, and T. Voinier. Computational modeling of stiff piano strings using digital waveguides and finite differences. *Acta Acustica united with Acustica*, 91(2):289–298, 2005.

[35] J. Bensoam, R. Caussé, C. Vergez, N. Misdariis, and N. Ellis. Sound synthesis for three-dimensional objects: Dynamic contact between two arbitrary elastic bodies. In *Proceedings of the Stockholm Musical Acoustics Conference*, pages 369–372, Stockholm, Sweden, August 2003.

[36] J. Bensoam, N. Misdariis, C. Vergez, and R. Caussé. Musical application with Modalys sound synthesis program based in modal representation. In *Systemics, Cybernetics and Informatics*, Orlando, Florida, 2001.

[37] H. Berger. A new approach to the analysis of large deflections of plates. *Journal of Applied Mathematics*, 22:465–472, 1955.

[38] D. Berners. *Acoustics and Signal Processing Techniques for Physical Modelling of Brass Instruments*. PhD thesis, Department of Electrical Engineering, Stanford University, 1999.

[39] S. Bilbao. Energy-conserving finite difference schemes for tension-modulated strings. In *Proceedings of the IEEE International Conference on Acoustics, Speech, and Signal Processing*, volume 4, pages 285–288, Montreal, Canada, May 2004.

[40] S. Bilbao. Parameterized families of finite difference schemes for the wave equation. *Numerical Methods for Partial Differential Equations*, 20(3):463–480, 2004.

[41] S. Bilbao. *Wave and Scattering Methods for Numerical Simulation*. John Wiley and Sons, Chichester, UK, 2004.

[42] S. Bilbao. Conservative numerical methods for nonlinear strings. *Journal of the Acoustical Society of America*, 118(5):3316–3327, 2005.

[43] S. Bilbao. Fast modal synthesis by digital waveguide extraction. *IEEE Signal Processing Letters*, 13(1):1–4, 2006.

[44] S. Bilbao. A digital plate reverberation algorithm. *Journal of the Audio Engineering Society*, 55(3): 135–144, 2007.

[45] S. Bilbao. Direct simulation for wind instrument synthesis. In *Proceedings of the 11th International Digital Audio Effects Conference*, Espoo, Finland, September 2008.

[46] S. Bilbao. A family of conservative finite difference schemes for the dynamical von Karman plate equations. *Numerical Methods for Partial Differential Equations*, 24(1):193–216, 2008.

[47] S. Bilbao, K. Arcas, and A. Chaigne. A physical model of plate reverberation. In *Proceedings of the IEEE International Conference on Acoustics, Speech, and Signal Processing*, volume 5, pages 165–168, Toulouse, France, 2006.

[48] S. Bilbao, L. Savioja, and J. O. Smith III. Parameterized finite difference schemes for plates: Stability, the reduction of directional dispersion and frequency warping. *IEEE Transactions on Audio, Speech and Language Processing*, 15(4):1488–1495, 2007.

[49] S. Bilbao and J. O. Smith III. Finite difference schemes and digital waveguide networks for the wave equation: Stability, passivity and numerical dispersion. *IEEE Transactions on Speech and Audio Processing*, 11(3):255–266, 2003.

[50] S. Bilbao and J. O. Smith III. Energy-conserving finite difference schemes for nonlinear strings. *Acta Acustica united with Acustica*, 91(2):299–311, 2005.

[51] I. Bisnovatyi. Flexible software framework for modal synthesis. In *Proceedings of the 3rd International Digital Audio Effects Conference*, pages 109–114, Verona, Italy, December 2000.

[52] G. Borin, G. DePoli, and A. Sarti. Algorithms and structures for synthesis using physical models. *Computer Music Journal*, 16(4):30–42, 1992.

[53] G. Borin, G. DePoli, and A. Sarti. Musical signal synthesis. In C. Roads, S. Pope, A. Piccialli, and G. DePoli, editors, *Musical Signal Processing*, pages 5–30. Swets and Zeitlinger, Lisse, The Netherlands, 1997.

[54] G. Borin, G. De Poli, and D. Rochesso. Elimination of delay-free loops in discrete-time models of nonlinear acoustic systems. *IEEE Transactions on Speech and Audio Processing*, 8(5):597–605, 2000.

[55] I. Bosmans, P. Mees, and G. Vermeir. Structure-borne sound transmission between thin orthotropic plates: Analytical solutions. *Journal of Sound and Vibration*, 191(1):75–90, 1996.

[56] D. Botteldooren. Finite-difference time-domain simulation of low-frequency room acoustic problems. *Journal of the Acoustical Society of America*, 98(6):3302–3308, 1995.

[57] R. Boulanger, editor. *The csound Book: Perspectives in Software Synthesis, Sound Design, Signal Processing, and Programming*. MIT Press, Cambridge, Massachusetts, 2001.

[58] X. Boutillon. Model for piano hammers: Experimental determination and digital simulation. *Journal of the Acoustical Society of America*, 83(2):746–754, 1988.

[59] J. Boyd. *Chebyshev and Fourier Spectral Methods*. Courier Dover, second edition, 2001.

[60] C. Brebbia and R. Ciskowski, editors. *Boundary Element Methods in Acoustics*. Kluwer Academic Publishers, 1991.

[61] J. Bretos, C. Santamaria, and J. Moral. Tuning process of xylophone and marimba bars analyzed by finite element modeling and experimental measurements. *Journal of the Acoustical Society of America*, 102(6):3815–3816, 1997.

[62] J. Bretos, C. Santamaria, and J. Moral. Vibrational patterns and frequency responses of the free plates and box of a violin obtained by finite element analysis. *Journal of the Acoustical Society of America*, 105(3):1942–1950, 1999.

[63] A. Bruckstein and T. Kailath. An inverse scattering framework for several problems in signal processing. *IEEE ASSP Magazine*, 4(1):6–20, 1987.

[64] C. Bruyns. Modal synthesis for arbitrarily shaped objects. *Computer Music Journal*, 30(3):22–37, 2006.

[65] J. Butcher. *Numerical Methods for Ordinary Differential Equations*. John Wiley and Sons, second edition, 2008.

[66] C. Cadoz. Synthèse sonore par simulation de mécanismes vibratoires, 1979. Thèse de Docteur Ingénieur, I.N.P.G. Grenoble, France.

[67] C. Cadoz, A. Luciani, and J.-L. Florens. Responsive input devices and sound synthesis by simulation of instrumental mechanisms. *Computer Music Journal*, 8(3):60–73, 1983.

[68] C. Cadoz, A. Luciani, and J.-L. Florens. Cordis-anima: A modeling and simulation system for sound and image synthesis. *Computer Music Journal*, 17(1):19–29, 1993.

[69] J. Cage. *For The Birds: John Cage in Conversation with Daniel Charles*. Marion Boyers, London, UK, 1981.

[70] D. Campbell and C. Greated. *The Musician's Guide to Acoustics*. Oxford University Press, Oxford, UK, 1994.

[71] C. Canuto, M. Hussaini, A. Quarteroni, and T. Zang. *Spectral Methods in Fluid Dynamics*. Springer-Verlag, New York, New York, 1987.

[72] G. Carrier. On the nonlinear vibration problem of the elastic string. *Quarterly of Applied Mathematics*, 3:157–165, 1945.

[73] S. Cavaliere and A. Piccialli. Granular synthesis of musical signals. In C. Roads, S. Pope, A. Piccialli, and G. DePoli, editors, *Musical Signal Processing*, pages 155–186. Swets and Zeitlinger, Lisse, The Netherlands, 1997.

[74] A. Chaigne. On the use of finite differences for musical synthesis. Application to plucked stringed instruments. *Journal d'Acoustique*, 5(2):181–211, 1992.

[75] A. Chaigne and A. Askenfelt. Numerical simulations of struck strings. I. A physical model for a struck string using finite difference methods. *Journal of the Acoustical Society of America*, 95(2):1112–1118, 1994.

[76] A. Chaigne and A. Askenfelt. Numerical simulations of struck strings. II. Comparisons with measurements and systematic exploration of some hammer-string parameters. *Journal of the Acoustical Society of America*, 95(3):1631–40, 1994.

[77] A. Chaigne and V. Doutaut. Numerical simulations of xylophones. I. Time domain modeling of vibrating bars. *Journal of the Acoustical Society of America*, 101(1):539–557, 1997.

[78] A. Chaigne and J. Kergomard. *Acoustique des Instruments de Musique*. Belin, Paris, France, 2008.

[79] A. Chaigne and C. Lambourg. Time-domain simulation of damped impacted plates. I Theory and experiments. *Journal of the Acoustical Society of America*, 109(4):1422–1432, 2001.

[80] D. Cheng. *Field and Wave Electromagnetics*. Addison-Wesley, Reading, Massachusetts, second edition, 1989.

[81] C. Chien, S. Chang, and Z. Mei. Tracing the buckling of a rectangular plate with the block GMRES method. *Journal of Computational and Applied Mathematics*, 136(1–2):199–218, 2001.

[82] J. Chowning. The synthesis of complex audio spectra by means of frequency modulation. *Journal of the Audio Engineering Society*, 21(7):526–534, 1973.

[83] C. Christopoulos. *The Transmission-Line Modelling Method*. IEEE Press, New York, New York, 1995.

[84] G. Cohen and P. Joly. Construction and analysis of fourth-order finite difference schemes for the acoustic wave equation in non-homogeneous media. *SIAM Journal of Numerical Analysis*, 33(4):1266–1302, 1996.

[85] J. Coltman. Time-domain simulation of the flute. *Journal of the Acoustical Society of America*, 92(1): 69–73, 1992.

[86] H. Conklin. Design and tone in the mechanoacoustic piano. Part III. Piano strings and scale design. *Journal of the Acoustical Society of America*, 100(3):1286–1298, 1996.

[87] H. Conklin. Generation of partials due to nonlinear mixing in a stringed instrument. *Journal of the Acoustical Society of America*, 105(1):536–545, 1999.

[88] P. Cook. *Identification of Control Parameters in an Articulatory Vocal Tract Model with Applications to the Synthesis of Singing*. PhD thesis, Department of Electrical Engineering, Stanford University, 1990.

[89] P. Cook. Tbone: An interactive waveguide brass instrument synthesis workbench for the NeXT machine. In *Proceedings of the International Computer Music Conference*, pages 297–299, Montreal, Canada, 1991.

[90] P. Cook. Spasm: A real-time vocal tract physical model editor/controller and singer: The companion software synthesis system. *Computer Music Journal*, 17(1):30–44, 1992.

[91] P. Cook. *Real Sound Synthesis for Interactive Applications*. A. K. Peters, Natick, Massachusetts, 2002.

[92] P. Cook and G. Scavone. The synthesis tool kit. In *Proceedings of the International Computer Music Conference*, pages 164–166, Beijing, China, 1999.

[93] R. Cook, editor. *Concepts and applications of finite element analysis*. John Wiley and Sons, New York, New York, fourth edition, 2002.

[94] J. Cooley and J. Tukey. An algorithm for the machine computation of complex Fourier series. *Mathematical Computation*, 19:297–301, 1965.

[95] R. Courant, K. Friedrichs, and H. Lewy. Über die partiellen Differenzengleichungen de mathematischen Physik. *Mathematische Annalen*, 100:32–74, 1928.

[96] K. Cummings, J. Maloney, and M. Clements. Modelling speech production using Yee's finite difference method. In *Proceedings of the IEEE International Conference on Acoustics, Speech, and Signal Processing*, volume 1, pages 672–675, Detroit, Michigan, May 1995.

[97] A. da Silva, G. Scavone, and M. van Walstijn. Numerical simulations of fluid-structure interactions in single-reed mouthpieces. *Journal of the Acoustical Society of America*, 122(3):1798–1809, 2007.

[98] M. Dablain. The application of high-order differencing to the scalar wave equation. *Geophysics*, 51(1):54–66, 1986.

[99] G. Dahlquist. A special stability problem for linear multistep methods. *BIT*, 3:27–43, 1963.

[100] J.-P. Dalmont, J. Gilbert, and S. Ollivier. Nonlinear characteristics of single-reed instruments: Quasistatic volume flow and reed opening characteristics. *Journal of the Acoustical Society of America*, 114(4):2253–2262, 2003.

[101] P. Depalle and S. Tassart. State space sound synthesis and a state space synthesiser builder. In *Proceedings of the International Computer Music Conference*, pages 88–95, Banff, Canada, 1995.

[102] G. DePoli, A. Picialli, and C. Roads, editors. *Representations of Musical Signals*. MIT Press, Cambridge, Massachusetts, 1991.

[103] G. Derveaux, A. Chaigne, P. Joly, and E. Bécache. Time-domain simulation of a guitar: Model and method. *Journal of the Acoustical Society of America*, 114(6):3368–3383, 2003.

[104] B. Deutsch, C. Ramirez, and T. Moore. The dynamics and tuning of orchestral crotales. *Journal of the Acoustical Society of America*, 116(4):2427–2433, 2006.

[105] R. Dickey. Infinite systems of nonlinear oscillation equations related to the string. *Proceedings of the American Mathematics Society*, 23(3):459–468, 1969.

[106] R. Dickey. Stability of periodic solutions of the nonlinear string. *Quarterly of Applied Mathematics*, 38:253–259, 1980.

[107] C. Dodge and T. Jerse. *Computer Music: Synthesis, Composition and Performance*. Schirmer Books, New York, New York, 1985.

[108] M. Dolson. The phase vocoder: A tutorial. *Computer Music Journal*, 10(4):14–27, 1986.

[109] P. Doornbusch. Computer Sound Synthesis in 1951; The Music of CSIRAC. *Computer Music Journal*, 28(1):10–25, 2004.

[110] V. Doutaut, D. Matignon, and A. Chaigne. Numerical simulations of xylophones. II. Time domain modeling of the resonator and of the radiated sound pressure. *Journal of the Acoustical Society of America*, 104(3):1633–1647, 1998.

[111] V. Dubos, J. Kergomard, A. Khettabi, J.-P. Dalmont, D. Keefe, and C. Nederveen. Theory of sound propagation in a duct with a branched tube using modal decomposition. *Acta Acustica united with Acustica*, 85(2):153–169, 1999.

[112] E. Ducasse. A physical model of a single reed wind instrument, including actions of the player. *Computer Music Journal*, 27(1):59–70, 2003.

[113] G. Eckel, F. Iovino, and R. Caussé. Sound synthesis by physical modelling with Modalys. In *Proceedings of the International Symposium on Musical Acoustics*, pages 479–482, Dourdan, France, 1995.

[114] M. Elejabarrieta, A. Ezcurra, and C. Santamaria. Coupled modes of the resonance box of the guitar. *Journal of the Acoustical Society of America*, 111(5):2283–2292, 2002.

[115] W. Elmore and M. Heald. *Physics of Waves*. McGraw-Hill, New York, New York, 1969.

[116] C. Erkut. *Aspects in Analysis and Model-Based Sound Synthesis of Plucked String Instruments*. PhD thesis, Laboratory of Acoustics and Audio Signal Processing, Helsinki University of Technology, 2002.

[117] C. Erkut, M. Karjalainen, P. Huang, and V. Välimäki. Acoustical analysis and model-based sound synthesis of the kantele. *Journal of the Acoustical Society of America*, 112(4):1681–1691, 2002.

[118] G. Essl, S. Serafin, P. Cook, and J. O. Smith III. Musical applications of banded waveguides. *Computer Music Journal*, 28(1):51–63, 2004.

[119] G. Essl, S. Serafin, P. Cook, and J. O. Smith III. Theory of banded waveguides. *Computer Music Journal*, 28(1):37–50, 2004.

[120] G. Evangelista. Wavelet representations of musical signals. In C. Roads, S. Pope, A. Piccialli, and G. DePoli, editors, *Musical Signal Processing*, pages 127–153. Swets and Zeitlinger, Lisse, The Netherlands, 1997.

[121] G. Evans, J. Blackledge, and P. Yardley. *Numerical Methods for Partial Differential Equations*. Springer, London, UK, 1999.

[122] M. Facchinetti, X. Boutillon, and A. Constantinescu. Compliances of wood for violin top plates. *Journal of the Acoustical Society of America*, 113(5):2874–2883, 2003.

[123] G. Fant. *Acoustic theory of speech production, with calculations based on X-ray studies of Russian articulations. Description and analysis of contemporary standard Russian*. Mouton, The Hague, the Netherlands, second edition, 1970.

[124] G. Fant. *Speech Acoustics and Phonetics, Selected Writings*. Kluwer Academic Publishers—Springer, Boston, Massachusetts, 2004.

[125] S. Fels, J. Lloyd, I. Stavness, F. Vogt, A. Hannam, and E. Vatikiotis-Bateson. Artisynth: A 3d biome-chanical simulation toolkit for modeling anatomical structures. *Journal of the Society for Simulation in Healthcare*, 2(2):148, 2007.

[126] A. Fettweis. Digital filters related to classical structures. *AEU: Archive für Elektronik und Über-tragungstechnik*, 25:79–89, 1971. (See also U.S. Patent 3,967,099, 1976, now expired.).

[127] A. Fettweis. Wave digital filters: Theory and practice. *Proceedings of the IEEE*, 74(2):270–327, 1986.

[128] A. Fettweis. Discrete passive modelling of physical systems described by PDEs. In *Proceedings of EUSIPCO-92, Sixth European Signal Processing Conference*, volume 1, pages 55–62, Brussels, Belgium, August 1992.

[129] A. Fettweis. Discrete passive modelling of viscous fluids. In *Proceedings of the IEEE International Symposium on Circuits and Systems*, pages 1640–1643, San Diego, California, May 1992.

[130] A. Fettweis and K. Meerkötter. On adaptors for wave digital filters. *IEEE Transactions on Acoustics, Speech, and Signal Processing*, ASSP-23(6):516–525, 1975.

[131] A. Fettweis and G. Nitsche. Transformation approach to numerically integrating PDEs by means of WDF principles. *Multidimensional Systems and Signal Processing*, 2(2):127–159, 1991.

[132] H. Fischer. Wave digital filters for numerical integration. *ntz-Archiv*, 6:37–40, 1984.

[133] J. Flanagan. *Speech Analysis, Synthesis and Perception*. Springer-Verlag, New York, New York, second edition, 1972.

[134] J. Flanagan and R. Golden. The phase vocoder. *Bell System Technical Journal*, 45:1493–1509, 1966.

[135] H. Fletcher. Normal vibration frequencies of a stiff string. *Journal of the Acoustical Society of America*, 36(1):203–209, 1964.

[136] N. Fletcher and T. Rossing. *The Physics of Musical Instruments*. Springer-Verlag, New York, New York, 1991.

[137] N. Fletcher, T. Tarnopolskaya, and F. de Hoog. Wave propagation on helices and hyperhelices: A fractal regression. *Proceedings of the Royal Society*, 457:33–43, 2001.

[138] J.-L. Florens and C. Cadoz. The physical model: Modeling and simulating the instrument universe. In G. DePoli, A. Picialli, and C. Roads, editors, *Representations of Musical Signals*, pages 227–268. MIT Press, Cambridge, Massachusetts, 1991.

[139] F. Fontana and D. Rocchesso. Physical modelling of membranes for percussion instruments. *Acta Acustica united with Acustica*, 84(3):529–542, 1998.

[140] F. Fontana and D. Rocchesso. Signal-theoretic characterization of waveguide mesh geometries for models of two-dimensional wave propagation in elastic media. *IEEE Transactions on Speech and Audio Processing*, 9(2):152–61, 2001.

[141] B. Fornberg. *A Practical Guide to Pseudospectral Methods*. Cambridge Monographs on Applied and Computational Mathematics, Cambridge, UK, 1995.

[142] L. Franzoni, D. Bliss, and J. Rouse. An acoustic boundary element method based on energy and intensity variables for prediction of high-frequency broadband sound fields. *Journal of the Acoustical Society of America*, 110(6):3071–3080, 2001.

[143] D. Freedman. Analysis of musical instrument tones. *Journal of the Acoustical Society of America*, 41:793–806, 1967.

[144] F. Friedlander. On the oscillations of the bowed string. *Proceedings of the Cambridge Philosophical Society*, 49:516, 1953.

[145] D. Furihata. Finite difference schemes for nonlinear wave equation that inherit energy-conservation property. *Journal of Computational and Applied Mathematics*, 134(1–2):37–57, 2001.

[146] P. Garabedian. *Partial Differential Equations*. Chelsea Publishing Company, New York, New York, second edition, 1986.

[147] M. Garber. Computer modeling of a vibrating piano string. Master's thesis, Massachusetts Institute of Technology, 1982.

[148] Y. Genin. An algebraic approach to A-stable linear multistep-multiderivative integration formulas. *BIT*, 14(4):382–406, 1974.

[149] B. Geveci and D. Walker. Nonlinear resonance of rectangular plates. *Proceedings of the Royal Society A*, 457(2009):1215–1240, 2001.

[150] J. Gilbert, J. Kergomard, and J. Polack. On the reflection functions associated with discontinuities in conical bores. *Journal of the Acoustical Society of America*, 87(4):1773–1780, 1990.

[151] F. Gillan and S. Eliot. Measurement of the torsional modes of vibration of the strings on instruments of the violin family. *Journal of Sound and Vibration*, 130(2):347–351, 1989.

[152] N. Giordano. Simple model of a piano soundboard. *Journal of the Acoustical Society of America*, 102(2):1159–1168, 1997.

[153] N. Giordano. Sound production by a vibrating piano soundboard: Experiment. *Journal of the Acoustical Society of America*, 104(3):1648–1653, 1998.

[154] N. Giordano and M. Jiang. Physical modeling of the piano. *EURASIP Journal on Applied Signal Processing*, 2004(1):926–933, 2004.

[155] C. Gough. The nonlinear free vibration of a damped elastic string. *Journal of the Acoustical Society of America*, 75(6):1770–1776, 1984.

[156] K. Graff. *Wave Motion in Elastic Solids*. Dover, New York, New York, 1975.

[157] D. Greenspan. Conservative numerical methods for $\ddot{x} = f(x)$. *Journal of Computational Physics*, 56: 28–41, 1984.

[158] P. Guillemain. A digital synthesis model of double-reed wind instruments. *EURASIP Journal on Applied Signal Processing*, 2004(7):990–1000, 2004.

[159] P. Guillemain, J. Kergomard, and T. Voinier. Real-time synthesis of clarinet-like instruments using digital impedance models. *Journal of the Acoustical Society of America*, 118(1):483–494, 2005.

[160] B. Guo and W. Guo. Adaptive stabilization for a Kirchhoff-type nonlinear beam under boundary output feedback control. *Nonlinear Analysis*, 66:427–441, 2007.

[161] B. Gustaffson, H.-O. Kreiss, and J. Oliger. *Time Dependent Problems and Difference Methods*. John Wiley and Sons, New York, New York, 1995.

[162] B. Gustaffson, H.-O. Kreiss, and A. Sundstrom. Stability theory of difference approximations for mixed initial boundary value problems. II. *Mathematics of Computation*, 26(119):649–686, 1972.

[163] D. Hall. Piano string excitation II: General solution for a hard narrow hammer. *Journal of the Acoustical Society of America*, 81(2):535–546, 1987.

[164] A. Hannukainen, T. Lukkari, Malinen J, and P. Palo. Vowel formants from the wave equation. *Journal of the Acoustical Society of America*, 122(1):EL1–EL7, 2007.

[165] T. Hélie. On the use of Volterra series for real-time simulations of weakly nonlinear analog audio devices: Application to the Moog ladder filter. In *Proceedings of the 9th International Digital Audio Effects Conference*, pages 7–12, Montreal, Canada, September 2006.

[166] T. Hélie and D. Matignon. Diffusive representations for the analysis and simulation of flared acoustic pipes with visco-thermal losses. *Mathematical Models and Methods in Applied Sciences*, 16(4):503–536, 2006.

[167] T. Hélie and D. Roze. Sound synthesis of a nonlinear string using Volterra series. *Journal of Sound and Vibration*, 314(1–2):275–306, 2008.

[168] H. Hilber, T. Hughes, and R. Taylor. Improved numerical dissipation for time integration algorithms in structural dynamics. *Earthquake Engineering and Structural Dynamics*, 5:283–292, 1977.

[169] L. Hiller and P. Ruiz. Synthesizing musical sounds by solving the wave equation for vibrating objects: Part I. *Journal of the Audio Engineering Society*, 19(6):462–470, 1971.

[170] L. Hiller and P. Ruiz. Synthesizing musical sounds by solving the wave equation for vibrating objects: Part II. *Journal of the Audio Engineering Society*, 19(7):542–550, 1971.

[171] M. Hirsch and S. Smale. *Differential Equations, Dynamical Systems and Linear Algebra*. Academic Press, New York, New York, 1974.

[172] A. Hirschberg, J. Gilbert, R. Msallam, and A. Wijnands. Shock waves in trombones. *Journal of the Acoustical Society of America*, 99(3):1754–1758, 1996.

[173] A. Hirschberg, J. Kergomard, and G. Weinreich, editors. *Mechanics of Musical Instruments*. Springer, New York, New York, 1995.

[174] W. Hoefer. *The Electromagnetic Wave Simulator*. John Wiley and Sons, Chichester, UK, 1991.

[175] M. Horn. Nonlinear boundary stabilization of a von Kármán plate via bending moments only. In *Lecture Notes in Control and Information Sciences: System Modelling and Optimization*, pages 706–715. Springer, Berlin/Heidelberg, Germany, 1994.

[176] R. Horn and C. Johnson. *Matrix Analysis*. Cambridge University Press, Cambridge, UK, 1985.

[177] S. Ilanko. Vibration and post-buckling of in-plane loaded rectangular plates using a multiterm Galerkin's method. *Journal of Applied Mechanics*, 69(5):589–592, 2002.

[178] K. Ishizaka and J. Flanagan. Synthesis of voiced sounds from a two-mass model of the vocal cords. *Bell System Technical Journal*, 51(6):1233–1268, 1972.

[179] D. Jaffe and J. O. Smith III. Extensions of the Karplus-Strong plucked string algorithm. *Computer Music Journal*, 7(2):56–68, 1983.

[180] H. Järveläinen, T. Verma, and V. Välimäki. Perception and adjustment of pitch in inharmonic string instrument tones. *Journal of New Music Research*, 31(4):311–319, 2002.

[181] W. Jin and L. Ruxun. A new approach to design high-order schemes. *Journal of Computational and Applied Mathematics*, 134:59–67, 2001.

[182] P. Johns and R. Beurle. Numerical solution of 2-dimensional scattering problems using a transmission-line matrix. *Proceedings of the IEE*, 118:1203–1208, 1971.

[183] J. Johnson and A. Bajaj. Amplitude modulated and chaotic dynamics in resonant motion of strings. *Journal of Sound and Vibration*, 128(1):87–107, 1989.

[184] J.-M. Jot and A. Chaigne. Digital delay networks for designing artificial reverberators. Presented at the 90th Audio Engineering Society Convention, Paris, France, February, 1991. Preprint 3030.

[185] M. Junk. A finite difference interpretation of the lattice Boltzmann method. *Numerical Methods for Partial Differential Equations*, 17(4):383–402, 2001.

[186] W. Kaegi and S. Tempelaars. VOSIM—a new sound synthesis system. *Journal of the Audio Engineering Society*, 26(6):418–426, 1978.

[187] T. Kailath. *Linear Systems*. Prentice Hall, Englewood Cliffs, New Jersey, 1980.

[188] T. Kailath and A. Sayed. Displacement structure: Theory and applications. *SIAM Review*, 37(3):297–386, 1995.

[189] M. Karjalainen. Block-compiler: Efficient simulation of acoustic and audio systems. Presented at the 114th Audio Engineering Society Convention, Amsterdam, the Netherlands, May, 2003. Preprint 5756.

[190] M. Karjalainen. Time-domain physical modelling and real-time synthesis using mixed modelling paradigms. In *Proceedings of the Stockholm Musical Acoustics Conference*, volume 1, pages 393–396, Stockholm, Sweden, August 2003.

[191] M. Karjalainen and C. Erkut. Digital waveguides vs. finite difference schemes: Equivalence and mixed modeling. *EURASIP Journal on Applied Signal Processing*, 7:978–989, 2004.

[192] M. Karjalainen, V. Välimäki, and Z. Janosy. Towards high-quality sound synthesis of the guitar and string instruments. In *Proceedings of the International Computer Music Conference*, pages 56–63, Tokyo, Japan, September 1993.

[193] M. Karjalainen, V. Välimäki, and T. Tolonen. Plucked-string synthesis: From the Karplus-Strong algorithm to digital waveguides and beyond. *Computer Music Journal*, 22(3):17–32, 1998.

[194] K. Karplus and A. Strong. Digital synthesis of plucked-string and drum timbres. *Computer Music Journal*, 7(2):43–55, 1983.

[195] A. Kathnelson. A complete asymptotic analogue of Timoshenko's beam vibration equation. *Journal of Sound and Vibration*, 187(4):713–716, 1995.

[196] W. Kausel. *A Musical Acoustician's Guide to Computational Physics*. Institute für Wiener Klangstil, Vienna, Austria, 2003.

[197] D. Keefe. Experiments on the single woodwind tone hole. *Journal of the Acoustical Society of America*, 72(3):688–699, 1982.

[198] D. Keefe. Theory of the single woodwind tone hole. *Journal of the Acoustical Society of America*, 72(3):676–687, 1982.

[199] D. Keefe. Woodwind air column models. *Journal of the Acoustical Society of America*, 88(1):35–51, 1990.

[200] D. Keefe. Physical modeling of wind instruments. *Computer Music Journal*, 16(4):57–73, 1992.

[201] J. Kelly and C. Lochbaum. Speech synthesis. In *Proceedings of the Fourth International Congress on Acoustics*, pages 1–4, Copenhagen, Denmark, 1962. Paper G42.

[202] J. Kergomard. Elementary considerations on reed-instrument oscillations. In A. Hirschberg, J. Kergomard, and G. Weinreich, editors, *Mechanics of Musical Instruments, Lecture notes CISM*. Springer, New York, New York, 1995.

[203] J. Kim and D. Lee. Optimized compact finite difference schemes with maximum resolution. *American Institute of Aeronautics and Astronautics*, 34(5):887–892, 1996.

[204] R. Kirby and Z. Yosibash. Dynamic response of various von Karman non-linear plate models and their 3-D counterparts. *International Journal of Solids and Structures*, 193(6–8):575–599, 2004.

[205] R. Kirby and Z. Yosibash. Solution of von Karman dynamic non-linear plate equations using a pseudo-spectral method. *Computer Methods in Applied Mechanics and Engineering*, 193(6–8):575–599, 2004.

[206] G. Kirchhoff. *Vorlesungen über Mechanic*. Tauber, Leipzig, 1883.

[207] M. Kob. Eigenmodes of a flue organ pipe. *Acta Acustica united with Acustica*, 86(4):755–757, 2000.

[208] K. Kowalczyk and M. van Walstijn. Modeling frequency-dependent boundaries as digital impedance filters in FDTD and K-DWM room acoustics simulations. *Journal of the Audio Engineering Society*, 56(7/8):569–583, 2008.

[209] H.-O. Kreiss. Initial boundary value problems for hyperbolic systems. *Communications on Pure and Applied Mathematics*, 23:277–298, 1970.

[210] E. Kreyszig. *Introductory Functional Analysis with Applications*. John Wiley and Sons, New York, New York, 1978.

[211] G. Kron. Equivalent circuit of the field equations of Maxwell. *Proceedings of the IRE*, 32(5):284–299, 1944.

[212] W. Kuhl. The acoustical and technological properties of the reverberation plate. *E. B. U. Review*, A(49), 1958.

[213] E. Kurmyshev. Transverse and longitudinal mode coupling in a free vibrating soft string. *Physics Letters A*, 310(2–3):148–160, 2003.

[214] M. Kurz and B. Feiten. Physical modeling of a stiff string by numerical integration. In *Proceedings of the International Computer Music Conference*, pages 361–364, Hong Kong, August 1996.

[215] T. Laakso, V. Välimäki, M. Karjalainen, and U. Laine. Splitting the unit delay—tools for fractional delay filter design. *IEEE Signal Processing Magazine*, 13(1):30–60, 1996.

[216] J. Laird. *The Physical Modeling of Drums Using Digital Waveguides*. PhD thesis, University of York, 2001.

[217] C. Lambourg, A. Chaigne, and D. Matignon. Time-domain simulation of damped impacted plates. II Numerical model and results. *Journal of the Acoustical Society of America*, 109(4):1433–1447, 2001.

[218] M. Laurson, C. Erkut, V. Välimäki, and M. Kuuskankare. Methods for modeling realistic playing in acoustic guitar synthesis. *Computer Music Journal*, 25(3):38–49, 2001.

[219] M. LeBrun. Digital waveshaping synthesis. *Journal of the Audio Engineering Society*, 27(4):250–266, 1979.

[220] K. Legge and N. Fletcher. Nonlinear generation of missing modes on a vibrating string. *Journal of the Acoustical Society of America*, 76(1):5–12, 1984.

[221] A. Leissa. *Vibration of Shells*. Acoustical Society of America, 1993.

[222] S. Lele. Compact finite difference schemes with spectral-like resolution. *Journal of Computational Physics*, 103:16–42, 1992.

[223] A. Leung and S. Mao. A symplectic Galerkin method for nonlinear vibration of beams and plates. *Journal of Sound and Vibration*, 183(3):475–491, 1995.

[224] R. Leveque. *Finite Volume Methods for Hyperbolic Problems*. Cambridge University Press, Cambridge, UK, 2002.

[225] S. Li and L. Vu-Quoc. Finite difference calculus invariant structure of a class of algorithms for the nonlinear Klein Gordon equation. *SIAM Journal of Numerical Analysis*, 32:1839–1875, 1995.

[226] M. Little, I. Moroz, P. McSharry, and S. Roberts. Variational integration for speech signal processing. In *Proceedings of IMA Conference on Mathematics in Signal Processing VI*, Cirencester, UK, December 2004.

[227] D. Lockard, K. Brentner, and H. Atkins. High-accuracy algorithms for computational aeroacoustics. *American Institute of Aeronautics and Astronautics*, 33(2):247–251, 1995.

[228] A. Lyapunov. *Stability of Motion*. Academic Press, New York, New York, 1966.

[229] A. Mamoumani, J. Frelat, and C. Bensainou. Numerical simulation of a piano soundboard under downbearing. *Journal of the Acoustical Society of America*, 123(4):2401–2406, 2008.

[230] P. Manning. *Electronic and Computer Music*. Clarendon Press, Oxford, UK, 1985.

[231] J. Markel and A. Gray, Jr. *Linear Prediction of Speech*. Springer-Verlag, New York, New York, 1976.

[232] J. Martinez and J. Agulló. Conical bores. Part I: Reflection functions associated with discontinuities. *Journal of the Acoustical Society of America*, 84(5):1613–1619, 1988.

[233] R. McAulay and T. Quatieri. Speech analysis/synthesis based on a sinusoidal representation. *IEEE Transactions on Acoustics, Speech and Signal Processing*, 34(4):744–754, 1986.

[234] B. McCartin. An alternative analysis of Duffing's equation. *SIAM Review*, 34(3):482–491, 1992.

[235] J. McCartney. Supercollider: A new real-time sound synthesis language. In *Proceedings of the International Computer Music Conference*, pages 257–258, Hong Kong, August 1996.

[236] M. McIntyre, R. Schumacher, and J. Woodhouse. On the oscillations of musical instruments. *Journal of the Acoustical Society of America*, 74(5):1325–1345, 1983.

[237] M. McIntyre and J. Woodhouse. On the fundamentals of bowed string dynamics. *Acustica*, 43(2):93–108, 1979.

[238] L. McNeil and S. Mitran. Vibrational frequencies and tuning of the african mbira. *Journal of the Acoustical Society of America*, 123(2):1169–1178, 2008.

[239] R. Mindlin. Influence of rotatory inertia and shear on flexural motions of isotropic elastic plates. *Journal of Applied Mechanics*, 18:31–38, 1951.

[240] R. Moore. *Elements of Computer Music*. Prentice Hall, Englewood Cliffs, New Jersey, 1990.

[241] D. Morrill. Trumpet algorithms for computer composition. *Computer Music Journal*, 1(1):46–52, 1977.

[242] D. Morrison and J.-M. Adrien. Mosaic: A framework for modal synthesis. *Computer Music Journal*, 17(1):45–56, 1993.

[243] P. Morse. *Vibration and Sound*. Acoustical Society of America, New York, New York, second edition, 1981.

[244] P. Morse and U. Ingard. *Theoretical Acoustics*. Princeton University Press, Princeton, New Jersey, 1968.

[245] R. Msallam, S. Dequidt, S. Tassart, and R Caussé. Physical model of the trombone including nonlinear effects. Application to the sound synthesis of loud tones. *Acta Acustica united with Acustica*, 86(4):725–736, 2000.

[246] J. Mullen, D. Howard, and D. Murphy. Waveguide physical modeling of vocal tract acoustics: Flexible formant bandwidth control from increased model dimensionality. *IEEE Transactions in Audio Speech and Language Processing*, 14(3):964–971, 2006.

[247] J. Mullen, D. Howard, and D. Murphy. Real-time dynamic articulations in the 2-d waveguide mesh vocal tract model. *IEEE Transactions in Audio Speech and Language Processing*, 15(2):577–585, 2007.

[248] A. Muradova. Numerical technique for linear and nonlinear eigenvalue problems in the theory of elasticity. In *12th Biennial Computational Techniques and Applications Conference*, Melbourne, Australia, September 2004.

[249] D. Murphy and D. Howard. 2-D digital waveguide mesh topologies in room acoustic modelling. In *Proceedings of the COST G-6 Conference on Digital Audio Effects*, pages 211–216, Verona, Italy, December 2000.

[250] D. Murphy, A. Kelloniemi, J. Mullen, and S. Shelley. Acoustic modelling using the digital waveguide mesh. *IEEE Signal Processing Magazine*, 24(2):55–66, 2007.

[251] R. Narasimha. Nonlinear vibration of an elastic string. *Journal of Sound and Vibration*, 8(1):134–146, 1968.

[252] A. Nayfeh and D. Mook. *Nonlinear Oscillations*. John Wiley and Sons, New York, New York, 1979.

[253] C. Nederveen. *Acoustical Aspects of Woodwind Instruments*. Northern Illinois University Press, DeKalb, Illinois, second edition, 1998.

[254] C. Nederveen. Influence of a toroidal bend on wind instrument tuning. *Journal of the Acoustical Society of America*, 104(3):1616–1626, 1998.

[255] C. Nederveen, J. Jansen, and R. van Hassel. Corrections for woodwind tone-hole calculations. *Acta Acustica united with Acustica*, 84(5):957–966, 1998.

[256] N. Newmark. A method of computation for structural dynamics. *ACSE Journal of the Engineering Mechanics Division*, 85:67–94, 1959.

[257] A. Noor and W. Pilkey. *State-of-the-Art Surveys on Finite Element Technology*. ASME, New York, New York, 1983.

[258] D. Noreland. A numerical method for acoustic waves in horns. *Acta Acustica united with Acustica*, 88(4):576–586, 2002.

[259] B. Noye and J. Rankovic. An accurate explicit finite difference technique for solving the one-dimensional wave equation. *Communications in Applied Numerical Methods*, 2:557–561, 1986.

[260] B. Noye and J. Rankovic. An accurate five-point implicit finite difference method for solving the one-dimensional wave equation. *Communications in Applied Numerical Methods*, 5:247–252, 1989.

[261] A. Oppenheim and R. Schafer. *Digital Signal Processing*. Prentice-Hall, Englewood Cliffs, New Jersey, 1975.

[262] O. O'Reilly and P. Holmes. Non-linear, non-planar and non-periodic vibrations of a string. *Journal of Sound and Vibration*, 153(3):413–435, 1992.

[263] S. Osher. Stability of difference approximations of dissipative type for mixed initial boundary value problems. I. *Mathematics of Computation*, 23:335–340, 1969.

[264] J. Pakarinen, V. Välimäki, and M. Karjalainen. Physics-based methods for modeling nonlinear vibrating strings. *Acta Acustica united with Acustica*, 91(2):312–325, 2005.

[265] J. Pan, X. Li, J. Tian, and T. Lin. Short sound decay of ancient chinese music bells. *Journal of the Acoustical Society of America*, 112(6):3042–3045, 2002.

[266] J. Parker. Spring reverberation: A finite difference approach. Master's thesis, University of Edinburgh, 2008.

[267] M. Pearson. TAO: a physical modelling system and related issues. *Organized Sound*, 1(1):43–50, 1996.

[268] F. Pedersini, A. Sarti, S. Tubaro, and R. Zattoni. Towards the automatic synthesis of nonlinear wave digital models for musical acoustics. In *Proceedings of EUSIPCO-98, Ninth European Signal Processing Conference*, volume 4, pages 2361–2364, Rhodes, Greece, 1998.

[269] H. Penttinen, C. Erkut, J. Pölkki, V. Välimäki, and M. Karjalainen. Design and analysis of a modified kantele with increased loudness. *Acta Acustica united with Acustica*, 91(2):261–268, 2005.

[270] S. Petrausch, J. Escolano, and R. Rabenstein. A general approach to block-based physical modeling. with mixed modeling strategies for digital sound synthesis. In *Proceedings of the IEEE International Conference on Acoustics, Speech, and Signal Processing*, volume 3, pages 21–24, Philadelphia, Pennsylvania, 2005.

[271] S. Petrausch and R. Rabenstein. Tension modulated nonlinear 2D models for digital sound synthesis with the functional transformation method. In *Proceedings of EUSIPCO-05, Thirteenth European Signal Processing Conference*, Antalya, Turkey, September 2005.

[272] R. Pitteroff and J. Woodhouse. Mechanics of the contact area between a violin bow and a string. Part II: Simulating the bowed string. *Acta Acustica united with Acustica*, 84(4):744–757, 1998.

[273] M. Portnoff. A quasi-one-dimensional digital simulation for the time-varying vocal tract. Master's thesis, Massachusetts Institute of Technology, 1973.

[274] M. Portnoff. Implementation of the digital phase vocoder using the fast Fourier transform. *IEEE Transactions on Acoustics, Speech, and Signal Processing*, 24(3):243–248, 1976.

[275] J. Proakis. *Digital Signal Processing*. Prentice-Hall, Englewood Cliffs, New Jersey, third edition, 1996.

[276] M. Puckette. Pure data. In *Proceedings of the International Computer Music Conference*, pages 269–272, Hong Kong, August 1996.

[277] M. Puckette. *The Theory and Techniques of Electronic Music*. World Scientific Press, 2007.

[278] A. Quarteroni and A. Valli. *Numerical Approximation of Partial Differential Equations*. Springer, Berlin, 1997.

[279] R. Rabenstein, S. Petrausch, A. Sarti, G. De Sanctis, C. Erkut, and M. Karjalainen. Block-based physical modeling for digital sound synthesis. *IEEE Signal Processing Magazine*, 24(2):42–54, 2007.

[280] L. Rabiner and R. Schafer. *Digital Processing of Speech Signals*. Prentice-Hall, Englewood Cliffs, New Jersey, 1978.

[281] J. Rao. *Dynamics of Plates*. CRC Press, Boca Raton, Florida, 1999.

[282] M. Rath, F. Avanzini, and D. Rocchesso. Physically based real-time modeling of contact sounds. In *Proceedings of the International Computer Music Conference*, Goteborg, Sweden, September 2002.

[283] L. Rhaouti, A. Chaigne, and P. Joly. Time-domain modeling and numerical simulation of a kettledrum. *Journal of the Acoustical Society of America*, 105(6):3545–3562, 1999.

[284] R. Richtmyer and K. Morton. *Difference Methods for Initial-Value Problems*. Krieger Publishing Company, Malabar, Florida, second edition, 1994.

[285] J.-C. Risset. Computer study of trumpet tones. Technical report, Bell Technical Laboratories, Murray Hill, New Jersey, 1966.

[286] J. Rivera, H. Oquendo, and M. Santos. Asymptotic behavior to a von Kármán plate with boundary memory conditions. *Nonlinear Analysis*, 62:1183–1205, 2005.

[287] C. Roads. Granular synthesis of sound. In C. Roads and J. Strawn, editors, *Foundations of Computer Music*, pages 145–159. MIT Press, Cambridge, Massachusetts, 1985.

[288] C. Roads. A tutorial on nonlinear distortion or waveshaping synthesis. In C. Roads and J. Strawn, editors, *Foundations of Computer Music*, pages 83–94. MIT Press, Cambridge, Massachusetts, 1985.

[289] C. Roads. *The Computer Music Tutorial*. MIT Press, Cambridge, Massachusetts, 1996.

[290] C. Roads, S. Pope, A. Piccialli, and G. DePoli, editors. *Musical Signal Processing*. Swets and Zeitlinger, Lisse, The Netherlands, 1997.

[291] C. Roads and J. Strawn, editors. *Foundations of Computer Music*. MIT Press, Cambridge, Massachusetts, 1985.

[292] D. Rocchesso. The ball within the box: A sound processing metaphor. *Computer Music Journal*, 19(4):47–57, 1995.

[293] D. Rocchesso. Maximally diffusive yet efficient feedback delay networks for artificial reverberation. *IEEE Signal Processing Letters*, 4(9):252–255, 1997.

[294] D. Rocchesso and F. Fontana, editors. *The Sounding Object*. Mondo Estremo, 2003. Available online at http://www.mondo-estremo.com/info/publications/public.html.

[295] D. Rocchesso and J. O. Smith III. Circulant and elliptic feedback delay networks for artificial reverberation. *IEEE Transactions on Speech and Audio Processing*, 5(1):51–63, 1997.

[296] X. Rodet. Time-domain formant-wave-function synthesis. *Computer Music Journal*, 8(3):9–14, 1980.

[297] X. Rodet and C. Vergez. Nonlinear dynamics in physical models: From basic models to true musical-instrument models. *Computer Music Journal*, 23(3):35–49, 1999.

[298] X. Rodet and C. Vergez. Nonlinear dynamics in physical models: Simple feedback loop systems and properties. *Computer Music Journal*, 23(3):18–34, 1999.

[299] T. Rossing. Acoustics of percussion instruments: Recent progress. *Acoustical Science and Technology*, 22(3):177–188, 2001.

[300] T. Rossing and N. Fletcher. Nonlinear vibrations in plates and gongs. *Journal of the Acoustical Society of America*, 73(1):345–351, 1983.

[301] T. Rossing, F. Moore, and P. Wheeler. *The Science of Sound*. Addison Wesley, Reading, Massachusetts, third edition, 2002.

[302] D. Rowland. Parametric resonance and nonlinear string vibrations. *American Journal of Physics*, 72(6):758–765, 2004.

[303] D. Roze and T. Hélie. Sound synthesis of nonlinear strings using Volterra series. Presented at the International Congress on Acoustics, Madrid, Spain, September, 2007. Available on CD-ROM.

[304] M. Rubin and O. Gottlieb. Numerical solutions of forced vibration and whirling of a nonlinear string using the theory of a Cosserat point. *Journal of Sound and Vibration*, 197(1):85–101, 1996.

[305] P. Ruiz. A technique for simulating the vibrations of strings with a digital computer. Master's thesis, University of Illinois, 1969.

[306] J. Russ. *The Image Processing Handbook*. CRC Press, Boca Raton, Florida, fifth edition, 2006.

[307] J. Sanz-Serna. An explicit finite-difference scheme with exact conservation properties. *Journal of Computational Physics*, 47:199–210, 1982.

[308] J. Sanz-Serna. Symplectic integrators for Hamiltonian problems: An overview. *Acta Numerica*, 1:243–286, 1991.

[309] A. Sarti and G. DePoli. Toward nonlinear wave digital filters. *IEEE Transactions on Signal Processing*, 47(6):1654–1658, 1999.

[310] L. Sasaki and K. Smith. A simple data reduction scheme for additive synthesis. *Computer Music Journal*, 4(1):22–24, 1980.

[311] G. Sathej and R. Adhikari. The eigenspectra of Indian musical drums. *ArXiv e-prints*, September 2008.

[312] L. Savioja and V. Välimäki. Reduction of the dispersion error in the interpolated digital waveguide mesh using frequency warping. In *Proceedings of the IEEE International Conference on Acoustics, Speech, and Signal Processing*, volume 2, pages 973–976, New York, New York, March 1999.

[313] L. Savioja and V. Välimäki. Reducing the dispersion error in the digital waveguide mesh using interpolation and frequency-warping techniques. *IEEE Transactions on Speech and Audio Processing*, 8(2):184–194, 2000.

[314] G. Scavone. *An Acoustic Analysis of Single-Reed Woodwind Instruments with an Emphasis on Design and Performance Issues and Digital Waveguide Techniques*. PhD thesis, Department of Music, Stanford University, 1997.

[315] D. Schaeffer and M. Golubitsky. Boundary conditions and mode jumping in the buckling of a rectangular plate. *Communications in Mathematical Physics*, 69:209–236, 1979.

[316] S. Schedin, C. Lambourg, and A. Chaigne. Transient sound fields from impacted plates: Comparison between numerical simulations and experiments. *Journal of Sound and Vibration*, 221(32):471–490, 1999.

[317] W. Schottstaedt. The simulation of natural instrument tones using frequency modulation with a complex modulating wave. *Computer Music Journal*, 1(4):46–50, 1977.

[318] R. Schumacher. Compliances of wood for violin top plates. *Journal of the Acoustical Society of America*, 84(4):1223–1235, 1988.

[319] S. Serafin, F. Avanzini, and D. Rocchesso. Bowed string simulation using an elasto-plastic friction model. In *Proceedings of the Stockholm Musical Acoustics Conference*, volume 1, pages 95–98, Stockholm, Sweden, August 2003.

[320] S. Serafin and J. O. Smith III. A multirate, finite-width, bow-string interaction model. In *Proceedings of the COST-G6 Digital Audio Effects Conference*, pages 207–210, Verona, Italy, December 2000.

[321] S. Serafin, J. O. Smith III, and J. Woodhouse. An investigation of the impact of torsion waves and friction characteristics on the playability of virtual bowed strings. In *Proceedings of the IEEE Workshop*

1
2
3
4
5
6
7
8
9
10
11
12
13
14
15
16
17
18
19
20
21
22
23
24
25
26
27
28
29
30
31
32
33
34
35
36
37
38
39
40
41
42
43
44
45
46
47
48
49
50
51

on Applications of Signal Processing to Audio and Acoustics, pages 87–99, New Paltz, New York, October 1999.

[322] X. Serra and J. O. Smith III. Spectral modeling synthesis: A sound analysis/synthesis system based on a deterministic plus stochastic decomposition. *Computer Music Journal*, 14(4):12–24, 1990.

[323] G. R. Shubin and J. B. Bell. A modified equation approach to constructing fourth order methods for acoustic wave propagation. *SIAM Journal of Scientific and Statistical Computing*, 8:135–51, 1987.

[324] J. Simo, N. Tarnow, and K. Wong. Exact energy-momentum conserving algorithms for symplectic schemes for nonlinear dynamics. *Computer Methods in Applied Mechanics and Engineering*, 100:63–116, 1992.

[325] G. Smith. *Numerical Solution of Partial Differential Equations: Finite Difference Methods*. Clarendon Press, Oxford, UK, third edition, 1985.

[326] J. O. Smith III. A new approach to digital reverberation using closed waveguide networks. In *Proceedings of the International Computer Music Conference*, Vancouver, Canada, September 1985. Appears in Technical Report STAN-M-39, pp. 1–7, Center for Computer Research in Music and Acoustics (CCRMA), Department of Music, Stanford University.

[327] J. O. Smith III. Efficient simulation of the reed-bore and bow-string mechanisms. In *Proceedings of the International Computer Music Conference*, pages 275–280, The Hague, The Netherlands, October 1986.

[328] J. O. Smith III. Viewpoints on the history of digital synthesis. In *Proceedings of the International Computer Music Conference*, pages 1–10, Montreal, Canada, October 1991.

[329] J. O. Smith III. Waveguide simulation of non-cylindrical acoustic tubes. In *Proceedings of the International Computer Music Conference*, pages 304–307, Montreal, Canada, October 1991.

[330] J. O. Smith III. Physical modelling using digital waveguides. *Computer Music Journal*, 16(4):74–91, 1992.

[331] J. O. Smith III. Efficient synthesis of stringed musical instruments. In *Proceedings of the International Computer Music Conference*, pages 64–71, Tokyo, Japan, September 1993.

[332] J. O. Smith III. Acoustic modeling using digital waveguides. In C. Roads, S. Pope, A. Piccialli, and G. DePoli, editors, *Musical Signal Processing*, pages 221–263. Swets and Zeitlinger, Lisse, The Netherlands, 1997.

[333] J. O. Smith III. On the equivalence of digital waveguides and finite difference time domain schemes, 2004. Available onlne at http://arxiv.org/abs/physics/0 407 032/.

[334] J. O. Smith III. *Physical Audio Signal Procesing*. Stanford, CA, 2004. Draft version. Available online at http://ccrma.stanford.edu/˜jos/pasp04/.

[335] J. O. Smith III and P. Cook. The second-order digital waveguide oscillator. In *Proceedings of the International Computer Music Conference*, pages 150–153, San Jose, California, September 1992.

[336] J. O. Smith III and G. Scavone. The one-filter Keefe clarinet tonehole. In *Proceedings of the IEEE Workshop on Applications of Signal Processing to Audio and Acoustics*, New Paltz, New York, October 1997.

[337] J. O. Smith III, S. Serafin, and D. Berners. Doppler simulation and the Leslie. In *Proceedings of the 5th International Conference on Digital Audio Effects*, pages 13–20, Hamburg, Germany, 2002.

[338] J. O. Smith III and S. van Duyne. Commuted piano synthesis. In *Proceedings of the International Computer Music Conference*, pages 319–326, Banff, Canada, 1995.

[339] M. Sondhi. Model for wave propagation in a lossy vocal tract. *Journal of the Acoustical Society of America*, 55(5):1070–1075, 1974.

[340] T. Stilson and J. O. Smith III. Analyzing the Moog VCF with considerations for digital implementation. In *Proceedings of the International Computer Music Conference*, pages 398–401, Hong Kong, August 1996.

[341] B. Story. A parametric model of the vocal tract area function for vowel and consonant simulation. *Journal of the Acoustical Society of America*, 117(5):3231–3254, 2005.

[342] J. Strikwerda. *Finite Difference Schemes and Partial Differential Equations*. Wadsworth and Brooks/Cole Advanced Books and Software, Pacific Grove, California, 1989.

[343] H. Strube. Time-varying wave digital filters and vocal-tract models. In *Proceedings of the IEEE International Conference on Acoustics, Speech, and Signal Processing*, volume 2, pages 923–926, Paris, France, May 1982.

[344] H. Strube. Time-varying wave digital filters for modelling analog systems. *IEEE Transactions on Acoustics, Speech, and Signal Processing*, ASSP-30(6):864–868, 1982.

1
2
3
4
5
6
7
8
9
10
11
12
13
14
15
16
17
18
19
20
21
22
23
24
25
26
27
28
29
30
31
32
33
34
35
36
37
38
39
40
41
42
43
44
45
46
47
48
49
50
51

[345] H. Strube. The meaning of the Kelly-Lochbaum acoustic-tube model. *Journal of the Acoustical Society of America*, 108(4):1850–1855, 2000.

[346] A. Stulov. Hysteretic model of the grand piano felt. *Journal of the Acoustical Society of America*, 97(4):2577–2585, 1995.

[347] H. Suzuki. Vibration and sound radiation of a piano soundboard. *Journal of the Acoustical Society of America*, 80(6):1573–1582, 1986.

[348] R. Szilard. *Theory and Analysis of Plates*. Prentice Hall, Englewood Cliffs, New Jersey, 1974.

[349] N. Szilas and C. Cadoz. Analysis techniques for physical modeling networks. *Computer Music Journal*, 22(3):33–48, 1998.

[350] T. Tachibana and K. Takahashi. Sounding mechanism of a cylindrical pipe fitted with a clarinet mouthpiece. *Progress of Theoretical Physics*, 104(2):265–288, 2000.

[351] A. Taflove. *Computational Electrodynamics*. Artech House, Boston, Massachusetts, 1995.

[352] A. Taflove. *Advances in Computational Electrodynamics*. Artech House, Boston, Massachusetts, 1998.

[353] C. Tao, J. Jiang, and Y. Zhang. Simulation of vocal fold impact pressures with a self-oscillating finite-element model. *Journal of the Acoustical Society of America*, 119(6):3987–3994, 2006.

[354] L. Thomas. Elliptic problems in linear difference equations over a network. Technical report, Watson Scientific Computing Laboratory, Columbia University, New York, 1949.

[355] O. Thomas and S. Bilbao. Geometrically nonlinear mechanics of plates: An intrinsic formulation and a symmetry property of the nonlinear operator. *Journal of Sound and Vibration*, 315(3):569–590, 2008.

[356] O. Thomas, C. Touzé, and A. Chaigne. Asymmetric nonlinear forced vibrations of free-edge circular plates. Part II. Experiments. *Journal of Sound and Vibration*, 265:1075–1101, 2003.

[357] O. Thomas, C. Touzé, and A. Chaigne. Non-linear vibrations of free-edge thin spherical shells: Modal interaction rules and 1:1:2 internal resonance. *International Journal of Solids and Structures*, 42:3339–3373, 2005.

[358] T. Tolonen, V. Välimäki, and M. Karjalainen. Evaluation of modern sound synthesis methods. Technical Report 48, Laboratory of Acoustics and Audio Signal Processing, Helsinki University of Technology, March 1998.

[359] T. Tolonen, V. Välimäki, and M. Karjalainen. Modeling of tension modulation nonlinearity in plucked strings. *IEEE Transactions on Speech and Audio Processing*, 8(3):300–310, 2000.

[360] C. Touzé, O. Thomas, and A. Chaigne. Asymmetric nonlinear forced vibrations of free-edge circular plates. Part I. Theory. *Journal of Sound and Vibration*, 258(4):649–676, 2002.

[361] L. Trautmann and R. Rabenstein. *Digital Sound Synthesis by Physical Modeling Using the Functional Transformation Method*. Kluwer Academic/Plenum Publishers, New York, New York, 2003.

[362] L. Trefethen. Group velocity in finite difference schemes. *SIAM Review*, 24:113–136, 1982.

[363] L. Trefethen. Instability of finite difference models for hyperbolic initial boundary value problems. *Communications on Pure and Applied Mathematics*, 37:329–367, 1984.

[364] L. Trefethen. *Spectral Methods in Matlab*. SIAM, Philadelphia, Pennsylvania, USA, 2000.

[365] J. Tuomela. A note on high-order schemes for the one-dimensional wave equation. *BIT*, 35(3):394–405, 1995.

[366] J. Tuomela. On the construction of arbitrary order schemes for the many-dimensional wave equation. *BIT*, 36(1):158–165, 1996.

[367] A. Tveito and R. Winther. *Introduction to Partial Differential Equations*. Springer, New York, 1998.

[368] V. Välimäki. *Discrete-Time Modelling of Acoustic Tubes Using Fractional Delay Filters*. PhD thesis, Helsinki University of Technology, Faculty of Electrical Engineering, Laboratory of Acoustics and Audio Signal Processing, Espoo, Finland, 1995.

[369] V. Välimäki, R. Hänninen, and M. Karjalainen. An improved digital waveguide model of a flute—Implementation issues. In *Proceedings of the International Computer Music Conference*, pages 1–4, Hong Kong, August 1996.

[370] V. Välimäki and M. Karjalainen. Digital waveguide modeling of wind instrument bores constructed of truncated cones. In *Proceedings of the International Computer Music Conference*, pages 423–430, Århus, Denmark, September 1994.

[371] V. Välimäki and M. Karjalainen. Improving the Kelly-Lochbaum vocal tract model using conical tube sections and fractional delay filtering techniques. In *Proceedings of the International Conference on Spoken Language Processing*, volume 2, pages 615–618, Yokohama, Japan, September 1994.

[372] V. Välimäki and M. Karjalainen. Implementation of fractional delay waveguide models using allpass filters. In *Proceedings of the IEEE International Conference on Acoustics, Speech, and Signal Processing*, pages 8–12, Detroit, Michigan, May 1995.

[373] V. Välimäki, M. Karjalainen, Z. Janosz, and U. Laine. A real-time dsp implementation of a flute model. In *Proceedings of the IEEE International Conference on Acoustics, Speech and Signal Processing*, volume 2, pages 249–252, San Francisco, California, March 1992.

[374] V. Välimäki, M. Karjalainen, and T. Laakso. Modeling of woodwind bores with finger holes. In *Proceedings of the International Computer Music Conference*, pages 32–39, Tokyo, September 1993.

[375] V. Välimäki, M. Laurson, and C. Erkut. Commuted waveguide synthesis of the clavichord. *Computer Music Journal*, 27(1):71–82, 2003.

[376] V. Välimäki, J. Pakarinen, C. Erkut, and M. Karjalainen. Discrete time modeling of musical instruments. *Reports on Progress in Physics*, 69:1–78, 2006.

[377] V. Välimäki, H. Penttinen, J. Knif, M. Laurson, and C. Erkut. Sound synthesis of the harpsichord using a computationally efficient physical model. *EURASIP Journal on Applied Signal Processing*, 69(7):934–948, 2004.

[378] V. Välimäki, T. Tolonen, and M. Karjalainen. Plucked-string synthesis algorithms with tension modulation nonlinearity. In *Proceedings of the IEEE International Conference on Acoustics, Speech, and Signal Processing*, volume 2, pages 977–980, Phoenix, Arizona, March 1999.

[379] C. Vallette. The mechanics of vibrating strings. In A. Hirschberg, J. Kergomard, and G. Weinreich, editors, *Mechanics of Musical Instruments*, pages 116–183. Springer, New York, New York, 1995.

[380] K. van den Doel. Modal synthesis for vibrating objects. In K. Greenebaum, editor, *Audio Anecdotes III*. A. K. Peters, Natick, Massachusetts, 2007.

[381] K. van den Doel and U. Ascher. Real-time numerical solution of Webster's equation on a non-uniform grid. *IEEE Transactions on Audio, Speech and Language Processing*, 16(6):1163–1172, 2008.

[382] S. van Duyne. *Digital Filter Applications to Modeling Wave Propagation in Springs, Strings, Membranes and Acoustical Space*. PhD thesis, Music Department, Stanford University, 2007.

[383] S. van Duyne, J. Pierce, and J. O. Smith III. Travelling wave implementation of a lossless mode-coupling filter and the wave digital hammer. In *Proceedings of the International Computer Music Conference*, pages 411–418, Århus, Denmark, September 1994.

[384] S. van Duyne and J. O. Smith III. Physical modelling with the 2D digital waveguide mesh. In *Proceedings of the International Computer Music Conference*, pages 40–47, Tokyo, Japan, September 1993.

[385] S. van Duyne and J. O. Smith III. A simplified approach to modelling dispersion caused by stiffness in strings and plates. In *Proceedings of the International Computer Music Conference*, pages 407–410, Århus, Denmark, September 1994.

[386] S. van Duyne and J. O. Smith III. The 3D tetrahedral digital waveguide mesh with musical applications. In *Proceedings of the International Computer Music Conference*, pages 9–16, Hong Kong, August 1996.

[387] M. van Valkenburg. *Network Analysis*. Dover, New York, New York, 1975.

[388] M. van Walstijn. Wave-based simulation of wind instrument resonators. *IEEE Signal Processing Magazine*, 24(2):21–31, 2007.

[389] M. van Walstijn and F. Avanzini. Modeling the mechanical response of the reed-mouthpiece-lip system of a clarinet. Part II: A lumped model approximation. *Acta Acustica united with Acustica*, 93(3):435–446, 2007.

[390] M. van Walstijn and D. Campbell. Discrete-time modeling of woodwind instrument bores using wave variables. *Journal of the Acoustical Society of America*, 113(1):575–585, 2003.

[391] M. van Walstijn and G. Scavone. The wave digital tonehole model. In *Proceedings of the International Computer Music Conference*, pages 465–468, Berlin, Germany, August 2000.

[392] E. Varèse. The liberation of sound. *Perspectives of New Music*, 5(1):11–19, 1966.

[393] R. Verfürth. A posteriori error estimates for nonlinear problems. *Mathematics of Computation*, 67(224): 1335–1360, 1998.

[394] M.-P. Verge. *Aeroacoustics of confined jets with applications to the physical modeling of recorder-like instruments*. PhD thesis, Eindhoven University of Technology, 1995.

[395] M.-P. Verge, A. Hirschberg, and R. Caussé. Sound production in recorderlike instruments: II A simulation model. *Journal of the Acoustical Society of America*, 101(5):2925–2939, 1997.

[396] C. Vergez. *Trompette et Trompettiste: Un système dynamique non linéaire à analyser, modéliser et simuler dans un contexte musical*. PhD thesis, Université de Paris VI, 2000.

[397] C. Vergez, A. Almeida, R. Caussé, and X. Rodet. Toward a simple physical model of double-reed musical instruments: Influence of aero-dynamical losses in the embouchure on the coupling. *Acta Acustica united with Acustica*, 89(6):964–973, 2003.

[398] C. Vergez and X. Rodet. Dynamic systems and physical models of trumpet-like instruments: A study and asymptotical properties. *Acta Acustica united with Acustica*, 86(1):147–162, 2000.

[399] C. Vergez and X. Rodet. A new algorithm for nonlinear propagation of sound wave: Application to a physical model of a trumpet. *Journal of Signal Processing*, 4:79–88, 2000.

[400] C. Vergez and P. Tisserand. The brass project, from physical models to virtual musical instruments: Playability issues. In R. Kronland-Martinet, T. Voinier, and S. Ystad, editors, *Lecture Notes in Computer Science: Computer Music Modeling and Retrieval*, volume 3902, pages 24–33. Springer, Berlin/Heidelberg, Germany, 2006.

[401] W. Verplank, M. Mathews, and R. Shaw. Scanned synthesis. In *Proceedings of the International Computer Music Conference*, pages 368–371, Berlin, Germany, August 2000.

[402] R. Vichnevetsky and J. Bowles. *Fourier Analysis of Numerical Approximations of Hyperbolic Equations*. SIAM, Philadelphia, Pennsylvania, 1982.

[403] V. Vijayakumar and C. Eswaran. Synthesis of audio spectra using a diffraction model. *Journal of the Acoustical Society of America*, 120(6):EL70–EL77, 2006.

[404] L. Vu-Quoc and S. Li. Invariant-conserving finite difference algorithms for the nonlinear Klein-Gordon equation. *Computer Methods in Applied Mechanics and Engineering*, 107:341–391, 1993.

[405] A. Watzky. Non-linear three-dimensional large-amplitude damped free vibration of a stiff elastic stretched string. *Journal of Sound and Vibration*, 153(1):125–142, 1992.

[406] A. Webster. Acoustical impedance, and the theory of horns and of the phonograph. *Proceedings of the National Academy of Sciences of the United States of America*, 5(7):275–282, 1919.

[407] L. Weinberg. *Network Analysis and Synthesis*. McGraw-Hill, New York, New York, 1962.

[408] G. Weinreich. Mechanical oscillations. In A. Hirschberg, J. Kergomard, and G. Weinreich, editors, *Mechanics of Musical Instruments*, pages 79–114. Springer, New York, New York, 1995.

[409] W. Wittrick. On elastic wave propagation in helical springs. *International Journal of Mechanical Sciences*, 8:25–47, 1966.

[410] J. Woodhouse. Physical modeling of bowed strings. *Computer Music Journal*, 16(4):43–56, 1992.

[411] J. Woodhouse. Self-sustained musical oscillators. In A. Hirschberg, J. Kergomard, and G. Weinreich, editors, *Mechanics of Musical Instruments*. Springer, New York, New York, 1995.

[412] K. Yee. Numerical solution of initial boundary value problems involving Maxwell's equations in isotropic media. *IEEE Transactions on Antennas and Propagation*, 14:302–307, 1966.

[413] D. Yeh, J. Abel, A. Vladimirescu, and J. O. Smith III. Numerical methods for simulation of guitar distortion circuits. *Computer Music Journal*, 32(2):23–42, 2008.

[414] J. Yoo and T. Rossing. Geometrical effects on the tuning of Chinese and Korean stone chimes. *Journal of the Acoustical Society of America*, 120(6):EL78–EL73, 2006.

[415] S. Zambon, H.-M. Lehtonen, and B. Bank. Simulation of piano sustain-pedal effect by parallel second-order filters. In *Proceedings of the 11th International Digital Audio Effects Conference*, pages 199–204, Espoo, Finland, September 2008.

[416] Q. Zhang, L. Ye, and Z. Pan. Physically-based sound synthesis on GPUs. In *Lecture Notes in Computer Science*, volume 3711/2005, pages 328–333. Springer, Berlin/Heidelberg, Germany, 2005.

[417] Y. Zhiming. A nonlinear dynamical theory of non-classical plates. *Journal of Shangai University*, 1(2):1–17, 1997.

[418] D. Zicarelli. How I learned to love a program that does nothing. *Computer Music Journal*, 26(4):44–51, 2002.

[419] D. Zingg. Comparison of high-accuracy finite-difference methods for linear wave propagation. *SIAM Journal of Scientific Computing*, 22(2):476–502, 2000.

[420] D. Zingg and H. Lomax. Finite-difference schemes on regular triangular grids. *Journal of Computational Physics*, 108:306–313, 1993.

[421] E. Zwicker and H. Fastl. *Psychoacoustics: Facts and Models*. Springer-Verlag, Berlin-Heidelberg, Germany, 1990.

Index

1
2
3
4
5
6
7
8
9
10
11
12
13
14
15
16
17
18
19
20
21
22
23
24
25
26
27
28
29
30
31
32
33
34
35
36
37
38
39
40
41
42
43
44
45
46
47
48
49
50
51

1
2
3
4
5
6
7
8
9
10
11
12
13
14
15
16
17
18
19
20
21
22
23
24
25
26
27
28
29
30
31
32
33
34
35
36
37
38
39
40
41
42
43
44
45
46
47
48
49
50
51

1
2
3
4
5
6
7
8
9
10
11
12
13
14
15
16
17
18
19
20
21
22
23
24
25
26
27
28
29
30
31
32
33
34
35
36
37
38
39
40
41
42
43
44
45
46
47
48
49
50
51

1
2
3
4
5
6
7
8
9
10
11
12
13
14
15
16
17
18
19
20
21
22
23
24
25
26
27
28
29
30
31
32
33
34
35
36
37
38
39
40
41
42
43
44
45
46
47
48
49
50
51

Printed and bound in the UK by
CPI Antony Rowe, Eastbourne

Printed and bound by CPI Group (UK) Ltd, Croydon, CR0 4YY

27/10/2024

14580292-0003